Hands-On Unity 2022 Game Development

Third Edition

Learn to use the latest Unity 2022 features to create your first video game in the simplest way possible

Nicolas Alejandro Borromeo

BIRMINGHAM—MUMBAI

Hands-On Unity 2022 Game Development
Third Edition

Senior Publishing Product Manager: Manish Nainani

Acquisition Editor – Peer Reviews: Gaurav Gavas

Project Editor: Amisha Vathare

Content Development Editor: Grey Murtagh

Copy Editor: Safis Editing

Technical Editor: Srishty Bhardwaj

Proofreader: Safis Editing

Indexer: Pratik Shirodkar

Presentation Designer: Pranit Padwal

First published: July 2020
Second edition: August 2021
Third edition: October 2022

Production reference: 1211022

Published by Packt Publishing Ltd.
Livery Place
35 Livery Street
Birmingham
B3 2PB, UK.

ISBN 978-1-80323-691-9

www.packt.com

Contributors

About the author

Nicolas Alejandro Borromeo is a Game Developer currently working for Unity Technologies as a Senior Software Development Consultant and Unity Certified Instructor in London, helping Unity clients with their projects all around the globe. He started using Unity in 2008 and teaching it in 2012 at several universities and educational institutions.

I want to say thanks to my father who always encouraged my love for computers and games; I miss you. Also to my wife Edith, for always reminding me what I'm capable of, and supporting me in my career.

About the reviewer

Rafael J. M. Ocariz is currently an Expert Software Engineer living in Quebec City, Canada. With 11 years of experience in software development, 8 of those developing games in Unity, he has developed products for mobile, PC, and VR platforms. His portfolio includes big titles from the Call of Duty franchise, Crash Bandicoot, Tony Hawk's, and WWE. He also has solid skills in several other technologies, such as distributed systems, modern C++, Unreal Engine, Lua, Python, and native app development for Android and iOS.

I'd like to thank God and my wife, Giovanna N. Barbero, for all the support they gave me during this project.

Table of Contents

Preface xv

Chapter 1: Creating a Unity Project 1

Installing Unity 1

Unity's technical requirements • 2

Unity versioning • 2

Installing Unity with Unity Hub • 3

Creating projects 11

Creating a project • 12

Project structure • 14

Summary 16

Chapter 2: Editing Scenes and Game Objects 17

Manipulating scenes 17

The purpose of a scene • 18

The Scene View • 18

Adding our first GameObject to the scene • 20

Navigating the Scene View • 21

Manipulating GameObjects • 22

GameObjects and components 27

Understanding components • 27

Manipulating components • 29

Object Hierarchies 34

Parenting of objects • 34

Possible uses • 36

Prefabs 37

Creating Prefabs • 38

Prefab-instance relationship • 39

Prefab variants • 43

Saving scenes and projects 44

Summary 45

Chapter 3: Grayboxing with Terrain and ProBuilder 47

Defining our game concept 47

Creating a landscape with Terrain 48

Discussing Height Maps • 49

Creating and configuring Height Maps • 50

Authoring Height Maps • 53

Adding Height Map details • 57

Creating shapes with ProBuilder 60

Installing ProBuilder • 61

Creating a shape • 64

Manipulating the mesh • 65

Adding details • 72

Summary 76

Chapter 4: Importing and Integrating Assets 79

Importing assets 79

Importing assets from the internet • 80

Importing assets from the Asset Store • 82

Importing assets from Unity Packages • 90

Integrating assets 91

Integrating terrain textures • 91

Integrating meshes • 94

Integrating textures • 95

Configuring assets 99

Configuring meshes • 99

Configuring textures • 101

Assembling the scene • 103

Summary 106

Chapter 5: Introduction to C# and Visual Scripting 107

Creating scripts 108

Initial setup • 109

Creating a C# script • 112

Adding fields • 116

Creating a Visual Script • 118

Using events and instructions 121

Events and instructions in C# • 122

Events and instructions in Visual Scripting • 126

Using fields in instructions • 129

Common beginner C# script errors • 132

Summary 135

Chapter 6: Implementing Movement and Spawning 137

Implementing movement 137

Moving objects through Transform • 138

Using Input • 141

Understanding Delta Time • 148

Implementing spawning 150

Spawning objects • 151

Timing actions • 161

Destroying objects • 166

Using the new Input System 168

Installing the new Input System • 168

Creating Input Mappings • 170

Using Mappings in our scripts • 174

Summary 179

Chapter 7: Physics Collisions and Health System 181

Configuring physics 182

Setting shapes • 182

Physics object types • 186

Filtering collisions • 190

Detecting collisions 193

Detecting Trigger events • 193

Modifying the other object • 196

Moving with physics 200

Applying forces • 200

Tweaking physics • 203

Summary 206

Chapter 8: Win and Lose Conditions 207

Creating object managers 207

Sharing variables with the Singleton design pattern • 208

Sharing variables with Visual Scripting • 213

Creating managers • 216

Creating Game Modes 224

Improving our code with events 231

Summary 241

Chapter 9: Implementing Game AI for Building Enemies 243

Gathering information with sensors 243

Creating three-filter sensors with C# • 244

Creating Three-Filters sensors with Visual Scripting • 251
Debugging with Gizmos • 255
Making decisions with FSMs 264
Creating the FSM in C# • 264
Creating transitions • 267
Creating the FSM in Visual Scripting • 272
Executing FSM actions 283
Calculating our scene's NavMesh • 283
Using Pathfinding • 286
Adding the final details 291
Summary 298

Chapter 10: Materials and Effects with URP and Shader Graph 299

Introducing shaders and URP 299
Shader Pipeline • 300
Render Pipeline and URP • 303
URP built-in shaders • 305
Creating shaders with Shader Graph 310
Creating our first Shader Graph • 310
Using Textures 316
Combining Textures 325
Applying transparency 328
Creating Vertex Effects 331
Summary 334

Chapter 11: Visual Effects with Particle Systems and Visual Effect Graph 335

Introduction to Shuriken particle systems 335
Creating a basic particle system with Shuriken • 336
Using advanced modules • 342
Creating fluid simulations 344
Creating a waterfall effect • 344

Creating a bonfire effect • 346

Creating complex simulations with Visual Effect Graph 349

Installing Visual Effect Graph • 350

Creating and analyzing a Visual Effect Graph • 352

Creating a rain effect • 356

Scripting Visual Effects 363

Summary 370

Chapter 12: Lighting Using the Universal Render Pipeline 371

Applying lighting 371

Discussing lighting methods • 372

Configuring ambient lighting with skyboxes • 377

Configuring lighting in URP • 382

Applying shadows 386

Understanding shadow calculations • 386

Configuring performant shadows • 391

Optimizing lighting 395

Understanding static lighting • 395

Baking lightmaps • 396

Applying static lighting to static objects • 404

Summary 408

Chapter 13: Full-Screen Effects with Post-Processing 411

Using post-processing 411

Setting up a profile • 412

Using basic effects • 414

Using advanced effects 418

High Dynamic Range (HDR) and Depth Map • 418

Applying advanced effects • 421

Summary 428

Chapter 14: Sound and Music Integration 429

Importing audio ... 429

Audio types • 430

Configuring import settings • 432

Integrating and mixing audio ... 436

Using 2D and 3D AudioSources • 436

Using an Audio Mixer • 441

Scripting audio feedback ... 446

Summary ... 449

Chapter 15: User Interface Design 451

Understanding the Canvas and RectTransform ... 452

Creating a UI with the Canvas • 452

Positioning elements with RectTransform • 453

Canvas object types ... 456

Integrating assets for the UI • 456

Creating UI controls • 465

Creating a responsive UI ... 473

Adapting object positions • 474

Adapting object sizes • 477

Scripting the UI ... 480

Showing information in the UI • 480

Programming the Pause menu • 495

Summary ... 504

Chapter 16: Creating a UI with the UI Toolkit 507

Why learn UI Toolkit? ... 507

Creating a UI with UI Toolkit ... 508

Creating UI Documents • 508

Editing UI Documents • 510

Creating UI Stylesheets • 519

Making a responsive UI 524

Dynamic positioning and sizing • 524

Dynamic scaling • 528

Using relative positions • 530

Summary 536

Chapter 17: Creating Animations with Animator, Cinemachine, and Timeline 537

Using Skinning Animation with Animator 537

Understanding skinning • 538

Importing skeletal animations • 541

Integration using Animation Controllers • 545

Using Avatar Masks • 552

Scripting animations 557

Scripting player shooting animations • 557

Scripting movement animations • 567

Creating dynamic cameras with Cinemachine 570

Creating camera behaviors • 571

Creating dolly tracks • 575

Creating cutscenes with Timeline 578

Creating animation clips • 578

Sequencing our intro cutscene • 581

Summary 587

Chapter 18: Optimization with Profiler, Frame Debugger, and Memory Profiler 589

Optimizing graphics 590

Introduction to graphics engines • 590

Using Frame Debugger • 591

Using batching • 593

Other optimizations • 598

Optimizing processing 602

Detecting CPU- and GPU-bound • 603

Using the CPU Usage Profiler • 605

General CPU optimization techniques • 609

Optimizing memory 613

Memory allocation and the garbage collector • 613

Using the Memory Profiler • 619

Summary 624

Chapter 19: Generating and Debugging an Executable 627

Building a project 627

Debugging the build 632

Debugging code • 633

Profiling performance • 635

Summary 638

Chapter 20: Augmented Reality in Unity 639

Using AR Foundation 640

Creating an AR Foundation project • 640

Using tracking features • 644

Building for mobile devices 651

Building for Android • 651

Building for iOS • 659

Creating a simple AR game 663

Spawning the player and enemies • 663

Coding the player and enemy behavior • 666

Summary 672

Other Books You May Enjoy 675

Index 679

Preface

I still remember that moment of my life when I was afraid of telling my parents that I was going to study game development. At that time, in my region, that was considered a childish desire by most parents, and a career with no future, but I was stubborn enough not to care and to follow my dream. Today, game development is one of the biggest industries, generating more revenue than film.

Of course, following my dream was more difficult than I thought. Anyone with the same dream as me sooner or later faces the fact that developing games is a difficult task that requires a deep level of knowledge in different areas. Sadly, most people give up due to this difficulty level, but I strongly believe that with the proper guidance and tools, you can make your career path easier. In my case, what helped me to flatten the learning curve was learning to use Unity.

Welcome to this book about Unity 2022. Here, you will learn how to use the most recent Unity features to create your first videogame in the simplest way possible nowadays. Unity is a tool that provides you with powerful but simple-to-use features to solve the most common problems in game development, such as rendering, animation, physics, sound, and effects. We will be using all these features to create a simple but complete game, learning all the nuances needed to handle Unity.

If you have read the 2021 edition of this book, you will find that not only have the contents been updated to the latest Unity and Packages versions, but also new content has been introduced in 2022, such as coverage of the new Input System.

By the end of this book, you will be able to use Unity in a way that will allow you to start studying in depth the areas of game development that you are interested in to build your career or simply create hobby games just for the joy of doing it. Unity is a versatile tool that can be used in both professional and amateur projects, and is being used every day by more and more people.

It is worth mentioning that Unity can be used not only for creating games but for any kind of interactive apps, from simple mobile apps to complex training or educative applications (known as **Serious Gaming**), using the latest technologies such as Augmented or Virtual Reality. So, even if we are creating a game here, you are starting a learning path that can end in lots of possible specializations.

Who this book is for

People with different backgrounds can take advantage of the whole book or parts of it thanks to the way it is structured. If you have basic OOP knowledge but have never created a game before, or have never created one in Unity, you will find the book a nice introduction to game development and Unity basic to advanced concepts. You could also find most parts of this book useful even if you are a seasoned Unity developer who wants to learn how to use its latest features.

On the other side, if you don't have any programming knowledge, you can also take advantage of the book, as most of the chapters don't require programming experience to learn from them. Those chapters will give you a robust skillset to start learning coding in Unity, making the process easier than before reading them, and once you learn the basics of coding, you can take advantage of the scripting chapters of this book. Also, with the introduction of Visual Scripting, you will have an alternative language if you are more comfortable with node-based scripting.

What this book covers

Chapter 1, Creating a Unity Project, teaches you how to install and set up Unity on your computer, and also how to create your first project.

Chapter 2, Editing Scenes and GameObjects, teaches you the concepts of Scenes and GameObjects, the Unity way to describe what your game world is composed of.

Chapter 3, Grayboxing with Terrain and ProBuilder, is where we will be creating our first level layout, prototyping it with the Terrain and ProBuilder Unity features.

Chapter 4, Importing and Integrating Assets, is where we will be creating our first level layout, prototyping it with the Terrain and ProBuilder Unity features.

Chapter 5, Introduction to C# and Visual Scripting, is the first programming chapter of the book. We will learn how to create our first script using C# in the Unity way, and then we will explore how to do the same with Visual Scripting, the new node-based coding language of Unity. The rest of the programming chapters will show how to code the game in both languages.

Chapter 6, Implementing Movement and Spawning, teaches you how to program the movement of your objects and how to spawn them. This chapter introduces the new Unity Input System. General programming knowledge is assumed from now on.

Chapter 7, Physics Collisions and Health System, teaches you how to configure the Physics settings of objects to detect when two of them collide and react to the collision, creating a health system, in this case.

Chapter 8, Win and Lose Condition, covers how to detect when the game should end, both when the player wins and loses.

Chapter 9, Implementing Game AI for Building Enemies, covers creating a basic AI using several Unity features for creating challenging enemies in our game.

Chapter 10, Materials and Effects with URP and Shader Graph, shows how to use one of the latest Unity render systems (Universal Render Pipeline, or URP) and how to create effects with the Shader Graph feature.

Chapter 11, Visual Effects with Particle Systems and Visual Effect Graph, teaches you how to create visual effects such as water and fire using the two main Unity tools for doing so, Particle Systems and VFX Graph, and how to make scripts that control them according to what's happening in the game.

Chapter 12, Lighting Using the Univeral Render Pipeline, looks at lighting, which is a concept big enough to have its own chapter. Here, we will deepen our knowledge of the Universal Render Pipeline, specifically its lighting capabilities.

Chapter 13, Fullscreen Effects with Postprocessing, teaches you how to add a layer of effects on top of your scene graphics using the postprocessing feature of the Universal Render Pipeline to get that film effect most modern games have today.

Chapter 14, Sound and Music Integration, covers a topic that is underestimated by most beginner developers; here we will learn how to properly add sound and music to our game, taking into consideration its impact on performance. This also covers how to script the sound.

Chapter 15, User Interface Design, looks at the User Interface (UI). Of all the graphical ways to communicate information to the user, the UI is the most direct one. We will learn how to display information in the form of text, images, and life bars using the Unity UI system, and also how to script the UI.

Chapter 16, Creating a UI with the UI Toolkit, looks at UI Toolkit, which is the successor of Canvas, the UI system we learned about in *Chapter 15, User Interface Design*. We will explore it to get ahead and be prepared for Unity's use of this HTML-based toolkit in the future.

Chapter 17, Creating Animations with Animator, Cinemachine, and Timeline, takes us further than the static scene we have created so far. In this chapter, we will start moving our characters and creating cutscenes with the latest Unity features to do so, and how to script them.

Chapter 18, Optimization with Profiler, Frame Debugger, and Memory Profiler, discusses how making our game perform well is no easy task, but is certainly needed to release it. Here, we will be learning how to profile our game's performance and tackle the most common performance issues.

Chapter 19, Generating and Debugging an Executable, teaches you how to convert your Unity project into an executable format to distribute it to other people and run it without Unity installed.

Chapter 20, Augmented Reality in Unity, teaches you how to create an AR application with Unity's AR Foundation package, one of the most recent ways to create AR applications with Unity.

To get the most out of this book

You will be developing a full project through the chapters of this book, and while you can just read the chapters, I highly recommend you practice all the steps in this project as you advance through the book, to get the experience needed to properly learn the concepts demonstrated here. The chapters are designed so you can customize the game and not create the exact game shown in the book. However, consider not deviating too much from the main idea.

The project files are split into a folder per chapter and are designed in a cumulative way, each folder having just the new files introduced by the chapter or the changed ones. This means, for example, that if a file hasn't change since Chapter 1, you won't find it in Chapter 2 onward; those chapters will just use the file introduced in Chapter 1. This allows you to see just what we changed in each chapter, easily identifying the needed changes, and if for some reason you can't finish, for example, Chapter 3, you can just continue with Chapter 4's steps on top of Chapter 3. Also note that Chapters 15 to 19 will have two versions of the files, the C# ones and the Visual Scripting ones.

Software/hardware covered in the book	OS requirements
Unity 2022.1	Windows, macOS X or Linux (any)
Visual Studio 2022 Community	Windows or macOS X (any)
XCode 13	macOS X

While we will see how to use XCode 13, is not required for most of the chapters. Also, there are alternatives to Visual Studio in Linux, like Visual Studio Code.

If you are using the digital version of this book, we advise you to type the code yourself or access the code via the GitHub repository (link available in the next section). Doing so will help you avoid any potential errors related to the copying and pasting of code.

Download the example code files

The code bundle for the book is hosted on GitHub at `https://github.com/PacktPublishing/Hands-On-Unity-2022-Game-Development-Third-Edition`. We also have other code bundles from our rich catalog of books and videos available at `https://github.com/PacktPublishing/`. Check them out!

Download the color images

We also provide a PDF file that has color images of the screenshots/diagrams used in this book. You can download it here: `https://static.packt-cdn.com/downloads/9781803236919_ColorImages.pdf`.

Conventions used

There are a number of text conventions used throughout this book.

`CodeInText`: Indicates code words in text, database table names, folder names, filenames, file extensions, pathnames, dummy URLs, user input, and Twitter handles. For example: "Set its shader to `Universal Render Pipeline/Particles/Unlit`."

Bold: Indicates a new term, an important word, or words that you see on the screen. For instance, words in menus or dialog boxes appear in the text like this. For example: "Create a new empty GameObject (**GameObject** | **Create Empty**)."

Warnings or important notes appear like this.

Tips and tricks appear like this.

Get in touch

Feedback from our readers is always welcome.

General feedback: Email `feedback@packtpub.com` and mention the book's title in the subject of your message. If you have questions about any aspect of this book, please email us at `questions@packtpub.com`.

Errata: Although we have taken every care to ensure the accuracy of our content, mistakes do happen. If you have found a mistake in this book, we would be grateful if you reported this to us. Please visit `http://www.packtpub.com/submit-errata`, click Submit Errata, and fill in the form.

Piracy: If you come across any illegal copies of our works in any form on the internet, we would be grateful if you would provide us with the location address or website name. Please contact us at `copyright@packtpub.com` with a link to the material.

If you are interested in becoming an author: If there is a topic that you have expertise in and you are interested in either writing or contributing to a book, please visit `http://authors.packtpub.com`.

Share your thoughts

Once you've read *Hands-On Unity 2022 Game Development, Third Edition*, we'd love to hear your thoughts! Scan the QR code below to go straight to the Amazon review page for this book and share your feedback.

https://packt.link/r/1803236914

Your review is important to us and the tech community and will help us make sure we're delivering excellent quality content.

Download a free PDF copy of this book

Thanks for purchasing this book!

Do you like to read on the go but are unable to carry your print books everywhere?

Is your eBook purchase not compatible with the device of your choice?

Don't worry, now with every Packt book you get a DRM-free PDF version of that book at no cost.

Read anywhere, any place, on any device. Search, copy, and paste code from your favorite technical books directly into your application.

The perks don't stop there, you can get exclusive access to discounts, newsletters, and great free content in your inbox daily

Follow these simple steps to get the benefits:

1. Scan the QR code or visit the link below

`https://packt.link/free-ebook/9781803236919`

2. Submit your proof of purchase
3. That's it! We'll send your free PDF and other benefits to your email directly

1

Creating a Unity Project

In this chapter, we will learn how to install Unity and create a project with Unity Hub, a tool that manages different Unity installations and projects, among other tasks. Unity Hub gives easy access to community blogs, forums, resources, and learning portals; it also manages your licenses, and allows you to change the building platform before opening the project on top of managing different installs and projects.

Specifically, we will examine the following concepts in this chapter:

- Installing Unity
- Creating projects

Let's start by talking about how to get Unity up and running.

Installing Unity

We'll begin with a simple but necessary first step: installing Unity. It seems like a straightforward first step, but we can discuss the proper ways to do this. In this section, we will be looking at the following concepts:

- Unity's technical requirements
- Unity versioning
- Installing Unity with Unity Hub

First, we will discuss what is necessary to run Unity on our computers.

Unity's technical requirements

To run Unity 2022, your computer will need to meet the following operating system requirements:

- If you use Windows, you need Windows 7 Service Pack 1 or greater, Windows 10, or Windows 11. Unity will run only on 64-bit versions of those systems; there is no 32-bit support unless you are willing to work with Unity versions before 2017.x, but that's outside the scope of this book.
- For Mac, you need Big Sur 11.0 to run Apple silicon versions of the editor. In any other case, you can run Intel versions of the editor from High Sierra 10.13 or superior.
- For Linux, you need exactly Ubuntu 20.04, 18.04, or CentOS 7.

Regarding the CPU, these are the requirements:

- Your CPU needs to support 64 bits
- Your CPU needs to support SSE2 (most CPUs support it)
- In the case of Macs with Apple silicon, M1 or above is needed

Finally, regarding graphics cards, these are the supported ones:

- On Windows, we need a graphics card with DirectX 10, 11, or 12 support (most modern GPUs support it)
- On Mac, any Metal-capable Intel or AMD GPU will be enough
- On Linux, OpenGL 3.2 or any superior version, or a Vulkan-compatible card from Nvidia and AMD is supported

Now that we know the requirements, let's discuss the Unity installation management system.

Unity versioning

Unity releases a new major version each year—at the time of writing, 2022.1—and during that year it receives an update with new features, which is planned to be 2022.2 at the time of writing this book. Near the end of the year or during the beginning of the next one, an **LTS (long-term support)** version is released, which will be 2022.3 for this edition of the book, marking the end of new features being added to that year's version of the engine. After that, the next year's edition of the engine is released, and the cycle repeats.

LTS versions have the benefit that they are planned to be updated bi-weekly with bug fixes for 2 years, while new major versions of Unity release. That's the reason most companies stick to LTS versions of the engine: because of its stability and long-term support. In this book we will be using 2022.1 just to explore the new features of the engine, but consider sticking to LTS versions when developing commercial game titles.

Considering this, you may need to have several versions of Unity installed in case you work on different projects made with different versions. You may be wondering why you can't just use the latest version of Unity for every project, but there are some problems with that.

In newer versions of Unity, there are usually lots of changes to how the engine works, so you may need to rework lots of pieces of the game to upgrade it, including third-party plugins. It can take lots of time to upgrade the whole project, and that can push the release date back. Maybe you need a specific feature that comes with an update that will help you. In such a case, the cost of upgrading may be worthwhile. For projects that are maintained and updated for several years, developers are used to updates only to the latest LTS versions of the editor, although this policy may vary from case to case.

Managing different projects made with different Unity versions, and installing and updating new Unity releases, all used to be a huge hassle. Thus, **Unity Hub** was created to help us with this, and it has become the default way to install Unity. Despite this, it is not necessary for installing Unity, but we will keep things simple for now and use it. Let's look closer into it.

Installing Unity with Unity Hub

Unity Hub is a small piece of software that we will install before installing Unity. It centralizes the management of all your Unity projects and installations. You can get it from the official Unity website. The steps to download it change frequently, but at the time of writing this book, you need to do the following:

1. Go to `unity.com`.
2. Click on the **Get started** button, as shown in the following screenshot:

Figure 1.1: The Get started button on Unity's website

3. Click on the **Student and hobbyist** tab; then, under the **Personal** section, click on the **Get started** button, as illustrated in the following screenshot:

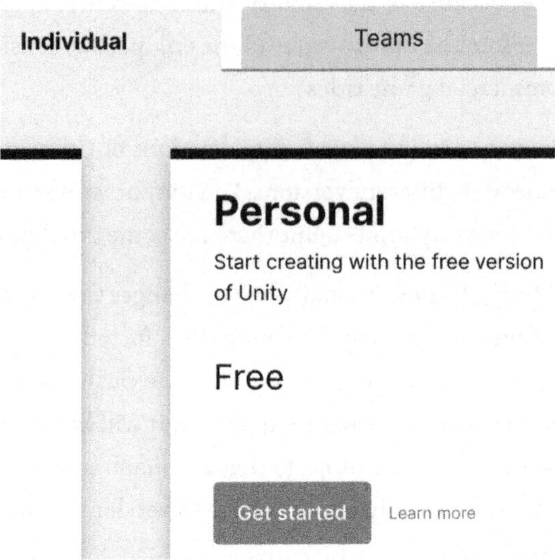

Figure 1.2: Choosing an individual/free license

4. Scroll down to the section saying **1. Download the Unity Hub** and click on the **Download** button according to your operating system. For Windows, click **Download for Windows**, and for Mac, click on **Download for Mac**. For Linux, there is an **Instructions for Linux** button with further info about how to install on that platform, but we won't be covering Unity in Linux in this book:

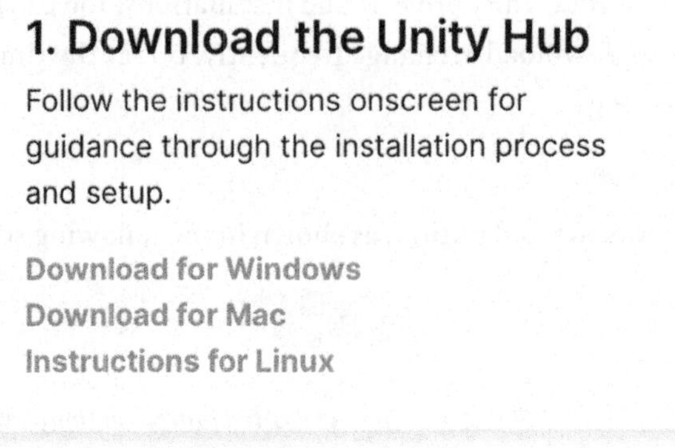

Figure 1.3: Starting the download

5. Execute the downloaded installer.
6. Follow the instructions of the installer, which will mostly be clicking **Next** all the way to the end.

Now that we have Unity Hub installed, we must use it to install a specific Unity version. You can do this with the following steps:

1. Start **Unity Hub**.
2. If prompted to install a Unity version and/or create a license, please skip these steps with the corresponding **Skip** buttons (which may vary according to the Unity Hub version). This way to install Unity and licenses is only available the first time you run Unity Hub, but we are going to learn the way to do this that works after the first time.
3. Log in to your account by clicking on the "person" icon at the top-left part of the window and selecting **Sign in**:

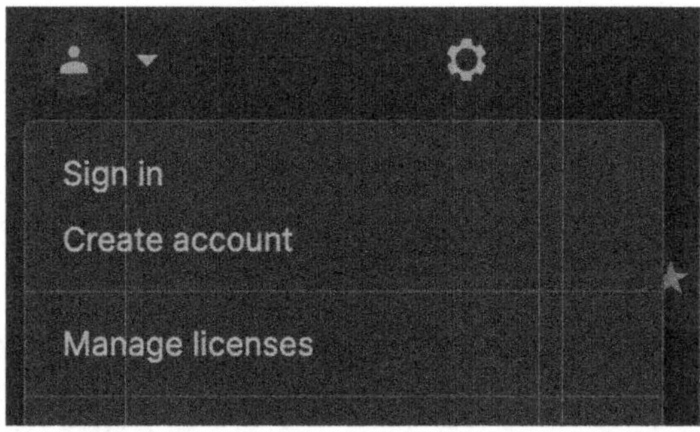

Figure 1.4: Signing into Unity Hub

4. Here, you also have the option to create a Unity account if you haven't already, as illustrated in the link labeled **create one** that appears in the Unity login prompt in the following screenshot:

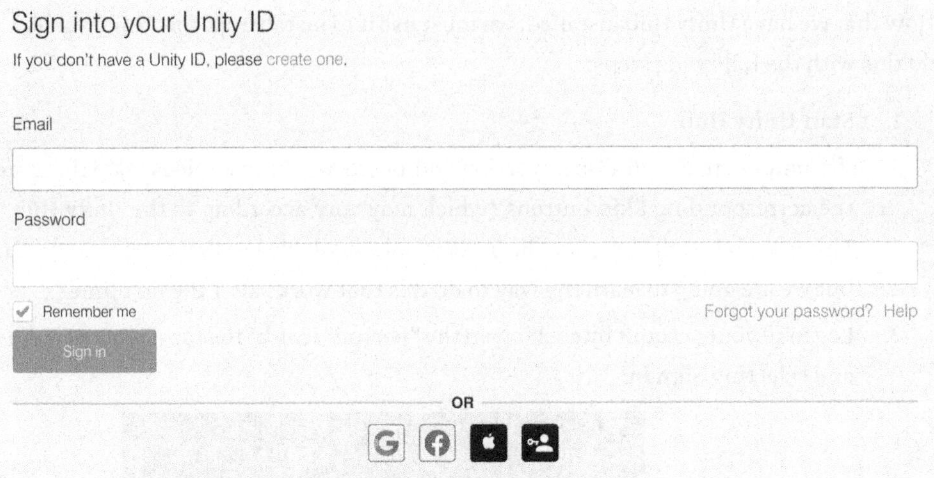

Figure 1.5: Logging into Unity Hub

5. Follow the steps on the installer and then you should see a screen like the one in the next image. If it is not the same, try clicking the **Learn** button at the top-left part of the screen:

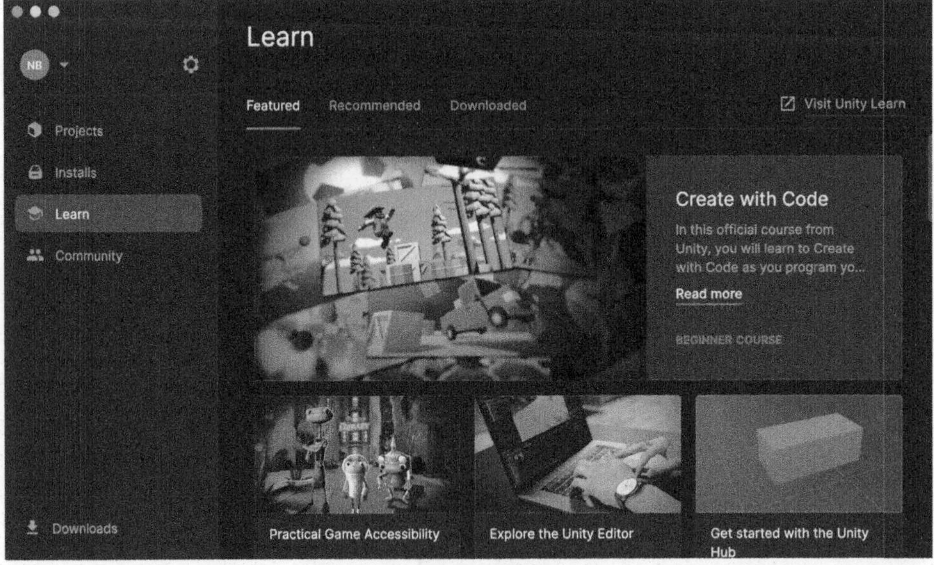

Figure 1.6: The Unity Hub window

6. Click on the **Installs** button and check if you have **Unity 2022** listed there.
7. If not, press the **Install Editor** button at the top-right corner. This will show a list of Unity versions that can be installed from here:

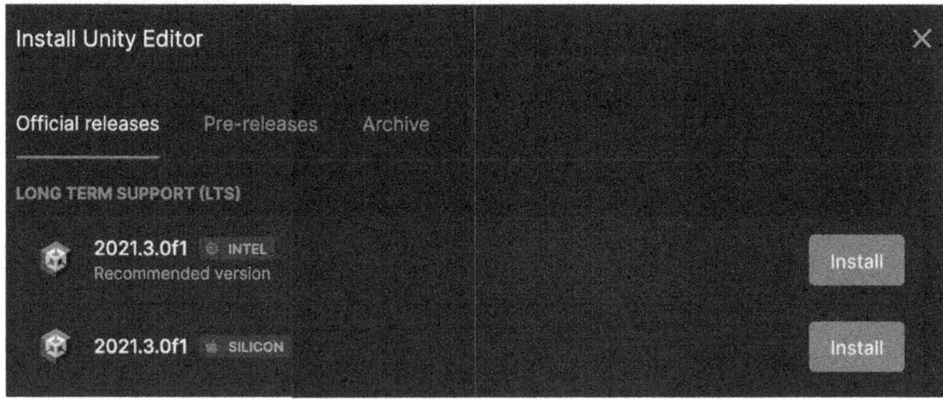

Figure 1.7: Unity versions available to install

8. You will see three tabs here. **Official releases** contains the latest versions of each major release already released. **Pre-releases** contains alpha and beta releases of Unity, so you can participate in these programs and test new features before they are officially released. **Archive** contains a link to the **Unity Download Archive** that contains every single Unity version released. For example, the official release at the moment of writing this is 2022.1.20, but the project is being developed in 2022.1.14, so you can install the correct version from the archive.
9. Locate Unity 2022.1 in the **Official releases** tab.
10. Click on the **Install** button at the right of Unity 2022.1.XXf1, where XX will vary according to the latest available version. At the moment of writing this book we are using 2022.1.14f1. You might need to scroll down to find this version. If not present, install the latest 2022 version available (for example, 2022.2.XX or 2022.3.XX). Newer versions might vary of what is seen in the book, if you find the images of the book being too different consider looking for Unity 2022.1.14 in the archive.
11. A modules selection window will show up. Make sure the **Visual Studio** feature is checked. While this program is not needed to work in Unity, we will be using it later in the book. If you already have a C# IDE installed, feel free to skip it.

12. Now, click the **Continue** button:

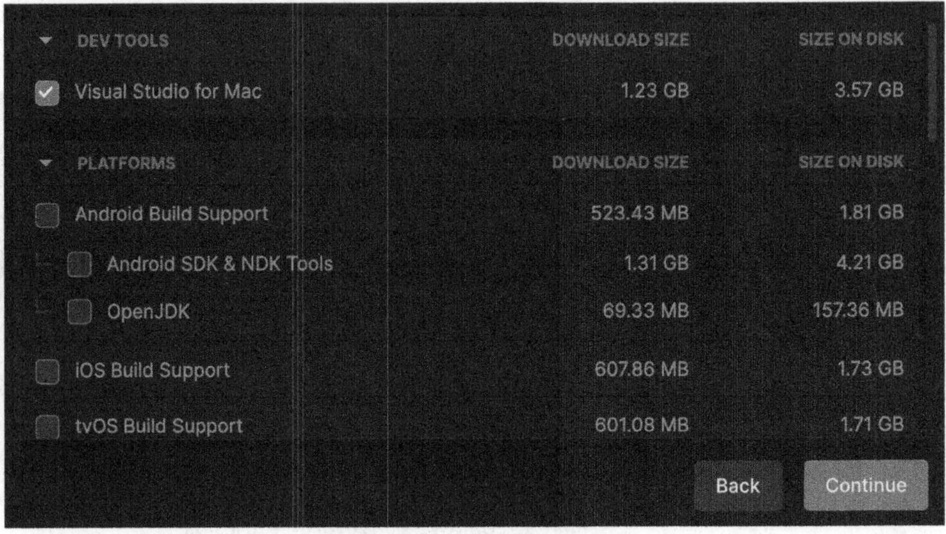

Figure 1.8: Selecting Visual Studio

13. Accept Visual Studio's terms and conditions and then click **Install**:

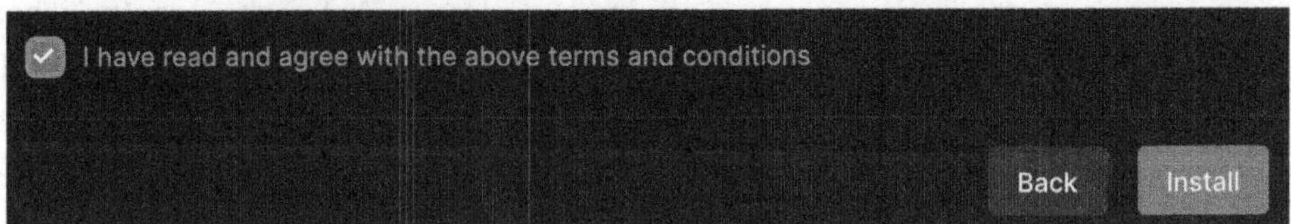

Figure 1.9: Accepting Visual Studio's terms and conditions

It is important to note that Visual Studio is the program we will use in *Chapter 5, Introduction to Scripting with C# and Visual Scripting*, to create our code. We do not need the other Unity features right now, but you can go back later and install them if you need them.

14. You will see the selected Unity version downloading and installing. Wait for this to finish. If you don't see it, click the **Downloads** button to reopen it:

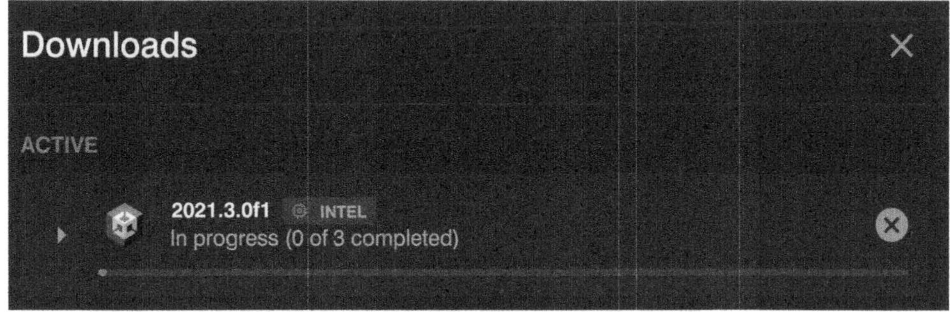

Figure 1.10: Currently active Unity Hub downloads

15. If you decided to install Visual Studio, after Unity has finished installing, the Visual Studio Installer will automatically execute. It will download an installer that will download and install Visual Studio Community:

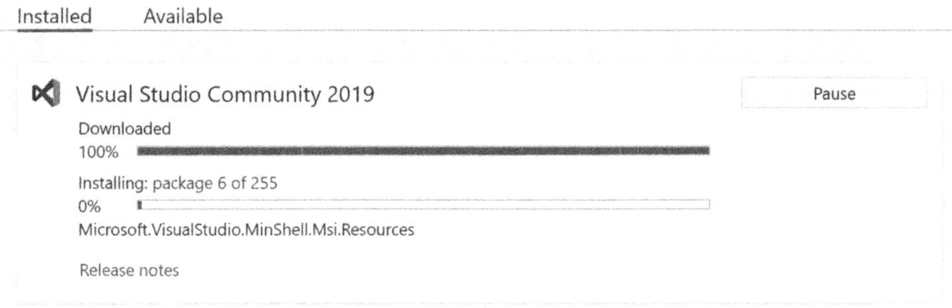

Figure 1.11: Installing Visual Studio

16. To confirm everything worked, you must see the selected Unity version in the list of **Installs** of Unity Hub:

Figure 1.12: Available Unity versions

Now, before using Unity, we need to acquire and install a free license to make it work by doing the following:

1. Click the **Manage licenses** button at the top-right corner of the Unity Hub. If you don't see it, click your account icon at the top-left corner and click **Manage licenses** there:

Figure 1.13: The Manage licenses button to press in order to acquire a free license

2. Click the **Add** button in the **Licenses** list window:

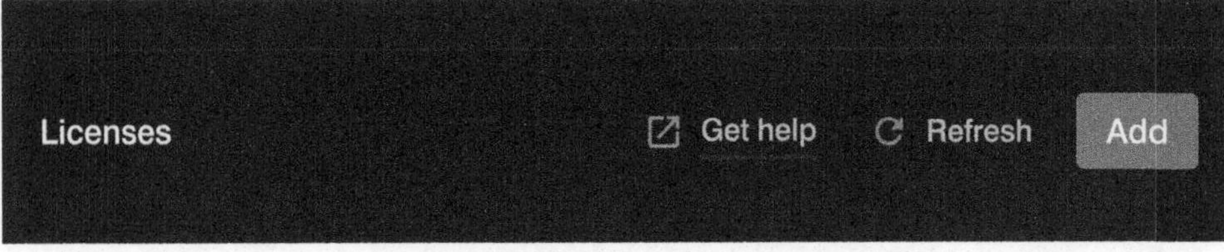

Figure 1.14: The Licenses list window's Add button

3. Click the **Get a free personal license** button:

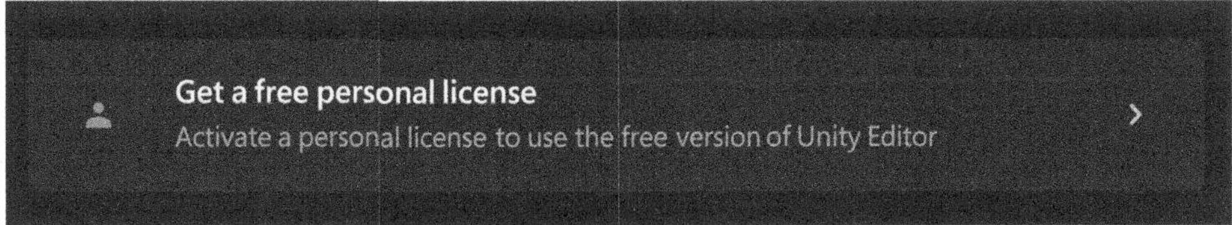

Figure 1.15: Option to get a free personal license

4. Read and accept the terms and conditions if you agree with them by clicking the **Agree and get personal edition license** button:

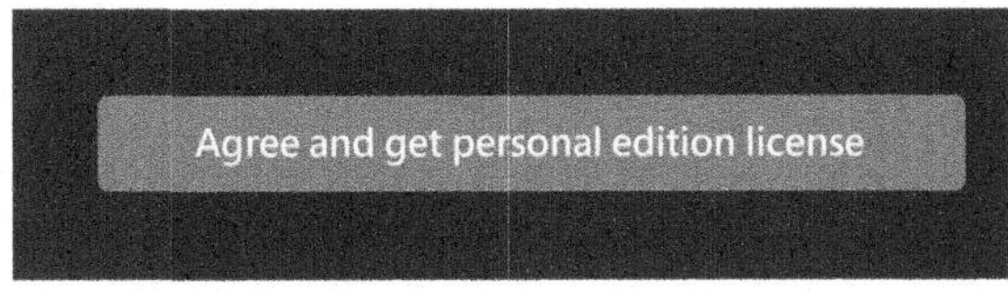

Figure 1.16: The button to accept the terms and conditions

Remember that the preceding steps may be different in new Unity Hub versions, so just try to follow the flow that Unity designed—most of the time, it is intuitive.

Now it is time to create a project using Unity.

Creating projects

Now that we have Unity installed, we can start creating our game. To do so, we first need to create a project, which is basically a folder containing all the files that your game will be composed of. These files are called **assets** and there are different types of them, such as images, audio, 3D models, script files, and so on. In this section, we will see how to manage a project, addressing the following concepts:

- Creating a project
- Project structure

Let's learn first how to create a blank project to start developing our project.

Creating a project

As with Unity installations, we will use the Unity Hub to manage projects. We need to follow these next steps to create one:

1. Open the Unity Hub and click on the **Projects** button, and then click on **New project**:

Figure 1.17: Creating a new project in Unity Hub

2. Pick the **3D (URP)** template as we will be creating a 3D game with simple graphics, prepared to run on every device Unity can be executed on, so the **Universal Render Pipeline** (or **URP**) is the better choice for that. In *Chapter 10, Materials and Effects with URP and Shader Graph*, we will be discussing exactly why.
3. If you see a **Download template** button, click it; if not, that means you already have the template:

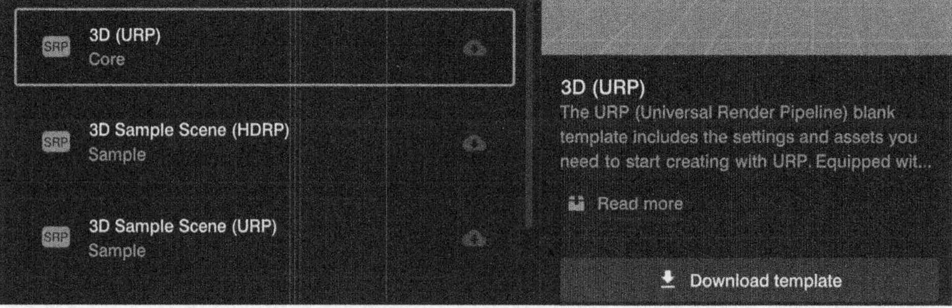

Figure 1.18: Downloading the 3D URP template

4. Choose a **Project name** and a **Location**, and click **Create project**:

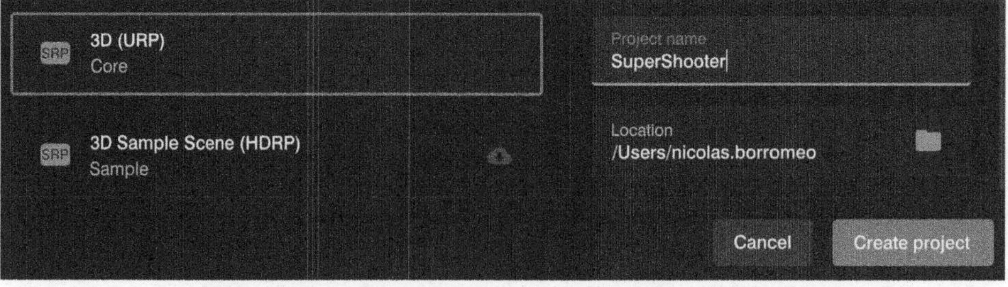

Figure 1.19: Selecting the Universal Render Pipeline template

5. Unity will create and automatically open the project. This can take a while, but after that you will see a window similar to the one in the following image. You might see the dark-themed editor instead, but for better clarity we will use the light theme throughout the book. Feel free to keep the dark theme:

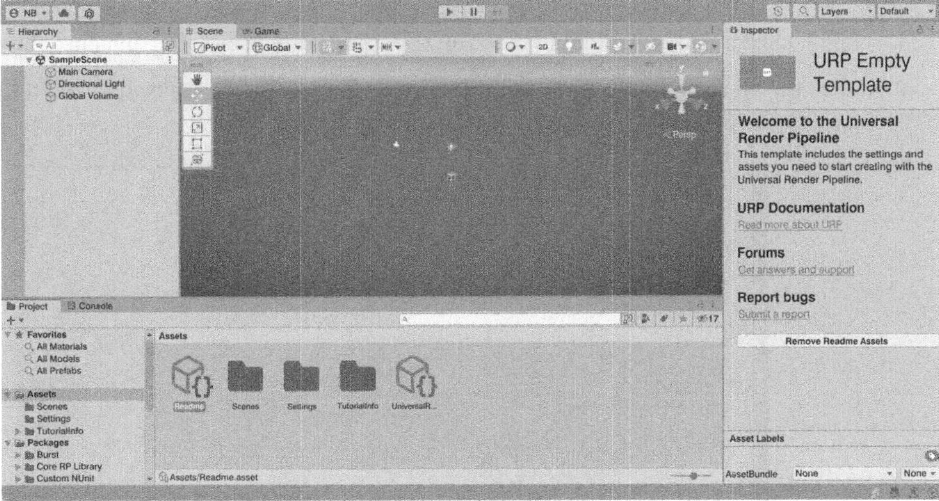

Figure 1.20: The Unity Editor window

6. Close the window, then go back to Unity Hub and pick the project from the list to open it again:

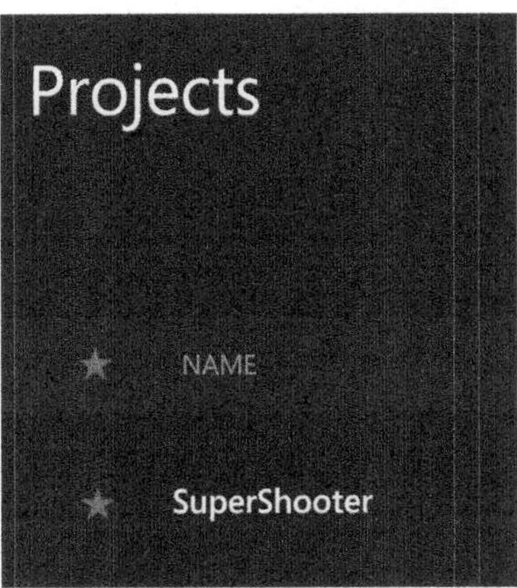

Figure 1.21: Reopening the project

Now that we have created the project, let's explore its structure.

Project structure

We have just opened Unity, but we won't start using it until the next chapter. Now, it's time to see how the project folder structure is composed. To do so, we need to open the folder in which we created the project. If you don't remember where this is, you can do the following:

1. Right-click the **Assets** folder in the **Project** panel, located at the bottom part of the editor.
2. Click the **Show in Explorer** option (if you are using a Mac, the option is called **Reveal in Finder**). The following screenshot illustrates this:

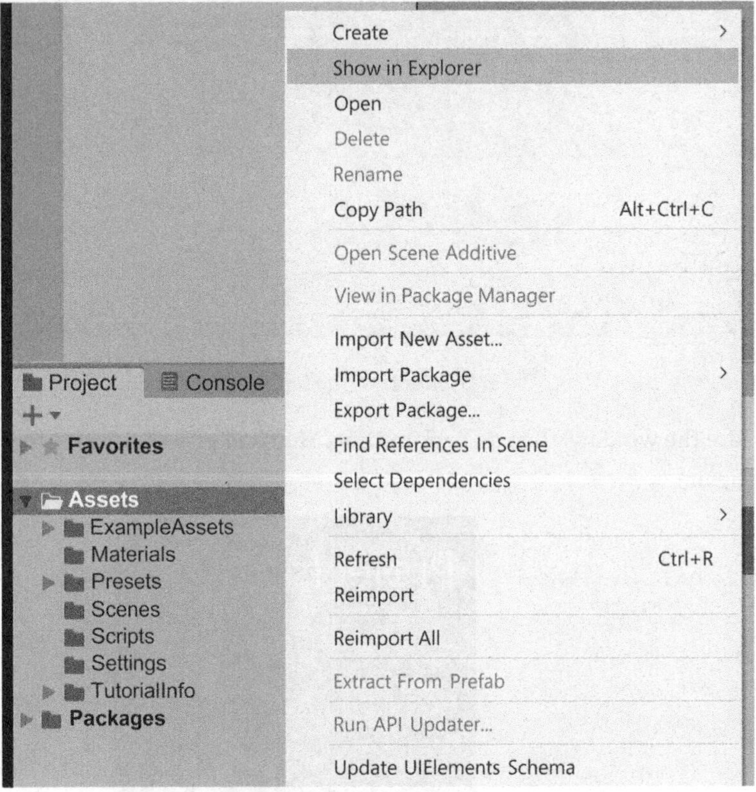

Figure 1.22: Opening the project folder in Explorer

3. Then, you will see a folder structure similar to this one (some files or folders may vary):

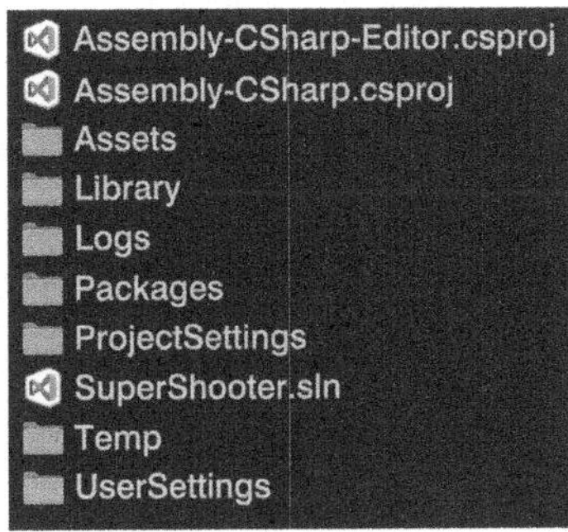

Figure 1.23: Unity project folder structure

If you want to move this project to another PC or send it to a colleague, you can just compress all those files and send it to them as a ZIP file, but not all the folders are necessary all of the time. The important folders are **Assets**, **Packages**, and **ProjectSettings**. **Assets** will hold all the files we will create and use for our game, so this is a must. We will also configure different Unity systems to tailor the engine to our game; all the settings related to this are in the **ProjectSettings** and **UserSettings** folders. Finally, we will install different Unity modules or packages to expand its functionality, so the **Packages** folder will hold which ones we are using.

It's not necessary to copy the rest of the folders if you need to move the project elsewhere or add it to any versioning system, but let's at least discuss what the **Library** folder is, especially considering it's usually a huge size. Unity needs to convert the files we will use to its own format in order to operate, and an example would be audio and graphics. Unity supports **MPEG Audio Layer 3** (**MP3**), **Waveform Audio File Format** (**WAV**), **Portable Network Graphics** (**PNG**), and **Joint Photographic Experts Group** (**JPG**) files (and much more), but prior to using them, they need to be converted to Unity's internal formats, a process called **Importing Assets**. Those converted files will be in the **Library** folder. If you copy the project without that folder, Unity will simply take the original files in the **Assets** folder and recreate the **Library** folder entirely. This process can take time, and the bigger the project, the more time involved.

Keep in mind that you want to have all the folders Unity created while you are working on the project, so don't delete any of them while you work on it, but if you need to move an entire project, you now know exactly what you need to take with you.

Summary

In this chapter, we reviewed how the Unity versioning system works. We also saw how to install and manage different Unity versions using Unity Hub. Finally, we created and managed multiple projects with the same tool. We will use Unity Hub a lot, so it is important to know how to use it initially. Now, we are prepared to dive into the Unity Editor.

In the next chapter, we will start learning the basic Unity tools to author our first level prototype.

Join us on Discord!

Read this book alongside other users, Unity game development experts, and the author himself.

Ask questions, provide solutions to other readers, chat with the author via Ask Me Anything sessions, and much more.

Scan the QR code or visit the link to join the community.

`https://packt.link/handsonunity22`

2

Editing Scenes and Game Objects

In this chapter, we will develop some base knowledge of Unity in order to edit a project, and learn how to use several Unity editor windows to manipulate our first scene and its objects. We will also learn how an object, or GameObject, is created and composed, and how to manage complex scenes with multiple objects using Hierarchies and Prefabs. Finally, we will review how we can properly save all our work to continue working on it later.

Specifically, we will examine the following concepts in this chapter:

- Manipulating scenes
- GameObjects and components
- Object Hierarchies
- Prefabs
- Saving scenes and projects

Manipulating scenes

A **scene** is one of the several types of files (also known as **assets**) in our project. A “scene” can be used for different things according to the type of project, but the most common use case is to separate your game into whole sections, the most common ones being the following:

- Main menu
- Level 1, Level 2, Level 3, etc.

- Victory screen and lose screen
- Splash screen and loading screen

In this section, we will cover the following concepts related to scenes:

- The purpose of a scene
- The Scene View
- Adding our first GameObject to the scene
- Navigating the Scene View
- Manipulating GameObjects

So, let's take a look at each of these concepts.

The purpose of a scene

The idea of separating your game into scenes is so that Unity can process and load just the data needed for the scene. Let's say you are in the main menu; in such a case, you will have only the textures, music, and objects that the main menu needs loaded in **random-access memory (RAM)**, the device's main memory. In that case, there's no need for your game to have loaded the Level 10 boss if you don't need it right now. That's why loading screens exist, just to fill the time between unloading the assets needed in one scene and loading the assets needed in another. Maybe you are thinking that open-world games such as *Grand Theft Auto* don't have loading screens while you roam around in the world, but they are actually loading and unloading chunks of the world in the background as you move, and those chunks are different scenes that are designed to be connected to each other.

The difference between the Main Menu and a regular level scene is the objects (also known as **GameObjects** in the Unity lingo) they have. In a menu, you will find objects such as backgrounds, music, buttons, and logos, and in a level, you will have the player, enemies, platforms, health boxes, and so on. So, the meaning of your scene depends on what GameObjects are put into it. But how can we create a scene? Let's start with the Scene View.

The Scene View

When you open a Unity project, you will see the Unity editor. It will be composed of several windows or **panels**, each one helping you to change different aspects of your game. In this chapter, we will be looking at the windows that help you create scenes. The Unity editor is shown in the following screenshot:

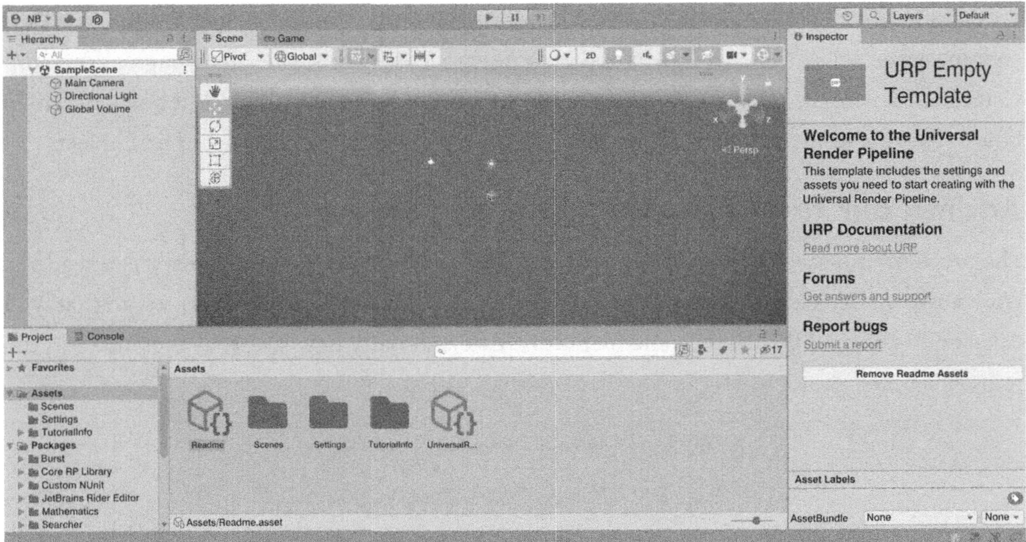

Figure 2.1: The Unity editor

If you have ever programmed any kind of application before, you are probably used to having a starting function such as **Main**, where you start writing code to create several objects needed for your app. If we are talking about games, you probably create all the objects for the scene there. The problem with this approach is that in order to ensure all objects are created properly, you will need to run the program to see the results, and if something is misplaced, you will need to manually change the coordinates of the object, which is a slow and painful process. Luckily, in Unity, we have the Scene View, an example of which is shown in the following screenshot:

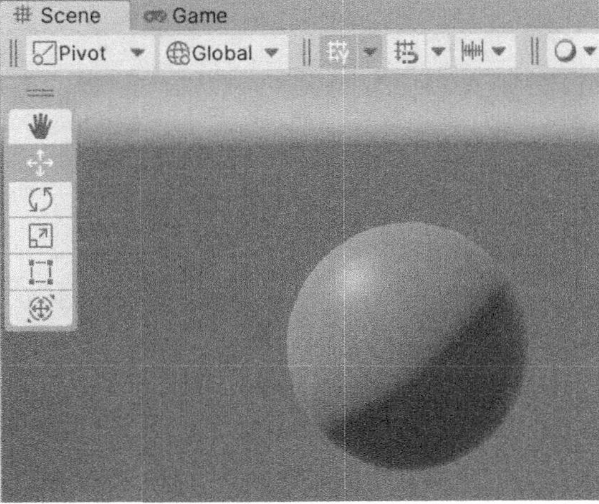

Figure 2.2: The Scene View

This window is an implementation of the classic **WYSIWYG (What You See Is What You Get)** concept. Here, you can create objects and place them all over the scene, all through a scene pre-visualization where you can see how the scene will look when you hit **Play**. But before learning how to use this scene, we need to have an object in the scene, so let's create our first object.

Adding our first GameObject to the scene

The project template we chose when creating the project comes with a blank scene ready to work with, but let's create our own empty scene to see how to do it ourselves. To do that, you can simply use the **File** | **New Scene** menu to create an empty new scene, as illustrated in the following screenshot:

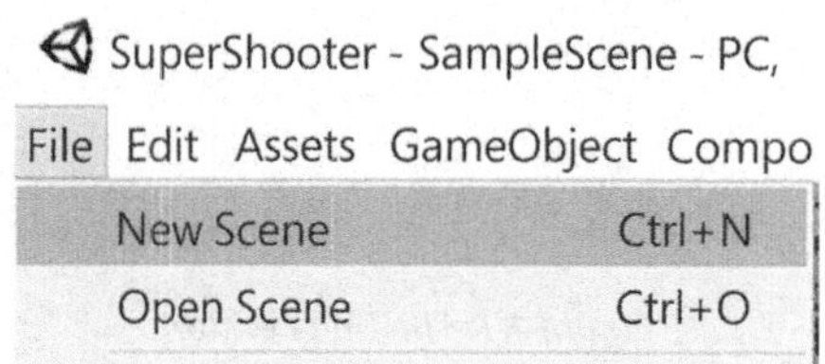

Figure 2.3: Creating a new scene

After clicking **New Scene**, you will see a window to pick a scene template; here, select the **Basic (URP)** template. A template defines which objects the new scene will have, and in this case, our template will come with a basic light and a camera, which will be useful for the scene we want to create. Once selected, just click the **Create** button:

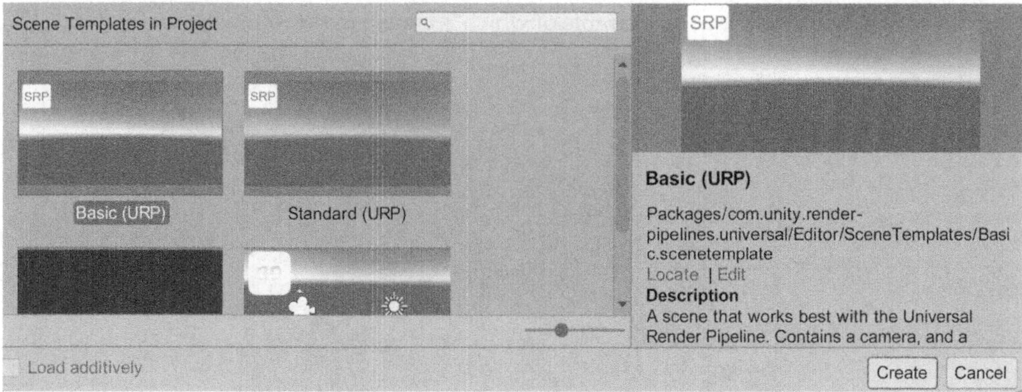

Figure 2.4: Selecting the scene template

Now that we have our empty scene, let's add GameObjects to it. We will learn several ways of creating GameObjects throughout the book, but for now, let's start using some basic templates Unity provides us. In order to create them, we will need to open the **GameObject** menu at the top of the Unity window, and it will show us several template categories, such as **3D Object**, **2D Object**, **Effects**, and so on, as illustrated in the following screenshot:

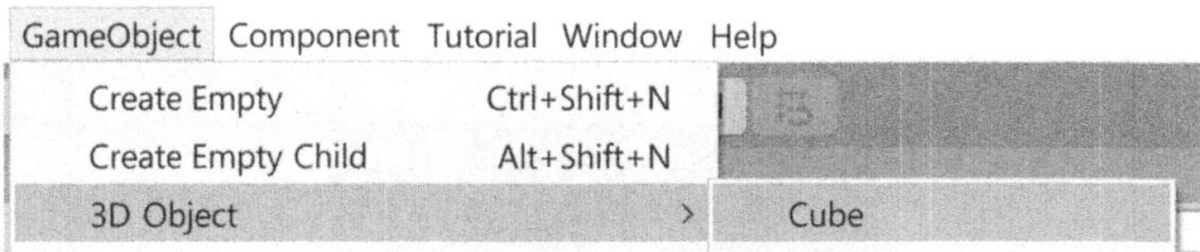

Figure 2.5: Creating a cube

Under the **3D Object** category, we will see several 3D primitives such as **Cube**, **Sphere**, **Cylinder**, and so on, and while using them is not as exciting as using beautiful, downloaded 3D models, remember that we are only prototyping our level at the moment. This is called **gray-boxing**, which means that we will use lots of prototyping primitive shapes to model our level so that we can quickly test it and see if our idea is good enough to start the complex work of converting it to a final version.

I recommend you pick the **Cube** object to start because it is a versatile shape that can represent lots of objects. So, now that we have a scene with an object to edit, the first thing we need to learn to do with the Scene View is to navigate through the scene.

Navigating the Scene View

In order to manipulate a scene, we need to learn how to move through it to view the results from different perspectives. There are several ways to navigate the scene, so let's start with the most common one, the first-person view. This view allows you to move through the scene using a first-person-shooter-like navigation, using the mouse and the *WASD* keys. To navigate like this, you will need to press and hold the right mouse button, and while doing so, you can:

- Move the mouse to rotate the camera around its current position
- Press the *WASD* keys to move the position of the camera, always holding the right click
- You can also press *Shift* to move faster
- Press the *Q* and *E* keys to move up and down

Another common way of moving is to click an object to select it (the selected object will have an orange outline), and then press the *F* key to focus on it, making the Scene View camera immediately move into a position where we can look at that object more closely. After that, we can press and hold the left *Alt* key on Windows, or *Option* on Mac, along with the left mouse click, to finally start moving the mouse and "orbit" around the object. This will allow you to see the focused object from different angles to check every part of it is properly placed, as demonstrated in the following screenshot:

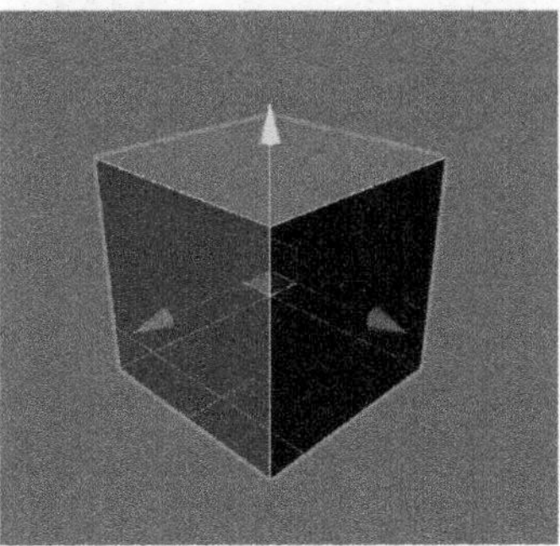

Figure 2.6: Selecting an object

Now that we can move freely through the scene, we can start using the Scene View to manipulate GameObjects.

Manipulating GameObjects

Another use of the **Scene** view is to manipulate the locations of the objects. In order to do so, we first need to select an object, and then press the **Transform** tool in the top-left corner of the Scene View. You can also press the *Y* key on the keyboard once an object is selected to do the same:

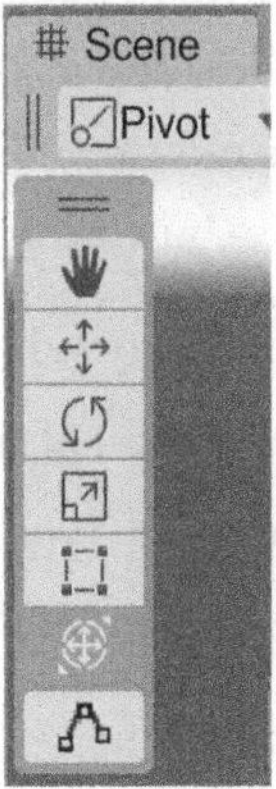

Figure 2.7: The transformation tool

This will show what is called the **Transform** gizmo over the selected object. A **gizmo** is a visual tool overlaid on top of the selected object, used to modify different aspects of it. In the case of the **Transform Gizmo,** it allows us to change the position, rotation, and scale of the object, as illustrated in *Figure 2.8*. Don't worry if you don't see the cube-shaped arrows outside the sphere—we will be enabling them in a moment:

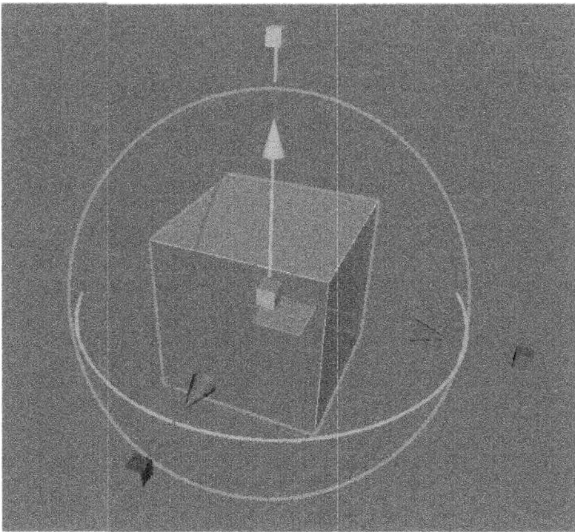

Figure 2.8: The Transform gizmo

Let's start translating the object, which is accomplished by dragging the red, green, and blue arrows inside the gizmo's sphere. While you do this, the object will be moving along the selected axis. An interesting concept to explore here is the meaning of the colors of these arrows. If you pay attention to the top-right area of the Scene View, you will see an axis gizmo that serves as a reminder of those colors' meaning, as illustrated in the following screenshot:

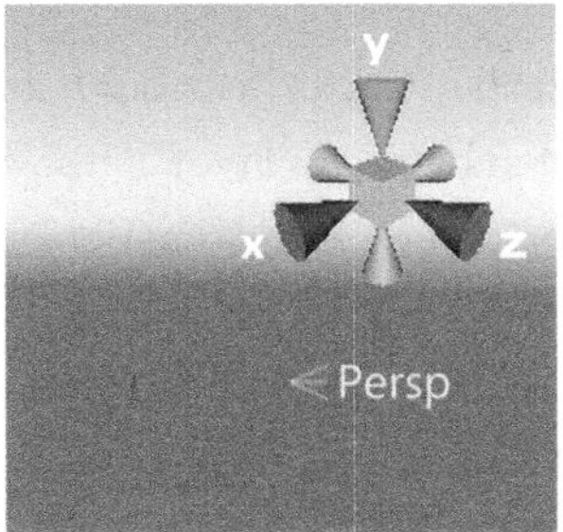

Figure 2.9: The axis gizmo

Computer graphics use the classic 3D **Cartesian coordinate system** to represent objects' locations. The red color is associated with the x axis of the object, green with the y axis, and blue with the z axis.

But what does each axis mean? If you are used to another 3D authoring program, this can be different, but in Unity, the *z* axis represents the **Forward Vector**, which means that the arrow is pointing along the front of the object; the *x* axis is the **Right Vector**, and the *y* axis represents the **Up Vector**.

These directions are known as **local** coordinates, and that's because every object can be rotated differently, meaning each object can be pointing its forward, up, and right vectors elsewhere according to its orientation. The local coordinates will make more sense when used later in the *Object Hierarchies* section of the chapter, so bear with me on that, but it's worth discussing **global** coordinates now. The idea is to have a single origin point (the zero point) with a single set of forward, right, and up axes that are common across the scene. This way, when we say the object has a global position of `5,0,0`, we know that we are referring to a position 5 meters along the global *x*-axis, starting from the global zero position. The global axes are the ones you see in the top-right axis gizmos previously mentioned.

In order to be sure that we are working with local coordinates, meaning we will move the object along its local axes, make sure the **Local** mode is activated in the Scene View, as shown in the following screenshot:

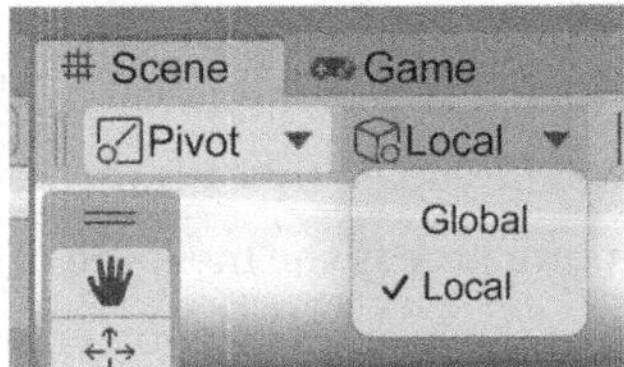

Figure 2.10: Switching pivot and local coordinates

If the right button says **Global** instead of **Local**, just click it and select **Local** from the dropdown options. By the way, try to keep the left button as **Pivot**. If it says **Center**, click and select **Pivot**. The pivot of the object is not necessarily its center, and that depends entirely on the 3D model we are using, where the author of it will specify where the object rotation center is located. For example, a car could have its pivot in the middle of its back wheels, so when we rotate, it will respect the real car's rotation center. Editing based on the object's pivot will simplify our understanding of how rotating via C# scripts will work later in *Chapter 6, Implementing Movement and Spawning*. Also, now that we have enabled **Local** coordinates, you should see the cube-shaped arrows seen in *Figure 2.8*; we will use them in a moment to scale the cube.

I know—we are editing a cube, so there is no clear front or right side, but when you work with real 3D models such as cars and characters, they will certainly have those sides, and they must be properly aligned with those axes. If by any chance in the future you import a car into Unity and the front of the car is pointing along the *x* axis, you will need to make that model aligned along the *z* axis because the code that we will create to move our object will rely on that convention (but let's keep that for later).

Now, let's use this **Transform** gizmo to rotate the object using the three colored circles around it. If you click and drag, for example, the red circle, you will rotate the object along the *x* axis. If you want to rotate the object horizontally, based on the color-coding we previously discussed, you will probably pick the *x* axis—the one that is used to move horizontally—but, sadly, that's wrong. A good way to look at the rotation is like the accelerator of a motorcycle: you need to take it and roll it. If you rotate the *x* axis like this, you will rotate the object up and down. So, in order to rotate horizontally, you would need to use the green circle or the *y* axis. The process is illustrated in the following screenshot:

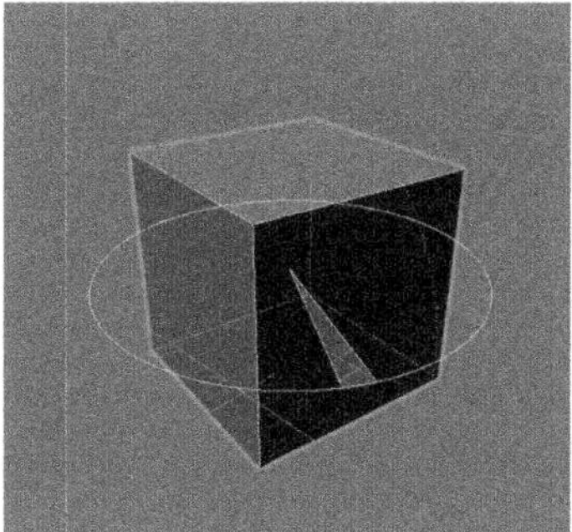

Figure 2.11: Rotating an object

Finally, we have scaling, and we have two ways to accomplish that, one of them being through the gray cube at the center of the **Transform** gizmo shown in *Figure 2.8*. This allows us to change the size of the object by clicking and dragging that cube. Now, as we want to prototype a simple level, sometimes we want to stretch the cube to create, for example, a column, or a flat floor, and here's where the second way comes in.

If you click and drag the colored cubes in front of the translation arrows instead of the gray one in the center, you will see how our cube is stretched over those axes, allowing you to change the shape of the object. If you don't see those cube-shaped arrows, remember to enable **Local** coordinates as stated earlier in this section.

The process to stretch is illustrated in the following screenshot:

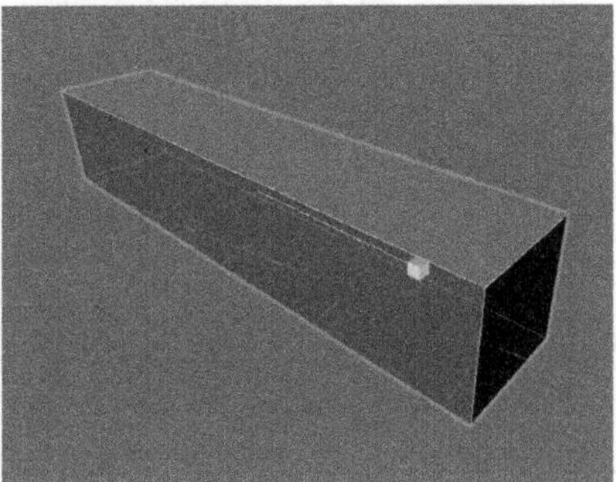

Figure 2.12: Scaling an object

Remember you can also use the gray cube in the middle to scale all axes at the same time if desired, also known as **uniform scaling**, the same gray cube we had in the **Transform** gizmo.

Finally, something to consider here is that several objects can have the same scale values but have different sizes, given how they were originally designed. **Scale** is a multiplier we can apply to the original size of the object, so a building and a car both with scale 1 makes perfect sense; the relative size of one against the other seems correct. The main takeaway here is that scale is not size, but a way to multiply it.

Consider that scaling objects is usually a bad practice in many cases. In the final versions of your scene, you will use models with the proper size and scale, and they will be designed in a modular way so that you can plug them one next to the other. If you scale them, several bad things can happen, such as textures being stretched and becoming pixelated, and modules that no longer plug properly. There are some exceptions to this rule, such as placing lots of instances of the same tree in a forest and changing its scale slightly to simulate variation. Also, in the case of gray-boxing, it is perfectly fine to take cubes and change the scale to create floors, walls, ceilings, columns, and so on, because in the end, those cubes will be replaced with real 3D models.

Here's a challenge! Create a room composed of a floor, three regular walls, and the fourth wall with a hole for a door (three cubes), and no need for a roof. In the next image you can see how it should look:

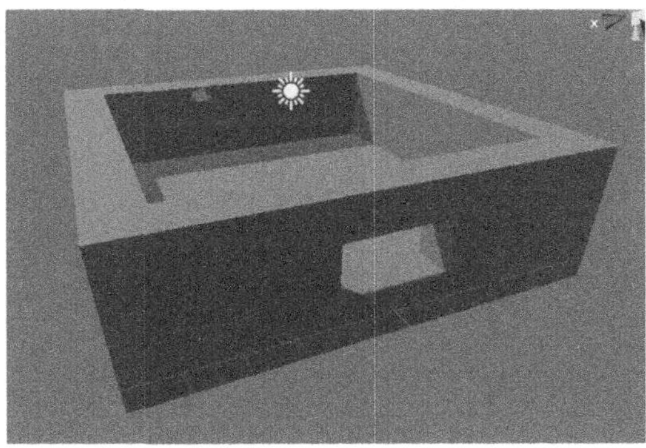

Figure 2.13: Room task finished

Now that we can edit an object's location, let's see how we can edit all its other aspects.

GameObjects and components

We talked about our project being composed of **assets** (the project's files), and that a scene (which is a specific type of asset) is composed of GameObjects; so, how can we create an object? Through a composition of **components**.

In this section, we will cover the following concepts related to components:

- Understanding components
- Manipulating components

Let's start by discussing what a component is.

Understanding components

A **component** is one of several pieces that make up a GameObject; each one is in charge of different features of the object. There are several components that Unity already includes that solve different tasks, such as playing a sound, rendering a mesh, applying physics, and so on; however, even though Unity has a large number of components, we will eventually need to create custom components sooner or later.

In the next image you can see what Unity shows us when we select a GameObject:

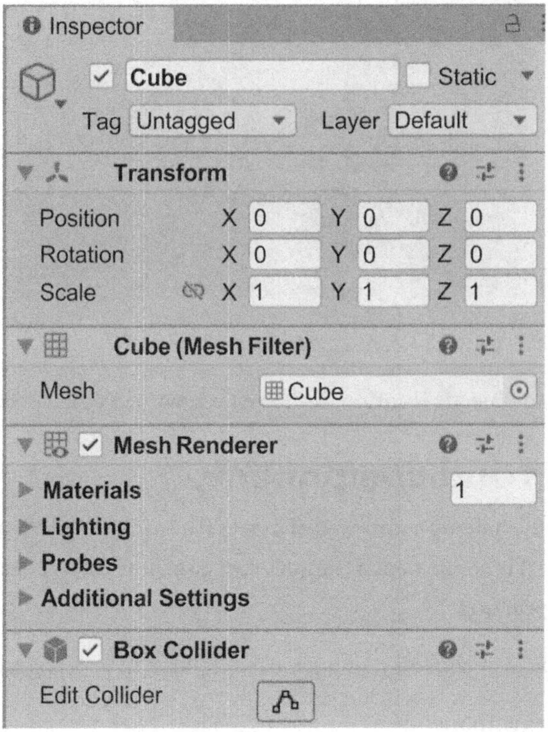

Figure 2.14: The Inspector panel

In the previous screenshot, we can see the **Inspector** panel. If we needed to guess what it does right now, we could say it shows all the properties of objects selected either via the Hierarchy or the Scene View, and allows us to configure those options to change the behavior of the object (i.e. the position and rotation, if it will project shadows or not, and so on). That is true, but we are missing a key element: those properties don't belong to the object; they belong to the components of the object. We can see some titles in bold before a group of properties, such as **Transform** and **Box Collider**, and so on. Those are the components of the object.

In this case, our object has a **Transform**, a **Mesh Filter**, a **Mesh Renderer**, and a **Box Collider** component, so let's review each one of those.

Transform just holds the position, rotation, and scale of the object, and by itself it does nothing—it's just a point in our game—but as we add components to the object, that position starts to have more meaning. That's because some components will interact with **Transform** and other components, each one affecting the other.

An example of that would be the case of **Mesh Filter** and **Mesh Renderer**, both of those being in charge of rendering a 3D model. **Mesh Renderer** will render the 3D model, also known as mesh, specified by the **Mesh Filter** in the position specified in the **Transform** component, so **Mesh Renderer** needs to get data from those other components and can't work without them.

Another example would be the **Box Collider**. This represents the physics shape of the object, so when the physics calculates collisions between objects, it checks if that shape is colliding with other shapes based on the position specified in the **Transform** component.

We will explore rendering and physics later in the book, but the takeaway from this section is that a GameObject is a collection of components, each component adding a specific behavior to our object, and each one interacting with the others to accomplish the desired task. To further reinforce this, let's see how we can convert a cube into a sphere that will fall due to gravity applied via physics.

Manipulating components

The tool to edit an object's components is the **Inspector**. It not only allows us to change the properties of our components but also lets us add and remove components. In this case, we want to convert a cube to a sphere, so we need to change several aspects of those components.

We can start by changing the visual shape of the object, so we need to change the rendered model or **mesh**. The component that specifies the mesh to be rendered is the **Mesh Filter** component. If we look at it, we can see a **Mesh** property that says **Cube**, with a little circle and a dot on its right:

Figure 2.15: The Mesh filter component

If you don't see a particular property, such as the **Mesh** we just mentioned, try to click the triangle at the left of the component's name. Doing this will expand and collapse all the component's properties.

If we click the button with a circle and a dot inside, the one at the right of the **Mesh** property, the **Select Mesh** window will pop up, allowing us to pick several **mesh** options. In this case, select the **Sphere** mesh. In the future, we will add more 3D models to our project so that the window will have more options.

The mesh selector is shown in the following screenshot:

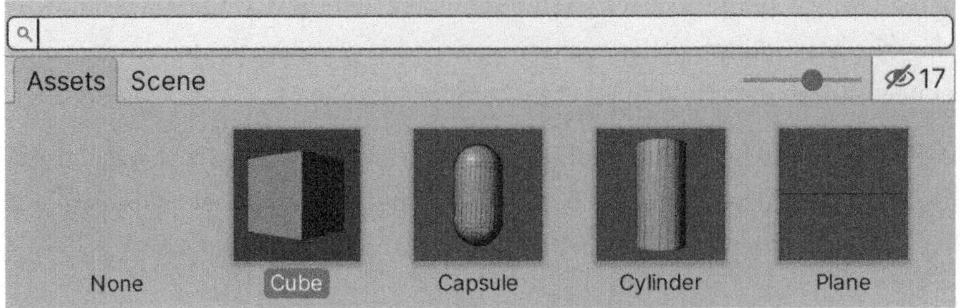

Figure 2.16: The Mesh selector

Okay—the object now looks like a sphere, but will it behave like a sphere? Let's find out. In order to do so, we can add a component named **Rigidbody** to our sphere, which will add physics to it. We will talk more about Rigidbody and physics later in *Chapter 7, Physics Collisions and Health System*, but for now, let's stick to the basics.

In order to do so, we need to click the **Add Component** button at the bottom of the Inspector. It will show a **Component Selector** window with lots of categories; in this case, we need to click on the **Physics** category. The window will show all the **Physics** components, and there we can find the **Rigidbody**. Another option would be to type `Rigidbody` in the search box at the top of the window. The following screenshot illustrates how to add a component:

Figure 2.17: Adding components

If you hit the **Play** button in the top-middle part of the editor, you can test your sphere physics using the **Game** panel. That panel will be automatically focused when you hit **Play** and will show you how the player will see the game. The playback controls are shown in the following screenshot:

Figure 2.18: Playback controls

Here, you can just use the **Transform** gizmo to rotate and position your camera in such a way that it looks at our sphere. This is important as one problem that can happen is that maybe you won't see anything during **Play** mode, and that can happen if the game camera is not pointing to where our sphere is located. While you are moving, you can check the little preview in the bottom-right part of the scene window to check out the new camera perspective. Another alternative would be to select the camera in the **Hierarchy** and use the shortcut *Ctrl* + *Shift* + *F* (or *Command* + *Shift* + *F* on a Mac). The camera preview is shown in the following screenshot:

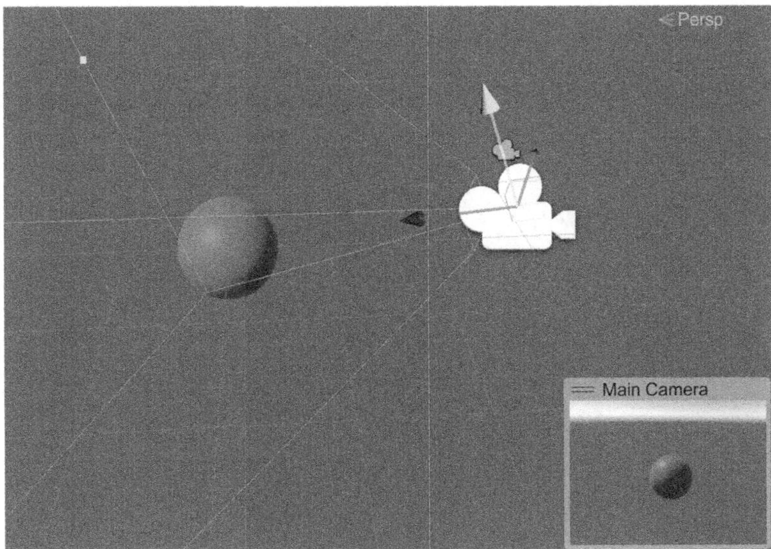

Figure 2.19: The camera preview

Now, to test if physics collisions are executing properly, let's create a cube, scale it until it has the shape of a ramp, and put that ramp below our sphere, as shown here:

Figure 2.20: Ball and ramp objects

If you hit **Play** now, you will see the sphere colliding with our ramp, but in a strange way. It looks like it's bouncing, but that's not the case. If you expand the **Box Collider** component of our sphere, you will see that even if our object looks like a sphere, the green box gizmo is showing us that our sphere is actually a box in the physics world, as illustrated in the following screenshot:

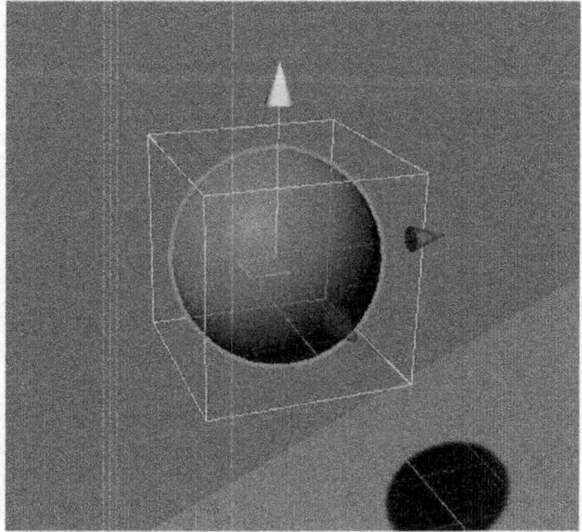

Figure 2.21: Object with sphere graphic and box collider

Nowadays, video cards (GPUs) can handle rendering highly detailed models (models with a high polygon count), but the physics system is executed in the **central processing unit** (**CPU**) and it needs to do complex calculations in order to detect collisions. To get a decent performance in our game, it needs to run at least 30 **frames per second** (**FPS**), the minimum accepted by the industry to provide a smooth experience. The physics system considers that, and hence it works using simplified collision shapes that may differ from the actual shape the player sees on the screen.

That's why we have **Mesh Filter** and the different types of **Collider** components separated—one handles the visual shape and the other the physics shape.

Again, the idea of this section is not to deep-dive into those Unity systems, so let's just move on for now. How can we solve our sphere actually being a box? Simple: by modifying our components! In this case, the **Box Collider** component already present in our cube GameObject can just represent a box physics shape, unlike **Mesh Filter**, which supports any rendering shape. So, first, we need to remove it by right-clicking the component's title and selecting the **Remove Component** option, as illustrated in the following screenshot:

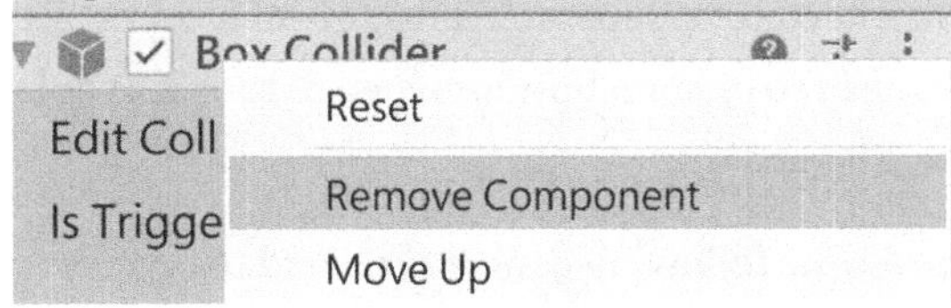

Figure 2.22: Removing components

Now, we can again use the **Add Component** menu to select a **Physics** component, this time selecting the **Sphere Collider** component. If you look at the **Physics** components, you will see other types of colliders that can be used to represent other shapes, but we will look at them later in *Chapter 7, Physics Collisions and Health System*. The **Sphere Collider** component can be seen in the following screenshot:

Figure 2.23: Adding a Sphere Collider component

So, if you hit **Play** now, you will see that our sphere not only looks like a sphere but also behaves like one. Remember: the main idea of this section of the book is understanding that in Unity you can create whatever object you want just by adding, removing, and modifying components, and we will be doing a lot of this throughout the book.

Now, components are not the only thing needed in order to create objects. Complex objects may be composed of several sub-objects, so let's see how that works.

Object Hierarchies

Some complex objects may need to be separated into sub-objects, each one with its own components. Those sub-objects need to be somehow attached to the main object and work together to create the necessary object behavior.

In this section, we will cover the following concepts related to objects:

- Parenting of objects
- Possible uses

Let's start by discovering how to create a parent-child relationship between objects.

Parenting of objects

Parenting consists of making an object the child of another, meaning that those objects will be related to each other. One type of relationship that happens is a **Transform relationship**, meaning that a child object will be affected by the parent's Transform. In simple terms, the child object will follow the parent, as if it is attached to it. For example, imagine a player with a hat on their head. The hat can be a child of the player's head, making the hat follow the head while they are attached.

In order to try this, let's create a capsule that represents an enemy and a cube that represents the weapon of the enemy. Remember that in order to do so, you can use the **GameObject | 3D Object | Capsule** and **Cube** options and then use the **Transform** tool to modify them. An example of a capsule and a cube can be seen in the following screenshot:

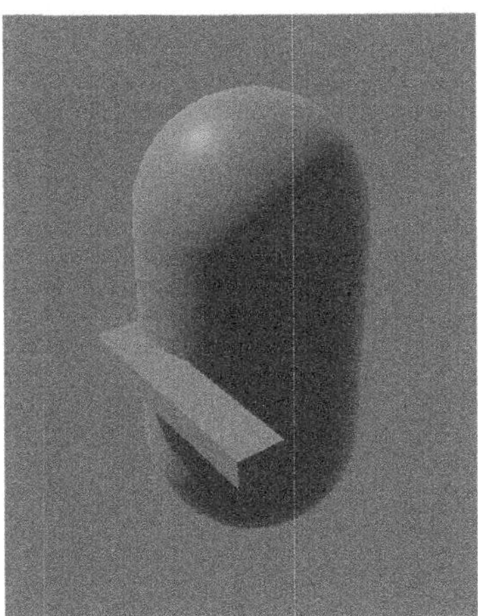

Figure 2.24: A capsule and a cube representing an enemy and a weapon

If you move the enemy object (the capsule), the weapon (the cube) will keep its position, not following our enemy. So, to prevent that, we can simply drag the weapon to the enemy object in the **Hierarchy** window, as illustrated in the following screenshot:

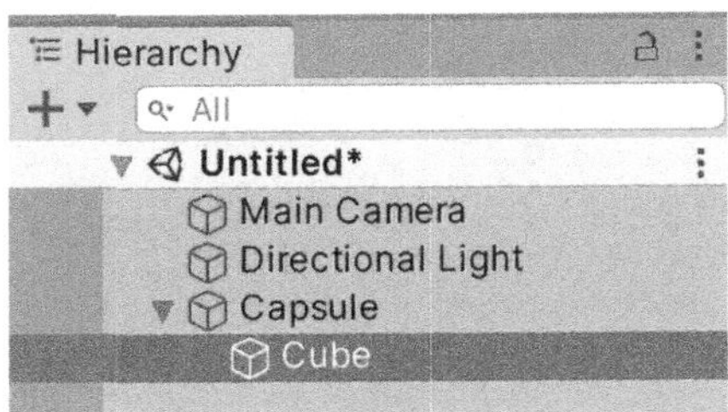

Figure 2.25: Parenting the cube weapon to the capsule character

Now, if you move the enemy, you will see the gun moving, rotating, and being scaled along with it. So, basically, the gun Transform also has the effects of the enemy Transform component.

Now that we have done some basic parenting, let's explore other possible uses.

Possible uses

There are some other uses of parenting aside from creating complex objects. Another common usage for it is to organize the project Hierarchy. Right now, our scene is simple, but in time it will grow, so keeping track of all the objects will become difficult. To prevent this, we can create empty GameObjects (in **GameObject | Create Empty**) that only have the Transform component to act as containers, putting objects into them just to organize our scene. Try to use this with caution because this has a performance cost if you abuse it. Generally, having one or two levels of parenting when organizing a scene is fine, but more than that can have a performance hit. Consider that you can—and will—have deeper parenting for the creation of complex objects; the proposed limit is just for scene organization.

To keep improving on our previous example, duplicate the enemy a couple of times all around the scene, create an empty GameObject and name it `Enemies`, and drag all the enemies into it so that it will act as a container. This is illustrated in the following screenshot:

Figure 2.26: Grouping enemies in a parent object

Another common usage of parenting is to change the **pivot** (or center) of an object. Right now, if we try to rotate our gun with the **Transform** gizmo, it will rotate around its center because the creator of that cube decided to put the center there. Normally, that's okay, but let's consider the case where we need to make the weapon aim at the point where our enemy is looking. In this case, we need to rotate the weapon around the weapon handle; so, in the case of this cube weapon, it would be the closest end to the enemy. The problem here is that we cannot change the center of an object, so one solution would be to create another "weapon" 3D model or mesh with another center, which will lead to lots of duplicated versions of the weapon if we consider other possible gameplay requirements such as a rotating weapon pickup. We can fix this easily using parenting.

The idea is to create an empty GameObject and place it where we want the new pivot of our object to be. After that, we can simply drag our weapon inside this empty GameObject, and, from now on, consider the empty object as the actual weapon.

If you rotate or scale this weapon container, you will see that the weapon mesh will apply those transformations around this container, so we can say the pivot of the weapon has changed (actually, it hasn't, but our container simulates the change). The process is illustrated in the following screenshot:

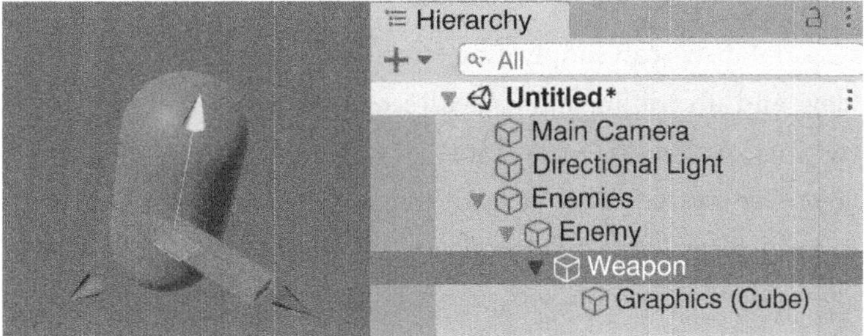

Figure 2.27: Changing the weapon pivot

Now, let's continue seeing different ways of managing GameObjects, using Prefabs this time.

Prefabs

In the previous example, we created lots of copies of our enemy around the scene, but in doing so, we have created a new problem. Let's imagine we need to change our enemy and add a **Rigidbody** component to it, but because we have several copies of the same object, we need to take them one by one and add the same component to all of them. Maybe later, we will need to change the mass of each enemy, so again, we need to go over each one of the enemies and make the change, and here we can start to see a pattern. One solution could be to select all the enemies using the *Ctrl* key (*Command* on a Mac) and modify all of them at once, but that solution won't be of any use if we have enemy copies in other scenes. So, here is where Prefabs come in.

In this section, we will cover the following concepts related to Prefabs:

- Creating Prefabs
- Prefab-instance relationship
- Prefab variants

Let's start by discussing how to create and use Prefabs.

Creating Prefabs

Prefabs are a Unity tool that allows us to convert custom-made objects, such as our enemy, into an asset that defines how they can be created. We can use them to create new copies of our custom object easily, without needing to create its components and sub-objects all over again.

In order to create a Prefab, we can simply drag our custom object from the Hierarchy window to the project window, and after doing that you will see a new asset in your project files. The project window is where you can navigate and explore all your project files; so, in this case, our Prefab is the first Asset we ever created. Now, you can simply drag the Prefab from the project window into the scene to easily create new Prefab copies, as illustrated in the following screenshot:

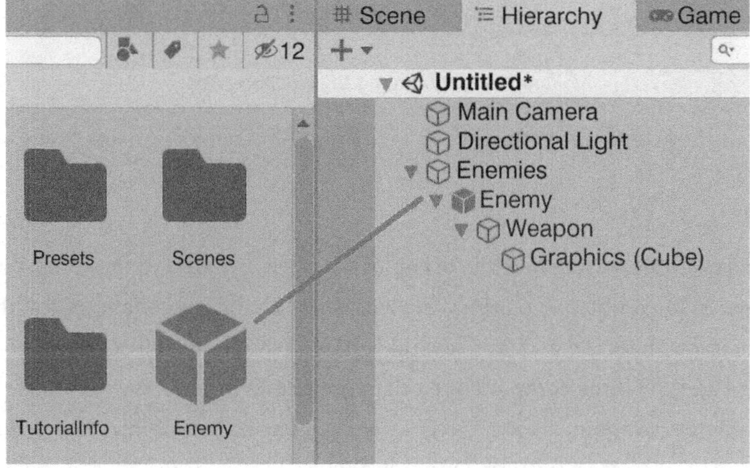

Figure 2.28: Creating a Prefab

Now, we have a little problem here. If you pay attention to the Hierarchy window, you will see the original Prefab objects and all the new copies with their names in the color blue, while the enemies created before the Prefab will have their names in black. The blue color in a name means that the object is an **instance** of a prefab, meaning that the object was created based on a Prefab. We can select those blue-named objects and click the **Select** button in the **Inspector** to select the original Prefab that created that object. This is illustrated in the following screenshot:

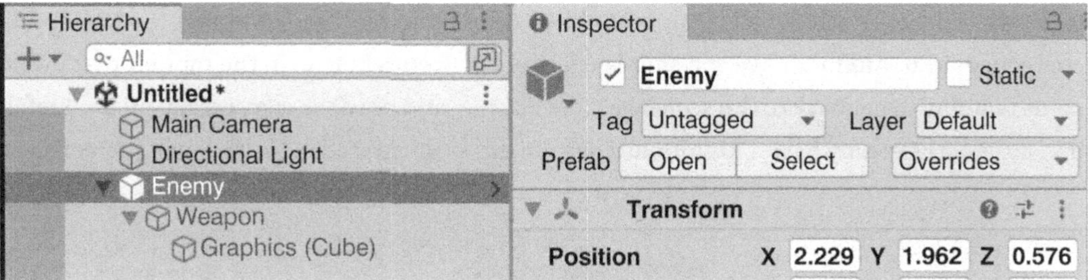

Figure 2.29: Detecting prefabs in the Hierarchy

So, the problem here is that the previous copies of the Prefab are not instances of the Prefab we just created, and sadly there's no way to connect them to it. So, in order to make that happen, we need to simply destroy the old copies and replace them with copies created with the Prefab. At first, not having all copies as instances doesn't seem to be a problem, but it will be in the next section of this chapter, where we will explore the relationship between the Prefabs and their instances.

Prefab-instance relationship

An instance of a Prefab, the GameObject created when dragging the Prefab to the scene, has a binding to it that helps to revert and apply changes easily between the prefab and the instance. If you take a Prefab and make some modifications to it, those changes will be automatically applied to all instances across all the scenes in the project, so we can easily create a first version of the Prefab, use it all around the project, and then experiment with changes.

To practice this, let's say we want to add a **Rigidbody** component to the enemies so that they can fall. In order to do so, we can simply double-click the Prefab file in the **Project** panel and we will enter the **Prefab Edit Mode**, where we can edit the Prefab isolated from the rest of the scene.

Here, we can simply take the Prefab root object (**Enemy** in our case) and add the **Rigidbody** component to it. After that, we can simply click on the **Scenes** button in the top-left part of the scene window to get back to the scene we were editing, and now, we can see that all the Prefab instances of the enemy have a **Rigidbody** component, as illustrated in the following screenshot:

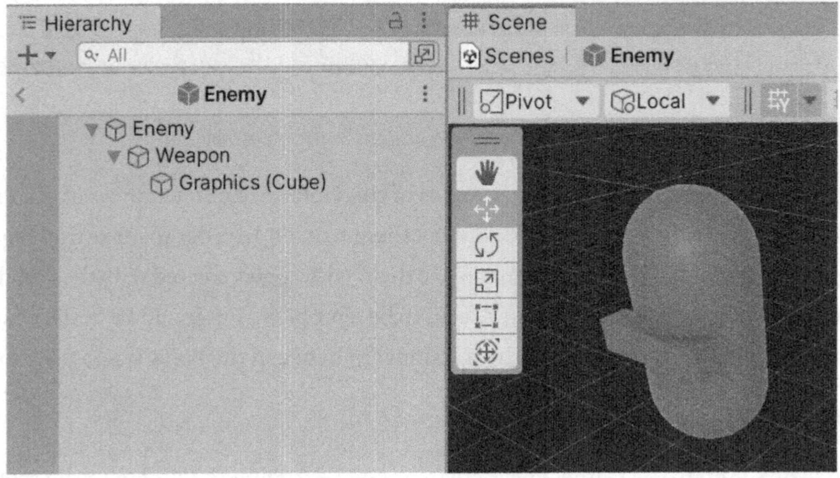

Figure 2.30: Prefab edit mode

Now, what happens if we change a Prefab instance (the one in the scene) instead? Let's say we want one specific enemy to fly, so they won't suffer the effect of gravity. We can do that by simply selecting the specific Prefab and unchecking the **Use Gravity** checkbox in the **Rigidbody** component. After doing that, if we play the game, we will see that only that specific instance will float. That's because changes to an instance of a Prefab become an **override**, a set of differences the instance has compared to the original prefab. We can see how the **Use Gravity** property is bold in the Inspector, and also has a blue bar displayed to its left, meaning it's an override of the original Prefab value. Let's take another object and change its **Scale** property to make it bigger. Again, we will see how the **Scale** property becomes bold and the blue bar at its left will appear. The **Use Gravity** checkbox can be seen in the following screenshot:

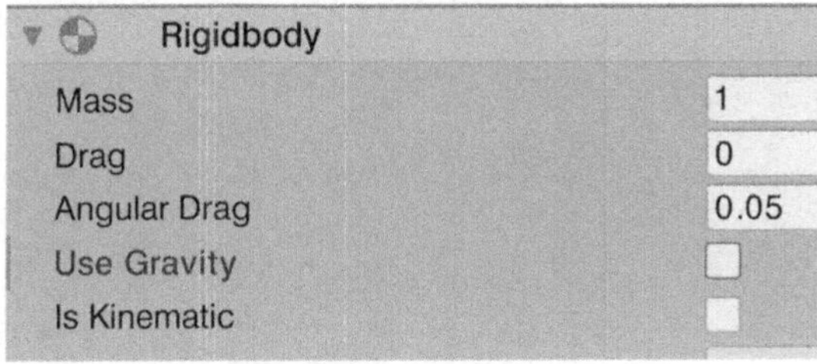

Figure 2.31: Use Gravity being highlighted as an override

The overrides have precedence over the Prefab, so if we change the scale of the original Prefab, the one that has a scale override won't change, keeping its own version of the scale, as illustrated in the following screenshot:

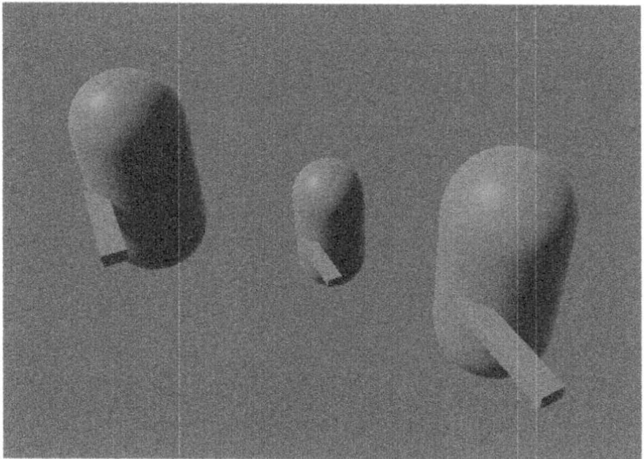

Figure 2.32: One Prefab instance with a scale override

We can easily locate all overrides of an instance using the **Overrides** dropdown in the Inspector after selecting the Prefab instance (the one in the scene, outside **Prefab Edit Mode**) in the Hierarchy, locating all changes our object has. It not only allows us to see all the overrides but also reverts any override we don't want and applies the ones we do want. Let's say we regretted the lack of gravity of that specific Prefab—no problem! We can just locate the override and revert it using the **Revert** button after clicking on the component with the override. The process is illustrated in the following screenshot:

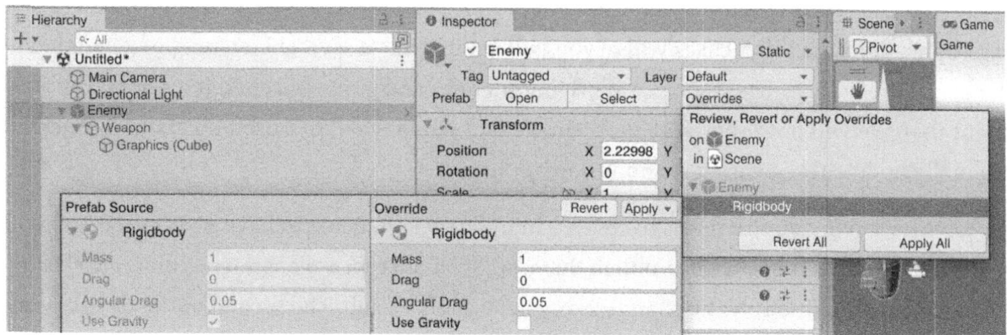

Figure 2.33: Reverting a single override

Also, let's imagine that we really liked the new scale of that instance, so we want all instances to have that scale—great! We can simply select the specific override, hit the **Apply** button, and then the **Apply to Prefab** option; now, all instances will have that scale (except the ones with an override), as illustrated in the following screenshot:

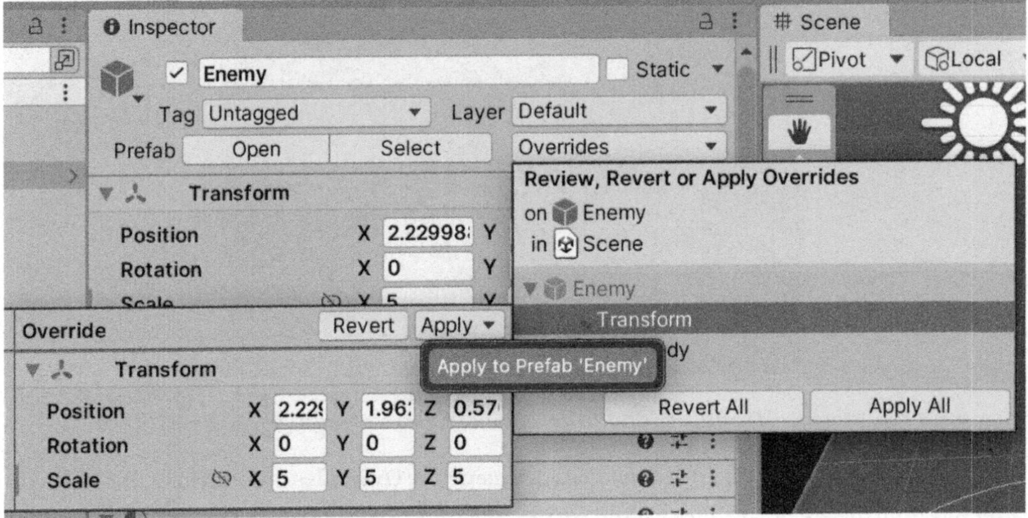

Figure 2.34: The Apply button

Also, we have the **Revert All** and **Apply All** buttons, but use them with caution, because you can easily revert and apply changes that you are not aware of.

So, as you can see, Prefabs are a really useful Unity tool to keep track of all similar objects and apply changes to all of them, and also have specific instances with few variations. Talking about variations, there are other cases where you will want to have several instances of a Prefab with the same set of variations—for example, flying enemies and grounded enemies—but if you think about that, we will have the same problem we had when we didn't use Prefabs, so we need to manually update those varied versions one by one.

Here, we have two options: one is to create a brand new Prefab just to have another version with that variation. This leads to the problem that if we want all types of enemies to undergo changes, we need to manually apply the changes to each possible Prefab. The second option is to create a Prefab variant. Let's review the latter.

Prefab variants

A **Prefab variant** is a new Prefab created based on an existing one, so the new one **inherits** the features of the base Prefab. This means that our new Prefab can have differences from the base one, but the features that they have in common are still connected.

To illustrate this, let's create a variation of the enemy Prefab that can fly: the flying enemy Prefab. In order to do that, we can select an existing enemy Prefab instance in the Hierarchy window, name it `Flying Enemy`, and drag it again to the project window, and this time we will see a prompt, asking which kind of Prefab we want to create. This time, we need to choose **Prefab Variant**, as illustrated in the following screenshot:

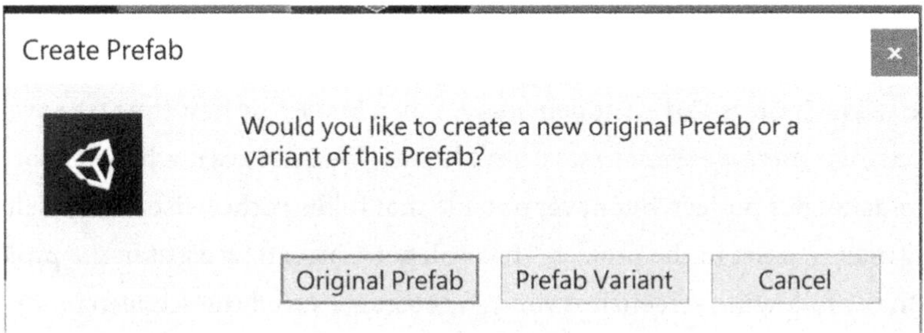

Figure 2.35: Creating Prefab Variants

Now, we can enter the Prefab Edit Mode of the variant by double-clicking the new Prefab file created in the project panel, and then add a cube as the jetpack of our enemy, and also uncheck the **Use Gravity** property for the enemy. If we get back to the scene, we will see the variant instance being changed, and the base enemies aren't changed. You can see this in the following screenshot:

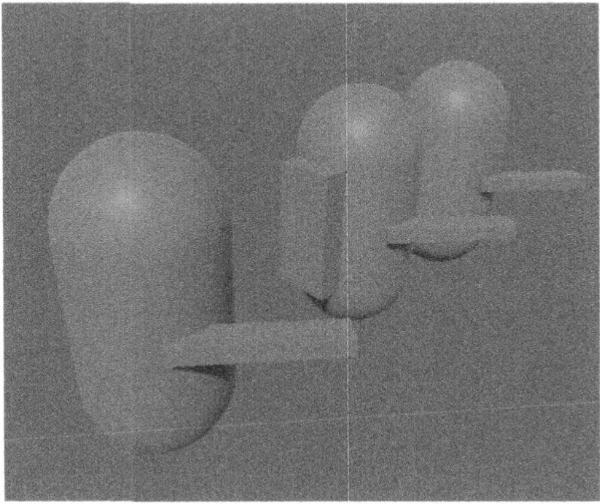

Figure 2.36: A Prefab variant instance

Now, imagine you want to add a hat to all our types of enemies. We can simply enter the **Prefab Edit Mode** of the base enemy Prefab by double-clicking it and adding a cube as a hat. Now, we will see that change applied to all the enemies, because remember: the **Flying Enemy** Prefab is a variant of the base enemy Prefab, meaning that it will inherit all the changes of that one.

We have created lots of content so far, but if our PC turns off for some reason, we will certainly lose it all, so let's see how we can save our progress.

Saving scenes and projects

As in any other program, we need to save our progress. The difference here is that we don't have just one giant file with all the project assets, but several files for each asset.

Let's start saving our progress by saving the scene, which is pretty straightforward. We can simply go to **File | Save** or press *Ctrl + S* (*Command + S* on a Mac). The first time we save our scene, a window will ask us where we want to save our file, and you can save it wherever you want inside the `Assets` folder of our project, but never outside that folder; otherwise, Unity will not be capable of finding it as an asset in the project. That will generate a new asset in the project window: a scene file. In the following screenshot you can see how I saved the scene, naming it `test`, and now it shows up in the **Project** panel:

Figure 2.37: Scene files

We can create a folder to save our scene in the save dialog, or, if you already saved the scene, you can create a folder using the **plus (+)** icon in the project window and then click the **Folder** option. Finally, drag the created scene to that folder. Now, if you create another scene with the **File | New Scene** menu option, you can get back to the previous scene just by double-clicking the scene asset in the project window. Try it!

This only saved the scene, but any change in Prefabs and other kinds of assets are not saved with that option. Instead, if you want to save every change of the assets except scenes, you can use the **File | Save Project** option. It can be a little bit confusing, but if you want to save all your changes, you need to both save the scenes and the project, as saving just the project won't save the changes to scenes. Sometimes, the best way to be sure everything is saved is just by closing Unity, which is recommended when you try to move your project between computers or folders. This will show you a prompt to save the changes on the scene, and will automatically save any change made to other assets, like Prefabs.

Summary

In this chapter, we saw a quick introduction to essential Unity concepts. We reviewed the basic Unity windows and how we can use all of them to edit a full scene, from navigating it, then creating premade objects (Prefabs), to manipulating them to create our own types of objects using GameObjects and components. We also discussed how to use the Hierarchy window to parent GameObjects to create complex object Hierarchies, as well as creating Prefabs to reutilize and manipulate large amounts of the same type of objects. Finally, we discussed how we can save our progress.

In the next chapter, we will learn different tools like the Terrain system and ProBuilder to create the first prototype of our game's level. This prototype will serve as a preview of where our scene will be headed, testing some ideas before going into full production.

3

Grayboxing with Terrain and ProBuilder

Now that we've grasped all the necessary concepts to use Unity, let's start designing our first level. The idea in this chapter is to learn how to use Terrain Tools to create the landscape of our game and then use ProBuilder to create the 3D mesh of the base with greater detail than using cubes. At the end of the chapter, you will be able to create a prototype of any kind of scene and try out your idea before actually implementing it with final graphics.

Specifically, we will examine the following concepts in this chapter:

- Defining our game concept
- Creating a landscape with Terrain
- Creating shapes with ProBuilder

Let's start by talking about our game concept, which will help us draft the first level environment.

Defining our game concept

Before even adding the first cube to our scene, it is good to have an idea of what we are going to create, as we will need a basic concept of our game to start designing the first level. Throughout this book, we will be creating a shooter game, in which the player will be fighting against waves of enemies trying to destroy the player's base.

This base will be a complex in a (not so) secret location bordered by mountains:

Figure 3.1: Our finished game

We will be defining the mechanics of our game as we progress through the book, but with this basic high-level concept of the game we can start thinking about how to create a mountainous landscape and a placeholder player's base to start.

With that in mind, in the next section of this chapter we will learn how to use Unity's Terrain Tools to create our scene's landscape.

Creating a landscape with Terrain

So far, we have used cubes to generate our level prototype, but we also learned that those shapes sometimes cannot represent all possible objects we could need. Imagine something irregular, such as a full terrain with hills, canyons, and rivers. This would be a nightmare to create using cubes given the irregular shapes you find in the terrain. Another option would be to use 3D modeling software, but the problem with that is that the generated model will be so big and so detailed that it won't perform well, even on high-end PCs. In this scenario, we need to learn how to use Unity's Terrain system, which we will do in this first section of the chapter.

In this section, we will cover the following concepts related to terrains:

- Discussing Height Maps
- Creating and configuring Height Maps
- Authoring Height Maps
- Adding Height Map details

Let's start by talking about Height Maps, whose textures help us define the heights of our terrain.

Discussing Height Maps

If we create a giant area of the game with hills, canyons, craters, valleys, and rivers using regular 3D modeling tools, we will have a problem in that we will use fully detailed models for objects at all possible distances, thus wasting resources on rendering details that we won't see when the object is far away. We will see lots of parts of the terrain from a great distance, so this is a serious issue.

Unity Terrain Tools uses a technique called Height Maps to generate the terrain in a performant and dynamic way. Instead of generating large 3D models for the whole terrain, it uses an image called a **Height Map**, which looks like a top-down black and white photo of the terrain.

In the following image, you can see a black and white top-down view of a region of Scotland, with white being higher and black being lower:

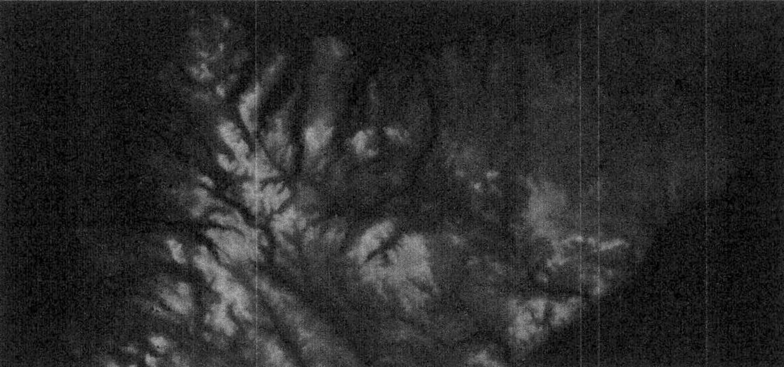

Figure 3.2: Scotland's Height Map

In the preceding image, you can easily spot the peaks of the mountains by looking for the whitest areas of the image. Everything below sea level becomes black, while anything in the middle uses gradients of gray, representing different heights between the minimum and maximum heights. The idea is that each pixel of the image determines the height of that specific area of the terrain.

Unity Terrain Tools can automatically generate a 3D mesh from that image, saving us the hard drive space of having full 3D models of that terrain. Also, Unity will create the terrain as we move, generating high-detail models for nearby areas and low-detail models for faraway areas, making it a performant solution.

In the following image, you can see the mesh that was generated for the terrain. You can appreciate that the nearer parts of the terrain have more polygons than further away parts:

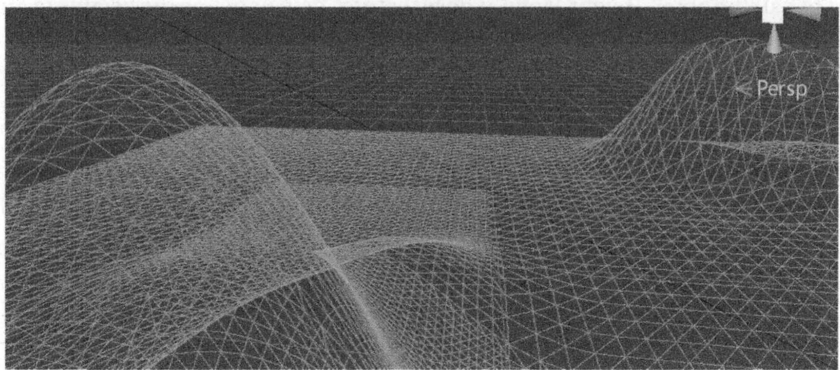

Figure 3.3: Height Map generated mesh

Take into account that this technology has its cons, such as the time it takes for Unity to generate those 3D models while we play and the inability to create caves, but for now, that's not a problem for us.

Now that we know what a Height Map is, let's see how we can use Unity Terrain Tools to create our own Height Maps.

Creating and configuring Height Maps

If you click on **GameObject | 3D Object | Terrain**, you will see a giant plane appear on your scene, and a **Terrain** object appears on your Hierarchy window. That's our terrain, and it is plain because its Height Map starts all black, so no height whatsoever is in its initial state.

In the following image, you can see what a brand-new **Terrain** object looks like:

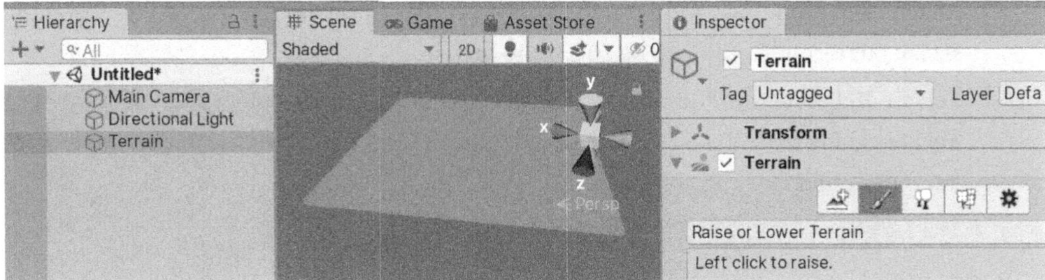

Figure 3.4: Terrain with no heights painted yet

Before you start editing this Terrain, you must configure different settings such as the size and resolution of the Terrain's Height Map, and that depends on what you are going to do with it. This is not the same as generating a whole world. Our game will feature the player's base, which they will defend, so the terrain will be small. In this case, an area that's 200 x 200 meters in size surrounded by mountains will be enough.

In order to configure our terrain for those requirements, we need to do the following:

1. Select **Terrain** from the **Hierarchy** or **Scene** window.
2. Look at the **Inspector** for the **Terrain** component and expand it if it is collapsed.
3. Click on the mountain and gear icon (the furthest right option) to switch to configuration mode. In the following screenshot, you can see where that button is located:

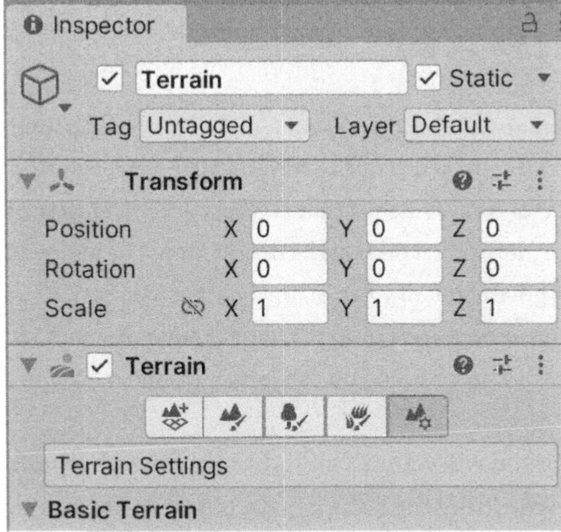

Figure 3.5: Terrain Settings button

4. Look for the **Mesh Resolution (On Terrain Data)** section.
5. Change **Terrain Width** and **Terrain Length** to `200` in both settings. This will say that the size of our terrain is going to be 200 x 200 meters.
6. **Terrain Height** determines the maximum height possible. The white areas of our Height Map are going to be that size. We can reduce it to `500` just to limit the maximum peak of our mountains:

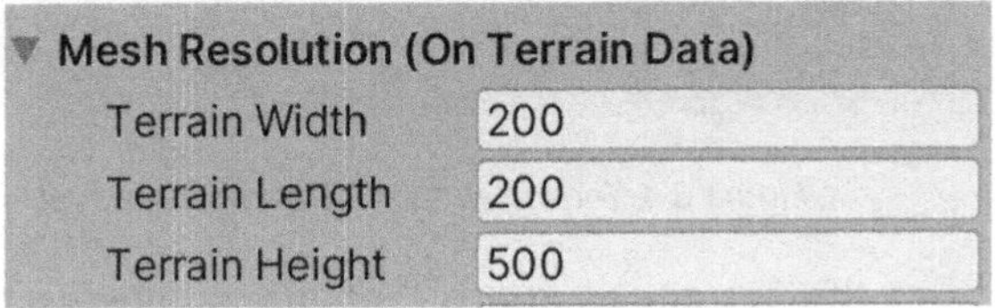

Figure 3.6: Terrain resolution settings

7. Look for the **Texture Resolutions (On Terrain Data)** section.
8. Change **Heightmap Resolution** to **257 x 257**:

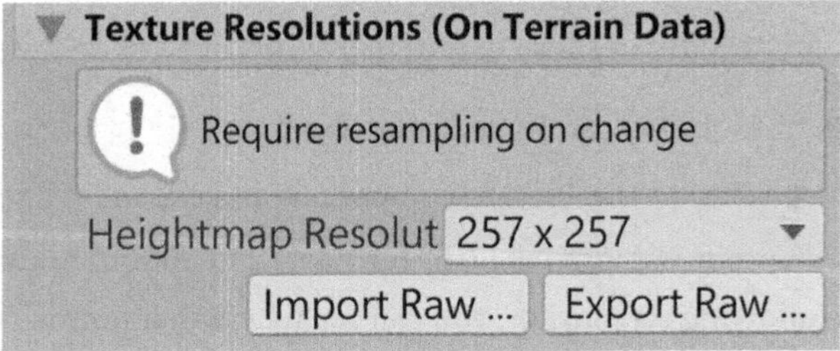

Figure 3.7: Height Map resolution settings

Heightmap Resolution is the size of the Height Map image that will hold the heights of the different parts of the terrain. Using a resolution of 257 x 257 in our 200 x 200-meter terrain means that each square meter in the terrain will be covered by a little bit more than 1 pixel of the Height Map. The higher the resolution per square meter, the greater detail you can draw in that area size. Usually, terrain features are big, so having more than 1 pixel per square meter is generally a waste of resources. Find the smallest resolution you can have that allows you to create the details you need.

Another initial setting you will want to set is the initial terrain height. By default, this is 0, so you can start painting heights from the bottom part, but this way, you can't make holes in the terrain because it's already at its lowest point. Setting up a little initial height allows you to paint river paths and pits in case you need them.

In order to do so, do the following:

1. Select our **Terrain** in the **Hierarchy** panel.
2. Click on the **Paint Terrain** button (the second button).
3. Set the dropdown to **Set Height** if it's not already there.
4. Set the **Height** property to `50`. This will state we want all the terrain to start at `50` meters in height, allowing us to make holes with a maximum depth of `50` meters:

Figure 3.8: Set Height Terrain tool location

5. Click the **Flatten All** button. You will see all the terrain has been raised to the `50` meters we specified. This leaves us with 450 more meters to go up, based on the maximum of 500 meters we specified earlier.

Now that we have properly configured our Height Map, let's start editing it.

Authoring Height Maps

Remember that the Height Map is just an image of the heights, so in order to edit it, we need to paint the heights in that image. Luckily, Unity has tools that allow us to edit the terrain directly in the editor and see the results of the modified heights directly. In order to do this, we must follow these steps:

1. Select our **Terrain** in the **Hierarchy** panel.
2. Click the **Paint Terrain** button (the second button, the same as in the previous section).

3. Set the dropdown to **Raise or Lower Terrain**:

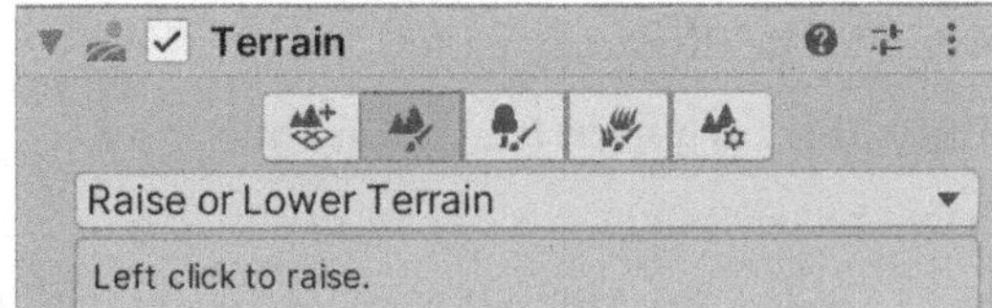

Figure 3.9: Raise or Lower Terrain tool location

4. Select the second brush in the Brushes selector. This brush has blurred borders to allow us to create softer heights.
5. Set **Brush Size** to **30** so that we can create heights that span 30-meter areas. If you want to create subtler details, you can reduce this number.
6. Set **Opacity** to **10** to reduce the amount of height we paint per second or click:

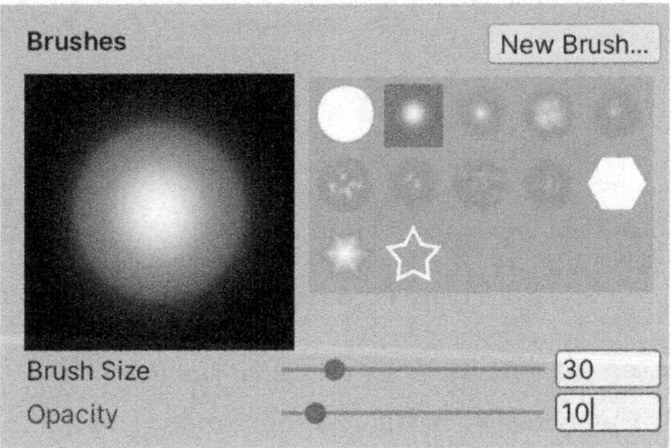

Figure 3.10: Smooth edges brush

7. Now, if you move the mouse in the **Scene** view, you will see a little preview of the height you will paint if you click on that area. Maybe you will need to navigate closer to the terrain to see it in detail:

Figure 3.11: Previsualization of the area to raise the terrain

That checked pattern you can see allows you to see the actual size of the objects you are editing. Each cell represents a square meter. Remember that having a reference to see the actual size of the objects you are editing helps to prevent you from creating terrain features that are too big or too small. Maybe you can put in other kinds of references, such as a big cube with accurate sizes representing a building to get a notion of the size of the mountain or lake you are creating. Remember that the cube has a default size of 1 x 1 x 1 meters, so scaling to 10,10,10 will give you a cube of 10 x 10 x 10 meters.

8. Hold, left-click, and drag the cursor over the terrain to start painting your terrain heights. Remember that you can press *Ctrl* + *Z* (*Command* + *Z* on Mac) to reverse any undesired change.

9. Try to paint the mountains all around the borders of our area, which will represent the background hills of our base:

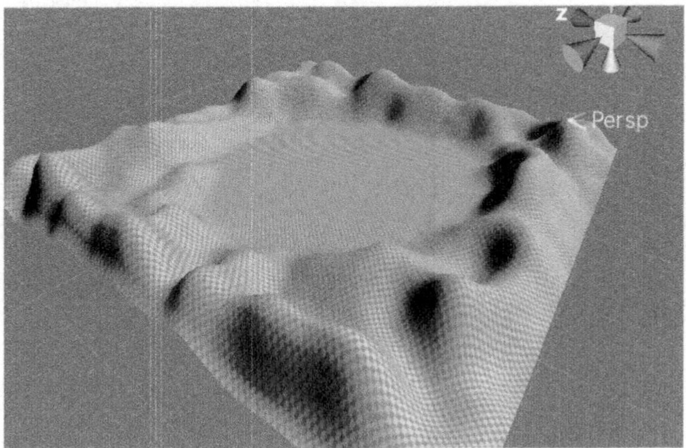

Figure 3.12: Painted mountains around the edges of the terrain

We now have decent starter hills around our future base. We can also draw a moat around our future base. To do so, follow these steps:

1. Place a cube with a scale of `50,10,50` in the middle of the terrain. This will act as a placeholder for the base we are going to create:

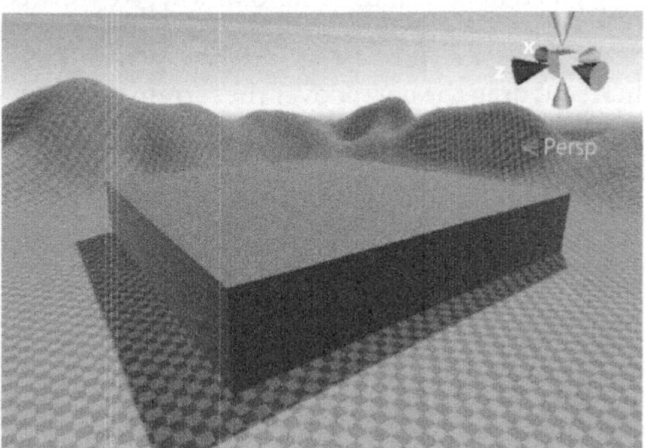

Figure 3.13: Placeholder cube for the base area

2. Select **Terrain** and the **Brush** button once more.
3. Reduce **Brush Size** to `10`.

4. Holding the *Shift* key, left-click and drag the mouse over the terrain to paint the basin around our base placeholder. Doing this will lower the terrain instead of raising it:

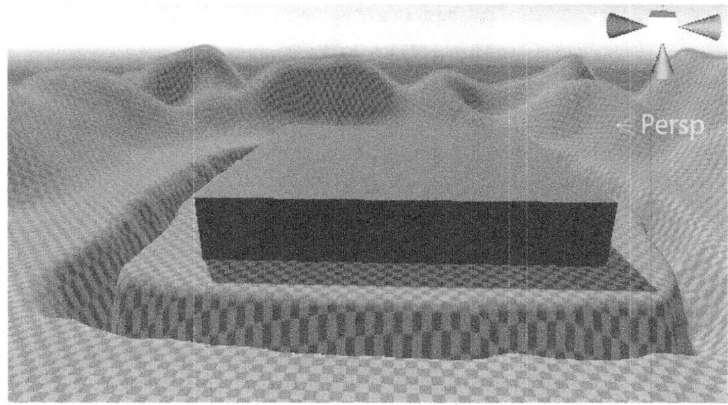

Figure 3.14: Moat around our placeholder base

Now, we have a simple but good starter terrain that gives us a basic idea of how our base and its surroundings will look. Before moving on, we will apply some finer details to make our terrain look a little bit better. In the next section, we will discuss how to simulate terrain erosion with different tools.

Adding Height Map details

In the previous section, we created a rough outline of the terrain. If you want to make it look a little bit more realistic, then you need to start painting lots of tiny details here and there. Usually, this is done later in the level design process, but let's take a look now since we are exploring Terrain Tools. Right now, our mountains look very smooth. In real life, they are generally sharper, so let's improve that:

1. Select the **Terrain** and click the **Brush** button as in the previous sections.
2. Set the dropdown to **Raise or Lower Terrain** if it's not already set.
3. Pick the fifth brush, as shown in *Figure 3.15*. This brush has an irregular shape so that we can paint a little bit of noise here and there.

4. Set **Brush Size** to `50` so that we can cover a greater area:

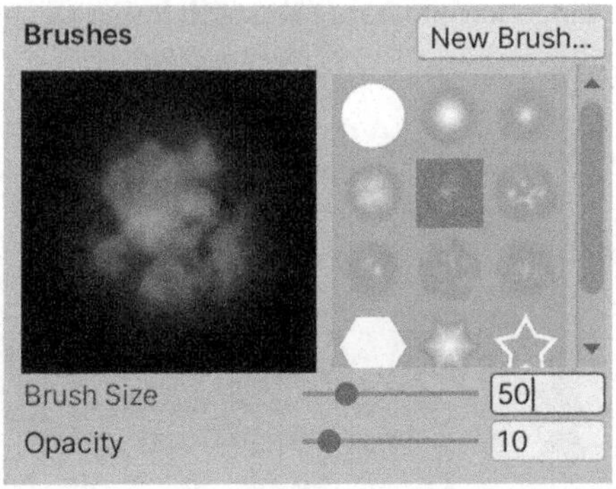

Figure 3.15: Cloud pattern brush for randomness

5. Hold *Shift* and do small clicks over the hills of the terrain without dragging the mouse. Remember to zoom in to the areas you are applying finer details to because they can't be seen at great distances:

Figure 3.16: Erosion generated with the aforementioned brush

This has added some irregularity to our hills. Now, let's imagine we want to have a flat area on the hills to put a decorative observatory or antenna. Follow these steps to do so:

1. Select **Terrain, Brush Tool**, and **Set Height** from the dropdown.
2. Set **Height** to `60`.
3. Select the full circle brush (the first one).

4. Paint an area over the hills. You will see that the terrain will rise if it's lower than 60 meters or drop in areas higher than 60 meters:

Figure 3.17: Flattened hill

5. You can see that the borders have some rough corners that need to be smoothed:

Figure 3.18: Non-smoothed terrain edges

6. Change the dropdown to **Smooth Height**.

7. Select the second brush, as shown in *Figure 3.19*, with a size of `5` and an opacity of `10`:

Figure 3.19: Smooth Height brush selected

8. Click and drag over the borders of our flat area to make them smoother:

Figure 3.20: Smoothed terrain edges

We could keep adding details here and there, but we can settle with this for now. The next step is to create our player's base, but first, let's explore ProBuilder in order to generate our geometry.

Creating shapes with ProBuilder

So far, we have created simple scenes using cubes and primitive shapes, and that's enough for most of the prototypes you will create, but sometimes, you will have tricky areas of the game that would be difficult to model with regular cubes, or maybe you want to have some deeper details in certain parts of your game to get an idea of how the player will experience that area.

In this case, we can use any 3D modeling tool for this, such as 3D Studio Max, Maya, or Blender, but they can be difficult to learn and you probably won't need all their power at this stage in your development. Luckily, Unity has a simple 3D model creator called ProBuilder, so let's explore it.

In this section, we will cover the following concepts related to ProBuilder:

- Installing ProBuilder
- Creating a shape
- Manipulating the mesh
- Adding details

ProBuilder is not included by default in our Unity project, so let's start by learning how to install it.

Installing ProBuilder

Unity is a powerful engine full of features, but adding all those tools to our project if we are not using all of them can make the engine run more slowly, so we need to manually specify which Unity tools we are using. To do so, we will use **Package Manager**, a tool that we can use to select which Unity Packages we are going to need. As you may recall, earlier, we talked about the `Packages` folder. This is basically what Package Manager is modifying.

In order to install ProBuilder in our project with this tool, we need to do the following:

1. Click the **Window | Package Manager** option:

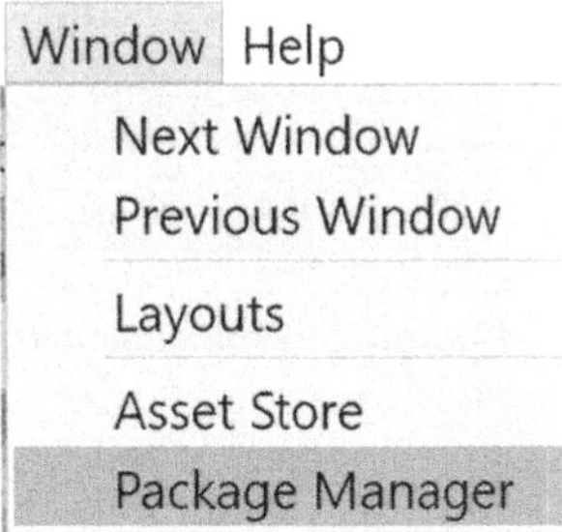

Figure 3.21: Package Manager option

2. In the window that just opened, ensure the **Packages** mode is in **Unity Registry** mode by clicking on the button saying **Packages** in the top-left part of the window and selecting **Unity Registry**. Unlike the **In Project** option, which will show only the packages our project already has, **Unity Registry** will show all the official Unity packages you can install:

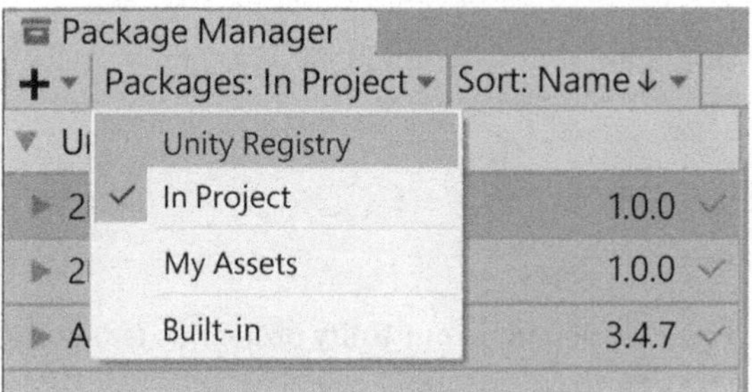

Figure 3.22: Showing all packages

3. Wait a moment for the left list of packages to fill. Make sure you are connected to the internet to download and install the packages.
4. Look at the **ProBuilder** package in that list and select it. You can also use the search box in the top-right corner of the **Package Manager** window:

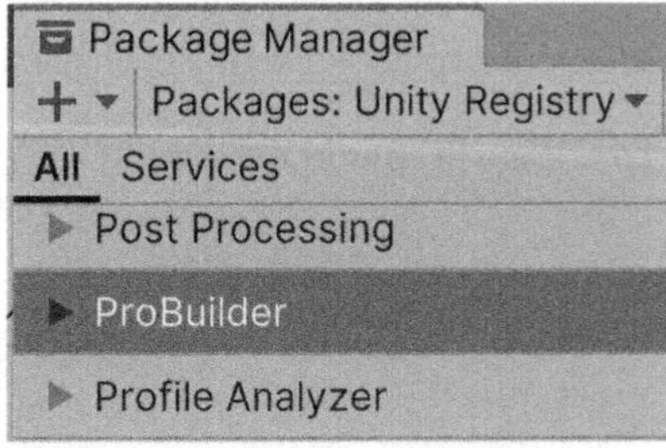

Figure 3.23: ProBuilder in the packages list

I'm using ProBuilder version 5.0.6, the newest version available at the time of writing this book. While you can use a newer version, the process of using it may differ. You can look at older versions using the arrow to the left of the title.

5. Click on the **Install** button in the bottom-right-hand corner of the **Package Manager**:

Figure 3.24: Install button

6. Wait for the package to install; this can take a while. You can tell that the process has ended when the **Install** button has been replaced with the **Remove** label, after the **Importing** popup finishes. If for some reason Unity freezes or takes more than 10 minutes, feel free to restart it.
7. Go to **Edit | Preferences** on Windows (**Unity | Preferences** on Mac).
8. Select the **ProBuilder** option from the left list.
9. Set **Vertex Size** to 2 and **Line Size** to 1. This will help you to better visualize the 3D model we are going to create while editing its different parts:

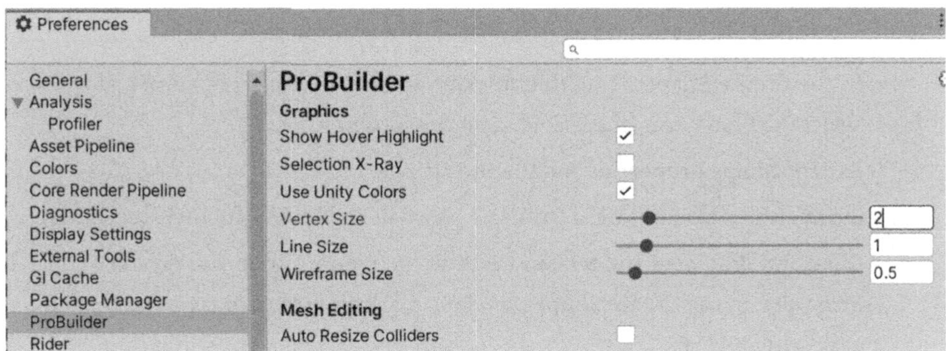

Figure 3.25: Configuring ProBuilder

The **Vertex Size** and **Line Size** values are big (2 and 1 meters respectively) due to the fact we are not going to edit little details of a model, but big features like walls. Consider you might want to modify it later depending on what you are editing.

Although this is all we need to know about **Package Manager** to install ProBuilder, if you want to know more about it, you can review its documentation here: `https://docs.unity3d.com/Manual/upm-ui.html`. Now that we have installed ProBuilder in our project, let's use it!

Creating a shape

We will start the player's base by creating a plane for our floor. We will do this by doing the following:

1. Delete the cube we placed as the base placeholder. You can do that by right-clicking on the cube in the Hierarchy and then pressing **Delete**.
2. Open ProBuilder and go to **Tools | ProBuilder | ProBuilder Window**:

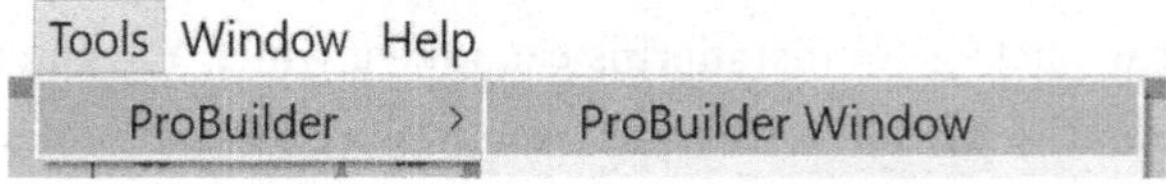

Figure 3.26: ProBuilder Window option

3. In the window that has opened, click the **New Shape** button:

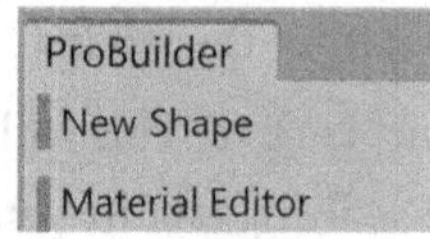

Figure 3.27: New Shape option

4. In the **Create Shape** panel that appears in the bottom-right corner of the Scene View, select the **Plane** icon (the first icon on the second row).
5. Expand **Shape Properties** and **Plane Settings**.
6. Set **Width Cuts** and **Height Cuts** to 2. We will need those subdivisions later.
7. Click and drag over the terrain to draw the plane. While you do that, check how the **Size** value in the **Create Shape** panel changes, and try to make it have *x* and *z* values of approximately `50`.
8. Release the mouse button and see the resulting plane:

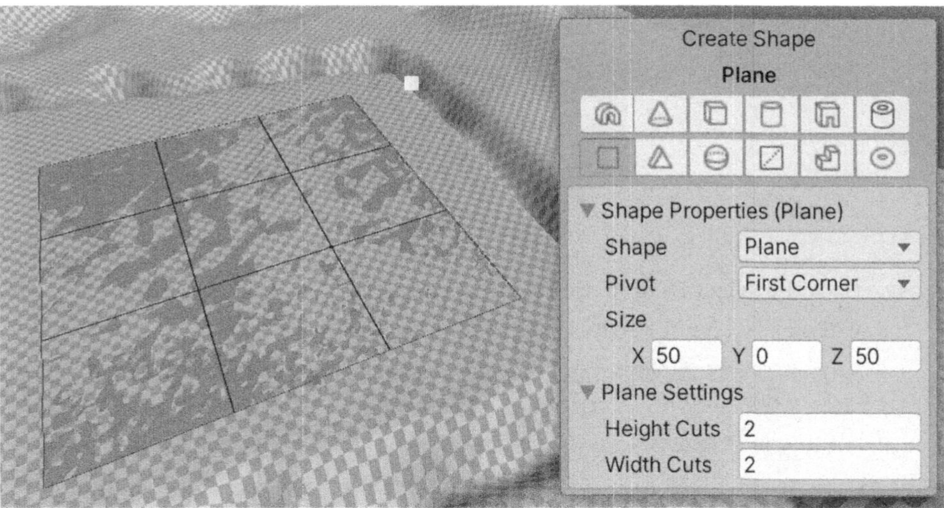

Figure 3.28: New shape created

9. Select the newly-created **Plane** object in the Hierarchy and drag it a little bit upwards using the **Transform** tool.

We needed to move the plane upwards because it was created at exactly the same height as the terrain. That caused an effect called **Z-Fighting**, where the pixels that are positioned in the same position are fighting to determine which one will be rendered and which won't.

Now that we have created the floor, let's learn how we can manipulate its vertices to change its shape.

Manipulating the mesh

If you select the plane, you will see that it is subdivided into a 3 x 3 grid because we set up the width and height cuts to 2. We did that because we will use the outer cells to create our walls, thus raising them. The idea is to modify the size of those cells to outline the wall length and width before creating the walls. In order to do so, we will do the following:

1. Select the plane in the Hierarchy.
2. Open ProBuilder if it's not already open, and go to the **Tools | ProBuilder | ProBuilder Window** option.

3. Select the second button (vertex) from the four new buttons that appear in the Scene View:

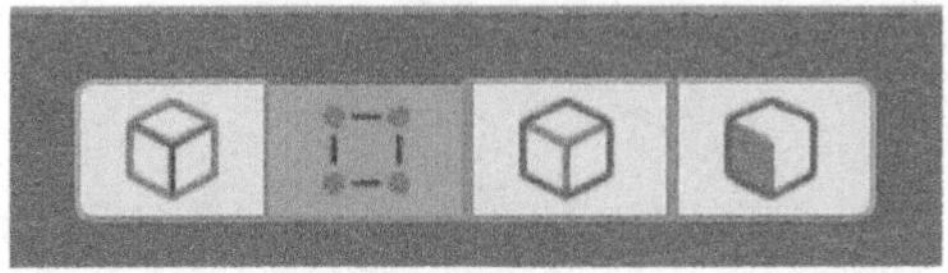

Figure 3.29: Select vertices tool

4. Click the **Select Hidden** option until it says **On**, as shown in the following image. This will make selecting vertices easier:

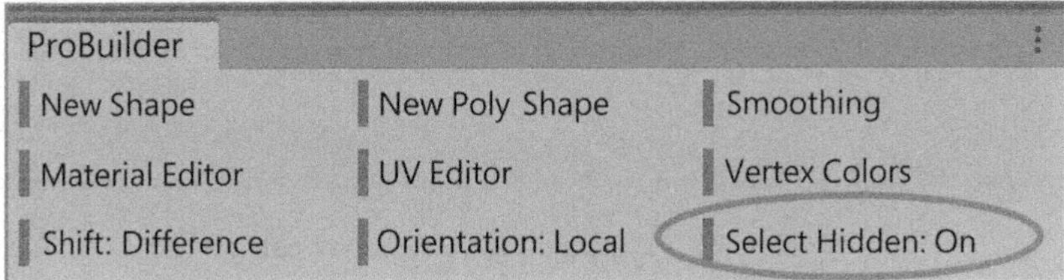

Figure 3.30: Enabling Select Hidden

5. Click and drag the mouse to create a selection box that picks the four vertices on the second row of vertices:

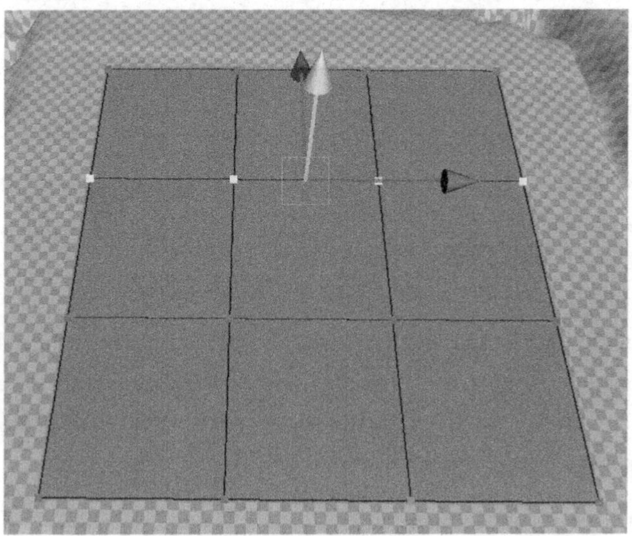

Figure 3.31: Vertex selection

6. Click on the second button in the top-left of the buttons of the Unity Editor to enable the **Move Tool**, which will allow us to move vertices. Like the **Transform Tool**, this can be used to move any object, but to move vertices, this is our only option. Remember to do this once you have selected the vertices. You can also press the *W* key to enable the **Move Tool**.

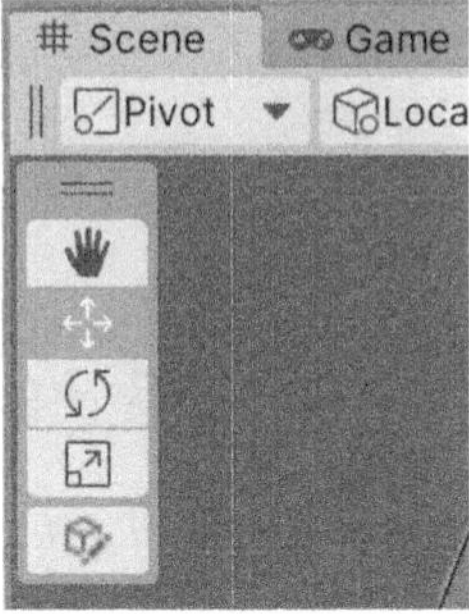

Figure 3.32: Move Tool

7. Move the row of vertices to make the subdivision of the plane thinner. You can use the checker pattern on the terrain to get a notion of the size of the wall in meters (remember, each square is one square meter):

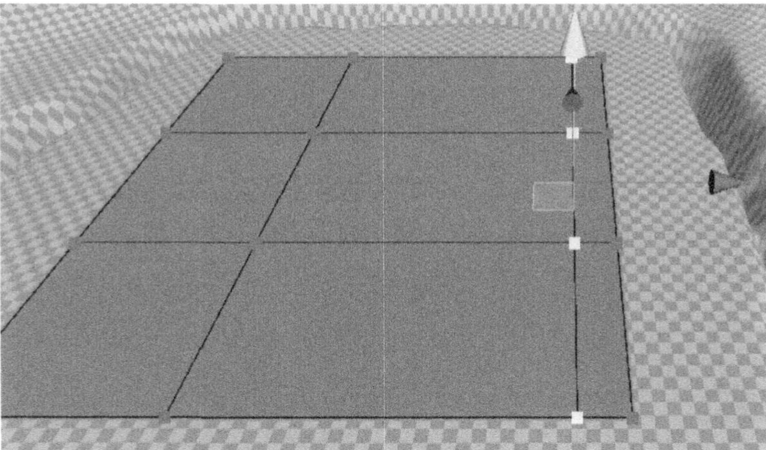

Figure 3.33: Moved vertices

8. Repeat *steps 3* to *5* for each row of vertices until you get wall outlines with similar sizes:

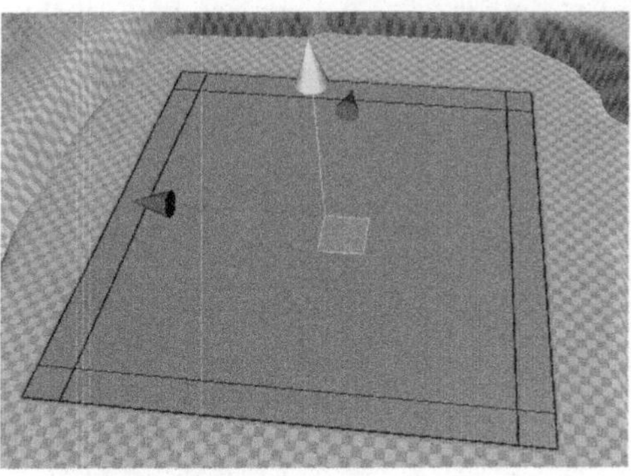

Figure 3.34: Moved vertices to reduce edges cell width

Now that we have created the outline for our walls, let's add new faces to our mesh to create them. In order to use the subdivisions, or **faces**, we have created to make our walls; we must pick and extrude them. Follow these steps to do so:

1. Select the plane.
2. Select the fourth button of the **ProBuilder** buttons in the Scene View:

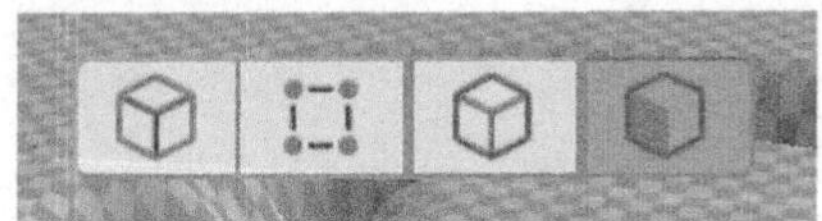

Figure 3.35: Select Face tool

3. While holding *Ctrl* (*Command* on Mac), click on each of the faces of the wall outlines:

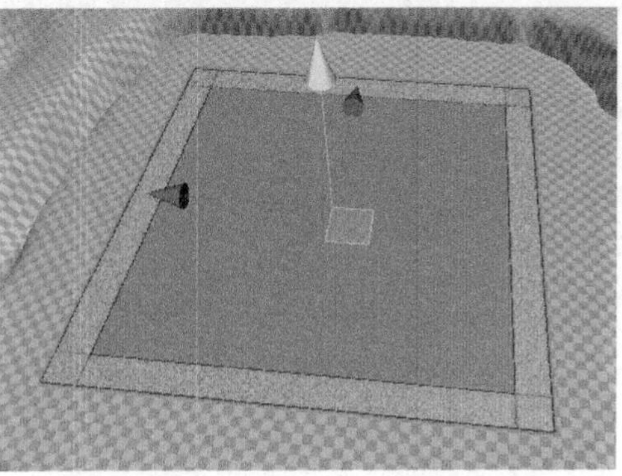

Figure 3.36: Edge faces being selected

4. In the **ProBuilder** window, look for the **plus (+)** icon to the right of the **Extrude Faces** button. It is located in the red section of the window:

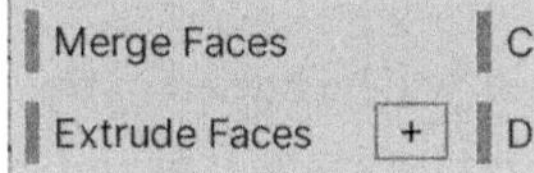

Figure 3.37: Extrude Faces option

5. Set **Distance** to 5 in the window that appears after we click the plus button.
6. Click the **Extrude Faces** button in that window:

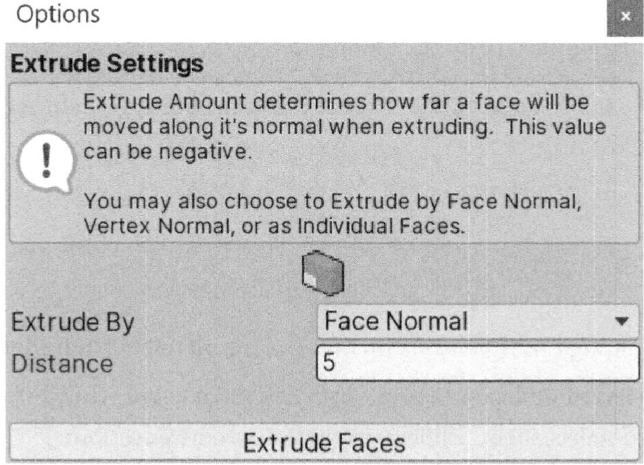

Figure 3.38: Extrude distance option

7. Now, you should see that the outline of the walls has just raised from the ground:

Figure 3.39: Extruded grid edges

Now, if you pay attention to how the base floor and walls touch the terrain, there's a little gap. We can try to move the base downward, but the floor will probably disappear because it will be buried under the terrain. A little trick we can do here is to push the walls downward, without moving the floor, so that the walls will be buried in the terrain but our floor will stay a little distance from it. You can see an example of how it would look in the following image:

Figure 3.40: Slice of the expected result

In order to do this, we need to do the following:

1. Select the third **ProBuilder** button in the Scene View to enable edge selection:

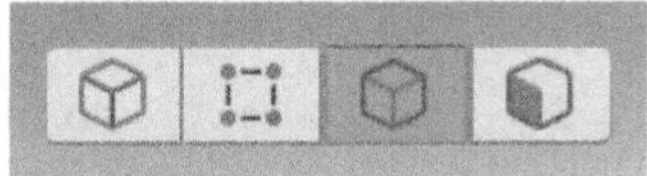

Figure 3.41: Select edges tool

2. While holding *Ctrl* (*Command* on Mac), select all the bottom edges of the walls.
3. If you selected undesired edges, just click them again while holding *Ctrl* (*Command* on Mac) to deselect them, while keeping the current selection:

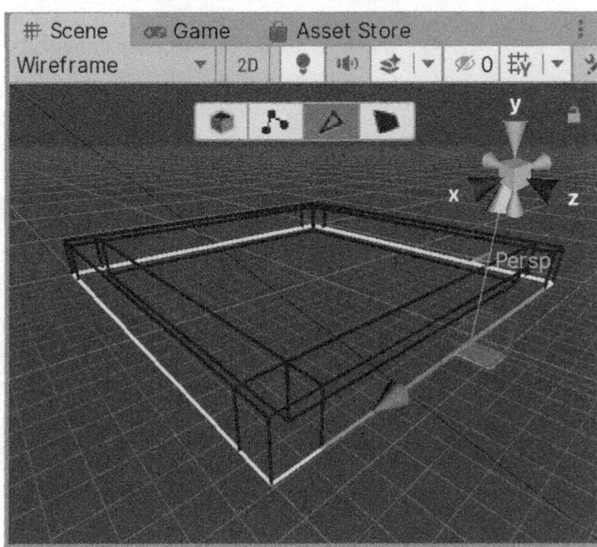

Figure 3.42: Selecting floor edges

If you want to use **Wireframe** mode in the **sphere** icon, go to the left of the 2D button in the top-right corner of the Scene View and select the **Wireframe** option from the drop-down menu, as shown in the following image. You can get back to normal by selecting **Shaded.**

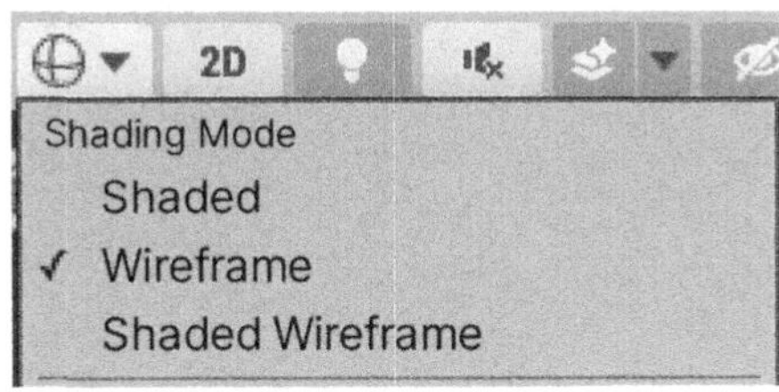

Figure 3.43: Enabling Wireframe mode

4. Enable the **Move** tool by pressing the second button (or the *W* key on the keyboard) in the top-left corner of the **Scene** panel:

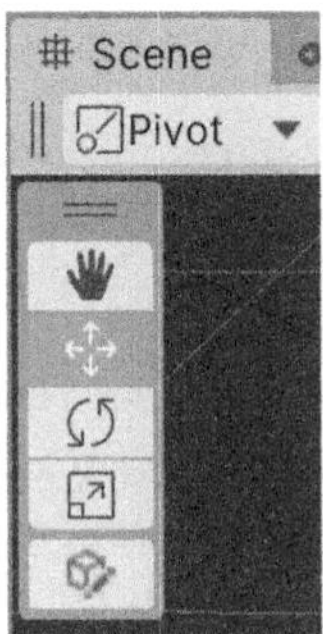

Figure 3.44: Object Move tool

5. Move the edges down until they are fully buried in the terrain:

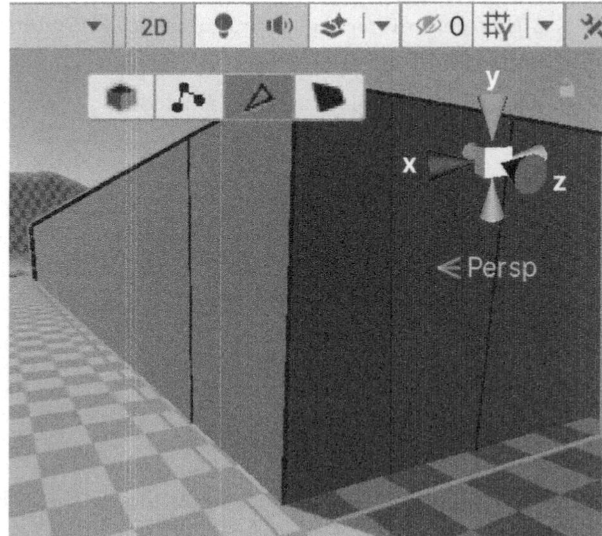

Figure 3.45: Overlapping faces

Now that we have a base mesh, we can start adding details to it using several other ProBuilder tools.

Adding details

Let's start adding details to the base by applying a little bevel to the walls, a little cut in the corners so they are not so sharp. To do so, follow these steps:

1. Using the edge selection tool (the third of the **ProBuilder** buttons), select the top edges of our model:

Figure 3.46: Top wall edges being selected

2. In the **ProBuilder** window, press the plus (+) icon to the right of the **Bevel** button.
3. Set a distance of `0.5`:

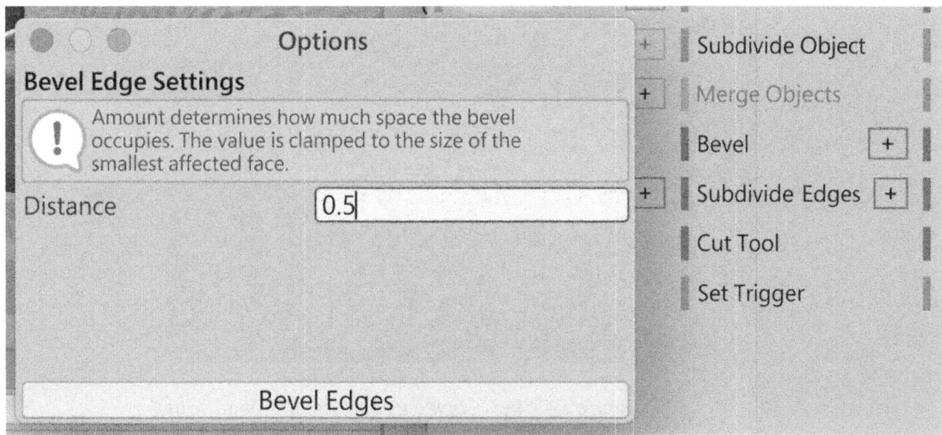

Figure 3.47: Bevel distance to generate

4. Click on **Bevel Edges**. Now you can see the top parts of our walls have a little bevel:

Figure 3.48: Result of the bevel process

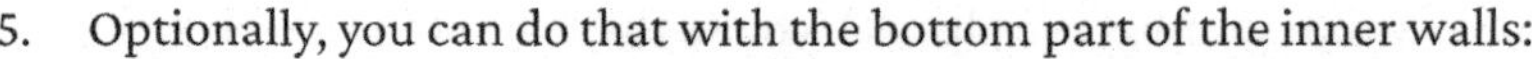

5. Optionally, you can do that with the bottom part of the inner walls:

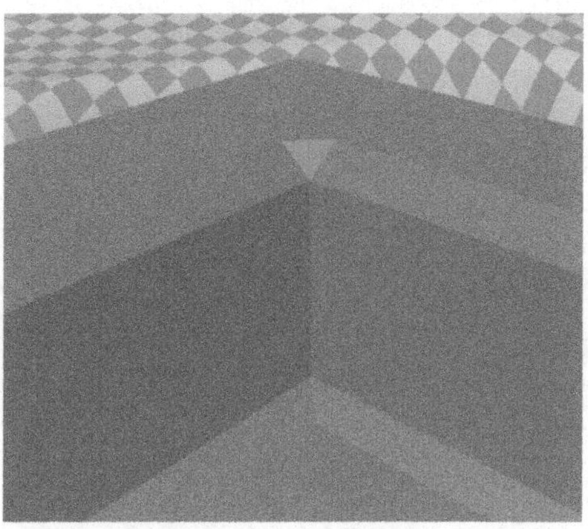

Figure 3.49: Bevel being applied to floor-wall edges

Another detail to add could be a pit in the middle of the ground as a hazard we need to avoid falling into and to make the enemies avoid it using AI. In order to do that, follow these steps:

1. Enable the **Face** selection mode by clicking the fourth ProBuilder Scene view button.
2. Select the floor.
3. Click the **Subdivide Faces** option in the **ProBuilder** window. You will end up with the floor split into four.
4. Click that button again to end up with a 4 x 4 grid:

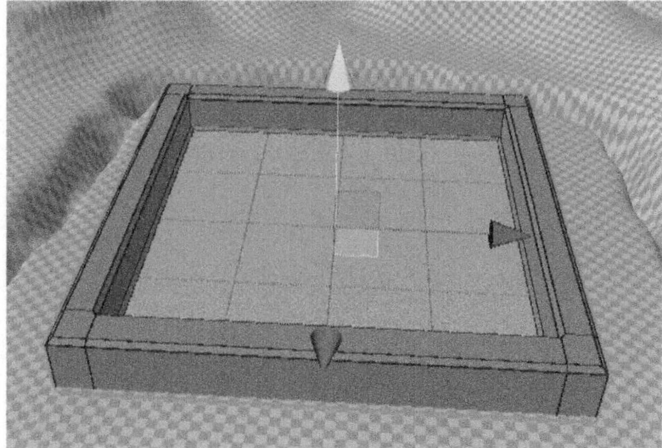

Figure 3.50: Subdividing the floor

5. Select the four inner floor tiles while holding *Ctrl* (*Command* on Mac) using the **Select Face** tool (the third of the ProBuilder buttons in the top part of the Scene View).
6. Enable the **Scale** tool by clicking the fourth button in the top-left part of the Scene View, or pressing the *R* key on the keyboard. As with the **Move** tool, this can be used to scale any object, not only vertices:

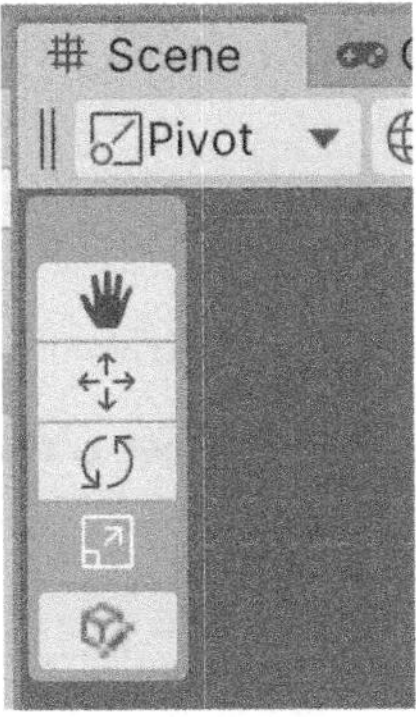

Figure 3.51: Scale tool

7. Using the gray cube at the center of the gizmo, scale down the center tiles:

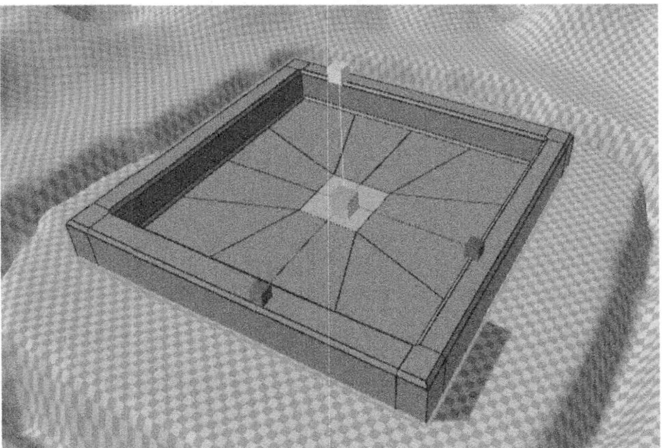

Figure 3.52: Inner cells being scaled down

8. Click the **Extrude Faces** button in the **ProBuilder** window.
9. Push the extruded faces downward with the **Move Tool**.

10. Right-click on the **ProBuilder** window tab and select **Close Tab**. We need to get back to terrain editing and having **ProBuilder** open won't allow us to do that comfortably:

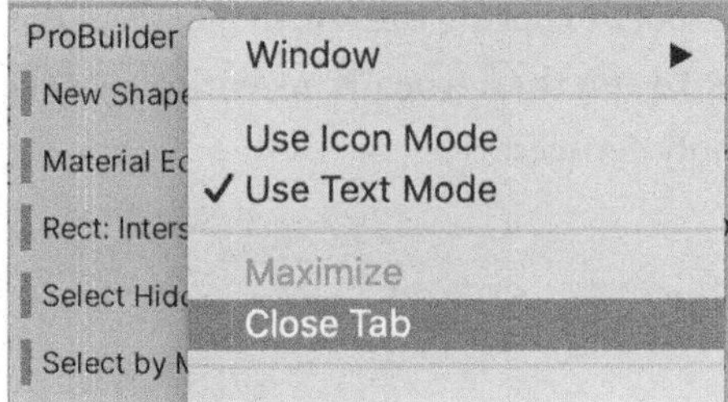

Figure 3.53: Close Tab option

11. Select the terrain and lower it so that we can see the pit:

Figure 3.54: Terrain being lowered for the pit to be visible

Summary

In this chapter, we learned how to create large terrain meshes using Height Maps and Unity Terrain Tools such as **Paint Height** and **Set Height** to create hills and rivers. Also, we saw how to create our own 3D meshes using ProBuilder, as well as how to manipulate the vertices, edges, and faces of a model to create a prototype base model for our game. We didn't discuss any performance optimizations we can apply to our meshes or advanced 3D modeling concepts as that would require entire chapters and is beyond the scope of this book. Right now, our main focus is prototyping, so we are fine with our level's current status.

In the next chapter, we will learn how to download and replace these prototyping models with final art by integrating assets (files) we have created with external tools. This is the first step to improving the graphics quality of our game, which we will finish by the end of *Part 3, Improving Graphics*.

Join us on Discord!

Read this book alongside other users, Unity game development experts, and the author himself.

Ask questions, provide solutions to other readers, chat with the author via Ask Me Anything sessions, and much more.

Scan the QR code or visit the link to join the community.

`https://packt.link/handsonunity22`

4

Importing and Integrating Assets

In the previous chapter, we created the prototype of our level. Now, let's suppose that we have coded the game and tested it, confirming the game idea is fun. With that, it's time to replace the prototype art with the real finished art. We are going to actually code the game in the next chapter, *Chapter 5, Introduction to C# and Visual Scripting*, but for learning purposes, let's just skip that part for now. In order to use the final assets, we need to learn how to get them (images, 3D models, and so on), how to import them into Unity, and how to integrate them into our scene.

In this chapter, we will examine the following topics:

- Importing assets
- Integrating assets
- Configuring assets

Let's start by learning how to get assets in Unity, such as 3D models and textures.

Importing assets

We have different sources of assets we can use in our project. We can simply receive a file from our artist, download them from different free and paid assets sites, or we can use the **Asset Store**, Unity's official asset virtual store, where we can get free and paid assets ready to use with Unity. We will use a mix of downloading assets from the internet and from the Asset Store, just to use all possible resources.

In this section, we will cover the following concepts related to importing assets:

- Importing assets from the internet
- Importing assets from the Asset Store
- Importing assets from Unity Packages
- Let's start by exploring the first source of assets, the internet.

Importing assets from the internet

In terms of getting art assets for our project, let's start with our terrain textures. Remember that we have our terrain painted with a grid pattern, so the idea is to replace that with grass, mud, rock, and other kinds of textures. To do that, we need images. In this case, these kinds of images are usually top-down views of different terrain patterns, and they have the requirement of being "tileable," meaning you can repeat them with no noticeable pattern in their connections. You can see an example of this in the following image:

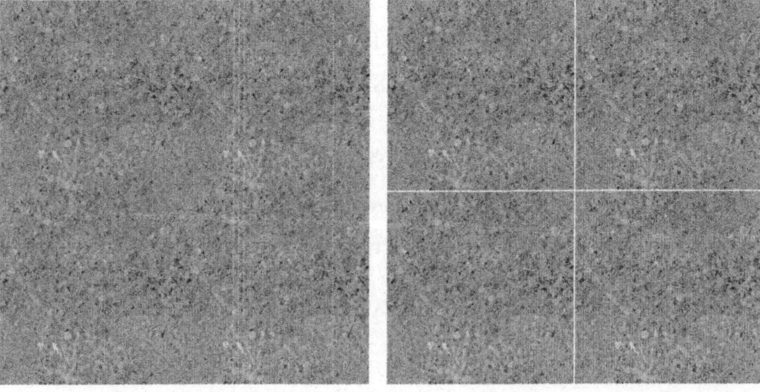

Figure 4.1: Left - grass patch; Right - the same grass patch separated to highlight the texture tiling

The grass on the left seems to be one single big image, but if you pay attention, you should be able to see some patterns repeating themselves. In this case, this grass is just a single image repeated four times in a grid, like the one on the right. This way, you can cover large areas by repeating a single small image, saving lots of RAM on the user's computer.

The idea is to get these kinds of images to paint our terrain. You can get them from several places, but the easiest way is to use *Google Images* or any image search engine. Always check for copyright permissions before using something from these sources. To do this, follow these steps:

1. Open your browser (Chrome, Safari, Edge, etc.).
2. Go to your preferred search engine. In this case, I will use Google.
3. Use the keywords `PATTERN tileable texture`, replacing `PATTERN` with the kind of terrain you are looking for, such as `grass tileable texture` or `mud tileable texture`. In this case, I am going to type `grass tileable texture` and then press *Enter* to search.
4. Switch to image search mode:

Figure 4.2: Google search for images

5. Choose any texture you find suitable for the kind of grass you need and click it. Remember that the texture must be a top-down view of the grass and must repeat.

Try to check the image's resolution before picking it. Try to select squared images that have a resolution less than 1024 x 1024 for now.

6. Right-click the opened image and select **Save image as...**:

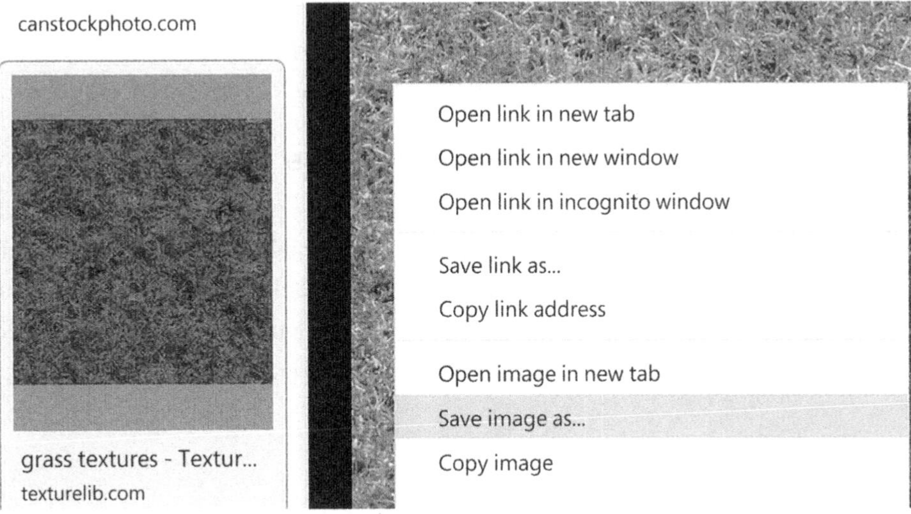

Figure 4.3 Save image as... option

7. Save the image in any folder you will remember.

Now that you have downloaded the image, you can add it to your project in several ways. The simplest one would be by doing the following:

1. Locate your image using **File Explorer** (**Finder** on Mac).
2. Locate or create the `Textures` folder in the Project window in Unity.
3. Put both the **File Explorer** and the **Unity Project Window** next to each other.
4. Drag the file from **File Explorer** to the `Textures` folder in the **Unity Project Window**:

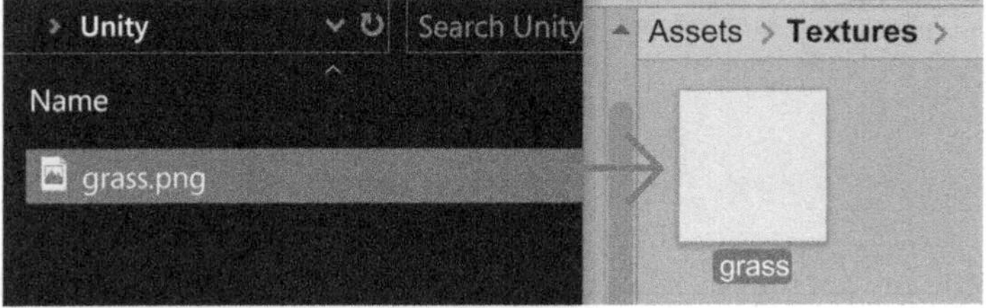

Figure 4.4: Texture being dragged from Windows File Explorer to Unity's Project view

For simple textures like these ones, any search engine can be helpful, but if you want to replace the player's base geometry with detailed walls and doors or place enemies in your scene, you need to get 3D models. If you search for those in any search engine using keywords such as "free zombie 3D model," you will find endless free and paid 3D models sites such as TurboSquid and Mixamo, but those sites can be problematic because those meshes are usually not prepared for being used in Unity, or even games. You will find models with very high polygon counts, incorrect sizes or orientations, unoptimized textures, and so on. To prevent those problems, we'll want to use a better source, and in this case, we will use Unity's Asset Store, so let's explore it.

Importing assets from the Asset Store

The Asset Store is Unity's official asset marketplace where you can find lots of models, textures, sounds, and even entire Unity plugins to extend the capabilities of the engine. In this case, we will limit ourselves to downloading 3D models to replace the player's base prototype. You will want to get 3D models with a modular design, meaning that you will get several pieces, such as walls, floors, corners, and so on. You can connect them to create any kind of scenario.

In order to do that, you must follow these steps:

1. Click on **Window | Asset Store** in Unity, which will open a new window saying the Asset Store has moved. In previous versions of Unity, you could see the Asset Store directly inside the editor, but now, it is recommended to open it in a regular web browser, so just click the **Search Online** button, which will open the site `https://assetstore.unity.com/` in your preferred browser. Also, you can check the **Always open in browser from menu** to directly open the page whenever you click on **Window | Asset Store**:

Figure 4.5: Asset Store moved message

2. In the top menu, click on the **3D** category to browse 3D assets:

Figure 4.6: 3D assets menu

3. In the recently opened page, click the arrow to the right of the **3D** category in the **All Categories** panel on the right, and then open **Environments** and check the **Sci-Fi** mark, as we will make a future-themed game:

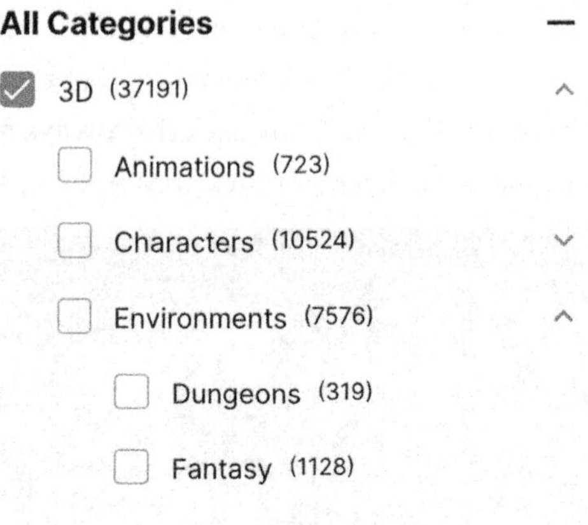

Figure 4.7: 3D assets menu

As you can see, there are several categories for finding different types of assets, and you can pick another one if you want to. In **Environments**, you will find 3D models that can be used to generate the scenery for your game.

4. If you need to, you can pay for an asset, but let's hide the paid ones for now. You can do that by clicking the **Sort by Price** option in the top-left section and selecting the **Free Assets** option:

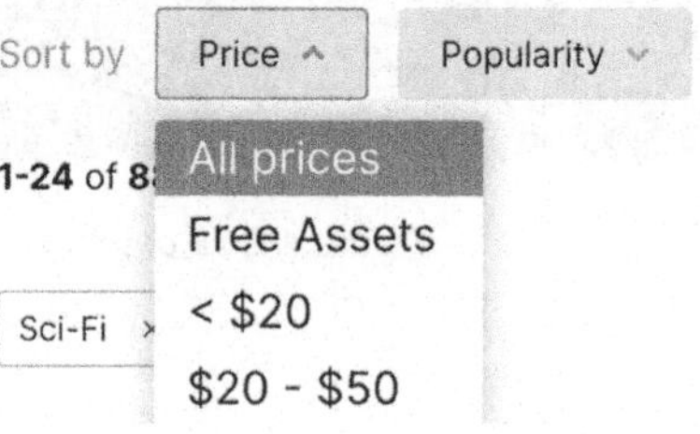

Figure 4.8: Free Assets option

5. In the search area, find any asset that seems to have the aesthetic you are looking for and click it. Remember to look out for outdoor assets, because most environment packs are usually interiors only. In my case, I have picked one called **Sci-Fi Styled Modular Pack**, which serves for both interiors and exteriors. Take into account that that package might not exist by the time you are reading this, so you might need to choose another one. If you don't find a suitable package, you can download and pick the asset files we used in the GitHub repository:

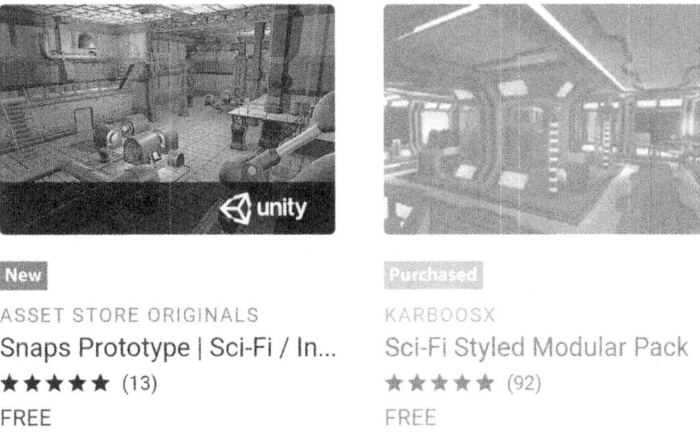

Figure 4.9: Preview of Asset Store searched packages

6. Now, you will see the package details in the **Asset Store** window. Here, you can find information regarding the package's description, videos/images, the package's contents, and the most important part, the reviews, where you can see whether the package is worth getting:

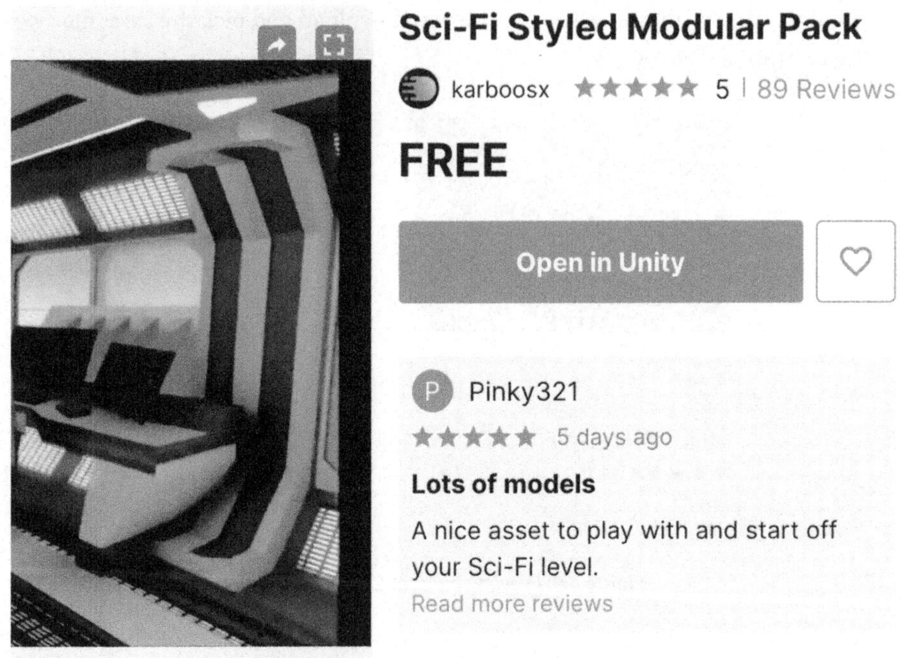

Figure 4.10: Asset Store package details

7. If you are OK with this package, click the **Add To My Assets** button, log in to Unity if requested, and then click the **Open In Unity** button. You might be prompted to accept the browser to open Unity; if so, just accept:

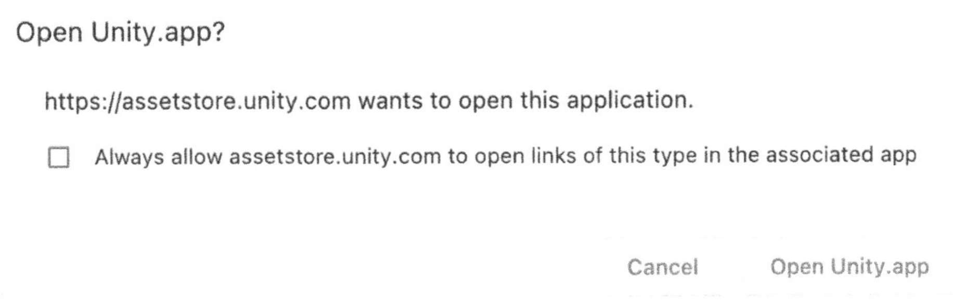

Open Unity.app?

https://assetstore.unity.com wants to open this application.

☐ Always allow assetstore.unity.com to open links of this type in the associated app

Cancel Open Unity.app

Figure 4.11: Switching apps

8. This will open the **Package Manager** again, but this time in the **My Assets** mode, showing a list of all assets you have ever downloaded from the Asset Store, and the one you just selected highlighted in the list:

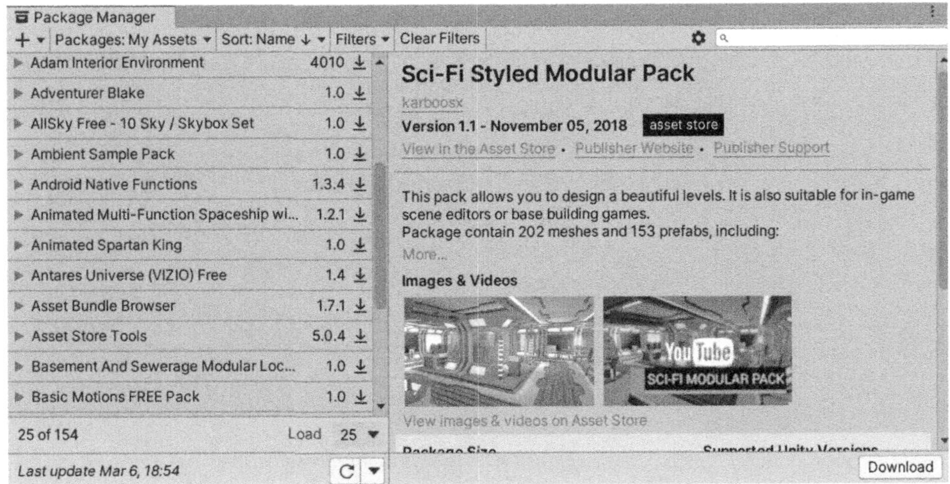

Figure 4.12: Package Manager showing assets

9. Click on **Download** on the bottom-right part of the window and wait for it to finish. Then hit **Import**.
10. After a while, the **Package Contents window** will show up, allowing you to select exactly which assets of the package you want in your project. For now, leave it as-is and click **Import**:

Figure 4.13: Assets to import selection

11. After some importing time, you will see all the package files in your **Project window**.

Take into account that importing lots of full packages will increase your project's size considerably, and that, later, you will probably want to remove the assets that you didn't use. Also, if you import assets that generate errors that prevent you from playing the scene, just delete all the `.cs` files that come with the package. They are usually in folders called `Scripts`. Those are code files that might not be compatible with your Unity version:

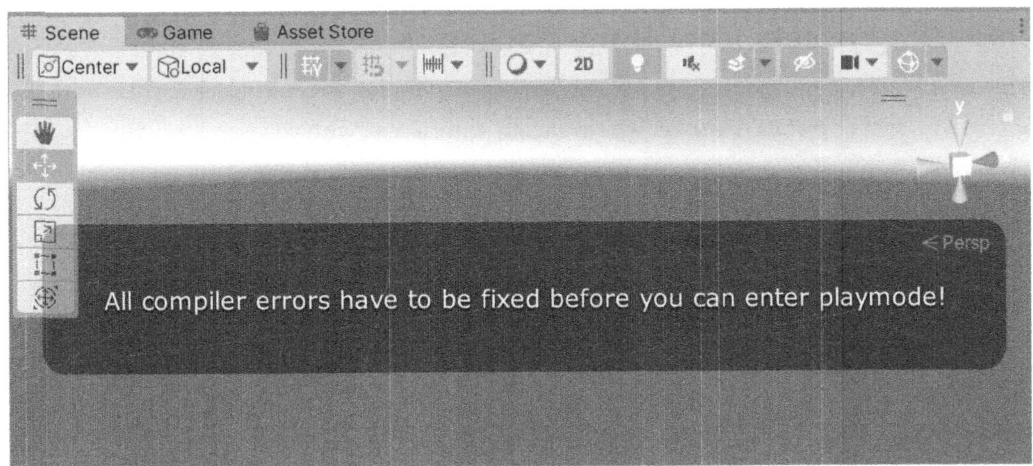

Figure 4.14: Code error warning when hitting play

Before you continue with this chapter, try to download a character 3D model using the Asset Store, following the previous steps. In order to do this, you must complete the same steps as we did with the level environment pack but look in the **3D | Characters | Humanoid** category of the Asset Store. In my case, I picked the **Robot Hero: PBR HP Polyart** package:

Figure 4.15: Character package used in our game

Now, let's explore yet another source of Unity Assets: **Unity Packages**.

Importing assets from Unity Packages

The Asset Store is not the only source of asset packages; you can get .unitypackage files from the internet, or maybe from a coworker who wants to share assets with you.

In order to import a `.unitypackage` file, you need to do the following:

1. Go to the **Assets | Import Package | Custom Package** option:

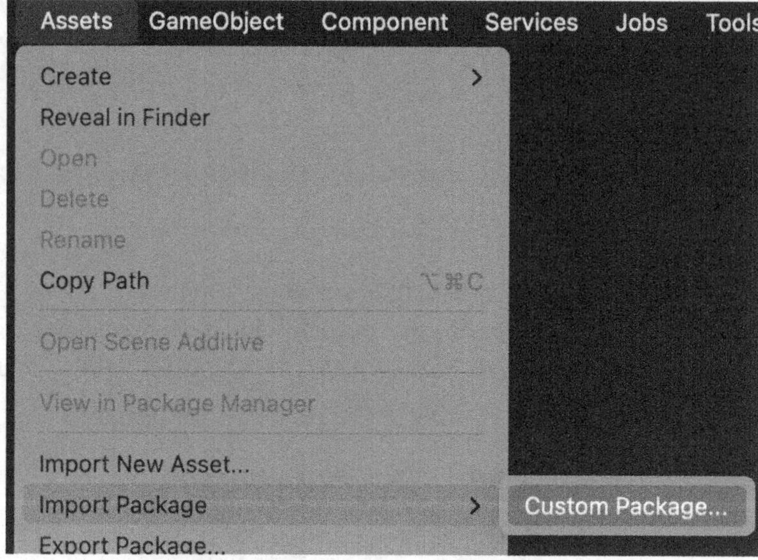

Figure 4.16: Importing custom packages

2. Search for the `.unitypackage` file in the displayed dialog.
3. Click the **Import** option in the **Import Unity Package** window that appeared, the same that we saw earlier in the Asset Store section.

Now that we have imported lots of art assets, let's learn how to use them in our scene.

Integrating assets

We have just imported lots of files that can be used in several ways, so the idea of this section is to see how Unity integrates those assets with the GameObjects and components that need them.

In this section, we will cover the following concepts related to importing assets:

- Integrating terrain textures
- Integrating meshes
- Integrating materials

Let's start by using the tileable textures to cover the terrain.

Integrating terrain textures

In order to apply textures to our terrain, do the following:

1. Select the **Terrain** object.
2. In the **Inspector**, click the brush icon of the **Terrain** component (second button).
3. From the drop-down menu, select **Paint Texture**:

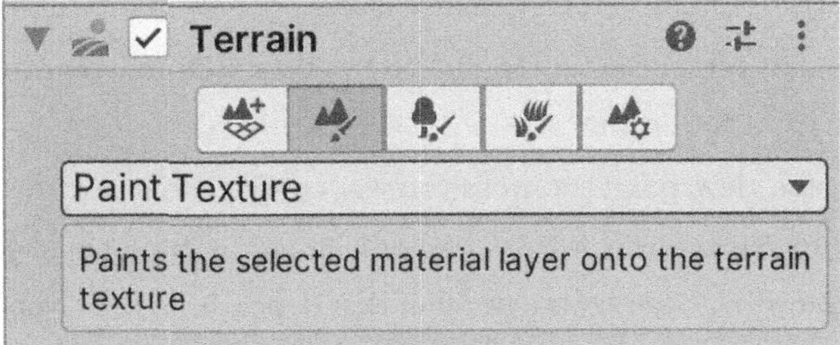

Figure 4.17: Terrain Paint Texture option

4. Click the **Edit Terrain Layers... | Create Layer** option.

5. Find and double-click the terrain texture you downloaded previously in the **Texture Picker** window that appears:

Figure 4.18: Texture to paint picker

6. You will see how the texture will be immediately applied to the whole terrain.
7. Repeat *steps 4* and *5* to add other textures. This time, you will see that that texture is not immediately applied.
8. In the **Terrain Layers** section, select the new texture you have created to start painting with that. I used a mud texture in my case.
9. As when you edited the terrain, in the **Brushes** section, you can select and configure a brush to paint the terrain.
10. In the **Scene** view, paint the areas you want to have that texture applied to.
11. If your texture patterns are too obvious, open the **New Layer N** section on top of the **Brushes** section, where *N* is a number that depends on the layer you have created.

Each time you add a texture to the terrain, you will see that a new asset called **New Layer N** is created in the **Project** view. It holds data of the terrain layer you have created, and you can use that one on other terrains if you need to. You can also rename that asset to give it a meaningful name. Also, you can reorganize those assets in their own folder for organization purposes.

12. Open the section using the triangle to its left and increase the **Size** property in the **Tiling Settings** section until you find a suitable size where the pattern is not that obvious:

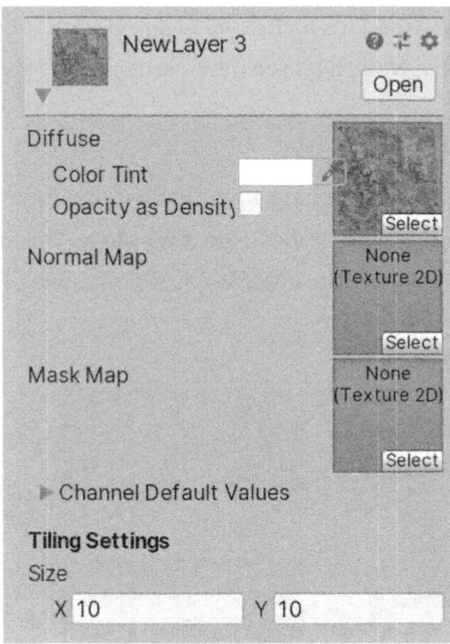

Figure 4.19: Painting texture options

13. Repeat *steps 4* to *12* until you have applied all the textures you wanted to add to your terrain. In my case, I applied the mud texture to the river basin and used a rock texture for the hills. For the texture of the rocks, I reduced the opacity property of the brush to blend it better with the grass in the mountains. You can try to add a layer of snow at the top just for fun:

Figure 4.20: Results of painting our terrain with three different textures

Of course, we can improve this a lot using lots of the advanced tools of the system, but let's just keep things simple for now. Now, let's see how we can integrate the 3D models into our game.

Integrating meshes

If you select one of the 3D assets we have downloaded previously and click the arrow to its right, one or more sub-assets will appear in the **Project window**. This means that the 3D model files we downloaded from the Asset Store (the FBX files) are containers of assets that define the 3D model:

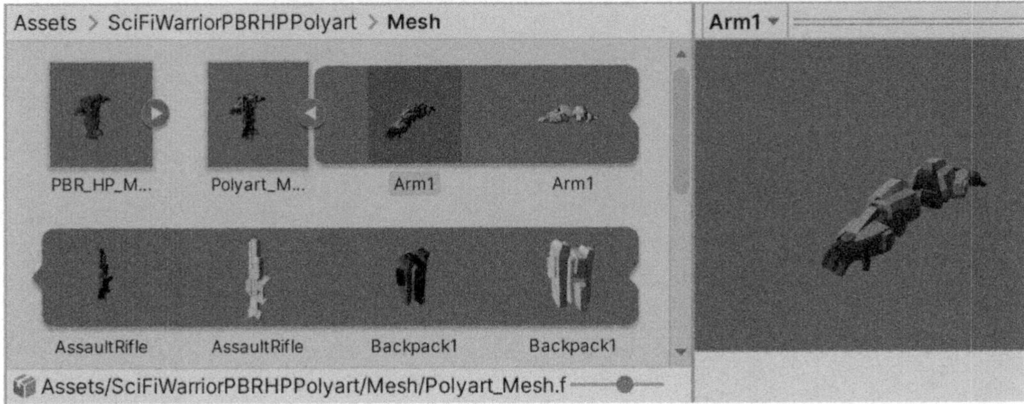

Figure 4.21: Mesh picker

Some of those sub-assets are meshes, which are a collection of triangles that define the geometry of your model. You can find at least one of these mesh sub-assets inside the file, but you can also find several, and that can happen if your model is composed of lots of pieces. For example, a car can be a single rigid mesh, but that won't allow you to rotate its wheels or open its doors; it will be just a static car, and that can be enough if the car is just a prop in the scene, but if the player will be able to control it, you will probably need to modify it. The idea is that all pieces of your car are different GameObjects parented to one another in such a way that if you move one, all of them will move, but you can still rotate its pieces independently.

When you drag the 3D model file to the scene (not the sub-asset), Unity will automatically create all the objects for each piece and its proper parenting based on how the artist created those. You can select the object in the Hierarchy and explore all its children to see this:

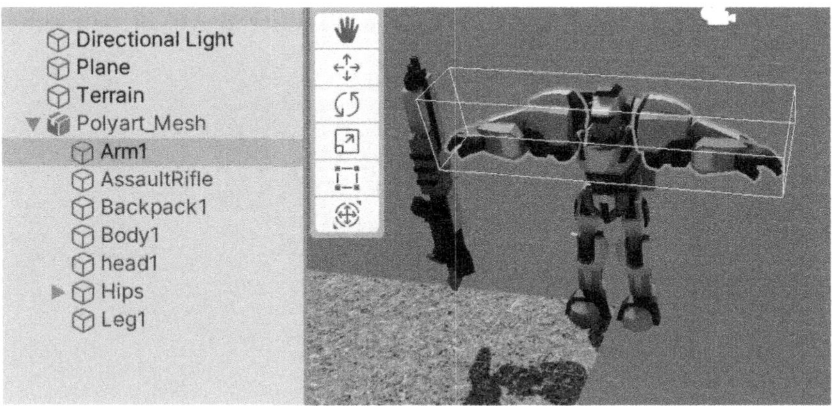

Figure 4.22: Sub-object selection

Also, you will find that each of those objects may have its own `Mesh Filter` and `Mesh Renderer` components, each one rendering just that piece of the model. Remember that the `Mesh Filter` is a component that has a reference to the mesh asset to render, so the `Mesh Filter` is the one using those mesh sub-assets we talked about previously. In the case of animated characters, you will find the `Skinned Mesh Renderer` component instead, but we will discuss that component later, in *Part 3, Improving Graphics*.

Now, when you drag the 3D model file into the scene, you will get a similar result as if the model were a Prefab and you were instancing it. But 3D model files are more limited than Prefabs because you can't apply changes to the model. If you've dragged the object onto the scene and edited it to have the behavior you want, I suggest that you create a Prefab to get all the benefits we discussed in *Chapter 2, Editing Scenes and GameObjects*, such as applying changes to all the instances of the Prefab and so on. Never create lots of instances of a model from its model file—always create them from the Prefab you created based on that file to allow you to add extra behavior to it.

That's the basic usage of 3D meshes. Now, let's explore the texture integration process, which will give our 3D models more detail.

Integrating textures

Maybe your model already has the texture applied but has a magenta color applied to all of it. If this is the case, that means the asset wasn't prepared to work with the **Universal Render Pipeline** (**URP**) template you selected when creating the project.

Some assets in the Asset Store are created by third-party editors and could be meant to be used in older versions of Unity:

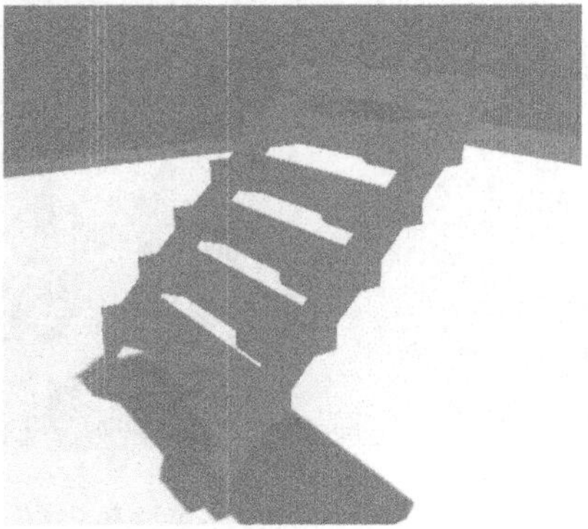

Figure 4.23: Mesh being rendered with erroneous or no material at all

One option to fix magenta assets is using the **Render Pipeline Converter**, a tool that will find them and reconfigure them (if possible) to work with URP. To do so, perform the following steps every time you import an asset that looks magenta:

1. Go to **Window | Rendering | Render Pipeline Converter.**
2. Select the **Built-in to URP** option from the dropdown:

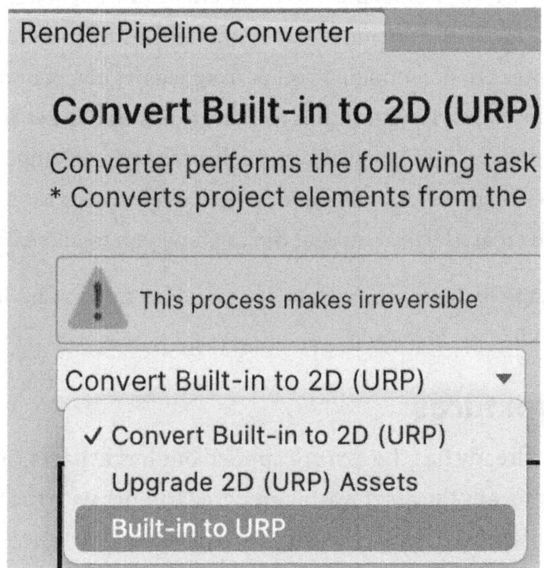

Figure 4.24: Upgrading older assets to URP

3. Scroll until you see the **Material Upgrade** checkbox and check it.
4. Click the **Initialize Converters** button in the bottom-left corner. This will display a list of all the materials that need to be upgraded. We will discuss materials more later:

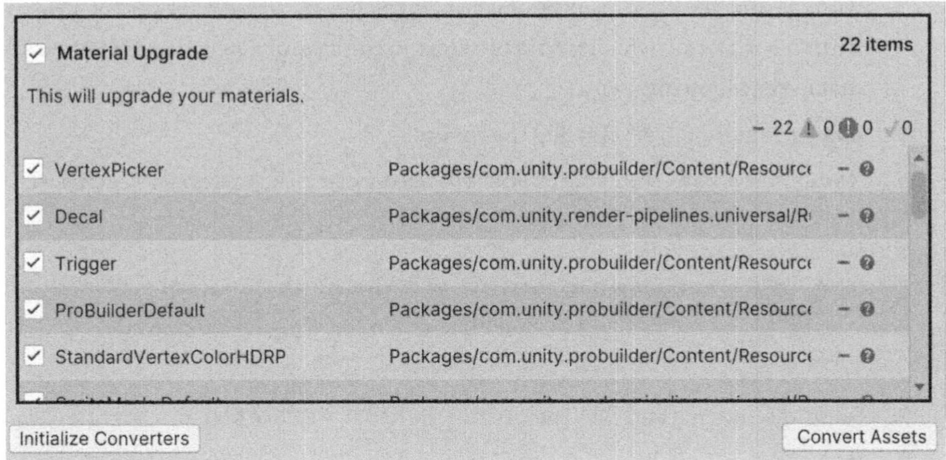

Figure 4.25: Fixing Material to work with URP

5. Click the **Convert Assets** button and see if the model was fixed.

You will need to close the window for it to detect new magenta assets that weren't there before opening it. The con of this method is that, sometimes, it won't upgrade the material properly. Luckily, we can fix this by reapplying the textures of the objects manually. Even if your assets work just fine, I suggest that you reapply your textures anyway, just to learn more about the concept of materials.

A texture is not applied directly to the object. That's because the texture is just one single configuration of all the ones that control the aspect of your model. In order to change the appearance of a model, you must create a **Material**. A material is a separate asset that contains lots of settings about how Unity should render your object. You can apply that asset to several objects that share the same graphics settings, and if you change the settings of the material, it will affect all the objects that are using it. It works like a graphics profile.

In order to create a material to apply the textures of your object, you need to follow these steps:

1. In the **Project Window**, click the plus (+) button in the top-left part of the window.
2. Click the **Material** option in that menu.

3. Name your material. This is usually the name of the asset we will be applying the material to (for example, `Car`, `Ship`, `Character`, and so on).
4. Drag the created material to the model instance on your scene. If you move the mouse with the dragged asset over the object, you will be able to see a preview of how it will look with that material, which would be white in the case of a new material. We will change that in the following steps.
5. Apply the material by releasing the mouse.
6. If your object has several parts, you will need to drag the material to each part.

Dragging the material will change the material's property of the `MeshRenderer` component of the object you have dragged.

7. Select the material and click the circle to the left of the **Base Map** property (see *Figure 4.23*).
8. In the **Texture Selector**, click on the texture of your model. It can be complicated to locate the texture just by looking at it. Usually, the name of the texture will match the model's name. If not, you will need to try different textures until you see one that fits your object. Also, you may find several textures with the same name as your model. Just pick the one that seems to have the proper colors instead of the ones that look black and white or light blue; we will use those later:

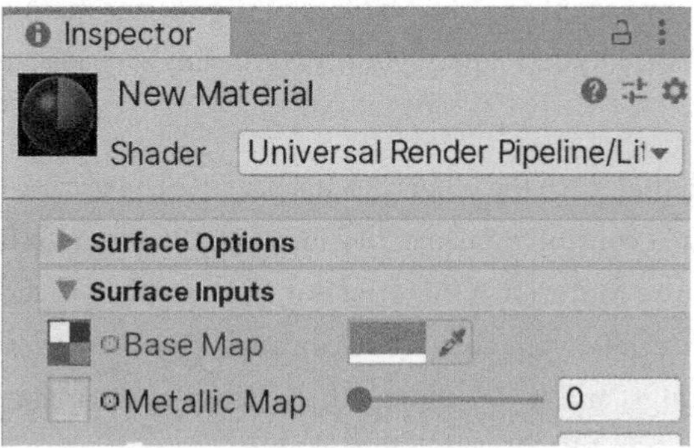

Figure 4.26: Base Map property of URP materials

With this, you have successfully applied the texture to the object through a material. For each object that uses the same texture, just drag the same material. Now that we have a basic understanding of how to apply the model textures, let's learn how to properly configure the import settings before spreading models all over the scene.

Configuring assets

As we mentioned earlier, artists are used to creating art assets outside Unity, and that can cause differences between how the asset is seen from that tool and how Unity will import it. As an example, 3D Studio Max can work in centimeters, inches, and so on, while Unity works in meters. We have just downloaded and used lots of assets, but we have skipped the configuration step to solve those discrepancies, so let's take a look at this now.

In this section, we will cover the following concepts related to importing assets:

- Configuring meshes
- Configuring textures

Let's start by discussing how to configure 3D meshes.

Configuring meshes

In order to change the model's import settings, you need to locate the model file you have downloaded. There are several file extensions that contain 3D models, with the most common one being the `.fbx` file, but you can encounter others such as `.obj`,`.3ds`, `.blender`, `.mb`, and so on. You can identify whether the file is a 3D mesh via its extension:

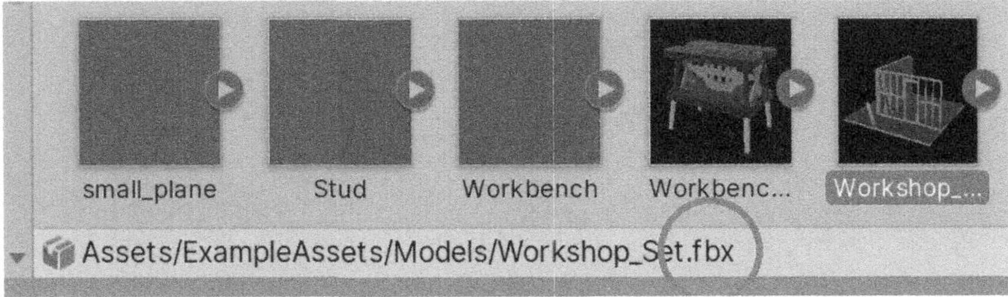

Figure 4.27: Selected asset path extension

Also, you can click the **asset** and check in the **Inspector** for the tabs you can see in the following screenshot:

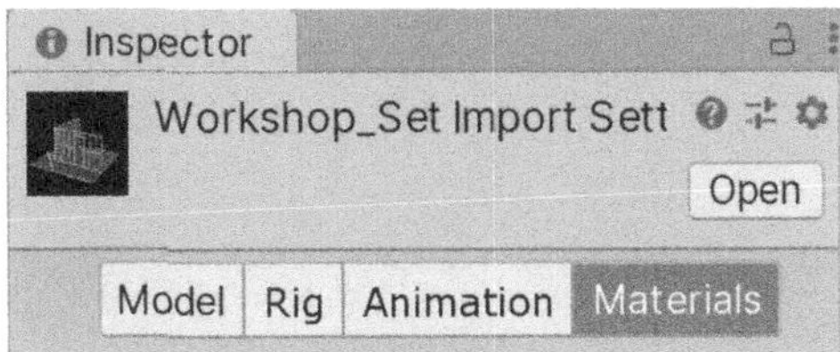

Figure 4.28: Mesh materials settings

Now that you have located the 3D mesh files, you can configure them properly. Right now, the only thing we should take into account is the proper scale of the model. Artists are used to working with different software with different setups; maybe one artist created the model using meters as its metric unit, while other artists used inches, feet, and so on. When importing assets that have been created in different units, they will probably be unproportioned, which means we will get results such as humans being bigger than buildings and so on.

The best solution is to just ask the artist to fix that. If all the assets were authored in your company, or if you used an external asset, you could ask the artist to fix it to the way your company works, but right now, you are probably a single developer learning Unity by yourself. Luckily, Unity has a setting that allows you to rescale the original asset before using it in Unity. In order to change the "**Scale Factor**" of an object, you must do the following:

1. Locate the 3D mesh in your **Project Window**.
2. Drag it to the scene. You will see that an object will appear in your scene.
3. Create a capsule using the **GameObject | 3D Object | Capsule** option.
4. Put the capsule next to the model you dragged into the editor. See if the scale has sense. The idea is that the capsule is representing a human being (2 meters tall) so that you have a reference for the scale:

Figure 4.29: Using a capsule as reference for scale

5. If the model is bigger or smaller than expected, select the mesh again in the Project window (not the GameObject instance you dragged to the editor) and you will see some import settings in the Inspector. In the image, we can say the model has good relative size, but just for learning purposes, do the next steps.
6. Look for the **Scale Factor** property and modify it, increasing it if your model is smaller than expected, or reducing it in the opposite case:

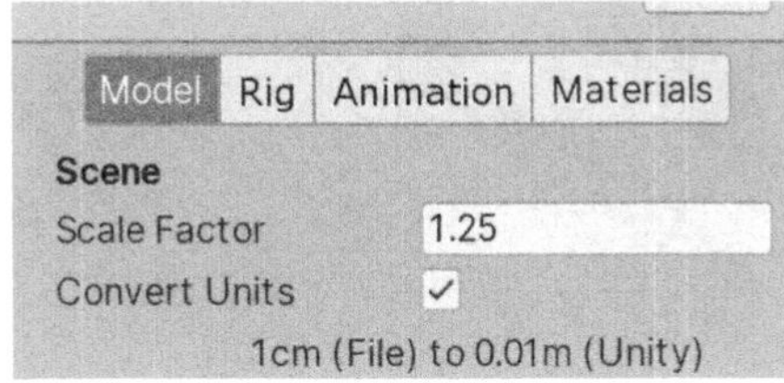

Figure 4.30: Model mesh options

7. Click the **Apply** button at the bottom of the Inspector.
8. Repeat *steps 6* and *7* until you get the desired result.

There are plenty of other options to configure, but let's stop here for now. Now, let's discuss how to properly configure the textures of our models.

Configuring textures

Again, there are several settings to configure here, but let's focus on the **Texture Size** for now. The idea is to use the size that best fits the usage of that texture, and that depends on lots of factors.

The first factor to take into account is the distance from which the object will be seen. If you are creating a first-person game, you will probably see lots of objects near enough to justify a big texture, but maybe you have lots of distant objects, such as billboards at the top of buildings, which you will never be near enough to see the details of, so you can use smaller textures for that.

Another thing to take into account is the importance of the object. If you are creating a racing game, you will probably have lots of 3D models that will be on screen for a few seconds and the player will never focus on them; they will be paying attention to the road and other cars. In this case, an object such as a trash can on the street can have a little texture and a low polygon model and the user will never notice that (unless they stop to appreciate the scenery, but that's acceptable).

Finally, you can have a game with a top-down view that will never zoom-in on the scene, so the same object that has a big texture in first-person games will have a less detailed texture here. In the following images, you can see that the smaller ship could use a smaller texture:

Figure 4.31: The same model seen at different distances

The ideal size of the texture is relative. The usual way to find it is by changing its size until you find the smallest possible size with a decent quality when the object is seen from the nearest position possible in the game. This is a trial-and-error method. In order to do that, you can do the following:

1. Locate the 3D model and put it into the scene.
2. Put the Scene view camera in a position that shows the object at its biggest possible in-game size. As an example, in a **first-person-shooter** (**FPS**) game, the camera can be almost right next to the object, while in a top-down game, it would be a few meters above the object. Again, that depends on your game. Remember our game is a third-person shooter.
3. Find and select the texture that the object is using in the folders that were imported with the package or from the material you created previously. They usually have the `.png`, `.jpg`, or `.tif` extensions.
4. In the Inspector, look at the **Max Size** property and reduce it, trying the next smaller value. For example, if the texture is **2048**, try **1024**.
5. Click **Apply** and check the Scene view to see if the quality has decreased dramatically or if the change isn't noticeable. You will be surprised.
6. Repeat *steps 4* to *5* until you get a bad-quality result. In that case, just increase the previous resolution to get an acceptable quality. Of course, if you are targeting PC games, you can expect higher resolutions than mobile games.

Now that you have imported, integrated, and configured your objects, let's create our player's base with those assets.

Assembling the scene

Let's start replacing our prototype base using the environment pack we have downloaded. To do that, you must do the following:

1. In the **Environment** pack we imported before, locate the folder that contains all the models for the different pieces of the scene and try to find a corner. You can use the search bar in the **Project Window** to search for the `corner` keyword:

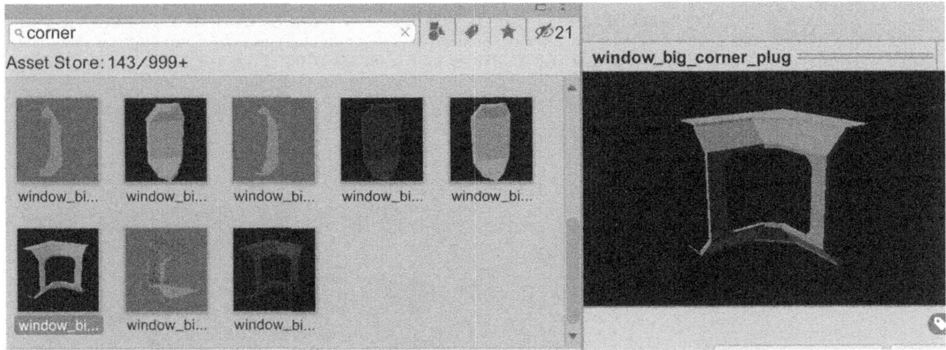

Figure 4.32: Mesh picker

2. In my specific case, I have the outer and inner sides of the corner as separate models, so I need to put them together.
3. Position it in the same position as any corner of your prototype base:

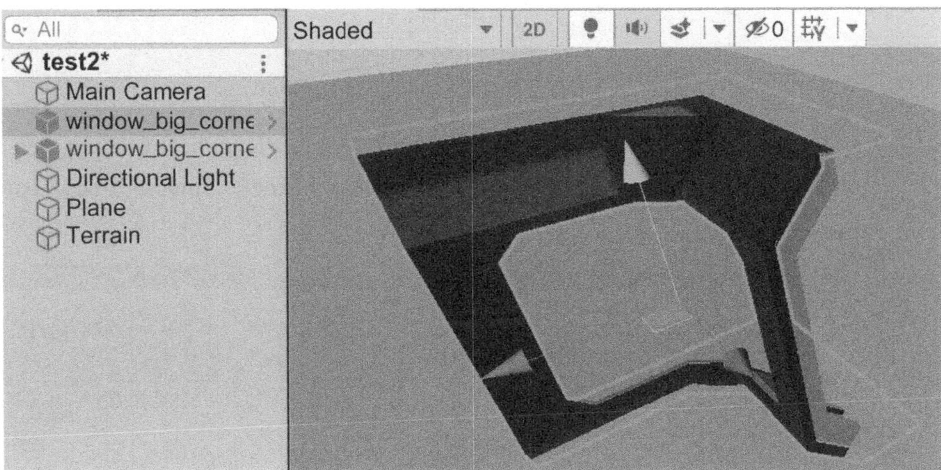

Figure 4.33: Positioning the mesh on a placeholder for replacement

4. Find the proper model that will connect with that corner to create walls. Again, you can try searching for the `wall` keyword in the **Project Window**.
5. Instance it and position it so that it's connected to the corner. Don't worry if it doesn't fit perfectly; you will go over the scene when necessary later.

You can select an object and press the *V* key to select a vertex of the selected object. Then you can drag it, click on the rectangle in the middle of the translate gizmo, and direct it to a vertex of another object. This is called **Vertex Snapping**. It allows you to connect two pieces of the scene exactly as intended.

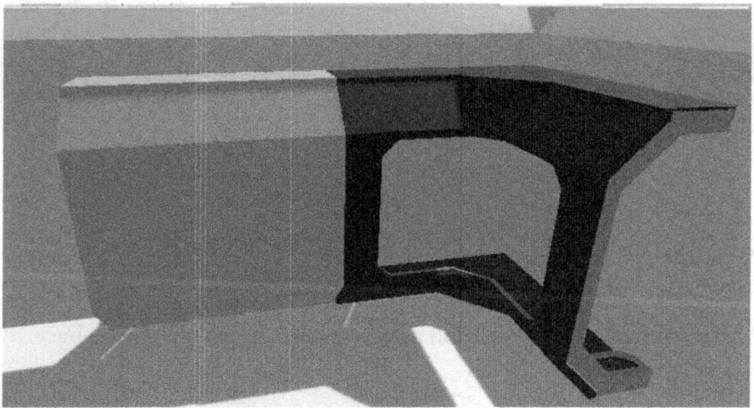

Figure 4.34: Connecting two modules

6. Repeat the walls until you reach the other end of the player base and position another corner. You might get a wall that's a little bit larger or smaller than the original prototype, but that's fine:

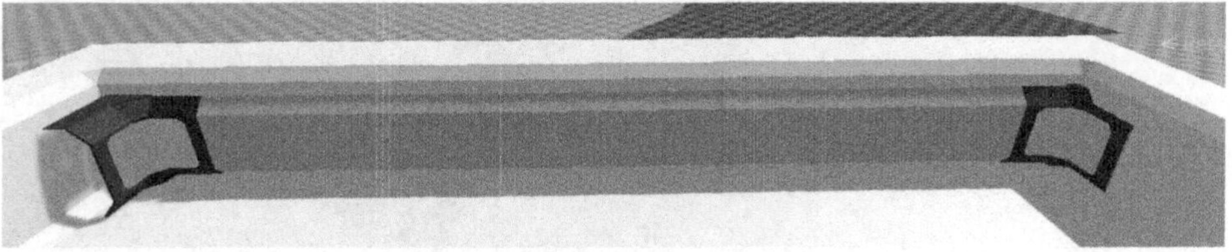

Figure 4.35: Chain of connected modules

You can move an object while pressing the *Ctrl* key (*Command* on Mac) to snap the object's position so that the clones of the wall can be easily located right next to the others. Another option is to manually set the `Position` property of the `Transform` component in the Inspector.

7. Complete the rest of the walls and destroy the prototype cube we made in ProBuilder. Remember that this process is slow and you will need to be patient.
8. Add floors by looking for floor tiles and repeating them all over the surface:

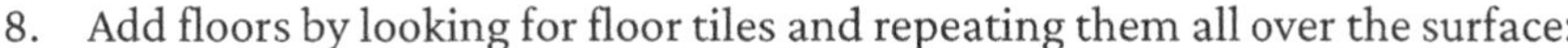

Figure 4.36: Floor modules with a hole for the pit

9. Add whatever details you want to add with other modular pieces in the package.
10. Put all those pieces in a container object called `Base`. Remember to create an empty object and drag the base pieces into it:

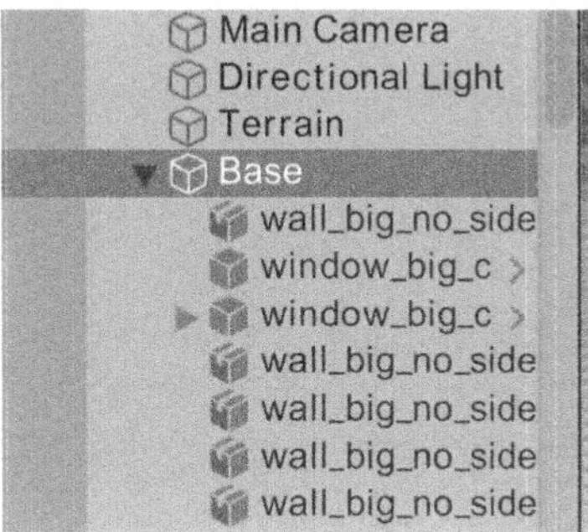

Figure 4.37: Mesh sub-assets

After a lot of practice doing this, you will slowly gain experience with the common pitfalls and good practices of modular scene design. All the packages have a different modular design in mind, so you will need to adapt to them.

Summary

In this chapter, we learned how to import models and textures and integrate them into our scene. We discussed how to apply textures to the terrain, how to replace our prototype mesh with modular models, how to apply textures to those, and how to properly configure the assets, all while taking several criteria into account according to the usage of the object.

With this, we have finished *Part 1* of this book and discussed several basic Unity concepts we will use throughout the book. In *Part 2,* we will start coding the gameplay of our game, like the player's movement and the health system. We will start learning how to create our own components to add behavior to our objects and the basic anatomy of a script.

5

Introduction to C# and Visual Scripting

Unity has a lot of great built-in tools to solve the most common problems in game development, such as the ones we have seen so far. Even two games of the same genre have their own little differences that make the game unique, and Unity cannot foresee that, so that's why we have scripting. Through coding, we can extend Unity's capabilities in several ways to achieve the exact behavior we need, all through a well-known language—C#. But aside from C#, Unity also has **Visual Scripting**, a way to generate code through a node graph tool. This means you can create scripts without writing code but by dragging **nodes**, boxes that represent actions that can be chained:

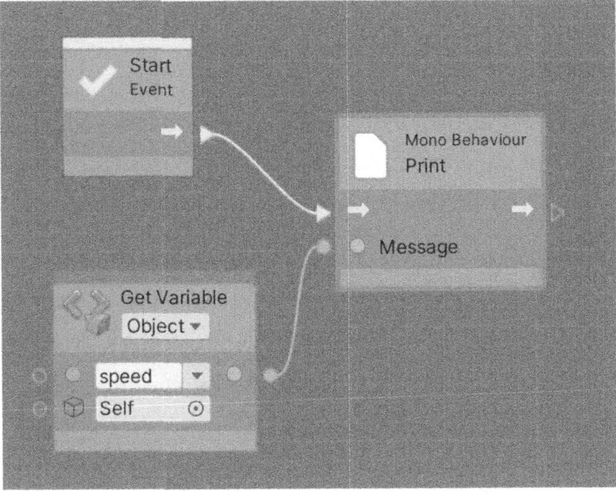

Figure 5.1: Example of a Visual Scripting graph

While essentially both ways can achieve the same result, we can use them for different things. Usually, the core logic of the game is written in C# due to it being usually huge and very performance sensitive. But sometimes using visual scripts instead allows non-programmer team members, like artists or game designers, to have more freedom to edit minor changes in the game, especially regarding balancing or visual effects.

Another example would be game designers prototyping ideas through visual scripts that later programmers will convert to C# scripts when the idea is approved. Also, C# programmers can create nodes for Visual Script programmers to use.

The way to mix these tools varies widely between teams, so while in the next chapters we are going to focus mainly on C#, we are going to also see the Visual Scripting equivalent version of the scripts we are going to create. This way you will have the opportunity to experiment when convenient to use one or the other according to your team structure.

In this chapter, we will examine the following scripting concepts:

- Creating scripts
- Using events and instructions

We are going to create our own Unity components, learning the basic structure of a script and the way that we can execute actions and expose properties to be configured, both with C# and Visual Scripting. We are not going to create any of our actual game codes here, just some example scripts to set the ground to start doing that in the next chapter. Let's start by discussing the basics of script creation.

Creating scripts

The first step to creating behavior is to create script assets; these are files that will contain the logic behind the behavior of our components. Both C# and Visual Scripting have their own type of asset to achieve that, so let's explore how to do that in both tools.

Having some programming knowledge is required in this book. However, in this first section, we are going to discuss a basic script structure to make sure you have a strong foundation to follow when we code the behaviors of our game in the following chapters. Even if you are familiar with C#, try not to skip this section because we will cover Unity-specific structures of the code.

In this section, we will examine the following script creation concepts:

- Initial setup
- Creating a C# script

- Adding fields
- Creating a Visual Script graph

We are going to create our first script, which will serve to create our component, discussing the tools needed to do so and exploring how to expose our class fields to the editor. Let's start with the basics of script creation.

Initial setup

Support for Visual Scripting is added by installing the **Visual Scripting** package in the **Package Manager** as we did with other packages in previous chapters, but as Unity does that automatically for us when we create the project, we don't need any further setup. That means the rest of this section will take care of setting up the tools needed to work with C#.

One thing to consider before creating our first C# script is how Unity compiles the code. While coding, we are used to having an **Integrated Development Environment** (**IDE**), which is a program to create our code and compile or execute it. In Unity, we will just use an IDE as a tool to create the scripts easily with coloring and auto-completion because Unity doesn't have a custom code editor (if you have never coded before, these are valuable tools for beginners). The scripts will be created inside the Unity project and Unity will detect and compile them if any changes are made, so you won't compile them in the IDE. Don't worry, even if not compiling and running the code in the IDE, it is possible to debug, add breakpoints, and check the data on the variables and structures using the IDE and Unity together.

We can use Visual Studio, Visual Studio Code, Rider, or whatever C# IDE you'd like to use, but when you install Unity, you will probably see an option to install Visual Studio automatically, which allows you to have a default IDE. This installs the free version of Visual Studio, so don't worry about the licenses here. If you don't have an IDE on your computer and didn't check the Visual Studio option while installing Unity, you can do the following:

1. Open **Unity Hub**.
2. Go to the **Installs** section.
3. Click on the wheel button in the top-right area of the Unity version you are using and click on **Add Modules**:

Figure 5.2: Adding a module to the Unity installation

4. Check the option that says **Visual Studio**; the description of the option will vary depending on the version of Unity and the platform you are using.
5. Hit the **Continue** button at the bottom-right:

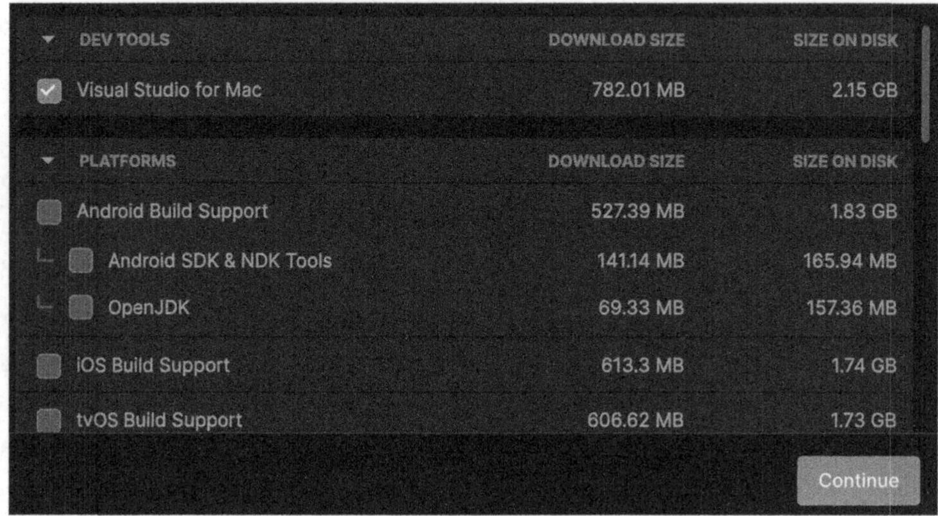

Figure 5.3: Installing Visual Studio

6. Check that you accept the terms and conditions and click **Install**:

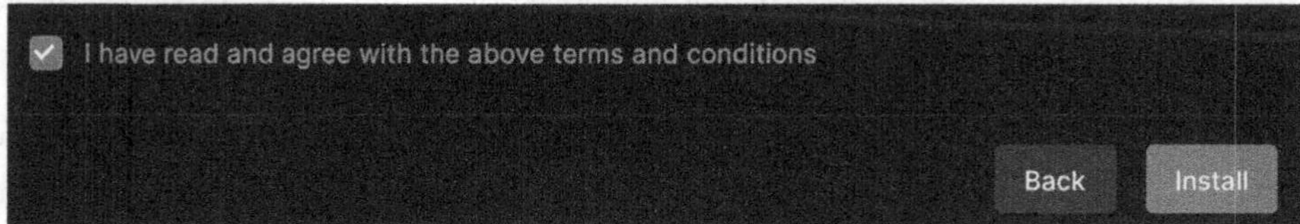

Figure 5.4: Accepting the terms and conditions

7. Wait for the operation to end. This might take a few minutes. There may be additional Visual Studio steps that vary between platform and version; if so, just follow them.

If you have a preferred IDE, you can install it yourself and configure Unity to use it. If you can afford it or you are a teacher or a student (as it is free in these cases), I recommend Rider. It is a great IDE with lots of C# and Unity features that you will love; however, it is not vital for this book. In order to set up Unity to use a custom IDE, do the following:

1. Open the project.
2. Go to **Edit | Preferences** in the top menu of the editor (**Unity | Preferences** on Mac).
3. Select the **External Tools** menu from the left panel.

4. From the external script editor, select your preferred IDE; Unity will automatically detect the supported IDEs:

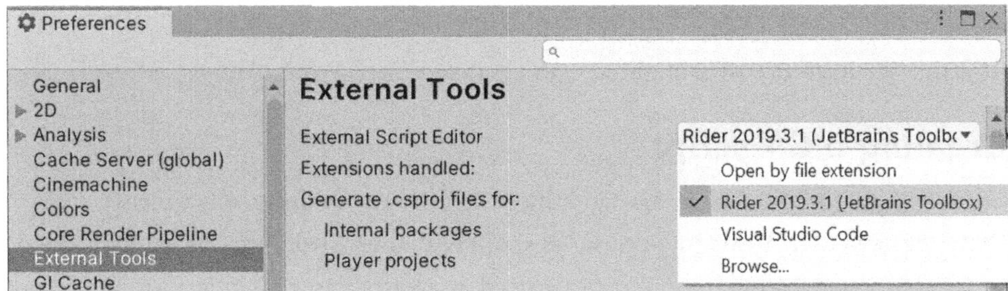

Figure 5.5: Selecting a custom IDE

5. If you don't find your IDE in the list, you can use the **Browse...** option. Note that usually, IDEs that require you to use this option are not very well supported—but it's worth a shot.

Finally, some IDEs, such as Visual Studio, Visual Studio Code, and Rider, have Unity integration tools that you need to install in your project, which is optional but can be useful. Usually, Unity installs these automatically, but if you want to be sure that they are installed, follow these steps:

1. Open **Package Manager** (**Window** | **Package Manager**).
2. Set the **Packages** dropdown to **Unity Registry** mode:

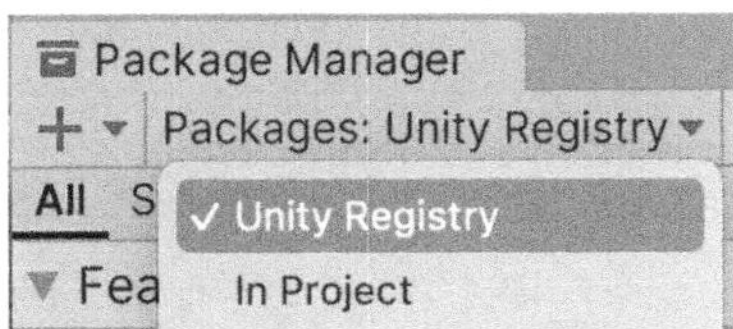

Figure 5.6: Enabling Unity Registry mode

3. Search the list for your IDE or filter the list by using the search bar. In my case, I used Rider, and I can find a package called **JetBrains Rider Editor**:

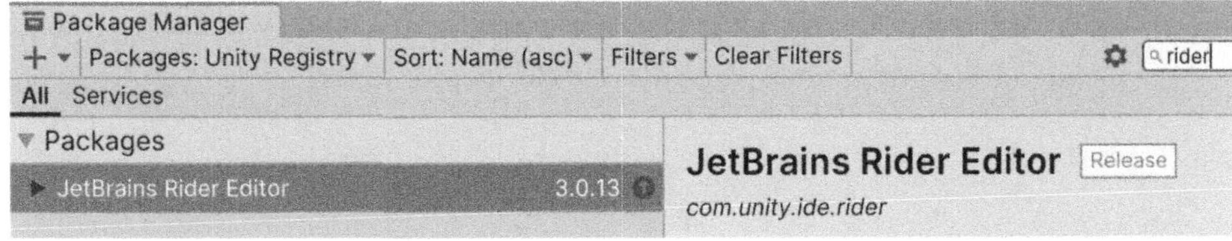

Figure 5.7: Custom IDE editor extension installation—in this case, the Rider one

4. Check whether your IDE integration package is installed by looking at the buttons at the bottom-right part of the package manager. If you see an **Install** or **Update** button, click on it, but if it says **Installed**, everything is set up.

Now that we have an IDE configured, let's create our first script.

Creating a C# script

C# is an object-oriented language, and this is no different in Unity. Any time we want to extend Unity, we need to create our own class—a script with the instructions we want to add to Unity. If we want to create custom components, we need to create a class that inherits from `MonoBehaviour`, the base class of every custom component.

We can create C# script files directly within the Unity project using the editor, and you can arrange them in folders right next to other `assets` folders. The easiest way to create a script is by following these steps:

1. Select any GameObject that you want to have the component we are going to create. As we are just testing this out, select any object.
2. Click on the **Add Component** button at the bottom of the Inspector and look for the **New script** option at the bottom of the list, displayed after clicking on **Add Component**:

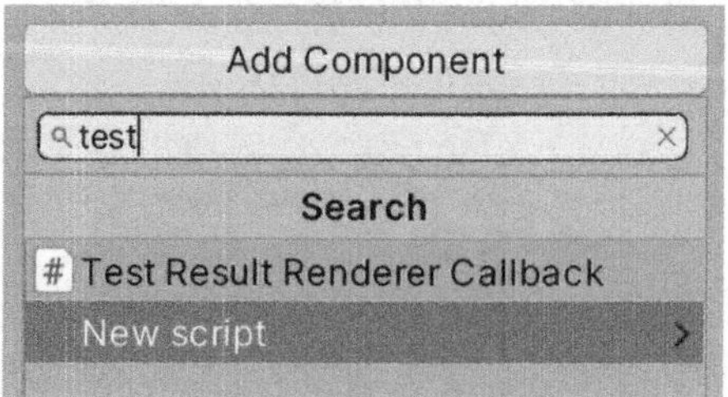

Figure 5.8: The New script option

3. In the **Name** field, enter the desired script name, and then click **Create and Add**. In my case, I will call it `MyFirstScript`, but for the scripts that you will use for your game, try to enter descriptive names, regardless of the length:

Figure 5.9: Naming the script

It is recommended that you use Pascal case for script naming. In Pascal case, a script for the player's shooting functionality would be called `PlayerShoot`. The first letter of each word of the name is in uppercase and you can't use spaces.

4. You can check how a new asset with the same name as your script is created in **Project View**. Remember that each component has its own asset, and I suggest you put each component in a `Scripts` folder:

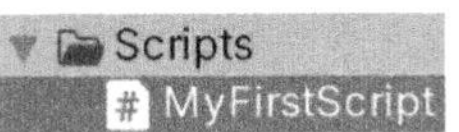

Figure 5.10: Script asset

5. Now, you will also see that your GameObject has a new component in the Inspector window, which has the same name as your script. So, you have now created your first `component` class:

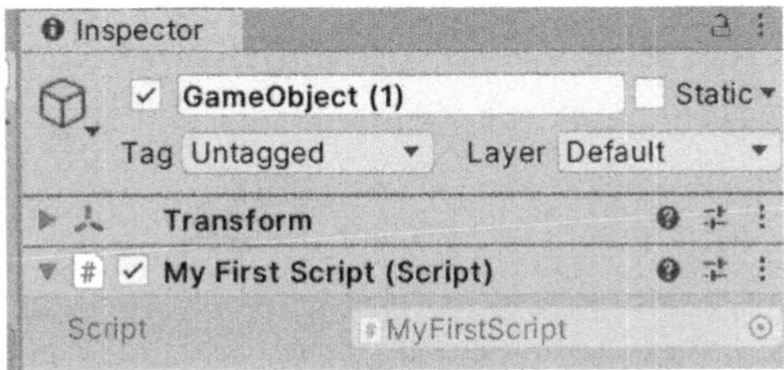

Figure 5.11: Our script added to a GameObject

Now that we have created a component class, remember that a class is not the component itself. It is a description of what the component should be—a blueprint of how a component should work. To actually use the component, we need to instantiate it by creating a component based on the class. Each time we add a component to an object using the editor, Unity is instantiating it for us. Generally, we don't instantiate components using the new C# keyword, but by using the editor or specialized functions.

Now, you can add your new empty component to other objects as you would any other component by using the **Add Component** button in the Inspector window. Then you can look for the component in the **Scripts** category or search it by name:

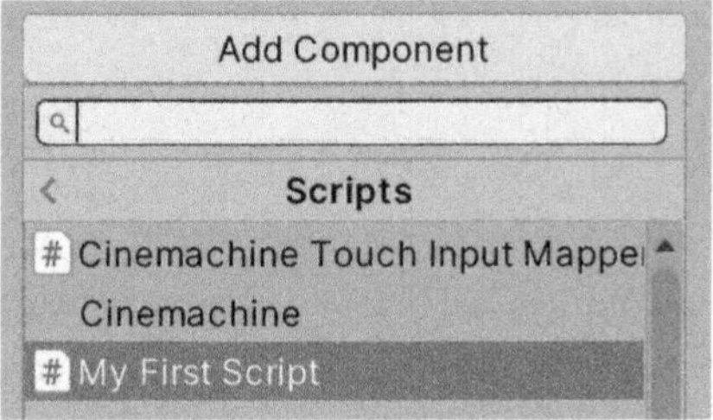

Figure 5.12: Adding a custom component in the Scripts category

Something that you need to consider here is that we can add the same component to several GameObjects. We don't need to create a class for each GameObject that uses the component. I know this is basic programmers' knowledge but remember that we are trying to recap the basics here.

Now that we have our component, let's explore how it looks and carry out a class structure recap by following these steps:

1. Locate the script asset in **Project View** and double-click on it. Remember that it should be in the `Scripts` folder you created previously.
2. Wait for the IDE to open; this can take a while. You will know that the IDE has finished the initialization when you see your script code and its keywords properly colored, which varies according to the desired IDE. In Rider, it looks like what is shown in *Figure 5.13*. In my case, I knew that Rider had finished initializing because the `MonoBehaviour` type and the script name are colored the same:

```
using System.Collections;
using System.Collections.Generic;
using UnityEngine;

public class MyFirstScript : MonoBehaviour
{
    // Start is called before the first frame update
    void Start()
    {

    }
```

Figure 5.13: A new script opened in the Rider IDE

3. The first three lines—the ones that start with the `using` keyword—include common namespaces. **Namespaces** are like code containers, which is, in this case, code created by others (such as Unity, C# creators, and so on). We will be using namespaces quite often to simplify our tasks; they already contain solved algorithms that we will use. We will be adding and removing the `using` component as we need; in my case, Rider is suggesting that the first two `using` components are not necessary because I am not using any code inside them, and so they are grayed out. But for now, keep them as you will use them in later chapters of this book. Remember, they should always be at the beginning of the file:

```
using System.Collections;
using System.Collections.Generic;
using UnityEngine;
```

Figure 5.14: The using sections

4. The next line, the one that starts with `public class`, is where we declare that we are creating a new class that inherits from `MonoBehaviour`, the base class of every custom component. We know this because it ends with `: MonoBehaviour`. You can see how the rest of the code is located inside brackets right below that line, meaning that the code inside them belongs to the component:

```
public class MyFirstScript : MonoBehaviour
```

Figure 5.15: The MyFirstScript class definition inherits from MonoBehaviour

Now that we have our C# script, let's add fields to configure it.

Adding fields

In previous chapters, when we added components as `Rigidbody` or as different kinds of colliders, adding the components wasn't enough. We needed to properly configure them to achieve the exact behavior that we need. For example, `Rigidbody` has the `Mass` property to control the object's weight, and the colliders have the `Size` property to control their shape. This way, we can reuse the same component for different scenarios, preventing the duplication of similar components. With a `Box` collider, we can represent a cube or rectangular box just by changing the size properties. Our components are no exception; if we have a component that moves an object and if we want two objects to move at different speeds, we can use the same component with different configurations.

Each configuration is a **field** or **variable** where we can hold the parameter's value. We can create class fields that can be edited in the editor in two ways:

- By marking the field as `public`, but breaking the encapsulation principle
- By making a private field and exposing it with an attribute

Now, we are going to cover both methods, but if you are not familiar with **Object-Oriented Programming (OOP)** concepts, such as encapsulation, I recommend you use the first method.

Suppose we are creating a movement script. We will add an editable number field representing the velocity using the first method—that is, by adding the `public` field. We will do this by following these steps:

1. Open the script by double-clicking it as we did before.
2. Inside the class brackets, but outside any brackets within them, add the following code:

```
public class MyFirstScript : MonoBehaviour
{
    public float speed;
```

Figure 5.16: Creating a speed field in our component

The `public` keyword specifies that the variable can be seen and edited beyond the scope of the class. The `float` part of the code says that the variable is using the decimal number type, and `speed` is the name we chose for our field—this can be whatever you want. You can use other value types to represent other kinds of data, such as `bool` to represent checkboxes or `Booleans` and `string` to represent text.

3. To apply the changes, just save the file in the IDE (usually by pressing *Ctrl* + *S* or *Command* + *S*) and return to Unity. When you do this, you will notice a little loading wheel at the bottom-right part of the editor, indicating that Unity is compiling the code. You can't test the changes until the wheel finishes:

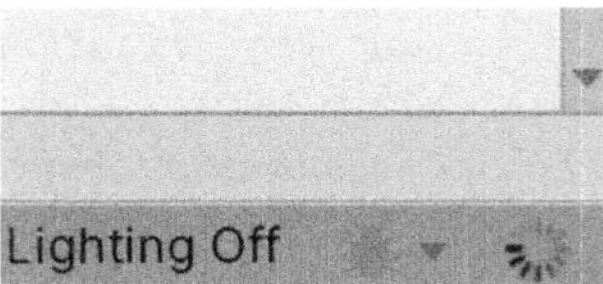

Figure 5.17: The loading wheel

Remember that Unity will compile the code; don't compile it in the IDE.

4. After the compilation is finished, you can see your component in the Inspector window and the **Speed** variable should be there, allowing you to set the speed you want. Of course, right now, the variables do nothing. Unity doesn't recognize your intention by the name of the variable; we need to set it for use in some way, but we will do that later:

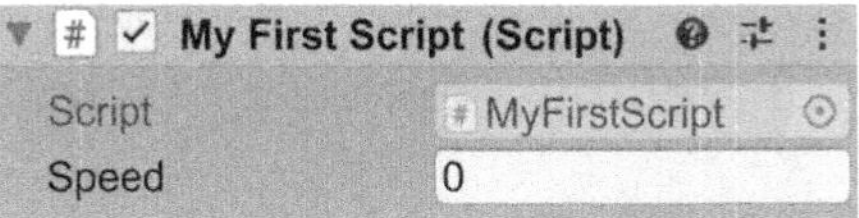

Figure 5.18: A public field to edit data that the component will use later

In case you don't see the speed variable, please check the section at the end of this chapter called *Common beginner C# script errors*, which will give you tips about how to troubleshoot compilation errors.

5. Try adding the same component to other objects and set a different speed. This will show you how components in different GameObjects are independent, allowing you to change some of their behaviors via different settings.
6. The second way to define properties is similar, but instead of creating a `public` field, we create a `private` field, encouraging encapsulation and exposing it using the `SerializeField` attribute, as shown in the following screenshot.

```
[SerializeField]
private float speed;
```

Figure 5.19: Exposing private attributes in the Inspector window

If you are not familiar with the OOP concept of encapsulation, just use the first method, which is more flexible for beginners. If you create a `private` field, it won't be accessible to other scripts because the `SerializeField` attribute only exposes the variable to the editor. Remember that Unity won't allow you to use constructors, so the only way to set initial data and inject dependencies is via serialized `private` fields or `public` fields and setting them in the editor (or using a dependency injection framework, but that is beyond the scope of this book). For simplicity, we will use the first method in most of the exercises in this book.

If you want, try to create other types of variables and check how they look in the Inspector. Try replacing `float` for `bool` or `string`, as previously suggested. Consider that not every possible C# type is recognized by Unity; through this book, we will learn the most commonly supported ones. Now that we know how to configure our components through data, let's use that data to create some behavior.

Now that we have our C# script, let's see how to do the same in Visual Scripting.

Creating a Visual Script

As we need to create a **Script Asset** for C# scripts, we need to create the Visual Scripting equivalent called **Script Graph** and also attach it to our GameObject, although using a different approach this time. Before continuing, it is worth noticing that our objects must only have C# or the Visual Scripting version, but not both, or the behavior will be applied twice, once per version.

Essentially, only do the steps for the version you want to try or do both steps in different objects if you want to experiment.

Let's create a Visual Script doing the following:

1. Create a new GameObject to which we will add the Visual Script.
2. Add the **Script Machine** component to it. This component will execute the **Visual Script Graph** we will be creating shortly:

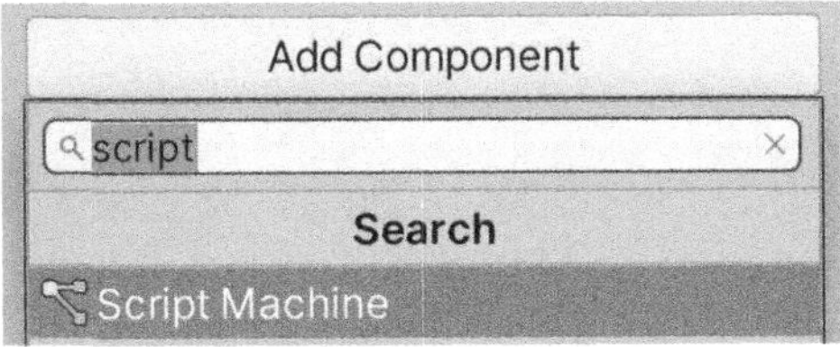

Figure 5.20: Adding a Script Machine component

3. In the **Script Machine** component, click the **New** button and select a folder and a name to save the **Visual Script Graph** asset. This asset will contain the instructions of our script, and the **Script Machine** component will execute those:

Figure 5.21: Using the New button to create a Visual Scripting Graph asset

4. If a warning appears, click the **Change now** option. This will prevent those changes on the script from affecting the game while its running, because as the warning says, it can cause instability of the code. Always stop the game, change the code, and then play again.

5. Click the **Edit Graph** Button to open the Visual Script editor window. You can drag the **Script Graph** tab to any part of the editor to merge that window:

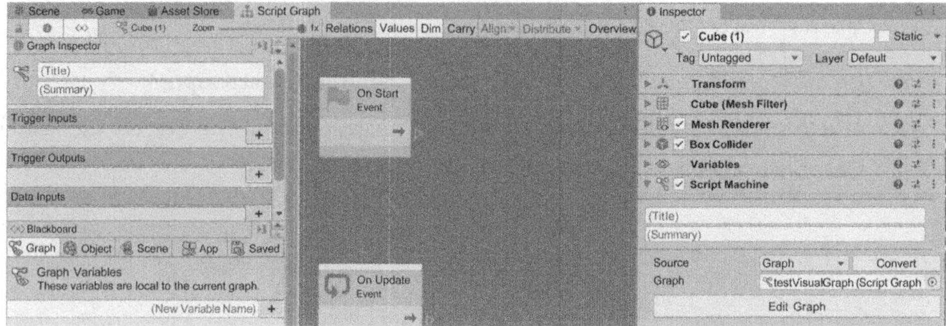

Figure 5.22: Visual Scripting asset editor

6. Put the mouse in an empty area in the grid of the **Visual Script** editor, and while holding the middle mouse button, move the mouse to scroll through the graph. On MacBooks and Apple Magic Mouses you can scroll using two fingers on the trackpad.

What we did is create the **Visual Graph** asset that will contain the code of our script, and attached it to a GameObject through the **Script Machine** component. Unlike C# scripts, we can't attach the **Graph Asset** directly; that's why we need the **Script Machine** to run the component for us.

Regarding fields, the ones we created in the C# scripts are contained in the script itself, but for **Visual Graph** they work a little bit differently. When we added the **Script Machine** component, another one was added: the **Variables** component. This will hold all the variables for all the **Visual Script Graph** that a GameObject can contain. That means that all graphs we add to our object will share those variables. You can create graph-specific variables if you want, but they won't be exposed in the Inspector, and this way also simplifies the access of variables from other objects' scripts. Also remember you will want to add several graphs to the object, given that each graph will take care of different behaviors, in a way in which we can mix and match them according to our needs.

In order to add a variable to our GameObject that can be used by our graph, let's do the following:

1. Select a GameObject with a **Visual Script** added (with the **Script Machine** component) and look at the **Variables** component.
2. Click the input field that says **(New Variable Name)** and type the name of the variable. In my case, this is `speed`. If you don't see that option, click the triangle at the left of the **Variables** component name.

3. Click the **Plus (+)** button of the **Variables** component.
4. In the **Type** dropdown, select **Float.**
5. Optionally you can set an initial value in the **Value** field:

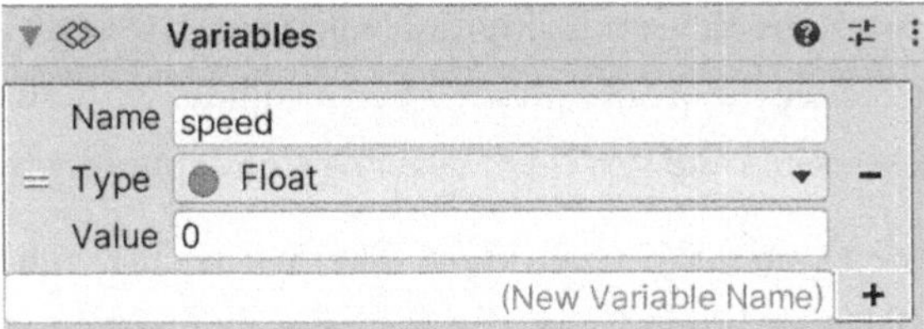

Figure 5.23: Creating variables for the Visual Graph

We created a `speed` variable that we can configure in the GameObject to alter the way all **Visual Scripts Graphs** attached to our GameObject will work, or at least the ones that use that `Variable` value. Consider that maybe you will have different kinds of speed, like movement and rotational speed, so in real cases you might want to be a little bit more specific with the variable name.

The `Variables` component used in Visual Scripting is also called **Blackboard**, a common programming technique. This Blackboard is a container of several values of our object, like a memory or database, that several other components of our object will then query and use. C# scripts usually contain their own variables inside instead. With our scripts created and ready to be configured, let's see how to make both of them do something.

Using events and instructions

Now that we have a script, we are ready to do something with it. We won't implement anything useful in this chapter, but we will settle the base concepts to add interesting behavior to the scripts we are going to create in the next chapters.

In this section, we are going to cover the following concepts:

- Events and instructions in C#
- Events and instructions in Visual Scripting
- Using fields in instructions
- Common beginner C# script errors

We are going to explore the **Unity event system**, which will allow us to respond to different situations by executing instructions. These instructions will also be affected by the value of the editor. Finally, we are going to discuss common scripting errors and how to solve them. Let's start by introducing the concept of Unity events in C#.

Events and instructions in C#

Unity allows us to create behavior in a cause-effect fashion, which is usually called an **event system**. An event is a situation that Unity is monitoring—for example, when two objects collide or are destroyed, Unity tells us about this situation, allowing us to react according to our needs. As an example, we can reduce the life of a player when it collides with a bullet. Here, we will explore how to listen to these events and test them by using some simple actions.

If you are used to event systems, you will know that they usually require us to subscribe to some kind of listener or delegate, but in Unity, there is a simpler method available. For C# scripts we just need to write a function with the exact same name as the event we want to use—and I mean *exactly*. If a letter of the name doesn't have the correct casing, it won't execute, and no warning will be raised. This is the most common beginner's error that is made, so pay attention. For Visual Scripting we will be adding a special kind of node, but will discuss that after the C# version.

There are lots of events or messages to listen to in Unity, so let's start with the most common one—`Update`. This event will tell you when Unity wants you to update your object, depending on the purpose of your behavior; some don't need them. The `Update` logic is usually something that needs to be executed constantly—to be more precise, in every frame. Remember that every game is like a movie—a sequence of images that your screen switches through fast enough to look like we have continuous motion. A common action to do in the `Update` event is to move objects a little bit, and by doing this, every frame will make your object constantly move.

We will learn about the sorts of things we can do with `Update` and other events or messages later. Now, let's focus on how to make our component at least listen to this event. Actually, the base script already comes with two event functions that are ready to use, one being `Update` and the other one `Start`. If you are not familiar with the concept of methods in C#, we are referring to the snippet of code in the following screenshot, which is already included in our script. Try to find it in yours:

```
// Update is called once per frame
void Update()
{

}
```

Figure 5.24: A function called Update, which will be executed with every frame

You will notice a (usually) green line of text (depending on the IDE) above the `void Update()` line—this is called a **comment**. These are basically ignored by the compiler. They are just notes that you can leave to yourself and must always begin with `//` to prevent Unity from trying to execute them and failing. We will use this to temporarily disable lines of code later.

Now, to test whether this actually works, let's add an instruction to be executed all the time. There's no better test function than `print`. This is a simple instruction that tells Unity to print a message to the console, where all kinds of messages can be seen by the developers to check whether everything is properly working. The user will never see these messages. They are similar to the classic log files that developers sometimes ask you for when something goes wrong in the game and you are reporting an issue.

In order to test events in C# using functions, follow these steps:

1. Open the script by double-clicking on it.
2. To test, add `print("test");` within the event function. In the following screenshot, you can see an example of how to do that in the `Update` event. Remember to write the instruction *exactly*, including the correct casing, spaces, and quote symbols:

```
void Update()
{
    print("test");
}
```

Figure 5.25: Printing a message in all the frames

3. Save the file, go to Unity, and play the game.

Remember to save the file before switching back to Unity from the IDE. This is the only way that Unity knows your file has changed. Some IDEs, such as Rider, save the file automatically for you, but I don't recommend you use auto-save, at least in big projects (you don't want accidental recompilations of unfinished work—that takes too long in projects with lots of scripts).

4. Look for the **Console** tab and select it. This is usually found next to the **Project View** tab. If you can't find it, go to **Window | General | Console**, or press *Ctrl* + *Shift* + *C* (*Command* + *Shift* + *C* on macOS).

5. You will see a new printed message saying "test" every frame on the **Console** tab. If you don't see this, remember to save the script file before playing the game.
6. You might see a single message but with a number increasing to its right; that means the same message is appearing several times. Try clicking the **Collapse** button of the **Console** to change that behavior.
7. Let's also test the `Start` function. Add `print("test Start");` to it, save the file, and play the game. The full script should look as follows:

```
using System.Collections;
using System.Collections.Generic;
using UnityEngine;

public class MyFirstScript : MonoBehaviour
{
    [SerializeField]
    private float speed;

    void Start()
    {
        print("test Start");
    }

    void Update()
    {
        print("test");
    }
}
```

Figure 5.26: The script that tests the Start and Update functions

If you check the console now and scroll all the way up, you will see a single `"test Start"` message and lots of `"test"` messages following it. As you can guess, the `Start` event tells you that the GameObject is created and allows you to execute the code that needs to happen just once at the beginning of its lifetime.

For the `void Update()` syntax, we will say to Unity that whatever is contained within the brackets below this line is a function that will be executed in all the frames. It is important to put the `print` instruction *inside* the `Update` brackets (the ones inside the brackets of the class). Also, the `print` function expects to receive a value to print inside its parenthesis, called an argument or parameter. In our example we want to print simple text, and in C# it must be enclosed with quotation marks. Finally, all instructions inside functions such as **Update** or **Start** *must* end with a semicolon.

Here, I challenge you to try to add another event called `OnDestroy` using a `print` to discover when it executes. A small suggestion is to play and stop the game and look at the bottom of the console to test this one.

For advanced users, you can also use breakpoints if your IDE allows you to do that. **Breakpoints** allow you to freeze Unity completely before executing a specific code line to see how our field's data changes over time and to detect errors. Here, I will show you the steps to use breakpoints in Rider, but the Visual Studio version should be similar:

1. Install the Unity package belonging to your IDE if not already installed. Check the **Package Manage** for the **JetBrains Rider Editor** package. In the case of Visual Studio, install the **Visual Studio Editor** package.
2. Click on the vertical bar at the left of the line where you want to add the breakpoint:

```
void Start()
{
    print( message: "test Start");
}
```

Figure 5.27: A breakpoint in the print instruction

3. Go to **Run | Attach to Unity Process**. If you are using Visual Studio, go to **Debug | Attach Unity Debugger**:

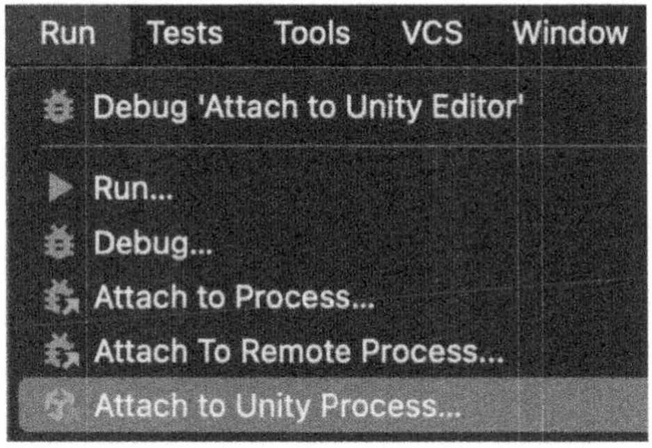

Figure 5.28: Attacking our IDE with a Unity process

4. From the list, look for the specific Unity instance you want to test. The list will show other opened editors or executing debugging builds if any.
5. If this doesn't work, check if the editor is in debug mode, looking at the bug icon at the bottom-right part of the editor. If the bug looks blue with a checkbox, then it is ok, but if it looks gray and crossed out, click it and click **Switch to debug mode**:

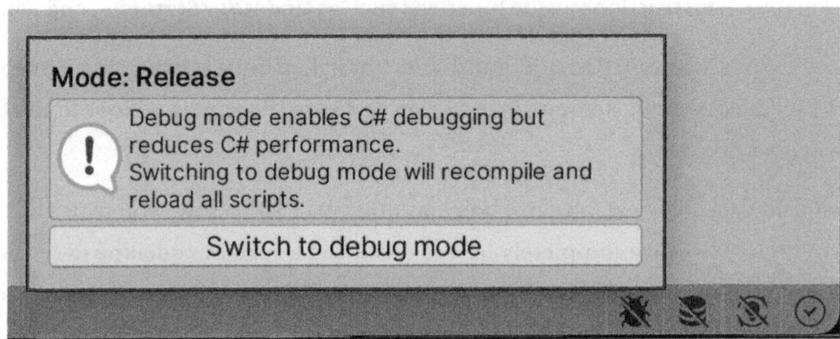

Figure 5.29: Changing from release mode to debug mode

Stopping the debugging process won't close Unity. It will just detach the IDE from the editor.

Now let's explore the Visual Scripting equivalent of using events and instructions.

Events and instructions in Visual Scripting

The same concept of events and instructions remains in Visual Scripting, but of course this will be done with nodes in the graph. Remember a node represents an instruction of the graph, and we can connect them to chain the effects of each instruction. In order to add events and the print instruction on our graph, do the following:

1. Open the **Visual Script Graph** (double-click the Visual Script asset).
2. Right-click the **On Start** and **On Update** nodes that are created by default and then click **Delete.** Even if those events are the ones we need, I want you to see how to create them from scratch:

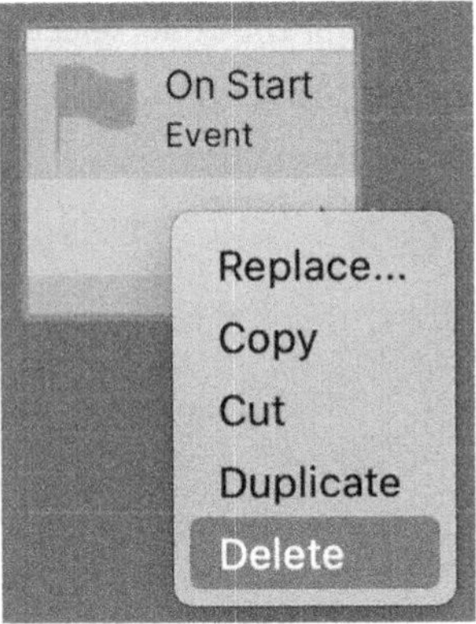

Figure 5.30: Deleting nodes

3. Right-click in any empty space of the **Graph** and type `start` inside the **Search** box. It can take a while the first time.
4. Select the **On Start** element in the list with the green checkbox to its left. In this case I knew this was an event because I was aware of it, but usually you will recognize it as an event because it won't have input pins (more on that in the next steps):

Figure 5.31: Searching the On Start event node

5. Drag the white arrow at the right of the event node, also known as the Output Flow Pin, and release the mouse button in any empty space.

6. In the **Search** box search for the `print` node, select the one that says **Mono Behaviour:Print**. This means that when the **On Start** event happens, the connected node will be executed, in this case **print**. This is how we start to chain instructions to events:

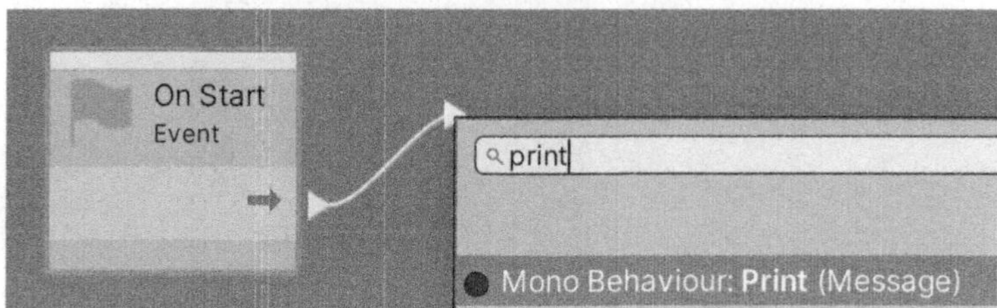

Figure 5.32: Creating a print node connected to the event

7. Drag the empty circle at the left of the **Message** input pin of the **Print** node and release it in any empty space. This pin has a circle indicating that is a parameter pin, data that will be used when executing the pin. The flow pins, the ones with a green arrow, represent the order in which the nodes will be executed.
8. Select the **String Literal** option, which will create a node to allow us to specify the message to print:

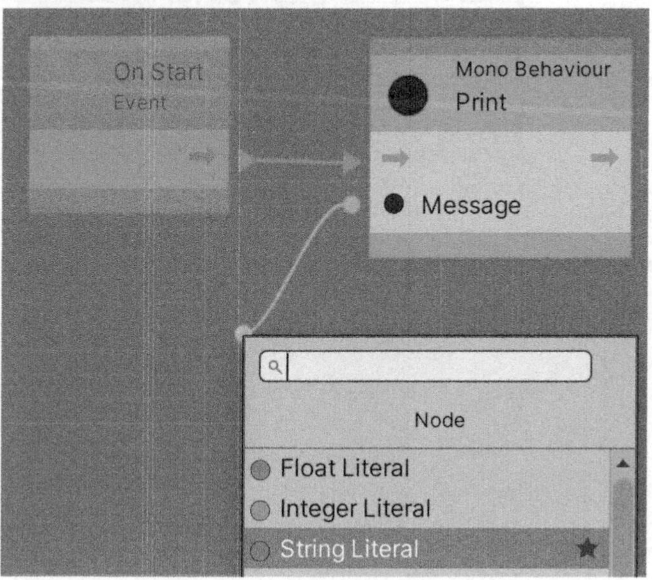

Figure 5.33: Creating a string literal node

9. In the empty white box write the message to be printed:

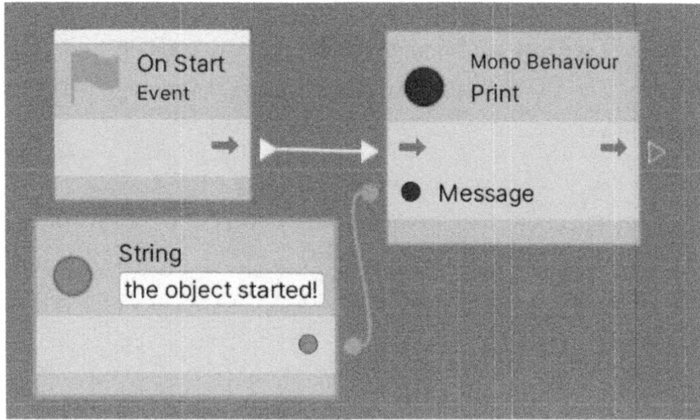

Figure 5.34: Specifying the message to print

10. Play the game and see the message printed in the console. Be sure you have only the Visual Scripting version in the scene to avoid confusing the message in the console with the C# version. You can also use different message texts in the Visual Scripts to be sure which ones are really executing.

You can chain more actions to the **On Start** by dragging the pin at the right (Flow Output Pin) of the **Print** node, and chaining new nodes, but we will do that later. Now that we have our scripts doing something, let's make the instructions use the fields we created so the scripts use their configurations.

Using fields in instructions

We have created fields to configure our components' behavior, but we have not used them so far. We will create meaningful components in the next chapter, but one thing we will often need is to use the fields we have created to change the behavior of the object. So far, we have no real use of the `speed` field that we created. However, following the idea of testing whether our code is working (also known as debugging), we can learn how to use the data inside a field with a function to test whether the value is the expected one, changing the output of `print` in the console according to the field's value.

In our current C# script, our `speed` value doesn't change during runtime. However, as an example, if you are creating a life system with shield damage absorption and you want to test whether the reduced damage calculation is working properly, you might want to print the calculation values to the console and check whether they are correct.

The idea here is to replace the fixed message inside the `print` functions with a field. When you do that, `print` will show the field's value in the console. So, if you set a value of `5` in `speed` and you print it, you will see lots of messages saying `5` in the console, and the output of the `print` function is governed by the field. To test this, your `print` message within the `Update` function should look as follows:

```
[SerializeField]
private float speed;

void Update()
{
    print(speed);
}
```

Figure 5.35: Using a field as a print function parameter

As you can see, we just put the name of the field without quotation marks. If you use quotation marks, you will print a `"speed"` message. In other scenarios, you can use this `speed` value within some moving functions to control how fast the movement will be, or you can perhaps create a field called `"fireRate"` (fields use **camel case** instead of Pascal case, with the first letter being in lowercase) to control the cooldown time between one bullet and the next:

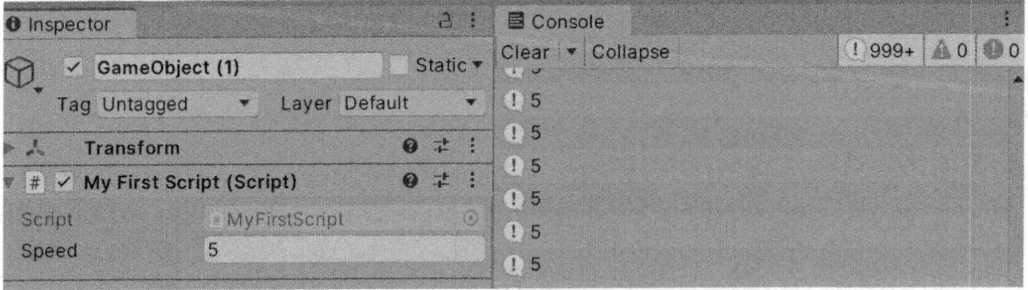

Figure 5.36: Printing the current speed

Now, to make the Visual Script graph print the value of the **speed** variable we created in the **Variables** component, let's do the following.

1. Open the Visual Scripting graph asset (double-click it).
2. In the panel at the left, select the **Object** tab to display all the variables our object has—essentially the ones we defined in the **Variables** component previously.

3. Drag the **speed** variable using the two lines to the left of the variable box to any empty area of the graph. This will create a **GetVariable** node in the graph to represent the variable. Consider the drag has a bug at the moment, so you might need to try a couple of times, trying to drag from the left part:

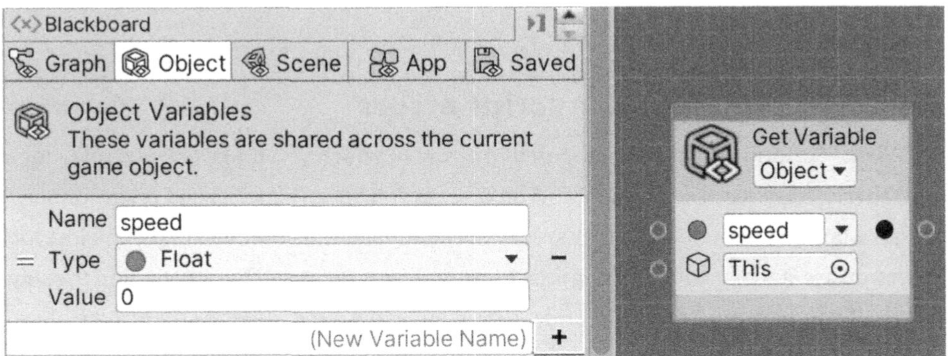

Figure 5.37: Dragging variables to the graph to be used in the nodes

4. Drag the empty circle at the right of the **Get Variable** node to the circle to the left of the **Message** input pin of the **Print** node. This will replace the previous connection to the **String Literal** node. This node doesn't have **Input** or **Output** flow nodes (the green arrow ones), as they are data-only nodes that provide data to other nodes. In this case, when `Print` needs to execute, it will execute `Get Variable` to get the text to read:

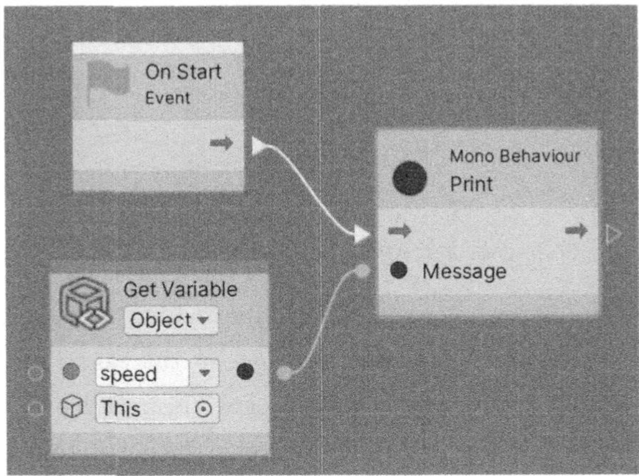

Figure 5.38: Connecting the speed variable to the print node

5. Right-click on the **String Literal** node and delete it.
6. Play the game and observe.

With all this, we now have the necessary tools to start creating actual components. Before moving on, let's recap some of the common errors that you will likely encounter if this is your first time creating scripts in C#.

Common beginner C# script errors

The Visual Scripting scripts are prepared in a way in which you make fewer errors, not allowing you to write incorrect syntax like C# script does. If you are an experienced programmer, I bet you are quite familiar with them, but let's recap the common errors that will make you lose lots of time when you are starting with C# scripting. Most of them are caused by not copying the shown code *exactly*. If you have an error in the code, Unity will show a red message in the console and won't allow you to run the game, even if you are not using the script. So, never leave anything unfinished.

Let's start with a classic error, a missing semicolon, which has resulted in many programmer memes and jokes. All fields and most instructions inside functions (such as `print`), when called, need to have a semicolon at the end. If you don't add a semicolon, Unity will show an error, such as the one in the screenshot on the left in *Figure 5.39*, in the console. You will also notice that this also has an example of bad code, where the IDE is showing a red icon suggesting something is wrong in that place:

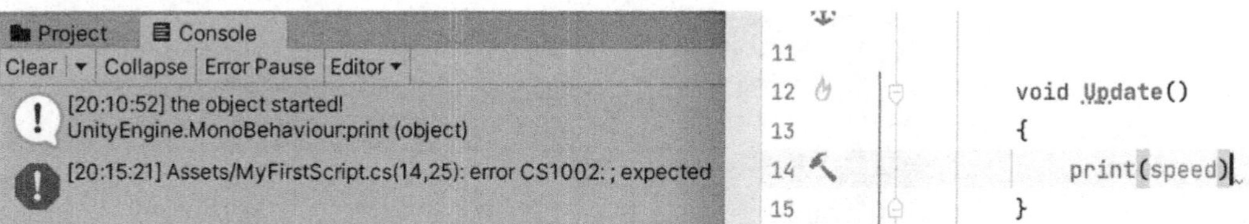

Figure 5.39: An error in the print line hinted by the IDE and the Unity console

You will notice that the error shows the exact script (`MyFirstScript.cs`), the exact line of code (14, in this case), and usually, a descriptive message—in this case, `; expected`–as a way to specify the instruction ends there, so the compiler can process the next instruction as a separate one. You can simply double-click the error and Unity will open the IDE highlighting the problematic line. You can even click on the links in the stack to jump to the line of the stack that you want.

I already mentioned why it is important to use the *exact* case for every letter of the instruction. However, based on my experience of teaching beginners, I need to stress this particular aspect more.

The first scenario where this can happen is in instructions. In the following screenshots, you can see how a badly written `print` function looks—that is, the error that the console will display and how the IDE will suggest that there is something wrong. First, in the case of Rider, the instruction is colored red, saying that the instruction is not recognized (in Visual Studio, it will show a red line instead). Then, the error message says that `Print` does not exist in the current context, meaning that Unity (or C#, actually) does not recognize any instruction named `Print`. In another type of script, `Print` in uppercase may be valid, but not in regular components, which is why the "**in the current context**" clarification exists:

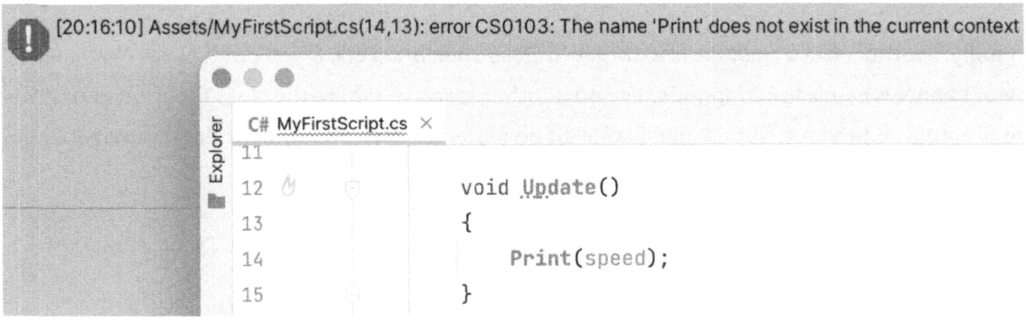

> [20:16:10] Assets/MyFirstScript.cs(14,13): error CS0103: The name 'Print' does not exist in the current context

```
void Update()
{
    Print(speed);
}
```

Figure 5.40: Error hints when writing an instruction wrong

Now, if you write an event with the wrong casing, the situation is worse. You can create functions such as `Start` and `Update` with whatever name you want for other purposes. Writing `update` or `start` is perfectly valid as C# will think that you are going to use those functions not as events but as regular functions. So, no error will be shown, and your code will just not work. Try to write `update` instead of `Update` and see what happens:

```
void update()
{
    print(speed);
}
```

Figure 5.41: The wrong casing in the Update function will compile the function but won't execute it

Another error is to put instructions outside the function brackets, such as inside the brackets of the class or outside them. Doing this will give no hint to the function as to when it needs to execute. So, a `print` function outside an `Event` function makes no sense, and it will show an error such as the ones in the following *Figures 5.42* and *5.43*.

This time, the error is not super descriptive. C# is expecting you to create a function or a field—the kind of structures that can be put directly inside a class:

[20:10:52] the object started!
UnityEngine.MonoBehaviour:print (object)

[20:17:55] Assets/MyFirstScript.cs(16,15): error CS1001: Identifier expected

```
void Update()
{
}

print("test");
```

Figure 5.42: Misplaced instruction or function call

Finally, another classic mistake is to forget to close open brackets. If you don't close a bracket, C# won't know where a function finishes and another starts or where the class function ends. This may sound redundant, but C# needs that to be perfectly defined. In the following screenshots, you can see how this would look:

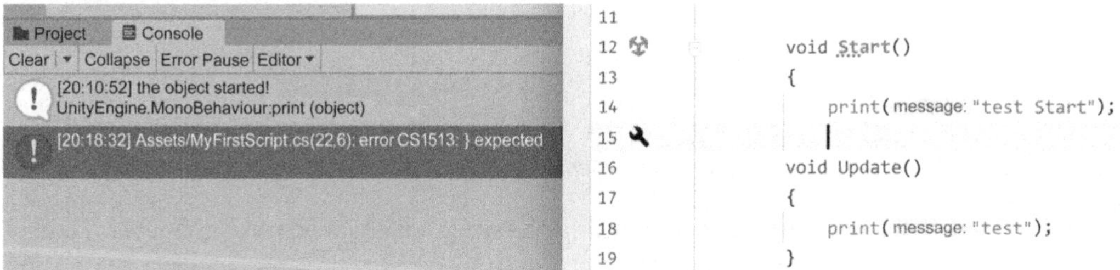

Figure 5.43: Missing closed brackets

This one is a little bit difficult to catch because the error in the code is shown way after the actual error. This is caused by the fact that C# allows you to put functions inside functions (not used often) and so C# will detect the error later, asking you to add a closing bracket. However, as we don't want to put `Update` inside `Start`, we need to fix the error before, at the end of `Start`. The error message will be descriptive in the console, but again, don't put the close bracket where the message suggests you do so unless you are 100% sure that position is correct.

You will likely face lots of errors aside from these ones, but they all work the same. The IDE will show you a hint and the console will display a message; you will learn them with time. Just have patience as every programmer experiences this. There are other kinds of errors, such as runtime errors, code that compiles but will fail when being executed due to some misconfiguration, or the worst: logic errors, where your code compiles and executes with no error but doesn't do what you intended.

Summary

In this chapter, we explored the basic concepts that you will use while creating scripts. We discussed the concept of a script's assets and how the C# ones must inherit from `MonoBehaviour` to be accepted by Unity to create our own scripts. We also saw how to mix events and instructions to add behavior to an object and how to use fields in instructions to customize what they do. All of this was done using both C# and Visual Scripting.

We just explored the basics of scripting to ensure that everyone is on the same page. However, from now on, we will assume that you have basic coding experience in some programming language, and you know how to use structures such as `if`, `for`, `array`, and so on. If not, you can still read through this book and try to complement the areas you don't understand with a C# introduction book as you need.

In the next chapter, we are going to start seeing how we can use what we have learned to create movement and spawning scripts.

Join us on Discord!

Read this book alongside other users, Unity game development experts, and the author himself.

Ask questions, provide solutions to other readers, chat with the author via Ask Me Anything sessions, and much more.

Scan the QR code or visit the link to join the community.

`https://packt.link/handsonunity22`

6

Implementing Movement and Spawning

In the previous chapter, we learned about the basics of scripting, so now let's create the first script for our game. We will see the basics of how to move objects through scripting using the `Transform` component, which will be applied to the movement of our player with the keyboard keys, the constant movement of bullets, and other object movements. Also, we will see how to create and destroy objects during the game, such as the bullets our player and enemy shoot and the enemy wave spawners. These actions can be used in several other scenarios, so we will explore a few to reinforce the idea.

In this chapter, we will examine the following scripting concepts:

- Implementing movement
- Implementing spawning
- Using the new Input System

We will start by scripting components to move our character through the keyboard, and then we will make our player shoot bullets. Something to consider is that we are going to first see the C# version and then show the Visual Scripting equivalent in each section.

Implementing movement

Almost every object in the game moves one way or another: the player character with the keyboard; the enemies through AI; the bullets that simply move forward; and so on. There are several ways of moving objects in Unity, so we will start with the simplest one, that is, through the `Transform` component.

In this section, we will examine the following movement concepts:

- Moving objects through `Transform`
- Using input
- Understanding Delta Time

First, we will explore how to access the `Transform` component in our script to drive the player movement, to later apply movement based on the player's keyboard input. Finally, we are going to explore the concept of Delta Time to make sure the movement speeds are consistent on every computer. We are going to start learning about the `Transform` API to make a simple movement script.

Moving objects through Transform

`Transform` is the component that holds the translation, rotation, and scale of the object, so every movement system such as physics or pathfinding will affect this component. Sometimes, we want to move the object in a specific way according to our game by creating our own script, which will handle the movement calculations we need and modify `Transform` to apply them.

One concept implied here is that components alter other components. The main way of coding in Unity is to create components that interact with other components. Here, the idea is to create one that accesses another and tells it to do something: in this case, to move. To create a script that tells `Transform` to move, do the following:

1. Create and add a script called `PlayerMovement` to our character, like we did in the previous chapter. In this case, it would be the animated 3D model we downloaded previously (drag the 3D asset from the **Project** view to the scene). Remember to move the script to the **Scripts** folder after creation:

Figure 6.1: Creating a Player Movement script in the character

2. Double-click the created script asset to open an IDE to edit the code.
3. We are moving, and the movement is applied to every frame. So this script will use only the `Update` function or method, and we can remove `Start` (it is a good practice to remove the unused functions):

```
using UnityEngine;

public class PlayerMovement : MonoBehaviour
{
    void Update()
    {

    }
}
```

Figure 6.2: A component with just the Update event function

4. To move our object along its local forward axis (z axis), add the `transform.Translate(0,0,1);` line to the `Update` function, as shown in *Figure 6.3*:

Every component inherits a `Transform` field (to be specific, a **getter**) that is a reference to the `Transform` of the GameObject the component is placed in; it represents the sibling `Transform` of our component. Through this field, we can access the `Translate` function of the `Transform`, which will receive the offset to apply to the x, y, and z local coordinates.

```
using UnityEngine;

public class PlayerMovement : MonoBehaviour
{
    void Update()
    {
        transform.Translate(0, 0, 1);
    }
}
```

Figure 6.3: A simple Move Forward script

5. Save the file and play the game to see the movement. Ensure the camera is pointing at the character to properly see the effect of the script.

You will notice that the player is moving too fast. That's because we are using a fixed speed of 1 meter, and because `Update` is executing all frames, we are moving 1 meter per frame. In a standard 30 FPS game, the player will move 30 meters per second, which is too much, but probably our computer is running the game with way more FPS than that. We can control the player's speed by adding a `speed` field and using the value set in the editor instead of the fixed value of 1. You can see one way to do this in the *Figure 6.4*, but remember the other options we discussed in *Chapter 5, Introduction to C# and Visual Scripting*:

```
public float speed;

void Update()
{
    transform.Translate(0, 0, speed);
}
```

Figure 6.4: Creating a speed field and using it as the z speed of the movement script

Now if you save the script to apply the changes and set the **Speed** of the player in the Editor, you can play the game and see the results. In my case, I used `0.1`, but you might need another value (more on this in the *Understanding Delta Time* section):

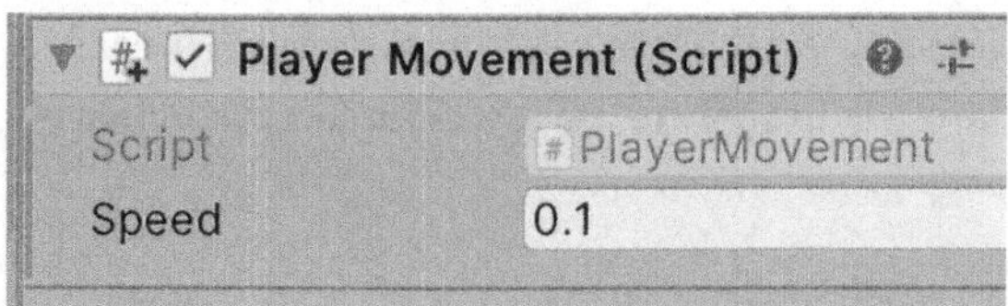

Figure 6.5: Setting speed of 0.1 meters per frame

Now, for the Visual Scripting version, first remember to not mix the C# and Visual Scripting versions of our scripts, not because it is not possible, but because we want to keep things simple for now. So, you can either delete the script from the player object and add the Visual Scripting version, or you can create two player objects and enable and disable them to try both versions. I recommend creating one project for the C# version of the scripts and then creating a second project to experiment with the Visual Script version.

The Visual Scripting Graph of this script will look like the following image:

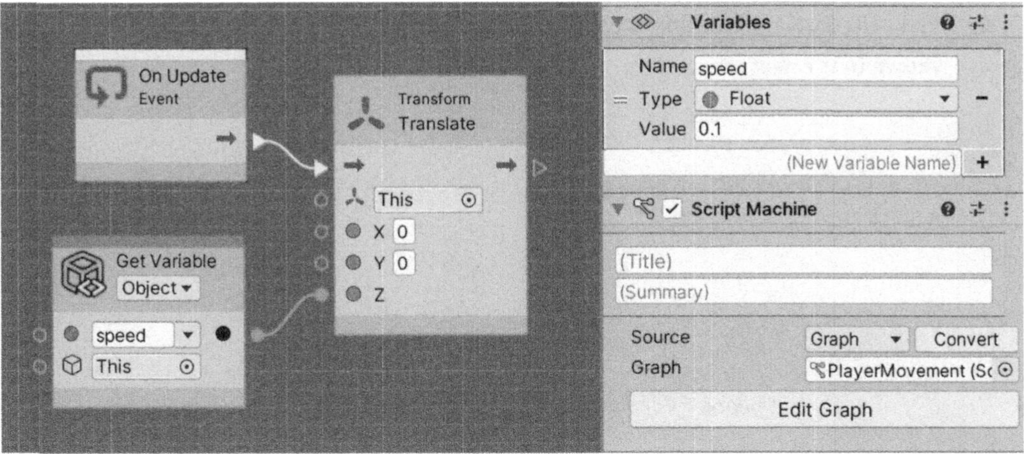

Figure 6.6: Setting a speed of 0.1 meters per frame

As you can see, we added a **Script Machine** component to our `Player` GameObject. Then, we pressed the **New** button in the **Script Machine** component to create a new **Graph** called `PlayerMovement`. We also created a **Float** variable called `speed` with the value of `0.1`. In the **Graph**, we added the **On Update** event node and attached it to the **Translate (X,Y,Z)** node of the **Transform**, which, similarly to the C# version, will move along the local axes of the object. Finally, we connected the **Z** parameter pin of **Translate** to the `GetVariable` node representing the speed we created in the GameObject. If you compare this **Graph** with the code we used in the C# version, they are essentially the same **Update** method and `Translate` function. If you don't remember how to create this **Graph**, you can go back to *Chapter 5, Introduction to C# and Visual Scripting*, to recap the process.

You will notice that the player will move automatically. Now let's see how to execute the movement based on **player input** such as the keyboard and mouse.

Using Input

Unlike NPCs, we want the player's movement to be driven by the player's input, based on which keys they press, the mouse movement, and so on. To know whether a certain key has been pressed, such as the *Up* arrow, we can use the `Input.GetKey(KeyCode.W)` line, which will return a Boolean, indicating whether the key specified in the `KeyCode` enum is pressed, which is *W* in this case. We can combine the `GetKey` function with an `If` statement to make the translation execute when the key is pressed.

Let's start by implementing the keyboard movement by following these steps:

1. Make the forward movement execute only when the *W* key is pressed with the code, as shown in the next screenshot:

```
void Update()
{
    if (Input.GetKey(KeyCode.W))
    {
        transform.Translate(0, 0, speed);
    }
}
```

Figure 6.7: Conditioning the movement until the W key is pressed

2. We can add other movement directions with more `If` statements to move backward and *A* and *D* to move left and right, as shown in the following screenshot. Notice how we used the minus sign to inverse the speed when we needed to move in the opposite axis direction:

```
if (Input.GetKey(KeyCode.W)) { transform.Translate(0, 0, speed); }
if (Input.GetKey(KeyCode.S)) { transform.Translate(0, 0, -speed); }
if (Input.GetKey(KeyCode.A)) { transform.Translate(-speed, 0, 0); }
if (Input.GetKey(KeyCode.D)) { transform.Translate(speed, 0, 0); }
```

Figure 6.8: Checking the W, A, S, and D key pressure

3. In case you also want to consider the arrow keys, you can use an `OR` inside `if`, as shown in the following screenshot:

```
if (Input.GetKey(KeyCode.W) || Input.GetKey(KeyCode.UpArrow)) { transform.Tra
if (Input.GetKey(KeyCode.S) || Input.GetKey(KeyCode.DownArrow)) { transform.T
if (Input.GetKey(KeyCode.A) || Input.GetKey(KeyCode.LeftArrow)) { transform.T
if (Input.GetKey(KeyCode.D) || Input.GetKey(KeyCode.RightArrow)) { transform.
```

Figure 6.9: Checking the W, A, S, D, and arrow key pressure

4. Save the changes and test the movement in **Play** mode.

Something to take into account is that, first, we have another way to map several keys to a single action by configuring the Input Manager—a place where action mappings can be created. Second, at the time of writing this, Unity has released a new Input System that is more extensible than this one.

For now, we will use this one because it is simple enough to make our introduction to scripting with Unity easier, but in games with complex input, it is recommended to look for more advanced tools.

Now, for the Visual Scripting version, the graph will look like this:

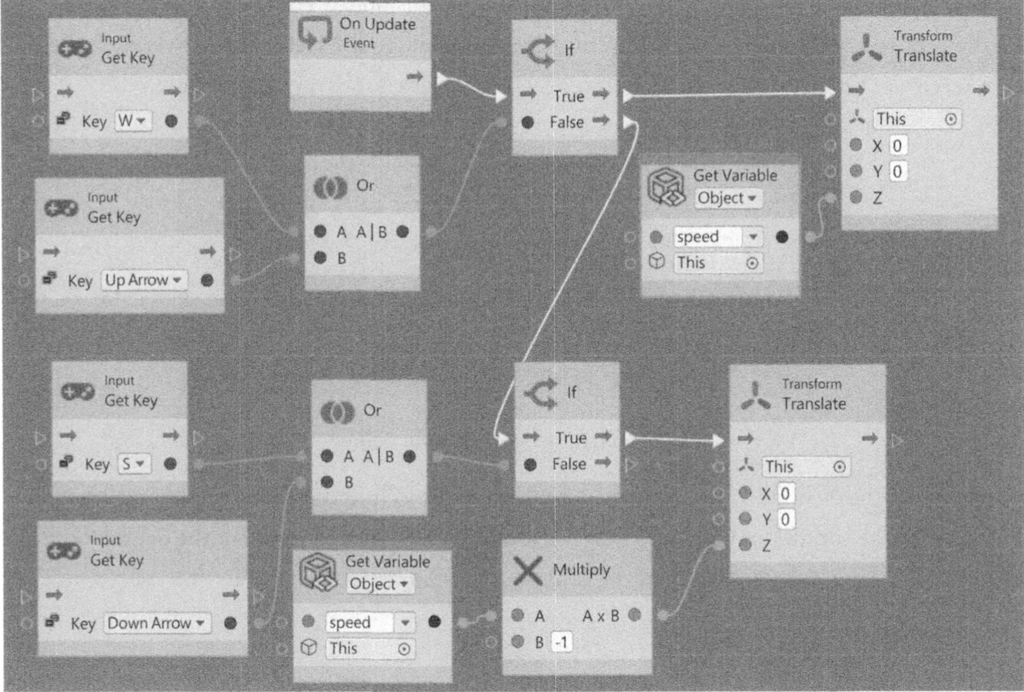

Figure 6.10: Input movement in Visual Scripting

As you can see, the graph has grown in size considerably compared to the C# version, which serves as an example of why developers prefer to code instead of using visual tools. Of course, we have several ways to split this graph into smaller chunks and make it more readable, and also consider I needed to squeeze the nodes together to be in the same image. Also, in the graph, we only see the example graph to move forward and backward, but you can easily extrapolate the necessary steps for lateral movement based on this one. As usual, you can also check the GitHub repository of the project to see the completed files.

Looking at the graph, you can quickly observe all the similarities to the C# version; we chained `If` nodes to the **On Update** event node in a way that if the first `If` node condition is true, it will execute the **Translate** in the player's forward direction. If that condition is false, we chained the **False** output node to another **If** that checks the pressure of the other keys, and in that case, we moved backward using the **Multiply (Scalar)** node to inverse the speed.

You can notice nodes like `If` that have more than one **Flow Output** pin to branch the execution of the code.

You can also notice the usage of the **GetKey (Key)** node, the Visual Scripting version of the same **GetKey** function we used previously. When looking at this node in the **Search** box, you will see all the versions of the function, and in this case, we selected the **GetKey(Key)** version; the one that receives a name (string) works differently, and we are not covering that one:

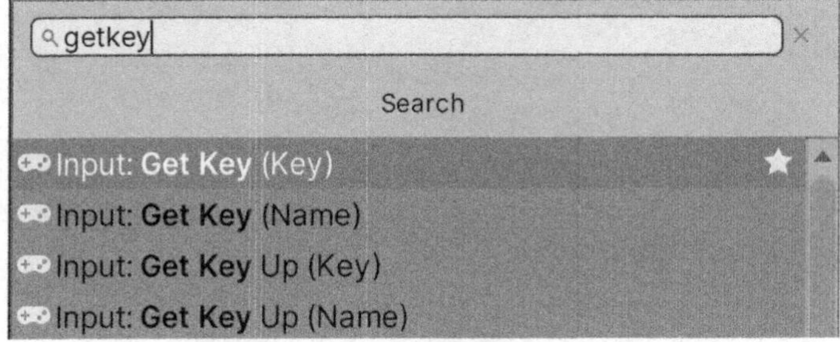

Figure 6.11: All versions of Input GetKey

We also used the `Or` node to combine the two **GetKey (Key)** functions into one condition to give to the `If`. These conditional operators can be found in the **Logic** category of the **Search** box:

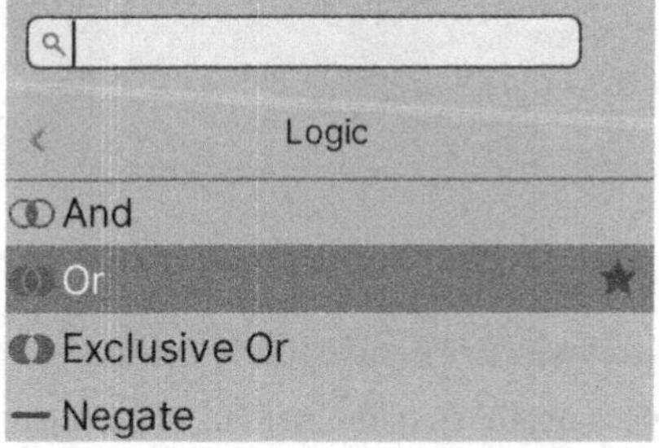

Figure 6.12: The Boolean Logic operators

One thing to highlight is the usage of the **Multiply** node to multiply the value of the speed variable by –1. We needed to create a **Float Literal** node to represent the –1 value. Next, surely all programmers will notice some limitations regarding how we used the `If` node's `True` and `False` output pins, but we will address that in a moment. Finally, consider that this implementation has the problem of blocking the second input read if the first is successful; we will discuss a way to fix this when we add rotation to our character later in this section.

Now, let's implement the mouse controls. In this section, we will only cover rotation with mouse movement; we will shoot bullets in the next section: *Implementing spawning*. In the case of mouse movement, we can get a value saying how much the mouse has moved both horizontally and vertically. This value isn't a Boolean but a number: a type of input usually known as an **axis**. The value of an axis will indicate the intensity of the movement, and the sign of that number will indicate the direction. For example, if Unity's `"Mouse X"` axis says `0.5`, it means that the mouse moved to the right with a moderate speed, but if it says `-1`, it moved quickly to the left, and if there is no movement, it will say `0`. The same goes for sticks in gamepads; the axis named **Horizontal** represents the horizontal movement of the left stick in common joysticks, so if the player pulls the stick fully to the left, it will say `-1`.

We can create our own axes to map other common joystick pressure-based controls, but for our game, the default ones are enough. To detect mouse movement, follow these steps:

1. Use the `Input.GetAxis` function inside `Update`, next to the movement `if` statements, as shown in the following screenshot, to store the value of this frame's mouse movement into a variable:

```
float mouseX = Input.GetAxis("Mouse X");
```

Figure 6.13: Getting the horizontal movement of the mouse

2. Use the `transform.Rotate` function to rotate the character. This function receives the degrees to rotate in the x, y, and z axes. In this case, we need to rotate horizontally, so we will use the mouse movement value as the y-axis rotation, as shown in the next screenshot:

```
float mouseX = Input.GetAxis("Mouse X");
transform.Rotate(0, mouseX, 0);
```

Figure 6.14: Rotating the object horizontally based on mouse movement

3. If you save and test this, you will notice that the character will rotate but very quickly or slowly, depending on your computer. Remember, this kind of value needs to be configurable, so let's create a `rotationSpeed` field to configure the speed of the player in the editor:

```
public float speed;
public float rotationSpeed;
```

Figure 6.15: The speed and rotation speed fields

4. Now we need to multiply the mouse movement value by the speed, so, depending on the `rotationSpeed`, we can increase or reduce the rotation amount. As an example, if we set a value of `0.5` in the rotation speed, multiplying that value by the mouse movement will make the object rotate at half the previous speed, as shown in the following screenshot:

```
float mouseX = Input.GetAxis("Mouse X");
transform.Rotate(0, mouseX * rotationSpeed, 0);
```

Figure 6.16: Multiplying the mouse movement by the rotation speed

5. Save the code and go back to the editor to set the rotation speed value. If you don't do this, the object won't rotate because the default value of the float type fields is `0`:

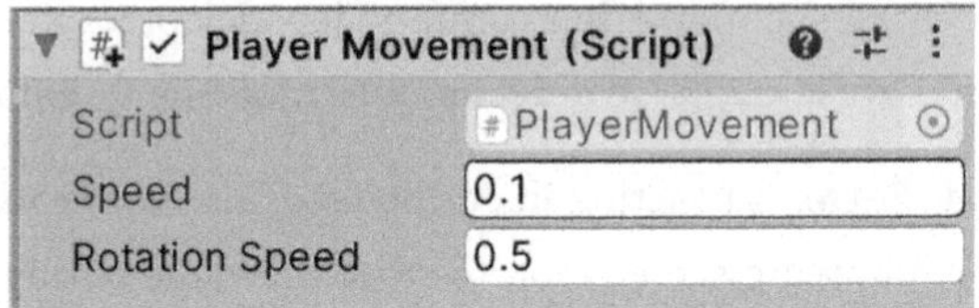

Figure 6.17: Setting the rotation speed

The Visual Scripting additions to achieve rotation will look like this:

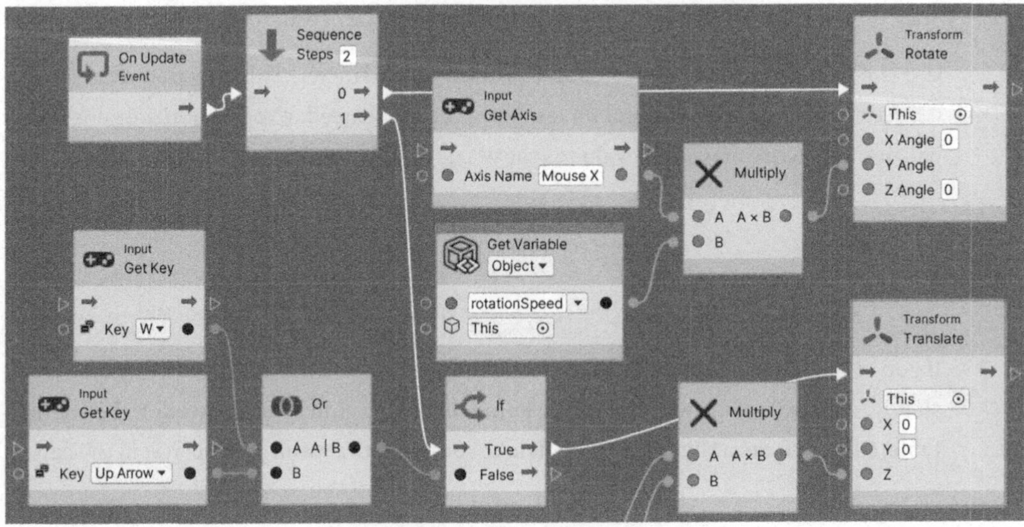

Figure 6.18: Rotating in Visual Scripting

The first thing to notice here is the usage of the **Sequence** node. An output pin can only be attached to one other node, but in this case, **On Update** needs to do two different things, to rotate and to move, each one being independent of the other. **Sequence** is a node that will execute all its output pins one after the other, regardless of the results of each one. You can specify the number of output pins in the **Steps** input box; in this example, two is enough.

In the output pin `0`, the first one, we added the rotation code, which is pretty self-explanatory given it is essentially the same as the movement code with slightly different nodes (**Rotate (X, Y, Z)** and **GetAxis**). Then, to `Output Pin 1`, we attached the `If` that checks the movement input—the one we did at the beginning of this section. This will cause the rotation to be executed first and the movement second.

Regarding the limitation we mentioned before, it's basically the fact we cannot execute both **Forward** and **Backward** rotations, given that if the forward movement keys are pressed, the first `If` will be true. Because the backward key rotation is checked in the false output pin, they won't be checked in such cases. Of course, as our first movement script it might be enough but consider the lateral movement. If we continue the `If` chaining using `True` and `False` output pins, we will have a scenario where we can only move in one direction. So we cannot combine, for example, `Forward` and `Right` to move diagonally.

A simple solution to this issue is to put the `If` nodes in the sequence instead of chaining them, so all the `If` nodes are checked, as the original C# did. You can see an example of this in the next image:

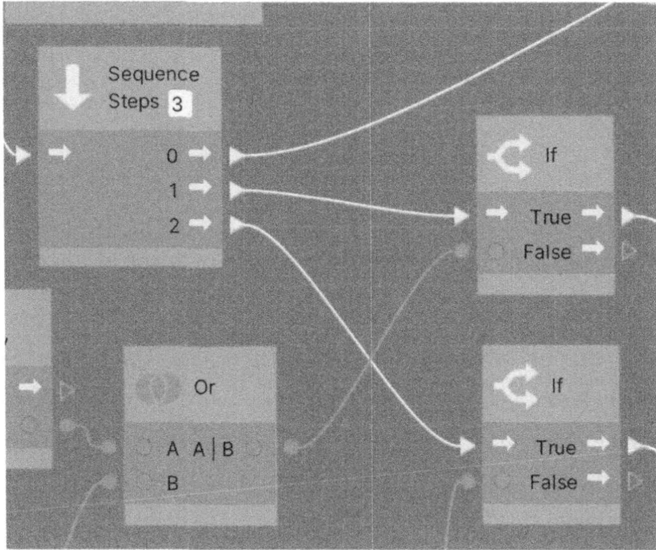

Figure 6.19: Sequencing Ifs

Something to consider here is that the chaining of the `Ifs` and any kind of node can be removed by right-clicking the circle pins on both ends of the line that connects them. Now that we have completed our movement script, we need to refine it to work in every machine by exploring the concept of Delta Time.

Understanding Delta Time

Unity's **Update** loop executes as fast as the computer can. You can specify in Unity the desired frame rate, but achieving that depends exclusively on whether your computer can reach that, which depends on lots of factors, not only hardware, so you cannot expect to always have consistent FPS. You must code your scripts to handle every possible scenario. Our current script is moving at a certain speed per frame, and the *per frame* part is important here.

We have set the movement speed to 0.1, so if my computer runs the game at 120 FPS, the player will move 12 meters per second. Now, what happens on a computer where the game runs at 60 FPS? As you may guess, it will move only 6 meters per second, making our game have inconsistent behavior across different computers. This is where Delta Time saves the day.

Delta Time is a value that tells us how much time has passed since the previous frame. This time depends a lot on our game's graphics, number of entities, physics bodies, audio, and countless aspects that will dictate how fast your computer can process a frame. As an example, if your game runs at 10 FPS, it means that, in a second, your computer can process the `Update` loop 10 times, meaning that each loop takes approximately `0.1` seconds; in the frame, Delta Time will provide that value. In the next diagram, you can see an example of 4 frames taking different times to process, which can happen in real-life cases:

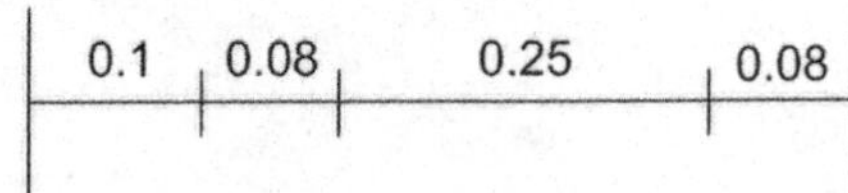

Figure 6.20: Delta Time values varying in different frames of the game

Here, we need to code in such a way as to change the *per frame* part of the movement to *per second*; we need to have consistent movement per second across different computers. A way to do that is to move proportionally to the Delta Time: the higher the Delta Time value, the longer that frame is, and the further the movement should be to match the real time that has passed since the last update. We can think about our `speed` field's current value in terms of `0.1` meters per second; our Delta Time saying `0.5` means that half a second has passed, so we should move half the speed, `0.05`.

After two frames a second have passed, the sum of the movements of the frames (2 x 0.05) matches the target speed, `0.1`. Delta Time can be interpreted as the percentage of a second that has passed.

To make the Delta Time affect our movement, we should simply multiply our speed by Delta Time every frame because the Delta Time can be different every frame, so let's do that:

1. We access Delta Time using Time.deltaTime. We can start affecting the movement by multiplying the Delta Time in every Translate:

```
if (Input.GetKey(KeyCode.W) || Input.GetKey(KeyCode.UpArrow))
{ transform.Translate(0, 0, speed * Time.deltaTime); }

if (Input.GetKey(KeyCode.S) || Input.GetKey(KeyCode.DownArrow))
{ transform.Translate(0, 0, -speed * Time.deltaTime); }

if (Input.GetKey(KeyCode.A) || Input.GetKey(KeyCode.LeftArrow))
{ transform.Translate(-speed * Time.deltaTime, 0, 0); }

if (Input.GetKey(KeyCode.D) || Input.GetKey(KeyCode.RightArrow))
{ transform.Translate(speed * Time.deltaTime, 0, 0); }
```

Figure 6.21: Multiplying speed by Delta Time

2. We can do the same with the rotation speed, by chaining the mouse and speed multiplications:

```
float mouseX = Input.GetAxis("Mouse X");
transform.Rotate(0, mouseX * rotationSpeed * Time.deltaTime, 0);
```

Figure 6.22: Applying Delta Time to the rotation code

3. If you save and play the game, you will notice that the movement will be slower than before. That's because now `0.1` is the movement per second, meaning `10` centimeters per second, which is pretty slow; try raising those values. In my case, `10` for speed and `180` for rotation speed was enough, but the rotation speed depends on the player's preferred sensibility, which can be configurable, but let's keep that for another time.

The Visual Scripting change for rotation will look like this:

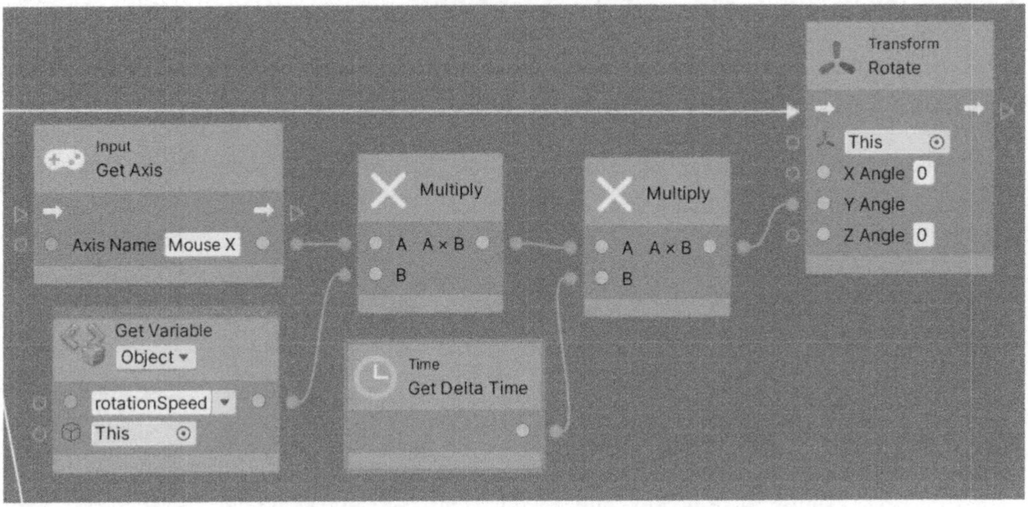

Figure 6.23: Applying Delta Time to Rotate Visual Script

For movement, you can easily extrapolate from this example or remember to check the project on GitHub. We simply chained another **Multiply** node with **Get Delta Time**.

We just learned how to mix the Input System of Unity, which tells us about the state of the keyboard, mouse, and other input devices, with the basic `Transform` movement functions. This way, we can start making our game feel more dynamic.

Now that we have finished the player's movement, let's discuss how to make the player shoot bullets using `Instantiate` functions.

Implementing spawning

We have created lots of objects in the editor that define our level, but once the game begins, and according to the player's actions, new objects must be created to better fit the scenarios generated by player interaction. Enemies might need to appear after a while, or bullets must be created according to the player's input; even when enemies die, there's a chance of spawning a power-up. This means that we cannot create all the necessary objects beforehand but should create them dynamically, and that's done through scripting.

In this section, we will examine the following spawning concepts:

- Spawning objects
- Timing actions
- Destroying objects

We will start seeing the Unity `Instantiate` function, which allows us to create instances of Prefabs at runtime, such as when pressing a key, or in a time-based fashion, such as making our enemy spawn bullets once every certain amount of time. Also, we will learn how to destroy these objects to prevent our scene from starting to perform badly due to too many objects being processed.

Let's start with how to shoot bullets according to the player's input.

Spawning objects

To spawn an object in runtime or **Play** mode, we need a description of the object, which components it has, and its settings and possible sub-objects. You might be thinking about Prefabs here, and you are right; we will use an instruction that will tell Unity to create an instance of a Prefab via scripting. Remember that an instance of a Prefab is an object created based on the Prefab—basically a clone of the original one.

We will start with shooting player's bullets, so first let's create the bullet Prefab by following these steps:

1. Create a sphere in GameObject | 3D Object | Sphere. You can replace the sphere mesh with another bullet model if you want, but we will keep the sphere in this example for now.
2. Rename the sphere `Bullet`.
3. Create a material by clicking on the + button of the Project window, choosing the option **Material**, and calling it `Bullet`. Remember to place it inside the `Materials` folder.

4. Check the **Emission** checkbox in the material and set the **Emission Map** and **Base Map** colors to red. Remember, the emission color will make the bullet shine, especially with the bloom effect in our post-processing volume:

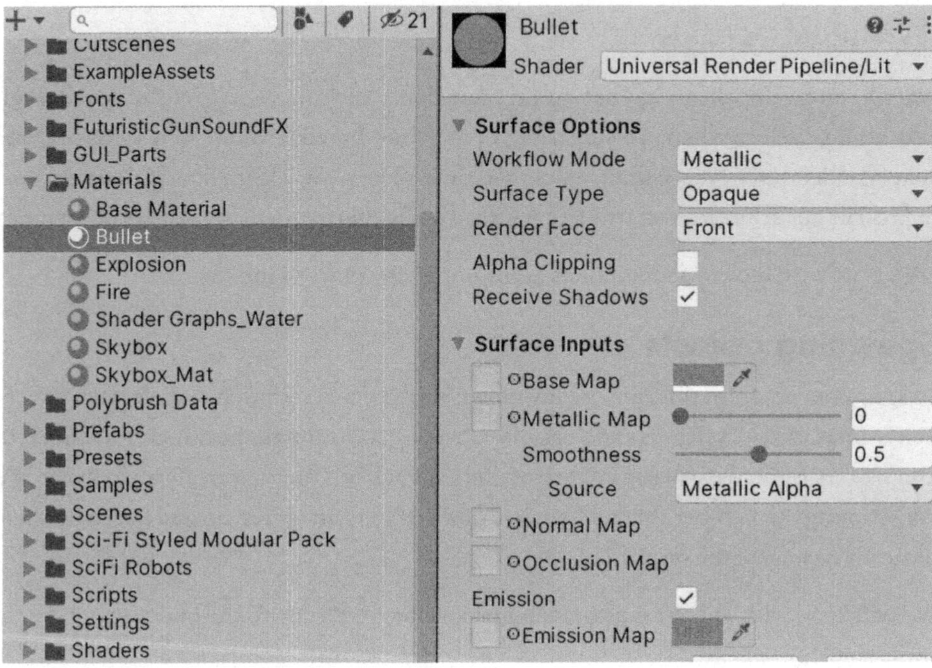

Figure 6.24: Creating a red bullet material with emission color

5. Apply the **Material** to the **Sphere** by dragging the material to it.
6. Set the Scale to a smaller value—`0.3, 0.3, 0.3` worked in my case.
7. Create a script called `ForwardMovement` to make the bullet constantly move forward at a fixed speed. You can create it both with C# and Visual Scripting, but for simplicity, we are only going to use C# in this case.

I suggest you try to solve this by yourself first and look at the screenshot in the next step with the solution later as a little challenge to recap the movement concepts we saw previously. If you don't recall how to create a script, please look at *Chapter 5, Introduction to C# and Visual Scripting*, and check the previous section to see how to move objects.

8. The next screenshot shows you what the script should look like:

```
using UnityEngine;

public class ForwardMovement : MonoBehaviour
{
    public float speed;

    void Update()
    {
        transform.Translate(0, 0, speed * Time.deltaTime);
    }
}
```

Figure 6.25: A simple ForwardMovement script

9. Add the script (if not already there) to the bullet and set the speed to a value you see fit. Usually, bullets are faster than the player but that depends on the game experience you want to get. In my case, `20` worked fine. Test it by placing the bullet near the player and playing the game:

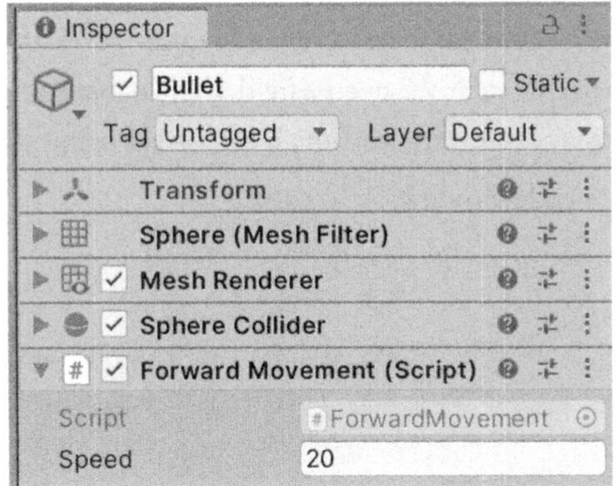

Figure 6.26: A ForwardMovement script in the bullet

10. Drag the bullet `GameObject` instance to the `Prefabs` folder to create a **Bullet** Prefab. Remember that the Prefab is an asset that has a description of the created bullet, like a blueprint of how to create a bullet:

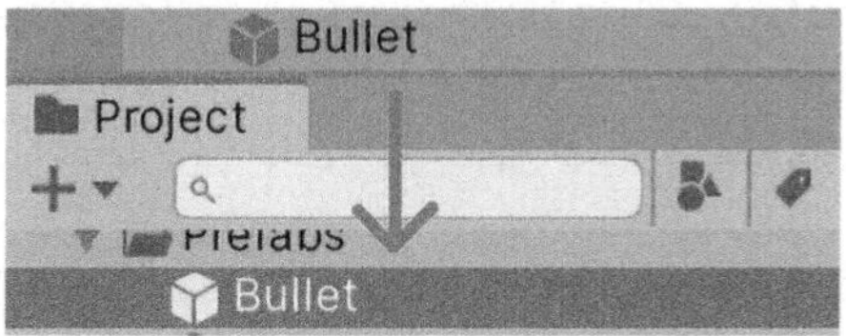

Figure 6.27: Creating a Prefab

11. Remove the original bullet from the scene; we will use the Prefab to create bullets when the player presses a key (if ever).

Now that we have our bullet Prefab, it is time to instantiate it (clone it) when the player presses a key. To do that, follow these steps:

1. Create and add a script to the player's `GameObject` called `PlayerShooting` and open it.
2. We need a way for the script to have access to the Prefab to know which Prefab to use from probably the dozens we will have in our project. All of the data our script needs, which depends on the desired game experience, is in the form of a field, such as the speed field used so far. So in this case, we need a field of the `GameObject` type—a field that can reference or point to a specific Prefab, which can be set using the editor.
3. Adding the field code would look like this:

```
using UnityEngine;

public class PlayerShooting : MonoBehaviour
{
    public GameObject prefab;
}
```

Figure 6.28: The Prefab reference field

> As you might have guessed, we can use the `GameObject` type to not only reference Prefabs but also other objects. Imagine an enemy AI needing a reference to the player object to get its position, using `GameObject` to link the two objects. The trick here is considering that Prefabs are just regular GameObjects that live outside the scene; you cannot see them, but they are in memory, ready to be copied or instantiated. You will only see them through copies or instances that are placed in the scene with scripting or via the editor, as we have done so far.

4. In the editor, click on the circle toward the right of the property and select the `Bullet` Prefab. Another option is to just drag the `Bullet` Prefab to the property. This way, we tell our script that the bullet to shoot will be that one. Remember to drag the Prefab and not the bullet in the scene (that one should be deleted by now):

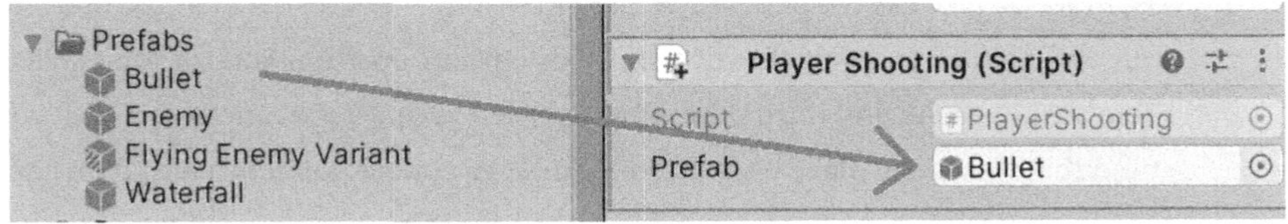

Figure 6.29: Setting the Prefab reference to point the bullet

5. We will shoot the bullet when the player presses the left mouse button, so place the proper if statement to handle that in the Update event function, like the one shown in the next screenshot:

```
void Update()
{
    if (Input.GetKeyDown(KeyCode.Mouse0)) { }
}
```

Figure 6.30: Detecting the pressure of the left mouse button

6. You will notice that this time, we used GetKeyDown instead of GetKey, the former being a way to detect the exact frame the pressure of the key started; this if statement will execute its code only in that frame, and until the key is released and re-pressed, it won't enter again. This is one way to prevent bullets from spawning in every frame, but just for fun, you can try using GetKey instead to check how it would behave. Also, KeyCode.Mouse0 is the mouse button number that belongs to left-click, KeyCode.Mouse1 is the right-click, and KeyCode.Mouse2 is the middle click.

7. Use the Instantiate function to clone the Prefab, passing the reference to it as the first parameter. This will create a clone of the previously mentioned Prefab that will be placed in the scene:

```
if (Input.GetKeyDown(KeyCode.Mouse0))
{
    Instantiate(prefab);
}
```

Figure 6.31: Instantiating the Prefab

If you save the script and play the game, you will notice that when you press the mouse, a bullet will be spawning, but probably not in the place you are expecting. If you don't see it, try to check the Hierarchy for new objects; it will be there. The problem here is that we didn't specify the desired spawn position, and we have two ways of setting that, which we will see in the next steps:

1. The first way is to use the `transform.position` and `transform.rotation` inherited fields from `MonoBehaviour`, which will tell us our current position and rotation. We can pass them as the second and third parameters of the `Instantiate` function, which will understand that this is the place we want our bullet to appear. Remember that it is important to set the rotation to make the bullet face the same direction as the player, so it will move that way:

```
Instantiate(prefab, transform.position, transform.rotation);
```

Figure 6.32: Instantiating the Prefab in our position and rotation

2. The second way is by using the previous version of `Instantiate`, but saving the reference returned by the function, which will be pointing to the clone of the Prefab. This allows us to change whatever we want from it. In this case, we will need the following three lines; the first will instantiate and capture the clone reference, the second will set the position, and the third the rotation. We will also use the `transform.position` field of the clone, but this time to change its value by using the = (assignment) operator:

```
GameObject clone = Instantiate(prefab);
clone.transform.position = transform.position;
clone.transform.rotation = transform.rotation;
```

Figure 6.33: The longer version of instantiating a Prefab in a specific position

Remember that you can check the project's GitHub repository linked in the *Preface* to see the full script finished. Now you can save the file with one of the versions and try to shoot.

If you try the script so far, you should see the bullet spawn in the player's position, but in our case, it will probably be the floor. The problem here is that the player's character pivot is there, and usually, every humanoid character has the pivot in their feet. We have several ways to fix that. The most flexible one is to create a **Shoot Point**, an empty GameObject child of the player, placed in the position we want the bullet to spawn. We can use the position of that object instead of the player's position by following these steps:

1. Create an empty `GameObject` in **GameObject | Create Empty**. Rename it `ShootPoint`.
2. Make it a child of the player's GameObject and place it where you want the bullet to appear, probably a little higher and further forward:

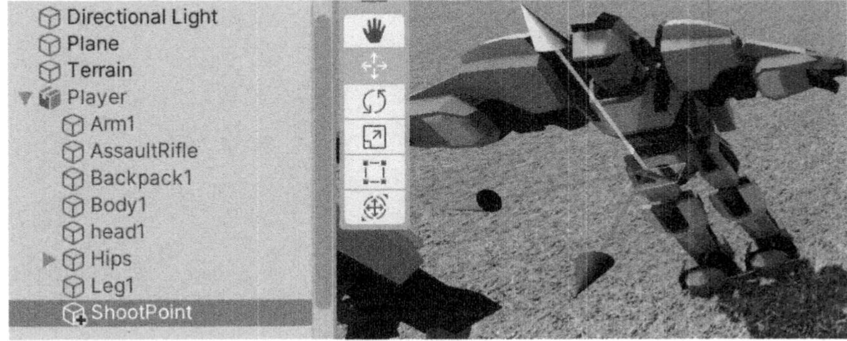

Figure 6.34: An empty ShootPoint object placed inside the character

3. As usual, to access the data of another object, we need a reference to it, such as the Prefab reference, but this time it needs to point to our shoot point. We can create another `GameObject` type field, but this time drag `ShootPoint` instead of the Prefab. The script and the object set would look as follows:

```
public GameObject prefab;
public GameObject shootPoint;
```

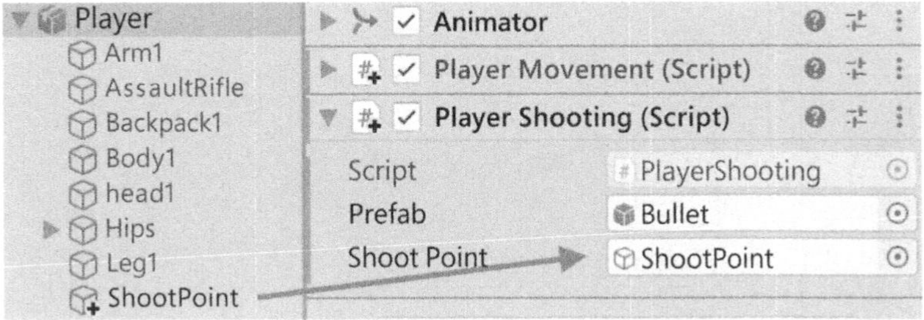

Figure 6.35: The Prefab and ShootPoint fields and how they are set in the editor

4. We can access the position of the ShootPoint by using the `transform.position` field of it again, as shown in the following screenshot:

```
clone.transform.position = shootPoint.transform.position;
clone.transform.rotation = shootPoint.transform.rotation;
```

Figure 6.36: The Prefab and ShootPoint fields and how they are set in the editor

The Visual Scripting version of **ForwardMovement** will look like this:

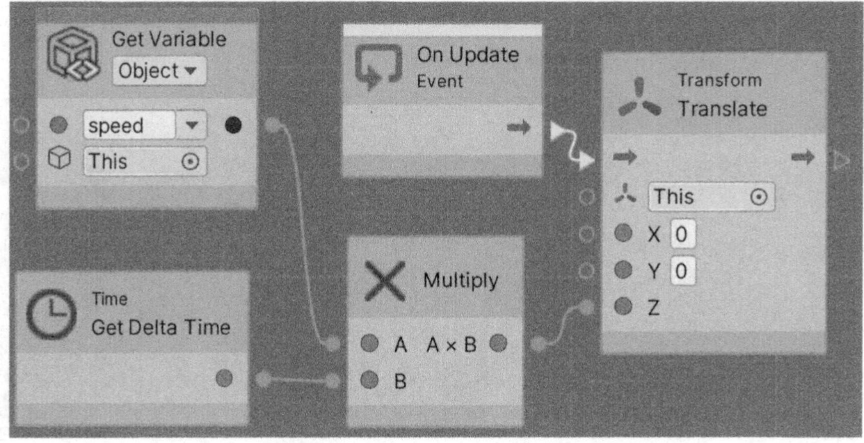

Figure 6.37: ForwardMovement with Visual Scripting

And `PlayerShooting` will look like this:

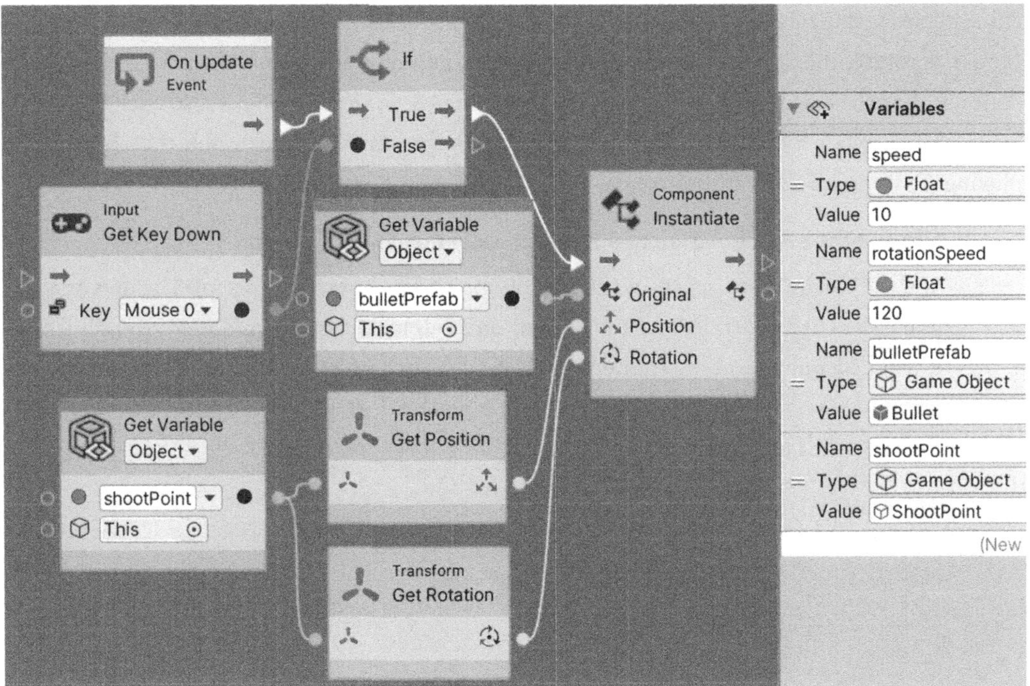

Figure 6.38: Instantiating in the PlayerShooting Visual Script

As you can see, we added a second **Script Machine** component with a new graph called **Player Shooting**. We also added a new variable, `bulletPrefab`, of type `GameObject` and dragged the **Bullet** Prefab to it, and a second `GameObject` typed variable called `shootPoint`, to have the reference to the bullet's spawn position. The rest of the script is essentially the counterpart of the C# version without any major differences. Something to highlight here is how we connected the `Transform GetPosition` and `Transform GetRotation` nodes to the `GetVariable` node belonging to the `shootPoint`; in this way, we are accessing the position and rotation of the shooting point. If you don't specify that, it will use the player's position and rotation, which in the case of our model is in the player's character's feet.

You will notice that now shooting and rotating with the mouse has a problem; when moving the mouse to rotate, the pointer will fall outside the **Game** View, and when clicking, you will accidentally click the editor, losing the focus on the **Game** View, so you will need to click the **Game** View again to regain focus and use input again. A way to prevent this is to disable the cursor while playing. To do this, follow these steps:

1. Add a `Start` event function to our Player Movement Script.
2. Add the two lines you can see in the following screenshot to your script. The first one will make the cursor visible, and the second one will lock it in the middle of the screen, so it will never abandon the **Game** View. Consider the latter; you will need to reenable the cursor when you switch back to the main menu or the pause menu, to allow the mouse to click the UI buttons:

```
void Start()
{
    Cursor.visible = false;
    Cursor.lockState = CursorLockMode.Locked;
}
```

Figure 6.39: Disabling the mouse cursor

3. Save and test this. If you want to stop the game, you could either press *Ctrl* + *Shift* + *P* (*Command* + *Shift* + *P* on Mac) or press the *Esc* key to reenable the mouse. Both options only work in the editor; in the real game, you will need to reset `Cursor.visible` to `true` and `Cursor.lockState` to `CursorLockMode.None`.
4. The Visual Scripting equivalent will look like this:

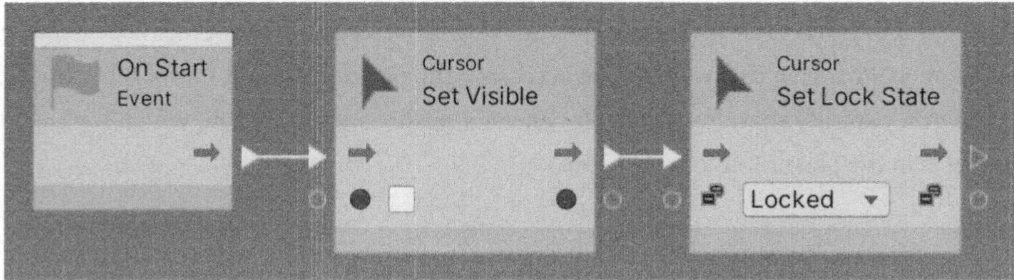

Figure 6.40: Disabling the mouse cursor in Visual Scripting

Now that we have covered the basics of object spawning, let's see an advanced example by combining it with timers.

Timing actions

Not entirely related to spawning, but usually used together, timing actions is a common task in video games. The idea is to schedule something to happen later; maybe we want the bullet to be destroyed after a while to prevent memory overflow, or we want to control the spawn rate of enemies or when they should spawn. That's exactly what we are going to do in this section, starting with the second, the **enemy waves.**

The idea is that we want to spawn enemies at a certain rate in different moments of the game; maybe we want to spawn enemies from second 1 to 5 at a rate of 2 per second, getting 10 enemies, and giving the player up to 20 seconds to finish them, programming another wave starting at 25 seconds. Of course, this depends a lot on the exact game you want, and you can start with an idea like this one and modify it after some testing to find the exact way you want the wave system to work. In our case, we will apply timing by implementing a simple wave system.

First of all, we need an enemy, and for now, we will simply use the same 3D model we used for the player, but add a Forward Movement script to simply make it move forward; later in this book, we will add AI behavior to our enemies. I suggest you try to create this Prefab by yourself and look at the following steps once you have tried it, to check the correct answer:

Drag the downloaded Character FBX model to the scene to create another instance of it, but rename it to `Enemy` this time:

1. Add the `ForwardMovement` script created for the bullets but this time to `Enemy`, and set it at a speed of `10` for now.
2. Drag the `Enemy` GameObject to the Project to create a Prefab based on that one; we will need to spawn it later. Remember to choose **Prefab Variant**, which will keep the Prefab linked with the original model to make the changes applied to the model automatically apply to the Prefab.
3. Remember also to destroy the original `Enemy` from the scene.

Now, to schedule actions, we will use the `Invoke` functions to create timers. They are basic but enough for our requirements. Let's use them by following these steps:

1. Create an empty GameObject at one end of the base and call it `Wave1a`.
2. Create and add a script called `WaveSpawner` to it.

3. Our spawner will need four fields: the Enemy Prefab to spawn, the startTime of the wave, the endTime, and the spawn rate of the enemies (how much time should be between each spawn). The script and the settings will look like the following screenshot:

```
public GameObject prefab;
public float startTime;
public float endTime;
public float spawnRate;
```

Figure 6.41: The fields of the wave spawner script

We will use the InvokeRepeating function to schedule a custom function to repeat periodically. You will need to schedule the repetition just once; Unity will remember that, so don't do it every frame. This is a good reason to use the Start event function instead. The first argument of the function is a string (text between the quotation marks) with the name of the other function to execute periodically, and unlike Start or Update, you can name the function whatever you want. The second argument is the time to start repeating, our startTime field, in this case. Finally, the third argument is the repetition rate of the function—how much time needs to happen between each repetition—this being the spawnRate field. You can find how to call that function in the next screenshot, along with the custom Spawn function:

```
void Start()
{
    InvokeRepeating("Spawn", startTime, spawnRate);
}

void Spawn() { }
```

Figure 6.42: Scheduling a Spawn function to repeat

1. Inside the Spawn function, we can put the spawning code as we know, using the Instantiate function. The idea is to call this function at a certain rate to spawn one enemy per call. This time, the spawn position will be in the same position as the spawner, so place it carefully:

```
void Spawn()
{
    Instantiate(prefab, transform.position, transform.rotation);
}
```

Figure 6.43: Instantiating in the Spawn function

If you test this script by setting the Prefab `startTime` and `spawnRate` fields to some values greater than 0, you will notice that the enemies will start spawning but never stop, and you can see that we didn't use the `endTime` field so far. The idea is to call the `CancelInvoke` function, the one function that will cancel all the `InvokeRepeating` calls we made, but after a while. We will delay the execution of `CancelInvoke` using the `Invoke` function, which works similarly to `InvokeRepeating`, but this one executes just once. In the next screenshot, you can see how we added an `Invoke` call to the `CancelInvoke` function in `Start`, using the `endTime` field as the time to execute `CancelInvoke`. This will execute `CancelInvoke` after a while, canceling the first `InvokeRepeating` call that spawns the Prefab:

```
InvokeRepeating("Spawn", startTime, spawnRate);
Invoke("CancelInvoke", endTime);
```

Figure 6.44: Scheduling a Spawn repetition but canceling after a while with CancelInvoke

This time, we used `Invoke` to delay the call to `CancelInvoke`. We didn't create a custom function because `CancelInvoke` doesn't receive arguments. If you need to schedule a function with arguments, you will need to create a wrapper function without parameters that calls the desired one and schedules it, as we did with `Spawn`, where the only intention is to call `Instantiate` with specific arguments.

2. Now you can save and set some real values to our spawner. In my case, I used the ones shown in the following screenshot:

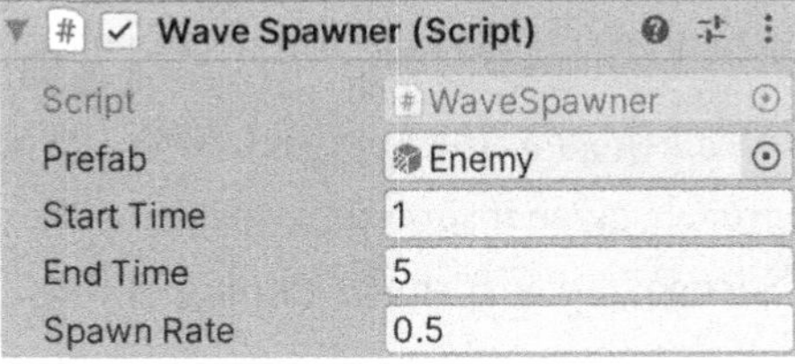

Figure 6.45: Spawning enemies from second 1 to 5 of the gameplay every 0.5 seconds, 2 per second

You should see the enemies being spawned one next to the other, and because they move forward, they will form a row of enemies. This behavior will change later with AI. Now, the Visual Scripting version will look like this:

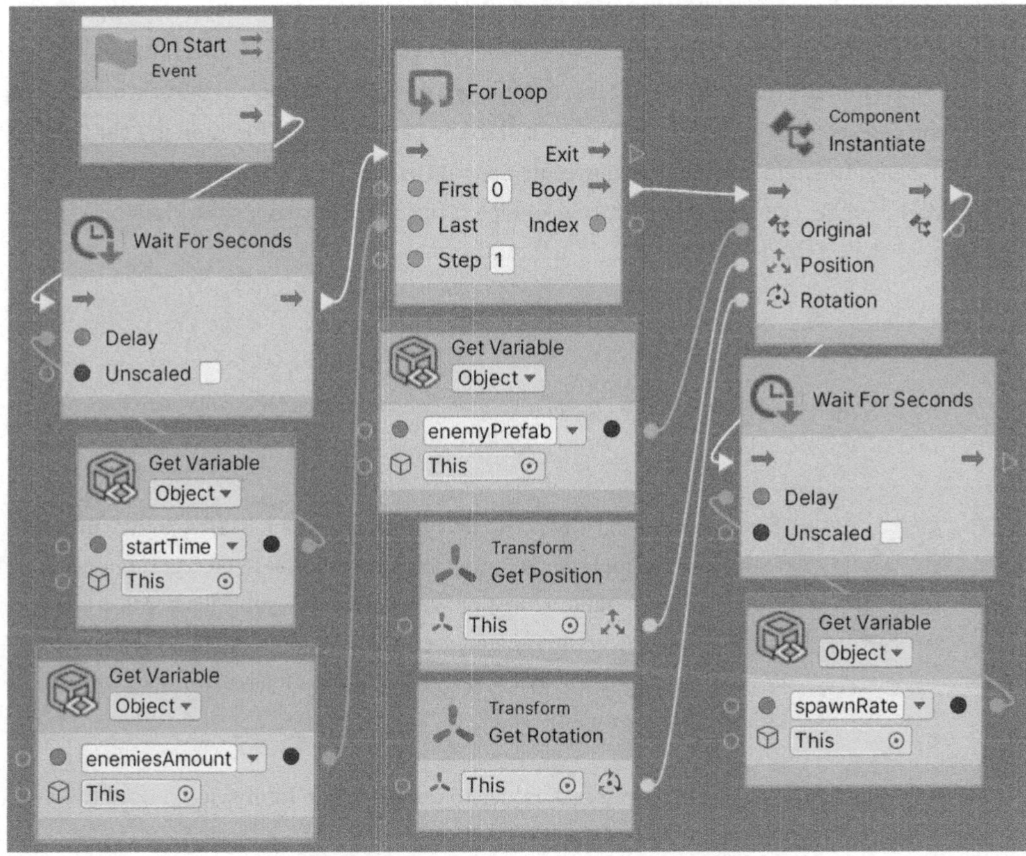

Figure 6.46: Spawning enemies in Visual Scripting

While we could use the `InvokeRepeating` approach in Visual Scripting, here we can see some benefits of the Visual approach, given it sometimes has more flexibility than coding. In this case, we used the `Wait For Seconds` node at the beginning of the `Start`, a node that basically will hold the execution of the flow for a couple of seconds. This will create the initial delay we had in the original script; that's why we used the `startTime` as the amount of `Delay`.

Now, after the wait, we used a `For` loop; for this example, we changed the concept of the script, as we want to spawn a specific number of enemies instead of spawning during a time. The `For` loop is essentially a classic `For` that will repeat whatever is connected to the `Body` output pin the number of times specified by the `Last` input pin.

We connected that pin to a variable to control the number of enemies we want to spawn. Then, we connected an `Instantiate` to the `Body` output pin of the `For` loop to instantiate our enemies, and then a `Wait For Seconds`, to stop the flow for a time before the loop can continue spawning enemies.

Something interesting is that if you play the game now, you will receive an error in the console that will look like this:

Figure 6.47: Error when using Wait nodes

You can even go back to the graph editor and see that the conflicting node will be highlighted in red:

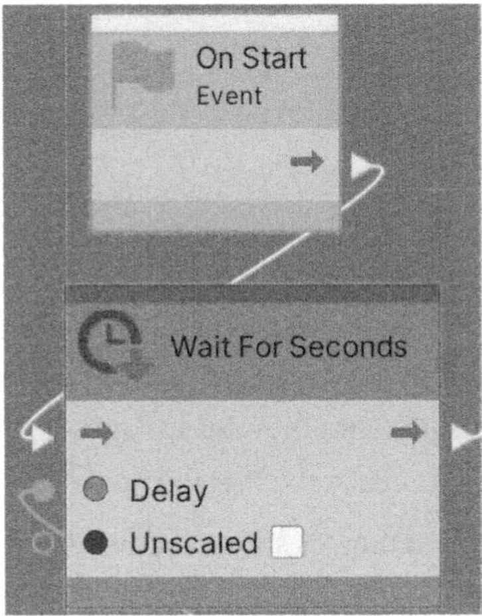

Figure 6.48: Node causing the error

The issue here is that in order for the `Wait For Seconds` nodes to work, you need to mark the `Start` event as a **Coroutine**. This will basically allow the event to be paused for an amount of time and be resumed later. The same concept exists in C#, but as it is simpler to implement here in Visual Scripting than in C#, we decided to go with this approach here.

To solve this error, just select the `On Start` event node and check the **Coroutine** checkbox in the **Graph Inspector** pane on the left of the **Script Graph** editor. If you don't see it, consider clicking the **Info** button (circle with *i*) in the top-left part of the editor.

A coroutine is a function that can be paused and resumed later, and that's exactly what the `Wait` node does. Coroutines also exist in `MonoBehaviours`, but let's keep things simple for now.

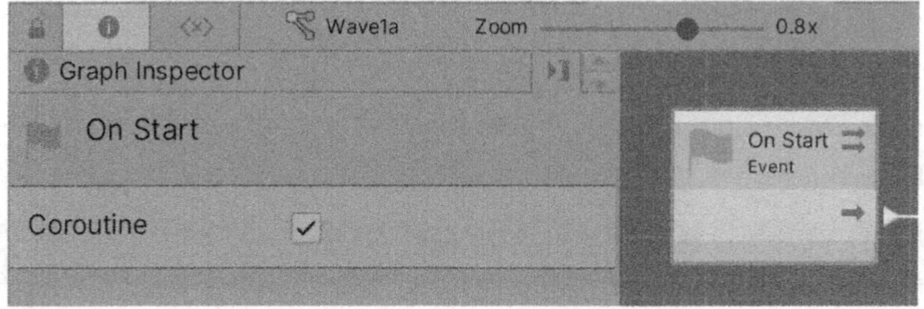

Figure 6.49: Marking Start as a coroutine

Now that we have discussed timing and spawn, let's discuss timing and `Destroy` to prevent our bullets from living forever in the memory.

Destroying objects

We can use the `Destroy` function to destroy object instances. The idea is to make the bullets have a script that schedules their own auto-destruction after a while to prevent them from living forever. We will create the script by following these steps:

1. Select the Prefab of `Bullet` and add a script called `Autodestroy` to it, as you did with other objects using the **Add Component > New Script** option. This time, the script will be added to the Prefab, and each instance of the Prefab you spawn will have it.
2. You can use the `Destroy` function, as shown in the next screenshot, to destroy the object just once in `Start`:

```
void Start()
{
    Destroy(gameObject);
}
```

Figure 6.50: Destroying an object when it starts

The `Destroy` function expects the object to destroy as the first argument, and here, we are using the `gameObject` reference; a way to point to the GameObject our script is placed into to destroy it. If you use the `this` pointer instead of `GameObject`, we will be destroying only the `Autodestroy` component we are creating.

Of course, we don't want the bullet to be destroyed as soon as it is spawned, so we need to delay the destruction. You may be thinking about using `Invoke`, but unlike most functions in Unity, `Destroy` can receive a second argument, which is the time to wait until destruction.

1. Create a delay field to use as the second argument of `Destroy`, as shown in the next screenshot:

```
public float delay;

void Start()
{
    Destroy(gameObject, delay);
}
```

Figure 6.51: Using a field to configure the delay to destroy the object

2. Set the `delay` field to a proper value; in my case, 5 was enough. Now check how the bullets despawn after a while by looking at them being removed from the Hierarchy.
3. The Visual Scripting equivalent will look like this:

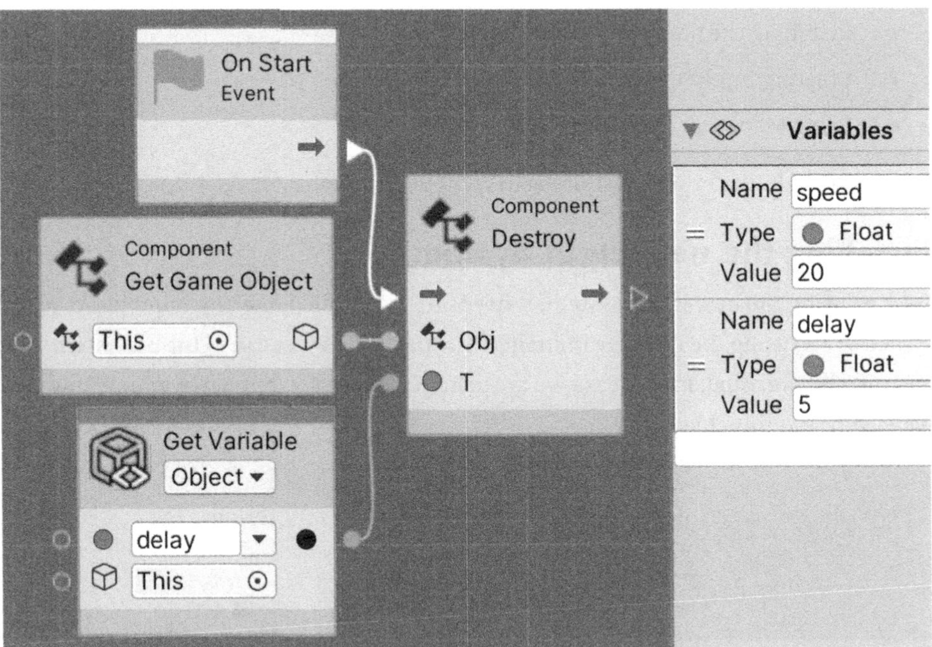

Figure 6.52: Destroying in Visual Scripting

Regarding this version, notice how we use the **Component Destroy (Obj, T)** version of the `Destroy` node, which includes the delay time.

Look for the `Object Pool` concept, which is a way to recycle objects instead of creating them constantly; you will learn that sometimes creating and destroying objects is not that performant.

Now, we can create and destroy objects at will, which is something very common in Unity scripting. In the next section, we will discuss how to modify the scripts we have done so far to support the new Unity Input System.

Using the new Input System

We have been using the **Input** class to detect the buttons and axes being pressed, and for our simple usage that is more than enough. But the default Unity input system has its limitations regarding extensibility to support new input hardware and mappings.

In this section, we will explore the following concepts:

- Installing the new Input System
- Creating Input Mappings
- Using Mappings in scripts

Let's start exploring how to install the new Input System.

Installing the new Input System

To start using the new Input System, it needs to be installed like any other package we have installed so far, using the **Package Manager**. The package is just called **Input System**, so go ahead and install it as usual. In this case we are using version 1.4.2, but a newer one may be available when you read this chapter.

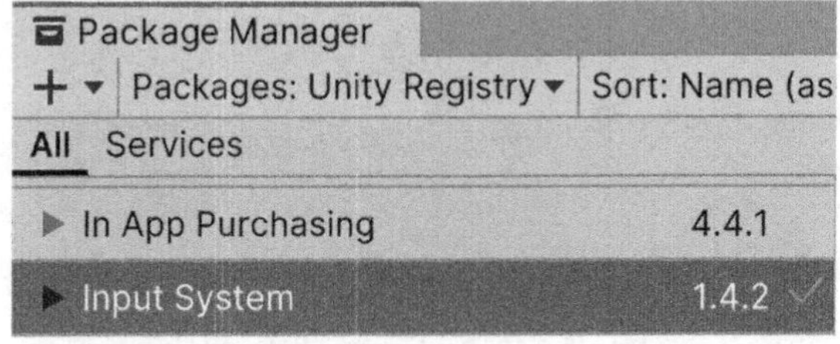

Figure 6.53: Installing the new Input System package

By default, when you install the Input System, it will prompt you to enable the new Input System with a window like the one in the following image. If that appears, just click **Yes** and wait for Unity to restart:

Warning
This project is using the new input system package but the native platform backends for the new input system are not enabled in the player settings. This means that no input from native devices will come through.
Do you want to enable the backends? Doing so will *RESTART* the editor and will *DISABLE* the old UnityEngine.Input APIs.
No
Yes

Figure 6.54: Switching the active Input System

If for some reason that didn't appear, the other alternative is going to **Edit | Project Settings** and then going to **Player | Other Settings | Configuration** to set the **Active Input Handling** property to **Input System Package (New)**.

There's an option called **Both** to keep both enabled, but let's stick with just one.

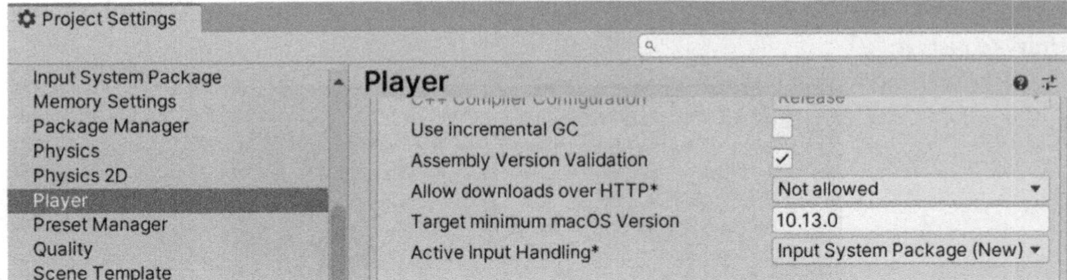

Figure 6.55: Switching the active Input System

Now that we have the system installed and set up, let's explore how to create the Input Mappings needed.

Creating Input Mappings

The new system has a way to directly request the current state of a button or thumbstick to the gamepad, mouse, keyboard, or whatever other device we have, like what we did so far with the previous Input System. But doing so would prevent us from using one of the best features of the system, the Input Mappings.

The idea of an Input Mapping is to abstract the Input Actions from the Physical Input. Instead of thinking about the space bar, the left thumbstick of a gamepad, or the right click of a mouse, you think in terms of actions, like move, shoot, or jump. In code, you will ask if the `Shoot` button has been pressed, or the current value of the `Move` axes, like we did with the mouse axes rotatation. While the previous system supported a certain degree of Input Mapping, the one in the new Input System is way more powerful and easier to configure.

Action	**Mappings**
Shoot	Left Mouse Button, Left Control, X button of the gamepad
Jump	Space, Y button of gamepad
Horizontal Movement	A and D keys, Left and Right arrows, gamepad Left Stick

Figure 6.56: Example of the Input Mapping table

The power of this idea is that the actual keys or buttons that will trigger these actions are configurable in the Unity editor, allowing any game designed to alter the exact keys to control the entire game without changing the code.

We can even map more than one button to the same action, even from different devices, so we can make the mouse, keyboard, and gamepad trigger the same action, greatly simplifying our code. Another benefit is that the user can also rebind the keys with some custom UI we can add to our game, which is very common in PC games.

The easiest way to start creating an Input Mapping is through the **Player Input** component. This component, as the name suggests, represents the input of a particular player, allowing us to have one of those on each player in our game to support split-screen multiplayer, but let's focus on single-player. Adding this script to our player will allow us to use the **Create Actions...** button to create a default Input Mapping asset. This asset, as a material, can be used by several players, so we modify it and it will affect all of them (for example, adding the `Jump` Input Mapping):

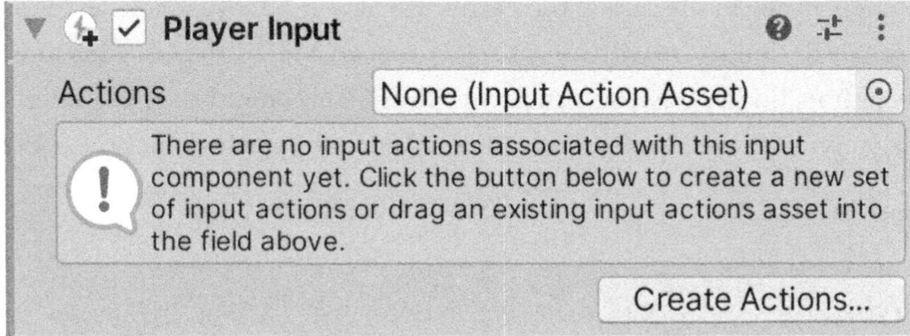

Figure 6.57: Creating Input Action assets using the Player Input component

After clicking that button and saving the asset location in the save prompt, you will see the following screen:

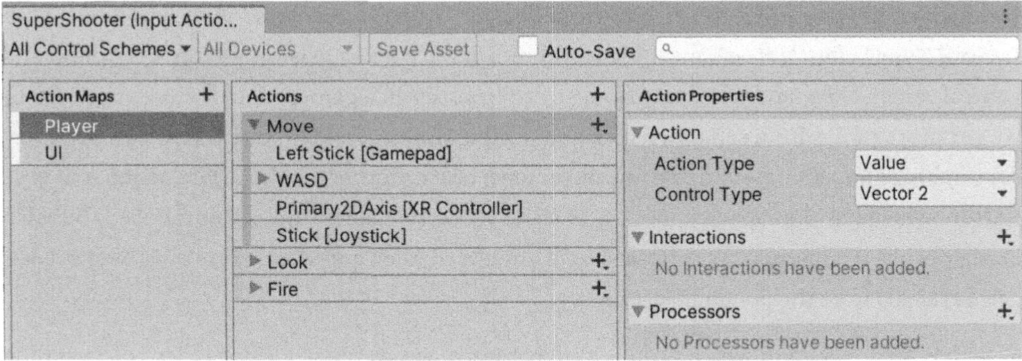

Figure 6.58: The default Input Mapping file

The first part to understand from this asset is the **Action Maps** section (left panel). This allows us to create separate Action Maps for different situations, for example, for driving and on-foot controls in games like GTA. By default, **Player** and **UI** mappings are created, to separate the mappings for the player controlling and navigating through the UI. If you check the **Player Input** component again, you will see that the **Default Map** property is set to **Player**, which means that we will only care for the player controlling the Input Mappings in this GameObject; any UI action pressed won't be considered. We can switch the active map in runtime at will, for example, to disable the character controller input when we are in the pause menu, or switch to the driving mappings while in a car, using the same buttons but for other purposes.

If you select an Action Map in the left panel, you will see all the actions it contains in the **Actions** list in the middle panel. In the case of the **Player**, we have the **Move**, **Look**, and **Fire** mappings, which are exactly the inputs we will use in our game. Bear in mind you can add more if you need to use the + button, but for now, let's stick with the default ones. When you select any action from the list, you will see their configurations in the **Action Properties** panel, the one on the right:

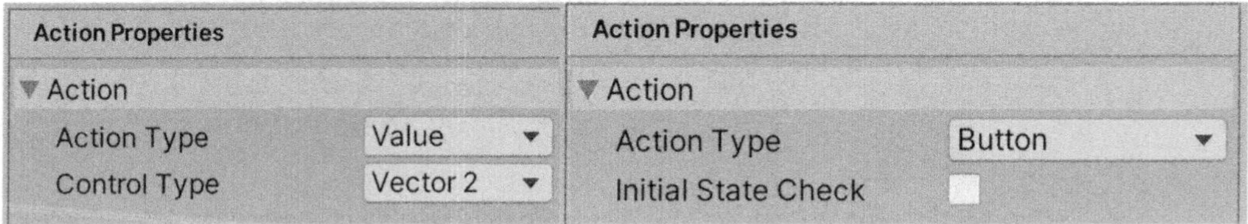

Figure 6.59: The Move (left) and Fire (right) action configurations

As you can see, there's a property called **Action Type** that will dictate which kind of input we are talking about. If you select **Move** in the middle panel, you can see it's a **Value** action type with **Control Type** being `Vector2`, meaning it will return the x and y axis values, the horizontal and vertical values—the kind we expect from any thumbstick in a gamepad. In the previous system, we got those values from separated 1D axes, like the **Mouse X** and **Mouse Y** axes, but here they are combined into a single variable for convenience. On the other hand, the **Fire** action is of type **Button**, which has the capacity not only to check its current state (pressed or released) but also do checks like if it has just been pressed or just released, the equivalents to `GetKey`, `GetKeyDown`, and `GetKeyUp` from the previous system.

Now that we understand which actions we have and of which type each one is, let's discuss how the Physical Input will trigger them. You can click the arrow on the left of each action in the middle panel to see its physical mappings. Let's start exploring the **Move** Action Mappings.

In this case, we have 4 mappings:

- **Left Stick [Gamepad]**: The left stick of the gamepad
- **Primary 2D Axis [XR Controller]**: The main stick of the VR controllers
- **Stick [Joystick]**: Main stick for arcade-like joysticks or even flight sticks
- **WASD**: A composite input simulating a stick through the W, A, S, and D keys

If you select any of them, you can check their configurations; let's compare the left stick and WASD as an example:

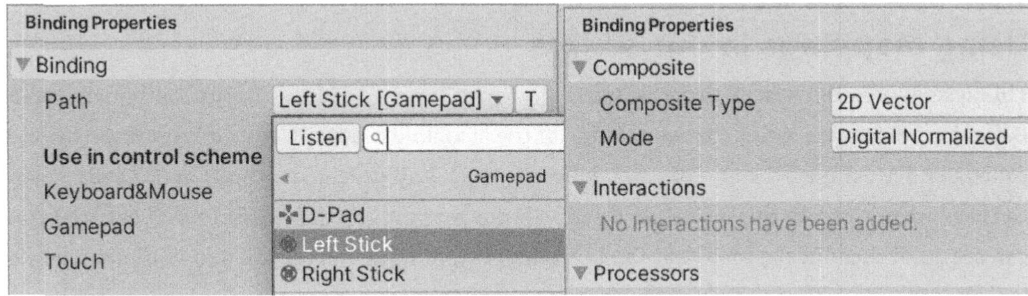

Figure 6.60: The left stick mapping (left) and the WASD key mapping (right)

In the case of the **Left Stick**, you can see the **Path** property that allows you to pick all the possible hardware physical controls that provide `Vector2` values (the x and y axes). In the case of the **WASD** key mapping, you can see it is a composite binding of type **2D Vector**, which, as stated previously, allows us to simulate a 2D Axis with other inputs—keys in this case. If you expand the **WASD** Input Mappings in the middle panel, you can see all inputs that are being composited for this 2D axis, and see their configurations by selecting them:

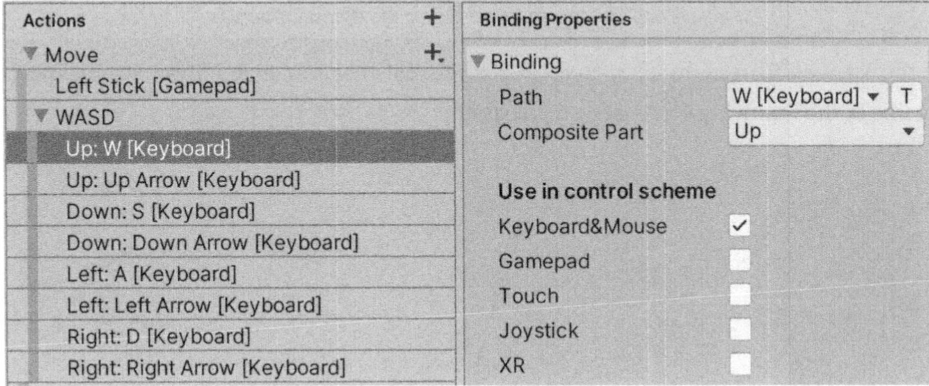

Figure 6.61: The inputs considered for the WASD composite 2D axis

In this case, it maps not only the W, A, S, and D buttons but also the 4 keyboard arrows. Each one of those mappings has a path to select the physical button, but also the **Composite Part** setting, allowing us to specify which direction this input will pull the simulated stick.

And with this, we have just scratched the surface of what this system is capable of, but for now, let's keep things simple and use these settings as they are. Remember a new asset was created with the same name as our game (*SuperShooter* in our case) in the root of the project. You can reopen this Action Mapping window by double-clicking it whenever you want. Now let's see how we can use these inputs in our code.

Using Mappings in our scripts

This system provides several ways to detect the input state. The **Player Input** component has a **Behavior** property to switch between some of the available modes. The simplest one is the one called **Send Messages**, the one that we will use, which will execute methods in our code when the keys are pressed. In this mode, each action in the mappings will have its own event, and you can see all of them in the tooltip at the bottom of the component. As you add mappings, more will appear.

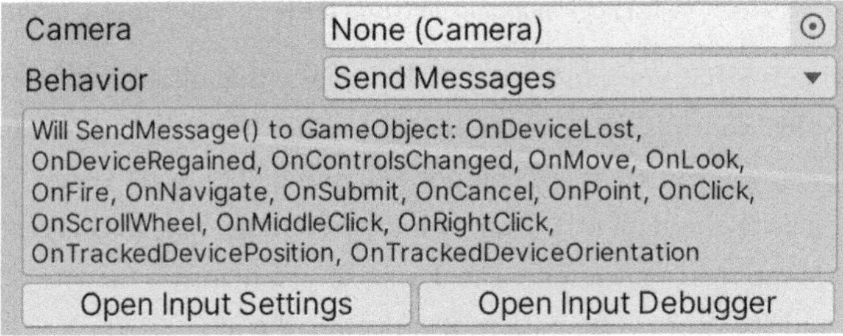

Figure 6.62: All the input events for the default mapping

From the list, we will need three, `OnMove`, `OnLook`, and `OnFire`. We can modify our `PlayerMovement` script like in the following screenshot to use them:

```
using UnityEngine;
using UnityEngine.InputSystem;

public class PlayerMovement : MonoBehaviour
{
    public float speed;
    public float rotationSpeed;
    private Vector2 movementValue;
    private float lookValue;

    private void Awake()
    {
        Cursor.visible = false;
        Cursor.lockState = CursorLockMode.Locked;
    }

    public void OnMove(InputValue value)
    {
        movementValue = value.Get<Vector2>() * speed;
    }

    public void OnLook(InputValue value)
    {
        lookValue = value.Get<Vector2>().x * rotationSpeed;
    }

    void Update()
    {
        transform.Translate(
            movementValue.x * Time.deltaTime,
            0,
            movementValue.y * Time.deltaTime);

        transform.Rotate(0, lookValue * Time.deltaTime, 0);
    }
}
```

Figure 6.63: Player movement with the new Input System

The first difference you will notice is that we don't request the status of the input in the `Update` method like we did before. Instead, we listen to the `OnMove` and `OnLook` events, which provide us with an `InputValue` parameter containing the current state of those axes. The idea is that every time these axes change value, these events will execute, and if the values didn't change, like when the player keeps pushing the stick all the way to the right, they won't be executed. That's why we need to store the current value in the `movementValue` and `lookValue` variables, to use the latest value of the axis later in the `Update` and apply the movement in every frame. Consider those are private, meaning they won't appear in the editor, but that's fine for our purposes. Also, observe that we added the `using UnityEngine.InputSystem` line at the top of the file to enable the usage of the new Input System in our script.

In this version of the `PlayerMovement` script, we used the axis input type like we did with the mouse before but also for movement, unlike the previous version that used buttons. This is the preferred option most of the time, so we will stick with that version. Observe how we use a single `transform.Translate` to move; we need to use the x axis of `movementValue` to move the x axis of our player but use the y axis of `movementValue` to move the z axis of our player. We don't want to move our player vertically, so that's why we needed to split the axis this way.

The `InputValue` parameter has the `Get<Vector2>()` method, which will give us the current value of both axes, given `Vector2` is a variable that contains the x and y properties. Then, we multiply the vector by the movement or rotation speed according to the case. You will notice that we don't multiply by `Time.deltaTime` in the axis events, but we do that in the `Update`. That's because `Time.deltaTime` can change between frames, so storing the movement value considering the `Time.deltaTime` of the last time we moved the stick won't be useful for us. Also, notice how `movementValue` is a `Vector2`, just a combination of the x and y axes, while `lookValue` is a simple float. We did it this way because we will rotate our character only following the lateral movement of the mouse; we don't want to rotate it up and down. Check that we do `value.Get<Vector2>().x`, with emphasis on the `.x` part, where we extract just the horizontal part of the axis for our calculations.

Regarding the `PlayerShooting` component, we need to change it to this:

```
public void OnFire()
{
    GameObject clone = Instantiate(prefab);

    clone.transform.position = shootPoint.transform.position;
    clone.transform.rotation = shootPoint.transform.rotation;
}
```

Figure 6.64: PlayerShooting script using the new Input System

This case is simpler, as we don't need to execute the shooting behavior each frame, we only need to execute something at the very same moment the input is pressed, which is exactly when the `OnFire` event will be executed. If you need to also detect when the key was released, you can add the `InputValue` parameter as we did with `OnMove` and `OnLook`, and consult the `isPressed` property:

```
public void OnFire(InputValue value)
{
    if (value.isPressed)
    {
        GameObject clone = Instantiate(prefab);

        clone.transform.position = shootPoint.transform.position;
        clone.transform.rotation = shootPoint.transform.rotation;
    }
}
```

Figure 6.65: Getting the state of the button

Regarding the Visual Script Machine version of our scripts, first, you will need to refresh the **Visual Script Node Library** by going to **Edit | Project Settings | Visual Scripting** and clicking the **Regenerate Nodes** button. If you don't do this, you won't see the new Input System nodes:

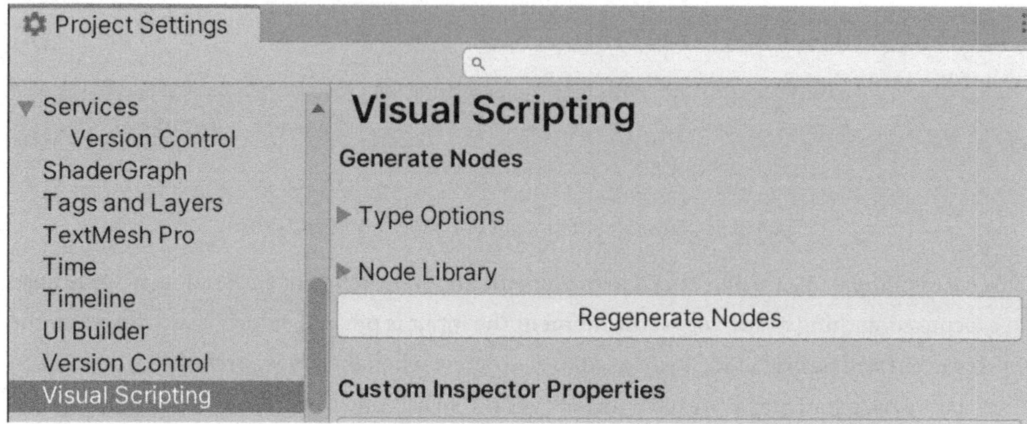

Figure 6.66: Regenerating Visual Scripting nodes to support the new Input System

Now, the `PlayerShooting` visual script would look like this:

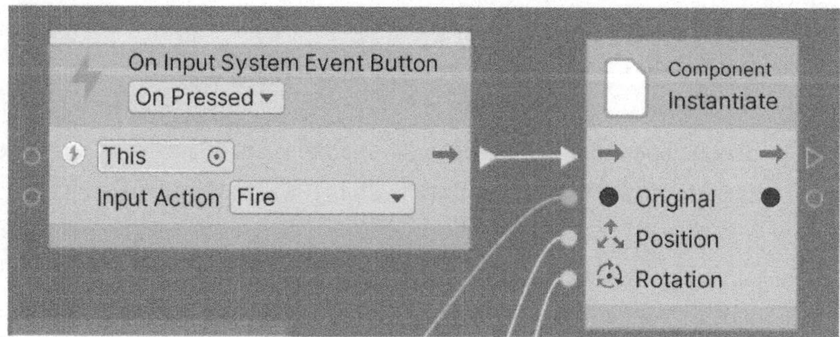

Figure 6.67: Instantiating bullets with the new input system

The new **On Input System Event Button** node allows us to detect when an action button has been pressed and react accordingly. You can pick the specific action in the **Input Action** parameter, and you can even make the node react to the pressure, release, or hold states of the button with the option right below the node's title. There is a bug where the **Input Action** property might not show any option; in such cases, try removing and adding the node again in the graph, and check that you added the `ScriptMachine` component to the same GameObject that has the `PlayerInput` component. Also check you have selected the Player GameObject in the hierarchy.

Regarding movement, it can be achieved this way:

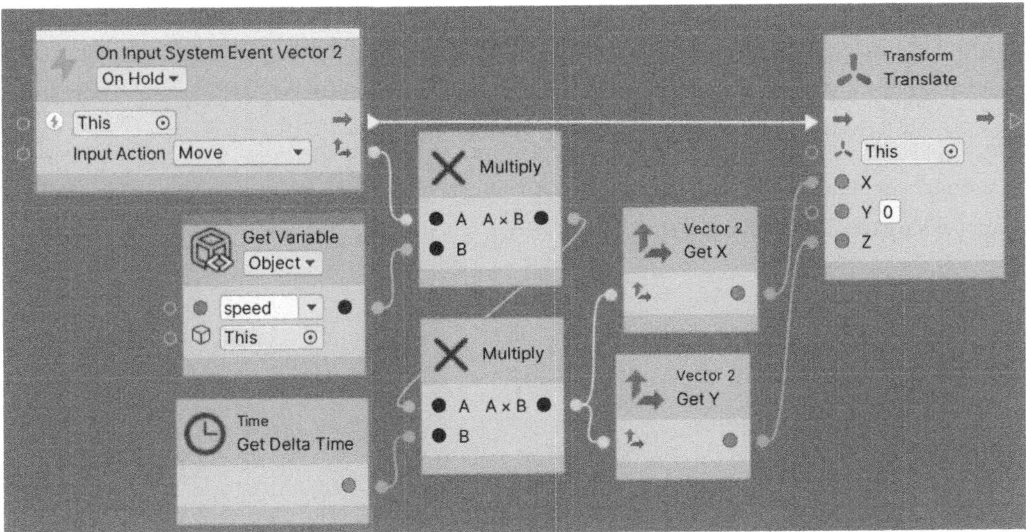

Figure 6.68: Moving with the new Input System

In this case, we used the **On Input System Event Vector2** node. This time, we used the `OnHold` mode, which means that, unlike the C# version, it won't execute just when the axis changes, but all the frames when the axis is pressed act like an `Update`; that, however, will only execute when the user is pressing the stick. The output pin of the node is the `Vector2` value, so we multiply it by the `speed` variable (declared in the `Variables` component of our player) and by `DeltaTime`. Finally, we use the `Vector2 GetX` and `Vector2 GetY` nodes to translate over the `x` and `z` axes. You may have trouble when rewiring the **Multiply** nodes with the new **Input System** node, given the return type is different compared to the previously used node (a `Vector2` instead of a single float). I recommend just deleting all nodes in this graph and redoing it to be sure everything is fine.

Summary

We created our first real scripts, which provide useful behavior. We discussed how to move a GameObject based on input and instantiate Prefabs via scripting to create objects at will according to the game situation. Also, we saw how to schedule actions, in this case, spawning, but this can be used to schedule anything. We saw how to destroy the created objects, to prevent increasing the number of objects to an unmanageable level. Finally, we explored the new Input System to provide maximum flexibility to customize our game's input. We will be using these actions to create other kinds of objects, such as sounds and effects, later in this book.

Now you are able to create any type of movement or spawning logic your objects will need and make sure those objects are destroyed when needed. You might think that all games move and create shooting systems the same way, and while they are similar, being able to create your own movement and shooting scripts allows you to customize those aspects of the game to behave as intended and create the exact experience you are looking for.

In the next chapter, we will be discussing how to detect collisions to prevent the player and bullets from passing through walls and much more.

7

Physics Collisions and Health System

As games try to simulate real-world behaviors, one important aspect to simulate is physics, which dictates how objects move and how they collide with each other, such as in the collision of players and walls, or bullets and enemies. Physics can be difficult to control due to the myriad of reactions that can happen after a collision, so we will learn how to properly configure our game to create physics as accurately as we can. This will generate the desired arcade movement feeling but get realistic collisions working—after all, sometimes, real life is not as interesting as video games!

In this chapter, we will examine the following collision concepts:

- Configuring physics
- Detecting collisions
- Moving with physics

First, we will learn how to properly configure physics, a step needed for the collisions between objects to be detected by our scripts, using new Unity events that we are also going to learn. All of this is needed in order to detect when our bullets touch our enemies and damage them. Then, we are going to discuss the difference between moving with `Transform`, as we have done so far, as well as moving with Rigidbody and the pros and cons of each version. This will be used to experiment with different ways of moving our player and let you decide which one you will want to use. Let's start by discussing physics settings.

Configuring physics

Unity's physics system is prepared to cover a great range of possible gameplay applications, so properly configuring it is important to get the desired result.

In this section, we will examine the following physics settings concepts:

- Setting shapes
- Physics object types
- Filtering collisions

We are going to start by learning about the different kinds of colliders that Unity offers, and then learn about different ways to configure those to detect different kinds of physics reactions (**collisions** and **triggers**). Finally, we will discuss how to ignore collisions between specific objects to prevent situations such as the player's bullets damaging the player.

Setting shapes

At the beginning of this book, we learned that objects usually have two shapes, the visual shape—which is basically the 3D mesh—and the physical one, the collider—the one that the physics system will use to calculate collisions. Remember that the idea of this is to allow you to have a highly detailed visual model while having a simplified physics shape to increase the performance.

Unity has several types of colliders, so here we will recap the common ones, starting with the primitive types, that is, **Box**, **Sphere**, and **Capsule**. These shapes are the cheapest ones (in terms of performance) to detect collisions due to the fact that the collisions between them are done via mathematical formulae, unlike other colliders such as the **Mesh Collider**, which allows you to use any mesh as the physics body of the object, but with a higher performance cost and some limitations. The idea is that you should use a primitive type to represent your objects or a combination of them, for example, an airplane could be done with two Box colliders, one for the body and the other one for the wings. You can see an example of this in the following screenshot, where you can see a weapons collider made from primitives:

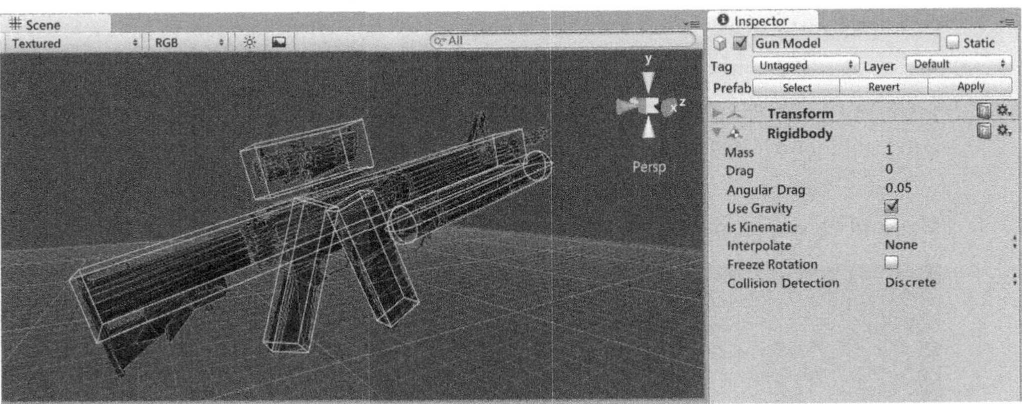

Figure 7.1: Compound colliders

Anyway, this is not always necessary; if we want the weapon to just fall to the ground, maybe a Box collider covering the entire weapon can be enough, considering those kinds of collisions don't need to be accurate, thereby increasing performance. Also, some shapes cannot be represented even with a combination of primitive shapes, such as ramps or pyramids, where your only solution is to use a Mesh collider, which asks for a 3D mesh to use for collisions, but we won't use them in this book given their high-performance impact; we will solve all of our physics colliders with primitives.

Now, let's add the necessary colliders to our scene to prepare it to calculate collisions properly. Consider that if you used an Asset Store environment package other than mine, you may already have the scene modules with colliders; I will be showing the work I needed to do in my case, but try to extrapolate the main ideas here to your scene. To add the colliders, follow these steps:

1. Select a wall in the base and check the object and possible child objects for collider components; in my case, I have no colliders. If you detect any Mesh collider, you can leave it if you want, but I would suggest you remove it and replace it with another option in the next step. The idea is to add the collider to it, but the problem I detected here is that, due to the fact my wall is not an instance of a Prefab, I need to add a collider to every wall in the scene.

2. One option is to create a Prefab and replace all of the walls with instances of the Prefab (the recommended solution) or to just select all walls in the Hierarchy (by clicking them while pressing *Ctrl* or *Cmd* on Mac) and, with them selected, use the **Add Component** button to add a collider to all of them. In my case, I will use the `Box Collider` component, which will adapt the size of the collider to the mesh. If it doesn't adapt, you can just change the **Size** and **Center** properties of the **Box Collider** to cover the entire wall:

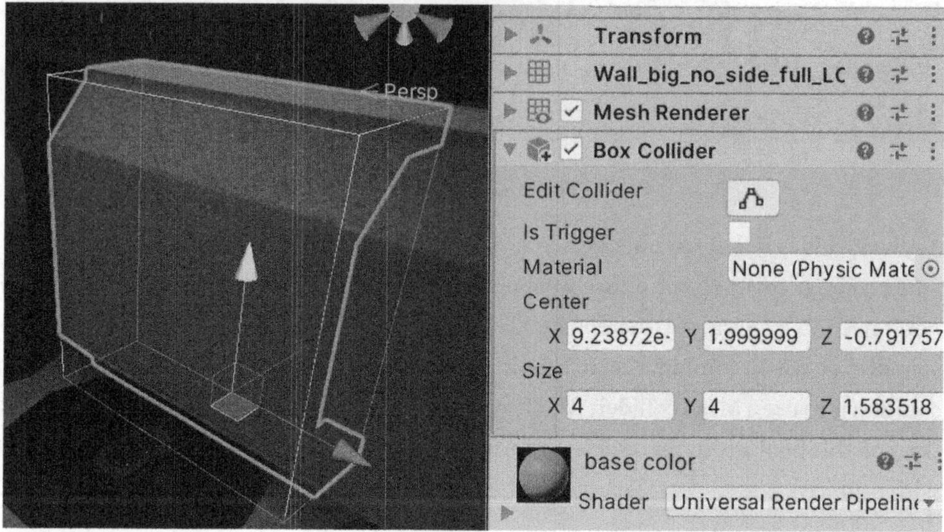

Figure 7.2: A Box Collider added to a wall

3. Repeat *steps 1* and *2* for the corners, floor tiles, and any other obstacle that will block player and enemy movement.

Now that we have added the needed colliders to the walls and floor, we can continue with the player and enemy. We will be adding the **Capsule Collider** to them, the usual collider to use in movable characters due to the fact that the rounded bottom will allow the object to smoothly climb ramps. Being horizontally rounded allows the object to easily rotate in corners without getting stuck, along with other conveniences of that shape. You might want to create an enemy Prefab based on one of the characters we downloaded before, so you can add the collider to that Prefab. Our player is a simple GameObject in the scene, so you will need to add the collider to that one, but consider also creating a Prefab for the player for convenience.

You may be tempted to add several Box colliders to the bones of the character to create a realistic shape of the object, and while we can do that to apply different damage according to the part of the body where the enemies were shot, we are just creating movement colliders; the capsule is enough. In advanced damage systems, both capsule and Bone colliders will coexist, one for the movement and the other for damage detection; but we will simplify this in our game.

Also, sometimes the collider won't adapt well to the visual shape of the object, and in my case, the Capsule collider didn't fit the character very well. I needed to fix its shape to match the character by setting its values as shown in the following screenshot: **Center** to `0,1,0`, **Radius** to `0.5`, and **Height** to `2`:

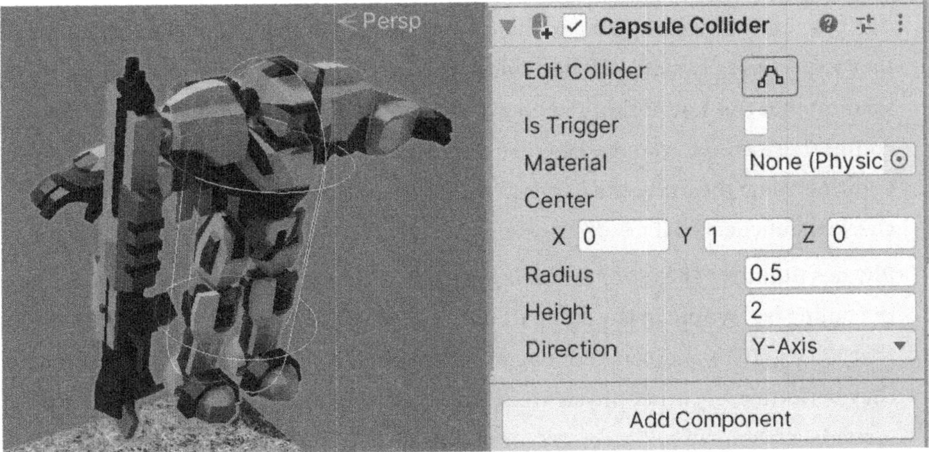

Figure 7.3: Character collider

The bullet we created with the Sphere already had a Sphere collider, but if you replaced the mesh of the bullet with another one, you might want to change the collider. For now, we don't need other objects in our game, so now that everything has its proper collider, let's see how to set the different physics settings to each object to enable proper collision detection.

If you check the Terrain's components, you will see that it has its own kind of collider, the **Terrain Collider**. For Terrains, that's the only collider to use.

Physics object types

Now that we have added colliders to every object by making the objects have a presence in the physics simulation, it is time to configure them to have the exact physics behavior we want. We have a myriad of possible combinations of settings, but we will discuss a set of common profiles that cover most situations. Remember, besides colliders, we saw the Rigidbody component at the beginning of this book, which is the one that applies physics to the object. The following profiles are done with a combination of colliders and Rigidbody settings:

- **Static Collider**: As the name suggests, this kind of collider is not supposed to move, aside from some specific exceptions. Most of the environment objects fall into this category, such as walls, floors, obstacles, and the terrain. These kinds of colliders are just colliders with no `Rigidbody` component, so they have a presence in the physics simulation but don't have any physics applied to them; they cannot be moved by other objects' collisions, they won't have physics, and they will be fixed in their position no matter what. Take into account that this has nothing to do with the **Static** checkbox at the top-right part of the editor; those are for systems we will explore later in several chapters (such as Chapter 12, Lighting Using the Universal Render Pipeline), so you can have a Static Collider with that checkbox unchecked if needed.
- **Physics Collider**: These are colliders with a `Rigidbody` component, like the example of the falling ball we did in the first part of this book. These are fully physics-driven objects that have gravity and can be moved through forces; other objects can push them and they perform every other physics reaction you can expect. You can use this for the player, grenade movement, falling crates, or in all objects in heavily physics-based games such as *The Incredible Machine*.
- **Kinematic Collider**: These are colliders that have a `Rigidbody` component but have the **Is Kinematic** checkbox checked. These don't have physics reactions to collisions and forces like **Static Colliders**, but they are expected to move, allowing **Physics Colliders** to properly handle collisions against them when moving. These can be used in objects that need to move using animations or custom scripting movements such as moving platforms.
- **Trigger Static Collider**: This is a regular Static Collider but with the **Is Trigger** checkbox of the collider checked. The difference is that kinematic and physics objects pass through it but by generating a `Trigger` event, an event that can be captured via scripting, which tells us that something is inside the collider.

This can be used to create buttons or trigger objects, in areas of the game when the player passes through something happening, such as a wave of enemies being spawned, a door being opened, or winning the game in case that area is the goal of the player. Note that regular Static Colliders won't generate a trigger event when passing through this type because those aren't supposed to move.

- **Trigger Kinematic Collider**: Kinematic Colliders don't generate collisions, so they will pass through any other object, but they will generate `Trigger` events, so we can react via scripting. This can be used to create moveable power-ups that, when touched, disappear and give us points, or bullets that move with custom scripting movements and no physics, just straight like our bullets, but damage other objects when they touch them.

Of course, other profiles can exist aside from the specified ones to use in some games with specific gameplay requirements, but it's down to you to experiment with all possible combinations of physics settings to see whether they are useful for your case; the described profiles will cover 99% of cases.

To recap the previous scenarios, I leave you with the following table showing the reaction of contact between all of the types of colliders. You will find a row per each profile that can move; remember that static profiles aren't supposed to move. Each column represents the reaction when they collide with the other types, `Nothing` meaning the object will pass through with no effect, `Trigger` meaning the object will pass through but raise `Trigger` events, and `Collision` meaning that the object won't be able to pass through the object:

	Collides with Static	**Collides with Dynamic**	**Collides with Kinematic**	**Collides with Trigger Static**	**Collides with Trigger Kinematic**
Dynamic	Collision	Collision	Collision	Trigger	Trigger
Kinematic	Nothing	Collision	Nothing	Trigger	Trigger
Trigger Kinematic	Trigger	Trigger	Trigger	Trigger	Trigger

Figure 7.4: Collision Reaction Matrix

Considering this, let's start configuring the physics of our scene's objects.

The walls, corners, floor tiles, and obstacles should use the Static Collider profile, so no `Rigidbody` component on them, and their colliders will have the **Is Trigger** checkbox unchecked:

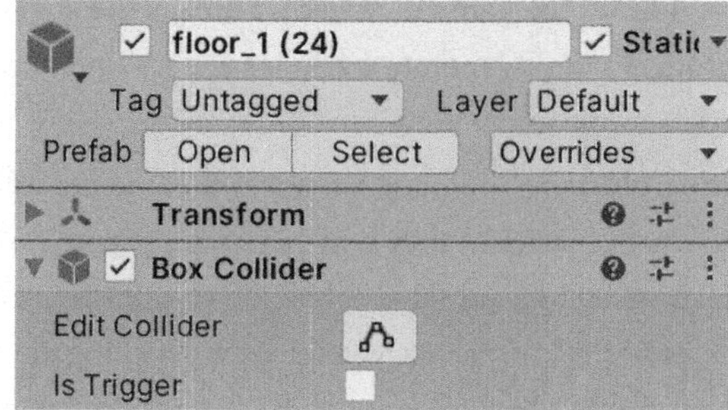

Figure 7.5: Configuration for floor tiles; remember the Static checkbox is for lighting only

The player should move and generate collisions against objects, so we need it to have a **Dynamic** profile. This profile will generate a funny behavior with our current movement script (which I encourage you to test), especially when colliding against walls, so it won't behave as you expected. We will deal with this later in this chapter:

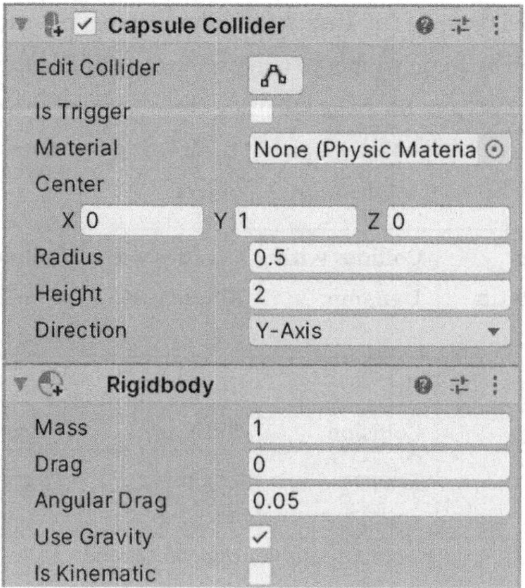

Figure 7.6: Dynamic settings on the player

The `Enemy` Prefab we suggested you create previously will be using the Kinematic profile because we will be moving this object with Unity's AI systems later, so we don't need physics here, and as we want the player to collide against them, we need a collision reaction there, so there's no `Trigger` here:

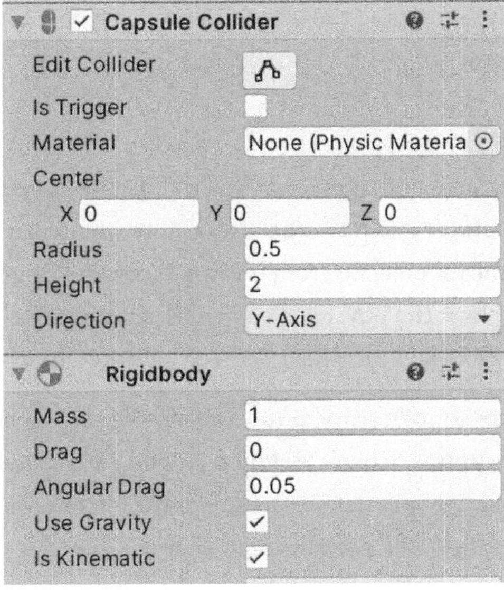

Figure 7.7: Kinematic setting for the enemy

For the `Bullet` Prefab, it moves with simplistic movement via scripting (it just moves forward), and not physics. We don't need collisions; we will code the bullet to destroy itself as soon as it touches something and will damage the collided object (if possible), so a Kinematic Trigger profile is enough for this one. We will use the `Trigger` event to script the contact reactions:

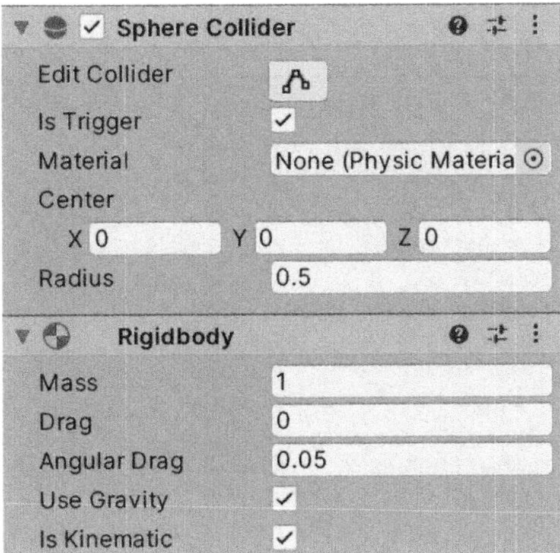

Figure 7.8: The Kinematic Trigger setting for our bullet; Is Trigger and Is Kinematic are checked

Now that we have properly configured the objects, let's check how to filter undesired collisions between certain object types.

Filtering collisions

Sometimes we want certain objects to ignore each other, like the bullets shot by the player, which shouldn't collide with the player itself. We can always filter that with an `if` statement in the C# script, checking whether the hit object is from the opposite team or whatever filtering logic you want, but by then, it is too late; the physics system wasted resources by checking a collision between objects that were never meant to collide. Here is where the Layer Collision Matrix can help us.

The **Layer Collision Matrix** sounds scary, but it is a simple setting of the physics system that allows us to specify which groups of objects should collide with other groups. For example, the player's bullets should collide with enemies, and enemy bullets should collide with the player. In this case the enemies' bullets will pass through enemies, but this is desired in our case. The idea is to create those groups and put our objects inside them, and in Unity, those groups are called **layers**. We can create layers and set the layer property of the GameObject (the top part of the Inspector) to assign the object to that group or layer. Note that you have a limited number of layers, so try to use them wisely.

We can achieve this by doing the following:

1. Go to **Edit | Project Settings** and, inside it, look for the **Tags and Layers** option from the left pane:

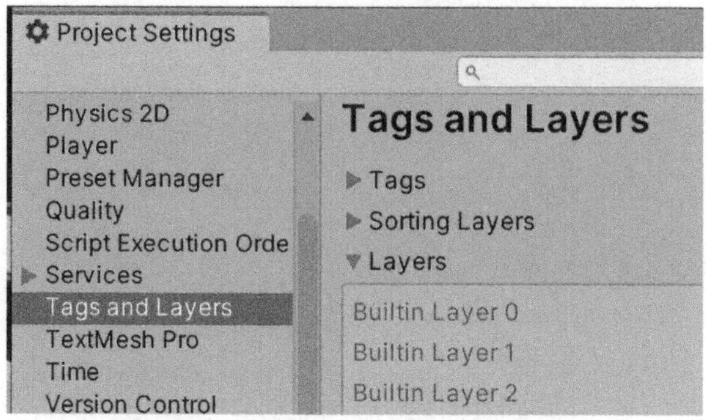

Figure 7.9: The Tags and Layers settings

2. From the **Layers** section, fill the empty spaces to create layers. We will use this for the bullet scenario, so we need four layers: `Player`, `Enemy`, `PlayerBullet`, and `EnemyBullet`:

Figure 7.10: Creating layers

3. Select the `Player` GameObject in the Hierarchy and, from the top part of the Inspector, change the **Layer** property to `Player`. Also, change the `Enemy` Prefab to have the `Enemy` layer. A window will show, asking you whether you want to also change the child objects; select **Yes**:

Figure 7.11: Changing the layers of the player and the enemy Prefab

4. In the case of the bullet, we have a problem; we have one Prefab but two layers, and a Prefab can only have one layer. We have two options: changing the layer according to the shooter via scripting, or having two bullet Prefabs with different layers. For simplicity, I will choose the latter, also taking the chance to apply another material to the enemy bullet to make it look different.
5. We will be creating a Prefab **Variant** of the player bullet. Remember that a Variant is a Prefab that is based on an original one like class inheritance. When the original Prefab changes, the Variant will change, but the Variant can have differences, which will make it unique.
6. Drop a bullet Prefab into the scene to create an instance.
7. Drag the instance again to the `Prefabs` folder, this time selecting the **Prefab Variant** option in the window that will appear.
8. Rename it `Enemy Bullet`.
9. Destroy the Prefab instance in the scene.
10. Create a second material similar to the player bullet with a different color and put it on the enemy bullet Prefab Variant.

11. Select the enemy bullet Prefab, set its layer to `EnemyBullet`, and do the same for the original Prefab (`PlayerBullet`). Even if you changed the original Prefab layer, as the Variant modified it, the modified version (or override) will prevail, allowing each Prefab to have its own layer.

Now that we have configured the layers, let's configure the physics system to use them:

1. Go to **Edit | Project Settings** and look for the **Physics** settings (not **Physics 2D**).
2. Scroll down until you see the **Layer Collision Matrix**, a half grid of checkboxes. You will notice that each column and row is labeled with the names of the layers, so each checkbox in the cross of a row and column will allow us to specify whether these two should collide. In our case, we configured it as shown in the following screenshot so that player bullets do not hit the player or other player bullets, and enemy bullets do not hit enemies or other enemy bullets:

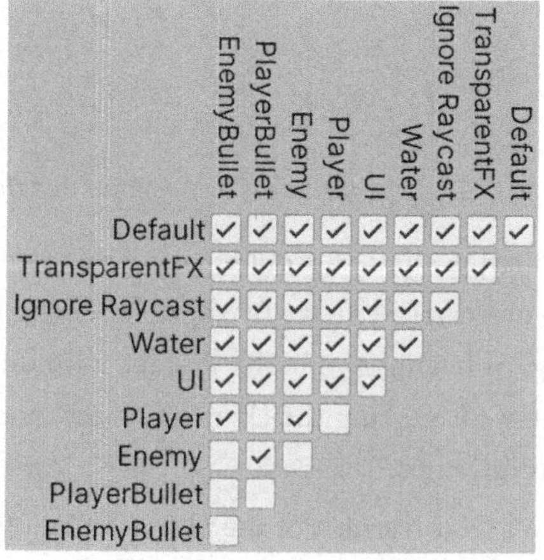

Figure 7.12: Making player bullets collide with enemies and enemy bullets with the player

It is worth noticing that sometimes filtering logic won't be that fixed or predictable, for example, only hit objects that have a certain amount of life, objects that don't have an invisibility temporal buff, or conditions that can change during the game and are difficult to generate for all possible layers for all possible groups. So, in these cases, we should rely on manual filtering after the **Trigger** or **Collision** event.

Now that we have filtered collisions, let's check whether our settings are working properly by reacting to collisions in the next section.

Detecting collisions

As you can see, proper physics settings can be complicated and very important, but now that we have tackled that, let's do something with those settings by reacting to the contact in different ways and creating a **health system** in the process.

In this section, we will examine the following collision concepts:

- Detecting Trigger events
- Modifying the other object

First, we are going to explore the different collision and trigger events Unity offers to react to contact between two objects through the Unity collision events. This allows us to execute any reaction code we want to place, but we are going to explore how to modify the contacted object components using the `GetComponent` function.

Detecting Trigger events

If objects are properly configured, as previously discussed, we can get two reactions: collisions or triggers. The **Collision** reaction has a default effect that blocks the movement of the objects, but we can add custom behavior on top of that using scripting; but with a **Trigger**, unless we add custom behavior, it won't produce any noticeable effect. Either way, we can script reactions to both possible scenarios such as adding a score, reducing health, and losing the game. To do so, we can use the suite of **Physics events**.

These events are split into two groups, **Collision events** and **Trigger events**, so according to your object setting, you will need to pick the proper group. Both groups have three main events, **Enter**, **Stay**, and **Exit**, telling us when a collision or trigger began (*Enter*), whether they are still happening or are still in contact (*Stay*), and when they stopped contacting (*Exit*). For example, we can script a behavior such as playing a sound when two objects first make contact in the Enter event, such as a friction sound, and stop it when the contact ends, in the Exit event.

Let's test this by creating our first contact behavior: the bullet being destroyed when coming into contact with something. Remember that the bullets are configured to be triggers, so they will generate `Trigger` events on contact with anything. You can do this with the following steps:

1. Create and add a script called `ContactDestroyer` on the **Player Bullet** Prefab; as the **Enemy Bullet** Prefab is a Variant of it, it will also have the same script.
2. To detect when a trigger happens, such as with **Start** and **Update**, create an event function named `OnTriggerEnter`.

3. Inside the event, use the `Destroy(gameObject);` line to make the bullet destroy itself when touching something:

```
public class ContactDestroyer : MonoBehaviour
{
    void OnTriggerEnter()
    {
        Destroy(gameObject);
    }
}
```

Figure 7.13: Auto-destroying on contact with something

4. Save the script and shoot the bullets against the walls to see how they disappear instead of passing through them. Here we don't have a collision, but a trigger that destroys the bullet on contact. So, this way, we are sure that the bullet will never pass through anything, but we are still not using physics movement.

For now, we won't need the other Collision events, but if you need them, they will work similarly; just create a function called `OnCollisionEnter` instead.

Now, let's explore another version of the same function. It not only tells us that we hit something but also what we came into contact with. We will use this to make our **Contact Destroyer** also destroy the other object. To do this, follow these steps:

1. Replace the `OnTriggerEnter` method signature with the one in the following screenshot. This one receives a parameter of the `Collider` type, indicating the exact collider that hit us:

```
void OnTriggerEnter(Collider other)
```

Figure 7.14: Version of the trigger event that tells us which object we collided with

2. We can access the GameObject of that collider using the `gameObject` property. We can use this to destroy the other one as well, as shown in the following screenshot. If we just use the `Destroy` function by passing the `other` variable, it will only destroy the `Collider` component:

```
void OnTriggerEnter(Collider other)
{
    Destroy(gameObject);
    Destroy(other.gameObject);
}
```

Figure 7.15: Destroying both objects

3. Save and test the script. You will notice that the bullet will destroy everything it touches. Remember to verify that your enemy has a Capsule collider for the bullet to detect collisions against it.

The equivalent version in Visual Scripting would be like the following figure:

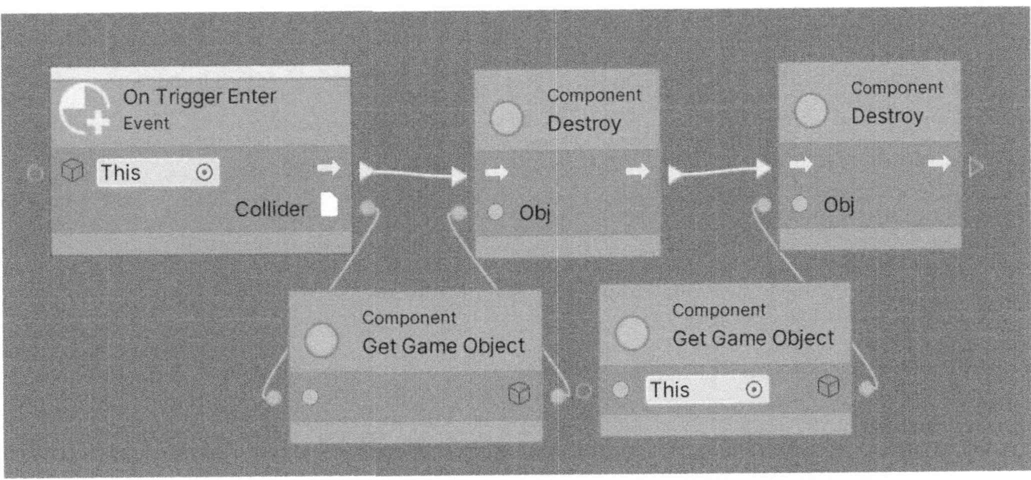

Figure 7.16: Destroying both objects with Visual Scripting

As you can see, we created an **On Trigger Enter** node and chained it to two **Destroy** nodes. To specify which object each **Destroy** node will destroy, we used the **Component: Get GameObject** node twice. The right one was created with no node connected to its left input pin, which means it will return the GameObject that is currently executing this script (hence, the **This** label in the node left pin), in this case, the bullet. For the second one we needed to connect the **Collider** output pin at the right of the **OnTriggerEnter** node to the **Get GameObject** node; this way we specify we want to obtain the GameObject that contains the collider our bullet collided with.

Now, in our game we don't want the bullet to destroy everything on contact; instead, we will make the enemies and the player have a life amount; the bullets will reduce that life amount until it reaches 0, so let's check how to do that.

Modifying the other object

For the bullet to damage the collided object, we will need to access a `Life` component to change its amount, so we will need to create this `Life` component to hold a float field with the amount of life. Every object with this component will be considered a damageable object. To access the `Life` component from our bullet scripts we will need the `GetComponent` function to help us.

If you have a reference to a GameObject or component, you can use `GetComponent` to access a specific component if the object contains it (if not, it will return `null`). Let's see how to use that function to make the bullet lower the amount of life of the other object:

1. Create and add a `Life` component with a `public float` field called `amount` to both the player and enemy Prefabs. Remember to set the value `100` (or whatever life amount you want to give them) in the **Amount** field for both in the Inspector:

```
public class Life : MonoBehaviour
{
    public float amount;
}
```

Figure 7.17: The Life component

2. Remove the `ContactDestroyer` component from the player bullet, which will also remove it from the **Enemy Bullet Variant**.
3. Add a new script called `ContactDamager` to both the enemy and player.
4. Add an `OnTriggerEnter` event that receives the `other` collider as a parameter and just add the `Destroy` function call that auto-destroys itself, not the one that destroys the other object; our script won't be responsible for destroying it, just reducing its life.
5. Add a float field called `damage`, so we can configure the amount of damage to inflict on the other object. Remember to save the file and set a value before continuing.
6. Use `GetComponent` on the reference to the other collider to get a reference to its `Life` component and save it in a variable:

```
Life life = other.GetComponent<Life>();
```

Figure 7.18: Accessing the collided object's Life component

7. Before reducing the life of the object, we must check that the `Life` reference isn't `null`, which would happen if the other object doesn't have the `Life` component, as in the case of walls and obstacles. The idea is that the bullet will destroy itself when anything collides with it and reduce the life of the other object if it is a damageable object that contains the `Life` component.

   In the following screenshot, you will find the full script:

```
public class ContactDamager : MonoBehaviour
{
    public float damage;

    void OnTriggerEnter(Collider other)
    {
        Destroy(gameObject);

        Life life = other.GetComponent<Life>();

        if (life != null)
        {
            life.amount -= damage;
        }
    }
}
```

Figure 7.19: Reducing the life of the collided object

8. Place an enemy in the scene and set its speed to `0` to prevent it from moving.
9. Select it in the Hierarchy before hitting **Play** and start shooting at it.

You can see how the life value reduces in the Inspector. You can also press the *Esc* key to regain control of the mouse and select the object while in **Play** mode to see the life field change during the runtime in the editor.

Now, you will notice that life is decreasing, but it will become negative; we want the object to destroy itself when life is below 0 instead. We can do this in two ways: one is to add an `Update` to the `Life` component, which will check all of the frames to see whether life is below 0, destroying itself when that happens. The second way is by encapsulating the life field and checking that inside the setter to prevent all frames from being checked. I would prefer the second way, but we will implement the first one to make our scripts as simple as possible for beginners.

To do this, follow these steps:

1. Add `Update` to the `Life` component.
2. Add `If` to check whether the amount field is below or equals `0`.
3. Add `Destroy` in case the `if` condition is `true`.
4. The full `Life` script will look like the following screenshot:

```
public class Life : MonoBehaviour
{
    public float amount;

    void Update()
    {
        if (amount <= 0)
        {
            Destroy(gameObject);
        }
    }
}
```

Figure 7.20: The Life component

5. Save and see how the object is destroyed once `Life` becomes `0`.

The Visual Scripting version for the `Life` component would look like this:

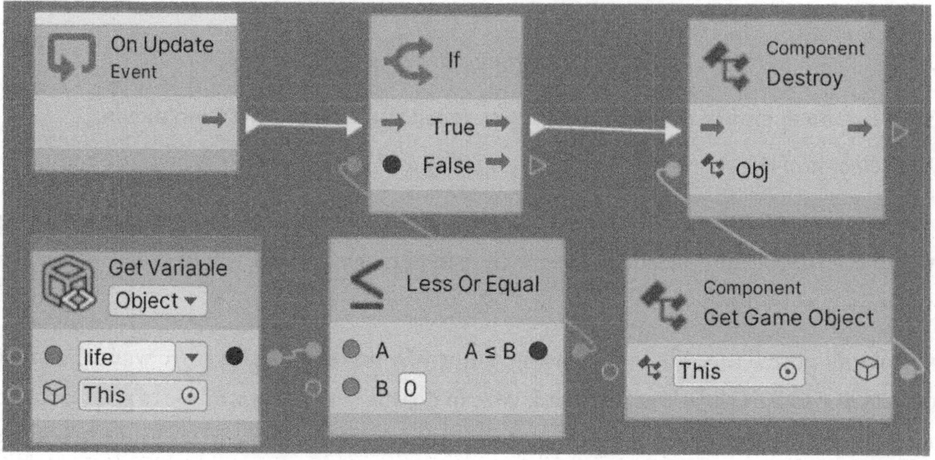

Figure 7.21: The Life component in Visual Scripting

The script is pretty straightforward—we check if our `Life` variable is less than 0 and then destroy ourselves as we did previously. Now, let's check the **Damager** script:

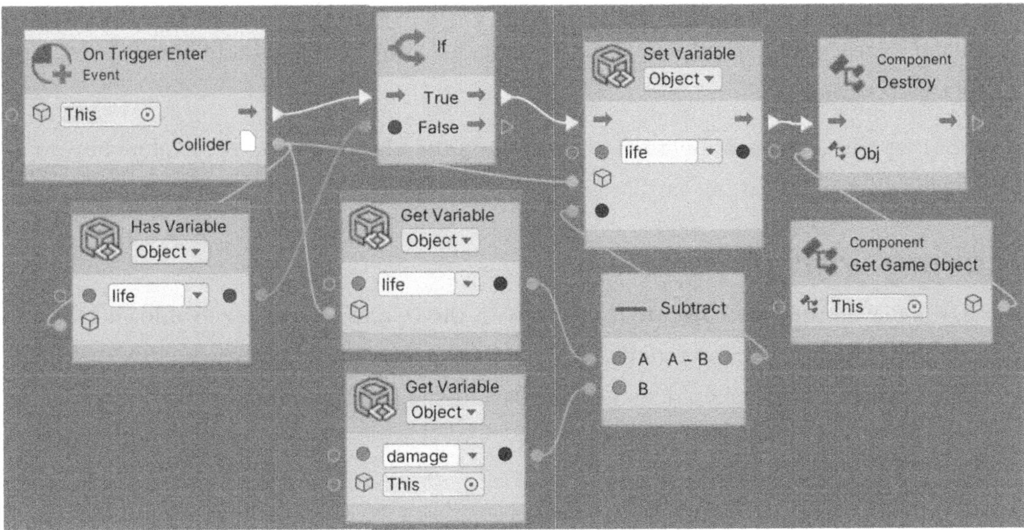

Figure 7.22: The Damager component in Visual Scripting

This version is a little bit different from our C# counterpart. At first glance it looks the same: we use **Get Variable** as before to read the life, then we use the **Subtract** node to subtract **damage** from **life**, and the result of that calculation becomes the new value of **life**, with the **Set Variable** node used to alter the current value of that variable.

The first difference we can see here is the absence of any `GetComponent` node. In C# we used that instruction to get the `Life` component on the collided object in order to read and alter its **amount** variable, reducing the remaining life. But as in Visual Scripting our node graphs don't have variables, so we don't need to access the component to read them. Instead, knowing that the enemy has a `Life` variable in its **Variables** component, we use the **Get Variable** node, connecting it to the collider we hit (the **Collider** output pin of **On Trigger Enter**), so essentially we are reading the value of the `Life` variable of the collided object.

The same goes for changing its value: we use the **Set Value** node, connecting it to the collider, specifying we want to alter the value of the `Life` variable of the collider object, not ours (as bullets, we even don't have a `Life` variable). Note that this can raise an error if the collided object doesn't have the `Life` variable, and that is why we added the **Object Has Variable** node, which checks if the object has a variable called `Life`. If it doesn't, we just do nothing, which is useful when we collide with walls or other non-destructible objects. Finally, we make the **Damager** (the bullet in this case) auto-destroy itself.

Optionally, you can instantiate an object when this happens such as a sound, a particle, or maybe a power-up. I will leave this as a challenge for you. By using a similar script, you can make a life power-up that increases the life value or a speed power-up that accesses the `PlayerMovement` script and increases the **Speed** field; from now on, use your imagination to create exciting behaviors using this.

Now that we have explored how to detect collisions and react to them, let's explore how to fix the player falling when hitting a wall.

Moving with physics

So far, the player, the only object that moves with the **Dynamic Collider Profile** and the one that will move with physics, is actually moving through custom scripting using the Transform API. Every dynamic object should instead move using the Rigidbody API functions in a way the physics system understands better. As such, here we will explore how to move objects, this time through the Rigidbody component.

In this section, we will examine the following physics movement concepts:

- Applying forces
- Tweaking physics

We will start by seeing how to move objects the correct physical way, through forces, and we will apply this concept to the movement of our player. Then, we will explore why real physics is not always fun, and how we can tweak the physics properties of our objects to have a more responsive and appealing behavior.

Applying forces

The physically accurate way of moving an object is through forces, which affect the object's velocity. To apply force, we need to access `Rigidbody` instead of `Transform` and use the `AddForce` and `AddTorque` functions to move and rotate respectively. These are functions where you can specify the amount of force to apply to each axis of position and rotation. This method of movement will have full physics reactions; the forces will accumulate on the velocity to start moving and will suffer drag effects that will make the speed slowly decrease, and the most important aspect here is that they will collide against walls, blocking the object's way.

To get this kind of movement, we can do the following:

1. Create a `Rigidbody` field in the `PlayerMovement` script, but this time, make it `private`, meaning, do not write the `public` keyword in the field, which will make it disappear in the editor; we will get the reference another way:

```
private Rigidbody rb;
```

Figure 7.23: The private Rigidbody reference field

2. Note that we named this variable `rb` just to prevent our scripts from being too wide, making the screenshots of the code in the book too small. It's recommended to call the variable properly in your scripts—in this case, it would be named `rigidbody`.
3. Using `GetComponent` in the `Start` event function, get our Rigidbody and save it in the field. We will use this field to cache the result of the `GetComponent` function; calling that function every frame to access the Rigidbody is not performant. Also, you can notice here that the `GetComponent` function can be used to retrieve not only components from other objects (like the collision example) but also your own:

```
private void Awake()
{
    Cursor.visible = false;
    Cursor.lockState = CursorLockMode.Locked;

    rb = GetComponent<Rigidbody>();
}
```

Figure 7.24: Caching the Rigidbody reference for future usage

4. Replace the `transform.Translate` calls with `rb.AddRelativeForce`. This will call the add force functions of the Rigidbody, specifically the relative ones, which will consider the current rotation of the object. For example, if you specify a force in the *z*-axis (the third parameter), the object will apply its force along with its forward vector.

5. Replace the `transform.Rotate` calls with `rb.AddRelativeTorque`, which will apply rotation forces:

```
void Update()
{
    rb.AddRelativeForce(
        movementValue.x * Time.deltaTime,
        0,
        movementValue.y * Time.deltaTime);

    rb.AddRelativeTorque(0, lookValue* Time.deltaTime, 0);
}
```

Figure 7.25: Using the Rigidbody forces API

6. Check that the player GameObject capsule collider is not intersecting with the floor, but just a little bit over it. If the player is intersecting, the movement won't work properly. If this is the case, move it upward.

In the Visual Scripting version, the change is the same; replace the **Transform** and **Rotate** nodes with **Add Relative Force** and **Add Relative Torque** nodes. An example of **Add Relative Force** would be the following one:

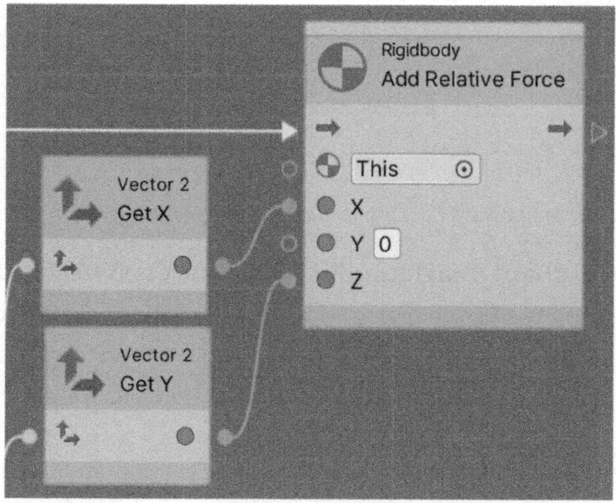

Figure 7.26: Using the Rigidbody forces API

And for rotation like this:

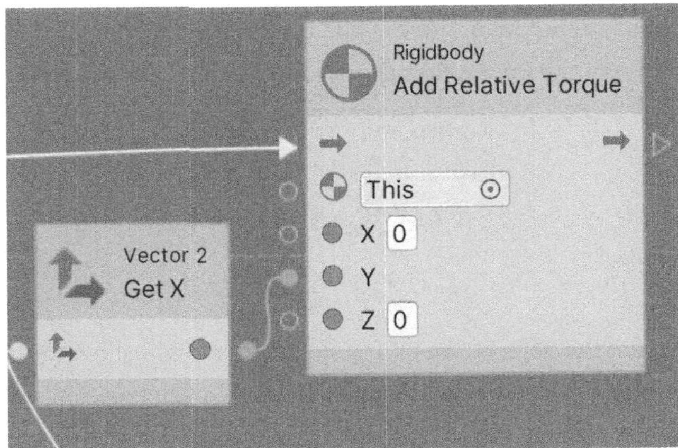

Figure 7.27: Using the Rigidbody torque API

You can see that we don't need to use **GetComponent** nodes here either, given that just using the **Add Relative Force** or **Torque** nodes makes Visual Scripting understand that we want to apply those actions on our own Rigidbody component (explaining again the **This** label). If in any other case we need to call those functions on a Rigidbody other than ours, we would need the **GetComponent** node there, but let's explore that later.

Now, if you save and test the results, you will probably find the player falling and that's because now we are using real physics, which contains floor friction, and due to the force being applied at the center of gravity, it will make the object fall. Remember that, in terms of physics, you are a capsule; you don't have legs to move, and here is where standard physics is not suitable for our game. The solution is to tweak physics to emulate the kind of behavior we need.

Tweaking physics

To make our player move like in a regular platformer game, we will need to freeze certain axes to prevent the object from falling. Remove the friction to the ground and increase the air friction (drag) to make the player reduce its speed automatically when releasing the keys.

To do this, follow these steps:

1. In the `Rigidbody` component, look at the **Constraints** section at the bottom and check the **X** and **Z** axes of the **Freeze Rotation** property:

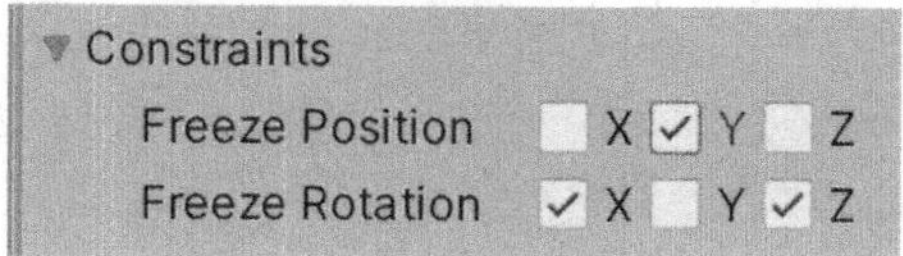

Figure 7.28: Freezing rotation axes

2. This will prevent the object from falling sideways but will allow the object to rotate horizontally. You might also freeze the *y*-axis of the **Freeze Position** property if you don't want the player to jump, preventing some undesired vertical movement on collisions.
3. You will probably need to change the speed values because you changed from a meters-per-second value to newtons-per-second, the expected value of the **Add Force** and **Add Torque** functions. Using 1,000 in speed and 160 in rotation speed was enough for me.
4. Now, you will probably notice that the speed will increase a lot over time, as will the rotation. Remember that you are using forces, which affects your velocity. When you stop applying forces, the velocity is preserved, and that's why the player kill keeps rotating even if you are not moving the mouse. The fix to this is to increase the **Drag** and **Angular Drag**, which emulates air friction, and will reduce the movement and rotation respectively when no force is applied. Experiment with values that you see suitable; in my case, I used `2` for **Drag** and `10` for **Angular Drag**, needing to increase **Rotation Speed** to `150` to compensate for the drag increase:

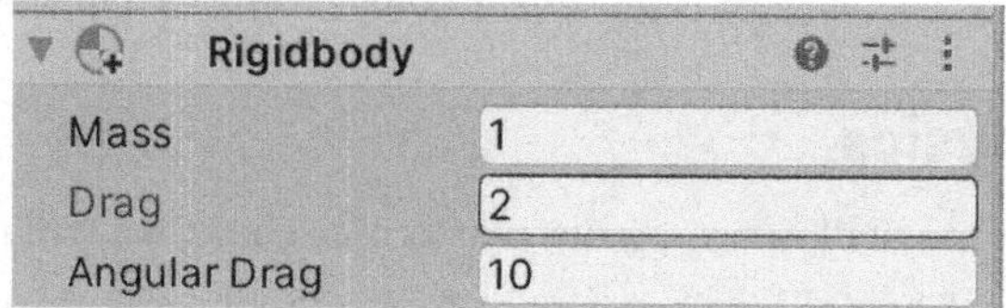

Figure 7.29: Setting air friction for rotation and movement

5. Now, if you move while touching the wall, instead of sliding, like in most games, your Player will stick to the obstacles due to contact friction. We can remove this by creating a `Physics Material`, an asset that can be assigned to the colliders to control how they react in those scenarios.

6. Start creating one by clicking on the + button from the **Project** window and selecting **Physics Material** (not the 2D version). Call it `Player` and remember to put it in a folder for those kinds of assets.
7. Select it and set **Static Friction** and **Dynamic Friction** to `0`, and **Friction Combine** to `Minimum`, which will make the **Physics** system pick the minimum friction of the two colliding objects, which is always the minimum—in our case, zero:

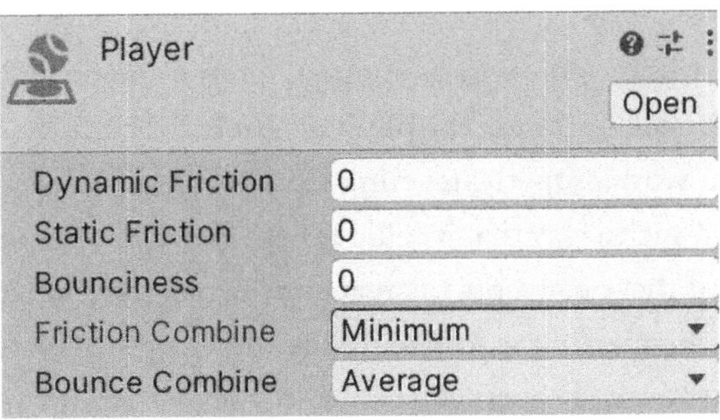

Figure 7.30: Creating a physics material

8. Select the player and drag this asset to the **Material** property of the **Capsule Collider**:

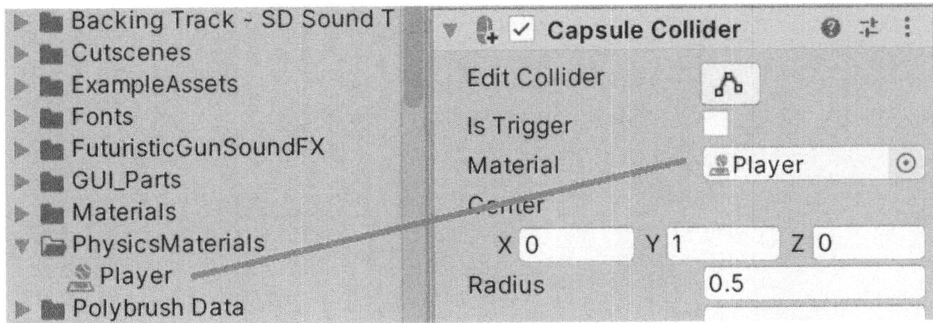

Figure 7.31: Setting the physics material of the player

9. If you play the game now, you may notice that the player will move faster than before because now we don't have any kind of friction on the floor, so you may need to reduce the movement force.

As you can see, we needed to bend the physics rules to allow a responsive player movement. You can get more responsiveness by increasing drags and forces, so the speeds are applied faster and reduced faster, but that depends, again, on the experience you want your game to have.

Some games want an immediate response with no velocity interpolation, going from 0 to full speed and vice versa from one frame to the other, and in these cases, you can override the velocity and rotation vectors of the player directly at your will or even use other systems instead of physics, such as the `Character Controller` component, which have special physics for platformer characters; but let's keep things simple for now.

Summary

Every game has physics in some way or another, for movement, collision detection, or both. In this chapter, we learned how to use the physics system for both, being aware of proper settings to make the system work properly, reacting to collisions to generate gameplay systems, and moving the player in such a way that it collides with obstacles, keeping its physically inaccurate movement. We used these concepts to create our player and bullet movement and make our bullets damage the enemies, but we can reuse the knowledge to create a myriad of other possible gameplay requirements, so I suggest you play a little bit with the physics concepts seen here; you can discover a lot of interesting use cases.

In the next chapter, we will be discussing how to program the visual aspects of the game, such as effects, and make the UI react to the input.

8

Win and Lose Conditions

Now that we have a basic gameplay experience, it's time to make the game end with the outcomes of winning or losing. One common way to implement this is through separated components with the responsibility of overseeing a set of objects to detect certain situations that need to happen, such as the player life becoming 0 or all of the waves being cleared. We will implement this through the concept of **managers**, components that will manage and monitor several objects.

In this chapter, we will examine the following manager concepts:

- Creating object managers
- Creating game modes
- Improving our code with events

With this knowledge, you will be able to not only create the victory and lose conditions of the game, but also do this in a properly structured way using design patterns such as **Singleton** and **Event Listeners**. These skills are not only useful for creating the winning and losing code of the game but any code in general. First, let's begin by creating managers to represent concepts such as score or game rules.

Creating object managers

Not every object in your Scene should be something that can be seen, heard, or collided with. Some objects can also exist with a conceptual meaning, not something tangible. For example, imagine you need to keep a count of the number of enemies: where do you save that? You also need someplace to save the current score of the player, and you may be thinking it could be on the player itself, but what happens if the player dies and respawns?

The data would be lost! In such scenarios, the concept of a **manager** can be a useful way of solving this in our first games, so let's explore it.

In this section, we are going to see the following object manager concepts:

- Sharing variables with the Singleton design pattern
- Sharing variables in Visual Scripting
- Creating managers

We will start by discussing what the Singleton design pattern is and how it helps us simplify the communication of objects. With it, we will create manager objects that allow us to centralize information about a group of objects, among other things. Let's start by discussing the Singleton design pattern.

Sharing variables with the Singleton design pattern

Design patterns are usually described as common solutions to common problems. There are several coding design decisions you will have to make while you code your game, but luckily, the ways to tackle the most common situations are well known and documented. In this section, we are going to discuss one of the most common design patterns, the **Singleton**, a convenient one to implement in simple projects.

A Singleton pattern is used when we need a single instance of an object, meaning that there shouldn't be more than one instance of a class and that we want to be easily accessible (not necessarily, but useful in our scenario). We have plenty of cases in our game where this can be applied, for example, `ScoreManager`, a component that will hold the current score. In this case, we will never have more than one score, so we can take advantage of the benefits of the Singleton manager here.

One benefit is being sure that we won't have duplicated scores, which makes our code less error prone. Also, so far, we have needed to create public references and drag objects via the editor to connect two objects, or look for them using `GetComponent`; with this pattern, however, we will have global access to our Singleton component, meaning you can just write the name of the component in your script and you will access it. In the end, there's just one `ScoreManager` component, so specifying which one via the editor is redundant. This is similar to `Time.deltaTime`, the class responsible for managing time—we have just one time.

If you are an advanced programmer, you may be thinking about code testing and dependency injection now, and you are right, but remember, we are trying to write simple code so far, so we will stick to this simple solution.

Let's create a **Score Manager** object, responsible for handling the score, to show an example of a Singleton by doing the following:

1. Create an empty GameObject (**GameObject | Create Empty**) and call it `ScoreManager`; usually, managers are put in empty objects, separated from the rest of the scene's objects.
2. Add a script called `ScoreManager` to this object with an `int` field called `amount` that will hold the current score.
3. Add a field of the `ScoreManager` type called `instance`, but add the `static` keyword to it; this will make the variable global, meaning it can be accessed anywhere by just writing its name:

```
public class ScoreManager : MonoBehaviour
{
    public static ScoreManager instance;

    public int amount;
}
```

Figure 8.1: A static field that can be accessed anywhere in the code

4. In `Awake`, check whether the `instance` field is not `null`, and in that case, set this `ScoreManager` instance as the instance reference using the `this` reference.

5. In the `else` clause of the `null` checking `if` statement, print a message indicating that there's a second `ScoreManager` instance that must be destroyed:

```
void Awake()
{
    if (instance == null)
    {
        instance = this;
    }
    else
    {
        print("Duplicated ScoreManager, ignoring this one");
    }
}
```

Figure 8.2: Checking whether there's only one Singleton instance

The idea is to save the reference to the only `ScoreManager` instance in the instance static field, but if by mistake the user creates two objects with the `ScoreManager` component, this `if` statement will detect it and inform the user of the error, asking them to take action. In this scenario, the first `ScoreManager` instance to execute `Awake` will find that there's no instance set (the field is `null`) so it will set itself as the current instance, while the second `ScoreManager` instance will find the instance is already set and will print the message.

Remember that `instance` is a static field, shared between all classes, unlike regular reference fields, where each component will have its own reference, so in this case, we have two `ScoreManager` instances added to the scene, and they will share the same instance field.

To improve the example a little bit, it would be ideal to have a simple way to find the second `ScoreManager` in the game. It will be hidden somewhere in the Hierarchy and it may be difficult to find, but we fix this by doing the following:

1. Replace `print` with `Debug.Log`. `Debug.Log` is similar to `print` but has a second argument that expects an object to be highlighted when the message is clicked in the console. In this case, we will pass the `gameObject` reference to allow the console to highlight the duplicated object:

```
Debug.Log("Duplicated ScoreManager, ignoring this one", gameObject);
```

Figure 8.3: Printing messages in the console with Debug.Log

After clicking the log message, the GameObject containing the duplicated `ScoreManager` will be highlighted in the Hierarchy:

Figure 8.4: The highlighted object after clicking the message

2. Finally, a little improvement can be made here by replacing `Debug.Log` with `Debug.LogError`, which will also print the message but with an error icon. In a real game, you will have lots of messages in the console, and highlighting the errors over the information messages will help us to identify them quickly:

```
Debug.LogError("Duplicated
```

Figure 8.5: Using LogError to print an error message

3. Try the code and observe the error message in the console:

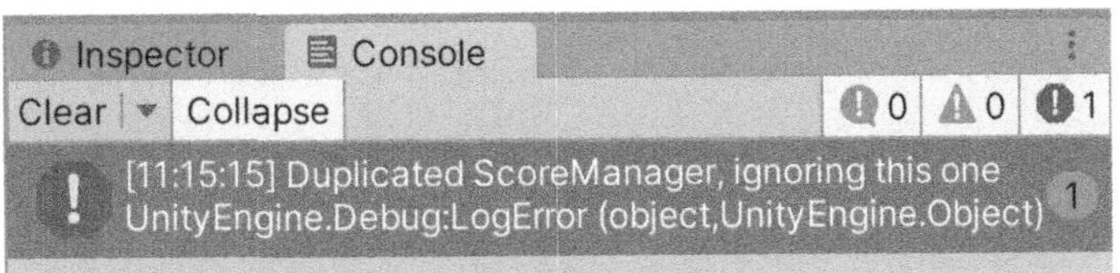

Figure 8.6: An error message in the console

The next step would be to use this Singleton somewhere, so in this case, we will make the enemies give points when they are killed by doing the following:

1. Add a script to the `Enemy` Prefab called `ScoreOnDeath` with an `int` field called `amount`, which will indicate the number of points the enemy will give when killed. Remember to set the value to something other than `0` in the editor for the Prefab.

2. Create the `OnDestroy` event function, which will be automatically called by Unity when this object is destroyed, in our case, the enemy:

```
void OnDestroy()
{

}
```

Figure 8.7: The OnDestroy event function

Consider that the `OnDestroy` function is also called when we change scenes or the game is quitting, so in this scenario, we might get points when changing scenes, which is not correct. So far, this is not a problem in our case, but later in this chapter, we will see a way to prevent this.

3. Access the Singleton reference in the `OnDestroy` function by writing `ScoreManager.instance`, and add the `amount` field of our script to the `amount` field of the Singleton to increase the score when an enemy is killed:

```
public class ScoreOnDeath : MonoBehaviour
{
    public int amount;

    void OnDestroy()
    {
        ScoreManager.instance.amount += amount;
    }
}
```

Figure 8.8: Full ScoreOnDeath component class contents

4. Select the `ScoreManager` in the Hierarchy, hit **Play**, and kill some enemies to see the score rise with every kill. Remember to set the `amount` field of the `ScoreOnDeath` component of the Prefab.

As you can see, the Singleton simplified a lot the way to access `ScoreManager` and have security measures to prevent duplicates of itself, which will help us to reduce errors in our code. Something to take into account is that now you will be tempted to just make everything a Singleton, such as the player's life or player's bullets and just to make your life easier when creating gameplay mechanics such as power-ups.

While that will totally work, remember that your game will change, and I mean change a lot; any real project will experience constant change. Maybe today, the game has just one player, but maybe in the future, you want to add a second player or an AI companion, and you want the power-ups to affect them too, so if you abuse the Singleton pattern, you will have trouble handling those scenarios and many more. Maybe a future player companion will try to get the health pickup but the main player will be healed instead!

The point here is to try to use the pattern as few times as you can, in case you don't have any other way to solve the problem. To be honest, there are always ways to solve problems without Singleton, but they are a little bit more difficult to implement for beginners, so I prefer to simplify your life a little bit to keep you motivated. With enough practice, you will reach a point where you will be ready to improve your coding standards.

Now, let's discuss how to achieve this in Visual Scripting, which deserves its own section given that it will be a little bit different. You may consider skipping the following section if you are not interested in the Visual Scripting side of these scripts.

Sharing variables with Visual Scripting

Visual Scripting has a mechanism that replaces Singleton as a holder of variables to be shared between objects: the **scene variables**. If you check the left panel in the **Script Graph** editor (the window where we edit the nodes of a script) under the `Blackboard` panel (the panel that shows the variables of our object), you will notice it will have many tabs: **Graph**, **Object**, **Scene**, **App** and **Saved**. If you don't see `Blackboard` panel, click the third button from left to right at the top-left part of the window, the button at the right of the **i** (information) button:

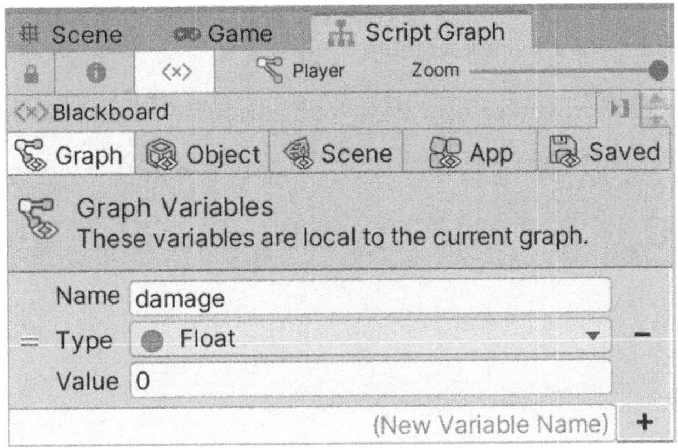

Figure 8.9: Blackboard (variables) editor in Script Graph

So far, when we created a variable in the **Variables** component of any object, we were actually creating **Object Variables**: variables that belongs to an object and are shared between all Visual Scripts in that one, but that's not the only scope a variable can have. Here's a list of the remaining scopes:

- **Graph**: Variables that can only be accessed by our current graph. No other script can read or write that variable. This is useful to save internal state, like private variables in C#.
- **Scene**: Variables that can be accessed by all objects in the current scene. When we change the scene, those variables are lost.
- **App**: Variables that can be accessed in any part of the game at any time. This is useful to move values from one scene to the other. For example, you can increase the score in one level and keep increasing it in the next, instead of restarting the score from 0.
- **Saved**: Variables whose values are kept between game runs. You can save persistent data such as the **Player Level** or **Inventory** to continue the quest, or simpler things such as the sound volume as set by the user in the **Options** menu (if you created one).

In this case, the **Scene** scope is the one we want, as the score we intend to increase will be accessed by several objects in the scene (more on that later) and we don't want it to persist if we reset the level to play again; it will need to be set again to 0 in each run of the level and game.

To create scene variables, you can simply select the **Scene** tab in the **Blackboard** pane of the **Script Graph** editor, while you are editing any **Script Graph**, or you can also use the **Scene Variables** GameObject that was created automatically when you started editing any graph. That object is the one that really holds the variables and must not be deleted. You will notice it will have a **Variables** component as we have used before, but it will also have the **Scene Variables** component, indicating those variables are scene variables.

In the following screenshot, you can see how we have simply added the **Score** variable to the **Scene Variables** tab to make it accessible in any of our Script Graphs.

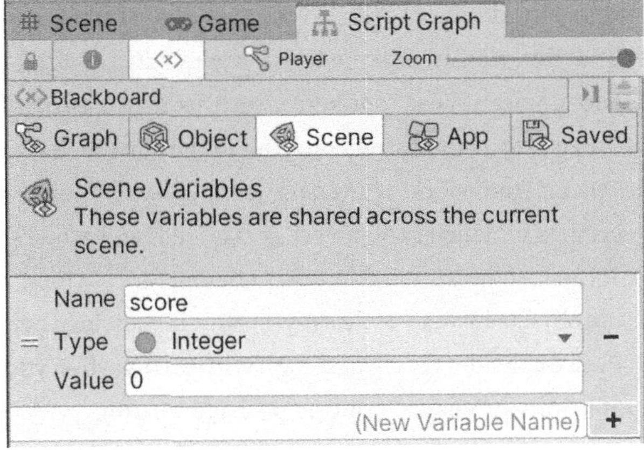

Figure 8.10: Adding scene variables to our game

Finally, for the score-increasing behavior, we can add the following graph to our enemy. Remember, as usual, to have the C# or the Visual Scripting version of the scripts, not both.

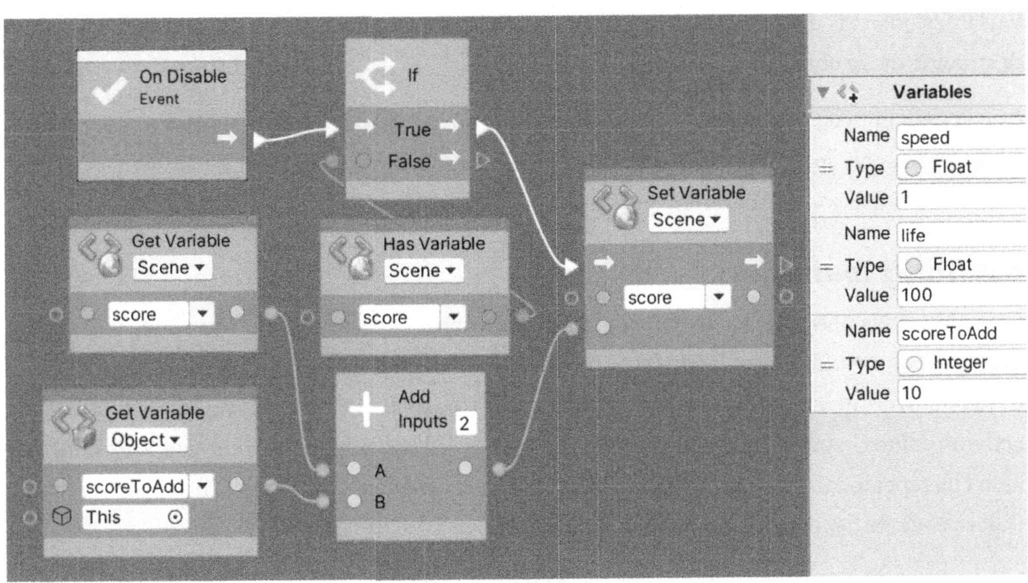

Figure 8.11: Adding score when this object is destroyed

At first, this script seems pretty similar to our C# version; we add our `scoreToAdd` variable of our object (**Object** scope) and then we add it to the whole scene's `score` variable, as specified in the node. The main difference you can see is that here we are using the **OnDisable** event instead of **OnDestroy**. Actually, **OnDestroy** is the correct one, but in the current version of Visual Scripting there is a bug that prevents it from working properly, so I replaced it for now. The problem with **OnDisable** is that it executes whenever the object is disabled, and while the object is disabled before it is destroyed, it can also be disabled in other circumstances (for example, using **Object Pooling**, a way to recycle objects instead of destroying and instancing them constantly), but so far it is enough for us. Please consider trying first with **OnDestroy** when you try this graph to see if it runs properly in your Unity or Visual Scripting package version.

Something to highlight is the usage of the **Has Variable** node to check if the **score variable** exists. This is done because **OnDisable** can be executed either at the moment of the enemy being destroyed, or when the scene changes, which we will do later this chapter with the lose/win screens. If we try to get a scene variable at that moment, we risk getting an error ourselves if the **Scene Variables** object is destroyed before the **GameMode** object, given the change of scene involves destroying every object in the scene first.

As you may noticed by now, even if Visual Scripting is mostly extremely similar to C#, one has concepts to solve certain scenarios that the other doesn't. Now that we know how to share variables, let's finish some other managers that we will need later in the game.

Creating managers

Sometimes, we need a place to put together information about a group of similar objects, for example, `EnemyManager`, to check the number of enemies and potentially access an array of them to iterate over them and do something, or maybe `MissionManager`, to have access to all of the active missions in our game. Again, these cases can be considered Singletons, single objects that won't be repeated (in our current game design), so let's create the ones we will need in our game, that is, `EnemyManager` and `WaveManager`.

In our game, `EnemyManager` and `WaveManager` will just be used as places to save an array of references to the existing enemies and waves in our game, just as a way to know their current amount. There are ways to search all objects of a certain type to calculate their count, but those functions are expensive and not recommended for use unless you really know what you are doing. So, having a Singleton with a separate updated list of references to the target object type will require more code but will perform better. Also, as the game features increase, these managers will have more functionality and helper functions to interact with those objects.

Let's start with the enemies manager by doing the following:

1. Add a script called `Enemy` to the **Enemy** Prefab; this will be the script that will connect this object with `EnemyManager` in a moment.
2. Create an empty `GameObject` called `EnemyManager` and add a script to it called `EnemiesManager`.
3. Create a `public` static field of the `EnemiesManager` type called `instance` inside the script and add the Singleton repetition check in `Awake` as we did in `ScoreManager`.
4. Create a public field of the `List<Enemy>` type called `enemies`:

```
public List<Enemy> enemies;
```

Figure 8.12: List of Enemy components

A list in C# represents a dynamic array, an array capable of adding and removing objects. You will see that you can add and remove elements to this list in the editor, but keep the list empty; we will add enemies another way. Take into account that `List` is in the `System.Collections.Generic` namespace; you will find the `using` sentence at the beginning of our script. Also, consider that you can make the list private and expose it to the code via a getter instead of making it a public field; but as usual, we will make our code as simple as possible for now:

```
using System;
using System.Collections.Generic;
using UnityEngine;
```

Figure 8.13: Using needed to use the List class

Consider that `List` is a class type, so it must be instantiated, but as this type has exposing support in the editor, Unity will automatically instantiate it. You must use the `new` keyword to instantiate it in cases where you want a non-editor-exposed list, such as a private one or a list in a regular non-component C# class.

The C# list internally is implemented as an array. If you need a linked list, use the `LinkedList` collection type instead.

5. In the `Start` function of the `Enemy` script, access the `EnemyManager` Singleton and using the `Add` function of the enemies list, add this object to the list. This will "register" this enemy as active in the manager, so other objects can access the manager and check for the current enemies. The `Start` function is called after all of the `Awake` function calls, and this is important because we need to be sure that the `Awake` function of the manager is executed prior to the `Start` function of the enemy to ensure that there is a manager set as the instance.

The problem we solved with the `Start` function is called a race condition, that is, when two pieces of code are not guaranteed to be executed in the same order, whereas `Awake` execution order can change due to different reasons. There are plenty of situations in code that this will happen, so pay attention to the possible race conditions in your code. Also, you might consider using more advanced solutions such as `lazy initialization` here, which can give you better stability, but again, for the sake of simplicity and exploring the Unity API, we will use the `Start` function approach for now.

6. In the `OnDestroy` function, remove the enemy from the list to keep the list updated with just the active ones:

```
public class Enemy : MonoBehaviour
{
    void Start()
    {
        EnemyManager.instance.enemies.Add(this);
    }

    void OnDestroy()
    {
        EnemyManager.instance.enemies.Remove(this);
    }
}
```

Figure 8.14: The enemy script to register ourselves as an active enemy

With this, now we have a centralized place to access all of the active enemies in a simple but efficient way. I challenge you to do the same with the waves, using `WaveManager`, which will have the collection of all active waves to later check whether all waves finished their work to consider the game as won. Take some time to solve this; you will find the solution in the following screenshots, starting with `WavesManager`:

```
using System.Collections.Generic;
using UnityEngine;

public class WavesManager : MonoBehaviour
{
    public static WavesManager instance;

    public List<WaveSpawner> waves;

    private void Awake()
    {
        if (instance == null)
            instance = this;
        else
            Debug.LogError("Duplicated WavesManager", gameObject);
    }
}
```

Figure 8.15: The full WavesManager script

You will also need the WaveSpawner script:

```
public class WaveSpawner : MonoBehaviour
{
    public GameObject prefab;
    public float startTime;
    public float endTime;
    public float spawnRate;

    private void Start()
    {
        WavesManager.instance.waves.Add(this);
        InvokeRepeating("Spawn", startTime, spawnRate);
        Invoke("EndSpawner", endTime);
    }

    void Spawn()
    {
        Instantiate(prefab, transform.position, transform.rotation);
    }

    void EndSpawner()
    {
        WavesManager.instance.waves.Remove(this);
        CancelInvoke();
    }
}
```

Figure 8.16: The modified WaveSpawner script to support WavesManager

As you can see, `WaveManager` is created the same way `EnemyManager` was, just a Singleton with a list of `WaveSpawner` references, but `WaveSpawner` is different. We execute the `Add` function of the list in the `Start` event of `WaveSpawner` to register the wave as an active one, but the `Remove` function needs more work.

The idea is to deregister the wave from the active waves list when the spawner finishes its work. Before this modification, we used `Invoke` to call the `CancelInvoke` function after a while to stop the spawning, but now we need to do more after the end time.

Instead of calling `CancelInvoke` after the specified wave end time, we will call a custom function called `EndSpawner`, which will call `CancelInvoke` to stop the spawner, `Invoke Repeating`, but also will call the remove-from-`WavesManager`-list function to make sure the removing-from-the-list function is called exactly when `WaveSpawner` finishes its work.

Regarding the Visual Scripting version, we can add two lists of GameObject type to the scene variables to hold the references to the existing waves and enemies so we can keep track of them. Just search `"List of GameObject"` in the search bar of the variable type selector and you will find it. In this case, the lists contain only GameObjects given that the Visual Scripting versions of **WaveSpawner** and enemy scripts are not types we can reference like C# ones. If you did both C# and Visual Scripting versions of these you will see you can reference the C# versions, but we are not going to mix C# and Visual Scripting as it is out of the scope of the book, so ignore them. Anyway, given how the **Variables** system of Visual Scripting works, we can still access variables inside if needed using the **GetVariable** node—remember the variables are not in the Visual Scripts but in the **Variables** node:

Figure 8.17: Adding lists to the Scene variables

Then, we can add the following to the **WaveSpawner** graph:

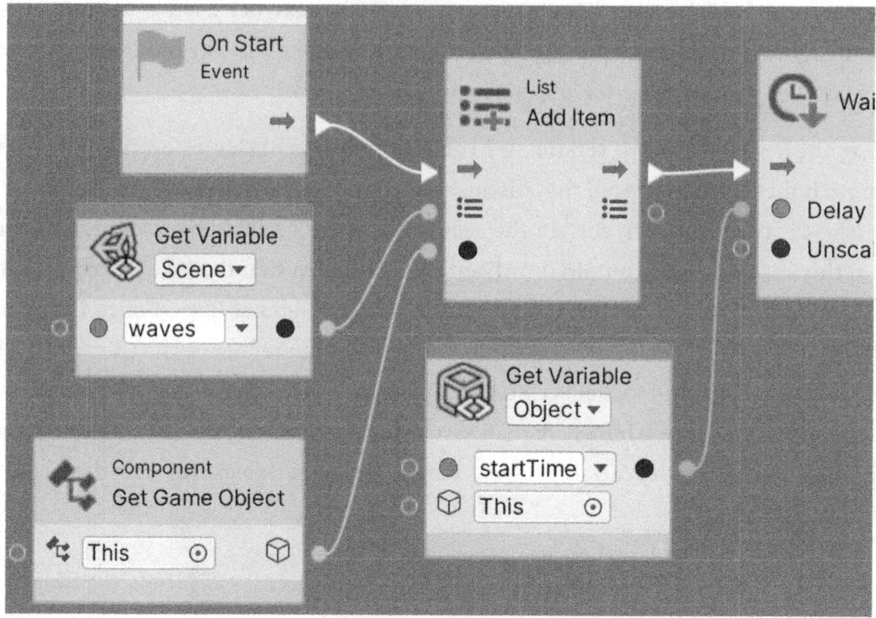

Figure 8.18: Adding elements to List

We used the **Add List Item** node to add our GameObject to the **waves** variable. We did this as the first thing to do in the **On Start** event node before anything. And to remove that wave from the active ones you will need to make the following change:

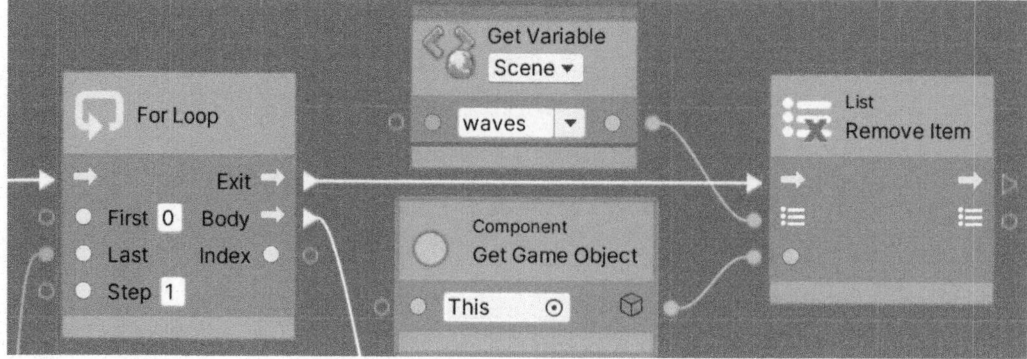

Figure 8.19: Removing elements from the List

We remove this spawner from the list using the **Exit** flow output pin of the **For Loop**, which is executed when the `for` loop finishes iterating.

Finally, regarding **Enemy**, you will need to create a new **Enemy Script** graph that will look similar:

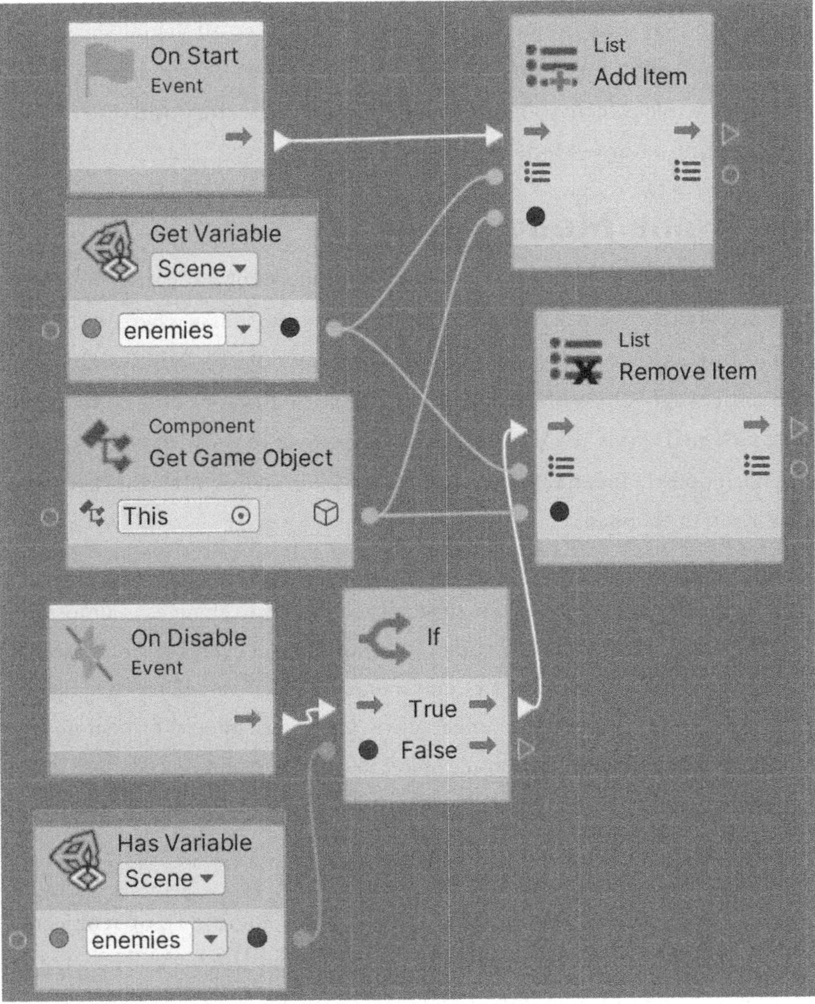

Figure 8.20: Enemy Adding and removing itself from the Lists

As you can see, we simply add the enemy on **OnStart** and remove it in **OnDisable**. Remember to try first using **OnDestroy** instead of **OnDisable** due to the bug we mentioned previously. You can check these changes by playing the game while having the **Scene Variables** GameObject selected and seeing how its value changes. Also remember the need to use the **Has Variable** node in case we are changing scenes.

Using Object managers, we now have centralized information about a group of objects, and we can add all sorts of object group logic here. We created the `EnemiesManager`, `WavesManager`, and `ScoreManager` as centralized places to store several game systems' information, such as the enemies and waves present in the scene, and the score as well. We also saw the Visual Scripting version, centralizing that data in the Scene Variables object, so all Visual Scripts can read that data. But aside from having this information for updating the UI (which we will do in the next chapter), we can use this information to detect whether the victory and lose conditions of our game are met, creating a **Game Mode** object to detect that.

Creating Game Modes

We have created objects to simulate lots of gameplay aspects of our game, but the game needs to end sometime, whether we win or lose. As always, the question is where to put this logic, and that leads us to further questions. The main questions would be, will we always win or lose the game the same way? Will we have a special level with different criteria than "kill all of the waves," such as a timed survival? Only you know the answer to those questions, but if right now the answer is no, it doesn't mean that it won't change later, so it is advisable to prepare our code to adapt seamlessly to changes.

To be honest, preparing code to adapt seamlessly to changes is almost impossible; there's no way to have code that takes into account every possible case, and we will always need to rewrite some code sooner or later. We will try to make the code as adaptable as possible to changes; always doing that doesn't consume lots of developing time and it's sometimes preferable to write simple code fast than complex code slow that might not be necessary, and so we suggest you balance your time budget wisely.

To do this, we will separate the Victory and Lose conditions' logic in its own object, which I like to call the "Game Mode" (not necessarily an industry standard). This will be a component that will oversee the game, checking conditions that need to be met in order to consider the game over. It will be like the referee of our game. The Game Mode will constantly check the information in the object managers and maybe other sources of information to detect the needed conditions. Having this object separated from other objects allows us to create different levels with different Game Modes; just use another Game Mode script in that level and that's all.

In our case, we will have a single Game Mode for now, which will check whether the number of waves and enemies becomes 0, meaning that we have killed all of the possible enemies and the game is won. Also, it will check whether the life of the player reaches 0, considering the game as lost in that situation. Let's create it by doing the following:

1. Create an empty `GameMode` object and add a `WavesGameMode` script to it. As you can see, we gave the script a descriptive name considering that we can add other Game Modes.
2. In its `Update` function, check whether the number of enemies and waves has reached `0` by using the `Enemy` and `Wave` managers; in that case, just `print` a message in the console for now. All lists have a `Count` property, which will tell you the number of elements stored inside.
3. Add a `public` field of the `Life` type called `PlayerLife` and drag the player to that one; the idea is to also detect the lose condition here.
4. In `Update`, add another check to detect whether the life amount of the `playerLife` reference reached `0`, and in that case, `print` a lose message in the console:

```
[SerializeField] Life playerLife;

void Update()
{
    if (EnemyManager.instance.enemies.Count <= 0 &&
        WavesManager.instance.waves.Count <= 0)
    {
        SceneManager.LoadScene("You win!");
    }

    if (playerLife.amount <= 0)
    {
        SceneManager.LoadScene("You lose!");
    }
}
```

Figure 8.21: Win and lose condition checks in WavesGameMode

5. Play the game and test both cases, whether the player life reaches 0 or whether you have killed all enemies and waves.

Now, it is time to replace the messages with something more interesting. For now, we will just change the current scene to a **Win Scene** or **Lose Scene**, which will only have a UI with a win or lose message and a button to play again. In the future, you can add a Main Menu scene and have an option to get back to it. Let's implement this by doing the following:

1. Create a new scene (**File | New Scene**) and save it, calling it `WinScreen`.
2. Add something to indicate that this is the win screen, such as simply a sphere with the camera pointing to it. This way we know when we changed to the win screen.
3. Select the scene in the **Project View** and press *Ctrl* + *D* (*Cmd* + *D* on Mac) to duplicate the scene. Rename it `LoseScreen`.
4. Double-click the `LoseScreen` scene to open it and change the sphere to something different, maybe a cube.
5. Go to **File | Build Settings** to open the **Scenes in Build** list inside this window.

   The idea is that Unity needs you to explicitly declare all scenes that must be included in the game. You might have test scenes or scenes that you don't want to release yet, so that's why we need to do this. In our case, our game will have `WinScreen`, `LoseScreen`, and the scene we have created so far with the game scenario, which I called `Game`, so just drag those scenes from the **Project View** to the list of the **Build Settings** window; we will need this to make the Game Mode script change between scenes properly. Also, consider that the first scene in this list will be the first scene to be opened when we play the game in its final version (known as the build), so you may want to rearrange the list according to that:

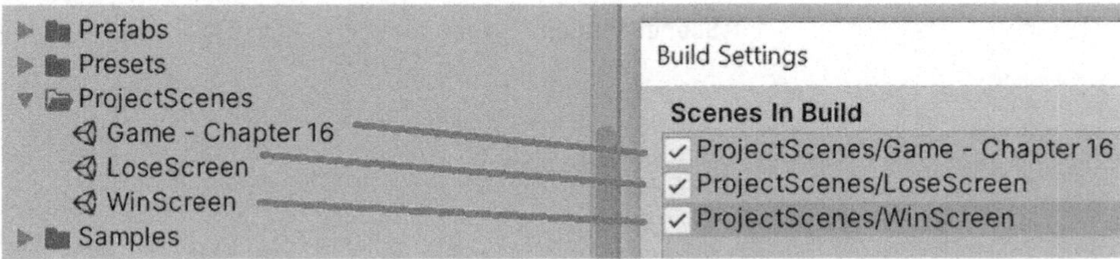

Figure 8.22: Registering the scenes to be included in the build of the game

6. In `WavesGameMode`, add a `using` statement for the `UnityEngine.SceneManagement` namespace to enable the scene changing functions in this script.
7. Replace the console `print` messages with calls to the `SceneManager.LoadScene` function, which will receive a string with the name of the scene to load; in this case, it would be `WinScreen` and `LoseScreen`. You just need the scene name, not the entire path to the file.

If you want to chain different levels, you can create a `public` string field to allow you to specify via editor which scenes to load. Remember to have the scenes added to the **Build Settings**, if not, you will receive an error message in the console when you try to change the scenes:

```
using UnityEngine;
using UnityEngine.SceneManagement;

public class WavesGameMode : MonoBehaviour
{
    [SerializeField] Life playerLife;

    void Update()
    {
        if (EnemyManager.instance.enemies.Count <= 0 &&
            WavesManager.instance.waves.Count <= 0)
        {
            SceneManager.LoadScene("WinScreen");
        }

        if (playerLife.amount <= 0)
        {
            SceneManager.LoadScene("LoseScreen");
        }
    }
}
```

Figure 8.23: Changing scenes with SceneManager

8. Play the game and check whether the scenes change properly.

Right now, we picked the simplest way to show whether we lost or won, but in the future, you may want something gentler than a sudden change of scene, such as maybe waiting a few moments with `Invoke` to delay that change or directly show the winning message inside the game without changing scenes. Bear this in mind when testing the game with people and checking whether they understood what happened when they were playing—game feedback is important to keep the player aware of what is happening and is not an easy task to tackle.

Regarding the Visual Scripting version, we added a new Script Graph to a separated object. Let's examine it piece by piece to see it clearly. Let's start with the win condition:

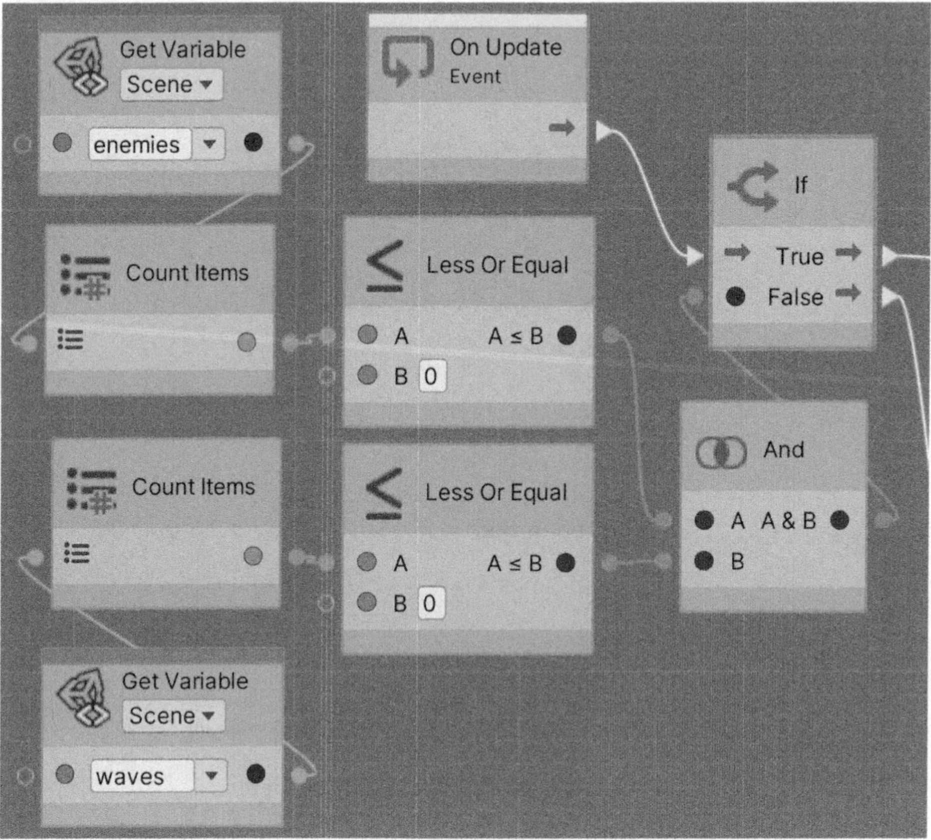

Figure 8.24: Win condition in Visual Scripting

Here, we are getting the **Enemies** list from the scene context (**GetVariable** node), and knowing that it contains a List, we are using the **Count Items** node to check how many enemies remain in this list. Remember we have a script that adds the enemy to the list when it's spawned and removes it when it is destroyed. We do the same for the waves, so combine the conditions with an **And** node and connect it with an **If** to then do something (more on that in a moment).

Now let's examine the Lose condition:

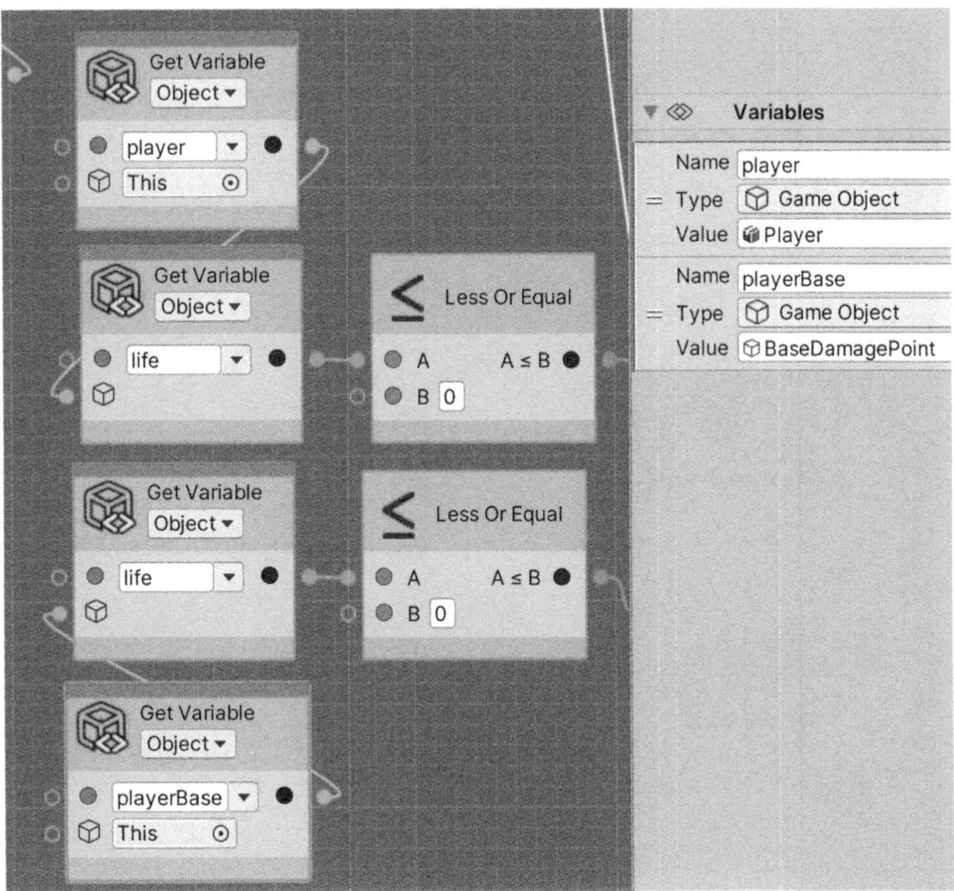

Figure 8.25: Lose condition in Visual Scripting

As the player's life is not in the scene context (and shouldn't be), and the player is a different GameObject from the one called `GameMode` (the one we created specifically for this script), we need a variable of type GameObject called **player** to reference it.

As you can see, we dragged our player to it in the **Variables** component. Finally, we used a **GetVariable** to access our player reference in the graph, and then another **GetVariable** to extract the life from it. We accomplished that by connecting the player reference to the **GetVariable** node of the life variable. Then we repeated this for the player's base.

Finally, we load the scenes by doing the following:

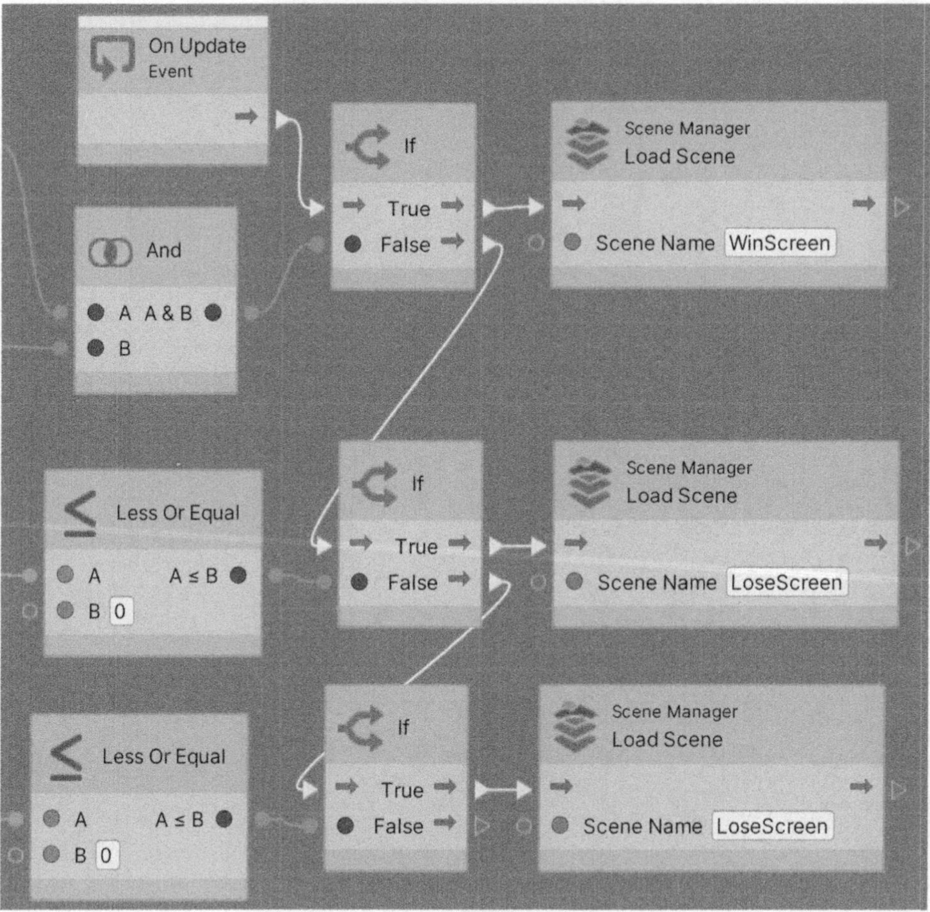

Figure 8.26: Loading scenes in Visual Scripting

As you can see, we use the **SceneManager LoadScene (SceneName)** node to load the scenes. Notice how we load scenes with the postfix `_VisualScripting` given we have two versions of the scenes in our GitHub, the C# version and the Visual Scripting version.

Now we have a fully functional simple game, with mechanics and win and lose conditions, and while this is enough to start developing other aspects of our game, I want to discuss some issues with our current manager approach and how to solve them with events.

Improving our code with events

So far, we used Unity event functions to detect situations that can happen in the game such as `Awake` and `Update`. There are other similar functions that Unity uses to allow components to communicate with each other, as in the case of `OnTriggerEnter`, which is a way for the Rigidbody to inform other components in the GameObject that a collision has happened. In our case, we are using `if` statements inside the `Update` method to detect changes on other components, such as `GameMode` checking whether the number of enemies has reached 0. But we can improve this if we are informed by the Enemy manager when something has changed, and just do the check at that moment, such as with the Rigidbody telling us when collisions occur instead of checking for collisions every frame.

Also, sometimes, we rely on Unity events to execute logic, such as the score being given in the `OnDestroy` event, which informs us when the object is destroyed, but due to the nature of the event, it can be called in situations we don't want to add to the score, such as when the scene is changed, or the game is closed. Objects are destroyed in those cases, but not because the player killed the enemy, leading to the score increasing when it shouldn't. In this case, it would be great to have an event that tells us that life reached 0 to execute this logic, instead of relying on the general-purpose `OnDestroy` event.

The idea of events is to improve the model of communication between our objects, with the assurance that at the exact moment something happens, the relevant parts in that situation are notified to react accordingly. Unity has lots of events, but we can create ones specific to our gameplay logic. Let's start by applying this in the score scenario we discussed earlier; the idea is to make the `Life` component have an event to communicate to the other components that the object was destroyed because life reached 0.

There are several ways to implement this, and we will use a little bit of a different approach than the **Awake** and **Update** methods; we will use the `UnityEvent` field type. This is a field type capable of holding references to functions to be executed when we want to, like C# delegates, but with other benefits, such as better Unity editor integration.

To implement this, do the following:

1. In the `Life` component, create a `public` field of the `UnityEvent` type called `onDeath`. This field will represent an event where other classes can subscribe to it to be made aware when `Life` reaches 0:

```
public class Life : MonoBehaviour
{
    public float amount;
    public UnityEvent onDeath;
```

Figure 8.27: Creating a custom event field

2. If you save the script and go to the editor, you can see the event in the Inspector. Unity events support being subscribed to methods in the editor so we can connect two objects together. We will use this in the UI scripting chapter, so let's just ignore this for now:

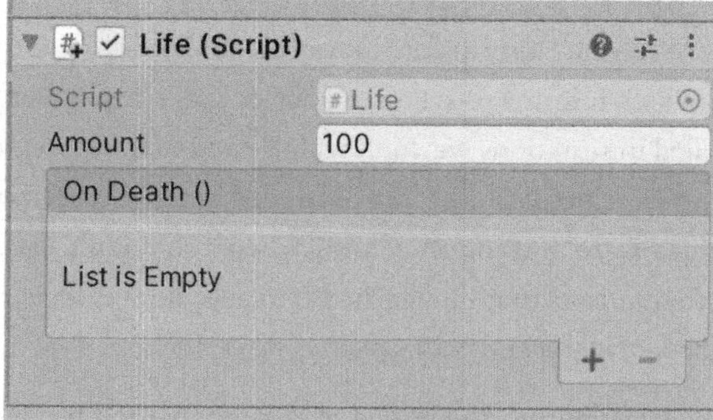

Figure 8.28: UnityEvents showing up in the Inspector

You can use the generic delegate action or a custom delegate to create events instead of using `UnityEvent`, and aside from certain performance aspects, the only noticeable difference is that `UnityEvent` will show up in the editor, as demonstrated in *step 2*.

3. When life reaches `0`, call the `Invoke` function of the event. This way, we will be telling any script interested in the event that it has happened:

```
public float amount;
public UnityEvent onDeath;

void Update()
{
    if (amount <= 0)
    {
        onDeath.Invoke();
        Destroy(gameObject);
    }
}
```

Figure 8.29: Executing the event

4. In `ScoreOnDeath`, rename the `OnDestroy` function to `GivePoints` or whatever name you prefer; the idea here is to stop giving points in the `OnDestroy` event.
5. In the `Awake` function of the `ScoreOnDeath` script, get the `Life` component using `GetComponent` and save it in a local variable.
6. Call the `AddListener` function of the `onDeath` field of the `Life` reference and pass the `GivePoints` function as the first argument. This is known as **subscribing** our `listener` method `GivePoints` to the event `onDeath`. The idea is to tell `Life` to execute `GivePoints` when the `onDeath` event is invoked. This way, `Life` informs us about that situation. Remember that you don't need to call `GivePoints`, but just pass the function as a field:

```
private void Awake()
{
    var life = GetComponent<Life>();
    life.onDeath.AddListener(GivePoints);
}

void GivePoints()
{
    ScoreManager.instance.amount += amount;
}
```

Figure 8.30: Subscribing to the OnDeath event to give points in that scenario

Consider calling `RemoveListener` in `OnDestroy`; as usual, it is convenient to unsubscribe listeners when possible to prevent any memory leak (reference preventing the GC to deallocate memory). In this scenario, it is not entirely necessary because both the `Life` and `ScoreOnDeath` components will be destroyed at the same time, but try to get used to this as a good practice.

7. Save, select `ScoreManager` in the editor, and hit **Play** to test this. Try deleting an enemy from the Hierarchy while in **Play** mode to check that the score doesn't rise because the enemy was destroyed for a reason other than their life becoming 0; you must destroy an enemy by shooting at them to see the score increase.

Now that `Life` has an `onDeath` event, we can also replace the player's `Life` check from the `WavesGameMode` to use the event by doing the following:

1. Create an `OnPlayerDied` function on the `WavesGameMode` script and move the loading of the `LoseScreen` scene from `Update` to this function. You will be removing the `if` that checks the life from the `Update` method, given that the event version will replace it.
2. In `Awake`, add this new function to the `onDeath` event of the player's `Life` component reference, called `playerLife` in our script:

```
void Awake()
{
    playerLife.onDeath.AddListener(OnPlayerDied);
}

void OnPlayerDied()
{
    SceneManager.LoadScene("LoseScreen");
}
```

Figure 8.31: Checking the lose condition with events

As you can see, creating custom events allows you to detect more specific situations other than the defaults in Unity, and keeps your code clean, without needing to constantly ask conditions in the `Update` function, which is not necessarily bad, but the event approach generates clearer code.

Remember that we can lose our game also by the player's base `Life` reaching 0, so let's create a cube that represents the object that enemies will attack to reduce the base `Life`. Taking this into account, I challenge you to add this second lose condition (player's base life reaching 0) to our script. When you finish, you can check the solution in the following screenshot:

```
[SerializeField] private Life playerLife;
[SerializeField] private Life playerBaseLife;

void Awake()
{
    playerLife.onDeath.AddListener(OnPlayerOrBaseDied);
    playerBaseLife.onDeath.AddListener(OnPlayerOrBaseDied);
}

void OnPlayerOrBaseDied()
{
    SceneManager.LoadScene("LoseScreen");
}
```

Figure 8.32: Complete WavesGameMode lose condition

As you can see, we just repeated the `life` event subscription, remember to create an object to represent the player's base damage point, add a `Life` script to it, and drag that one as the player base `Life` reference of the Waves Game Mode. Something interesting here is that we subscribed the same function called `OnPlayerOrBaseDied` to both player `Life` and base `Life` `onDeath` events, given that we want the same result in both situations.

Now, let's keep illustrating this concept by applying it to the managers to prevent the Game Mode from checking conditions every frame:

1. Add a `UnityEvent` field to `EnemyManager` called `onChanged`. This event will be executed whenever an enemy is added or removed from the list.
2. Create two functions, `AddEnemy` and `RemoveEnemy`, both receiving a parameter of the `Enemy` type. The idea is that instead of `Enemy` adding and removing itself from the list directly, it should use these functions.

3. Inside these two functions, invoke the `onChanged` event to inform others that the enemies list has been updated. The idea is that anyone who wants to add or remove enemies from the list needs to use these functions:

```
public List<Enemy> enemies;
public UnityEvent onChanged;

public void AddEnemy(Enemy enemy)
{
    enemies.Add(enemy);
    onChanged.Invoke();
}

public void RemoveEnemy(Enemy enemy)
{
    enemies.Remove(enemy);
    onChanged.Invoke();
}
```

Figure 8.33: Calling events when enemies are added or removed

Here, we have the problem that nothing stops us from bypassing those two functions and using the list directly. You can solve that by making the list private and exposing it using the `IReadOnlyList` interface. Remember that this way, the list won't be visible in the editor for debugging purposes.

4. Change the `Enemy` script to use these functions:

```
public class Enemy : MonoBehaviour
{
    void Start()
    {
        EnemyManager.instance.AddEnemy(this);
    }

    void OnDestroy()
    {
        EnemyManager.instance.RemoveEnemy(this);
    }
}
```

Figure 8.34: Making the Enemy use the add and remove functions

5. Repeat the same process for `WaveManager` and `WaveSpawner`, create an `onChanged` event, and create the `AddWave` and `RemoveWave` functions and call them in `WaveSpawner` instead of directly accessing the list. This way, we are sure the event is called when necessary as we did with `EnemyManager`. Try to solve this step by yourself and then check the solution in the following screenshot, starting with `WavesManager`:

```
public class WavesManager : MonoBehaviour
{
    public static WavesManager instance;

    public List<WaveSpawner> waves;
    public UnityEvent onChanged;

    private void Awake()
    {
        if (instance == null)
            instance = this;
        else
            Debug.LogError("Duplicated WavesManager", gameObject);
    }

    public void AddWave(WaveSpawner wave)
    {
        waves.Add(wave);
        onChanged.Invoke();
    }

    public void RemoveWave(WaveSpawner wave)
    {
        waves.Remove(wave);
        onChanged.Invoke();
    }
}
```

Figure 8.35: WaveManager OnChanged event implementation

6. Also, `WavesSpawner` needed the following changes:

```
public class WaveSpawner : MonoBehaviour
{
    public GameObject prefab;
    public float startTime;
    public float endTime;
    public float spawnRate;

    private void Start()
    {
        WavesManager.instance.AddWave(this);
        InvokeRepeating("Spawn", startTime, spawnRate);
        Invoke("EndSpawner", endTime);
    }

    void Spawn()
    {
        Instantiate(prefab, transform.position, transform.rotation);
    }

    void EndSpawner()
    {
        WavesManager.instance.RemoveWave(this);
        CancelInvoke();
    }
}
```

Figure 8.36: Implementing the AddWave and RemoveWave functions

7. In `WavesGameMode`, rename `Update` to `CheckWinCondition` and subscribe this function to the `onChanged` event of `EnemyManager` and the `onChanged` event of `WavesManager`. The idea is to check for the number of enemies and waves being changed only when necessary. Remember to do the subscription to the events in the `Start` function due to the Singletons being initialized in `Awake`:

```
void Start()
{
    playerLife.onDeath.AddListener(OnPlayerOrBaseDied);
    playerBaseLife.onDeath.AddListener(OnPlayerOrBaseDied);
    EnemyManager.instance.onChanged.AddListener(CheckWinCondition);
    WavesManager.instance.onChanged.AddListener(CheckWinCondition);
}

void OnPlayerOrBaseDied()
{
    SceneManager.LoadScene("LoseScreen");
}

void CheckWinCondition()
{
    if (EnemyManager.instance.enemies.Count <= 0 && WavesManager.instance.waves.Count <= 0)
    {
        SceneManager.LoadScene("WinScreen");
    }
}
```

Figure 8.37: Checking the win condition when the enemies or waves amount is changed

Regarding the Visual Scripting version, let's start checking the lose condition with events, checking first some changes needed in the **Life Script Graph**:

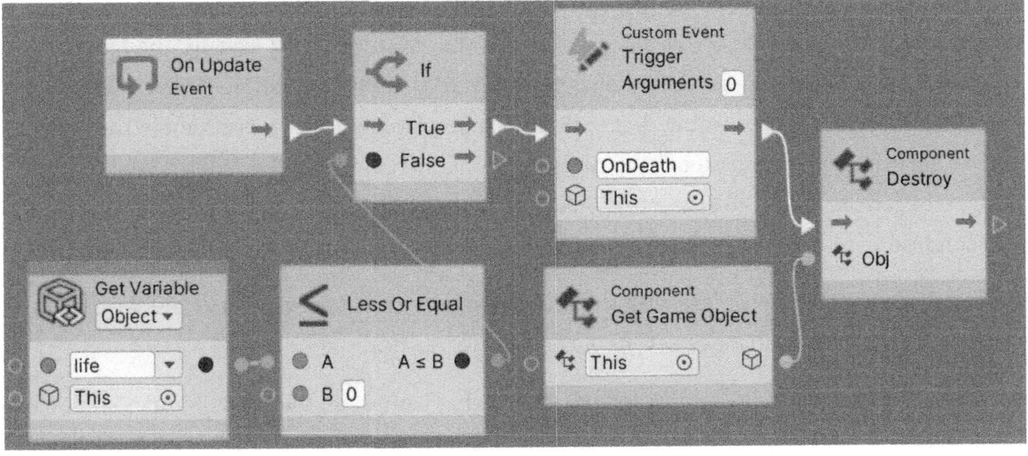

Figure 8.38: Triggering a Custom Event in our Life graph

First, after destroying the object when life reaches 0, we use the **Trigger Custom Event** node, specifying the name of our event is `OnDeath`. This will tell anyone waiting for the execution of the `OnDeath` event that we did. Remember, this is our **Life Script Graph**. Be sure to call destroy after triggering the event—while most of the time the order doesn't matter, given that the destroy action doesn't actually happen until the end of the frame, sometimes it can cause issues, so better be safe here. In this case, Game Mode should listen to the player's `OnDeath` event, so let's make the following change in our **Game Mode Graph**:

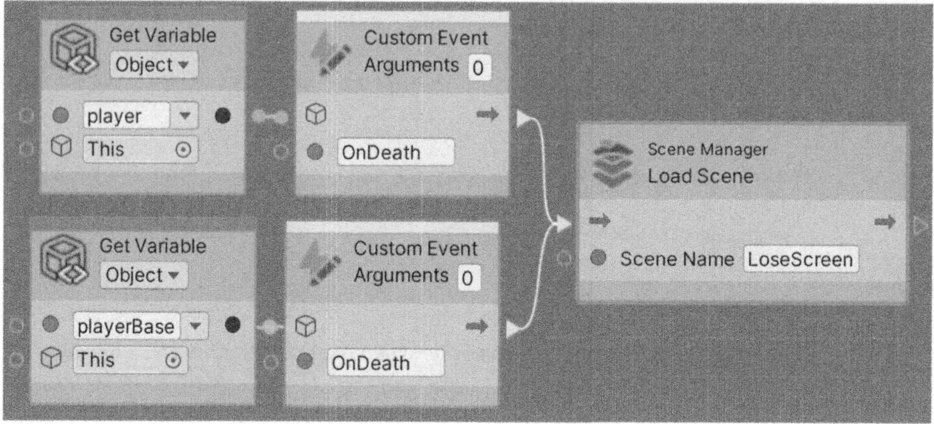

Figure 8.39: Listening to the OnDeath event of Player in Visual Scripting

We used the **CustomEvent** node connecting it to the player reference of our GameMode. This way we are specifying that if that player executes that event, we will execute the **Load Scene** node. Remember that the player reference is crucial to specify from whom we want to execute the `OnDeath` event, and remember that the **Life Visual Graph** will also be present in the enemies and we are not interested in them here. Also, remember to remove the `If` node and the condition nodes we used previously to detect this – the only `If` our Game Mode will have is the one for the win condition.

Essentially, we made any object with the `Life` script have an `OnDeath` event, and we made the GameMode listen to the `OnDeath` event of the player specifically.

We could also do events for enemies and waves, but that would complicate our graphs somewhat, given that we don't have `WaveManager` or `EnemyManager` in the Visual Scripting versions. We could certainly create those to accomplish this, but sometimes the point of using Visual Scripting is to create simple logic, and these kinds of changes tend to make a graph grow quite a bit.

Another possible solution is to make the enemy and wave directly inform the Game Mode. We could use **Trigger Custom Event** in the enemies and waves, connecting that node to the Game Mode, to finally let the Game Mode have a **Custom Event** node from which to listen. The issue is that that would violate the correct dependencies between our objects; lower-level objects such as enemies and waves shouldn't communicate with higher-level objects such as Game Mode. Essentially, Game Mode was supposed to be an overseer. If we apply the solution described in this paragraph, we won't be able to have an enemy in another scene or game without having a Game Mode. So, for simplicity and code decoupling purposes, let's keep the other conditions as they are—the more complex logic such as this will be probably handled in C# in full production projects.

Yes, using events means that we have to write more code than before, and in terms of functionality, we didn't obtain anything new, but in bigger projects, managing conditions through `Update` checks will lead to different kinds of problems as previously discussed, such as race conditions and performance issues. Having a scalable code base sometimes requires more code, and this is one of those cases.

Before we finish, something to consider is that Unity events are not the only way to create this kind of event communication in Unity; you will find a similar approach called **Action**, the native C# version of events, which I recommend you look into if you want to see all of the options out there.

Summary

In this chapter, we finished an important part of the game: the ending, both by victory and by defeat. We discussed a simple but powerful way to separate the different layers of responsibilities by using managers created through Singletons, to guarantee that there isn't more than one instance of every kind of manager and simplifying the connections between them through static access. Also, we visited the concept of events to streamline communication between objects to prevent problems and create more meaningful communication between objects.

With this knowledge, you are now able not only to detect the victory and lose conditions of the game but can also do it in a better-structured way. These patterns can be useful to improve our game code in general, and I recommend you try to apply them in other relevant scenarios.

In the next chapter, we are going to start *Part 3* of the book, where we are going to see different Unity systems to improve the graphics and audio aspects of our game, starting by seeing how we can create materials to modify aspects of our objects, and create shaders with Shader Graph.

Join us on Discord!

Read this book alongside other users, Unity game development experts, and the author himself.

Ask questions, provide solutions to other readers, chat with the author via Ask Me Anything sessions, and much more.

Scan the QR code or visit the link to join the community.

`https://packt.link/handsonunity22`

Implementing Game AI for Building Enemies

What is a game if not a great challenge to the player, who needs to use their character's abilities to tackle different scenarios? Each game imposes different kinds of obstacles on the player, and the main one in our game is the enemies. Creating challenging and believable enemies can be complex; they need to behave like real characters and be smart enough so as not to be easy to kill, but also easy enough that they are not impossible to kill. We are going to use basic but sufficient AI techniques to make an AI capable of sensing its surroundings and, based on that information, make decisions on what to do, using **FSMs** or **Finite State Machines**, along with other techniques. Those decisions will be executed using **intelligent pathfinding**.

In this chapter, we will examine the following AI concepts:

- Gathering information with sensors
- Making decisions with FSMs
- Executing FSM actions

By the end of the chapter, you will have a fully functional enemy capable of detecting the player and attacking them, so let's start by seeing first how to make the sensor systems.

Gathering information with sensors

An AI works by first taking in information about its surroundings. Then, that data is analyzed in order to choose an action, and finally, the chosen action is executed. As you can see, we cannot do anything without information, so let's start with that part.

There are several sources of information our AI can use, such as data about itself (life and bullets) or maybe some game state (winning condition or remaining enemies), which can easily be found with the code we've seen so far. One important source of information, however, is also the AI senses. According to the needs of our game, we might need different senses such as sight and hearing, but in our case, sight will be enough, so let's learn how to code that.

In this section, we will examine the following sensor concepts:

- Creating three-filter sensors with C#
- Creating three-filter sensors with Visual Scripting
- Debugging with gizmos

Let's start by seeing how to create a sensor with the three-filters approach.

Creating three-filter sensors with C#

The common way to code senses is through a three-filters approach to discard enemies out of sight. The first filter is a distance filter, which will discard enemies too far away to be seen, then the second filter would be the angle check, which will check enemies inside our viewing cone, and finally, the third filter is a raycast check, which will discard enemies that are being occluded by obstacles such as walls.

Before starting, a word of advice: we will be using vector mathematics here, and covering those topics in-depth is outside the scope of this book. If you don't understand something, feel free to just search online for the code in the screenshots.

Let's code sensors in the following way:

1. Create an empty `GameObject` called `AI` as a child of the **Enemy** Prefab. You need to first open the Prefab to modify its children (double-click the Prefab). Remember to set the transform of this `GameObject` to **Position 0,1.75,0**, **Rotation 0,0,0**, and **Scale 1,1,1** so it will be aligned to the enemy's eyes. This is done this way for the future sight sensors we will do. Consider your enemy prefab might have a different height for the eyes. While we can certainly just put all AI scripts directly in the **Enemy** Prefab root `GameObject`, we did this just for separation and organization:

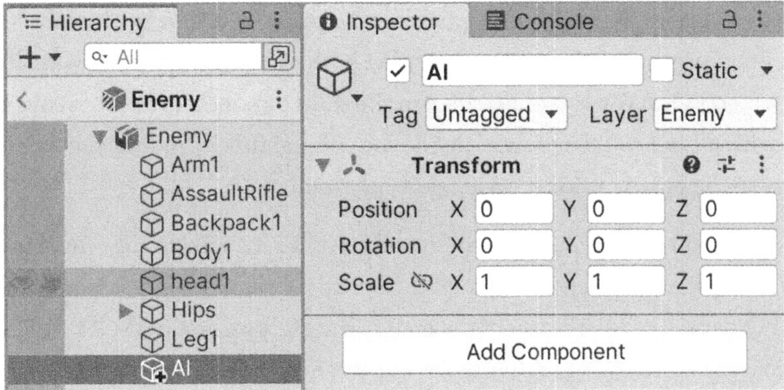

Figure 9.1: AI scripts container

2. Create a script called `Sight` and add it to the `AI` child object.
3. Create two fields of the `float` type called `distance` and `angle`, and another two of the `LayerMask` type called `obstaclesLayers` and `objectsLayers`. `distance` will be used as the vision distance, `angle` will determine the amplitude of the view cone, `obstacleLayers` will be used by our obstacle check to determine which objects are considered obstacles, and `objectsLayers` will be used to determine what types of objects we want the `Sight` component to detect.

   We just want the sight to see enemies; we are not interested in objects such as walls or power-ups. `LayerMask` is a property type that allows us to select one or more layers to use inside code, so we will be filtering objects by layer. In a moment, you will see how we use it:

```
using UnityEngine;

public class Sight : MonoBehaviour
{
    public float distance;
    public float angle;
    public LayerMask objectsLayers;
    public LayerMask obstaclesLayers;
}
```

Figure 9.2: Fields to parametrize our sight check

4. In `Update`, call `Physics.OverlapSphere` as in the *Figure 9.3*.

This function creates an imaginary sphere in the place specified by the first parameter (in our case, our position) and with a radius specified in the second parameter (the distance property) to detect objects with the layers specified in the third parameter (`ObjectsLayers`). It will return an array with all the colliders found inside the sphere; these functions use physics to carry out the check, so the objects must have at least one collider.

This is the method we will be using to find all enemies inside our view distance, and we will be further filtering them in the next steps. Note that we are passing our position to the first parameter, which is not actually the position of the enemy but the position of the `AI` child object, given our script is located there. This highlights the importance of the position of the AI object.

Another way of accomplishing the first check is to just check the distance from the objects we want to see to the player, or if looking for other kinds of objects, to a `Manager` component containing a list of them. However, the method we chose is more versatile and can be used for any kind of object.

Also, you might want to check the `Physics.OverlapSphereNonAlloc` version of this function, which does the same but is more performant by not allocating an array to return the results.

1. Iterate over the array of objects returned by the function using a `for` loop:

```
private void Update()
{
    Collider[] colliders = Physics.OverlapSphere(
        transform.position, distance, objectsLayers);

    for (int i = 0; i < colliders.Length; i++)
    {
        Collider collider = colliders[i];
    }
}
```

Figure 9.3: Getting all GameObjects at a certain distance

2. To detect whether the object falls inside the vision cone, we need to calculate the angle between our viewing direction and the direction from ourselves towards the object itself. If the angle between those two directions is less than our cone angle, we consider that the object falls inside our vision. We will do that in the following steps:

Start calculating the direction toward the object, which can be done by normalizing the difference between the object's position and ours, like in *Figure 9.4*. You might notice we used `bounds.center` instead of `transform.position`; this way, we check the direction to the center of the object instead of its pivot. Remember that the player's pivot is in the ground and the ray check might collide against it before the player:

```
Vector3 directionToController = Vector3.Normalize(
    collider.bounds.center - transform.position);
```

Figure 9.4: Calculating direction from our position toward the collider

3. We can use the `Vector3.Angle` function to calculate the angle between two directions. In our case, we can calculate the angle between the direction toward the enemy and our forward vector to see the angle:

```
float angleToCollider = Vector3.Angle(
    transform.forward, directionToController);
```

Figure 9.5: Calculating the angle between two directions

If you want, you can instead use `Vector3.Dot`, which will execute a dot product, a mathematics function to calculate the length of a vector projected to another (search online for more info). `Vector3.Angle` actually uses that one, but converts the result of the dot product into an angle, which needs to use trigonometry, and that can be time expensive to calculate. But our `Vector3.Angle` approach is simpler and faster to code, and given that we don't require many sensors because we won't have many enemies, optimizing the sensor using dot products is not necessary now, but consider that for games with larger scale.

4. Now check whether the calculated angle is less than the one specified in the `angle` field. Note that if we set an angle of `90`, it will actually be `180`, because if the `Vector3.Angle` function returns, as an example, `30`, it could be `30` to the left or to the right. If our angle says `90`, it could be both `90` to the left and to the right, so it will detect objects in a 180-degree arc.

5. Use the `Physics.Linecast` function to create an imaginary line between the first and the second parameter (our position and the collider position) to detect objects with the layers specified in the third parameter (the obstacle layers) and return `boolean` indicating whether that ray hit something or not.

   The idea is to use the line to detect whether there are any obstacles between ourselves and the detected collider, and if there is no obstacle, this means that we have a direct line of sight toward the object. Observe how we use the `!` or `not` operator in *Figure 9.6* to check if `Physics.Linecast` didn't detect any objects. Again, note that this function depends on the obstacle objects having colliders, which in our case, we have (walls, floor, and so on):

```
if (angleToCollider < angle)
{
    if (!Physics.Linecast(transform.position,
            collider.bounds.center, obstaclesLayers))
    {
    }
}
```

Figure 9.6: Using a Linecast to check obstacles between the sensor and the target object

6. If the object passes the three checks, that means that this is the object we are currently seeing, so we can save it inside a field of the `Collider` type called `detectedObject`, to save that information for later usage by the rest of the `AI` scripts.

   Consider using `break` to stop the `for` loop that is iterating the colliders to prevent wasting resources by checking the other objects, and to set `detectedObject` to `null` before `for` to clear the result from the previous frame. So if in this frame, we don't detect anything, it will keep the `null` value so we notice that there is nothing in the sensor:

```
public float distance;
public float angle;
public LayerMask objectsLayers;
public LayerMask obstaclesLayers;
public Collider detectedObject;

private void Update()
{
    Collider[] colliders = Physics.OverlapSphere(
        transform.position, distance, (int) objectsLayers);

    detectedObject = null;
    for (int i = 0; i < colliders.Length; i++)
    {
        Collider collider = colliders[i];

        Vector3 directionToController = Vector3.Normalize(
            collider.bounds.center - transform.position);

        float angleToCollider = Vector3.Angle(
            transform.forward, directionToController);

        if (angleToCollider < angle)
        {
            if (!Physics.Linecast(transform.position,
                    collider.bounds.center, (int) obstaclesLayers))
            {
                detectedObject = collider;
                break;
            }
        }
    }
}
```

Figure 9.7: Full sensor script

In our case, we are using the sensor just to look for the player, the only object the sensor is in charge of looking for, but if you want to make the sensor more advanced, you can just keep a list of detected objects, placing inside it every object that passes the three tests instead of just the first one. In our case, it's not necessary given we have only one player in the game.

7. In the editor, configure the sensor at your will. In this case, we will set `ObjectsLayer` to `Player` so our sensor will focus its search on objects with that layer, and `obstaclesLayer` to `Default`, the layer we used for walls and floors. Remember the `Sight` script is in the `AI` GameObject, which is a child of the `Enemy` prefab:

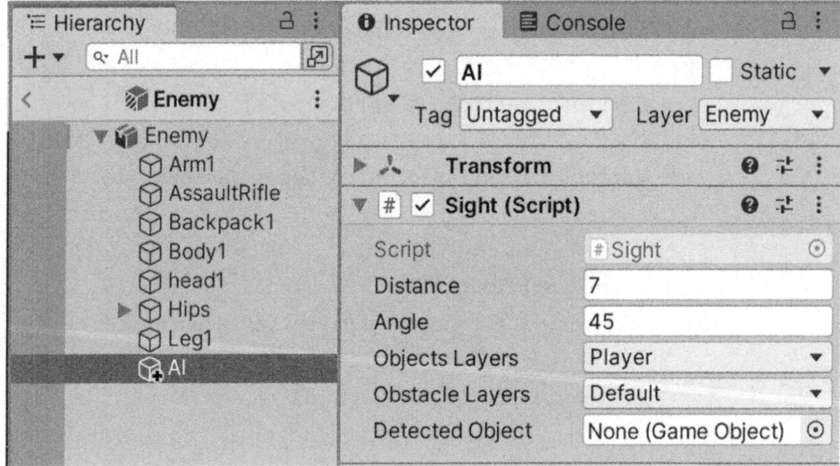

Figure 9.8: Sensor settings

8. To test this, just place an enemy with a movement speed of 0 in front of the player, select its `AI` child object and then play the game to see how the property is set in the Inspector. Also, try putting an obstacle between the two and check that the property says **None** (`null`). If you don't get the expected result, double-check your script, its configuration, and whether the player has the `Player` layer, and the obstacles have the `Default` layer. Also, you might need to raise the `AI` object a little bit to prevent the ray from starting below the ground and hitting it.

Given the size of the script, let's dedicate an entire section to the Visual Scripting version, given it also introduces some new Visual Scripting concepts needed here.

Creating Three-Filters sensors with Visual Scripting

Regarding the Visual Scripting version, let's check it part by part, starting with the **Overlap Sphere**:

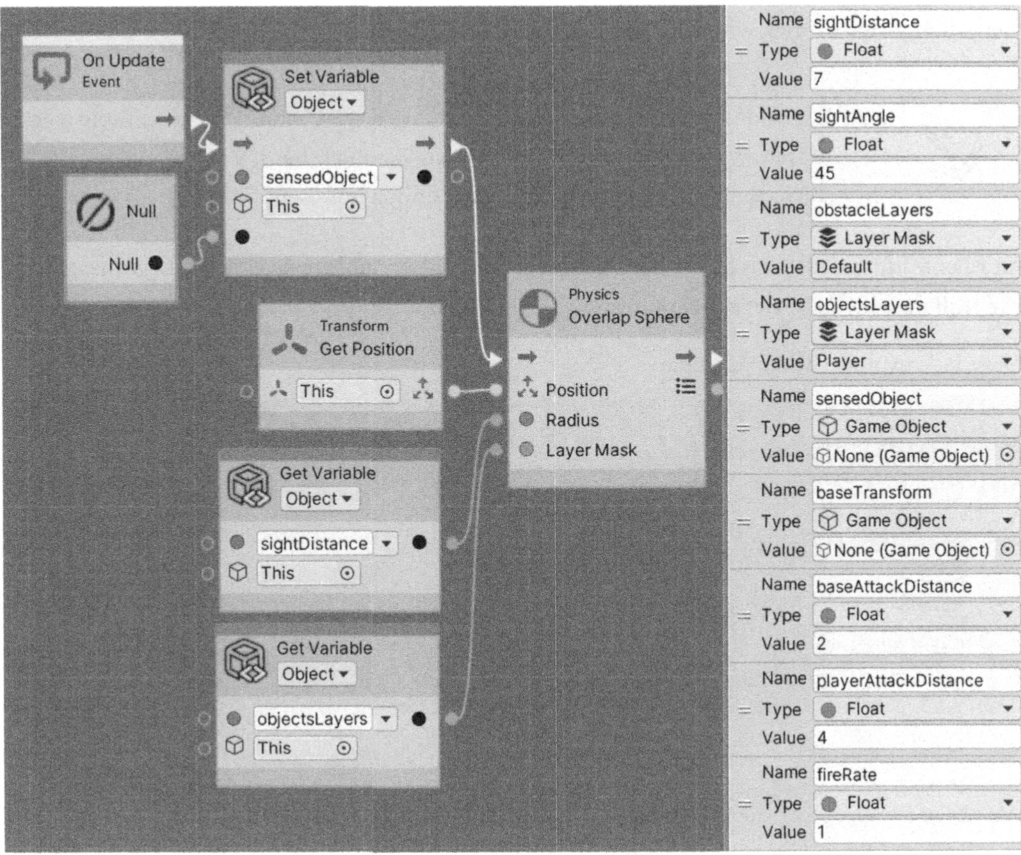

Figure 9.9: Overlap Sphere in Visual Scripting

So far, we just called **Overlap Sphere** after setting the `sensedObject` variable to `null`. Something to consider is how the `sensedObject` variable in the **Variables** component in the Inspector doesn't have a type (a **Null** type is no type in Visual Scripting). This can't be possible in C#—all variables must have a type—and while we could set the `sensedObject` variable to the proper type (**Collider**), we will keep the variable type to be set later via a script. Even if we set the type now, Visual Scripting tends to forget the type if no value is set, and we cannot set it until we detect something.

Don't worry about that for the moment; when we set the variable through our script it will acquire the proper type. Actually, all variables in Visual Scripting can switch types at runtime according to what we set them to, given how the **Variables** component works. I don't recommend doing that, though: try to stick with the intended variable type.

We just said that all variables in C# must have a type, but that's not entirely true. There are ways to create dynamically-typed variables, but it's not a good practice that I'd recommend using unless no other option is present.

Another thing to observe is how we set the `sensedObject` variable to `null` at the beginning using the **Null** node, which effectively represents the `null` value.

Now, let's explore the `Foreach` part:

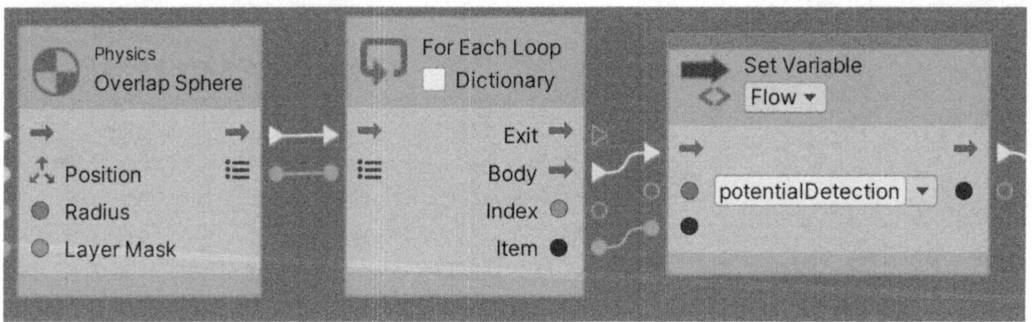

Figure 9.10: Iterating collections in Visual Scripting

We can see that one of the output pins of **Overlap Sphere** is a little list, which essentially represents the collider array returned by **Overlap Sphere**. We connect that pin to the **For Each Loop** node, which as you might imagine iterates over the elements of the provided collection (array, list, dictionary, etc.). The **Body** pin represents the nodes to execute in each iteration of the loop, and the **Item** output pin represents the item currently being iterated—in our case, one of the colliders detected in **Overlap Sphere**. Finally, we save that item in a **Flow** `potentialDetection` variable, **Flow** variables being the equivalent to local variables in C# functions.

The idea here is that, given the size of the graph and the number of times we will be needing to query the currently iterated item, we don't want the line connecting the output **Item** pin to the other nodes to cross the entire graph. Instead, we save that item in the **Flow** variable to reference it later, essentially naming that value to be referenced later in the graph, which you will see in the next parts of it.

Now let's explore the **Angle** check:

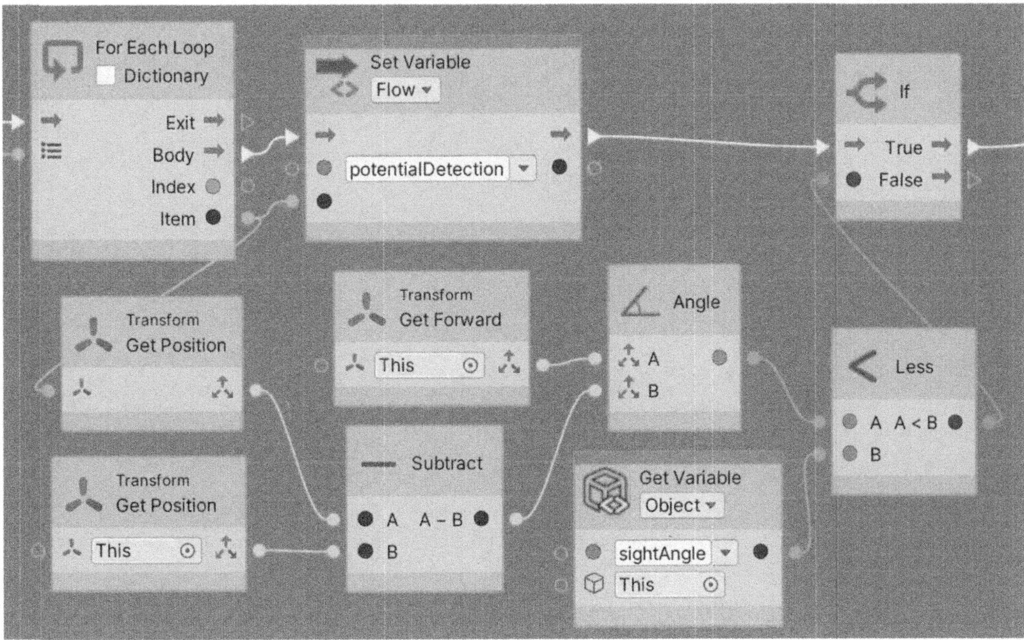

Figure 9.11: Angle check in Visual Scripting

Here, you can see a direct translation of what we did in C# to detect the angle, so it should be pretty self-explanatory. The only thing here is given the proximity of the **Item** output pin to the **Get Position** node where we query its position, we directly connected the node, but we will use the `potentialDetection` flow variable later.

Now, let's explore the **Linecast** part:

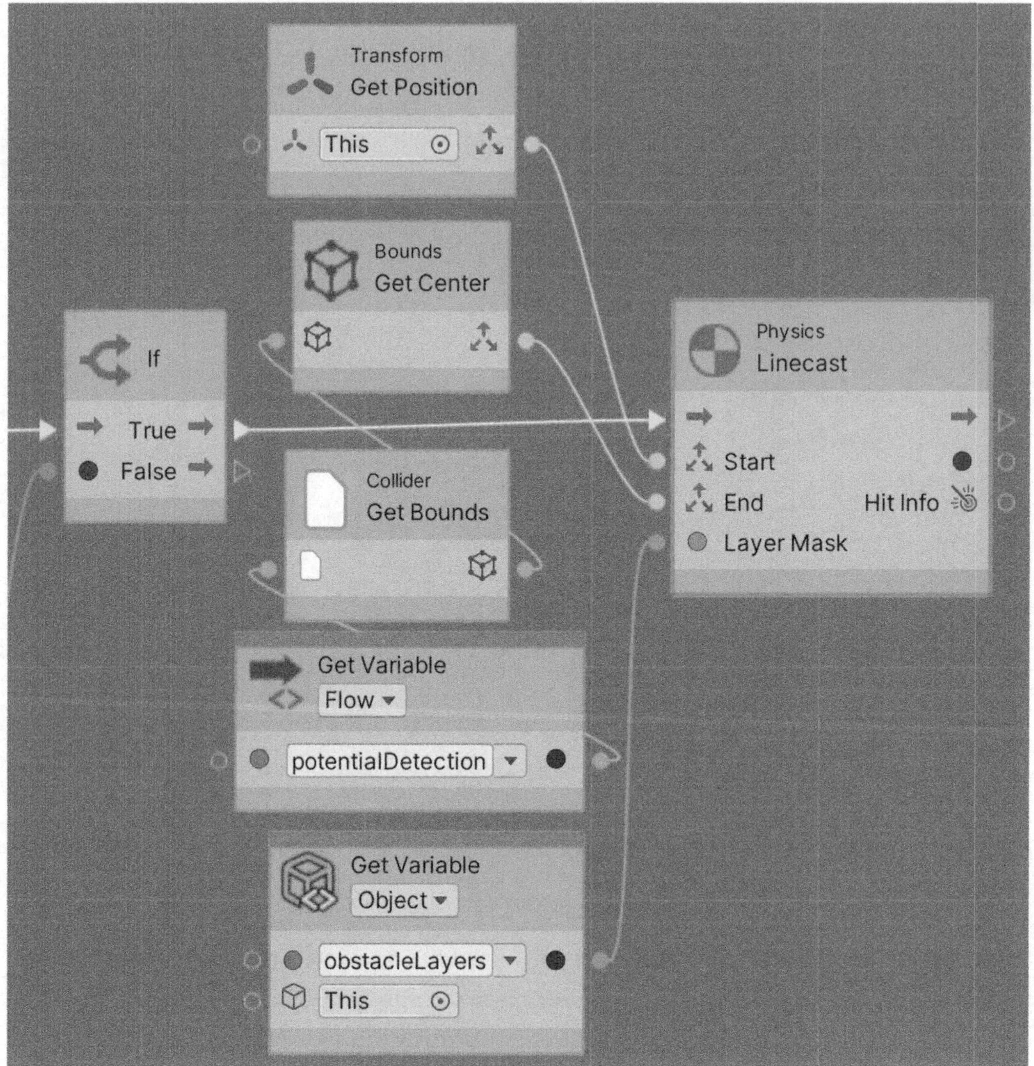

Figure 9.12: Linecast check in Visual Scripting

Again, essentially the same as we did before in C#. The only thing to highlight here is the fact we used the **Flow** variable `potentialDetection` to again get the position of the current item being iterated, instead of connecting the **Get Position** node all the way to the **Foreach Item** output pin.

Now, let's explore the final part:

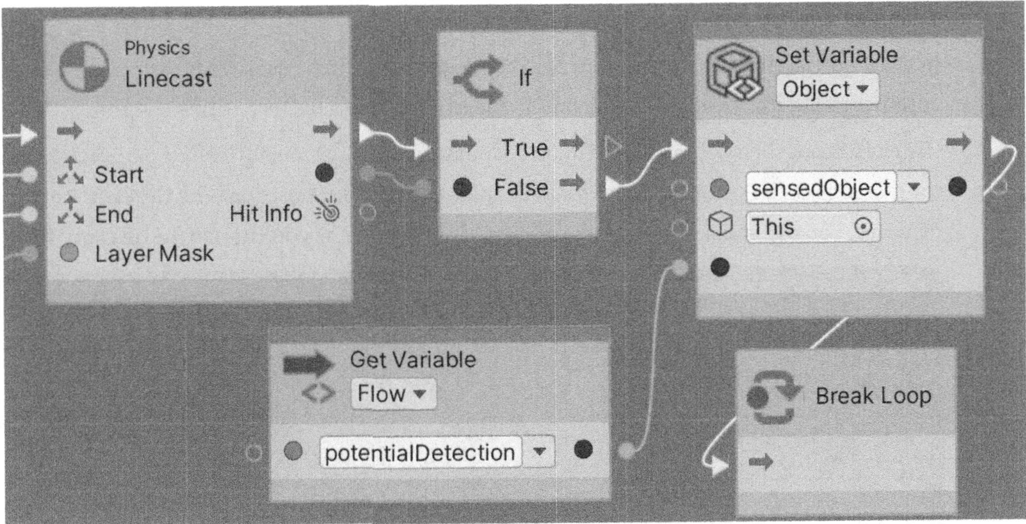

Figure 9.13: Setting the sensedObject

Again, pretty much self-explanatory; if the **Linecast** returns `false`, we set the `potentialDetection` variable (the currently iterated item) as the `sensedObject` variable (the one that will be accessed by other scripts later to query which is the object our AI can see right now). Something to consider here is the usage of the **Break Loop** node, which is the equivalent to the C# `break` keyword; essentially, we are stopping the **Foreach** loop we are currently in.

Now, even if we have our sensor working, sometimes checking whether it's working or configured properly requires some visual aids we can create using gizmos.

Debugging with gizmos

As we create our AI, we will start to detect certain errors in edge cases, usually related to misconfigurations. You may think that the player falls within the sight range of the enemy but maybe you cannot see that the line of sight is occluded by an object, especially as the enemies move constantly. A good way to debug those scenarios is through editor-only visual aids known as `Gizmos`, which allow you to visualize invisible data such as the sight distance or the `Linecasts` executed to detect obstacles.

Let's start seeing how to create `Gizmos` drawing a sphere representing the sight distance by doing the following:

1. In the `Sight` script, create an event function called `OnDrawGizmos`. This event is only executed in the editor (not in builds) and is the place Unity asks us to draw `Gizmos`.
2. Use the `Gizmos.DrawWireSphere` function, passing our position as the first parameter and the distance as the second parameter to draw a sphere in our position with the radius of our distance. You can check how the size of the `Gizmo` changes as you change the distance field:

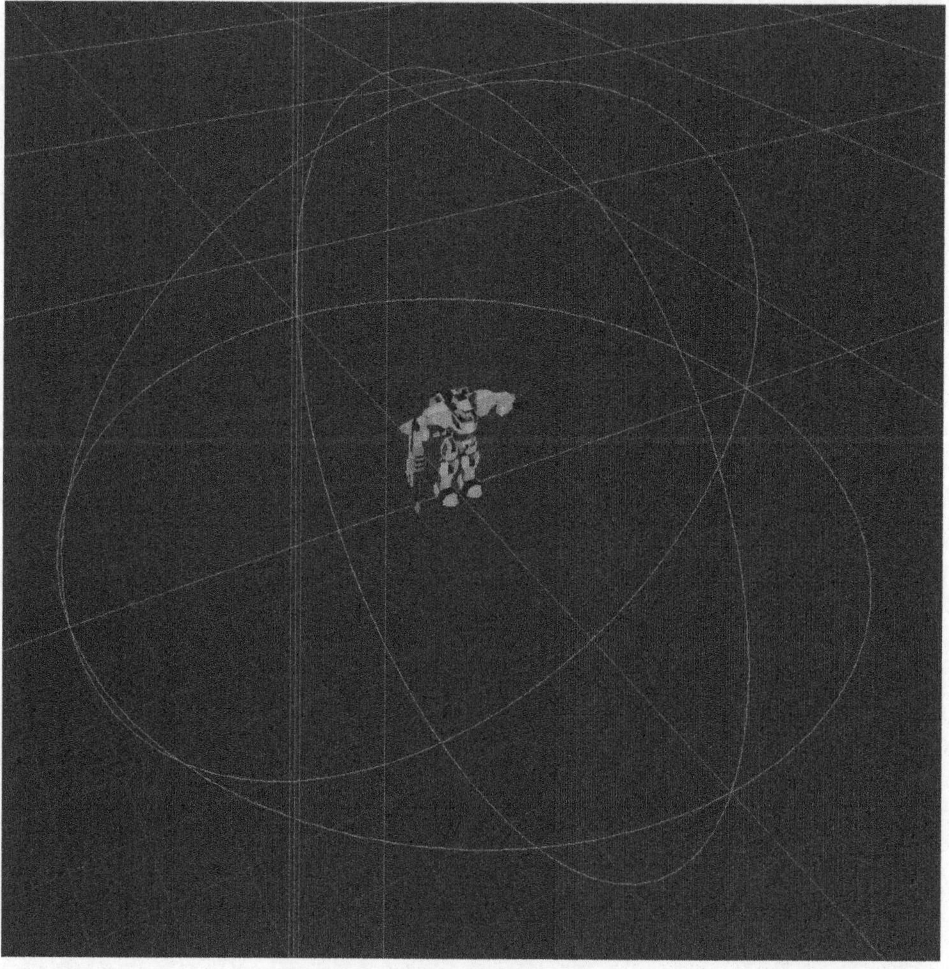

Figure 9.14: Sphere Gizmo

3. Optionally, you can change the color of the gizmo, setting `Gizmos.color` prior to calling the drawing functions:

```
void OnDrawGizmos()
{
    Gizmos.color = Color.red;
    Gizmos.DrawWireSphere(transform.position, distance);
}
```

Figure 9.15: Gizmos drawing code

Now you are drawing `Gizmos` constantly, and if you have lots of enemies, they can pollute the scene view with too many `Gizmos`. In that case, try the `OnDrawGizmosSelected` event function instead, which draws `Gizmos` only if the object is selected.

4. We can draw the lines representing the cone using `Gizmos.DrawRay`, which receives the origin of the line to draw and the direction of the line, which can be multiplied by a certain value to specify the length of the line, as in the following screenshot:

```
Vector3 rightDirection = Quaternion.Euler(0, angle, 0) * transform.forward;
Gizmos.DrawRay(transform.position, rightDirection * distance);

Vector3 leftDirection = Quaternion.Euler(0, -angle, 0) * transform.forward;
Gizmos.DrawRay(transform.position, leftDirection * distance);
```

Figure 9.16: Drawing rotated lines

5. In the screenshot, we used `Quaternion.Euler` to generate a quaternion based on the angles we want to rotate. A quaternion is a mathematical construct to represent rotations; please search for this term for more info on it. If you multiply this quaternion by a direction, we will get the rotated direction. We are taking our forward vector and rotating it according to the angle field to generate our cone vision lines.

Also, we multiply this direction by the sight distance to draw the line as far as our sight can see; you will see how the line matches the end of the sphere this way:

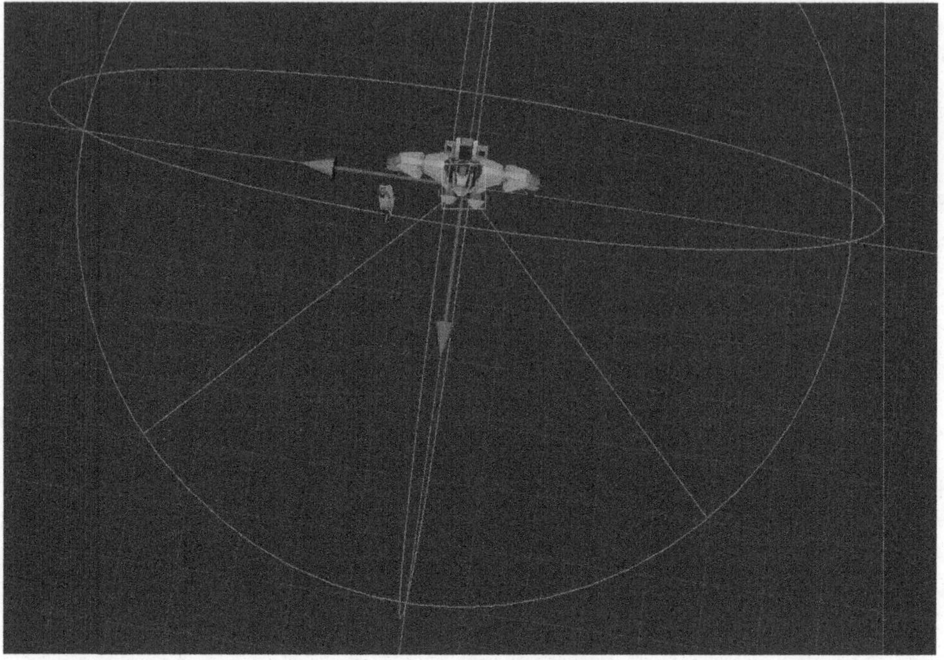

Figure 9.17: Vision angle lines

We can also draw the Linecasts, which check the obstacles, but as those depend on the current situation of the game, such as the objects that pass the first two checks and their positions, we can use `Debug.DrawLine` instead, which can be executed in the `Update` method. This version of `DrawLine` is designed to be used in runtime only. The `Gizmos` we saw also execute in the editor. Let's try them the following way:

1. First, let's debug the scenario where `Linecast` didn't detect any obstacles, so we need to draw a line between our sensor and the object. We can call `Debug.DrawLine` in the `if` statement that calls `Linecast`, as in the following screenshot:

```
if (angleToCollider < angle)
{
    if (!Physics.Linecast(transform.position,
            collider.bounds.center, obstaclesLayers))
    {
        Debug.DrawLine(transform.position,
            collider.bounds.center, Color.green);
        detectedObject = collider;
        break;
    }
}
```

Figure 9.18: Drawing a line in Update

2. In the next screenshot, you can see `DrawLine` in action:

Figure 9.19: Line toward the detected Object

3. We also want to draw a line in red when the sight is occluded by an object. In this case, we need to know where the `Linecast` hit, so we can use an overload of the function, which provides an `out` parameter that gives us more information about what the line collided with, such as the position of the hit and the normal and the collided object, as in the following screenshot:

```
if (!Physics.Linecast(
        transform.position, collider.bounds.center,
        out RaycastHit hit, obstaclesLayers))
{
```

Figure 9.20: Getting information about Linecast

Note that `Linecast` doesn't always collide with the nearest obstacle but with the first object it detects in the line, which can vary in order. If you need to detect the nearest obstacle, look for the `Physics.Raycast` version of the function.

4. We can use that information to draw the line from our position to the hit point in `else` of the `if` sentence when the line collides with something:

```
if (!Physics.Linecast(
        transform.position, collider.bounds.center,
        out RaycastHit hit, obstaclesLayers))
{
    Debug.DrawLine(transform.position,
        collider.bounds.center, Color.green);
    detectedObject = collider;
    break;
}
else
{
    Debug.DrawLine(transform.position, hit.point, Color.red);
}
```

Figure 9.21: Drawing a line if we have an obstacle

5. In the next screenshot, you can see the results:

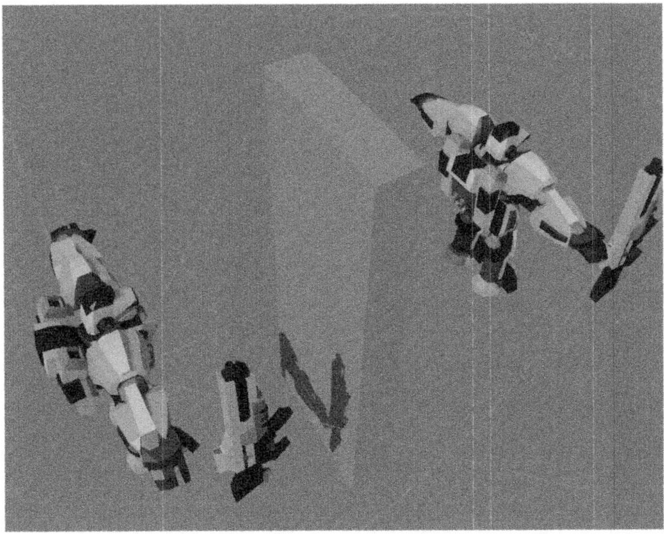

Figure 9.22: Line when an obstacle occludes vision

Regarding the Visual Scripting version, the first part will look like this:

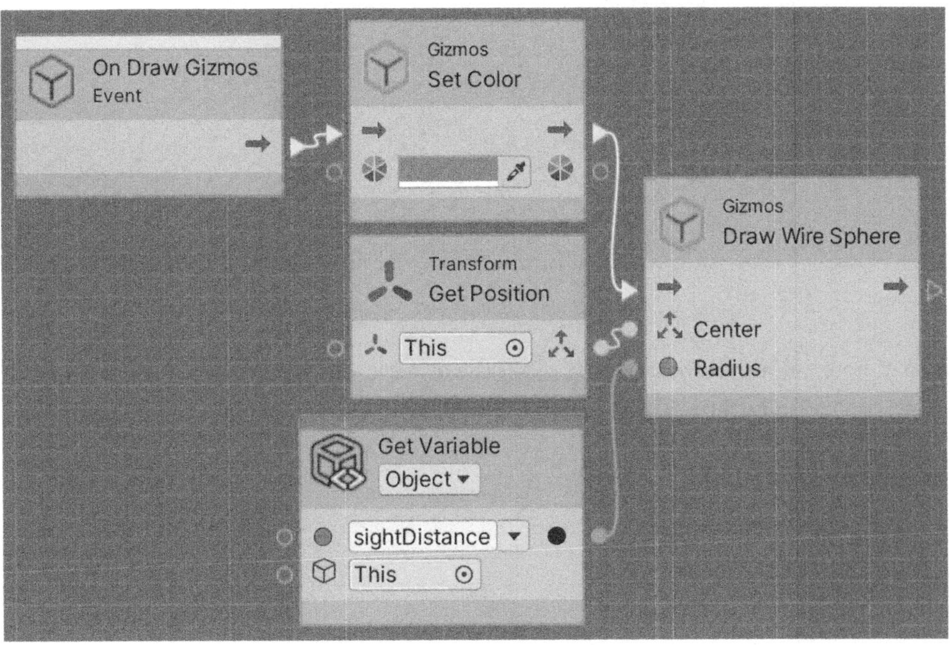

Figure 9.23: Drawing Gizmos with Visual Scripting

Then, the angle lines would look like this:

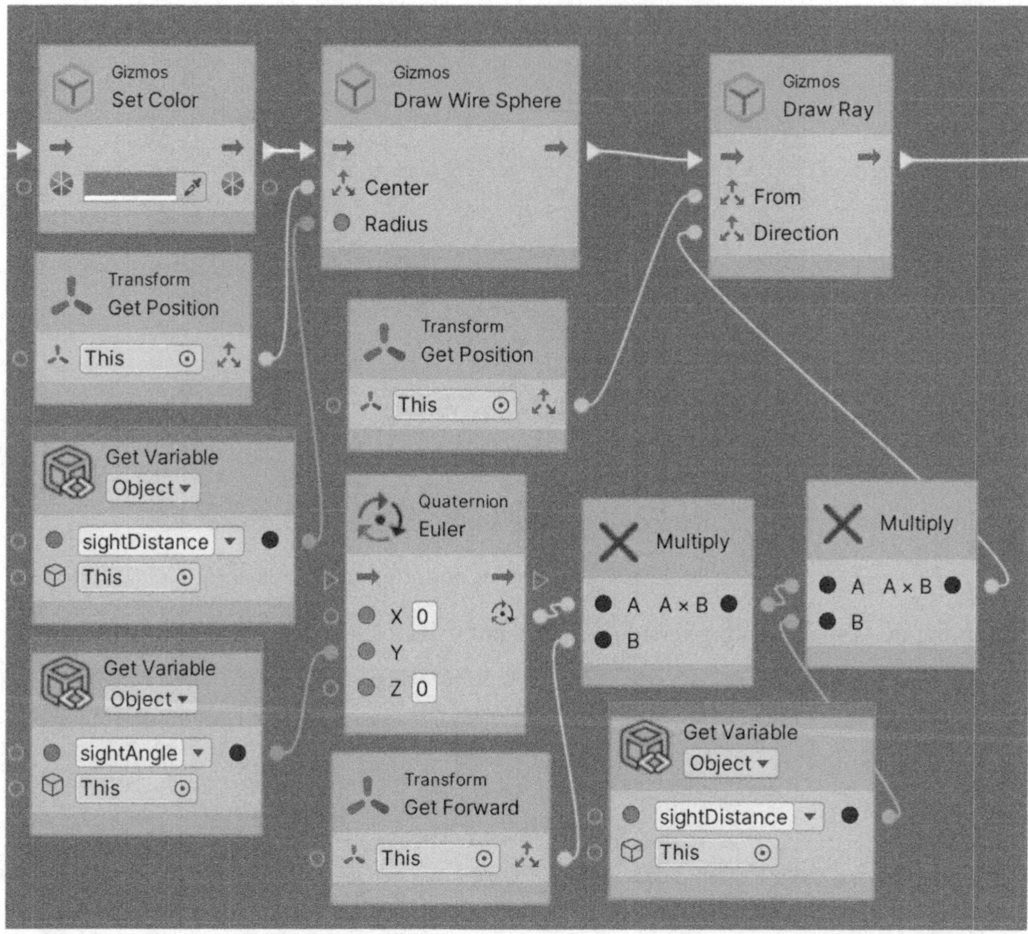

Figure 9.24: Drawing Angle lines of sight in Visual Scripting

Note that, here, we are showing just one, but the other is essentially the same but multiplying the angle by -1. Finally, the red lines towards the detected object and obstacles will look like this:

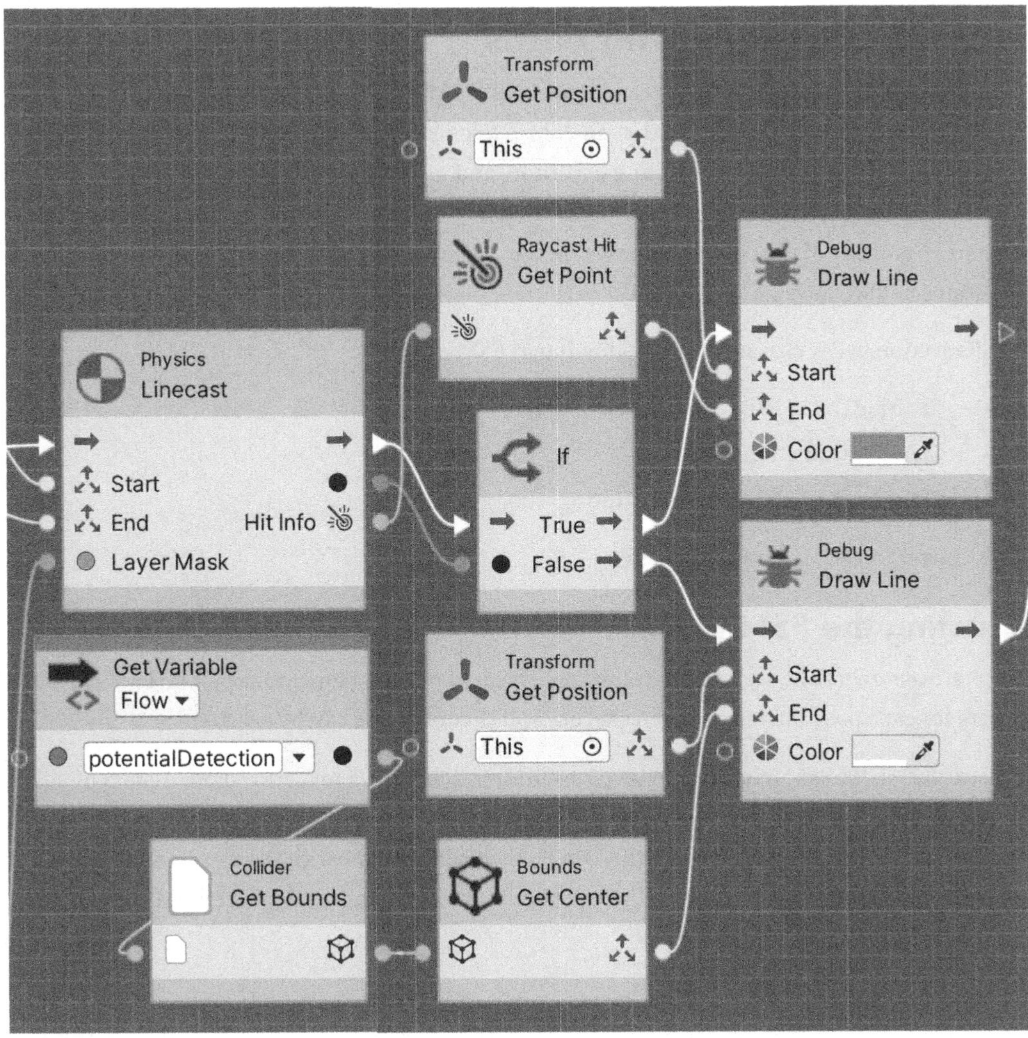

Figure 9.25: Drawing lines towards obstacles or detected objects in Visual Scripting

Note that, to accomplish this last one, we needed to change the previous **Linecast** node for the version that returns **Raycast Hit** info at the end.

With all of that, in this section, we created the sensors system that will give sight to our AI and plenty of info about what to do next. Now that we have our sensors completed, let's use the information provided by them to make decisions with FSMs.

Making decisions with FSMs

We explored the concept of **Finite State Machines (FSMs)** in the past when we used them in the `Animator` component. We learned that an FSM is a collection of states, each one representing an action that an object can be executing at a time, and a set of transitions that dictates how the states are switched. This concept is not only used in animation but in a myriad of programming scenarios, and one of the common ones is AI. We can just replace the animations with AI code in the states and we have an AI FSM.

In this section, we will examine the following AI FSM concepts:

- Creating the FSM in C#
- Creating transitions
- Creating the FSM in Visual Scripting

Let's start by creating our FSM skeleton.

Creating the FSM in C#

To create our own FSM, we need to recap some basic concepts. Remember that an FSM can have a state for each possible action it can execute and that only one can be executed at a time.

In terms of AI, for example, we can be patrolling, attacking, fleeing, and so on. Also, remember that there are transitions between states that determine conditions to be met to change from one state to another, and in terms of AI, this can be the user being near the enemy to start attacking or life being low to start fleeing. In the next figure, you can find a simple reminder example of the two possible states of a door:

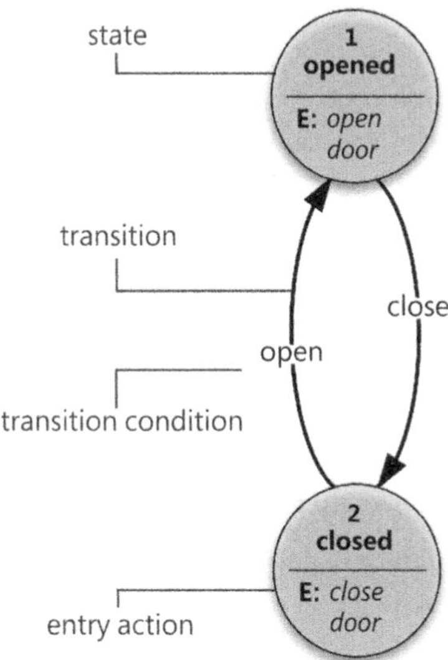

Figure 9.26: FSM example

1. There are several ways to implement FSMs for AI; you can even use the `Animator` component if you want to or download some FSM system from the Asset Store. In our case, we are going to take the simplest approach possible, a single script with a set of `If` sentences, which can be basic but is still a good start to understanding the concept. Let's implement it by doing the following:
2. Create a script called `EnemyFSM` in the `AI` child object of the enemy.
3. Create an `enum` called `EnemyState` with the `GoToBase`, `AttackBase`, `ChasePlayer`, and `AttackPlayer` values. We are going to have those states in our AI.

4. Create a field of the `EnemyState` type called `currentState`, which will hold the current state of our enemy:

```
public class EnemyFSM : MonoBehaviour
{
    public enum EnemyState { GoToBase, AttackBase, ChasePlayer, AttackPlayer }

    public EnemyState currentState;
}
```

Figure 9.27: EnemyFSM state definition

5. Create three functions named after the states we defined.
6. Call those functions in `Update` depending on the current state:

```
void Update()
{
    if (currentState == EnemyState.GoToBase) { GoToBase(); }
    else if (currentState == EnemyState.AttackBase) { AttackBase(); }
    else if (currentState == EnemyState.ChasePlayer) { ChasePlayer(); }
    else { AttackPlayer(); }
}

void GoToBase() { print("GoToBase"); }
void AttackBase() { print("AttackBase"); }
void ChasePlayer() { print("ChasePlayer"); }
void AttackPlayer() { print("AttackPlayer"); }
```

Figure 9.28: If-based FSM

Yes, you can totally use a switch here, but I just prefer the regular `if` syntax for this example.

7. Test in the editor how changing the `currentState` field will change which state is active, seeing the messages being printed in the console:

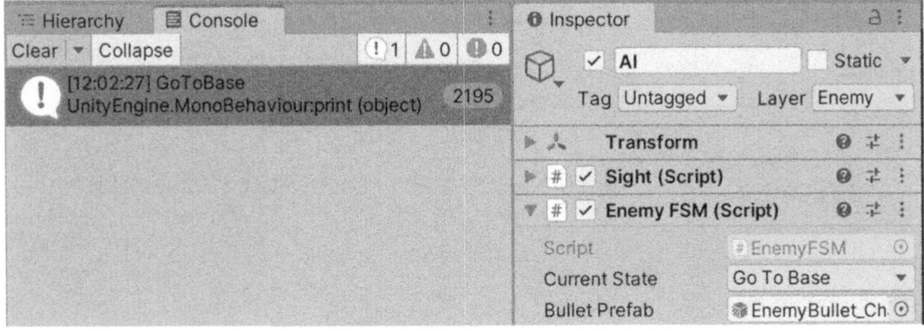

Figure 9.29: State testing

As you can see, it is a pretty simple but totally functional approach. In the future, you could face having to code enemies with many more states, and this approach will start to scale badly. In such a case, you could use any FSM plugin of the Asset Store you prefer to have more powerful and scalable tools, or even consider advanced techniques like Behavior Trees, but that's outside the scope of this book. Now let's continue with this FSM, creating its transitions.

Creating transitions

If you remember the transitions created in the `Animator Controller`, those were basically a collection of conditions that are checked if the state the transition belongs to is active. In our FSM approach, this translates simply as `If` sentences that detect conditions inside the states. Let's create the transitions between our proposed states as follows:

1. Add a field of the `Sight` type called `sightSensor` in our FSM script, and drag the AI `GameObject` to that field to connect it to the `Sight` component there. As the FSM component is in the same object as `Sight`, we can also use `GetComponent` instead, but in advanced AIs, you might have different sensors that detect different objects, so I prefer to prepare my script for that scenario. You should pick the approach you like the most.
2. In the `GoToBase` function, check whether the detected object of the `Sight` component is not `null`, meaning that something is inside our line of vision. If our AI is going toward the base but detects an object in the way, we must switch to the `Chase` state to pursue the player, so we change the state, as in the following screenshot:

```
public Sight sightSensor;

void GoToBase()
{
    if (sightSensor.detectedObject != null)
    {
        currentState = EnemyState.ChasePlayer;
    }
}
```

Figure 9.30: Creating transitions

3. Also, we must change to `AttackBase` if we are near enough to the object that must be damaged to decrease the base life. We can create a field of the `Transform` type called `baseTransform` and drag the player's base life object we created previously there so we can check the distance. Remember to add a float field called `baseAttackDistance` to make that distance configurable:

```
public Transform baseTransform;
public float baseAttackDistance;

void GoToBase()
{
    if (sightSensor.detectedObject != null)
    {
        currentState = EnemyState.ChasePlayer;
    }

    float distanceToBase = Vector3.Distance(
        transform.position, baseTransform.position);

    if (distanceToBase < baseAttackDistance)
    {
        currentState = EnemyState.AttackBase;
    }
}
```

Figure 9.31: GoToBase transitions

4. In the case of `ChasePlayer`, we need to check whether the player is out of sight to switch back to the `GoToBase` state or whether we are near enough to the player to start attacking it. We will need another distance field called `PlayerAttackDistance`, which determines the distance to attack the player, and we might want different attack distances for those two targets. Consider an early return in the transition to prevent getting `null` reference exceptions if we try to access the position of the sensor detected object when there are not any:

```
public float playerAttackDistance;

void ChasePlayer()
{
    if (sightSensor.detectedObject == null)
    {
        currentState = EnemyState.GoToBase;
        return;
    }

    float distanceToPlayer = Vector3.Distance(transform.position,
        sightSensor.detectedObject.transform.position);

    if (distanceToPlayer <= playerAttackDistance)
    {
        currentState = EnemyState.AttackPlayer;
    }
}
```

Figure 9.32: ChasePlayer transitions

5. For `AttackPlayer`, we need to check whether the player is out of sight to get back to `GoToBase` or whether it is far enough to go back to chasing it. You will notice how we multiplied `playerAttackDistance` to make the stop-attacking distance a little bit greater than the start-attacking distance; this will prevent switching back and forth rapidly between attacking and chasing when the player is near that distance.

You can make it configurable instead of hardcoding `1.1`:

```
void AttackPlayer()
{
    if (sightSensor.detectedObject == null)
    {
        currentState = EnemyState.GoToBase;
        return;
    }


    float distanceToPlayer = Vector3.Distance(transform.position,
        sightSensor.detectedObject.transform.position);

    if (distanceToPlayer > playerAttackDistance * 1.1f)
    {
        currentState = EnemyState.ChasePlayer;
    }
}
```

Figure 9.33: AttackPlayer transitions

6. In our case, `AttackBase` won't have any transition. Once the enemy is near enough to the base to attack it, it will stay like that, even if the player starts shooting at it. Its only objective once there is to destroy the base.
7. Remember you can use `Gizmos` to draw the distances:

```
private void OnDrawGizmos()
{
    Gizmos.color = Color.blue;
    Gizmos.DrawWireSphere(transform.position, playerAttackDistance);

    Gizmos.color = Color.yellow;
    Gizmos.DrawWireSphere(transform.position, baseAttackDistance);
}
```

Figure 9.34: FSM Gizmos

8. Test the script by selecting the AI Object prior to clicking play and then move the player around, checking how the states change in the inspector. You can also keep the original `print` messages in each state to see them changing in the console. Remember to set the attack distances and the references to the objects. In the screenshot, you can see the settings we use:

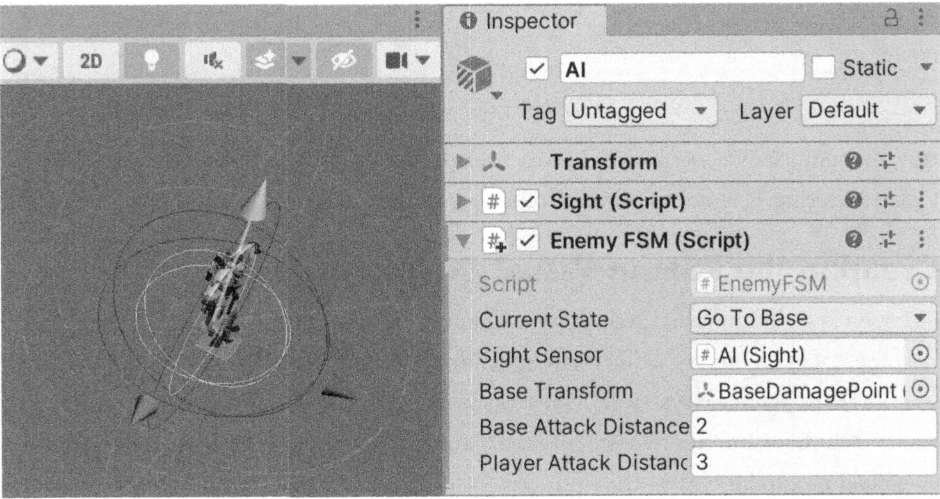

Figure 9.35: Enemy FSM settings

A little problem that we will have now is that the spawned enemies won't have the needed references to make the distance calculations to the player's base transform. You will notice that if you try to apply the changes on the enemy of the scene to the Prefab (**Overrides -> Apply All**), the **Base Transform** variable will say `None`. Remember that Prefabs cannot contain references to objects in the scene, which complicates our work here. One alternative would be to create `BaseManager`, a Singleton that holds the reference to the damage position, so our `EnemyFSM` can access it. Another one could be to make use of functions such as `GameObject.Find` to find our object.

In this case, we will see the latter. Even though it can be less performant than the `Manager` version, I want to show you how to use it to expand your Unity toolset. In this case, just set the `baseTransform` field in `Awake` to the return of `GameObject.Find`, using `BaseDamagePoint` as the first parameter, which will look for an object with the same name, as in the following screenshot.

You will see that now our wave-spawned enemies will change states:

```
private Transform baseTransform;

private void Awake()
{
    baseTransform = GameObject.Find("BaseDamagePoint").transform;
}
```

Figure 9.36: Searching for an object in the scene by name

Now that our FSM states are coded and execute transitions properly, let's see how to do the same in Visual Scripting. Feel free to skip the following section if you are only interested in the C# version.

Creating the FSM in Visual Scripting

So far, most scripts in Visual Scripting were almost a mirror of the C# version with some differences in some nodes. While regarding state machines we could do the same, instead, we are going to use the **State Machine** system of Visual Scripting. The concept is the same, you have states and can switch them, but how the states are organized and when the transitions trigger is managed visually, in a similar way as the Animator system does. So, let's see how we can use the system by creating our first `State Machine Graph` and some `states`. Follow these steps:

1. Add the **State Machine** component to our enemy. Remember it is called **State Machine** and not **Script Machine**, the latter being the component for regular Visual Scripts.
2. Click the **New** button in the component and select a place to save the `fixed` asset in a similar way to what we have done so far for regular Visual Scripts. In my case, I called it `EnemyFSM`.

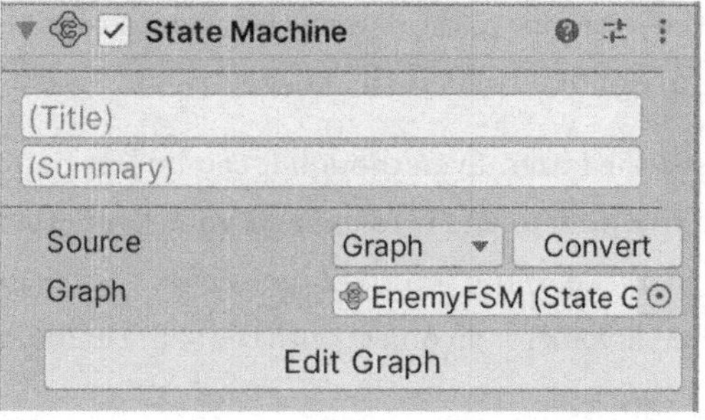

Figure 9.37: Creating a Visual State Machine

3. Double-click **State Machine Graph** to edit it as usual.
4. Right-click in any empty area of the **Graph** editor and select **Create Script State** in order to create a new state:

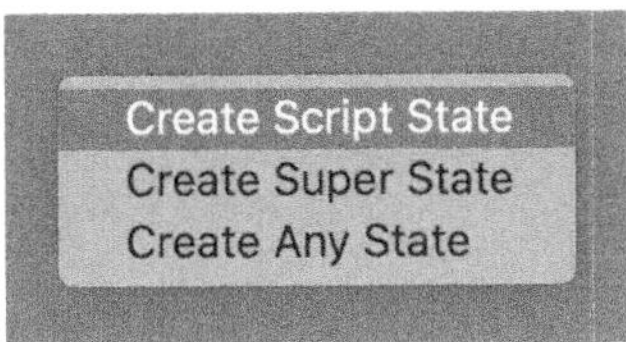

Figure 9.38: Creating our first Visual State Machine State

5. Repeat *step 4* until you end up having 4 states:

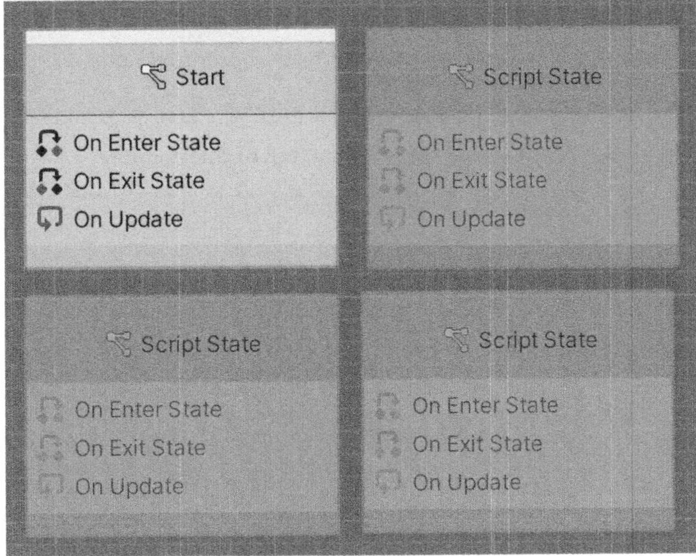

Figure 9.39: Visual states

6. Select any of them and in the **Info** panel on the left, fill the **Title** field (the first one) with the name of any of the states we created before (`GoToBase`, `AttackBase`, `ChasePlayer`, and `AttackPlayer`). If you don't see the **Info** panel, click the button with the **i** in the middle to display it:

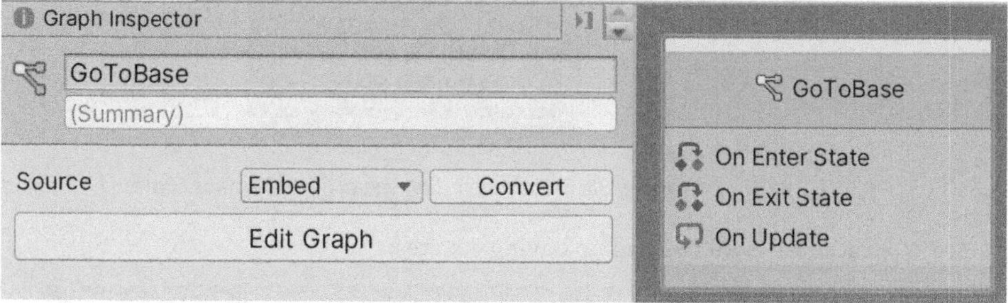

Figure 9.40: Renaming a Visual State

7. Repeat that for the rest of the state nodes until you have each node named after each state created in the *Creating the FSM in C#* section of this chapter:

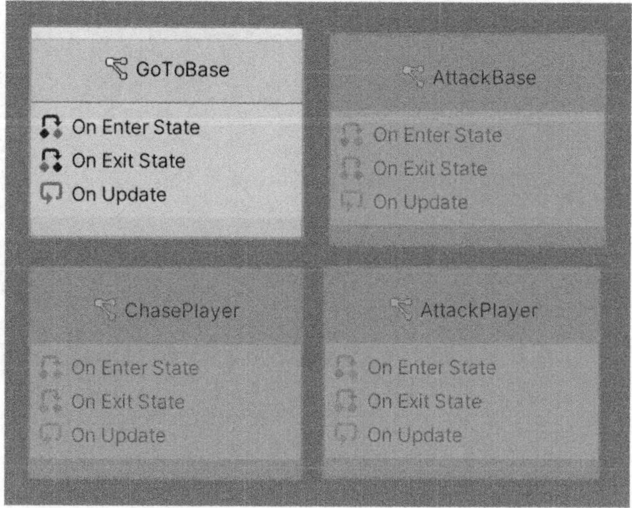

Figure 9.41: All needed states

8. You can see one of the states has a green bar at the top, which represents which node is supposed to be the first one. I renamed that initial state `GoToBase` as that's the one I prefer to be first. If you don't have that one as the starting one, right-click the node that currently has the green bar in your state machine, select **Toggle Start** to remove the green bar from it, and then repeat for the node that you want to be the first one (`GoToBase` in our scenario), adding the green bar to that one.

Something to consider is that you can have more than one start state in Visual Scripting, meaning you can have multiple states running at the same time and transitioning. If possible, I recommend avoiding having more than one state active at a time to make things simple.

9. Double-click `GoToBase` to enter the edit mode for these states. Connect a **String** node to the **print Message** input pin in the **OnUpdate** event node to print a message saying `GoToBase`:

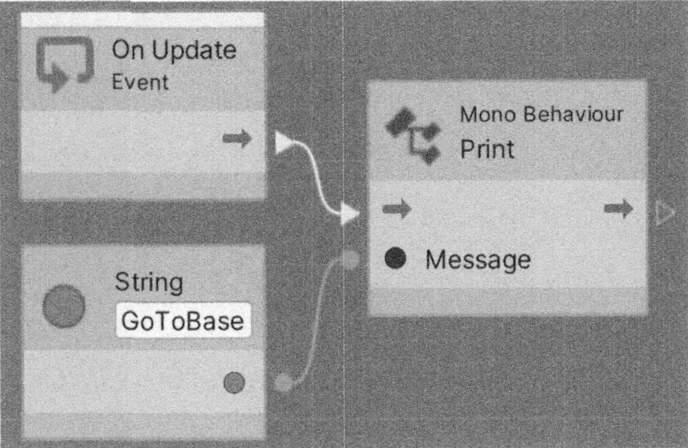

Figure 9.42: Our first state machine logic

10. In the top bar, click the **EnemyFSM** label at the left of **GoToBase** in order to return to the whole State Machine view. If you don't see it, click any text label at the right of the third button (the one that looks like *<x>*):

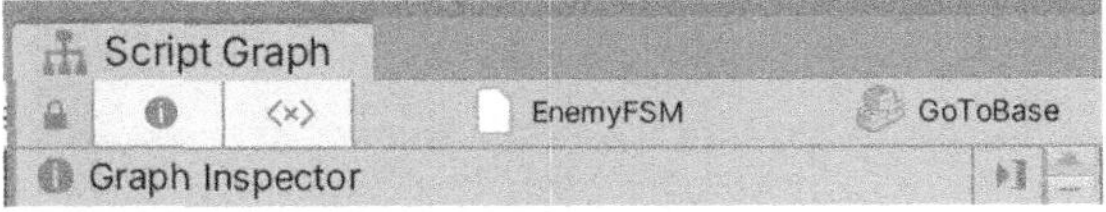

Figure 9.43: Returning to the State Machine editor mode

11. Feel free to delete the other event nodes if you are not planning to use them.
12. Repeat *steps 9-11* for each state until all of them print their names.

With this, we have created the nodes representing the possible states of our AI. In the next section, we will be adding logic for them to something meaningful, but before that, we need to create the transitions between the states and the conditions that need to be met to trigger them by doing the following:

1. Create variables in the **Variables** component of the enemy called `baseTransform`, `baseAttackDistance`, and `playerAttackDistance` as we are going to need them to do the transitions.
2. Don't set any type to `baseTransform` as we will fill it later via code, but regarding `baseAttackDistance`, make it using the **Float** type and put a value of 2, and finally for `playerAttackDistance`, also use **Float** and a value of `3`. Feel free to change those values if you prefer:

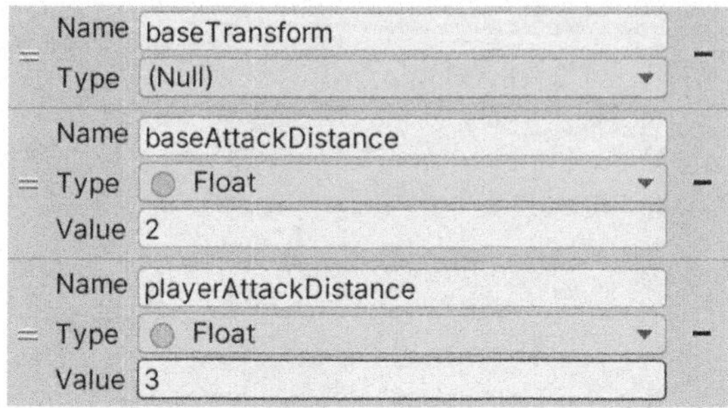

Figure 9.44: Variables needed for our transitions

3. Right-click the `GoToBase` node and select the **Make Transition** option, and then click the `ChasePlayer` node. This will create a transition between the two states:

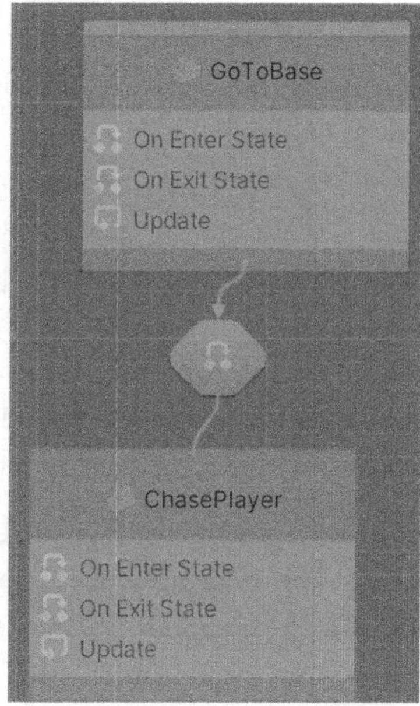

Figure 9.45: A transition between two states

4. Repeat *step 3* for each transition we created in the C# version. The `State Machine Graph` will need to look like the following screenshot:

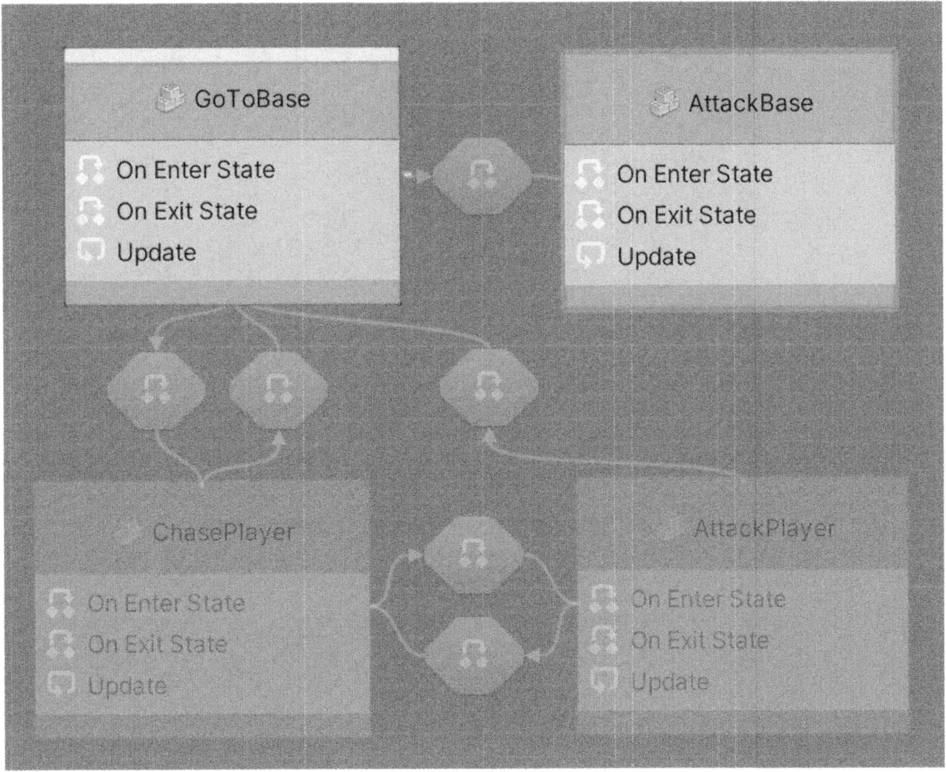

Figure 9.46: All the needed transitions

5. Double-click the yellow shape in the middle of the transition between **GoToBase** and **ChasePlayer** to enter the **Transition** mode. Here, you will be able to specify the condition that will trigger that transition (instead of using an `If` node during the state logic). Remember you have two yellow shapes, one for each transition direction, so check you are double-clicking the correct one based on the white arrows connecting them.

6. Modify the graph in order to check if the `sensedObject` variable is not `null`. It should look like this:

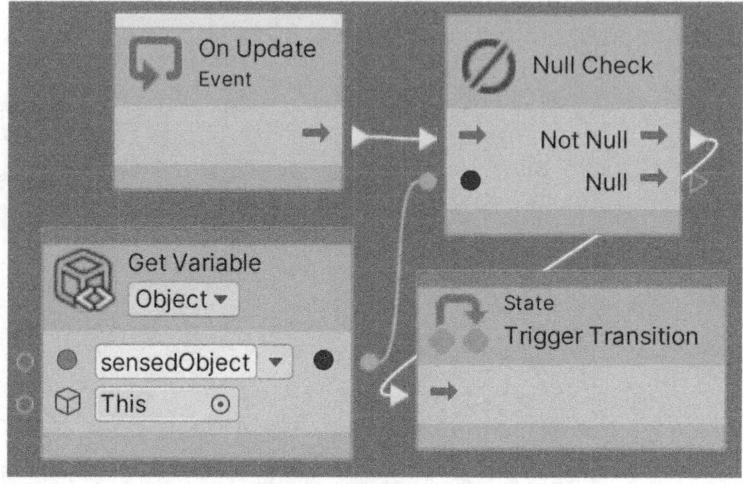

Figure 9.47: Adding a transition condition

7. The transition between **GoToBase** and **AttackBase** should look like this:

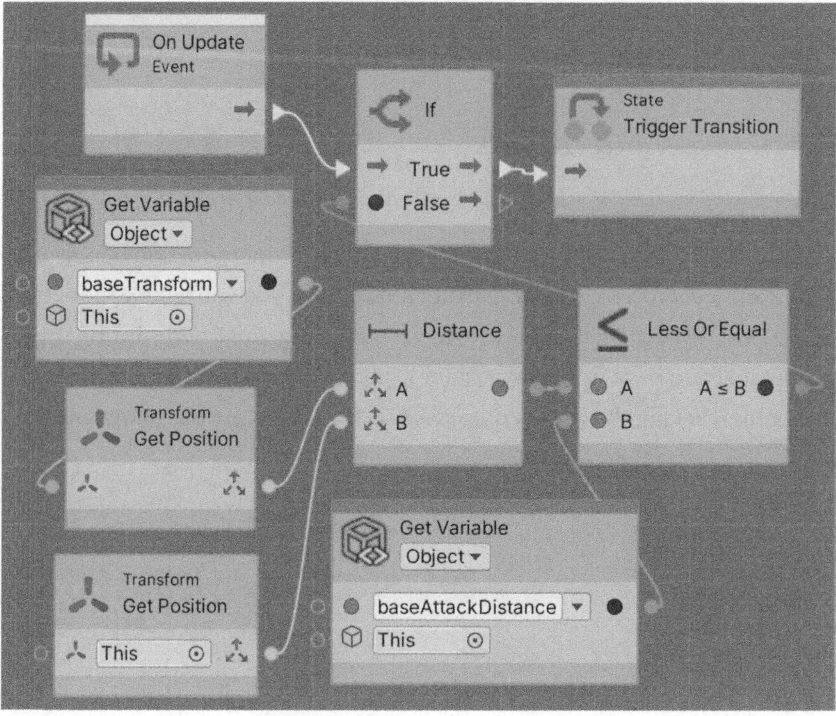

Figure 9.48: GoToBase to AttackBase transition condition

8. Now, **ChasePlayer** to **GoToBase** should be as follows:

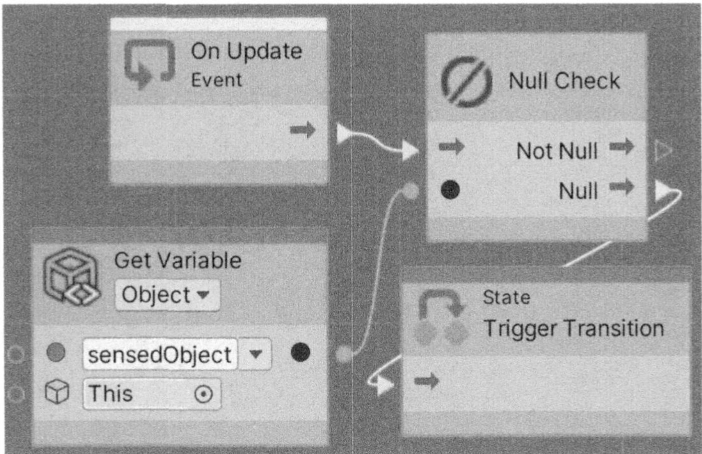

Figure 9.49: ChasePlayer to GoToBase transition condition

9. For the **ChasePlayer** to **AttackPlayer** transition, do as in *Figure 9.50*. This is essentially the same as **GoToBase** and **AttackBase**, a distance check, but with different targets:

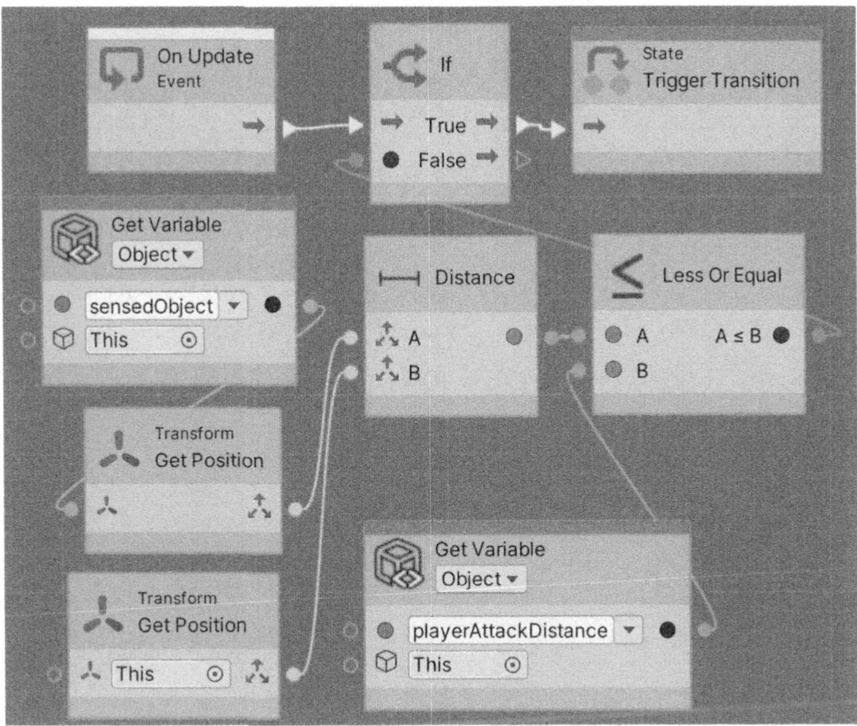

Figure 9.50: ChasePlayer to AttackPlayer transition condition

10. For the **AttackPlayer** to **ChasePlayer** transition, do as in *Figure 9.51*. This is another distance check but is now checking if the distance is greater and multiplying the distance by `1.1` (to prevent transition jittering as we explained in the C# version):

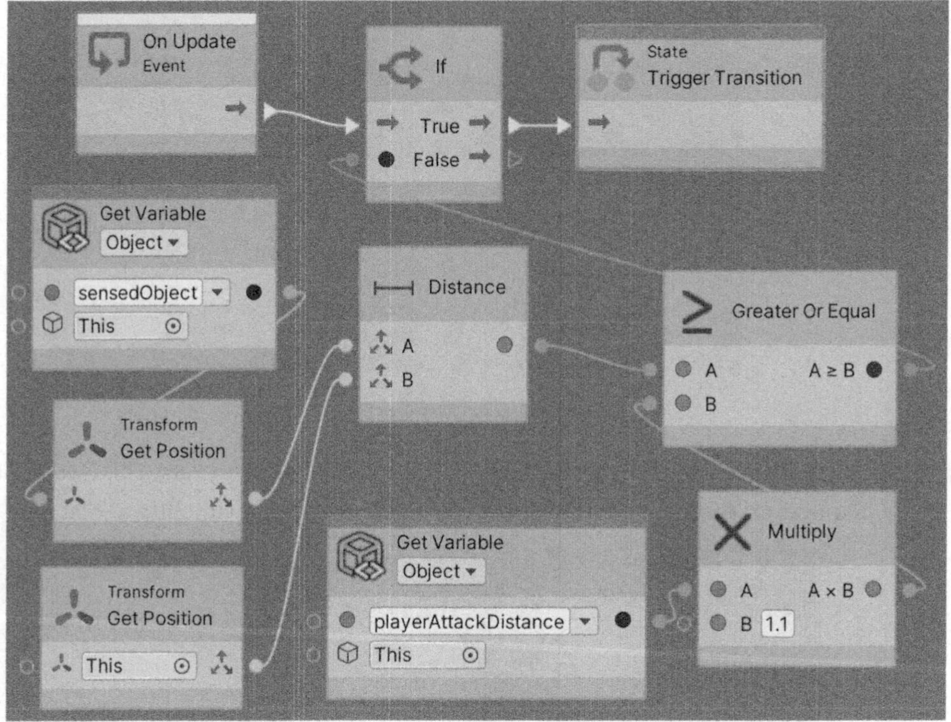

Figure 9.51: AttackPlayer to ChasePlayer transition condition

11. Finally, for **AttackPlayer** to **GoToBase** this is the expected graph:

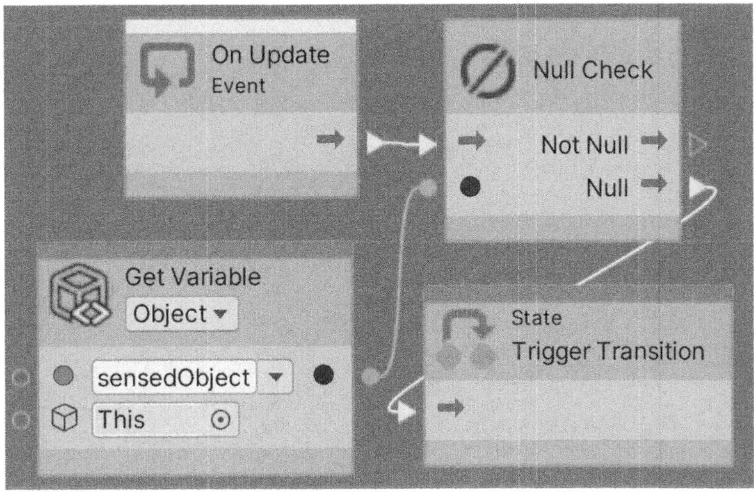

Figure 9.52: AttackPlayer to GoToBase transition condition

A little detail we need to tackle before moving on is the fact that we still don't have any value set in the `baseTransform` variable. The idea is to fill it via code as we did in the C# version. But something to consider here is that we cannot add an `Awake` event node to the whole state machine, but just to the states.

In this scenario, we could use the **OnEnterState** event, which is an exclusive event node for state machines. It will execute as soon as the state becomes active, which is useful for state initializations. We could add the logic to initialize the `baseTransform` variable in the **OnEnterState** event node of the **GoToBase** state, given it is the first state we execute.

This way, **GoToBase** logic will look as in *Figure 9.53*. Remember to double-click the state node to edit it:

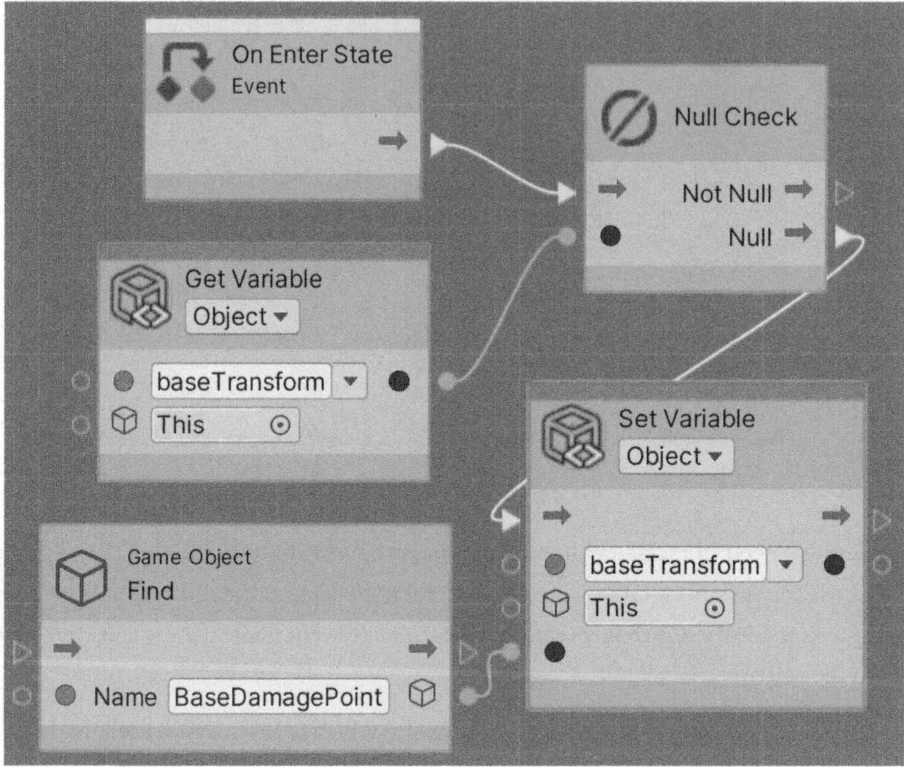

Figure 9.53: GoToBase initialization logic

Notice how, here, we set the result of the **Find** node into the variable only on the **Null** pin of **Null Check**. What **Null Check** does is check if our **baseTransform** variable is set, going through the `Not Null` pin if it is, and `Null` if it isn't. This way we avoid executing **GameObject.Find** every time we enter the **GoToBase** state, but only the first time. Also, note that in this case, we will be executing the **Set Variable** node not only when the object initializes, but also each time **GoToBase** becomes the current state. If, in any case, that results in unexpected behavior, other options could be to create a new initial state that initializes everything and then transitions to the rest of the states, or maybe do a classic Visual Script graph that initializes those variables in the **On Start** event node.

With all this, we learned how to create a decision-making system for our AI through FSMs. It will make decisions based on the info gathered via sensors and other systems. Now that our FSM states are coded and transition properly, let's make them do something.

Executing FSM actions

Now we need to complete the last step—make the FSM do something interesting. Here, we can do a lot of things such as shoot the base or the player and move the enemy toward its target (the base or the player). We will be handling movement with the Unity Pathfinding system called `NavMesh`, a tool that allows our AI to calculate and traverse paths between two points while avoiding obstacles, which needs some preparation to work properly.

In this section, we will examine the following FSM action concepts:

- Calculating our scene's NavMesh
- Using Pathfinding
- Adding final details

Let's start by preparing our scene for movement with Pathfinding.

Calculating our scene's NavMesh

Pathfinding algorithms rely on simplified versions of the scene. Analyzing the full geometry of a complex scene is almost impossible to do in real time. There are several ways to represent Pathfinding information extracted from a scene, such as Graphs and `NavMesh` geometries. Unity uses the latter—a simplified mesh similar to a 3D model that spans all areas that Unity determines are walkable. In the next screenshot, you can find an example of `NavMesh` generated in a scene, that is, the light blue geometry:

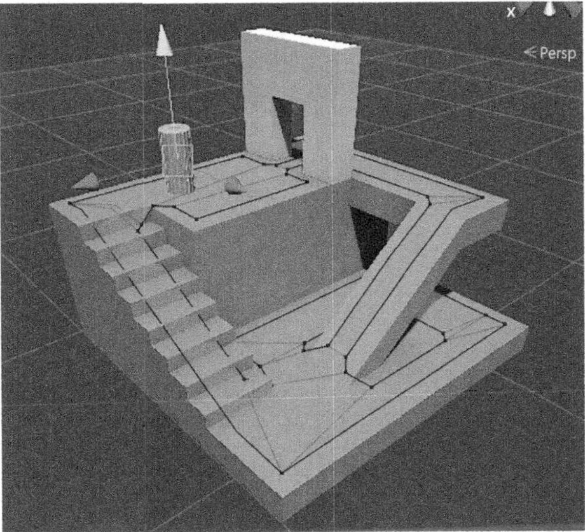

Figure 9.54: NavMesh of walkable areas in the scene

Generating NavMesh can take from seconds to minutes depending on the size of the scene. That's why Unity's Pathfinding system calculates the NavMesh once in the editor, so when we distribute our game, the user will use the pre-generated NavMesh. Just like Lightmapping, NavMesh is baked into a file for later usage. Like Lightmapping, the main caveat here is that NavMesh objects cannot change during runtime. If you destroy or move a floor tile, the AI will still walk over that area. The NavMesh on top of that didn't notice the floor isn't there anymore, so you are not able to move or modify those objects in any way. Luckily, in our case, we won't suffer any modification of the scene during runtime, but note that there are components such as NavMeshObstacle that can help us in those scenarios.

To generate NavMesh for our scene, do the following:

1. Select any walkable object and the obstacles on top of it, such as floors, walls, and other obstacles, and mark them as **Static**. You might remember that the **Static** checkbox also affects Lightmapping, so if you want an Object not to be part of Lightmapping but to contribute to the NavMesh generation, you can click the arrow at the left of the static check and select **Navigation Static** only. Try to limit Navigation Static GameObjects to only the ones that the enemies will actually traverse to increase NavMesh generation speed. Making the terrain navigable, in our case, will increase the generation time a lot and we will never play in that area.
2. Open the NavMesh panel in **Window | AI | Navigation**.
3. Select the **Bake** tab, click on the **Bake** button at the bottom of the window, and check the generated NavMesh:

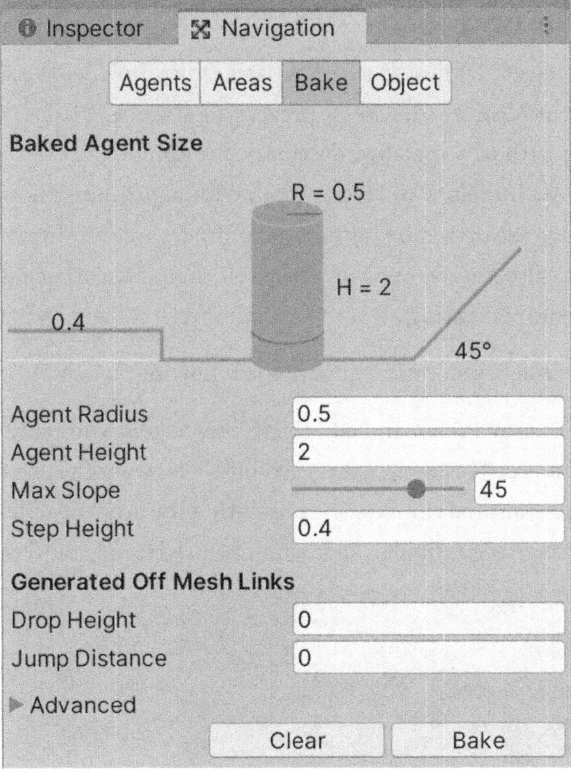

Figure 9.55: Generating a NavMesh

And that's pretty much everything you need to do. Of course, there are lots of settings you can fiddle around with, such as **Max Slope**, which indicates the maximum angle of slopes the AI will be able to climb, or **Step Height**, which will determine whether the AI can climb stairs, connecting the floors between the steps in `NavMesh`, but as we have a plain and simple scene, the default settings will suffice.

Now, let's make our AI move around `NavMesh`.

Using Pathfinding

For making an AI object that moves with `NavMesh`, Unity provides the `NavMeshAgent` component, which will make our AI stick to `NavMesh`, preventing the object from going outside it. It will not only calculate the path to a specified destination automatically but also will move the object through the path with the use of Steering behavior algorithms that mimic the way a human would move through the path, slowing down on corners and turning with interpolations instead of instantaneously. Also, this component is capable of evading other `NavMeshAgent GameObjects` running in the scene, preventing all of the enemies from collapsing in the same position.

Let's use this powerful component by doing the following:

1. Select the **Enemy** Prefab and add the `NavMeshAgent` component to it. Add it to the root object, the one called `Enemy`, not the AI child—we want the whole object to move. You will see a cylinder around the object representing the area the object will occupy in `NavMesh`. Note that this isn't a collider, so it won't be used for physical collisions:

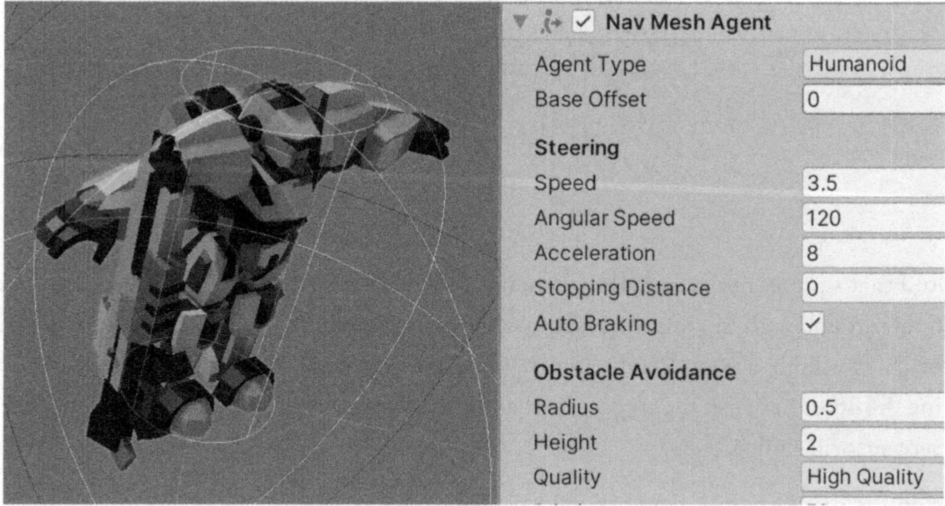

Figure 9.56: The NavMeshAgent component

2. Remove the `ForwardMovement` component; from now on, we will drive the movement of our enemy with `NavMeshAgent`.

3. In the Awake event function of the EnemyFSM script, use the GetComponentInParent function to cache the reference of NavMeshAgent. This will work similarly to GetComponent—it will look for a component in our GameObject, but if the component is not there, this version will try to look for that component in all parents. Remember to add the using UnityEngine.AI line to use the NavMeshAgent class in this script:

```
private NavMeshAgent agent;

private void Awake()
{
    baseTransform = GameObject.Find("BaseDamagePoint").transform;
    agent = GetComponentInParent<NavMeshAgent>();
}
```

Figure 9.57: Caching a parent component reference

As you can imagine, there is also the GetComponentInChildren method, which searches components in GameObject first and then in all its children if necessary.

4. In the GoToBase state function, call the SetDestination function of the NavMeshAgent reference, passing the position of the base object as the target:

```
void GoToBase()
{
    agent.SetDestination(baseTransform.position);
```

Figure 9.58: Setting a destination for our AI

5. Save the script and test this with a few enemies in the scene or with the enemies spawned by the waves. You will see the problem where the enemies will never stop going toward the target position, entering inside the object, if necessary, even if the current state of their FSMs changes when they are near enough. That's because we never tell NavMeshAgent to stop, which we can do by setting the isStopped field of the agent to true.

You might want to tweak the base attack distance to make the enemy stop a little bit closer or further away:

```
void AttackBase()
{
    agent.isStopped = true;
}
```

Figure 9.59: Stopping agent movement

6. We can do the same for `ChasePlayer` and `AttackPlayer`. In `ChasePlayer`, we can set the destination of the agent to the player's position, and in `AttackPlayer`, we can stop the movement. In this scenario, Attack Player can go back again to `GoToBase` or `ChasePlayer`, so you need to set the `isStopped` agent field to `false` in those states or before doing the transition. We will pick the former, as that version will cover other states that also stop the agent without extra code. We will start with the `GoToBase` state:

```
void GoToBase()
{
    agent.isStopped = false;
    agent.SetDestination(baseTransform.position);
```

Figure 9.60: Reactivating the agent

7. Then, continue with `ChasePlayer`:

```
void ChasePlayer()
{
    agent.isStopped = false;

    if (sightSensor.detectedObject == null)
    {
        currentState = EnemyState.GoToBase;
        return;
    }

    agent.SetDestination(sightSensor.detectedObject.transform.position);
```

Figure 9.61: Reactivating the agent and chasing the player

8. And finally, continue with `AttackPlayer`:

```
void AttackPlayer()
{
    agent.isStopped = true;
```

Figure 9.62: Stopping the movement

9. You can tweak the **Acceleration**, **Speed**, and **Angular Speed** properties of `NavMeshAgent` to control how fast the enemy will move. Also, remember to apply the changes to the Prefab for the spawned enemies to be affected.
10. Regarding the Visual Scripting versions, `GoToBase` will look like the following screenshot:

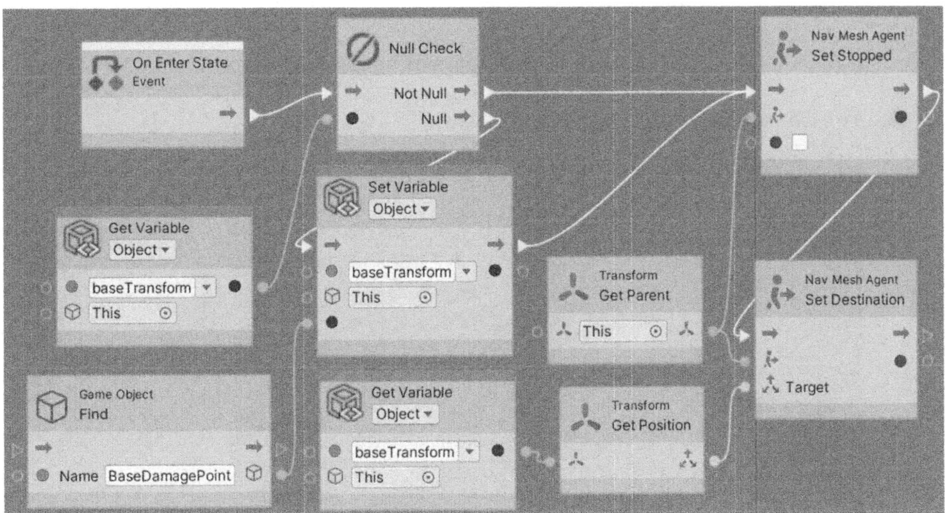

Figure 9.63: Making our agent move

11. We deleted the **OnUpdate** event node printing a message as we don't need it anymore. Also, we called the **Set Destination** node after setting the variable if `if` was `null`, and also when the variable wasn't `null` (**Not Null** pin of **Null** Check). Note that all of this happens in the **On Enter State** event, so we just need to do it once. We do it every frame in the C# version for simplicity but that's actually not necessary, so we will take advantage of the **OnEnterState** event. We can emulate that behavior in the C# version if we want, executing these actions at the moment we change the state (inside the `If` statements that check the transition conditions), instead of using the **Update** function. Finally, notice how we needed to use the **GetParent** node in order to access the `NavMeshAgent` component in the enemy's root object? This is needed because we are currently in the **AI** child object instead.

12. Now, the **AttackBase** state will look like this:

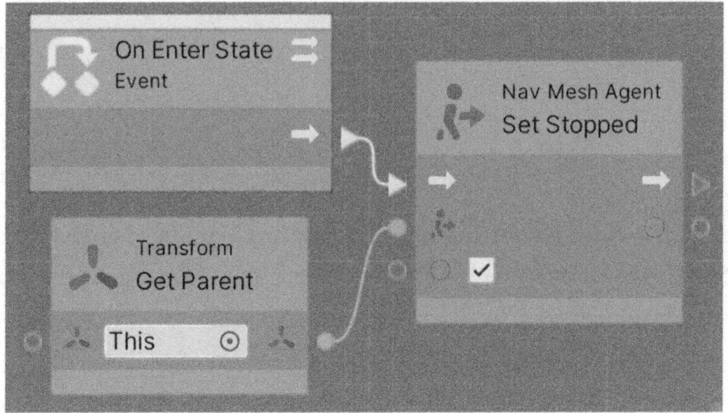

Figure 9.64: Making our agent stop

13. The **ChasePlayer** state will look like this:

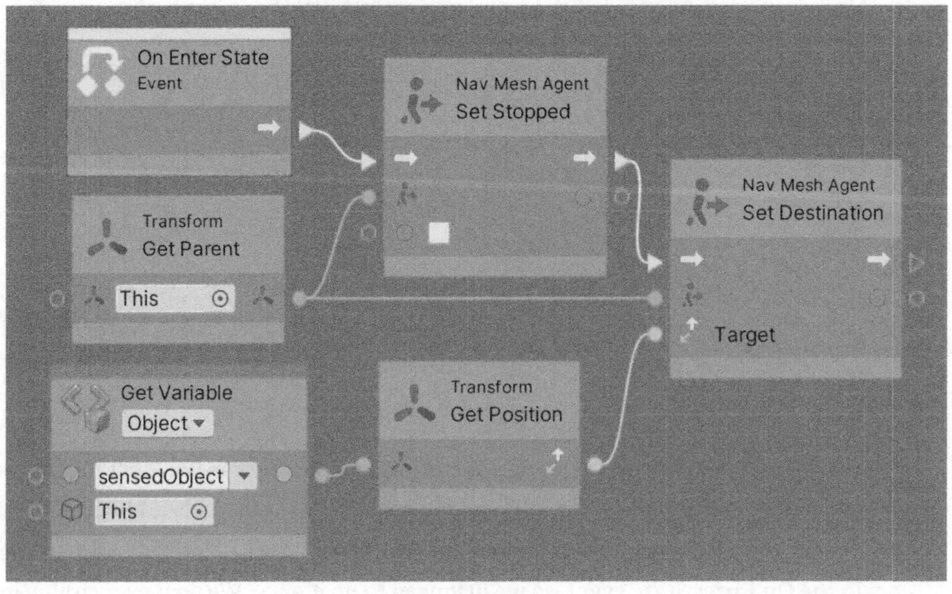

Figure 9.65: ChasePlayer logic

14. And finally, **AttackPlayer** like this:

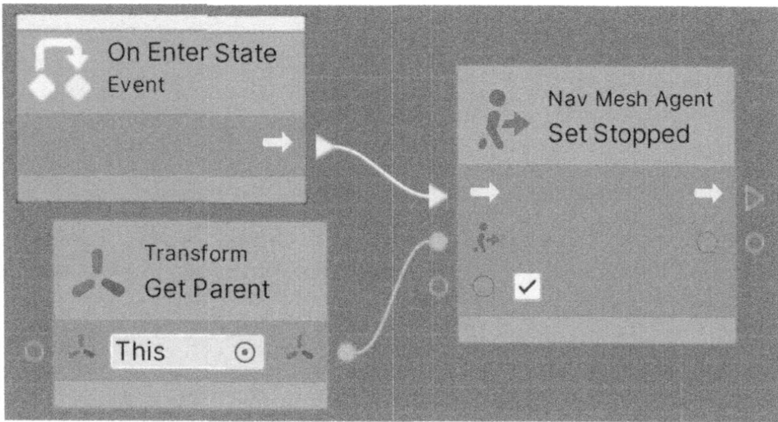

Figure 9.66: AttackPlayer logic

Now that we have movement in our enemy, let's finish the final details of our AI.

Adding the final details

We have two things missing here: the enemy is not shooting any bullets, and it doesn't have animations. Let's start with fixing the shooting by doing the following:

1. Add a `bulletPrefab` field of the `GameObject` type to our `EnemyFSM` script and a `float` field called `fireRate`.

2. Create a function called `Shoot` and call it inside `AttackBase` and `AttackPlayer`:

```
void AttackPlayer()
{
    agent.isStopped = true;

    if (sightSensor.detectedObject == null)
    {
        currentState = EnemyState.GoToBase;
        return;
    }

    Shoot();

    float distanceToPlayer = Vector3.Distance(transform.position,
        sightSensor.detectedObject.transform.position);

    if (distanceToPlayer > playerAttackDistance * 1.1f)
    {
        currentState = EnemyState.ChasePlayer;
    }
}

void AttackBase()
{
    agent.isStopped = true;
    Shoot();
}

void Shoot()
{

}
```

Figure 9.67: Shooting function calls

3. In the `Shoot` function, put similar code as that used in the `PlayerShooting` script to shoot bullets at a specific fire rate, as in *Figure 9.68*. Remember to set the **Enemy** layer in your **Enemy** Prefab, if you didn't before, to prevent the bullet from damaging the enemy itself. You might also want to raise the AI GameObject position a little bit to shoot bullets from a position other than the ground or, better, add a `shootPoint` transform field and create an empty object in the enemy to use as a spawn position. If you do that, consider making the empty object not be rotated so the enemy rotation affects the direction of the bullet properly:

```
public float lastShootTime;
public GameObject bulletPrefab;
public float fireRate;

void Shoot()
{
    var timeSinceLastShoot :float = Time.time - lastShootTime;
    if (timeSinceLastShoot > fireRate)
    {
        lastShootTime = Time.time;
        Instantiate(bulletPrefab,
            transform.position, transform.rotation);
    }
}
```

Figure 9.68: Shoot function code

Here, you find some duplicated shooting behavior between `PlayerShooting` and `EnemyFSM`. You can fix that by creating a **Weapon** behavior with a function called `Shoot` that instantiates bullets and takes into account the fire rate and call it inside both components to re-utilize it.

4. When the agent is stopped, not only does the movement stop but also the rotation. If the player moves while the enemy is being attacked, we still need the enemy to face the player to shoot bullets in its direction. We can create a `LookTo` function that receives the target position to look at and call it in `AttackPlayer` and `AttackBase`, passing the target to shoot at:

```
    LookTo(sightSensor.detectedObject.transform.position);
    Shoot();

    float distanceToPlayer = Vector3.Distance(transform.position,
        sightSensor.detectedObject.transform.position);

    if (distanceToPlayer > playerAttackDistance * 1.1f)
    {
        currentState = EnemyState.ChasePlayer;
    }
}

void AttackBase()
{
    agent.isStopped = true;
    LookTo(baseTransform.position);
    Shoot();
}

void LookTo(Vector3 targetPosition)
{

}
```

Figure 9.69: LookTo function calls

5. Complete the `LookTo` function by calculating the direction of our parent to the target position. We access our parent with `transform.parent` because, remember, we are the child AI object—the object that will move is our parent. Then, we set the `Y` component of the direction to `0` to prevent the direction from pointing upward or downward—we don't want our enemy to rotate vertically. Finally, we set the forward vector of our parent to that direction so it will face the target position immediately. You can replace that with interpolation through quaternions to have a smoother rotation if you want to, but let's keep things as simple as possible for now:

```
void LookTo(Vector3 targetPosition)
{
    Vector3 directionToPosition = Vector3.Normalize(
        targetPosition - transform.parent.position);
    directionToPosition.y = 0;
    transform.parent.forward = directionToPosition;
}
```

Figure 9.70: Looking toward a target

6. Regarding the Visual Scripting version, **AttackBase** actions look like this:

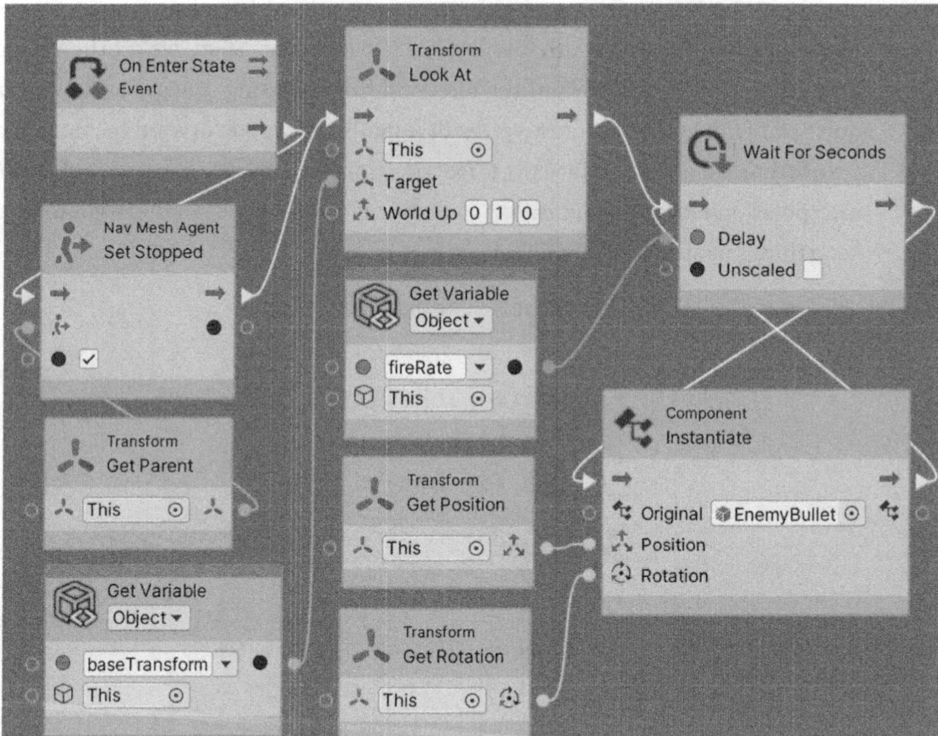

Figure 9.71: AttackBase state

In this state, we have some things to highlight. First, we are using the **LookAt** node in the **OnEnterState** event node after the **SetStopped** node. As you might imagine, this does the same as we did with math in C#. We specify a target to look at (our base transform) and then we specify that the **World Up** parameter is a vector pointing upwards `0,1,0`. This will make our object look at the base but maintain its up vector pointing to the sky, meaning our object will not look at the floor if the target is lower than him. We can use this exact function in C# if we want to (`transform.LookAt`); the idea was just to show you all the options. Also note that we execute `LookAt` only when the state becomes active—as the base doesn't move, we don't need to constantly update our orientation.

The second thing to highlight is that we used coroutines to shoot, the same idea we used in the `Enemy Spawner` to constantly spawn enemies. Essentially, we make an infinite loop between **Wait For Seconds** and **Instantiate**. We took this approach here because it was convenient given it takes fewer nodes in Visual Scripting.

Remember to select the **OnEnterState** node and check the **Coroutine** checkbox as we did before. Also, we need a new Float type variable called `fireRate` in the Enemy's AI child object:

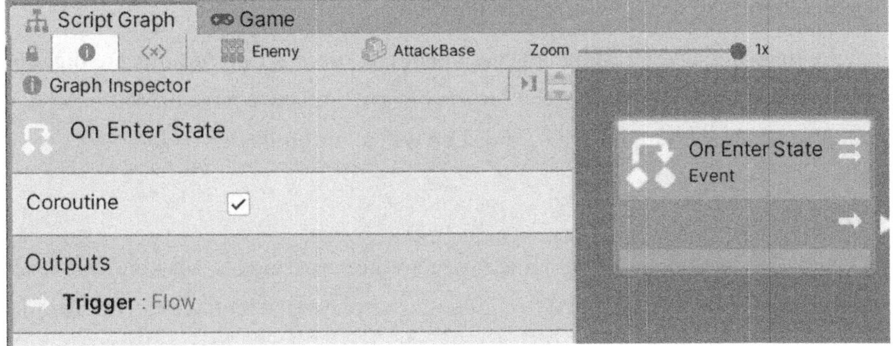

Figure 9.72: Coroutines

Then, **AttackPlayer** will look like this:

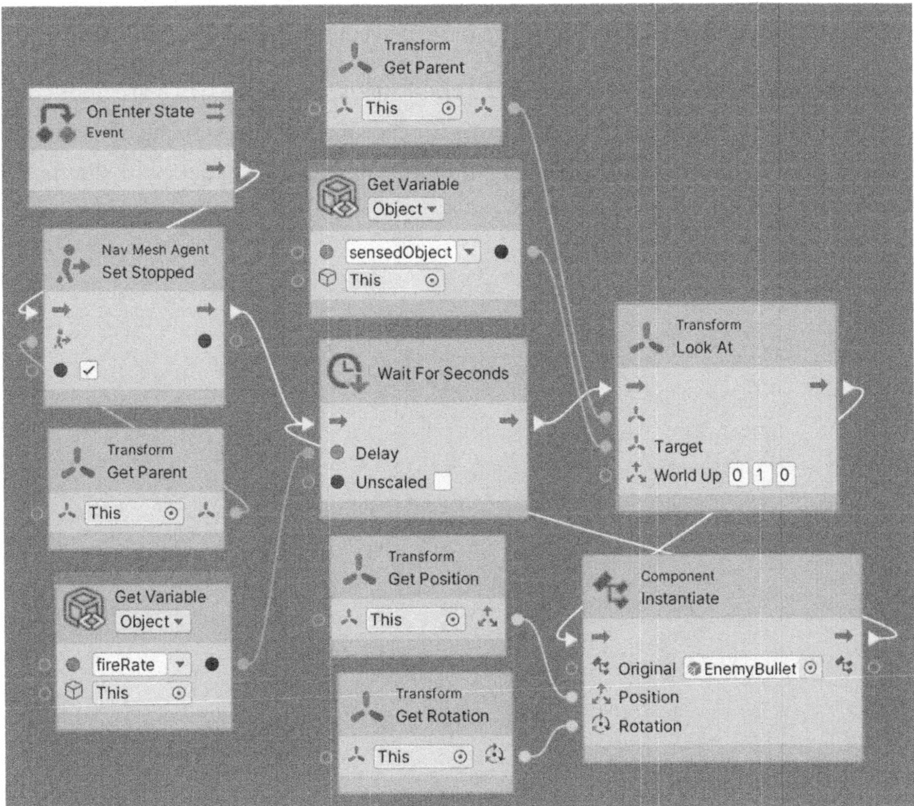

Figure 9.73: AttackPlayer state

Essentially it is the same as **AttackBase**, but that looks towards the `sensedObject` instead toward the player's base, and we also made the **LookAt** node part of the infinite loop, to correct the enemy's heading before shooting to target the player.

With that, we have finished all AI behaviors. Of course, these scripts/graphs are big enough to deserve some rework and splitting in the future, but with this, we have prototyped our AI, and we can test it until we are happy with it, and then we can improve this code.

Summary

I'm pretty sure AI is not what you imagined; you are not creating Skynet here, but we have accomplished a simple but interesting AI to challenge our players, which we can iterate and tweak to tailor to our game's expected behavior. We saw how to gather our surrounding information through sensors to make decisions on what action to execute using FSMs and using different Unity systems such as Pathfinding to make the AI execute those actions. We used those systems to diagram a State Machine capable of detecting the player, running to them, and attacking them, and if the player is not there, just going to the base to accomplish its task to destroy it.

In the next chapter, we are going to start *Part 3* of this book, where we will learn about different Unity systems to improve the graphics and audio aspects of our game, starting by seeing how we can create materials to modify the aspect of our objects and create Shaders with Shader Graph.

10

Materials and Effects with URP and Shader Graph

Welcome to the first chapter of *Part 3*. Here, we will dive deep into the different graphics and audio systems of Unity to dramatically improve the look and feel of the game. We will start by discussing what a shader is and how to create our own to achieve several custom effects that couldn't be accomplished using the default Unity Shaders. We will be creating a simple water animation effect using Shader Graph, a visual shader editor included in the Universal Render Pipeline. Also known as URP, this is one of the different rendering pipelines available in Unity, which provides rendering features oriented toward performance. We will be discussing some of its capabilities in this chapter.

In this chapter, we will examine the following shader concepts:

- Introducing shaders and URP
- Creating shaders with Shader Graph

Introducing shaders and URP

We created **Materials** in *Part 1* of the book, but we never discussed how they internally work and why their **Shader** property is important. In this first section of this chapter, we will be exploring the concept of a shader as a way to program the video card to achieve custom visual effects. We will also be discussing how URP works with those shaders, and the default shaders it provides.

In this section, we will cover the following concepts related to shaders:

- Shader Pipeline
- Render Pipeline and URP
- URP built-in shaders

Let's start by discussing how a shader modifies the Shader Pipeline to achieve effects.

Shader Pipeline

Whenever a video card renders a 3D model, it needs different information to process, such as a **Mesh**, **Textures**, the transform of the object (position, rotation, and scale), and lights that affect that object. With that data, the video card must output the pixels of the object into the **back-buffer**, an image where the video card will be drawing our objects, but the user won't see this yet. This is done to prevent the user from seeing unfinished results, given we can still be drawing at the time the monitor refreshes. That image will be shown when Unity finishes rendering all objects (and some effects) to display the finished scene, swapping the **Back-buffer** with the **front-buffer**, the image that the user actually sees. You can imagine this as having a page with an image that is being shown to the user while you draw a new image, and when you finish the new drawing, you just swap the pages and start drawing again on the page the user is not seeing, repeating this with every frame.

That's the usual way to render an object, but what happens between the input of the data and the output of the pixels can be handled in a myriad of different ways and techniques that depend on how you want your object to look; maybe you want it to be realistic or look like a hologram, maybe the object needs a disintegration effect or a toon effect—there are endless possibilities. The way to specify how our video card will handle the render of the object is through a shader.

A **shader** is a program coded in specific video card languages, such as:

- **HLSL**: The DirectX shading language, DirectX being a graphics library.
- **GLSL**: The OpenGL shading language, OpenGL also being a graphics library.
- **CG**: A language that can output either HLSL or GLSL, depending on which graphics library we use in our game.
- **Shader Graph**: A visual language that will be automatically converted into one of the previously mentioned languages according to our needs. This is the one we will be using given its simplicity (more on that later).

Any of those languages can be used to configure different stages of the render process necessary to render a given object, sometimes not only configuring them but also replacing them with completely custom code to achieve the exact effect we want. All of the stages to render an object make up what we call the Shader Pipeline, a chain of modifications applied to the input data until it is transformed into pixels.

Each stage of the pipeline is in charge of different modifications and depending on the video card shader model, this pipeline can vary a lot. In the next diagram, you can find a simplified Render Pipeline, skipping advanced/optional stages that are not important right now:

Figure 10.1: Common Shader Pipeline

Let's discuss each of the stages:

- **Input Assembler**: Here is where all of the mesh data, such as vertex position, UVs, and normals, is assembled to be prepared for the next stage.
- **Vertex Shader**: This stage used to be limited to applying the transformation of the object, the position and perspective of the camera, and simple lighting calculations. In modern GPUs, you are in charge of doing whatever you want. This stage receives each one of the vertexes of the object to render and outputs a modified one. You have the chance to modify the geometry of the object here. The usual code here is applying the transform of the object, but you can also apply several effects such as inflating the object along its normals to apply the old toon effect technique or apply distortion adding random offsets to each vertex to recreate a hologram. There's also the opportunity to calculate data for the next stages.
- **Culling**: Most of the models you are going to render have the particularity that you will never see the back side of a model face. In a cube, there's no way to look at its inner sides. Given that, rendering both sides of each face of the cube makes no sense, and this stage takes care of that. Culling will determine whether the face needs to be rendered based on the orientation of the face, saving lots of pixel calculation of occluded faces. You can change this to behave differently for specific cases; as an example, we can create a glass box that needs to be transparent to see all sides of the box.

- **Rasterizer**: Now that we have the modified and visible geometry of our model calculated, it's time to convert it into pixels. The rasterizer creates all pixels for the triangles of our mesh. Lots of things happen here but again, we have very little control of that; the usual way to rasterize is just to create all pixels inside the edges of the mesh triangles. We have other modes that just render the pixels on the edges to see a wireframe effect, but this is usually used for debugging purposes:

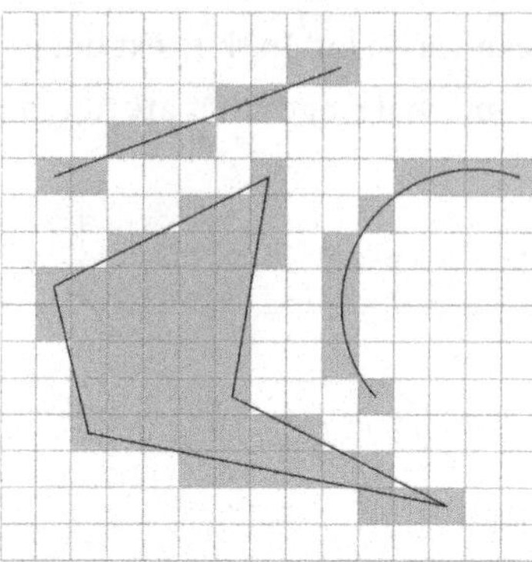

Figure 10.2: Example of figures being rasterized

- **Fragment Shader**: This is one of the most customizable stages of all. Its purpose is simple: just determine the color of each one of the fragments (pixels) that the rasterizer has generated. Here, lots of things can happen, from simply outputting a plain color or sampling a texture to applying complex lighting calculations such as normal mapping and PBR. Also, you can use this stage to create special effects such as water animations, holograms, distortions, disintegrations, and any special effects that require you to modify what the pixels look like. We will explore how we can use this stage in the next sections of this chapter.
- **Depth Testing**: Before showing a pixel on the screen, we need to check whether it can be seen. This stage checks whether the pixel's depth is behind or in front of the previous pixel rendered in the same position, guaranteeing that regardless of the rendering order of the objects, the nearest pixels to the camera are always being drawn on top of others. Again, usually, this stage is left in its default state, prioritizing pixels that are nearer to the camera, but some effects require different behavior. Also, nowadays we have **Early-Z testing**, which does this same test but before the Fragment shader, but let's keep things simple for now. As an example, in the next screenshot, you can see an effect that allows you to see objects that are behind other objects, like the one used in *Age of Empires* when a unit is behind a building:

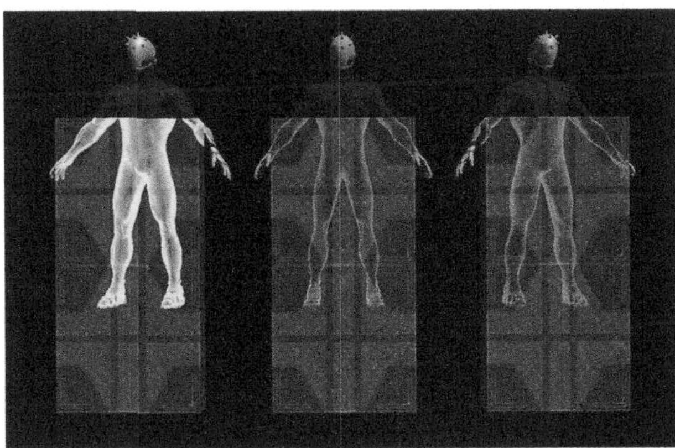

Figure 10.3: Rendering the occluded parts of the character

- **Blending**: Once the color of the pixel is determined and we are sure the pixel is not occluded by a previous pixel, the final step is to put it in the back-buffer (the frame or image you are drawing). Usually, we just override whatever pixel was in that position (because our pixel is nearer to the camera), but if you think about transparent objects, we need to combine our pixel with the previous one to make the transparent effect. Transparencies have other things to take into account aside from the blending, but the main idea is that blending controls exactly how the pixel will be combined with the previously rendered pixel in the back-buffer.

Shader Pipelines is a subject that would require an entire book, but for the scope of this book, the previous description will give you a good idea of what a shader does, and the possible effects that it can achieve. Now that we have discussed how a shader renders a single object, it is worth discussing how Unity renders all of the objects using Render Pipelines.

Render Pipeline and URP

We have covered how the video card renders an object, but Unity is in charge of asking the video card to execute its Shader Pipeline per object. To do so, Unity needs to do lots of preparations and calculations to determine exactly how and when each shader needs to be executed. The responsibility of doing this is with what Unity calls the Render Pipeline.

A Render Pipeline is a way to draw the objects of the scene. At first, it sounds like there should be just one simple way of doing this, for example, iterating over all objects in the scene and executing the Shader Pipeline with the shader specified in each object's Material, but it can be more complex than that.

Usually, the main difference between one Render Pipeline and another is the way in which lighting and some advanced effects are calculated, but they can differ in other ways.

In previous Unity versions, there was just one single Render Pipeline, which is now called the **Built-in Renderer Pipeline** (also known as **BIRP**). It was a pipeline that had all of the possible features you would need for all kinds of projects, from mobile 2D graphics and simple 3D to cutting-edge 3D like the ones you can find in consoles or high-end PCs. This sounds ideal, but actually, it isn't. Having one single giant renderer that needs to be highly customizable to adapt to all possible scenarios generates lots of overhead and limitations that cause more headaches than creating a custom Render Pipeline. Luckily, the last versions of Unity introduced **Scriptable Render Pipeline** (**SRP**), a way to create Render Pipeline adapted for your project.

Luckily, Unity doesn't want you to create your own Render Pipeline for each project (which is a complex task), so it has created two custom pipelines for you that are ready to use: **URP** (formerly called LWRP), which stands for **Universal Render Pipeline**, and **HDRP**, which stands for **High Definition Render Pipeline**. The idea is that you must choose one or the other based on your project's requirements (unless you really need to create your own).

URP, the one we selected when creating the project for our game, is a Render Pipeline suitable for most games that don't require lots of advanced graphics features, such as mobile games or simple PC games, while HDRP is packed with lots of advanced rendering features for high-quality games. The latter requires high-end hardware to run, while URP runs in almost every relevant target device. It is worth mentioning that you can swap between Built-in Renderer, HDRP, and URP whenever you want, including after creating the project (but this is not recommended):

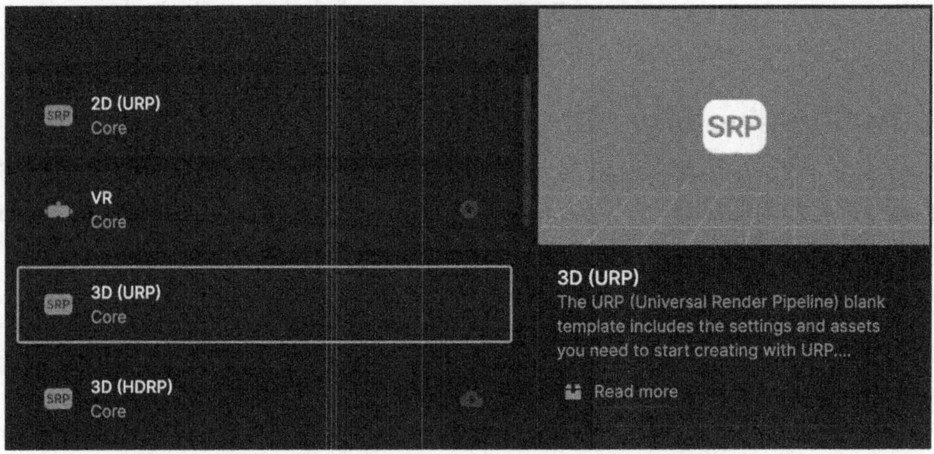

Figure 10.4: Project wizard showing HDRP and URP templates

We can discuss how each one is implemented and the differences between each, but again, this could fill entire chapters; right now, the idea of this section is for you to know why we picked URP when we created our project because it has some restrictions we will encounter throughout this book that we will need to take into account, so it is good to know why we accepted those limitations (to run our game on every relevant hardware).

Also, we need to know that we have chosen URP because it has support for Shader Graph, the Unity tool that we will be using in this chapter to create custom effects. Previous Unity built-in pipelines didn't provide us with such a tool (aside from third-party plugins). Finally, another reason to introduce the concept of URP is that it comes with lots of built-in shaders that we will need to know about before creating our own to prevent reinventing the wheel. This will allow us to get used to those shaders, because if you came from previous versions of Unity, the shaders you already know won't work here; actually, this is exactly what we are going to discuss in the next section of this chapter: the difference between the different URP built-in shaders.

URP built-in shaders

Now that we know the difference between URP and other pipelines, let's discuss which shaders come integrated into URP. Let's briefly describe the three most important shaders in this pipeline:

- **Lit**: This is the replacement of the old Standard Shader. This shader is useful for creating all kinds of realistic physics materials such as wood, rubber, metal, skin, and combinations of them (such as a character with skin and metal armor). It supports features like Normal Mapping, Occlusion, different lighting workflows like Metallic and Specular, and transparencies.
- **Simple Lit**: This is the replacement of the old Mobile/Diffuse Shader. As the name suggests, this shader is a simpler version of Lit, meaning that its lighting calculations are simpler approximations of how light works, getting fewer features than its counterpart. Basically, when you have simple graphics without realistic lighting effects, this is the best choice.
- **Unlit**: This is the replacement of the old Unlit/Texture Shader. Sometimes, you need objects with no lighting whatsoever, and in that case, this is the shader for you. No lighting doesn't mean an absence of light or complete darkness; it actually means that the object has no shadows at all, and it's fully visible without any shade. Some simplistic graphics can work with this, relying on shadowing being baked in the texture, meaning that the texture comes with the shadow.

This is extremely performant, especially for low-end devices such as mobile phones. Also, you have other cases such as light tubes or screens, objects that can't receive shadows because they emit light, so they will be seen at their full color even in complete darkness. In the following screenshot, you can see a 3D model using an Unlit Shader. It looks like it's being lit, but it's just the texture of the model that applied lighter and darker colors in different parts of the object:

Figure 10.5: Pod using an Unlit effect to simulate cheap lighting

Let's do an interesting disintegration effect with the Simple Lit Shader to demonstrate its capabilities. You must do the following:

1. Download and import a **Cloud Noise** texture from any search engine:

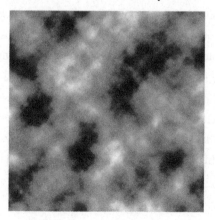

Figure 10.6: Noise texture

2. Select the recently imported texture in the **Project** panel.
3. In the Inspector, set the **Alpha Source** property to **From Gray Scale**. This will make the alpha channel of the texture be calculated based on the grayscale of the image:

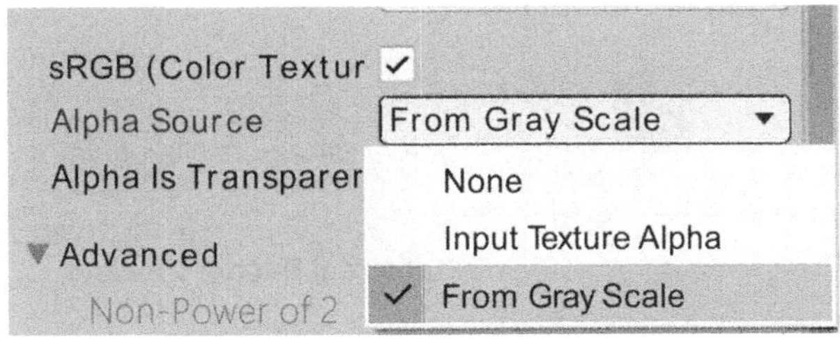

Figure 10.7: Generate Alpha From Gray Scale texture setting

The Alpha channel of a color is often associated with transparency, but you will notice that our object won't be transparent. The Alpha channel is extra color data that can be used for several purposes when creating effects. In this case, we will use it to determine which pixels are being disintegrated first.

4. Click the + icon in the Project view and select **Material**:

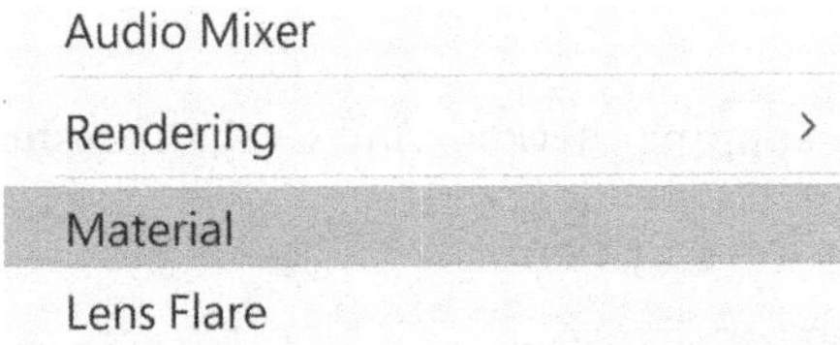

Figure 10.8: Material creation button

5. Create a cube by going to **GameObject | 3D Object | Cube**:

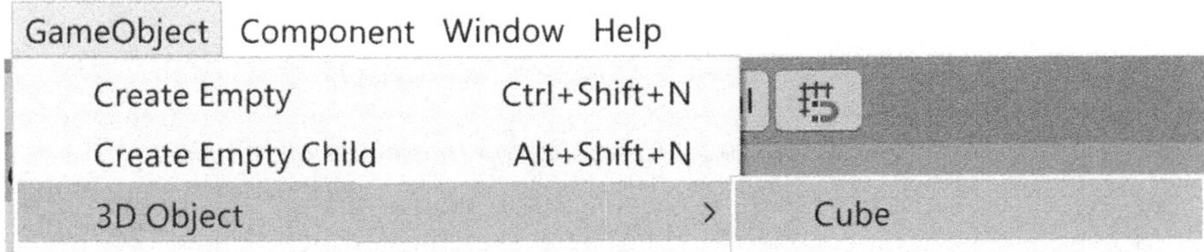

Figure 10.9: Cube primitive creation

6. Drag the Material from the Project window to the cube in the Scene window.

7. Click in the drop-down menu at the right of the **Shader** property in the Inspector and look for the **Universal Render Pipeline | Simple Lit** option. We could also work with the default shader (**Lit**), but **Simple Lit** is going to be easier on performance and we won't use the advanced features of Lit:

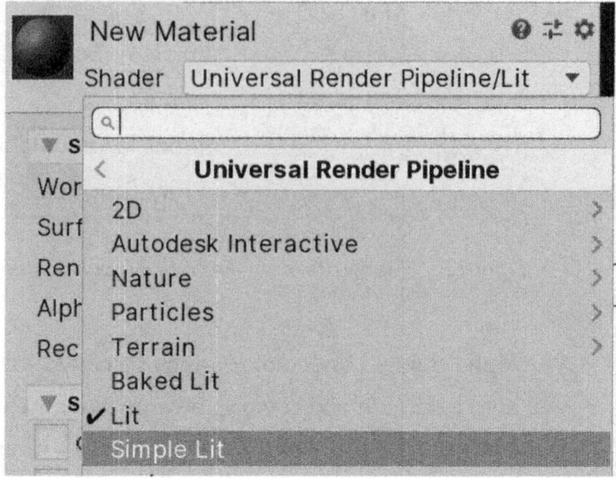

Figure 10.10: Simple Lit Shader selection

8. Select the **Material** and drag the downloaded cloud Texture to the rectangle at the left of **Base Map**.
9. Check the **Alpha Clipping** checkbox and set the **Threshold** slider to `0.5`:

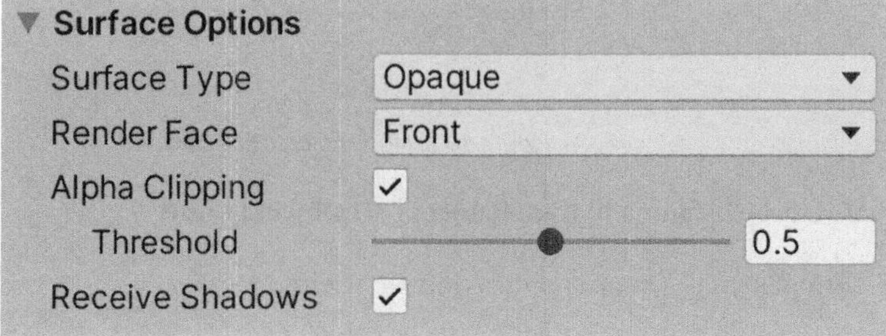

Figure 10.11: Alpha Clipping Threshold Material slider

10. As you move the **Threshold** slider, the object will start to disintegrate. **Alpha Clipping** discards pixels that have less Alpha intensity than the **Threshold** value:

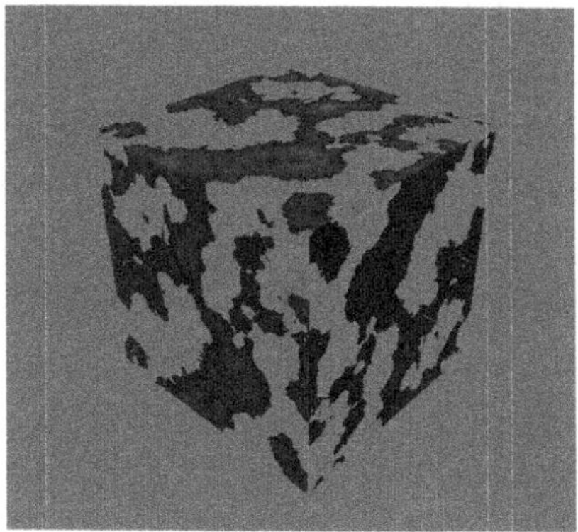

Figure 10.12: Disintegration effect with Alpha Clipping

11. Finally, set **Render Face** to **Both** to see both sides of the cube's faces:

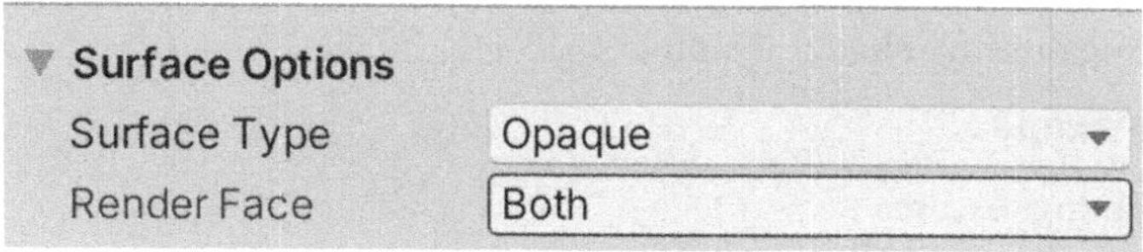

Figure 10.13: Double-sided render face

12. Take into account that the artist that creates the texture can configure the Alpha channel manually instead of calculating it from the grayscale, just to control exactly how the disintegration effect must look regardless of the texture's color distribution:

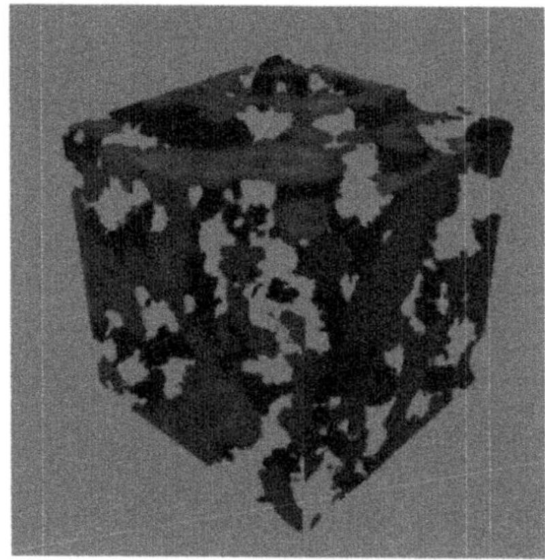

Figure 10.14: Double-sided Alpha Clipping

The idea of this section is not to give a comprehensive guide of all of the properties of all URP shaders, but to give you an idea of what a shader can do when properly configured and when to use each one of the integrated shaders. Sometimes, you can achieve the effect you need just by using existing shaders, probably in 99% of cases in simple games, so try to stick to them as much as you can. But if you really need to create a custom shader to create a very specific effect, the next section will teach you how to use the URP tool called Shader Graph.

Creating shaders with Shader Graph

Now that we know how shaders work and the existing shaders in URP, we have a basic notion of when it is necessary to create a custom shader and when it is not necessary. In case you really need to create one, this section will cover the basics of effects creation with Shader Graph, a tool to create effects using a visual node-based editor. This is an easy tool to use when you are not used to coding.

In this section, we will discuss the following concepts of the Shader Graph:

- Creating our first Shader Graph
- Using textures
- Combining textures
- Applying transparency
- Creating Vertex effects

Let's start by seeing how we can create and use a Shader Graph.

Creating our first Shader Graph

Shader Graph is a tool that allows us to create custom effects using a node-based system. An effect in the Shader Graph can look like in the following screenshot:

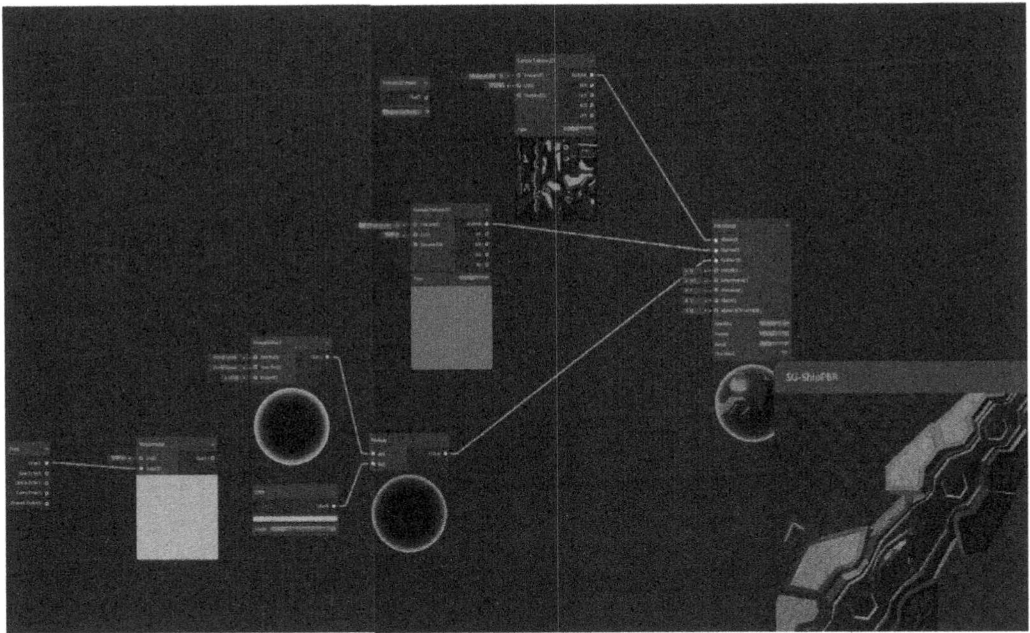

Figure 10.15: Shader Graph with nodes to create a custom effect

We will discuss later what those nodes do and we will be creating an example effect step by step, but in the screenshot, you can see how the author created and connected several nodes—the interconnected boxes—with each one executing a specific process to achieve the effect. The idea of creating effects with Shader Graph is to learn which specific nodes you need and how to connect them properly. This is similar to the way we code the gameplay of the game, but this Shader Graph is adapted and simplified just for effect purposes.

To create and edit our first Shader Graph, do the following:

1. In the Project window, click the + icon and find the **Shader Graph | URP | Lit Shader Graph** option. This will create a Shader Graph using the PBR mode, meaning that this shader will support lighting effects (unlike Unlit Graphs):

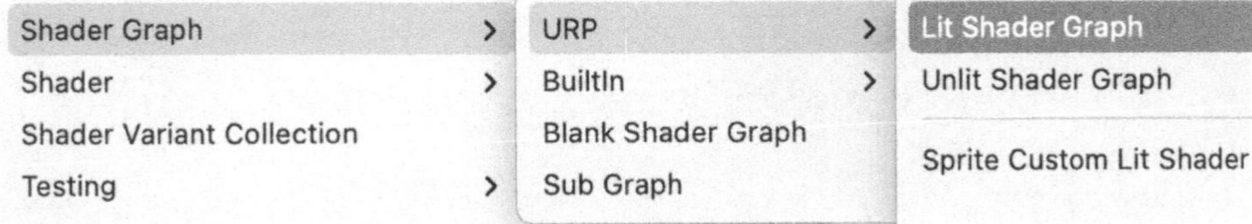

Figure 10.16: PBR Shader Graph creation

2. Name it `Water`. If you want the opportunity to rename the asset, remember that you can select the asset, right-click, and select **Rename**:

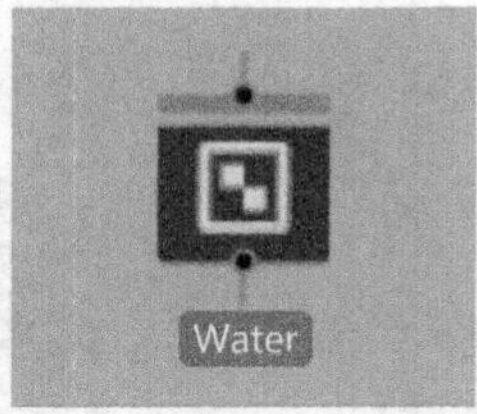

Figure 10.17: Shader Graph Asset

3. Create a new Material called `WaterMaterial` and set **Shader** to **Shader Graphs/Water**. If for some reason Unity doesn't allow you to do that, try right-clicking on the **Water Graph** and clicking **Reimport**. As you can see, the created Shader Graph now appears as a shader in the Material:

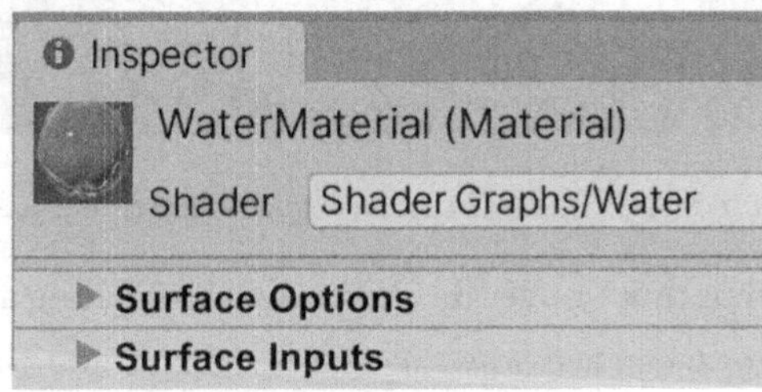

Figure 10.18: Setting a Shader Graph as a Material Shader

4. Create a plane with the **GameObject | 3D Object | Plane** option.
5. Drag the **Material** to the **Plane** to apply it.

Now, you have created your first custom shader and applied it to a Material. So far, it doesn't look interesting at all—it's just a gray effect—but now it's time to edit the graph to unlock its full potential. As the name of the graph suggests, we will be creating a water effect in this chapter to illustrate several nodes of the Shader Graph toolset and how to connect them, so let's start by discussing the Master node.

When you open the graph by double-clicking the shader asset, you will see the following:

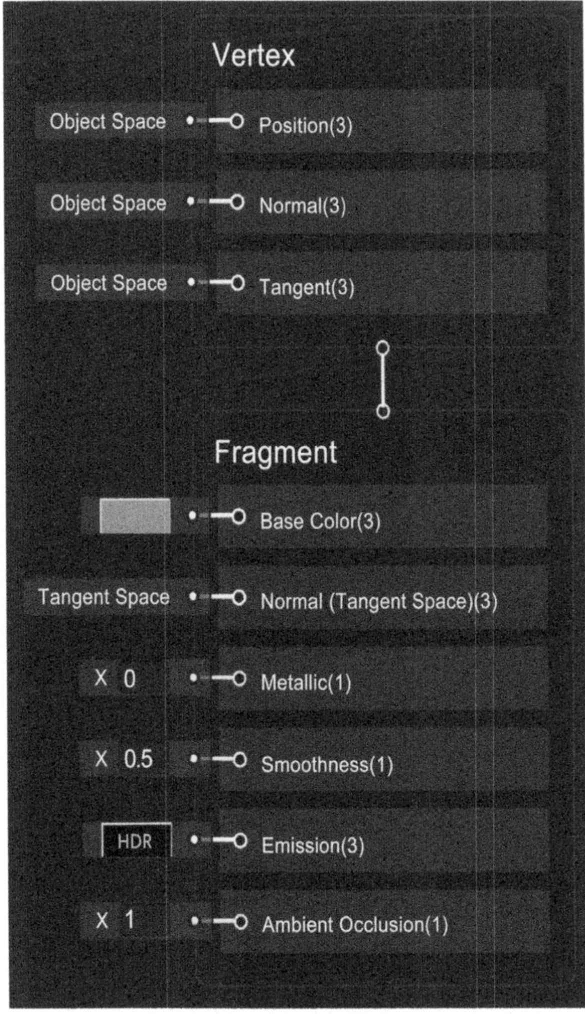

Figure 10.19: Master node with all of the properties needed to calculate object appearance

All nodes will have input pins, the data needed to work, and output pins, the results of its process. As an example, in a sum operation, we will have two input numbers and an output number, the result of the sum. In this case, you can see that the Master node only contains inputs, and that's because all data that enters the Master node will be used by Unity to calculate the rendering and lighting of the object, things such as the desired object color or texture (**Base Color** input pin), how smooth it is (**Smoothness** input pin), or how much metal it contains (**Metallic** input pin), properties that will affect how the lighting will be applied to the object.

You can see that the Master node is split between a **Vertex** section and a **Fragment** section. The first is capable of changing the mesh of the object we are modifying to deform it, animate it, etc., while the latter will change how it will look, which textures to use, how it will be illuminated, etc. Let's start exploring how we can change that data in the **Fragment** section by doing the following:

1. Double-click the **Shader Graph** asset in Project View to open its editor.
2. Click in the gray rectangle at the left of the **Base Color** input pin:

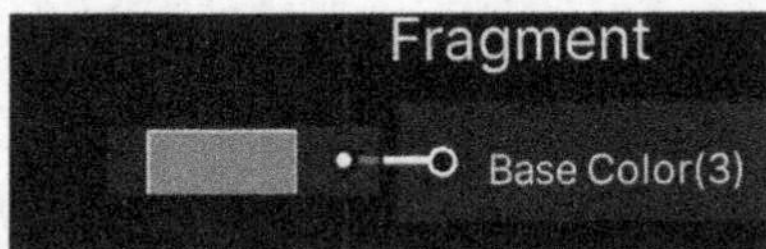

Figure 10.20: Base Color node input pin

3. In the color picker, select a light blue color, like water. Select the bluish part of the circle and then a shade of that color in the middle rectangle:

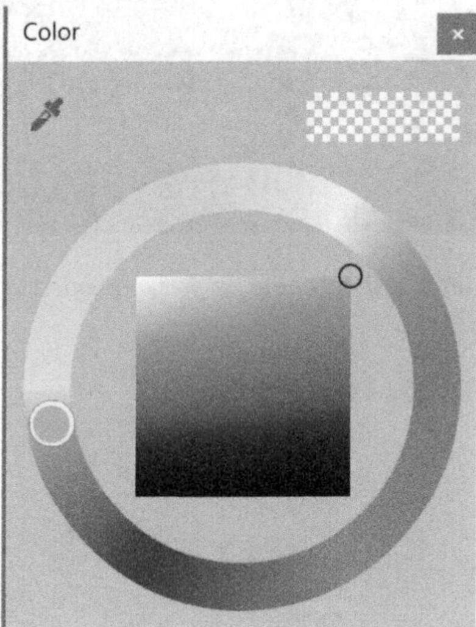

Figure 10.21: Color picker

4. Set **Smoothness** to `0.9`, which will make the object almost completely smooth (90% of the total smoothness possible). This will make our water reflect the sky almost completely:

Figure 10.22: Smoothness PBR Master node input pin

5. Click the **Save Asset** button at the top left of the window:

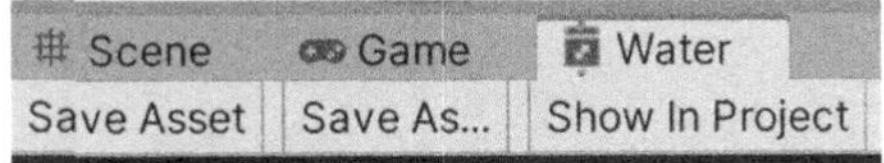

Figure 10.23: Shader Graph saving options

6. Go back to the Scene View and check the plane is light blue with the sun reflected on it:

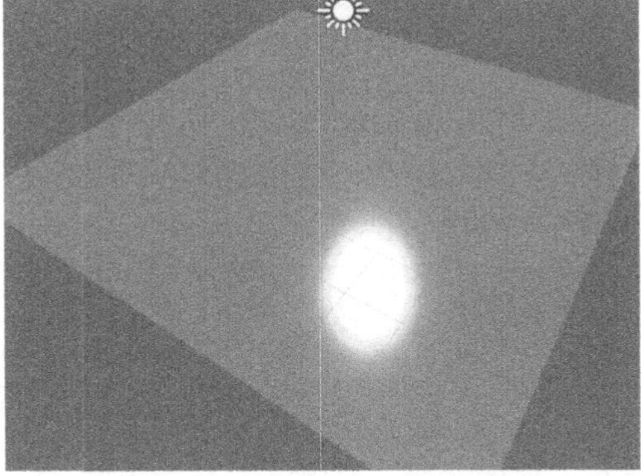

Figure 10.24: Initial Shader Graph results

As you can see, the behavior of the shader varies according to the properties you set in the **Master** node, but so far, doing this is no different than creating an Unlit Shader and setting up its properties; the real power of Shader Graph is when you use nodes that do specific calculations as inputs of the Master node. We will start looking at the texturing nodes, which allow us to apply Textures to our model.

Using Textures

The idea of using Textures is to have an image applied to the model in a way that we can paint different parts of the models with different colors. Remember that the model has a UV map, which allows Unity to know which part of the Texture will be applied to which part of the model:

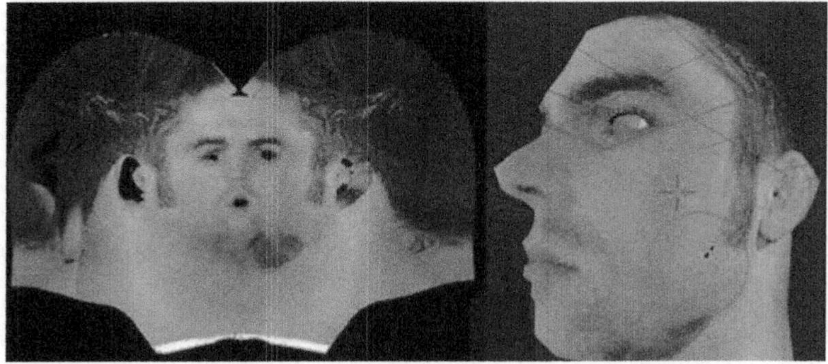

Figure 10.25: On the left, a face Texture; on the right, the same texture applied to a face mesh

We have several nodes to do this task, one of them being Sample Texture 2D, a node that has two main inputs. First, it asks us for the texture to sample or apply to the model, and then for the UV. You can see it in the following screenshot:

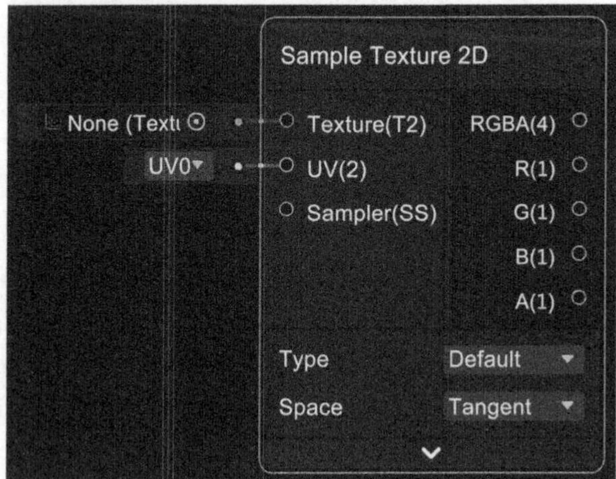

Figure 10.26: Sample Texture 2D node

As you can see, the default value of the **Texture** input node is **None**, so there's no texture by default, and we need to manually specify that. For **UV**, the default value is `UV0`, meaning that, by default, the node will use the main UV channel of the model, and yes, a model can have several UVs set. For now, we will stick with the main one. If you are not sure what that means, UV0 is the safest option. Let's try this node, doing the following:

1. Download and import a **tileable water texture** from the internet:

Figure 10.27: Water tileable Texture

2. Select the Texture and be sure that the **Wrap Mode** property of the Texture is set to **Repeat**, which will allow us to repeat the Texture as we did in the terrain because the idea is to use this shader to cover large water areas:

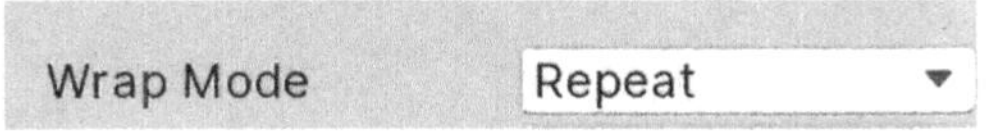

Figure 10.28: Texture Repeat mode

3. In the **Water Shader Graph**, right-click in an empty area of the **Shader Graph** and select **Create Node**:

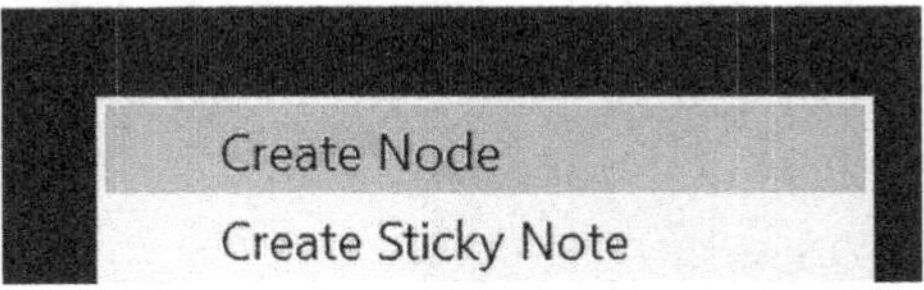

Figure 10.29: Shader Graph Create Node option

4. In the **Search** box, write `Sample texture` and all of the sampler nodes will show up. Double-click **Sample Texture 2D**. If for some reason you can't double-click the option, right-click on it first and then try again. There is a known bug on this tool and this is the workaround:

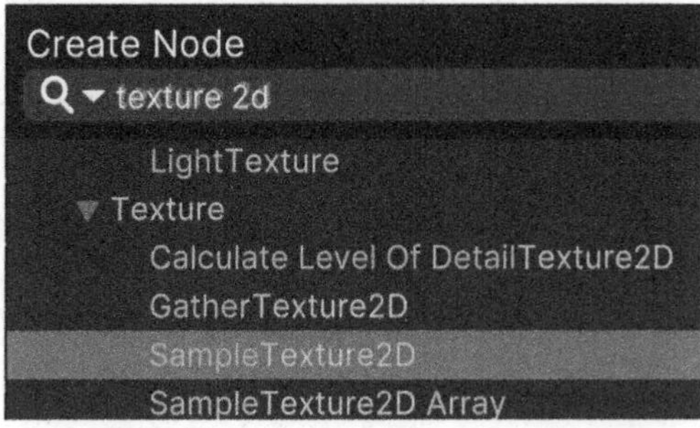

Figure 10.30: Sample texture node search

5. Click in the circle to the left of the **Texture** input pin of the **Sample Texture 2D** node. It will allow us to pick a Texture to sample—just select the water one. You can see that the Texture can be previewed in the bottom part of the node:

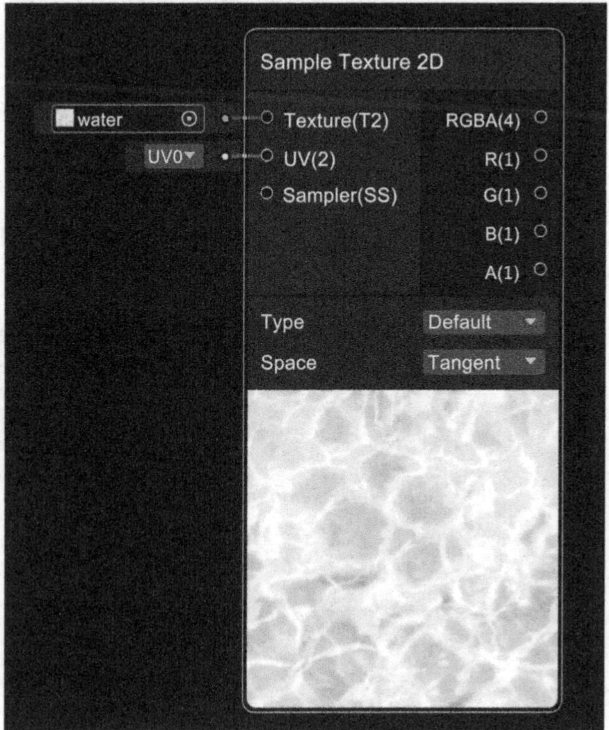

Figure 10.31: Sample Texture node with a Texture in its input pin

6. Drag the output pin **RGBA** from the **Sample Texture 2D** node to the **Base Color** input pin of the Master node:

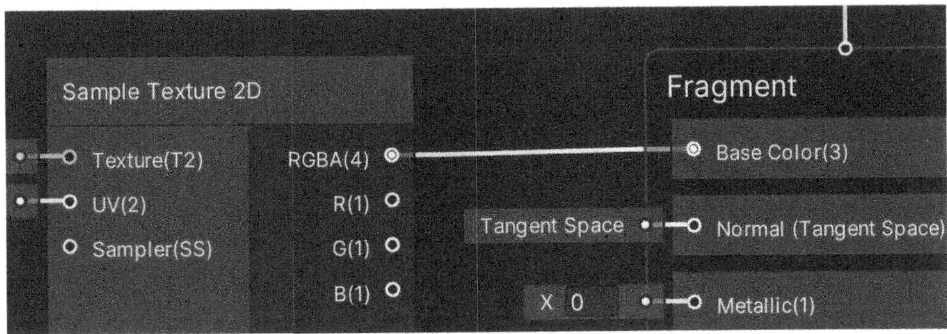

Figure 10.32: Connecting the results of a Texture sampling with the Base Color pin of the Master node

7. Click the **Save Asset** button at the top-left part of the Shader Graph editor and see the changes in the Scene view:

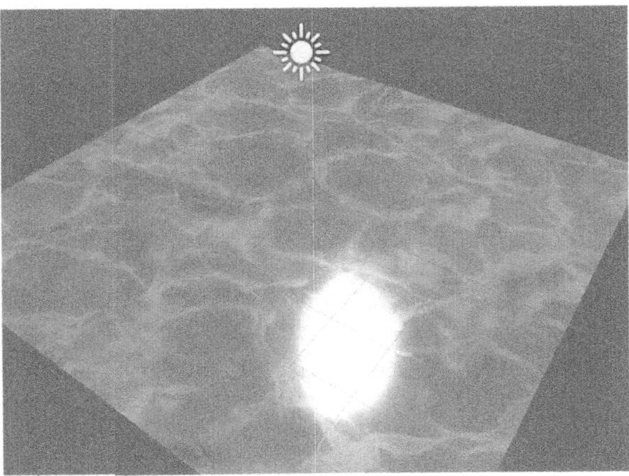

Figure 10.33: Results of applying a Texture in our Shader Graph

As you can see, the Texture is properly applied to the model, but if you take into account that the default plane has a size of 10x10 meters, the ripples of the water seem too big. So, let's tile the Texture!

To do this, we need to change the UVs of the model, making them bigger. You may imagine that bigger UVs mean the Texture should also get bigger, but take into account that we are not making the object bigger; we are just modifying the UV.

In the same object area, we will display more of the texture area, meaning that in the bigger texture sample area (achieved by bigger UVs), repetitions of the texture may appear. To do so, follow the next steps:

1. Right-click in any empty space and click **New Node** to search for the UV node:

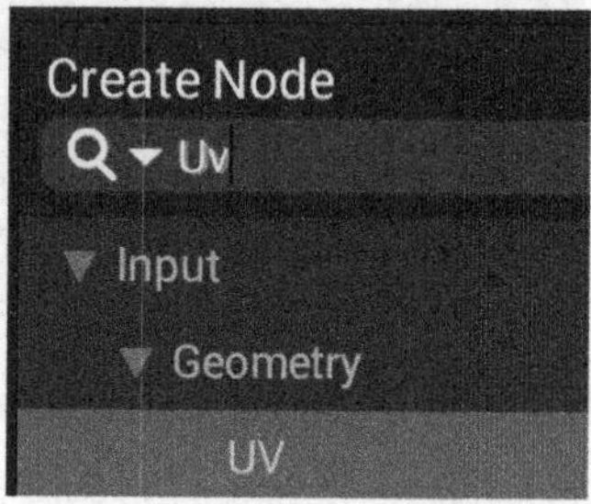

Figure 10.34: Searching for the UV node

2. Using the same method, create a **Multiply** node.
3. Drag the **Out** pin of the UV node to the **A** pin of the **Multiply** node to connect them.
4. Set the **B** pin input value of **Multiply** to 4,4,4,4:

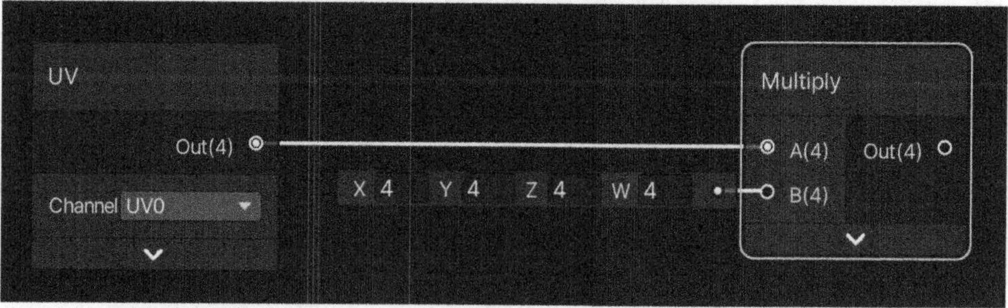

Figure 10.35: Multiplying the UVs by 4

5. Drag the **Out** pin of the **Multiply** node to the **UV** of the **Sample Texture 2D** node to connect them:

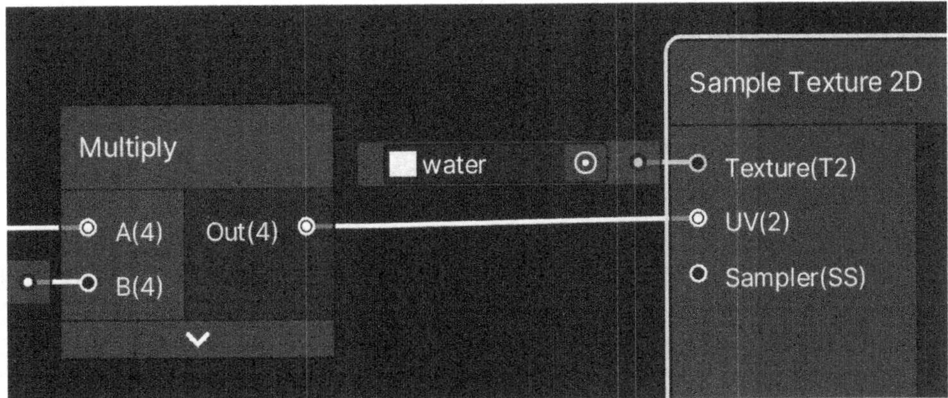

Figure 10.36: Using the multiplied UVs to sample the Texture

6. If you save the graph and go back to the Scene view, you can see that now the ripples are smaller, because we have tiled the UVs of our model. You can also see that in the preview of the **Sampler Texture 2D** node:

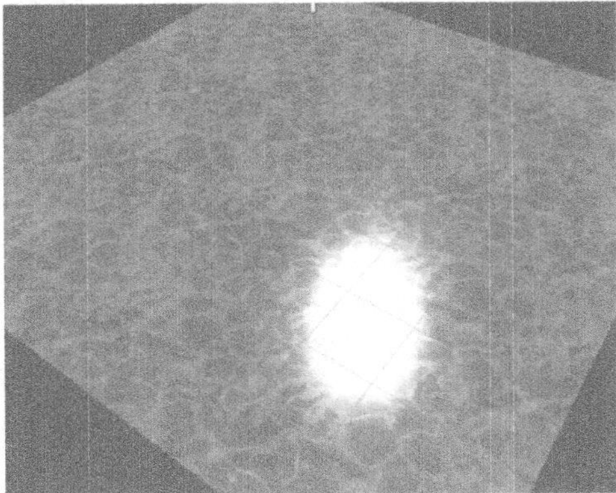

Figure 10.37: Results of the model's UV multiplication

Another interesting effect we can do now is to apply an offset to the Texture to move it. The idea is that even if the plane is not actually moving, we will simulate the flow of the water through it, moving just the Texture. Remember, the responsibility of determining the part of the Texture to apply to each part of the model belongs to the UV, so if we add values to the UV coordinates, we will be moving them, generating a Texture sliding effect. To do so, let's do the following:

1. Create an **Add** node to the right of the **UV** node.
2. Connect the **Out** pin of the **UV** to the **A** pin of the **Add** node:

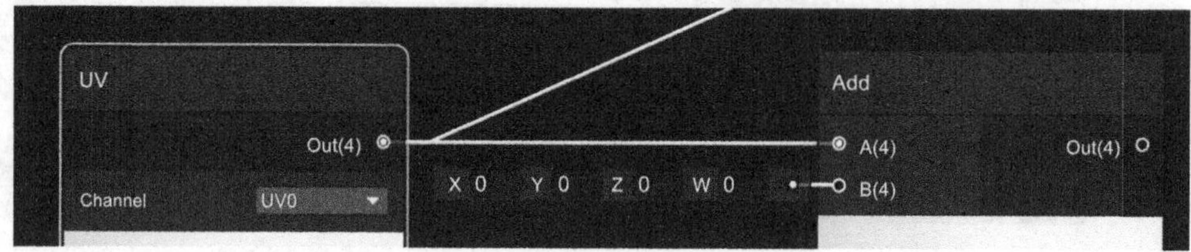

Figure 10.38: Adding values to the UVs

3. Create a **Time** node at the left of the **Add** node.
4. Connect the **Time** node to the **B** pin of the **Add** node:

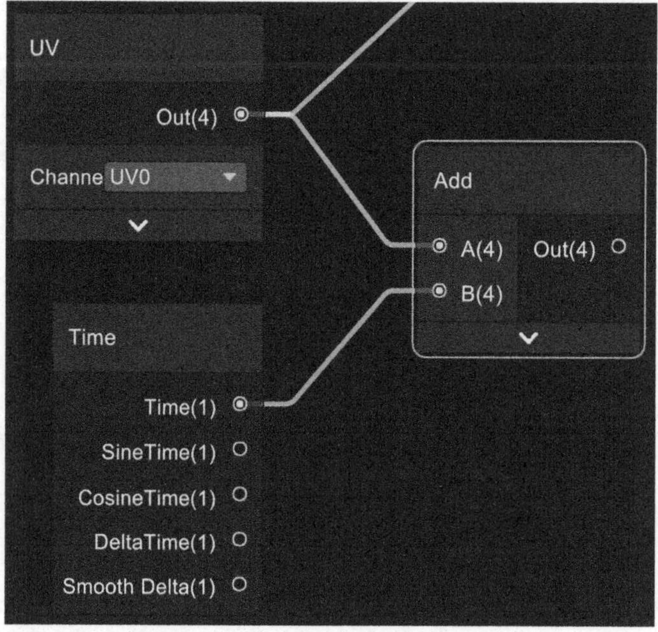

Figure 10.39: Adding time to the UVs

5. Connect the **Out** pin of the **Add** node to the **A** input pin of the **Multiply** node:

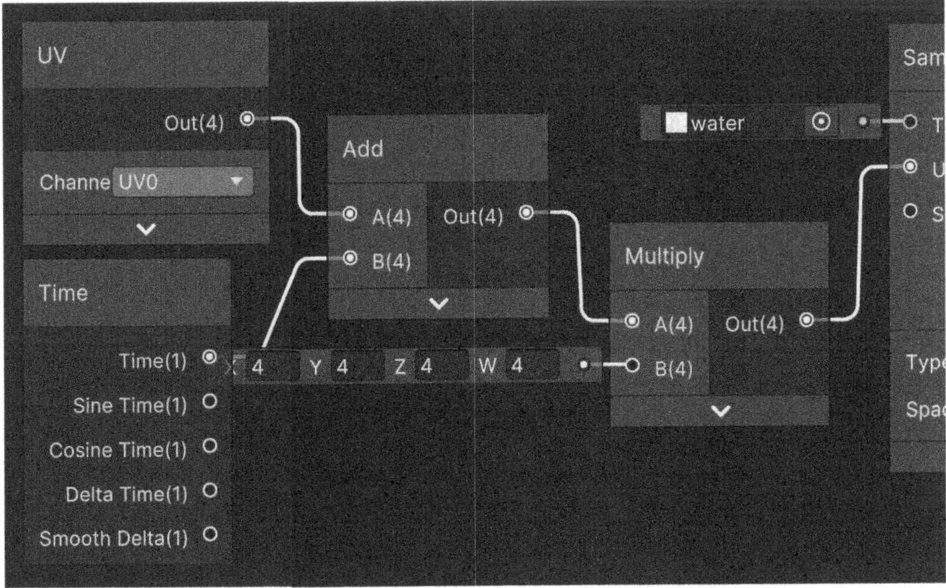

Figure 10.40: Added and multiplied UVs as an input of the sample Texture

6. Save and see the water moving in the Scene view. If you don't see it moving, click the layers icon in the top bar of the scene and check **Always Refresh**:

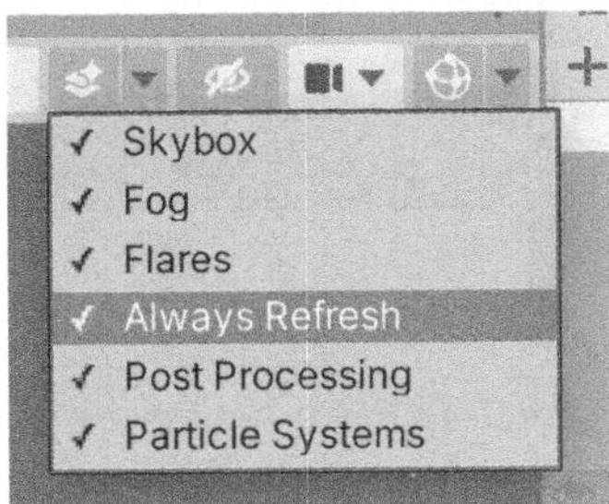

Figure 10.41: Enabling Always Refresh to preview the effect

7. If you feel the water is moving too fast, try using the multiplication node to make the time a smaller value. I recommend you try it by yourself before looking at the next screenshot, which has the answer:

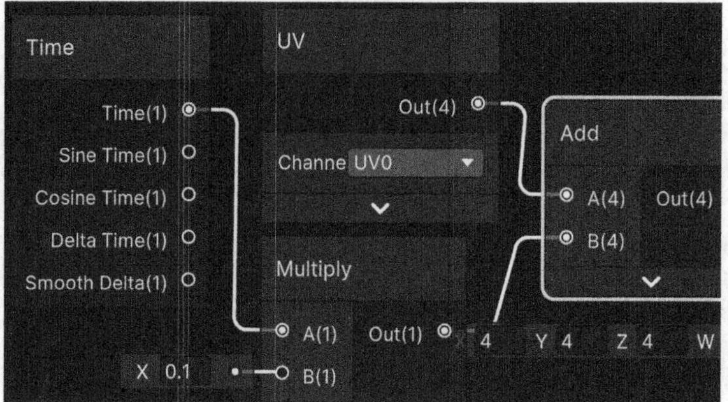

Figure 10.42: Multiplication of time to move the texture slower

8. If you feel the graph is too big, try to hide some of the node previews by clicking on the **up** (^) arrow that appears on the preview when you move the mouse over it:

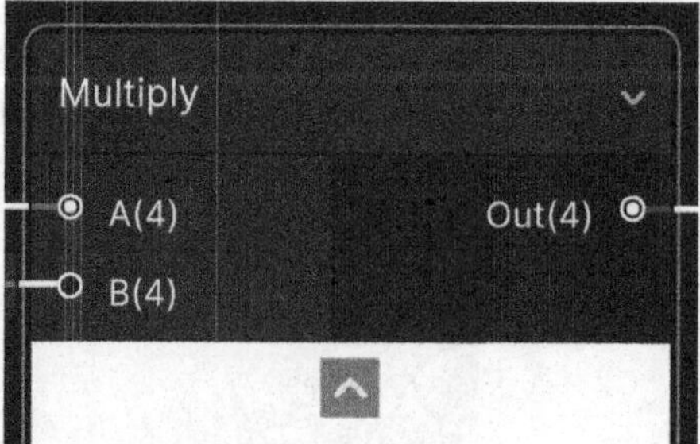

Figure 10.43: Hiding the preview from the graph nodes

9. Also, you can hide unused pins by selecting the node and clicking the arrow at its top right:

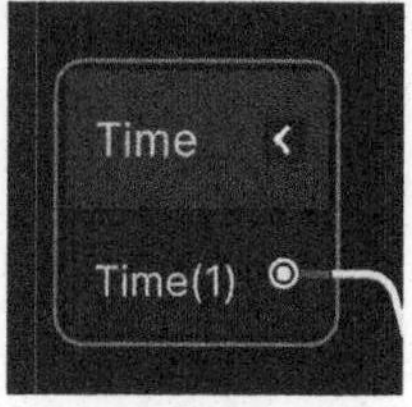

Figure 10.44: Hiding unused pins from the graph nodes

So, to recap, first we added the time to the UV to move it and then multiplied the result of the moved UV to make it bigger to tile the Texture. It is worth mentioning that there's a **Tiling and Offset** node that does all of this process for us, but I wanted to show you how a simple multiplication to scale the UV and an add operation to move it generates a nice effect; you can't imagine all of the possible effects you can achieve with other simple mathematical nodes! Actually, let's explore other usages of mathematical nodes to combine Textures in the next section.

Combining Textures

Even though we have used nodes, we haven't created anything that can't be created using regular shaders, but that's about to change. So far, we can see the water moving but it stills look static, and that's because the ripples are always the same. We have several techniques to generate ripples, and the simplest one would be to combine two water Textures moving in different directions to mix their ripples, and actually, we can simply use the same Texture just flipped to save some memory. To combine the Textures, we will sum them and then divide them by 2, so basically, we are calculating the average of the textures! Let's do that by doing the following:

1. Select all of the nodes between **Time** and **Sampler 2D** (including them) creating a selection rectangle by clicking in any empty space in the graph, holding and dragging the click, and then releasing when all target nodes are covered:

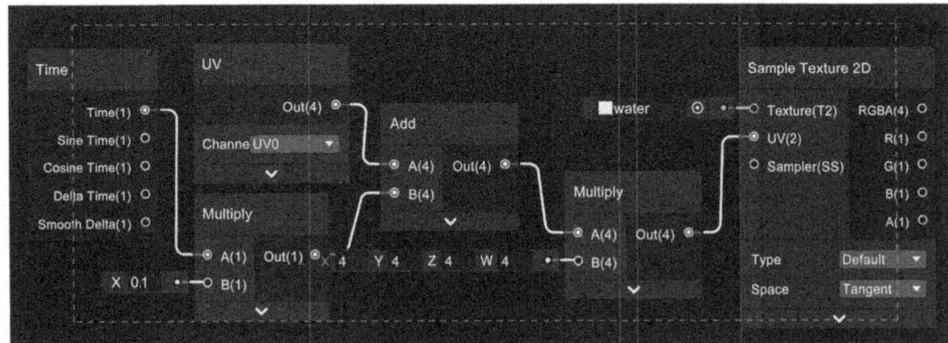

Figure 10.45: Selecting several nodes

2. Right-click and select **Copy**, and then again right-click and select **Paste**, or use the classic *Ctrl* + *C*, *Ctrl* + *V* commands (*Command* + *C*, *Command* + *V* on Mac).

3. Move the copied nodes below the original ones:

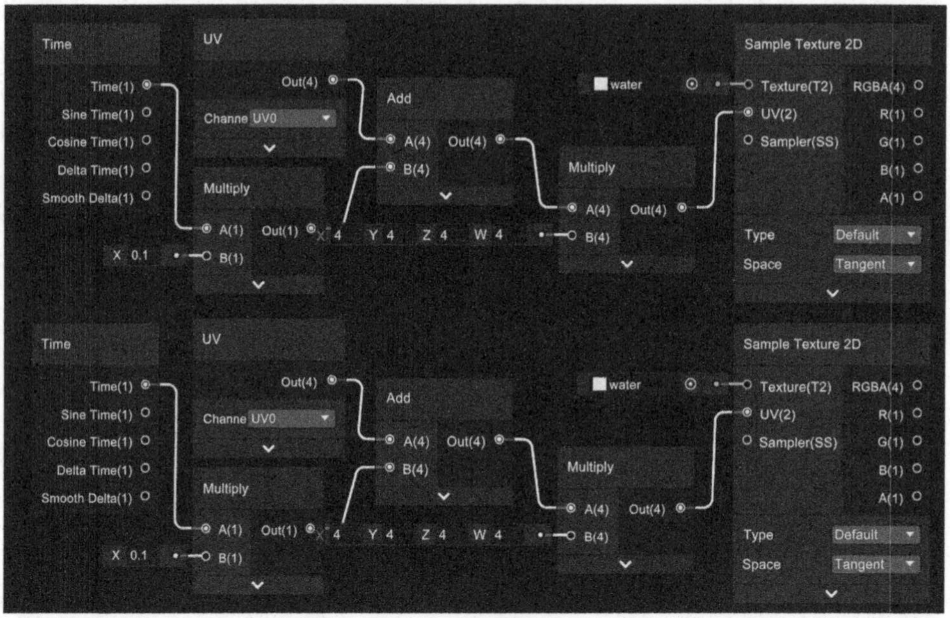

Figure 10.46: Duplication of nodes

4. For the copied nodes, set the **B** pin of the **Multiply** node connected to **Sample Texture 2D** to -4,-4,-4,-4. You can see that that flipped the texture.
5. Also, set the **B** pin of the **Multiply** node connected to the **Time** node to `-0.1`:

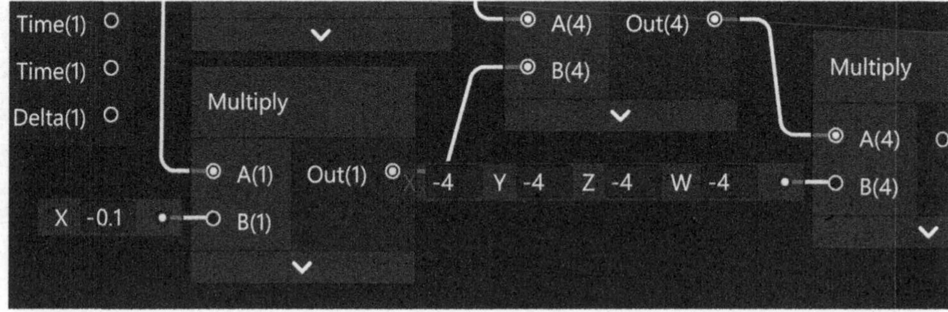

Figure 10.47: Multiplication of values

6. Create an **Add** node at the right of both **Sampler Texture 2D** nodes and connect the outputs of those nodes to the **A** and **B** input pins of the **Add** node:

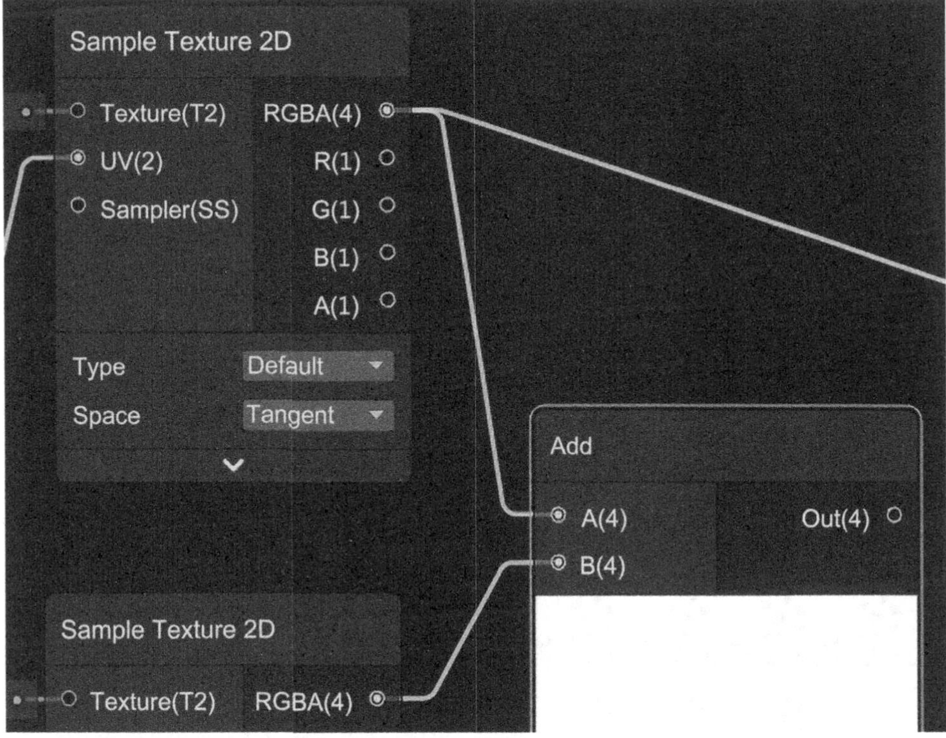

Figure 10.48: Adding two Textures

7. You can see that the resulting combination is too bright because we have summed up the intensity of both textures, so let's fix that by multiplying the **Out** of the **Add** node by `0.5,0.5,0.5,0.5`, which will divide each resulting color channel by 2, averaging the color. You can also experiment with what happens when you set different values to each channel if you want, but for our purposes, `0.5` is the proper value for each channel:

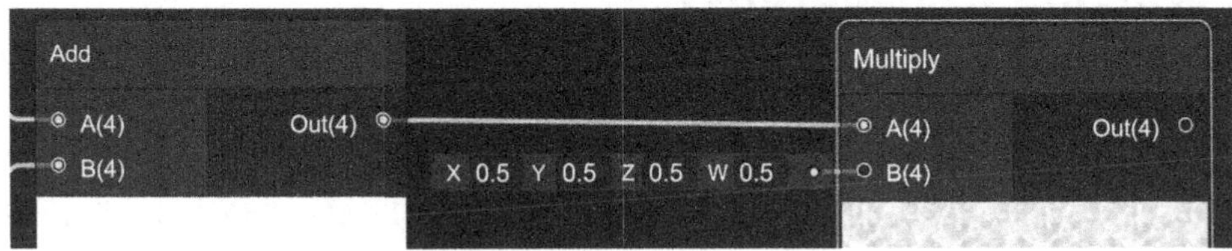

Figure 10.49: Dividing the sum of two Textures to get the average

8. Connect the **Out** pin of the **Multiply** node to the **Base Color** pin of the **Master** node to apply all of those calculations to the color of the object.
9. Save the **Asset** and see the results in the Scene view:

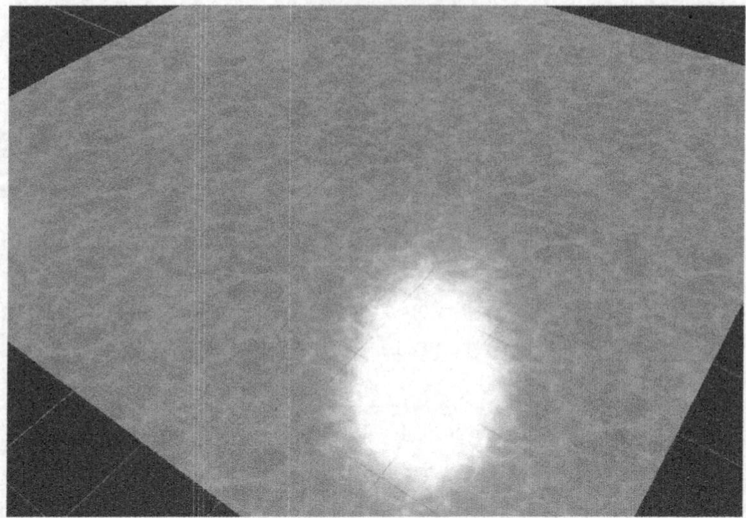

Figure 10.50: Results of texture blending

You can keep adding nodes to make the effect more diverse, such as using **Sine** nodes (which will execute the trigonometry sine operation) to apply non-linear movements and so on, but I will let you learn that by experimenting with this by yourself. For now, we will stop here. As always, this topic deserves a full book, and the intention of this chapter is to give you a small taste of this powerful Unity tool. I recommend you look for other Shader Graph examples on the internet to learn other usages of the same nodes and, of course, new nodes. One thing to consider here is that everything we just did is basically applied to the Fragment Shader stage of the Shader Pipeline we discussed earlier. Now, let's use the Blending Shader stage to apply some transparency to the water.

Applying transparency

Before declaring our effect finished, a little addition we can do is to make the water a little bit transparent. Remember that the Shader Pipeline has a blending stage, which has the responsibility of blending each pixel of our model into the image being rendered in this frame. The idea is to make our Shader Graph modify that stage to apply **Alpha Blending**, a blending mode that combines our model and the previously rendered models based on the Alpha value of our model.

To get that effect, take the following steps:

1. Look for the **Graph Inspector** window floating around. If you don't see it, click the **Graph Inspector** button at the top-right part of the Shader Graph editor.
2. Click the **Graph Settings** tab.
3. Set the **Surface Type** property to **Transparent**.
4. Set the **Blending Mode** property to **Alpha** if it isn't already at that value:

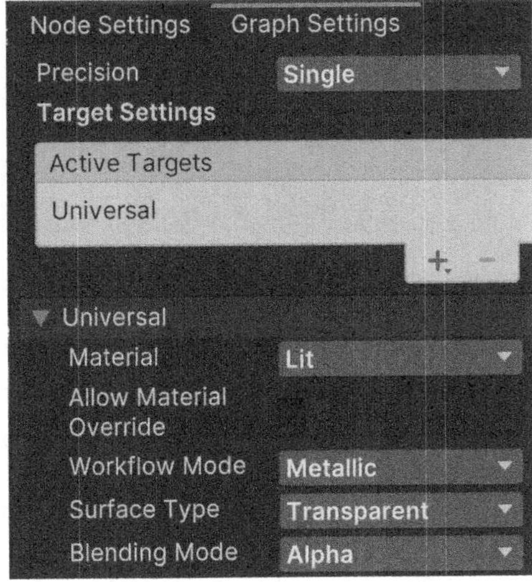

Figure 10.51: Graph Inspector Transparency settings

5. Set the **Alpha** input pin of the **Master** to `0.5`.

Figure 10.52: Setting Alpha of the Master node

6. Save the Shader Graph and see the transparency being applied in the Scene view. If you can't see the effect, just put a cube into the water to make the effect more evident:

Figure 10.53: Shadows from the water being applied to a cube

7. You can see the shadows that the water is casting on our cube because Unity doesn't know the object is transparent and hence casts shadows. Click on the water plane and look for the Mesh Renderer component in the Inspector. If you don't see the shadow, click the lightbulb at the top of the Scene view.

Figure 10.54: Enabling lights in the Scene View

8. In the **Lighting** section, set **Cast Shadows** to **Off**; this will disable shadow casting from the plane on the parts of the cube that are underwater:

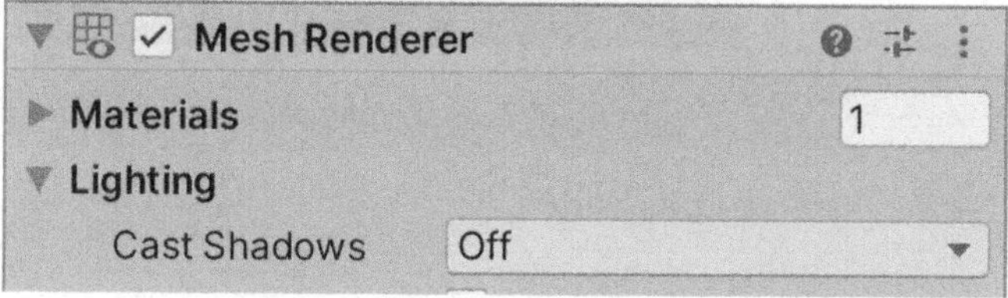

Figure 10.55: Disabling shadow casting

Adding transparency is a simple process but it has its caveats, like the shadow problem, and in more complex scenarios, it can have other problems, like increasing overdraw, meaning the same pixel needs to be drawn several times (the pixel belonging to the transparent object, and one of the objects behind). I would suggest you avoid using transparency unless it is necessary. Actually, our water can live without transparency, especially when we apply this water to the river basin around the base because we don't need to see the part under the water, but the idea is for you to know all of your options. In the next screenshot, you can see how we have put a giant plane with this effect below our base, big enough to cover the entire basin:

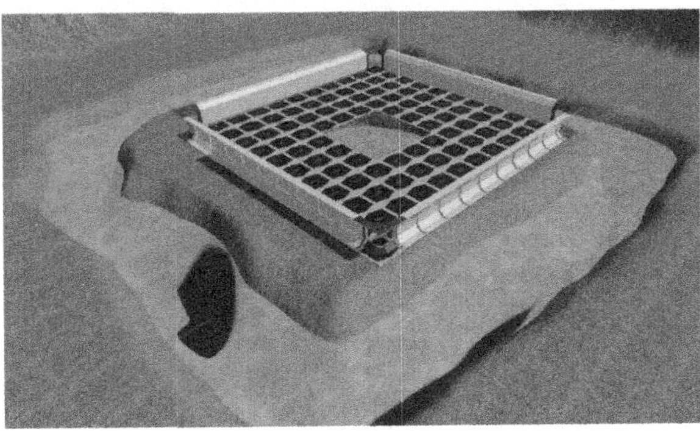

Figure 10.56: Using our water in the main scene

Now that we have modified how the object looks through the **Fragment** node section, let's discuss how to use the Vertex section to apply a mesh animation to our water.

Creating Vertex Effects

So far, we have applied water textures to our water, but it's still a flat plane. We can go further than that and make the ripples not only via textures but also by animating the mesh. To do so, we will apply the noise texture we used at the beginning of the chapter in the shader, but instead of using it as another color to add to the **Base Color** of the shader, we will instead use it to offset the **Y** position of the vertexes of our plane.

Due to the chaotic nature of the noise texture, the idea is that we will apply a vertical offset to different parts of the model, so we can emulate the ripples:

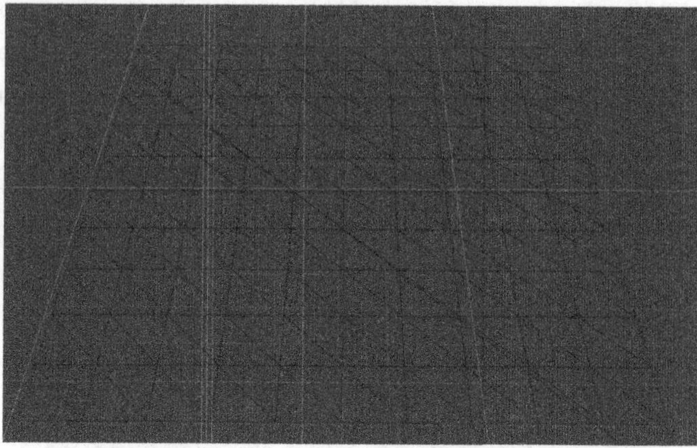

Figure 10.57: Default plane mesh subdivided into a grid of 10x10 with no offset

To accomplish something like this, you can modify the **Vertex** section of your shader to look like the following:

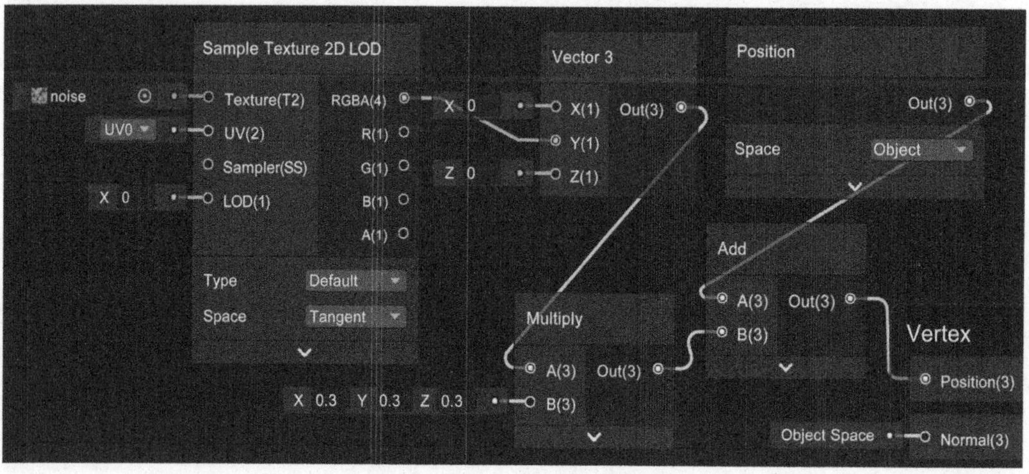

Figure 10.58: Ripples vertex effect

In the graph, you can see how we are creating a **Vector** whose *y* axis depends on the noise Texture we downloaded at the beginning of the chapter. The idea behind that is to create a **Vector** pointing upward whose length is proportional to the grayscale factor of the texture; the whiter the pixel of the texture, the longer the offset. This texture has an irregular yet smooth pattern so it can emulate the behavior of the tide.

Please notice that here we used **Sample Texture 2D LOD** instead of **Sample Texture 2D**; the latter does not work in the **Vertex** section, so keep that in mind.

Then we multiply the result by *0.3* to reduce the height of the offset to add, and then we add the result to the **Position** node.See that the **Space** property of the **Position** node is set to **Object** mode. We need that mode to work with the **Vertex** section of the Shader Graph (we discussed World and Local spaces before in *Chapter 2, Editing Scenes and GameObjects* but you can also search `Object vs World Space` on the internet for more info about this). Finally, the result is connected to the **Position** node of the **Vertex** section.

If you save, you will see something like the following image:

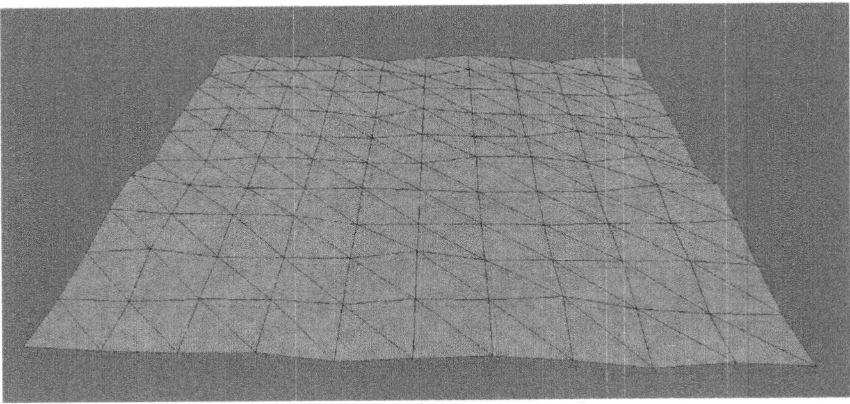

Figure 10.59: Ripples vertex effect applied

Of course, in this case, the ripples are static because we didn't add any time offset to the UV as we did before. In the following screenshot, you can see how to add that, but before looking at it I recommend you try to resolve it first by yourself as a personal challenge:

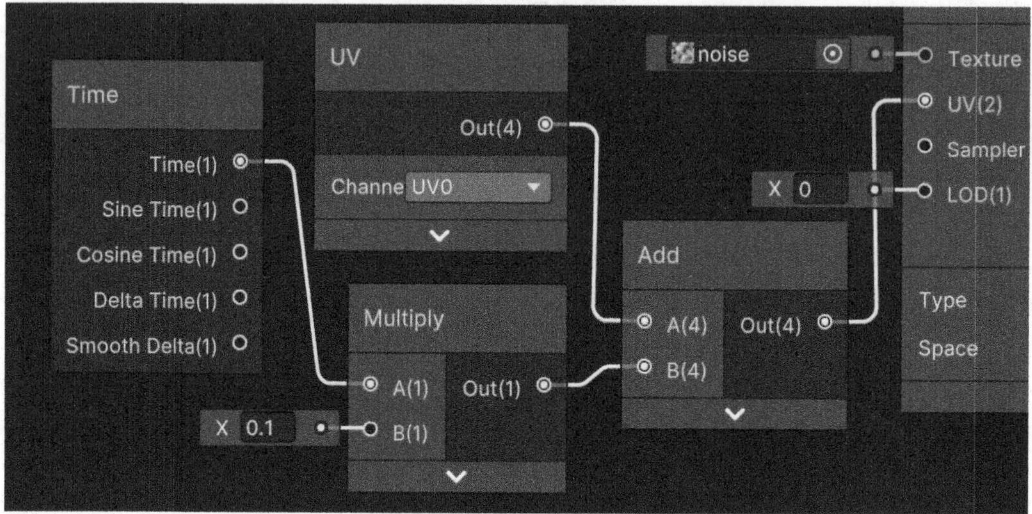

Figure 10.60: Animated ripples vertex effect graph

As you can see, we are again taking the original UV and adding the time multiplied by any factor so it will slowly move, the same as we did previously with our water texture. You can keep playing around with this, changing how this looks with different textures, multiplying the offset to increase or reduce the height of the ripples, applying interesting math functions like sine, and so much more, but for now, let's finish with this.

Summary

In this chapter, we discussed how a shader works in the GPU and how to create our first simple shader to achieve a nice water effect. Working with shaders is a complex and interesting job, and in a team, there is usually one or more people in charge of creating all of these effects, in a position called Technical Artist; so, as you can see, this topic can expand up to a whole career. Remember, the intention of this book is to give you a small taste of all the possible roles you can take in the industry, so if you really liked this role, I suggest you start reading shader-exclusive books. You have a long but super interesting road in front of you.

Enough shaders for now! In the next chapter, we will look at how to improve our graphics and create visual effects with particle systems!

11

Visual Effects with Particle Systems and Visual Effect Graph

In this chapter, we will continue learning about visual effects for our game. We will be discussing particle systems, a way to simulate fire, waterfalls, smoke, and all kinds of fluids. Also, we will see the two Unity **particle systems** to create these kinds of effects, **Shuriken**, and **Visual Effect Graph**, the latter being more powerful than the first but requiring more hardware.

In this chapter, we will cover the following particle system topics:

- Introduction to Shuriken particle systems
- Creating fluid simulations
- Creating complex simulations with Visual Effect Graph

Introduction to Shuriken particle systems

All graphics and effects we have created so far use static meshes—3D models that can't be skewed, bent, or deformed in any way. **Fluids** such as fire and smoke clearly can't be represented using this kind of mesh, but actually, we can simulate these effects with a combination of static meshes, and this is where particle systems are useful.

Particle systems are objects that emit and animate lots of **particles** or **billboards**, which are simple quad meshes that face the camera. Each particle is a static mesh, but rendering, animating, and combining lots of them can generate the illusion of a fluid.

In *Figure 11.1* you can see a smoke effect using particle systems on the left, and on the right, the **Wireframe** view of the same particles. There you can see the quads that create the illusion of smoke, which is done by applying a smoke texture to each of the particles and animating them, so they spawn at the bottom and move up in random directions:

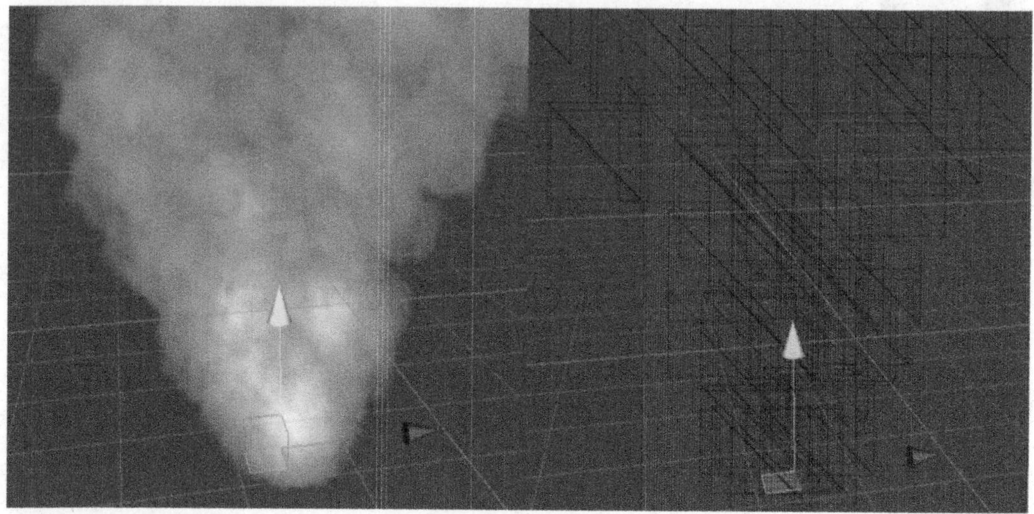

Figure 11.1: On the left side, a smoke particle system; on the right side, the wireframe of the same system

In this section, we will cover the following topics related to particles:

- Creating a basic particle system with Shuriken
- Using advanced modules

Let's start by discussing how to create our very first particle system using Shuriken.

Creating a basic particle system with Shuriken

To illustrate the creation of a particle system, let's create an explosion effect. The idea is to spawn lots of particles at once and spread them in all directions. Let's start with creating the Shuriken particle system and configuring the basic settings it provides to change its default behavior. To do so, follow these steps:

1. Select the **GameObject | Effects | Particle System** option:

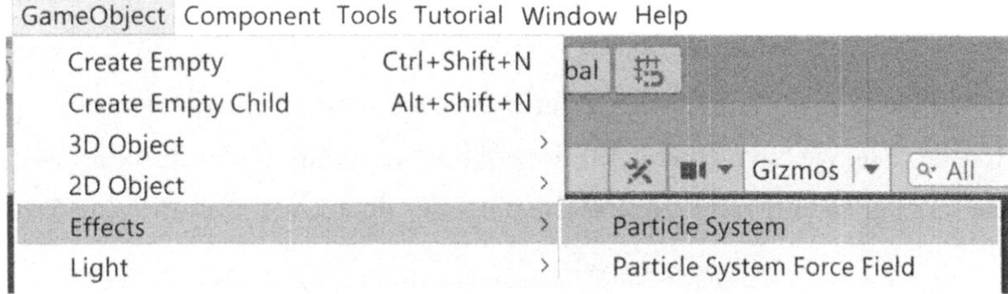

Figure 11.2: Particle System button

2. You should see the effect in the following screenshot. The default behavior is a column of particles going up, like the smoke effect shown previously. Let's change that:

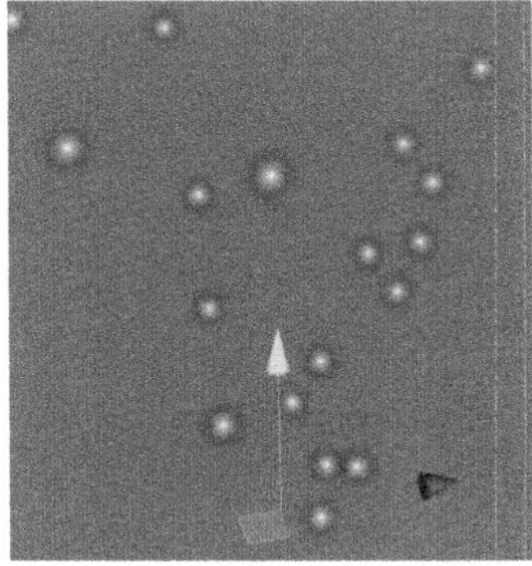

Figure 11.3: Default particle system appearance

3. Click the created object in the scene and look at the Inspector.
4. Open the **Shape** section by clicking on the title. Here you will be able to specify the particle emitter shape from where the particles are going to be spawned.
5. Change the **Shape** property to **Sphere**. Now the particles should move in all possible directions instead of following the default cone:

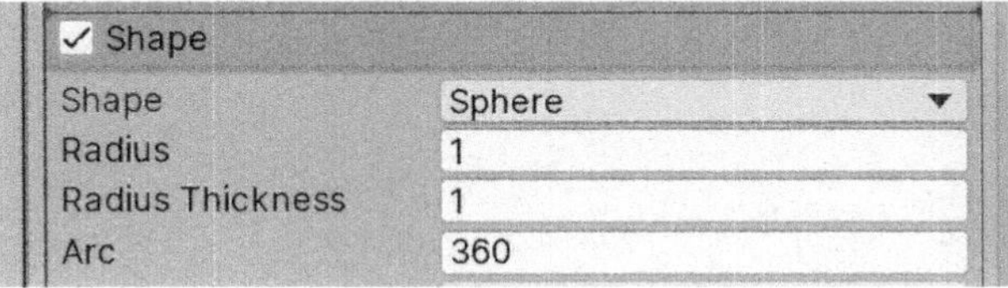

Figure 11.4: Shape properties

6. In the particle system **module** (usually known as **Main**) set **Start Speed** to `10`. This will make the particles move faster.
7. In the same module, set **Start Lifetime** to `0.5`. This specifies how long a particle will live. In this case, we have given a lifetime of half a second. In combination with the speed (10 meters per second), this makes the particles disappear after moving 5 meters:

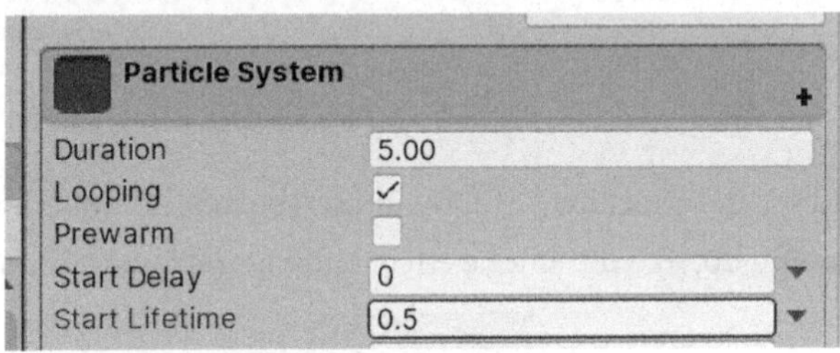

Figure 11.5: Main Particle System module

8. Open the **Emission** module and set **Rate over Time** to `0`. This property specifies how many particles will be emitted per second, but for an explosion, we actually need a burst of particles, so we won't emit particles constantly over time in this case.
9. In the **Bursts** list, click the + button at the bottom, and in the created item in the list, set the count column to `100`:

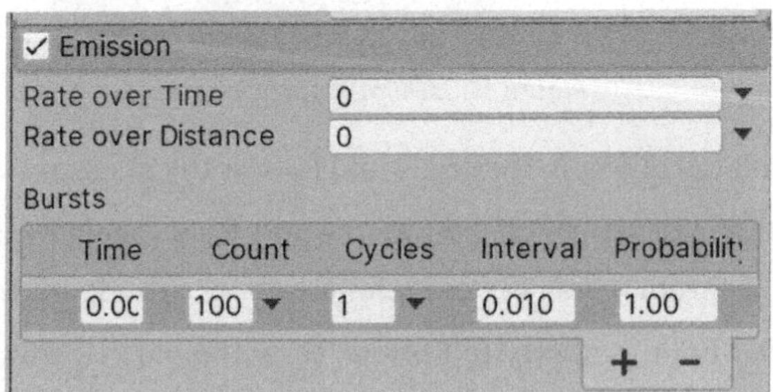

Figure 11.6: Emission module

10. In the **Main** module (the one titled **Particle System**) set **Duration** to 1 and uncheck **Looping**. In our case, the explosion won't repeat constantly; we just need one explosion:

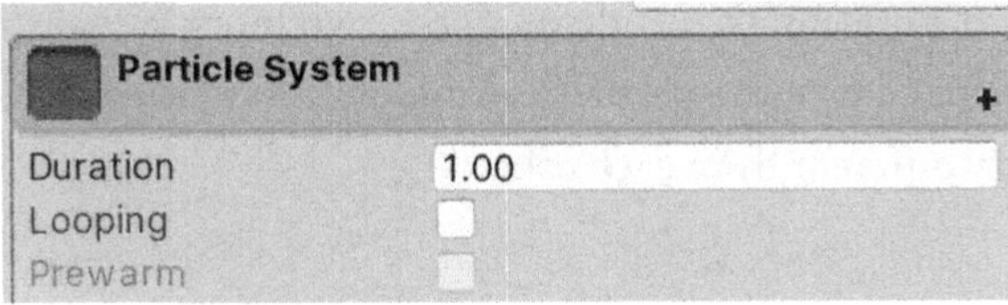

Figure 11.7: Looping checkbox

11. Now that the particle isn't looping, you need to manually hit the **Play** button that is shown in the **Particle Effect** window in the bottom-right part of the Scene view to see the system. If you don't see that window, remember to first select the GameObject with the Particle System in the Hierarchy.

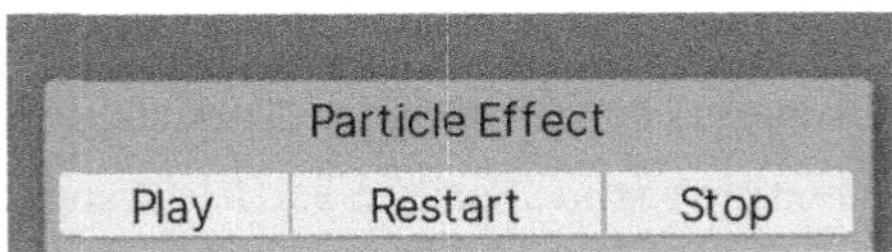

Figure 11.8: Particle system playback controls

12. Set **Stop Action** to **Destroy**. This will destroy the object when the **Duration** time has passed. This will just work when you are running the game, so you can safely use this configuration while editing your scene:

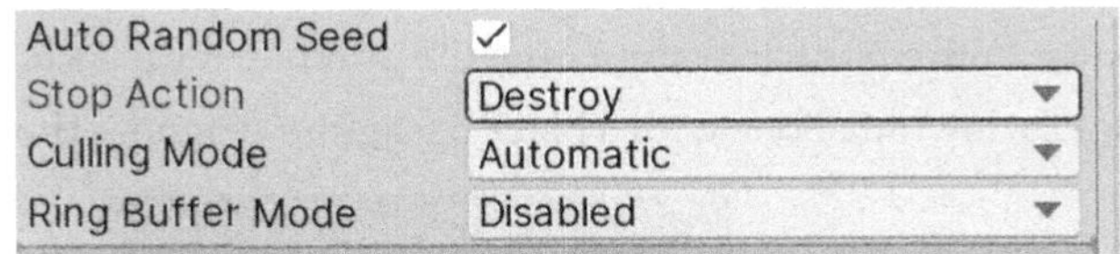

Figure 11.9: Stop Action set to Destroy

13. Set the **Start Size** of the **Main** module to 3. This will make the particles bigger so they seem denser:

Figure 11.10: Particle system Start Size

14. Click on the down-pointing arrow at the right of the **Start Rotation** property of the **Main** module and select **Random Between Two Constants.**
15. Set the **Start Rotation** to `0` and `360` in the two input values that appeared after *step 14*. This allows us to give the particles a random rotation when they spawn to make them look slightly different from each other:

Figure 11.11: Random Start Rotation

16. Now the particles behave as expected, but they don't look as expected. Let's change that. Create a new material by clicking on the + icon in the Project view and selecting **Material**. Call it `Explosion`.
17. Set its shader to **Universal Render Pipeline/Particles/Unlit**. This is a special shader that is used to apply a texture to the Shuriken particle system:

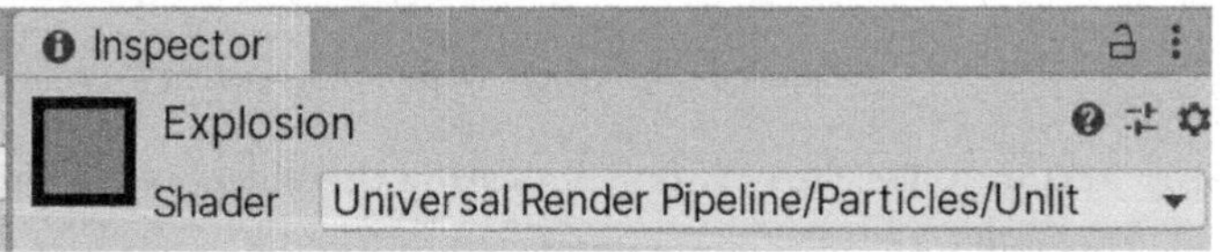

Figure 11.12: Particle system material shader

18. Download a smoke particle texture from the internet or the **Asset Store**. In this case, it is important to download one with a black background; ignore the others:

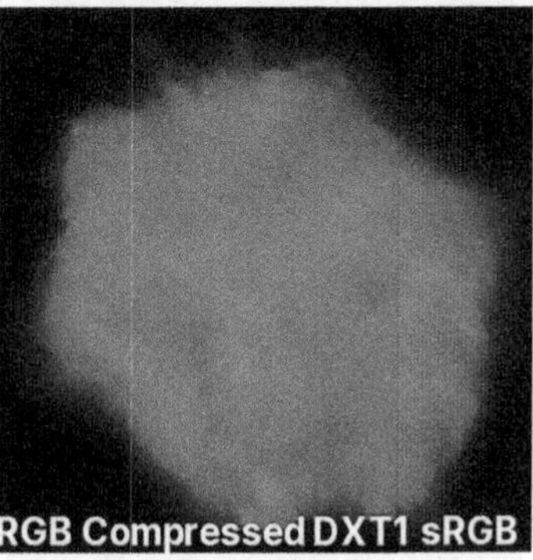

Figure 11.13: Smoke particle texture

19. Set this texture as the **Base Map** of the material.
20. Set the **Surface Type** to **Transparent** and the **Blending Mode** to **Additive**. Doing this will make the particles blend with each other, instead of being drawn on each other, to simulate a big mass of smoke instead of individual smoke puffs. We use **Additive** mode because our texture has a black background and because we want to create a lighting effect (the explosion will brighten the scene):

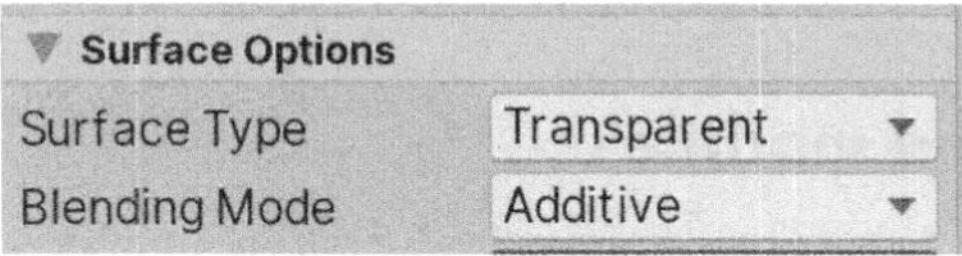

Figure 11.14: Surface options for particles

21. Drag your material to the **Material** property of the **Renderer** module:

Figure 11.15: Particle material settings

22. Now your system should look like the following figure:

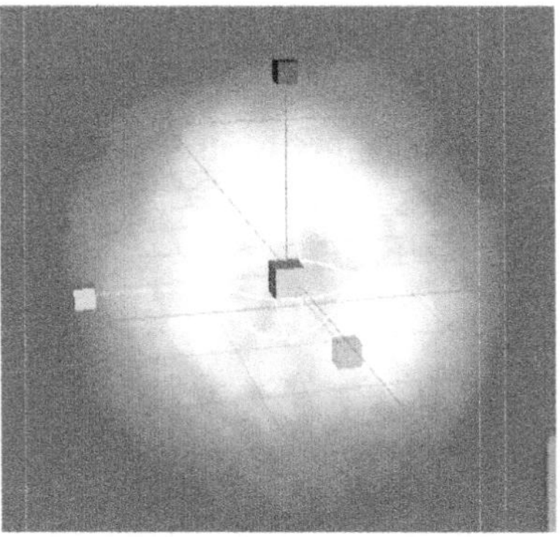

Figure 11.16: Result of the previous settings

With those steps, we have changed how the particles or billboards will spawn (using the **Emission** module), in which direction they will move (using the **Shape** module), how fast they will move, how long they will last, how big they will be (using the **Main** module), and what they will look like (using the **Renderer** module). Creating particle systems is a simple case of properly configuring their different settings. Of course, doing it properly is an art on its own; it requires creativity and knowledge of how to use all the settings and configurations they provide. So, to increase our skillset, let's discuss some advanced modules.

Using advanced modules

Our system looks nice, but we can improve it a lot, so let's enable some new modules to increase its quality:

1. Check the checkbox on the left of **Color over Lifetime** to enable it:

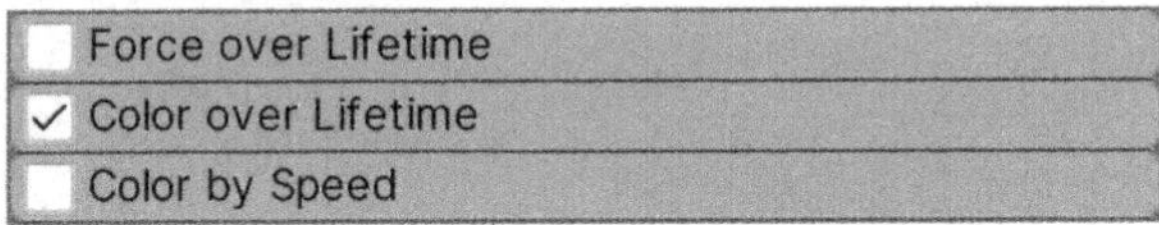

Figure 11.17: Enabling the Color over Lifetime module

2. Open the module by clicking on the title, and click the white bar on the right of the **Color** property. This will open the gradient editor.
3. Click slightly to the right of the top-left white marker in the bar to create a new marker. Also, click slightly to the left of the top-right white marker to create the fourth marker. These markers will allow us to specify the transparency of the particles during their life:

Figure 11.18: Color over Lifetime gradient editor

4. If you created unwanted markers, just drag them outside the window to remove them.
5. Click on the top-left marker (not the one we created, the one that was already there) and set the **Alpha** slider at the bottom to `0`. Do the same with the top-right marker, as shown in the following screenshot. Now you should see the particles fading away instead of popping out of existence when the explosion is finishing:

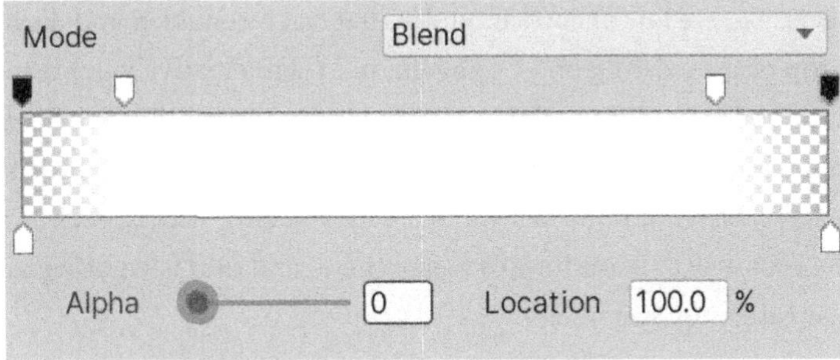

Figure 11.19: Fade-in and fade-out gradient

6. Enable the **Limit Velocity over Lifetime** module by clicking on its checkbox.
7. Set the **Dampen** setting to `0.1`. This will make the particles slowly stop instead of continuing to move:

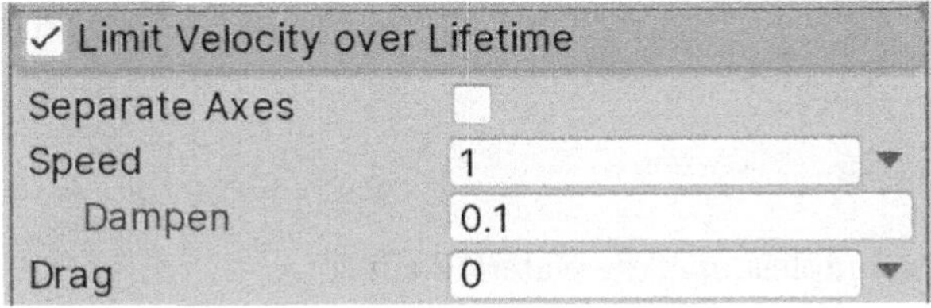

Figure 11.20: Dampen the velocity to make the particles stop

8. Enable **Rotation over Lifetime** and set the **Angular Velocity** between `-90` and `90`. Remember that you should set the value in **Random Between Two Constants** by clicking on the down-pointing arrow to the right of the property. Now the particles should rotate during their lives to simulate more motion:

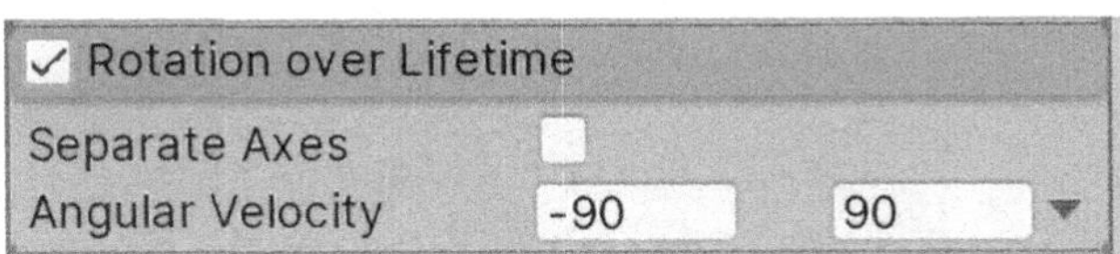

Figure 11.21: Random rotation velocity

Some of these effects will be very subtle given the short **Lifetime** we set in the **Main Module** when we just created the particle. Feel free to increase the **Lifetime** value to see those effects in more detail, but consider that this could lead to an excessive number of particles if you spawn them frequently, reducing performance. Just be wary about how they impact your performance when tweaking those values.

As you can see, there are lots of extra modules that can be enabled and disabled to add layers of behavior on top of the existing ones, so again, use them creatively to create all kinds of effects. Remember that you can create Prefabs of these systems to replicate them all over your scene. I also recommend searching for and downloading particle effects from the Asset Store to see how other people have used the same system to create amazing effects. Seeing a variety of different systems is the best way to learn how to create them, and that is what we are going to do in the next section: create more systems!

Creating fluid simulations

As we said, the best way to learn how to create particle systems is to keep looking for already-created particle systems and explore how people have used the various system settings to create completely different simulations.

In this section, we will learn how to create the following effects using particle systems:

- A waterfall effect
- A bonfire effect

Let's start with the simplest one, the waterfall effect.

Creating a waterfall effect

In order to do this, follow these steps:

1. Create a new particle system (**GameObject** | **Effects** | **Particle System**).
2. Set **Shape** to **Edge** and its **Radius** to 5 in the **Shape** module. This will make the particles spawn along a line of emission:

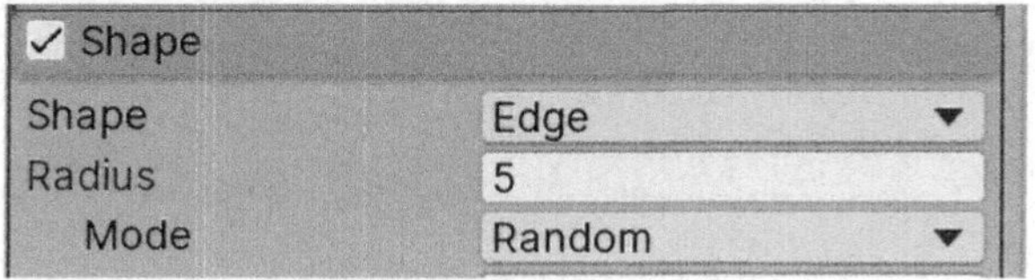

Figure 11.22: Edge shape

3. Set the **Rate over Lifetime** of the **Emission** module to `50`.

4. Set the **Start Size** of the **Main** module to 3 and the **Start Lifetime** to 3:

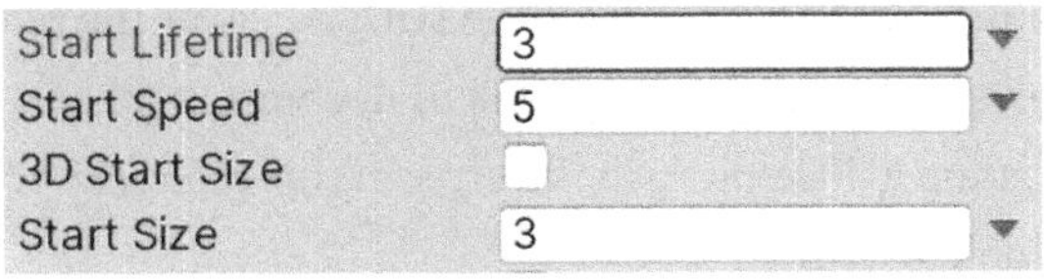

Start Lifetime 3
Start Speed 5
3D Start Size
Start Size 3

Figure 11.23: Main module settings

5. Set the **Gravity Modifier** of the Main module to `0.5`. This will make the particles fall down:

Figure 11.24: Gravity Modifier in the Main module

6. Use the same `Explosion` material we created previously for this system:

Figure 11.25: Explosion particle material

7. Enable **Color Over Lifetime** and open the **Gradient** editor.
8. Click the bottom-right marker, and this time you should see a color picker instead of an alpha slider. The top markers allow you to change the transparency over time, while the bottom ones change the color of the particles over time. Set a light blue color in this marker:

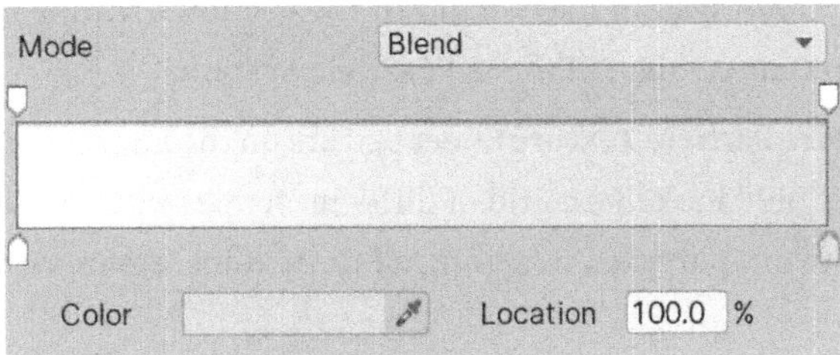

Figure 11.26: White to light blue gradient

As a challenge, I suggest you add a little particle system where this one ends to create some water splashes, simulating the water colliding with a lake at the bottom. Now we can add this particle system to one of the hills of our scene to decorate it, like in the following screenshot. I have adjusted the system a little bit to look better in this scenario. I challenge you to tweak it by yourself to make it look like this:

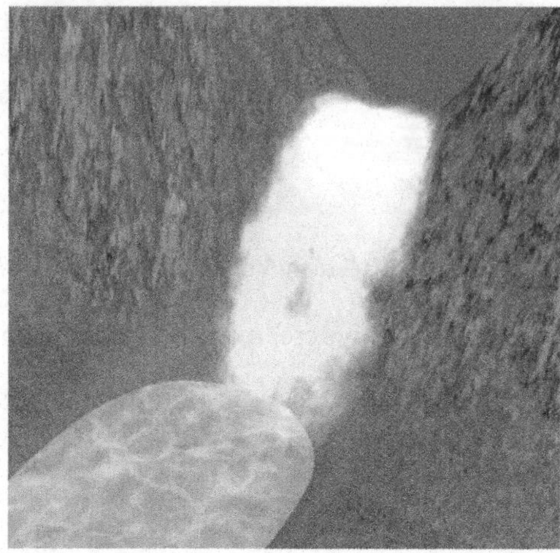

Figure 11.27: The waterfall particle system being applied to our current scene

Now, let's create another effect: a bonfire.

Creating a bonfire effect

In order to create a bonfire, do the following:

1. Create a particle system like we did in the section *Creating a basic particle system with Shuriken*, in **GameObject | Effects | Particle System**.
2. Look for a **Fire Particle Texture Sheet** texture on the internet or the Asset Store. This kind of texture should look like a grid of different flame textures. The idea is to apply a flame animation to our particles swapping all those mini textures:

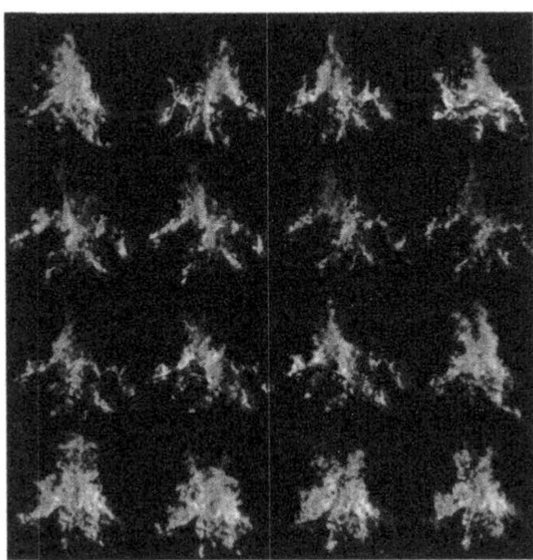

Figure 11.28: Particles texture sprite sheet

3. Create a particle **material** that uses the **Universal Render Pipeline/Particles/Unlit** shader.
4. Set the flames sprite sheet texture as the **Base Map**.
5. Set the color at the right of the **Base Map** to white.
6. Set this material as the particle material. Remember to set **Surface Type** to **Transparent** and **Blending Mode** to **Additive**:

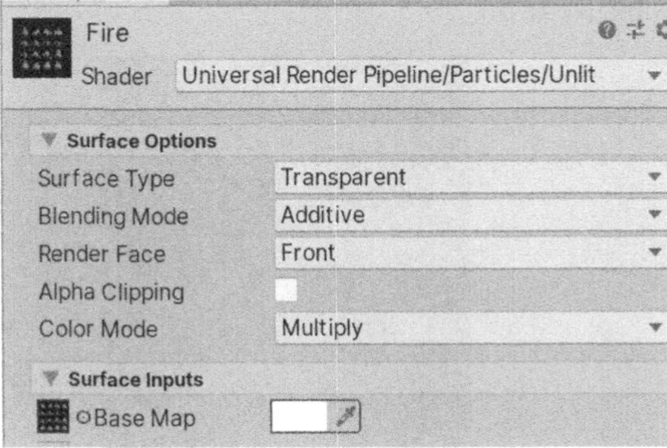

Figure 11.29: A material with a particle sprite sheet

7. Enable the **Texture Sheet Animation** module and set the **Tiles** property according to your fire sheet. In my case, I have a grid of 4x4 sprites, so I put 4 in **X** and 4 in **Y**. After this, you should see the particles swapping textures:

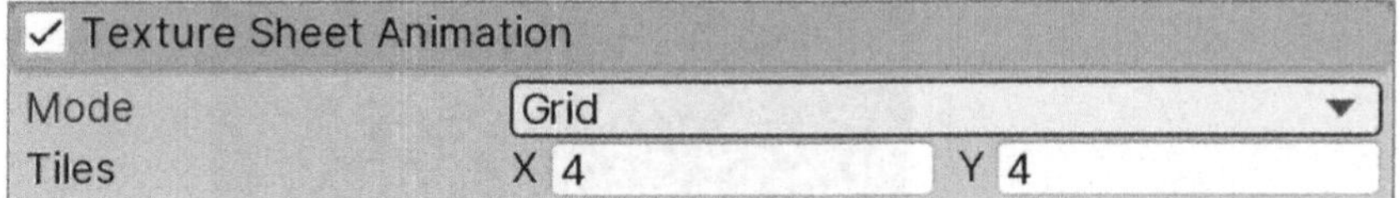

Figure 11.30: Enabling Texture Sheet Animation

8. Set **Start Speed** to `0` and **Start Size** to `1.5` in the Main module.
9. Set **Radius** to `0.5` in **Shape**.
10. Create a second particle system and make it a child of the fire system:

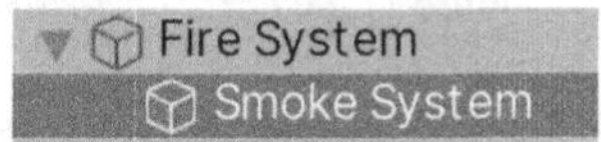

Figure 11.31: Parenting particle systems

11. Apply the **Explosion** material from the explosion example.
12. Set **Angle** to `0` and **Radius** to `0.5` in the **Shape** module.

The system should look like this:

Figure 11.32: Result of combining fire and smoke particle systems

As you can see, you can combine several particle systems to create a single effect. Take care when doing this because it's easy to emit too many particles and affect the game's performance. Particles are not cheap and may cause a reduction in the game's **FPS (Frames Per Second)** if you are not cautious with them.

So far, we have explored one of the Unity systems that you can use to create these kinds of effects, and while this system is enough for most situations, Unity recently released a new one that can generate more complex effects, called **Visual Effect Graph**. Let's see how to use it and see how it differs from Shuriken.

Creating complex simulations with Visual Effect Graph

The particle system we have used so far is called Shuriken, and it handles all calculations in the CPU. This has both pros and cons. A pro is that it can run on all possible devices that Unity supports, regardless of their capabilities (all of them have CPUs), but a con is that we can exceed CPU capabilities easily if we are not cautious with the number of particles we emit. Modern games require more complex particle systems to generate believable effects, and this kind of CPU-based particle system solution has started to reach its limit. This is where the Visual Effect Graph comes in:

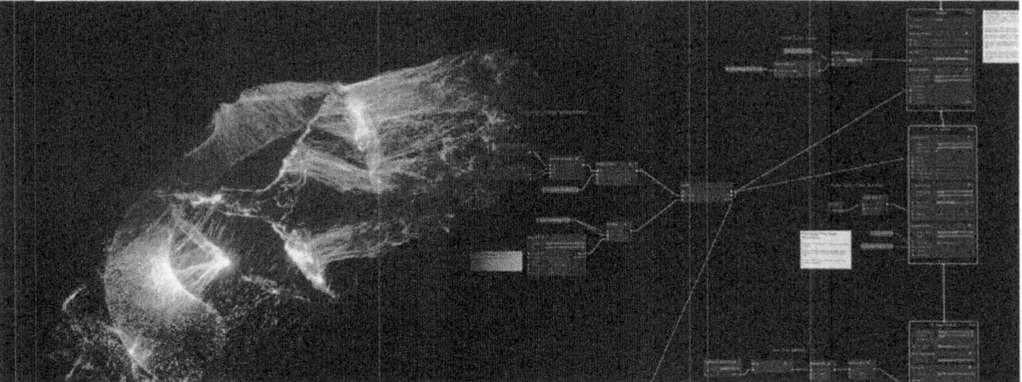

Figure 11.33: On the left, a massive particle system, and on the right, an example of a Visual Effect Graph

Visual Effect Graph is a GPU-based particle system solution, meaning that the system is executed in the video card instead of the CPU. That's because video cards are far more efficient at executing lots and lots of little simulations, like the ones each particle of a system needs, so we can reach far higher orders of magnitude in the number of particles with the GPU than we can with the CPU. The con here is that we need a fairly modern GPU that has **compute shader** capabilities to support this system, so we will exclude certain target platforms using this system (forget about most mobile phones), so use it if your target platform supports it (mid- to high-end PCs, consoles, and some high-end phones).

In this section, we will discuss the following topics of Visual Effect Graph:

- Installing Visual Effect Graph
- Creating and analyzing a Visual Effect Graph
- Creating a rain effect

Let's start by seeing how we can add support for Visual Effect Graph in our project.

Installing Visual Effect Graph

So far, we have used lots of Unity features that were already installed in our project, but Unity can be extended with a myriad of plugins, both official and third-party. Visual Effect Graph is one of those features that needs to be independently installed if you are using **Universal Render Pipeline (URP)**. We can do that using the Package Manager, a Unity window dedicated to managing official Unity plugins.

Something to think about when you are installing those packages is that each package or plugin has its own version, independent of the Unity version. That means that you can have Unity 2022.1 installed, but Visual Effect Graph 13.1.8 or whatever version you want, and you can actually update the package to a newer version without upgrading Unity. This is important because some versions of these packages require a minimum version of Unity—for example, Visual Effect Graph 13.1.8 requires Unity 2022.1 as a minimum. Moreover, some packages depend on other packages and specific versions of those packages, so we need to ensure we have the correct versions of every package to ensure compatibility. To be clear, the dependencies of a package are installed automatically, but sometimes we can have them installed separately, so in that scenario, we need to check the required version. It sounds complicated, but it is simpler than it sounds.

At the time of writing this book, in order to get Visual Effect Graph working properly we need version 13.1.8, and also we need the same version of **Universal RP**. Yes, Universal RP is another feature you can install using the Package Manager, but as we created the project using the Universal RP template, it was already installed for us with the proper version. With that in mind, let's install the Visual Effect Graph as follows:

1. In the top menu of Unity, go to **Window | Package Manager**:

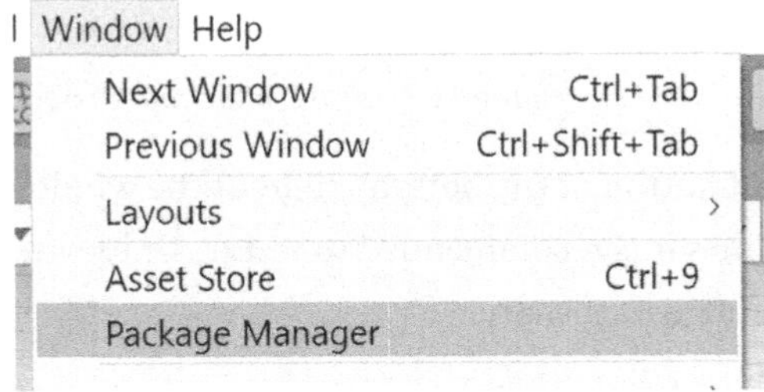

Figure 11.34: Package Manager location

2. Remember to be sure the **Packages** dropdown is in **Unity Registry** mode, to see the Unity official packages list:

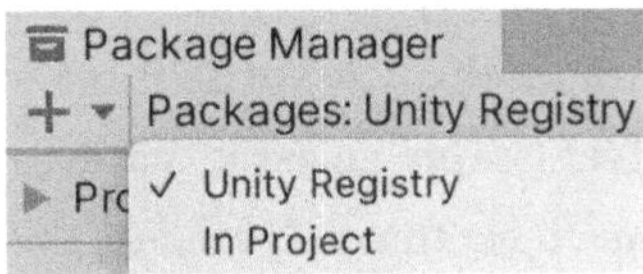

Figure 11.35: Package Manager Unity Registry mode

3. In the left column, locate **Universal RP** and check whether it says 13.1.8 or higher to the right. If it does, jump to *step 6*. Remember, though, that a higher version may look different or have different steps for use than the ones displayed in this chapter.
4. If you don't have version 13.1.8 or higher, click on the right-pointing arrow at the left to display a list of all possible versions to install. Locate 13.1.8 and click it. In my case it says **Currently installed** as I have that version already installed in the project, and there's no other one available for Unity 2022:

Figure 11.36: Package version selector

5. Click on the **Update to 13.1.8** button in the bottom-right part of the window and wait for the package to update.
6. Look for the **Visual Effect Graph** package on the left side of the window. As you did with Universal RP, make sure you select version 11.0.0 or the closest higher available:

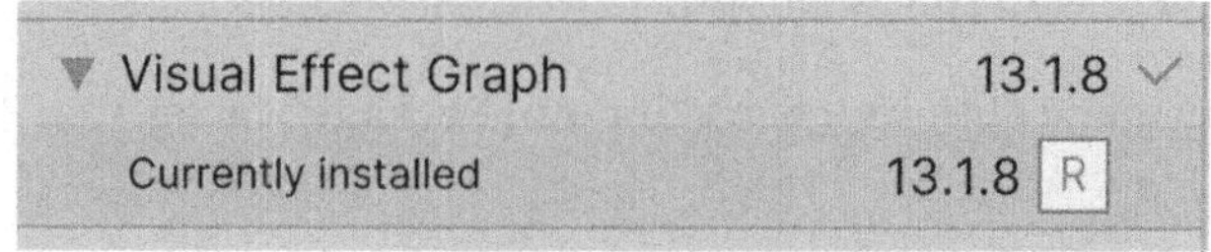

Figure 11.37: Visual Effect Graph package

7. Click the **Install** button at the bottom-right of the window and wait for the package to install. Sometimes it is recommended to restart Unity after installing packages, so save your changes and restart Unity.

Now that we have installed Visual Effect Graph, let's create our first particle system using it.

Creating and analyzing a Visual Effect Graph

The method to create a particle system using Visual Effect Graph is similar to a regular Particle System. We will chain and configure modules as parts of the behavior of the particles, each module adding some specific behavior, but the way we do it is very different than with Shuriken. First, we need to create a **Visual Effect Graph**, an asset that will contain all the modules and configurations, and then make a GameObject that will execute the Graph asset to spawn particles. Let's do that with the following steps:

1. In the Project window, click on the + button and look for **Visual Effects | Visual Effect Graph**:

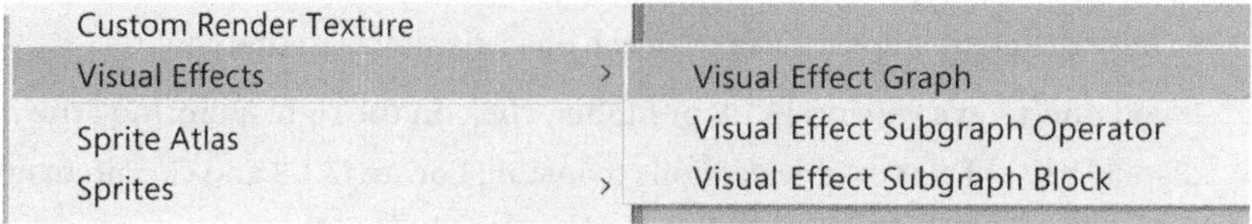

Figure 11.38: Visual Effect Graph

2. Create an **Empty** GameObject using the **GameObject | Create Empty** option:

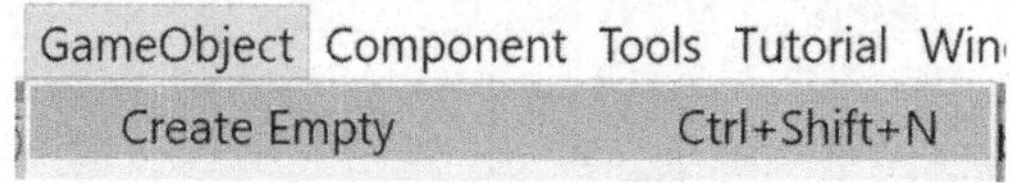

Figure 11.39: Empty GameObject creation

3. Select the created object and look at the **Inspector**.
4. Using the **Add Component** search bar, look for the **Visual Effect** component and click on it to add it to the object:

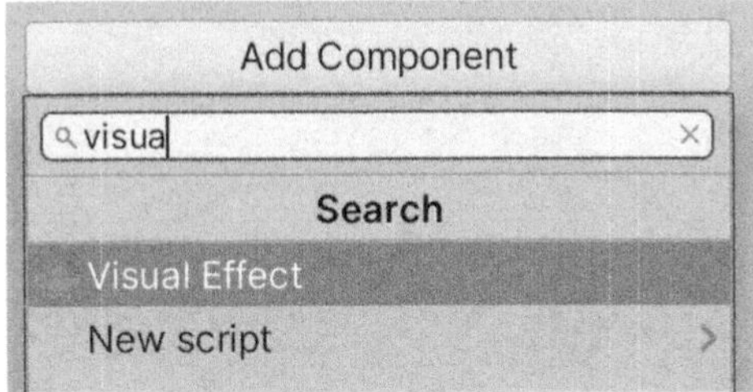

Figure 11.40: Adding a component to the Visual Effect Graph

5. Drag the **Visual Effect** asset we created to the **Asset Template** property of the **Visual Effect** component in our GameObject:

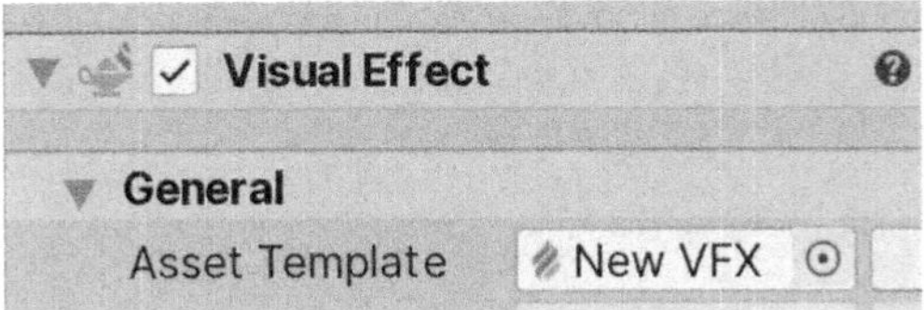

Figure 11.41: Visual Effect using the previously created Visual Effect asset

6. You should see clock particles being emitted from our object, which is the default behavior included in a new Visual Effect asset, meaning it's being executed correctly:

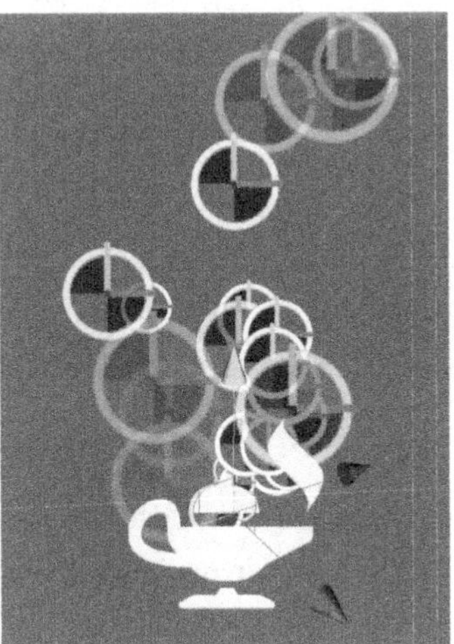

Figure 11.42: Default Visual Effect asset results

Now that we have a base effect, let's create something that requires a lot of particles, such as dense rain. Before doing so, we will explore some core concepts of Visual Effect Graph. If you double-click the Visual Effect asset, you will see the following editor:

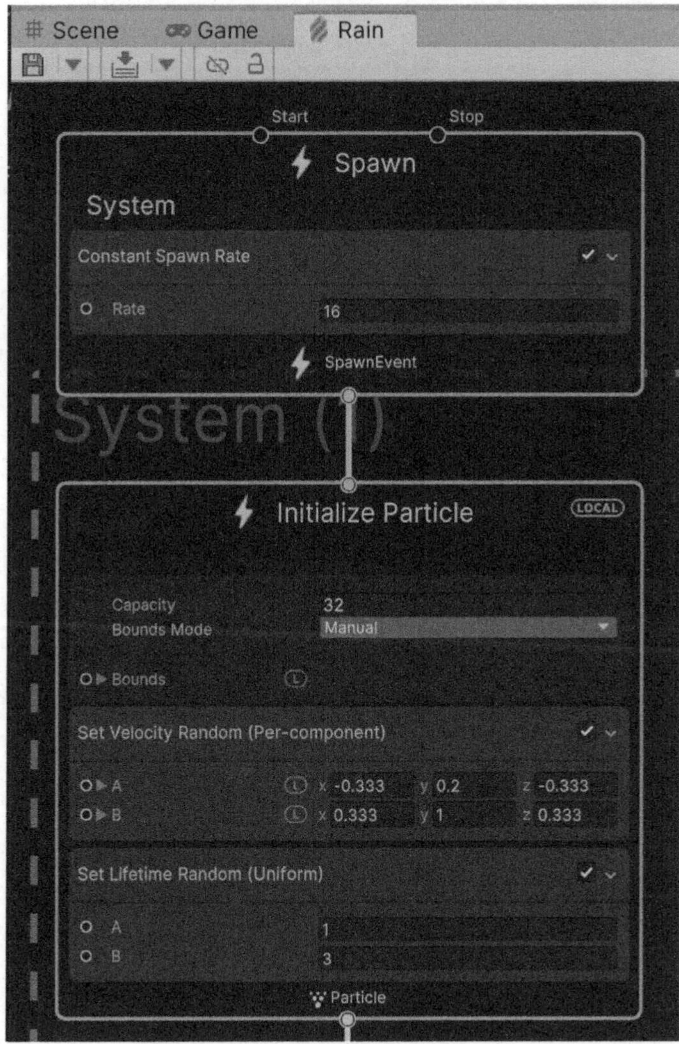

Figure 11.43: Visual Effect Graph editor window

This window is composed of several interconnected nodes, generating a flow of actions to be executed. As with the Shader Graph, you can navigate this window by keeping the *Alt* key (*Option* on Mac) pressed and dragging with the mouse the empty areas of the graph. At first, it seems similar to the Shader Graph, but it works a little bit differently, so let's study each section of the default graph.

The first area to explore is the dotted one that contains three nodes. This is what Unity calls a **System**. A System is a set of nodes that defines how a particle will behave, and you can have as many as you want, which is the equivalent of having several particle system objects. Each System is composed of **Contexts**, the nodes inside the dotted area, and in this case, we have **Initialize Particle**, **Update Particle**, and **Output Particle Quad**. Each Context represents a different stage of the particle system logic flow, so let's define what each Context in our graph does:

- **Initialize Particle**: This defines the initial data of each emitted particle, such as position, color, speed, and size. It is similar to the **Start** properties in the Main module of the particle system we saw at the beginning of this chapter. The logic in this node will only execute when a new particle is emitted.
- **Update Particle**: Here, we can apply modifications to the data of the living particles. We can change particle data such as the current velocity or particle size of all the frames. This is similar to the **Overtime** nodes of the Shuriken particle systems.
- **Output Particle Quad**: This Context will be executed when the particle needs to be rendered. It will read the particle data to see where to render, how to render, which texture and color to use, and the different visual settings. This is similar to the renderer module of the previous particle system.

Inside each Context, apart from some base configurations, we can add **Blocks**. Each Block is an action that will be executed in the Context. We have actions that can be executed in any Context and then some specific Context actions. As an example, we can use an **Add Position Block** in the Initialize Particle Context to move the initial particle position, but if we use the same Block in the Update Particle Context, it will move the particle constantly. So basically, Contexts are different situations that happen in the life of the particle, and Blocks are actions that are executed in those situations:

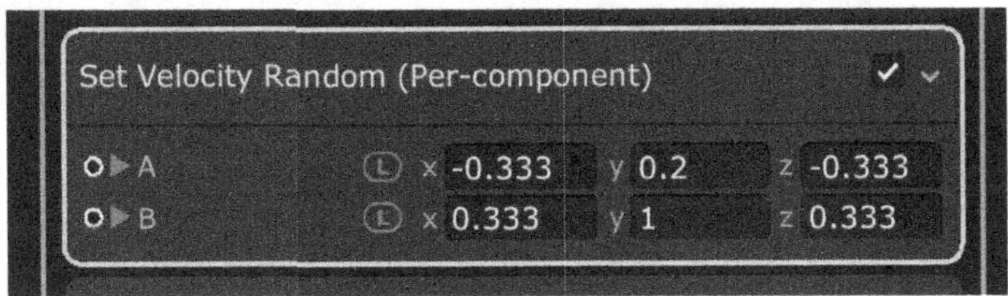

Figure 11.44: A Set Velocity Random Block inside the Initialize Particle Context. This sets the initial velocity of a particle

Also, we can have **Standalone Contexts**, Contexts outside Systems, such as **Spawn**. This Context is responsible for telling the System that a new particle needs to be created. We can add Blocks to specify when the context will tell the system to create the particle, such as at a fixed rate over time, bursts, and so on. The idea is that Spawn will create particles according to its Blocks, while a System is responsible for initializing, updating, and rendering each of them, again, according to the blocks we set up inside each one of those Contexts.

So, we can see that there are lots of similarities with Shuriken, but the way to create a system here is quite different. Let's reinforce this by creating a rain effect, which will require lots of particles—a nice use case for Visual Effect Graph.

Creating a rain effect

In order to create this effect, do the following:

1. Set the **Capacity** property of the **Initialize Particle** Context to `10000`:

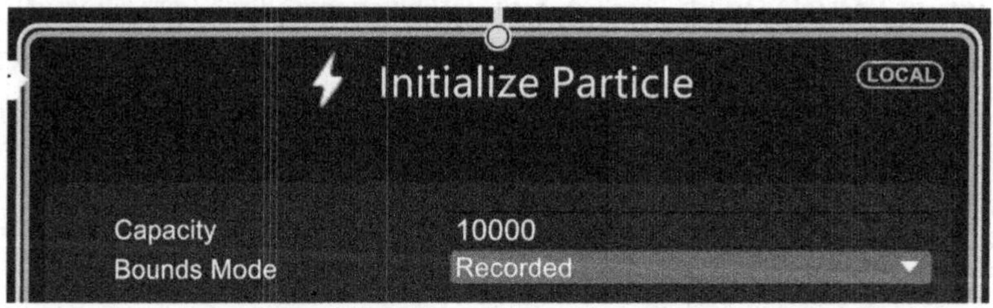

Figure 11.45: Initialize Particle Context

2. Set the **Rate** of the **Constant Spawn Rate** of the **Spawn** context to `10000`:

Figure 11.46: Constant Spawn Rate Block

3. Set the **A** and **B** properties to `0`, `-50`, and `0` and `0`, `-75`, and `0` respectively in the **Set Velocity Random** block in the **Initialize Particle** Context. This will set a random velocity pointing downward for our particles:

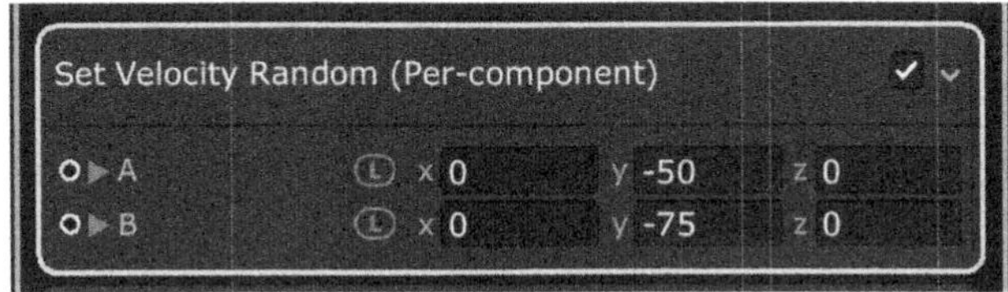

Figure 11.47: Set Velocity Random Block

4. Right-click the **Initialize Particle** title, and select **Create Block**.
5. Search for the **Set Position Random** block and click on it:

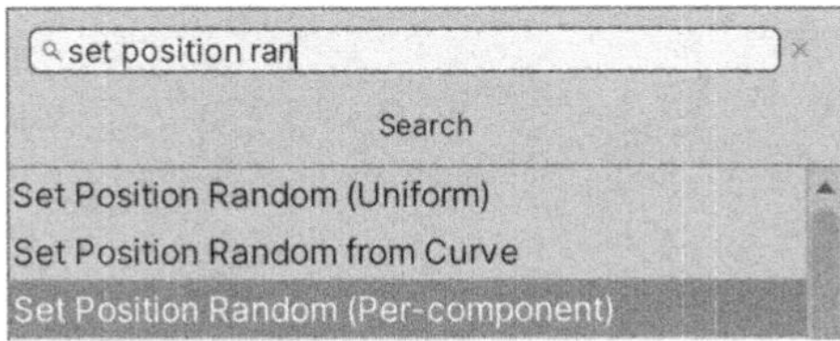

Figure 11.48: Adding blocks

6. Set the **A** and **B** properties of the **Set Position Random** Block to `-50`, `0`, and `-50` and `50`, `0`, and `50` respectively. This will define an initial area in which to randomly spawn the particle.
7. Click the arrow at the left of the **Bounds** property of the **Initialize Particle** Block to display its properties, and set **Center** and **Size** to `0`, `-12.5`, and `0` and `100`, `25`, and `100` respectively. This will define the area where the particles should be visible. Particles can actually move outside this area, but it is important to render the particles only in the areas we are interested in them being visible.

Search `Frustum culling` on the internet for more information about bounds.

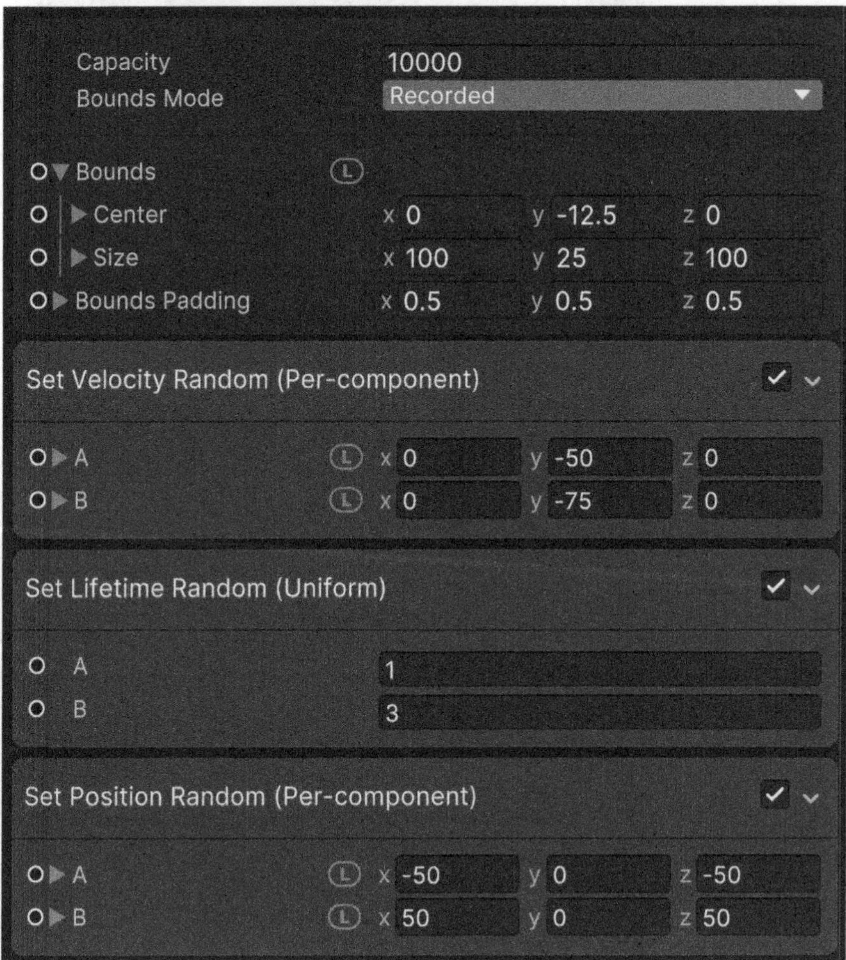

Figure 11.49: Configuring blocks

8. Select the GameObject that is executing the system, and in the bottom-right window in the Scene view check the **Show Bounds** checkbox to see the previously defined bounds:

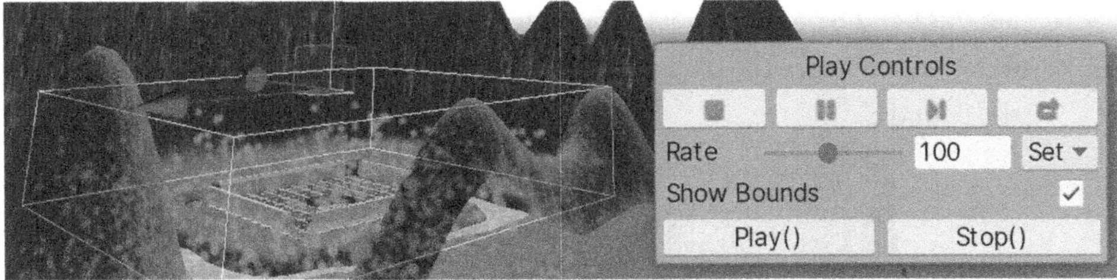

Figure 11.50: Visual Effect playback controls

9. If you don't see the window at the bottom right, click the **VE** (Visual Effect) button at the top-left side of the screen to display it. This button will be shown only if you have selected the **Rain** visual effect GameObject in the **Hierarchy**:

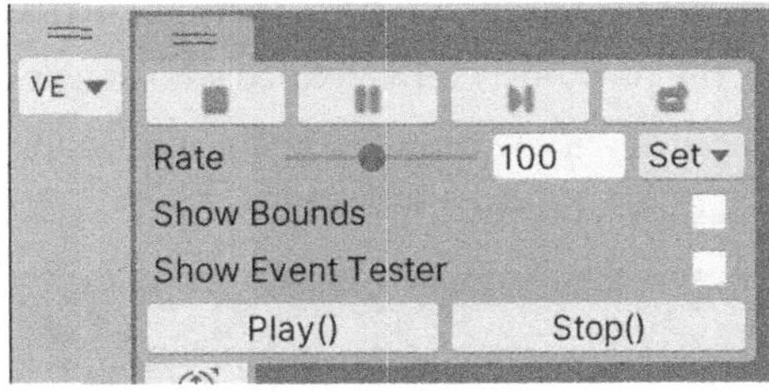

Figure 11.51: Another way to display the Visual Effect playback controls

10. If you can't see the changes being applied, click the **Compile** button in the top left of the window, the one that looks like a paper bin beneath a downward-pointing arrow. Also, you can save your changes using *Ctrl* + *S* (*Command* + *S* on Mac):

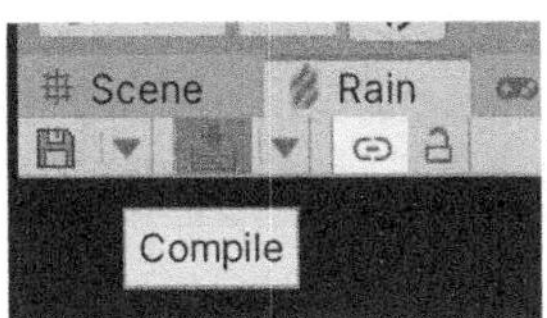

Figure 11.52: VFX asset saving controls

11. Set the object position to cover the whole base area. In my case, the position is `100`, `37`, and `100`. Remember that you need to change the **Position** of the **Transform** component for this:

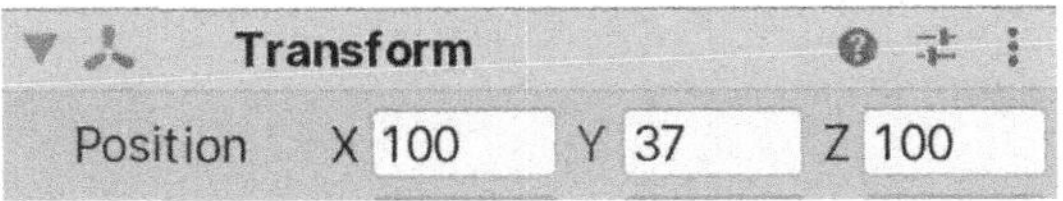

Figure 11.53: Setting a Transform position

12. Set the **A** and **B** properties of the **Set Lifetime Random** Block in the **Initialize Particle** to `0.5`. This will make the particles have a shorter life, ensuring that they are always inside the bounds:

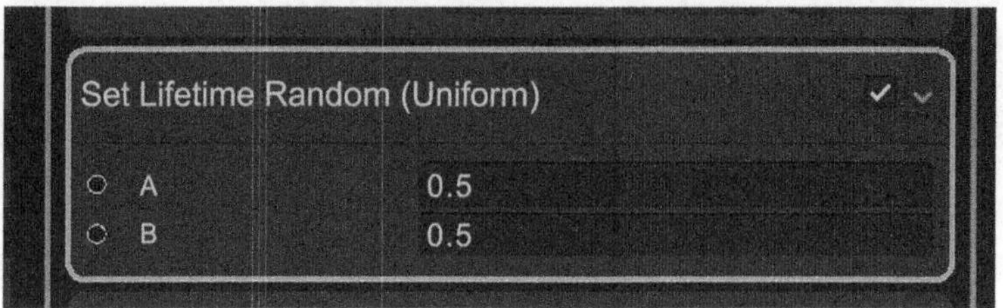

Figure 11.54: Set Lifetime Random Block

13. Change the **Main Texture** property of the **Output Particle Quad** Context to another texture. In this case, the previously downloaded smoke texture can work here, even though it's not water, because we will modify its appearance in a moment. Also, you can try to download a water droplet texture if you want to:

Figure 11.55: VFX Graph Main Texture

14. Set **Blend Mode** of the **Output Particle Quad** Context to **Additive**:

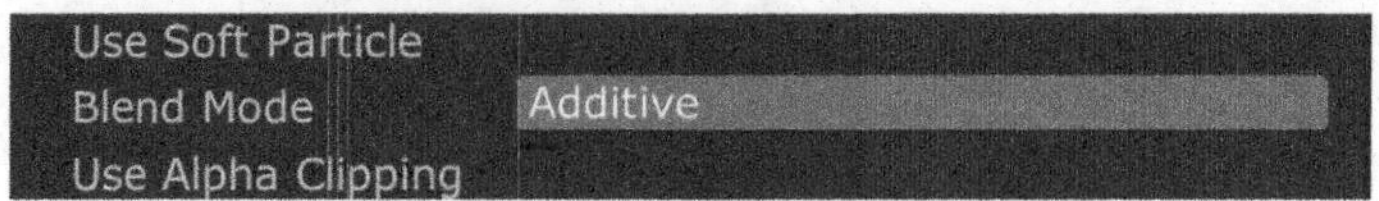

Figure 11.56: Additive mode of VFX Graph

15. We need to stretch our particles a little bit to look like actual raindrops instead of falling balls. Before accomplishing that, first we need to change the orientation of our particles, so they don't point at the camera all the time. In order to do this, right-click on the **Orient Block** in the **Output Particle Quad** Context and select **Delete** (or press *Delete* on PC or *Command* + *Backspace* on Mac):

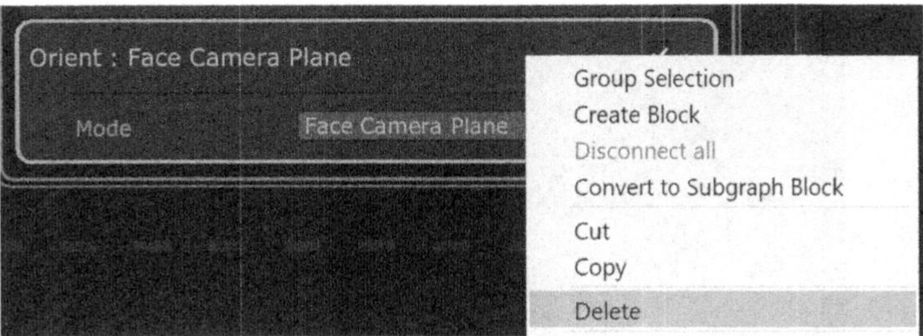

Figure 11.57: Deleting a block

16. We want to stretch our particles according to their velocity direction. Another preparation step before actually doing that is to select the title of the **Output Particle Quad** context and hit the space bar to look for a block to add. In this case, we need to search and add the **Orient Along Velocity** block.
17. Add a **Set Scale** Block to the **Initialize Particle** Context and set the **Scale** property to `0.25`, `1.5`, and `0.25`. This will stretch the particles to look like falling drops:

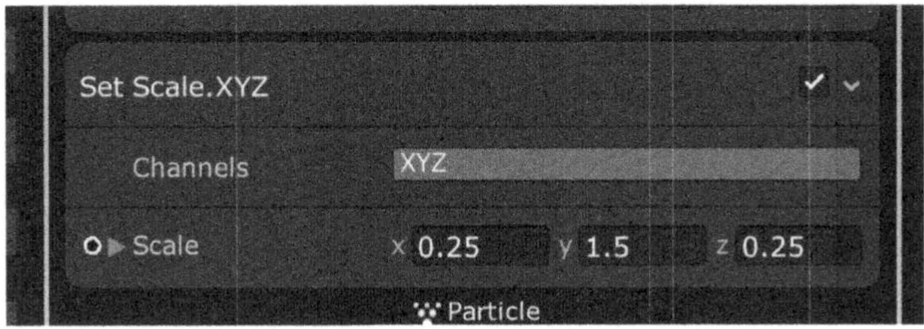

Figure 11.58: Set Scale Block

18. Click the **Compile** button in the top-left window again to see the changes. Your system should look like this:

Figure 11.59: Rain results

We have just modified lots of different properties of the Visual Effect Graph, but if you want to have two instances of the same Visual Effect Graph, but with slight differences, I recommend you look at the Blackboard feature, which will allow you to expose properties in the Inspector. For example, you can make less dense rain on another scene, making the spawn rate lower, or change the particle color to make acid rain, all using the same graph, but let's keep things simple for now.

The Blackboard feature is also present in Shader Graph.

From here, you can experiment by adding and removing Blocks from the Contexts as you wish, and again, I recommend you look for already-created Visual Effect Graphs to find ideas for other systems. Actually, you can get ideas for Visual Effect Graph by looking at effects made in Shuriken and using the analogous blocks. Also, I recommend you search for the Visual Effect Graph documentation online or at: `https://docs.unity3d.com/Packages/com.unity.visualeffectgraph@13.1/manual/index.html` to learn more about this system. You can also access the documentation of any Unity Package by clicking the **View Documentation** button in the Package Manager while the package is selected.

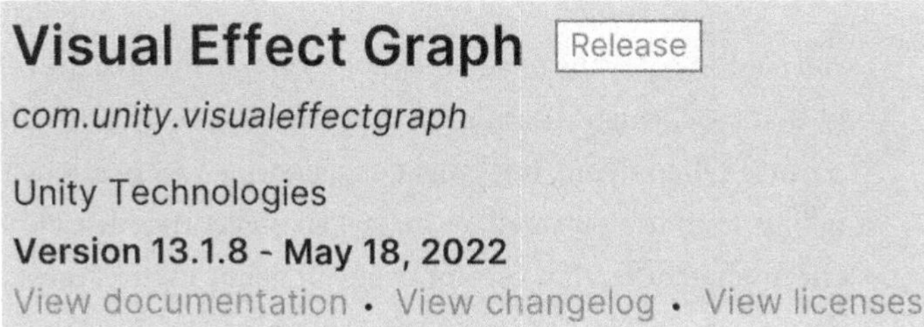

Figure 11.60: Package Manager documentation link

Now that we have learnt how to create different visual effects, let's see how to use them via scripting to achieve effects that react to what's happening in the game.

Scripting Visual Effects

Visual feedback is the concept of using different VFX, such as particles and a VFX graph, to reinforce what is happening. For example, say right now we are shooting our weapon, and we know that this is happening because we can see the bullets. However, it doesn't feel like a real shooting effect, because a proper shooting effect should have a muzzle effect on the tip of our gun. Another example would be the enemy dying—it just disappears with no animation! That doesn't feel as satisfying as it could be. We can instead add a little explosion (considering they are robots).

Let's start making our enemies spawn an explosion when they die by doing the following:

1. Create an explosion effect or download one from the Asset Store. It shouldn't loop and it needs to be destroyed automatically when the explosion is over (ensure **Looping** is unchecked and **Stop Action** is set to `Destroy` in the main module).
2. Some explosions in the Asset Store might use non-URP-compatible shaders. You can fix them by using **Window | Rendering | Render Pipeline Converter**, as we saw in *Chapter 4, Importing and Integrating Assets.*
3. Manually upgrade the materials that didn't upgrade automatically.
4. Add a script to the `Enemy` prefab called `ExplosionOnDeath`. This will be responsible for spawning the particles Prefab when the enemy dies.
5. Add a field of the `GameObject` type called `particlePrefab` and drag the explosion Prefab to it.

You may be expecting to add the explosion spawning to the `Life` component. In that case, you are assuming that anything to do with life will spawn a particle when dying, but consider scenarios where characters die with a falling animation instead, or maybe an object that just despawns with no effect whatsoever. If a certain behavior is not used in most scenarios, it is better to code it in a separate optional script to allow us to mix and match different components and get the exact behavior we want.

6. Make the script access the `Life` component and subscribe to its `onDeath` event.
7. In the `listener` function, spawn the particle system in the same location:

```
public class ExplosionOnDeath : MonoBehaviour
{
    public GameObject particlePrefab;

    void Awake()
    {
        var life = GetComponent<Life>();
        life.onDeath.AddListener(OnDeath);
    }

    void OnDeath()
    {
        Instantiate(particlePrefab,
            transform.position,
            transform.rotation);
    }
}
```

Figure 11.61: The explosion spawner script

The Visual Scripting version would look like this:

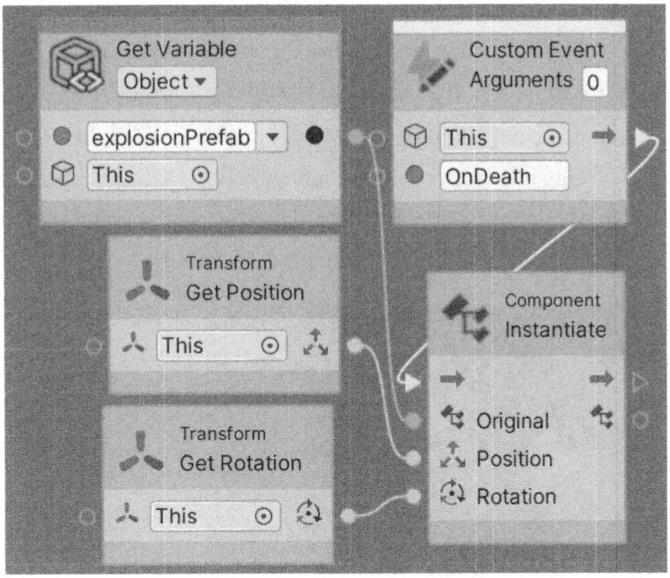

Figure 11.62: The explosion spawner visual script

As you can see, we are just using the same concepts we learned about in previous chapters but combining them in new ways. This is what programming is all about.

Let's continue with the muzzle effect, which will also be a particle system, but we will take another approach this time:

1. If you don't have one already, download a weapon model from the Asset Store. The character in the package we used in the book already comes with one, so we will use that one.
2. If it's not already in your character, instantiate the weapon so that it is the parent of the hand of the player. Remember that our character is rigged and has a hand bone, so you should put the weapon there.
3. The weapon that comes with the character we downloaded in this book is a special scenario where the weapon has a **SkinnedMeshRenderer**. This component uses the *Skinning Animation* system that we will learn to use in *Chapter 17, Create Animations with Animator, Cinemachine, and Timeline*. In this case, the movement of the weapon will be affected by the animations we will use in that chapter, so for now let's keep the weapon where it is located now, even if it looks odd.

4. Create or get a muzzle particle system. In this case, my muzzle particle system was created as a short particle system that has a burst of particles and then automatically stops. Try to get one with that behavior because there are others out there that will loop instead, and the script to handle that scenario would be different.
5. Create an instance of the particle system prefab in the editor and parent it inside the weapon, locating it in front of the weapon, aligned with the cannon of the gun. Make sure the **Play On Awake** property of the main module of the particle system is unchecked; we don't want the muzzle to fire until we press the fire key:

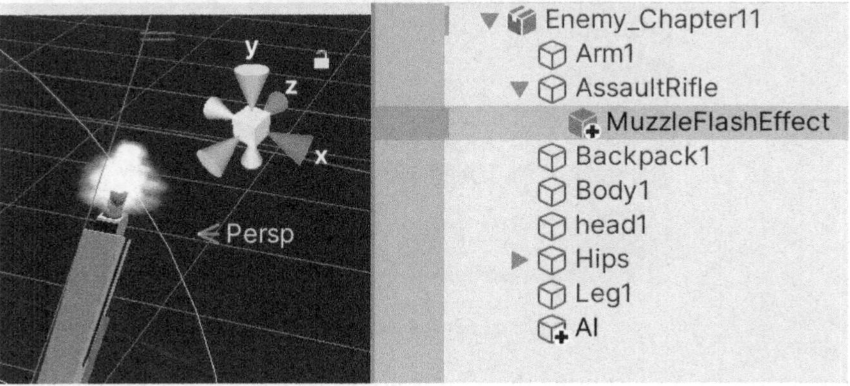

Figure 11.63: The muzzle parented to the weapon

6. Create a field of the `ParticleSystem` type called `muzzleEffect` in `PlayerShooting`.
7. Drag the muzzle effect GameObject that is parented in the gun to it in the Inspector. Now, we have a reference to the `ParticleSystem` component of the muzzle to manage it.
8. Inside the `if` statement that checks whether we are shooting, execute `muzzleEffect.Play();` to play the particle system. It will automatically stop and is short enough to finish between key presses:

```
public GameObject prefab;
public GameObject shootPoint;
public ParticleSystem muzzleEffect;

public void OnFire(InputValue value)
{
    if (value.isPressed)
    {
        GameObject clone = Instantiate(prefab);

        clone.transform.position = shootPoint.transform.position;
        clone.transform.rotation = shootPoint.transform.rotation;

        muzzleEffect.Play();
    }
}
```

Figure 11.64: The muzzle parented to the weapon

The Visual Scripting version's additional nodes and variables would be the following:

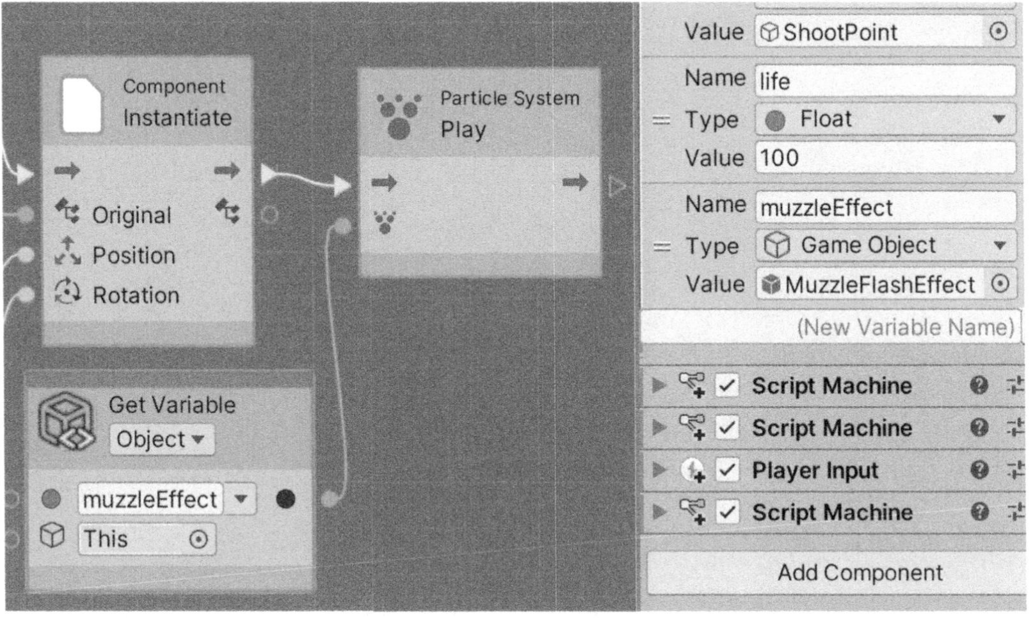

Figure 11.65: The muzzle playing visual script

Finally, we need to play the muzzle effect also on the AI while shooting by doing the following:

1. As we did with `PlayerShooting`, create a field of the `ParticleSystem` type called `muzzleEffect` in `EnemyFSM`.
2. Inside the `Shoot` method, add the line `muzzleEffect.Play();` at the end of the method to play the particle system:

```
public ParticleSystem muzzleEffect;

void Shoot()
{
    var timeSinceLastShoot :float = Time.time - lastShootTime;
    if(timeSinceLastShoot < fireRate)
        return;

    lastShootTime = Time.time;
    Instantiate(bulletPrefab, transform.position, transform.rotation);
    muzzleEffect.Play();
}
```

Figure 11.66: The muzzle playing C# script

The Visual Scripting version's additional nodes for the `Attack State` and `Attack Base` will be:

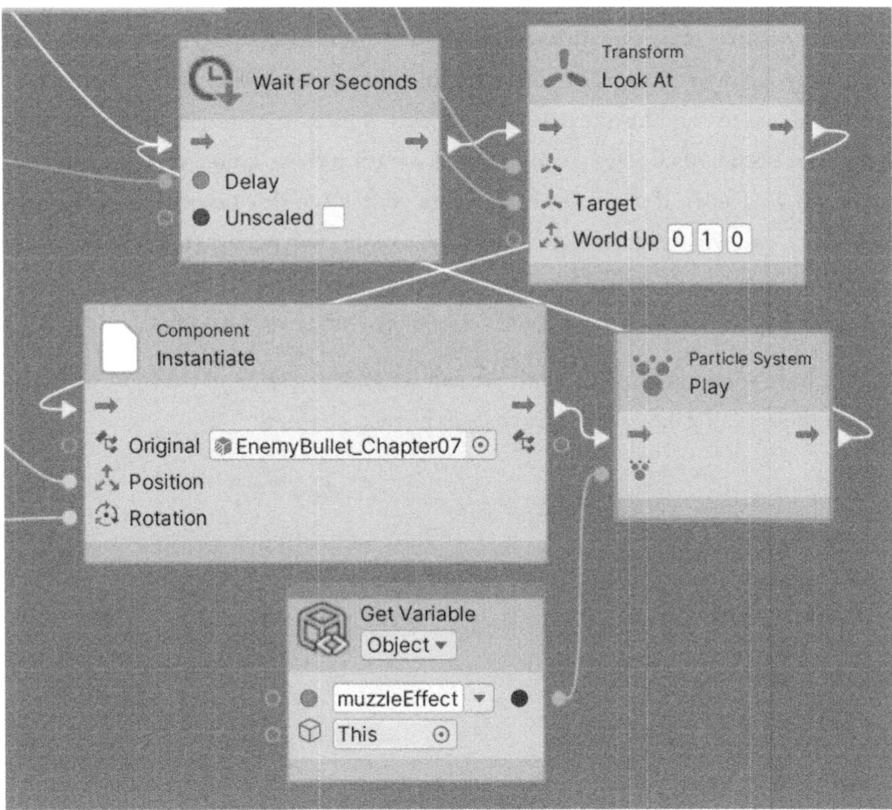

Figure 11.67: The muzzle playing script for the Attack State

Remember to add those nodes to both attack states and to add the `muzzleEffect` variable to the AI Variables component.

Summary

In this chapter, we discussed two different ways to create particle systems: using Shuriken and VFX Graph. We used them to simulate different fluid phenomena, such as fire, a waterfall, smoke, and rain. The idea is to combine particle systems with meshes to generate all the possible props needed for your scene. Also, as you can imagine, creating these kinds of effects professionally requires you to go deeper. If you want to dedicate yourself to this (another part of the job of a technical artist), you will need to learn how to create your own particle textures to get the exact look and feel you want, code scripts that control certain aspects of the systems, and several other aspects of particle creation. However, that is outside the scope of the book.

Now that we have some rain in our scene, we can see that the sky and the lighting in the scene don't really reflect a rainy day, so let's fix that in the next chapter!

12

Lighting Using the Universal Render Pipeline

Lighting is a complex topic and there are several possible ways to handle it, with each one having its pros and cons. In order to get the best possible quality and performance, you need to know exactly how your renderer handles lighting, and that is exactly what we are going to do in this chapter. We will discuss how lighting is handled in Unity's **Universal Render Pipeline** (**URP**), as well as how to properly configure it to adapt our scene's mood with proper lighting effects.

In this chapter, we will examine the following lighting concepts:

- Applying lighting
- Applying shadows
- Optimizing lighting

At the end of the chapter, we will have properly used the different Unity Illumination systems like Direct Lights and Lightmapping to reflect a cloudy and rainy night.

Applying lighting

When discussing ways to process lighting in a game, there are two main ways we can do so, known as **Forward Rendering** and **Deferred Rendering**. Both handle lighting in a different order, with different techniques, requirements, pros, and cons. Forward Rendering is usually recommended for performance, while Deferred Rendering is usually recommended for quality. The latter is used by the **High Definition Render Pipeline** of Unity, the renderer used for high-quality graphics in high-end devices.

At the time of writing this book, Unity is developing a performant version for URP. Also, in Unity, the Forward Renderer comes with two modes: **Multi-Pass Forward**, which is used in the Built-In Renderer (the old Unity Renderer), and **Single Pass Forward,** which is used in URP. Again, both have their pros and cons.

Choosing between them depends on the kind of game you are creating and the platform you need to run the game on. Your chosen option will change a lot due to the way you apply lighting to your scene, so it's crucial you understand which system you are dealing with.

In the next section, we will discuss the following real-time lighting concepts:

- Discussing lighting methods
- Configuring ambient lighting with skyboxes
- Configuring lighting in URP

Let's start by comparing the previously mentioned lighting methods.

Discussing lighting methods

To recap, we mentioned three main ways of processing lighting at the beginning of this chapter:

- Forward Rendering (Single Pass)
- Forward Rendering (Multi-Pass)
- Deferred Rendering

Before we look at the differences between each, let's talk about the things they have in common. Those three renderers start drawing the scene by determining which objects can be seen by the camera—that is, the ones that fall inside the camera's frustum, and provide a giant pyramid that can be seen when you select the camera:

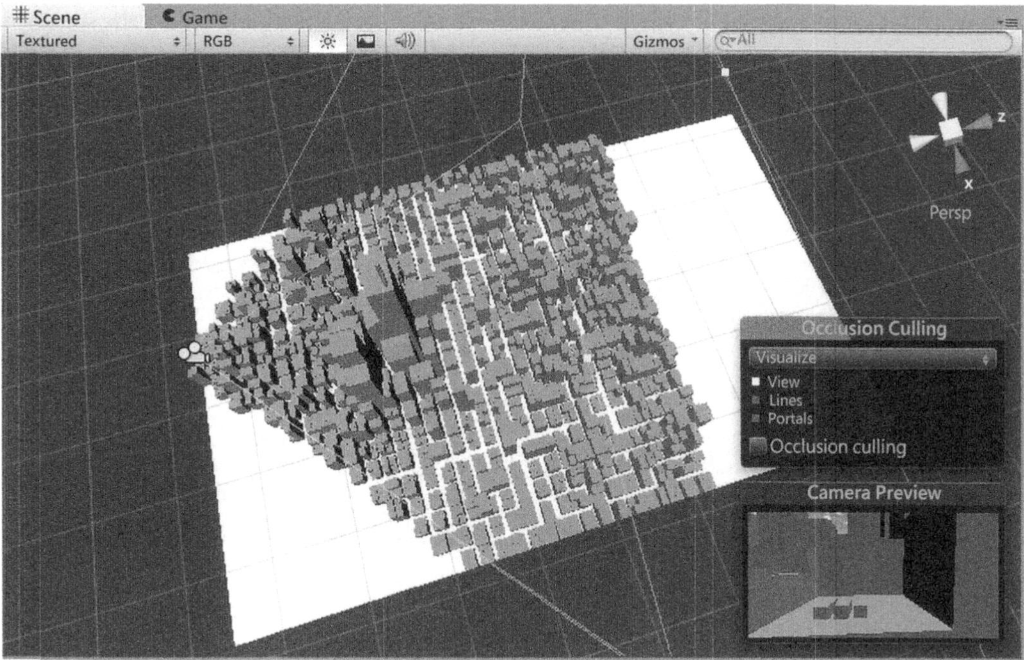

Figure 12.1: Camera's frustum showing only the objects that can be seen by it

After that, Unity will order them from the nearest to the camera to the farthest (transparent objects are handled a little bit differently, but let's ignore that for now). It's done like this because it's more probable that objects nearer to the camera will cover most of the camera, so they will occlude others (will block other objects from being seen), preventing us from wasting resources calculating pixels for the occluded ones.

Finally, Unity will try to render the objects in that order. This is where differences start to arise between lighting methods, so let's start comparing the two Forward Rendering variants. For each object, Single Pass Forward Rendering will calculate the object's appearance, including all the lights that are affecting the object, in one shot, or what we call a draw call.

A **draw call** is the exact moment when Unity asks the video card to actually render the specified object. All the previous work was just preparation for this moment. In the case of the Multi-Pass Forward Renderer, by simplifying a little bit of the actual logic, Unity will render the object once per light that affects the object; so, if the object is being lit by three lights, Unity will render the object three times, meaning that three draw calls will be issued, and three calls to the GPU will be made to execute the rendering process:

Figure 12.2: Left image, first draw call of a sphere affected by two lights in Multi-Pass; middle image, second draw call of the sphere; and right image, the combination of both draw calls

Now is when you are probably thinking, *"Why should I use Multi-Pass? Single Pass is more performant!"* And yes, you are right! Single Pass is much more performant than Multi-Pass, meaning our game will run at higher frames per second, and here comes the great but. A draw call in a GPU has a limited amount of operations that can be executed, so you have a limit to the complexity of the draw call. Calculating the appearance of an object and all the lights that affect it is very complex, and in order to make it fit in just one draw call, Single Pass executes simplified versions of lighting calculations, meaning less lighting quality and fewer features. They also have a limit on how many lights can be handled in one shot, which, at the time of writing this book, is eight per object, although you can configure fewer if you want, but the default value is good for us. This sounds like a small number, but it's usually just enough.

On the other side, Multi-Pass can apply any number of lights you want and can execute different logic for each light. Let's say our object has four lights that are affecting it, but there are two lights that are affecting it drastically because they are nearer or have higher intensity, while the remaining ones affecting the object are just enough to be noticeable. In this scenario, we can render the first two lights with higher quality and the remaining ones with cheap calculations—no one will be able to tell the difference.

In this case, Multi-Pass can calculate the first two lights using **Pixel Lighting** and the remaining ones using **Vertex Lighting**. The difference is in their names; Pixel calculates light per object's pixel, while Vertex calculates lighting per object vertex and fills the pixels between these vertexes, thereby interpolating information between vertexes. You can clearly see the difference in the following images:

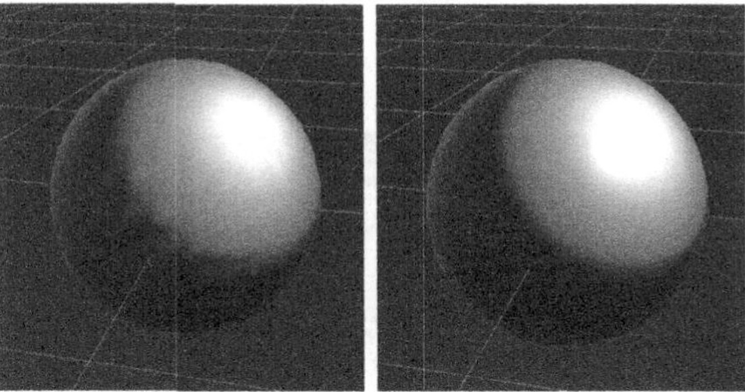

Figure 12.3: Left image, a sphere being rendered with Vertex Lighting; right image, a sphere being rendered with Pixel Lighting

In Single Pass, calculating everything in a single draw call forces you to use Vertex Lighting or Pixel Lighting; you cannot combine them.

So, to summarize the differences between Single and Multi-Pass, in Single, you have better performance because each object is just drawn once, but you are limited to the number of lights that can be applied, while in Multi-Pass, you need to render the object several times, but with no limits on the number of lights, and you can specify the exact quality you want for each light. There are other things to consider, such as the actual cost of a draw call (one draw call can be more expensive than two simple ones), and special lighting effects such as toon shading, but let's keep things simple.

Finally, let's briefly discuss Deferred. Even though we are not going to use it, it's interesting to know why we are not doing that. After determining which objects fall inside the frustum and ordering them, Deferred will render the objects without any lighting, generating what is called a **G-Buffer**. A G-Buffer is a set of several images that contain different information about the objects of the scene, such as the colors of their pixels (without lighting), the direction of each pixel (known as **Normals**), and how far from the camera the pixels are.

You can see a typical example of a G-Buffer in the following image:

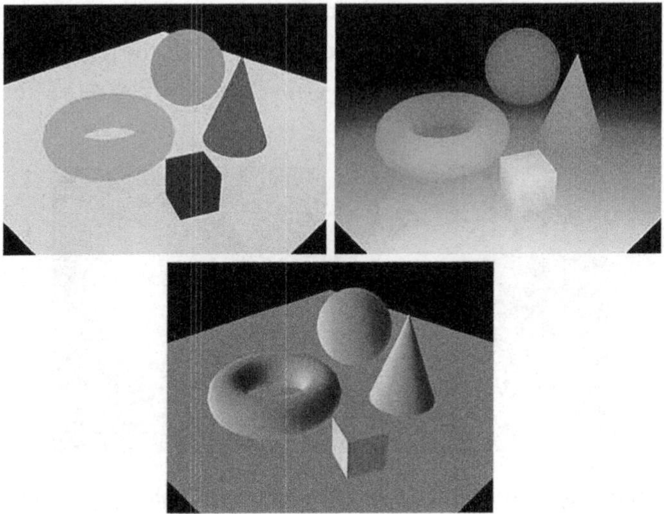

Figure 12.4: Left image, plain colors of the object; middle image, depths of each pixel; and right image, normals of the pixels

Normals are directions, and the *x*, *y*, and *z* components of the directions are encoded in the RGB components of the colors.

After rendering all the objects in the scene, Unity will iterate over all lights that can be seen in the camera, thus applying a layer of lighting over the G-Buffer, taking information from it to calculate that specific light. After all the lights have been processed, you will get the following result:

Figure 12.5: Combination of the three lights that were applied to the G-Buffer shown in the previous image

As you can see, the Deferred part of this method comes from the idea of calculating lighting as the last stage of the rendering process. This is better because you won't waste resources calculating lighting from objects that can potentially be occluded. If the floor of the image is being rendered first in **Forward** mode, the pixels that the rest of the objects are going to occlude were calculated in vain. Also, there's the pro that Deferred just calculates lighting in the exact pixels that the light can reach. As an example, if you are using a flashlight, Unity will calculate lighting only in the pixels that fall inside the cone of the flashlight. The con here is that Deferred is not supported by some relatively old video cards and that you can't calculate lighting with Vertex Lighting quality, so you will need to pay the price of Pixel Lighting, which is not recommended on low-end devices (or even necessary in simple graphics games).

So, why are we using URP with Single Pass Forward? Because it offers the best balance between performance, quality, and simplicity. In this game, we won't be using too many lights, so we won't worry about the light number limitations of Single Pass. If you need more lights, you can use Deferred, but consider the extra hardware requirements and the performance cost of not having per-vertex lighting options. Now that we have a very basic notion of how URP handles lighting, let's start using it!

Configuring ambient lighting with skyboxes

There are different light sources that can affect a scene, such as the sun, flashlights, light bulbs, and more. Those are known as **Direct Lights**—that is, objects that emit light rays. Then, we have **Indirect Light**, which represents how the Direct Light bounces on other objects, like walls. However, calculating all the bounces of all the rays emitted by all the lights is extremely costly in terms of performance and requires special hardware that supports ray tracing. The problem is that not having Indirect Light will generate unrealistic results, where you can observe places where the sunlight doesn't reach being completely dark because no light is bouncing from other places where light hits.

In the next image you can see an example of how this could look in a wrongly configured scene:

Figure 12.6: Shadows projected on a mountain without ambient lighting

If you ever experience this problem, the way to solve it performantly is using approximations of those bounces. These are what we call **Ambient Light**. This represents a base layer of lighting that usually applies a little bit of light based on the color of the sky, but you can choose whatever color you want. As an example, on a clear night, we can pick a dark blue color to represent the tint from the moonlight.

If you create a new scene in Unity 2022, usually this is done automatically, but in cases where it isn't, or the scene was created through other methods, it is convenient to know how to manually trigger this process by doing the following:

1. Click on **Window | Rendering | Lighting**. This will open the **Scene Lighting Settings** window:

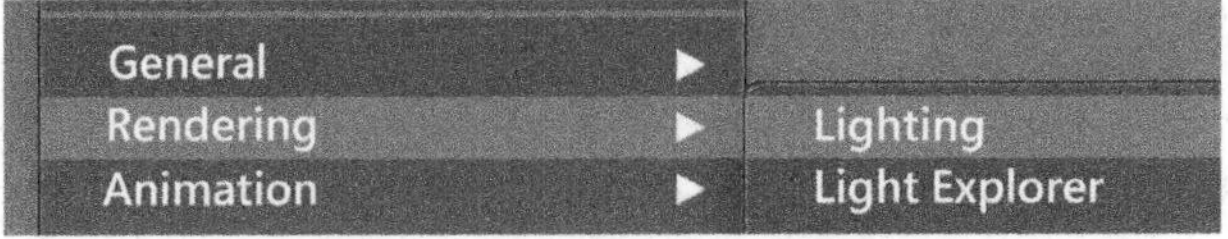

Figure 12.7: Lighting Settings location

2. Click the **Generate Lighting** button at the bottom of the window. If you haven't saved the scene so far, a prompt will ask you to save it, which is necessary:

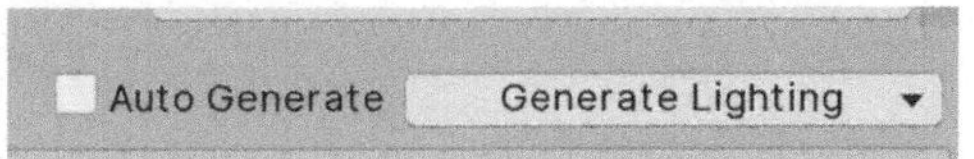

Figure 12.8: Generate Lighting button

3. See the bottom-right part of the Unity window to check the progress calculation bar to check when the process has finished:

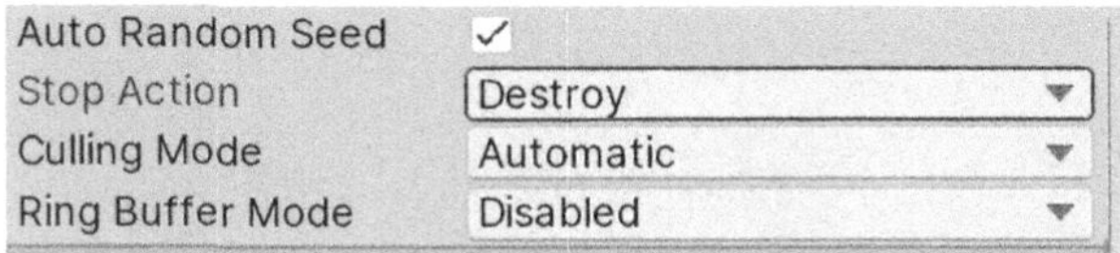

Figure 12.9: Lighting generation progress bar

4. You can now see how completely dark areas are now lit by the light being emitted by the sky:

Figure 12.10: Shadows with ambient lighting

Now, by doing this, we have better lighting, but it still looks like a sunny day. Remember, we want to have rainy weather. In order to do that, we need to change the default sky too so that it's cloudy. You can do that by downloading a **skybox**. The current sky you can see around the scene is just a big cube containing textures on each side, and those textures have a special projection to prevent us from detecting the edges of the cube. We can download six images for each side of the cube and apply them to have whatever sky you want, so let's do that:

1. You can download skybox textures from wherever you want, but here, I will choose the Asset Store. Open it by going to **Window | Asset Store** and going to the Asset Store website.

2. Look for **Categories | 2D | Textures & Materials | Sky** in the category list on the right. Remember that you need to make that window wider if you can't see the category list:

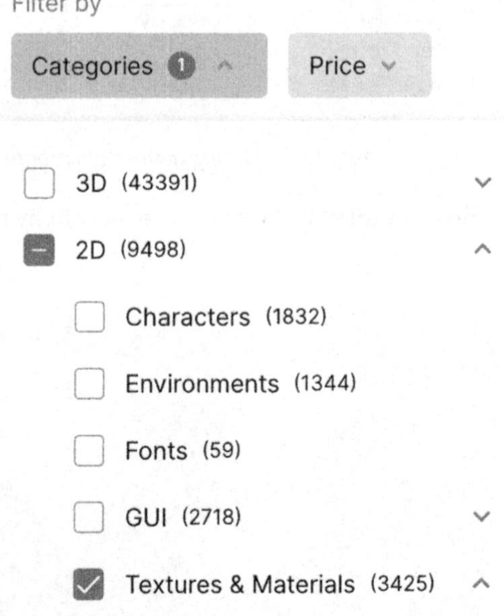

Figure 12.11: Textures & Materials

3. Remember to check the **Free Assets** checkbox in the **Price** options.
4. Pick any skybox you like for a rainy day. Take into account that there are different formats for skyboxes. We are using the six-image format, so check that before downloading one. There's another format called **Cubemap**, which is essentially the same, but we will stick with the six-image format as it is the simplest one to use and modify. In my case, I have chosen the skybox pack shown in *Figure 12.12*. Download and import it, as we did in *Chapter 5, Introduction to C# and Visual Scripting*:

Figure 12.12: Selected skybox set for this book

5. Create a new material by using the + icon in the **Project** window and selecting **Material**.
6. Set the **Shader** option of that material to **Skybox/6 sided**. Remember that the skybox is just a cube, so we can apply a material to change how it looks. The skybox shader is prepared to apply the six textures.
7. Drag the six textures to the **Front**, **Back**, **Left**, **Right**, **Up**, and **Down** properties of the material. The six downloaded textures will have descriptive names so that you know which textures go where:

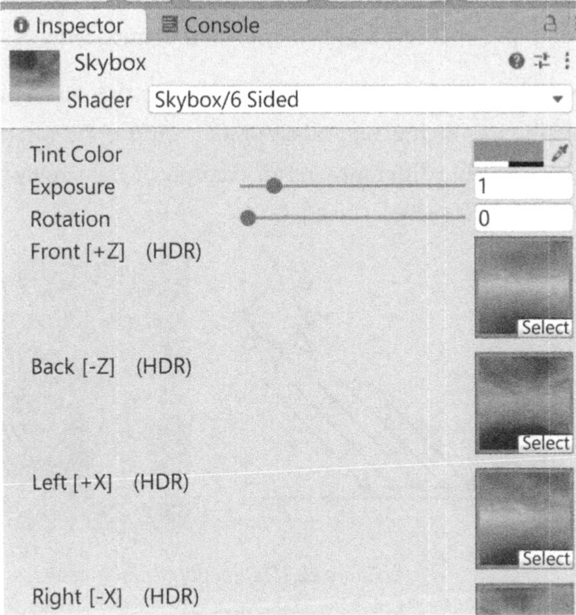

Figure 12.13: Skybox material settings

8. Drag the material directly into the sky in the Scene view. Be sure you don't drag the material into an object because the material will be applied to it.
9. Repeat *steps 1* to *4* of the ambient light calculation steps (**Lighting Settings | Generate Lighting**) to recalculate it based on the new skybox. In the following image, you can see the result of my project so far:

Figure 12.14: Applied skybox

Now that we have a good base layer of lighting, we can start adding light objects.

Configuring lighting in URP

We have three main types of Direct Lights we can add to our scene:

- **Directional Light**: This is a light that represents the sun. This object emits light rays in the direction it is facing, regardless of its position; the sun moving 100 meters to the right won't make a big difference. As an example, if you slowly rotate this object, you can generate a day/night cycle:

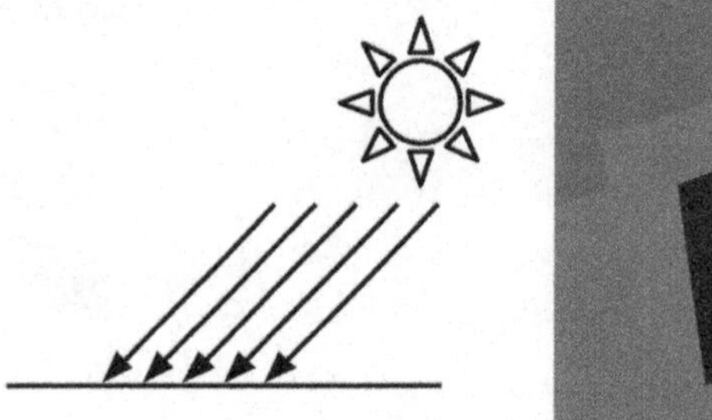

Figure 12.15: Directional Light results

- **Point Light**: This light represents a light bulb, which emits rays in an omnidirectional way. The difference it has compared to Directional Lights is that its position matters because it's closer to our objects. Also, because it's a weaker light, the intensity of this light varies according to the distance, so its effect has a range—the further the object from the light, the weaker the received intensity:

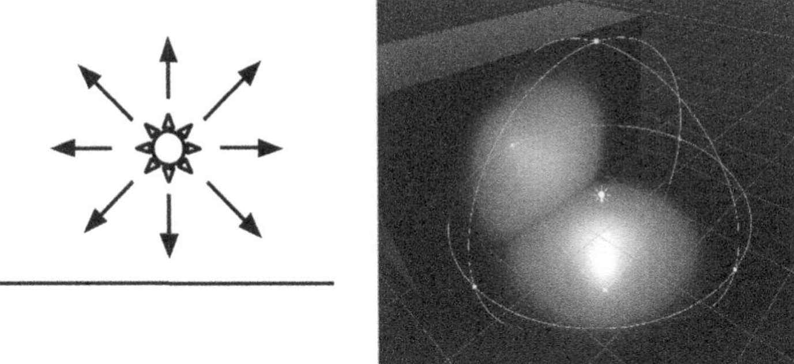

Figure 12.16: Point Light results

- **Spotlight**: This kind of light represents a light cone, such as the one emitted by a flashlight. It behaves similarly to point lights in that its position matters and the light intensity decays over a certain distance. But here the direction it points to (hence its rotation) is also important, given it will specify where to project the light:

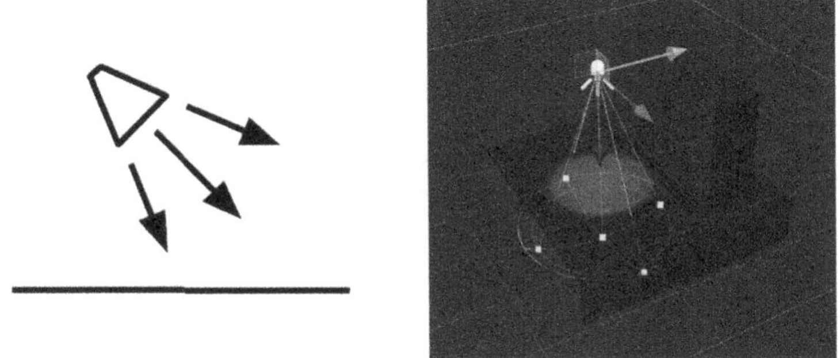

Figure 12.17: Spotlight results

So far, we have nice, rainy, ambient lighting, but the only Direct Light we have in the scene, the Directional Light, won't look like this, so let's change that:

1. Select the **Directional Light** object in the **Hierarchy** window and then look at the **Inspector** window.
2. Click the **Color** property in the **Emission** section to open the Color Picker.

3. Select a dark gray color to achieve sun rays partially occluded by clouds.
4. Set **Shadow Type** to **No Shadows**. Now that we have a cloudy day, the sun does not project clear shadows, but we will talk more about shadows in a moment:

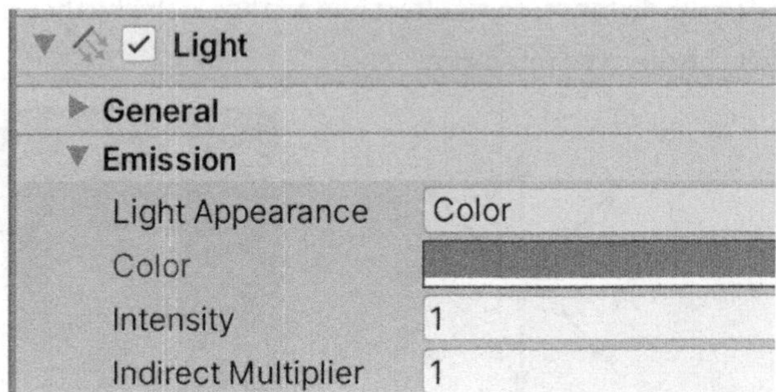

Figure 12.18: Soft directional light with no shadows

Now that the scene is darker, we can add some lights to light up the scene, as follows:

1. Create a Spotlight by going to **GameObject | Light | Spotlight**.
2. Select it. Then, in the Inspector window, set **Inner/Output Spot Angle** of the **Shape** section to 90 and 120, which will increase the angle of the cone.
3. Set **Range** in the **Emission** section to `50`, meaning that the light can reach up to 50 meters, decaying along the way.
4. Set **Intensity** in the **Emission** section to `1000`:

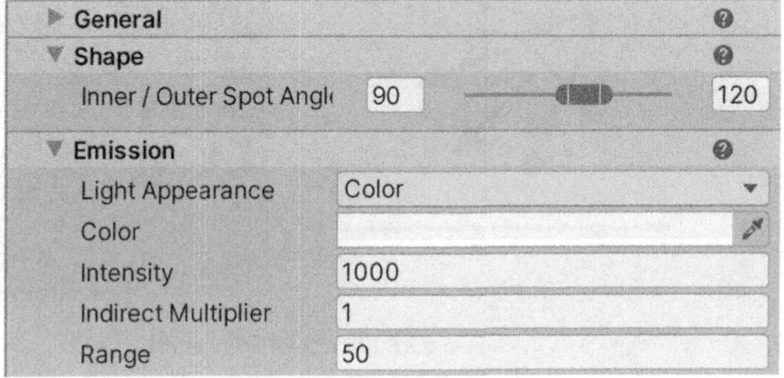

Figure 12.19: Spotlight settings

5. Position the light at one corner of your game's base, pointing it at the center:

Figure 12.20: Spotlight placement

6. Duplicate that light by selecting it and pressing *Ctrl+D* (*Command+D* on a Mac).
7. Put it in the opposite corner of the base:

Figure 12.21: Two Spotlight results

You can keep adding lights to the scene but take care that you don't go too far—remember the light's limits. Also, you can download some light posts to put in where the lights are located to visually justify the origin of the light. Now that we have achieved proper lighting, we can talk about shadows.

Applying shadows

Maybe you are thinking that we already have shadows in the scene, but actually, we don't. The darker areas of the object, the ones that are not facing the lights, don't have shadows—they are not being lit, and that's quite different from a shadow. In this case, we are referring to the shadows that are projected from one object to another—for example, the shadow of the player being projected on the floor, or from the mountains to other objects. Shadows can increase the quality of our scene, but they also cost a lot to calculate, so we have two options: not using shadows (recommended for low-end devices such as mobiles) or finding a balance between performance and quality according to our game and the target device.

In this section, we are going to discuss the following topics about shadows:

- Understanding shadow calculations
- Configuring performant shadows

Let's start by discussing how Unity calculates shadows.

Understanding shadow calculations

In game development, it is well-known that shadows are costly in terms of performance, but why? An object has a shadow when a light ray hits another object before reaching it. In that case, no lighting is applied to that pixel from that light. The problem here is the same problem we have with the light that ambient lighting simulates—it would be too costly to calculate all possible rays and its collisions. So, again, we need an approximation, and here is where Shadow Maps kick in.

A **Shadow Map** is an image that's rendered from the point of view of the light, but instead of drawing the full scene with all the color and lighting calculations, it will render all the objects in grayscale, where black means that the pixel is very far from the camera and whiter means that the pixel is nearer to the camera. If you think about it, each pixel contains information about where a **ray** of light hits. By knowing the position and orientation of the light, you can calculate the position where each "ray" hit using the Shadow Map.

In the following image, you can see the shadow map of our Directional Light:

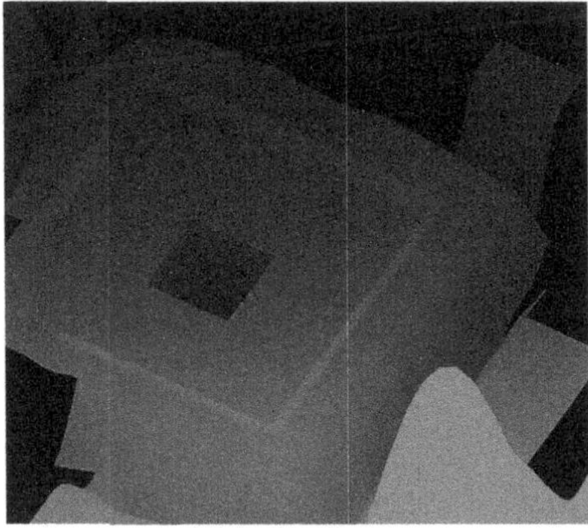

Figure 12.22: Shadow Map generated by the Directional Light of our scene

Each type of light calculates shadow maps slightly differently, especially the Point Light. Since it's omnidirectional, it needs to render the scene several times in all its directions (Front, Back, Left, Right, Up, and Down) in order to gather information about all the rays it emits. We won't talk about this in detail here, though, as we could talk about it all day.

Now, something important to highlight here is that shadow maps are textures, and as such, they have a resolution. The higher the resolution, the more "rays" our shadow map calculates. You are probably wondering what a low-resolution shadow map looks like when it has only a few rays in it. Take a look at the following image to see one:

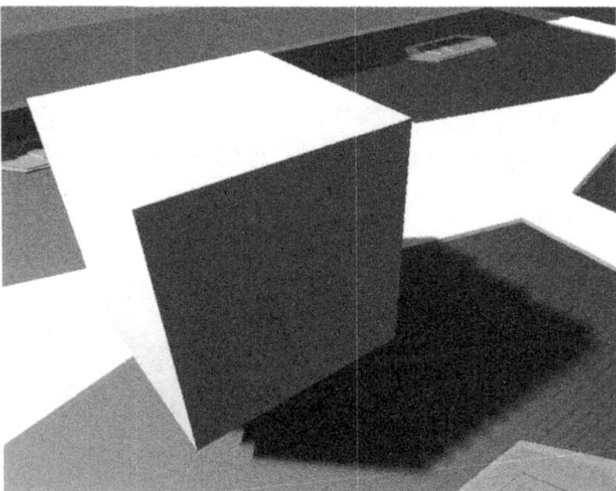

Figure 12.23: Hard Shadows rendered with a low-resolution Shadow Map

The problem here is that having fewer rays generates bigger shadow pixels, resulting in a pixelated shadow. Here, we have our first configuration to consider: what is the ideal resolution for our shadows? You will be tempted to just increase it until the shadows look smooth, but of course, that will increase how long it will take to calculate it, so it will impact the performance considerably unless your target platform can handle it (mobiles definitely can't). Here, we can use the **Soft Shadows** trick, where we can apply a blurring effect over the shadows to hide the pixelated edges, as shown in the following image:

Figure 12.24: Soft Shadows rendered with a low-resolution Shadow Map

Of course, the blurry effect is not free, but combining it with low-resolution shadow maps, if you accept its blurry result, can generate a nice balance between quality and performance.

Now, low-resolution shadow maps have another problem, which is called **Shadow Acne**. This is the lighting error you can see in the following image:

Figure 12.25: Shadow Acne from a low-resolution Shadow Map

A low-resolution shadow map generates false positives because it has fewer "rays" calculated. The pixels to be shaded between the rays need to interpolate information from the nearest ones. The lower the Shadow Map's resolution, the larger the gap between the rays, which means less precision and more false positives. One solution would be to increase the resolution, but again, there will be performance issues (as always). We have some clever solutions to this, such as using **depth bias**. An example of this can be seen in the following image:

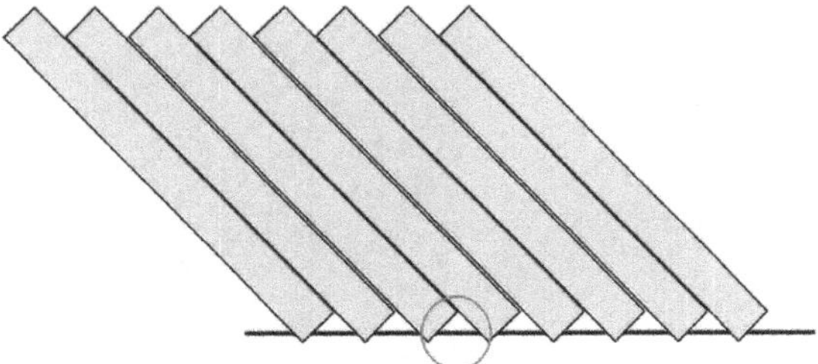

Figure 12.26: A false positive between two far "rays." The highlighted area thinks the ray hit an object before reaching it.

The concept of **depth bias** is simple—so simple that it seems like a big cheat, and actually, it is, but game development is full of them! To prevent false positives, we "push" the rays a little bit further, just enough to make the interpolated rays reach the surface being lit:

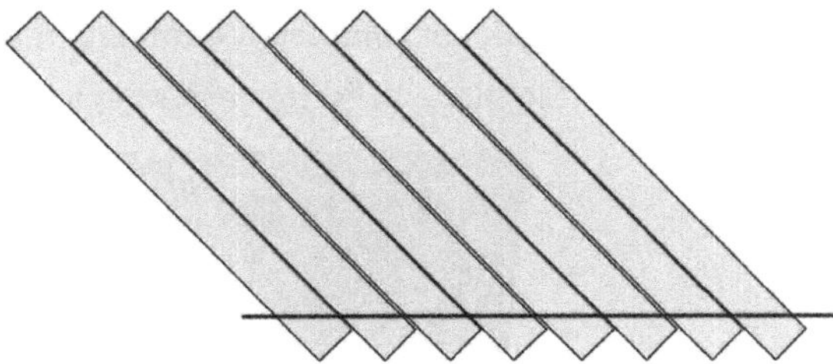

Figure 12.27: Rays with a depth bias to eliminate false positives

Of course, as you are probably expecting, they don't solve this problem easily without having a caveat. Pushing depth generates false negatives in other areas, as shown in the following image. It looks like the cube is floating, but actually, it is touching the ground—the false negatives generate the illusion that it is floating:

Figure 12.28: False negatives due to a high depth bias

Of course, we have a counter trick to this situation known as **normal bias**. This pushes the object's mesh along the direction they are facing, not the rays. This one is a little bit tricky, so we won't go into too much detail here, but the idea is that combining a little bit of depth bias and another bit of normal bias will reduce the false positives, but not completely eliminate them. Therefore, we need to learn how to live with that and hide these shadow discrepancies by cleverly positioning objects:

Figure 12.29: Reduced false positives, which is the result of combining depth and normal bias

There are several other aspects that affect how shadow maps work, with one of them being the light range. The smaller the light range, the less area the shadows will cover. The same shadow map resolution can add more detail to that area, so try to reduce the light ranges as much as you can, as we will do in the next section.

I can imagine your face right now, and yes, lighting is complicated, and we've only just scratched the surface! But keep your spirits up! After a little trial and error fiddling with the settings, you will understand it better. We'll do that in the next section.

If you are really interested in learning more about the internals of the shadow system, I recommend that you look at the concept of **Shadow Cascades**, an advanced topic about Directional Lights and shadow map generation.

Configuring performant shadows

Because we are targeting mid-end devices, we will try to achieve a good balance of quality and performance here, so let's start enabling shadows just for the spotlights. The Directional Light shadow won't be that noticeable, and actually, a rainy sky doesn't generate clear shadows, so we will use that as an excuse to not calculate those shadows. In order to do this, do the following:

1. Select both spotlights by clicking them in the Hierarchy while pressing *Ctrl* (*Command* on Mac). This will ensure that any changes made in the Inspector window will be applied to both:

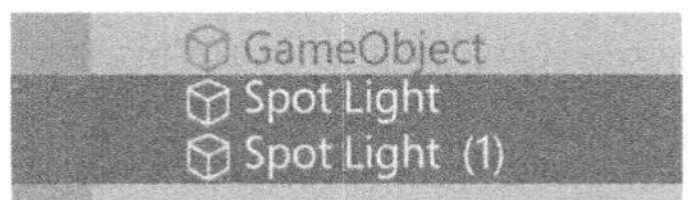

Figure 12.30: Selecting multiple objects

2. In the Inspector window, set **Shadow Type** in the **Shadows** section to **Soft Shadows**. We will be using low-resolution shadow maps here and the soft mode can help to hide the pixelated resolution:

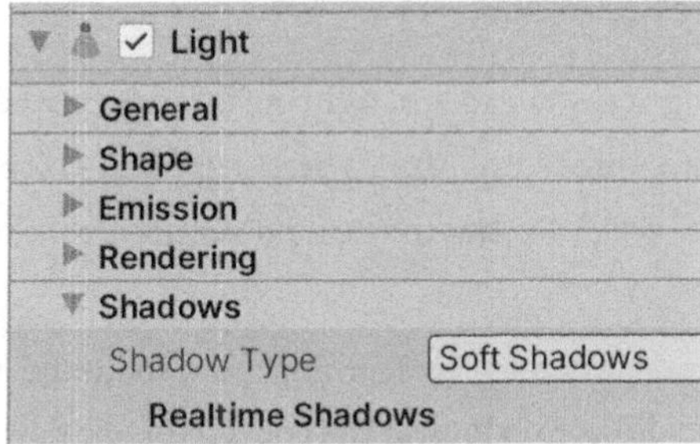

Figure 12.31: Soft Shadows setting

3. Select **Directional light** and set **Shadow Type** to **No Shadows** to prevent it from casting shadows:

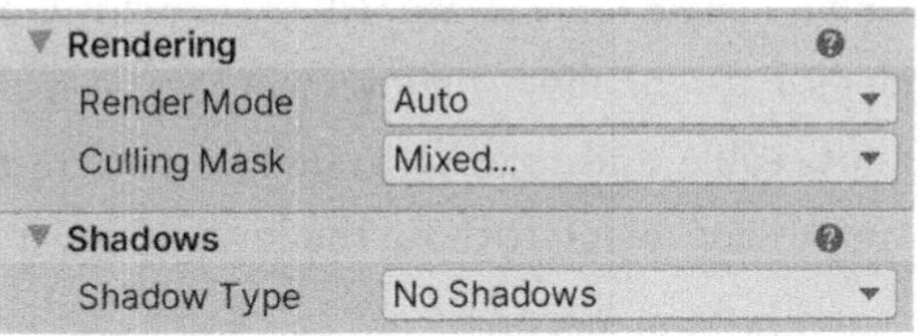

Figure 12.32: No Shadows setting

4. Create a cube (**GameObject** | **3D Object** | **Cube**) and place it near one of the lights, just to have an object that we can cast shadows on for testing purposes.

Now that we have a base test scenario, let's fiddle with the shadow maps resolution settings, preventing shadow acne in the process:

1. Go to **Edit** | **Project Settings**.
2. In the left-hand side list, look for **Graphics** and click it:

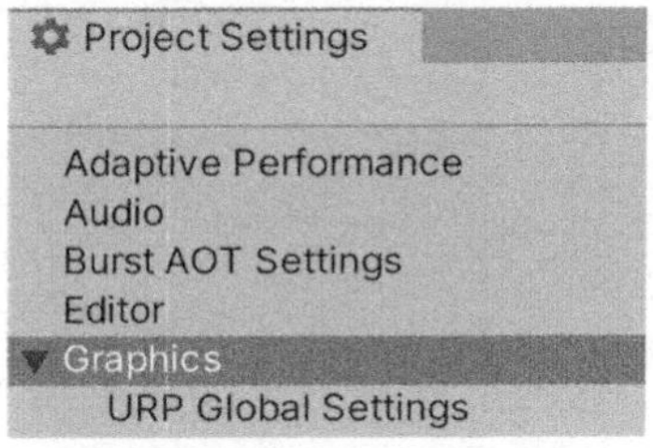

Figure 12.33: Graphics settings

3. In the properties that appear after selecting this option, click in the box below **Scriptable Render Pipeline Settings**—the one that contains a name. In my case, this is **URP-High-Fidelity**, but yours may be different if you have a different version of Unity:

Scriptable Render Pipeline Settings
URP-HighFidelity (Universal Render Pipeline Asset)

Figure 12.34: Current Render Pipeline setting

4. Doing that will highlight an asset in the Project window, so be sure that the window is visible before selecting it. Select the highlighted asset:

Figure 12.35: Current pipeline highlighted

5. This asset has several graphics settings related to how URP will handle its rendering, including lighting and shadows. Expand the **Lighting** section to reveal its settings:

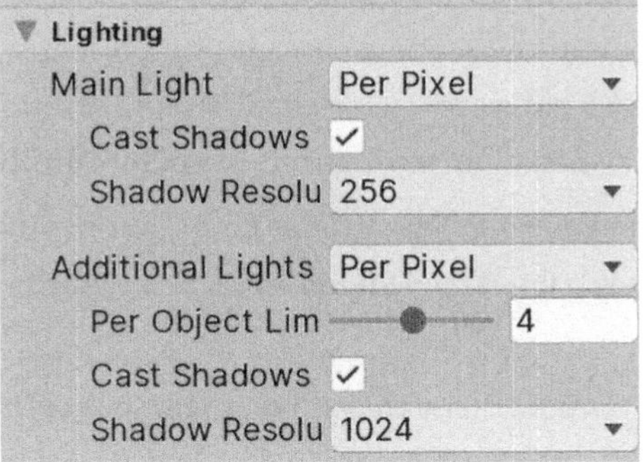

Figure 12.36: Pipeline lighting settings

6. The **Shadow Resolution** setting under the **Additional Lights** subsection represents the shadow map resolution for all the lights that aren't the Directional Light (since it's the Main Light). Set it to `1024` if it's not already at that value.

7. Under the **Shadows** section, you can see the **Depth** and **Normal Bias** settings, but those will affect all lights. Even if right now our Directional Light doesn't have shadows, we want only to affect Additional Lights bias values as they have a different Atlas Resolution compared to the Main one (Directional Light), so instead, select out spotlights and set **Bias** to **Custom** and **Depth** and **Normal Bias** to `0.25` in order to reduce them as much as we can before we remove the shadow acne:

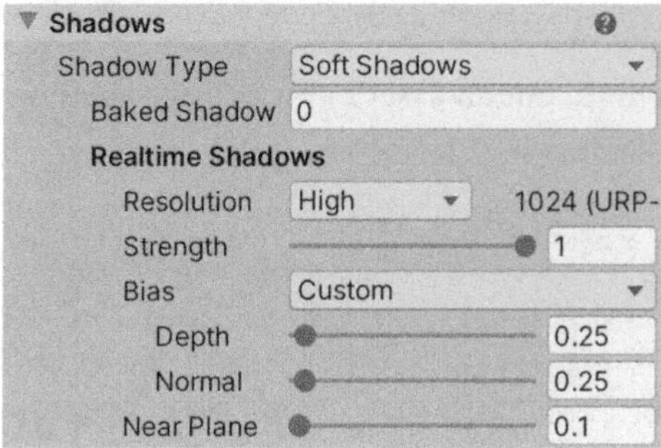

Figure 12.37: Bias settings

8. This isn't entirely related to shadows, but in the Univeral RP settings asset, you can change the **Per Object Light** limit to increase or reduce the number of lights that can affect the object (no more than eight). For now, the default is good as is.
9. In case you followed the shadow cascades tip presented earlier, you can play with the **Cascades** value a little bit to enable shadows for Directional Light to note the effect. Remember that those shadow settings only work for Directional Light.
10. We don't have shadows in **Directional Light**, but in any other case, consider reducing the **Max Distance** value in the **Shadows** section, which will affect the Directional Light shadows range.
11. Select both lights in the Hierarchy and set them so that they have a 40-meter **Range**. See how the shadows improve in quality before and after this change.

Remember that those values only work in my case, so try to fiddle with the values a little bit to see how that changes the result—you may find a better setup for your scene if it was designed differently from mine. Also, remember that not having shadows is always an option, so consider that if your game is running low on frames per second, also known as FPS (and there isn't another performance problem lurking).

You probably think that that is all we can do about performance in terms of lighting, but luckily, that's not the case! We have another resource we can use to improve it further known as static lighting.

Optimizing lighting

We mentioned previously that not calculating lighting is good for performance, but what about not calculating lights, but still having them? Yes, it sounds too good to be true, but it is actually possible (and, of course, tricky). We can use a technique called static lighting or baking, which allows us to calculate lighting once and use the cached result.

In this section, we will cover the following concepts related to static lighting:

- Understanding static lighting
- Baking lightmaps
- Applying static lighting to dynamic objects

Understanding static lighting

The idea is pretty simple: just do the lighting calculations once, save the results, and then use those instead of calculating lighting all the time.

You may be wondering why this isn't the default technique to use. This is because it has some limitations, with the big one being dynamic objects. **Precalculating shadows** means that they can't change once they've been calculated, but if an object that is casting a shadow is moved, the shadow will still be there, so the main thing to take into account here is that you can't use this technique with moving objects. Instead, you will need to mix **static** or **baked lighting** for static objects and **real-time lighting** for dynamic (moving) objects. Also, consider that aside from this technique being only valid for static objects, it is also only valid for static lights. Again, if a light moves, the precalculated data becomes invalid.

Another limitation you need to take into account is that precalculated data can have a huge impact on memory. That data occupies space in RAM, maybe hundreds of MB, so you need to consider if your target platform has enough space. Of course, you can reduce the precalculated lighting quality to reduce the size of that data, but you need to consider if the loss of quality deteriorates the look and feel of your game too much. As with all options regarding optimization, you need to balance two factors: performance and quality.

We have several kinds of precalculated data in our process, but the most important one is what we call **lightmaps**. A lightmap is a texture that contains all the shadows and lighting for all the objects in the scene, so when Unity applies the precalculated or baked data, it will look at this texture to know which parts of the static objects are lit and which aren't.

You can see an example of a lightmap in the following image:

Figure 12.38: Left, a scene with no lighting; middle, a lightmap holding precalculated data from that scene; and right, the lightmap being applied to the scene

Having lightmaps has its own benefits. The baking process is executed in Unity, before the game is shipped to users, so you can spend plenty of time calculating stuff that you can't do in runtime, such as improved accuracy, light bounces, light occlusion in corners, and light from emissive objects. However, that can also be a problem. Remember, dynamic objects still need to rely on real-time lighting, and that lighting will look very different compared to static lighting, so we need to tweak them a lot for the user to not notice the difference.

Now that we have a basic notion of what static lighting is, let's dive into how to use it.

Baking lightmaps

To use lightmaps, we need to make some preparations regarding the 3D models. Remember that meshes have **UVs**, which contain information about which part of the texture needs to be applied to each part of the model. Sometimes, to save texture memory you can apply the same piece of texture to different parts. For example, in a car's texture, you wouldn't have four wheels; you'd just have one, and you can apply that same piece of texture to all the wheels. The problem here is that static lighting uses textures the same way, but here, it will apply the lightmaps to light the object. In the wheel scenario, the problem would be that if one wheel receives shadows, all of them will have it, because all the wheels are sharing the same texture space. The usual solution is to have a second set of UVs in the model with no texture space being shared, just for use with lightmapping.

Sometimes, downloaded models are already prepared for lightmapping, and sometimes, they aren't, but luckily, Unity has us covered in those scenarios. To be sure a model will calculate lightmapping properly, let's make Unity automatically generate the **Lightmapping UVs** by doing the following:

1. Select the mesh asset (FBX) in the **Project** window.
2. In the **Model** tab, look for the **Generate Lightmap UVs** checkbox at the bottom and check it.
3. Click the **Apply** button at the bottom:

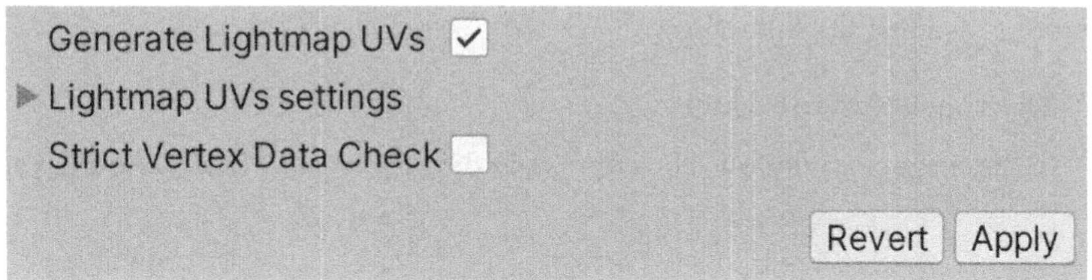

Figure 12.39: Generate Lightmap setting

4. Repeat this process for every model. Technically, you can only do this in the models where you get artifacts and weird results after baking lightmaps, but for now, let's do this in all the models just in case.

After preparing the models for being lightmapped, the next step is to tell Unity which objects are not going to move. To do so, do the following:

1. Select the object that won't move.
2. Check the **Static** checkbox in the top-right of the Inspector window:

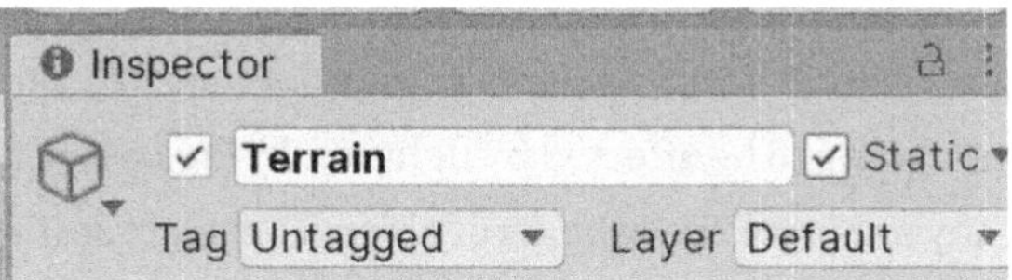

Figure 12.40: Static checkbox

3. Repeat this for every static object (this isn't necessary for lights; we will deal with those later).
4. You can also select a container of several objects, check the **Static** checkbox, and click the **Yes, All Children** button in the prompt to apply the checkbox to all child objects.

Consider that you may not want every object, even if it's static, to be lightmapped, because the more objects you lightmap, the more texture size you will require. As an example, the terrain could be too large and would consume most of the lightmapping's size. Usually, this is necessary, but in our case, the spotlights are barely touching the terrain. Here, we have two options: leave the terrain as dynamic, or better, directly tell the spotlights to not affect the terrain since one is only lit by ambient lighting and the Directional Light (which is not casting shadows). Remember that this is something we can do because of our type of scene; however, you may need to use other settings in other scenarios. You can exclude an object from both real-time and static lighting calculations by doing the following:

1. Select the object to exclude.
2. In the Inspector window, click the **Layer** dropdown and click on **Add Layer...**:

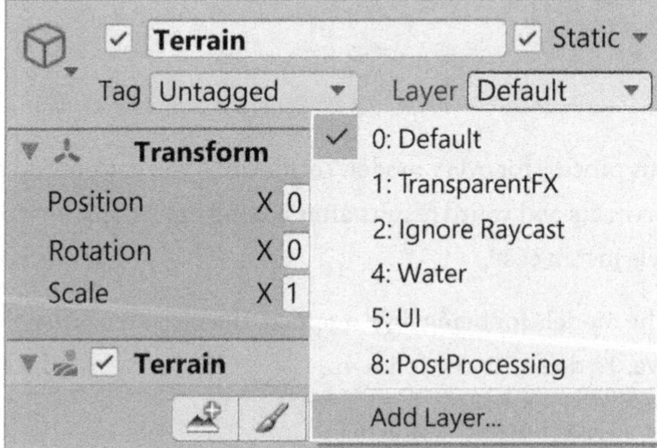

Figure 12.41: Layer creation button

3. Here, you can create a layer, which is a group of objects that are used to identify which objects are not going to be affected by lighting. In the **Layers** list, look for an empty space and type in any name for those kinds of objects. In my case, I will only exclude the terrain, so I have just named it **Terrain**:

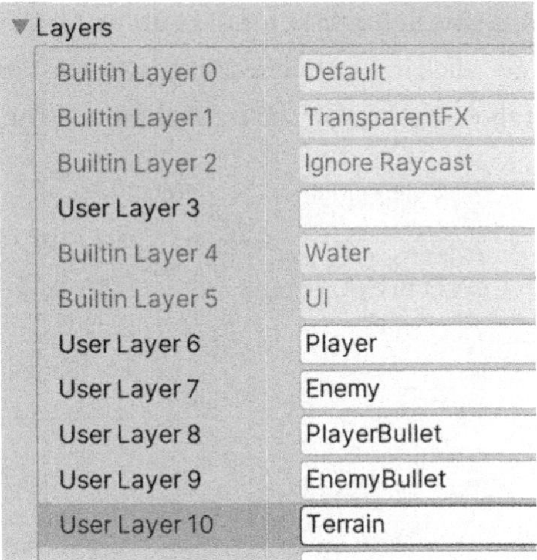

Figure 12.42: Layers list

4. Once again, select the terrain, go to the **Layer** dropdown, and select the layer you created in the previous step. This way, you can specify that this object belongs to that group of objects:

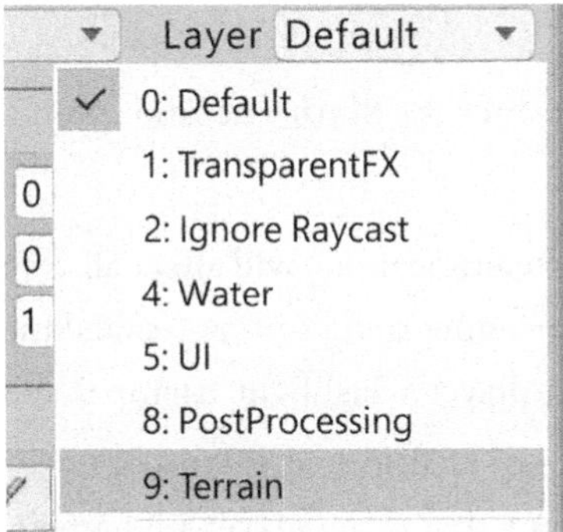

Figure 12.43: Changing a GameObject's layer

5. Select all the spotlights lights, look for the **Culling Mask** in the **Rendering** section in the Inspector window, click it, and uncheck the layer you created previously. This way, you can specify that those lights won't affect that group of objects:

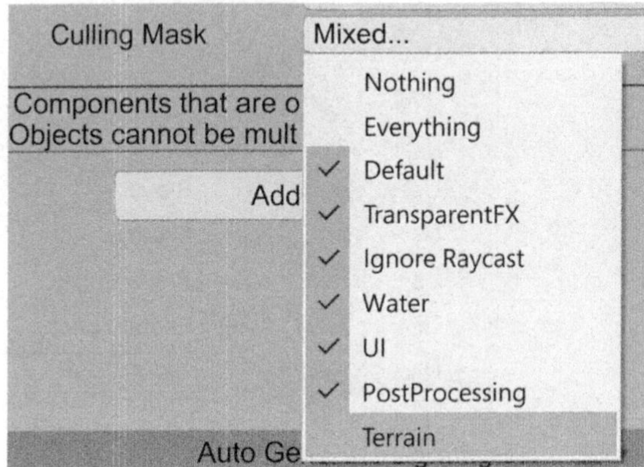

Figure 12.44: Light Culling Mask

6. Now, you can see how those selected lights are not illuminating or applying shadows to the terrain.

Now, it's time for the lights since the **Static** checkbox won't work for them. For them, we have the following three modes:

- **Realtime**: A light in Realtime mode will affect all objects, both static and dynamic, using real-time lighting, meaning there's no pre-calculation. This is useful for lights that are not static, such as the player's flashlight, a lamp that is moving due to the wind, and so on.
- **Baked**: The opposite of Realtime, this kind of light will only affect static objects with lightmaps. This means that if the player (dynamic) moves under a baked light on the street (static), the street will look lit, but the player will still be dark and won't cast any shadows on the street. The idea is to use this on lights that won't affect any dynamic object, or on lights that are barely noticeable on them, so that we can increase performance by not calculating them.
- **Mixed**: This is the preferred mode in case you are not sure which one to use. This kind of light will calculate lightmaps for static objects, but will also affect dynamic objects, combining its Realtime lighting with the baked one (like Realtime lights also do).

In our case, our Directional Light will only affect the terrain, and because we don't have shadows, applying lighting to it is relatively cheap in URP, so we can leave the Directional Light in Realtime so that it won't take up any lightmap texture area.

Our spotlights are affecting the base, but actually, they are only applying lighting to them—we have no shadows because our base is empty. In this case, it is preferable to not calculate lightmapping whatsoever, but for learning purposes, I will add a few objects as obstacles to the base to cast some shadows and justify the use of lightmapping, as shown in the following image:

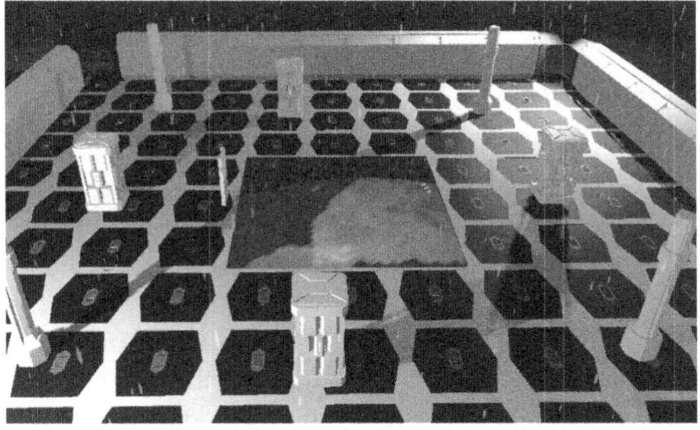

Figure 12.45: Adding objects to project light

Here, you can see how the original design of our level changes constantly during the development of the game, and that's something you can't avoid—bigger parts of the game will change over time. Now, we are ready to set up the Light Modes and execute the baking process, as follows:

1. Select the **Directional Light** in the **Hierarchy**.
2. Set the **Mode** property of the **General** section in the Inspector window to **Realtime** (if it's not already in that mode).
3. Select both Spotlights.
4. Set their **Render Mode** to **Mixed**:

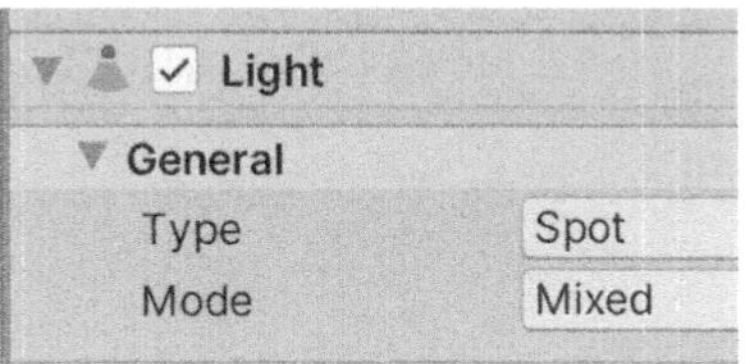

Figure 12.46: Mixed lighting setting for Spotlights, the mode will be Realtime for the Directional Light

5. Open the **Lighting Settings** window (**Window** | **Rendering** | **Lighting**).

6. We want to change some of the settings of the baking process. In order to enable the controls for this, click the **New Lighting Settings** button. This will create an asset with lightmapping settings that can be applied to several scenes in case we want to share the same settings multiple times:

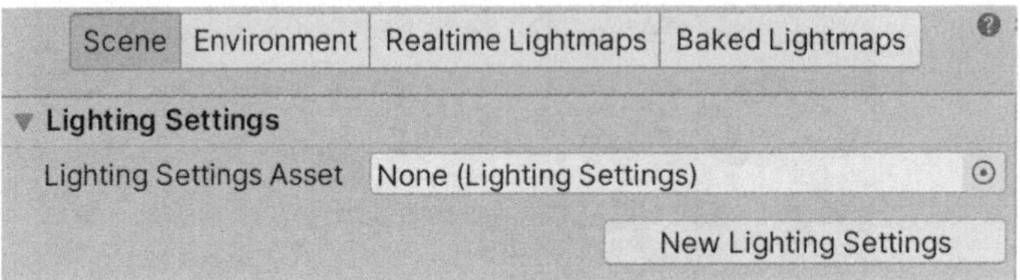

Figure 12.47: Creating lighting settings

7. Reduce the quality of lightmapping, just to make the process go faster. Just to iterate, the lighting can easily be reduced by using settings such as **Lightmap Resolution**, **Direct Samples**, **Indirect Samples**, and **Environment Samples**, all of them located under the **Lightmapping Settings** category. In my case, I have those settings applied, as shown in the following image. Note that even reducing those will take time; we have too many objects in the scene due to the modular level design:

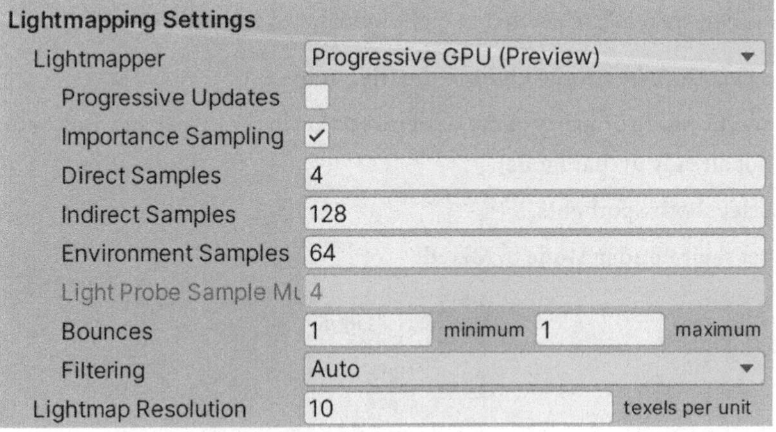

Figure 12.48: Scene lighting settings

8. Click **Generate Lighting**, which is the same button we used previously to generate ambient lighting.

9. Wait for the process to complete. You can do this by checking the progress bar at the bottom-right of the Unity editor. Note that this process could take even hours in large scenes, so be patient:

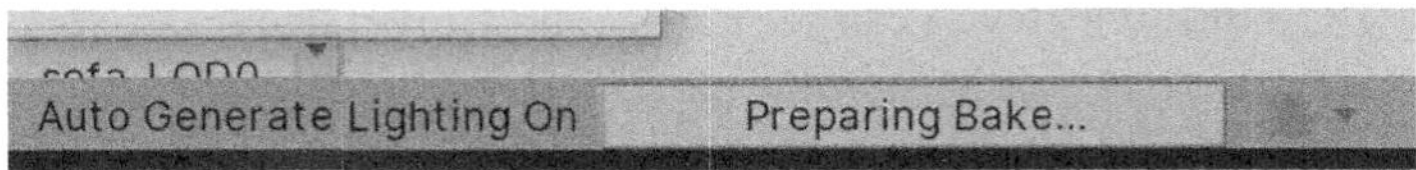

Figure 12.49: Baking progress bar

10. After the process has completed, you can check the bottom part of the **Lighting settings** window, where you can see how many lightmaps need to be generated. We have a maximum lightmap resolution, so we probably need several of them to cover the entire scene. Also, it informs us of their size so that we can consider their impact in terms of RAM. Finally, you can check out the **Baked Lightmaps** section to see them:

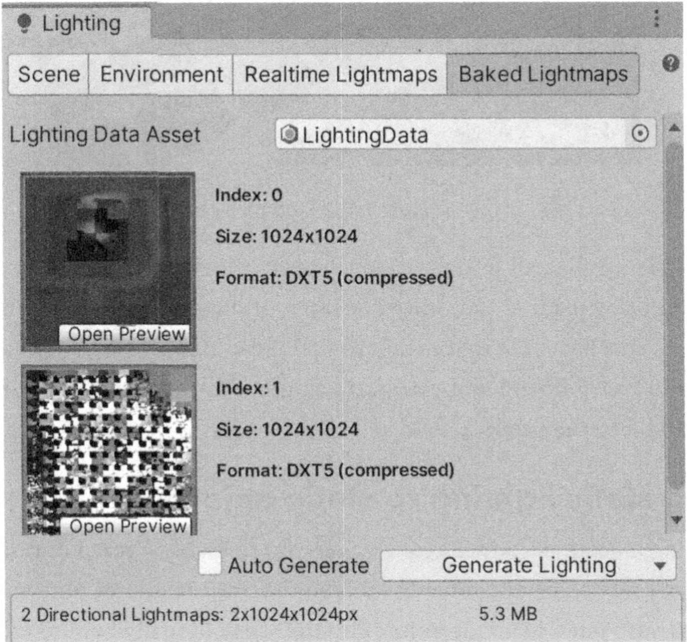

Figure 12.50: Generated lightmaps

11. Now, based on the results, you can move objects, modify light intensities, or make whatever correction you would need in order to make the scene look the way you want and recalculate the lighting every time you need to. In my case, those settings gave me good enough results, which you can see in the following image:

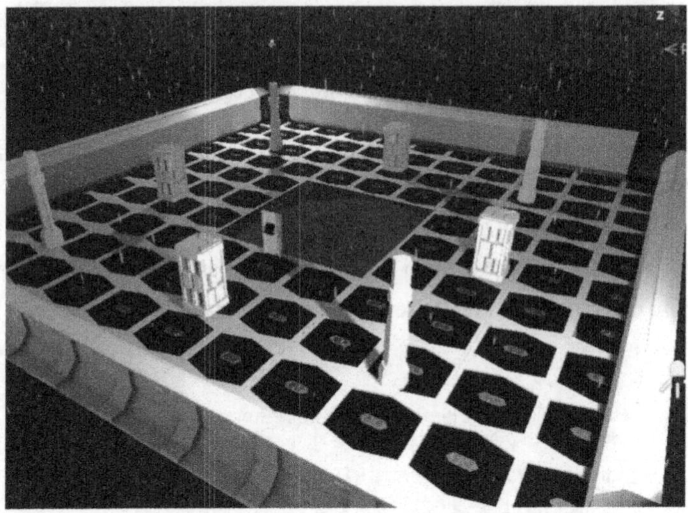

Figure 12.51: Lightmap result

We still have plenty of small settings to touch on, but I will leave you to discover those through trial and error or by reading the Unity documentation about lightmapping over at: `https://docs.unity3d.com/Manual/Lightmappers.html`. Reading the Unity manual is a good source of knowledge and I recommend that you start using it—any good developer, no matter how experienced, should read the manual.

Applying static lighting to static objects

When marking objects as static in your scene, you probably figured out that all the objects in the scene won't move, so you probably checked the static checkbox for everyone. That's ok, but you should always put a dynamic object into the scene to really be sure that everything works ok—no games have totally static scenes. Try adding a capsule and moving it around to simulate our player, as shown in the following image. If you pay attention to it, you will notice something odd—the shadows being generated by the lightmapping process are not being applied to our dynamic object:

Figure 12.52: Dynamic object under a lightmap's precalculated shadow

You may be thinking that Mixed Light Mode was supposed to affect both dynamic and static objects, and that is exactly what it's doing. The problem here is that everything related to static objects is pre-calculated into those lightmap textures, including the shadows they cast, and because our capsule is dynamic, it wasn't there when the pre-calculation process was executed. So, in this case, because the object that cast the shadow was static, its shadow won't affect any dynamic object.

Here, we have several solutions. The first would be to change the Static and Realtime mixing algorithm to make everything near the camera use Realtime lighting and prevent this problem (at least near the focus of attention of the player), which will have a big impact on performance. The alternative is to use **Light Probes**. When we baked information, we only did that on lightmaps, meaning that we have information on lighting just over surfaces, not in empty spaces. Because our player is traversing the empty spaces between those surfaces, we don't know exactly how the lighting would look in those spaces, such as the middle of a corridor. Light Probes are a set of points in those empty spaces where Unity also pre-calculates information, so when some dynamic object passes through the Light Probes, it will sample information from them. In the following image, you can see some Light Probes that have been applied to our scene. You will notice that the ones that are inside shadows are going to be dark, while the ones exposed to light will have a greater intensity.

This effect will be applied to our dynamic objects:

Figure 12.53: Spheres representing Light Probes

If you move your object through the scene now, it will react to the shadows, as shown in the following two images, where you can see a dynamic object being lit outside a baked shadow and being dark inside:

Figure 12.54: Dynamic object receiving baked lighting from Light Probes

In order to create Light Probes, do the following:

1. Create a group of **Light Probes** by going to **GameObject | Light | Light Probe Group**.

2. Fortunately, we have some guidelines on how to locate them. It is recommended to place them where the lighting changes, such as inside and outside shadow borders. However, that is complicated. The simplest and recommended approach is to just drop a grid of Light Probes all over your playable area. To do that, you can simply copy and paste the Light Grid Group several times to cover the entire base:

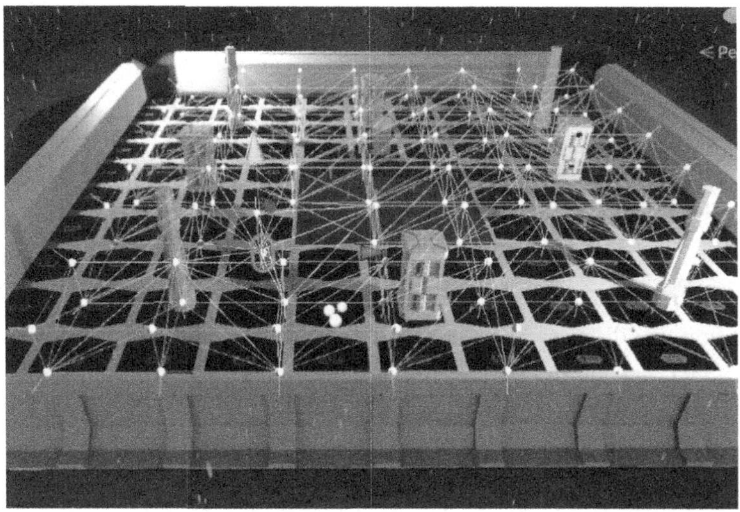

Figure 12.55: Light Probe grid

3. Another approach would be to select one group and click the **Edit Light Probes** button to enter Light Probe edit mode:

Figure 12.56: Light Probe Group edit button

4. Click the **Select All** button and then **Duplicate Selected** to duplicate all the previously existing probes.
5. Using the translate gizmo, move them next to the previous ones, extending the grid in the process. Consider that the nearer the probes are, you more you will need to cover the terrain, which will generate more data. However, Light Probes data is relatively cheap in terms of performance, so you can have lots of them, as seen in *Figure 12.55*.
6. Repeat *steps 4* and *5* until you've covered the entire area.
7. Regenerate lighting with the **Generate Lighting** button in **Lighting Settings**.

With that, you have pre-calculated lighting on the Light Probes affecting our dynamic objects, combining both worlds to get cohesive lighting.

Summary

In this chapter, we discussed several lighting topics, such as how Unity calculates lights and shadows, how to deal with different light sources such as direct and indirect lighting, how to configure shadows, how to bake lighting to optimize performance, and how to combine dynamic and static lighting so that the lights aren't disconnected from the world they affect. This was a long chapter, but lighting deserves that. It is a complex subject that can improve the look and feel of your scene drastically, as well as reduce your performance dramatically. It requires a lot of practice and here, we tried to summarize all the important knowledge you will need to start experimenting with it. Be patient with this topic; it is easy to get incorrect results, but you are probably just one checkbox away from solving it.

Now that we have improved all we can in the scene settings, in the next chapter, we will apply a final layer of graphic effects using the Unity Post-Processing Stack, which will apply full-screen image effects—the ones that will give us that cinematic look and feel that all games have nowadays.

Join us on Discord!

Read this book alongside other users, Unity game development experts, and the author himself.

Ask questions, provide solutions to other readers, chat with the author via Ask Me Anything sessions, and much more.

Scan the QR code or visit the link to join the community.

`https://packt.link/handsonunity22`

13

Full-Screen Effects with Post-Processing

So far, we have created different objects to alter the visuals of our scene, such as meshes, particles, and lights. We can tweak the settings of those objects here and there to improve our scene quality, but you will always feel that something is missing when comparing it with modern game scenes, and that is post-processing effects. In this chapter, you will learn how to apply effects to the final rendered frame, which will alter the look of the overall scene.

In this chapter, we will examine the following image effect concepts:

- Using post-processing
- Using advanced effects

Let's start by seeing how we can apply post-processing to our scene.

Using post-processing

Post-processing is a Unity feature that allows us to apply a stack of effects (several effects) one on top of the other that will alter the final look of an image. Each one will affect the finished frame, changing the colors in it based on different criteria. In *Figure 13.1*, you can see a scene before and after applying image effects. You will notice a dramatic difference, but that scene doesn't have any change in its objects, including lights, particles, or meshes.

The effects applied are based on a per-pixel level. Have a look at both scenes here:

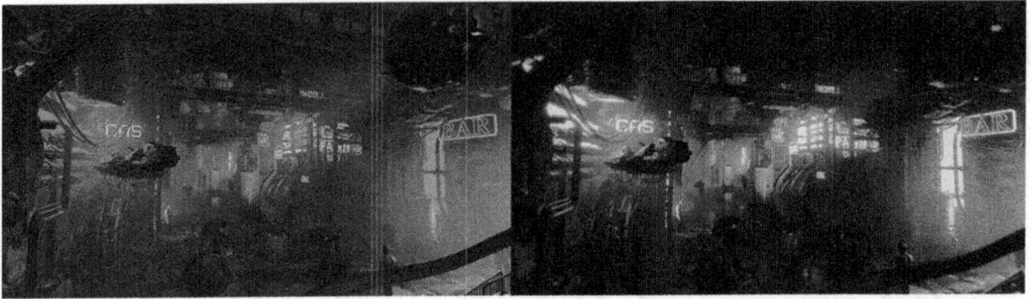

Figure 13.1: A scene without image effects (left) and the same scene with effects (right)

Something to take into account is that the previous post-processing solution, **Post Processing Stack version 2 (PPv2)** won't work on the **Universal Render Pipeline (URP)**; it has its own post-processing implementation, so we will see that one in this chapter. They are very similar, so even if you are using PPv2, you can still learn something from this chapter.

In this section, we will discuss the following URP Post-Processing concepts:

- Setting up a profile
- Using basic effects

Let's start preparing our scene to apply effects.

Setting up a profile

To start applying effects, we need to create a **profile**, which is an asset containing all the effects and settings we want to apply. This is a separate asset for the same reason the Material is: because we can share the same post-processing profile across different scenes and parts of scenes. When we refer to parts of the scenes, we are referring to volumes or areas of the game that have certain effects applied. We can define a global area that applies effects regardless of the position of the player, or we can apply different effects—for example, when we are outdoors or indoors.

In this case, we will use a global volume, one that we will use to apply a profile with our first effect, by doing the following:

1. Create a new empty GameObject (**GameObject | Create Empty**) named `PP Volume` (Post-Processing Volume).
2. Add the **Volume** component to it and make sure the **Mode** is set to **Global**.

3. Click on the **New** button at the right of the **Profile** setting, which will generate a new `Profile` asset with the same name as the GameObject that was selected when clicking the button (**PPVolume Profile**). Move that asset to its own folder, which is recommended for asset organization purposes. The process is illustrated in the following figure:

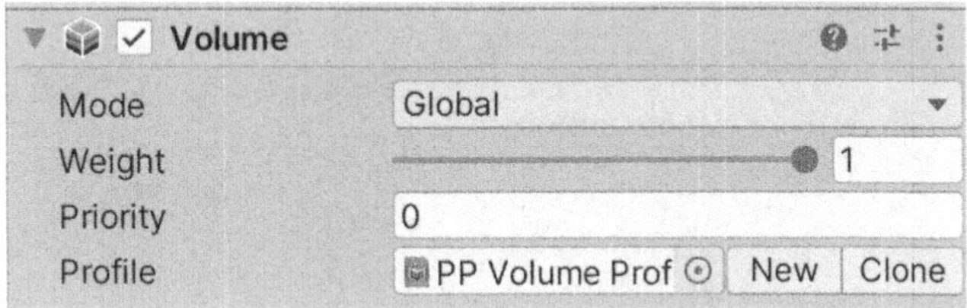

Figure 13.2: Volume component

4. To test if the volume is working, let's add an effect. Click the **Add Override** button and select the **Post-Processing | Chromatic Aberration** option.
5. Check the **Intensity** checkbox in the **Chromatic Aberration** effect and set the intensity to `0.25`, as illustrated in the following figure:

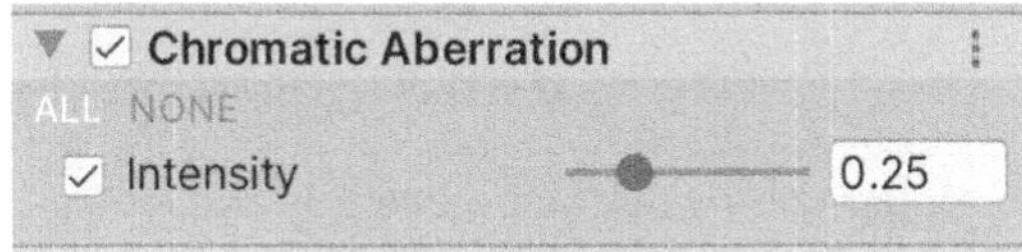

Figure 13.3: Chromatic aberration effect

6. Now, you will see an aberration effect being applied in the corners of the image. Remember to look at this in the **Scene** panel; we will make the effect applied to the Game view in the next step. This is illustrated in the following figure:

Figure 13.4: Chromatic aberration applied to the scene

7. Now, if you hit **Play** and see the game from the view of the Main Camera, you will see that the effect is not being applied, and that's because we need to check the **Post Processing** checkbox in the **Rendering** section of our Main Camera, as illustrated in the following figure:

Figure 13.5: Enabling post-processing

So, we have created a global volume, which will apply the effects specified as overrides to the entire scene regardless of the player's position.

Now that we have prepared our scene to use post-processing, we can start experimenting with different effects. Let's start with the simplest ones in the next section.

Using basic effects

Now that we have post-processing in our scene, the only thing needed is to start adding effects and set them up until we have the desired look and feel. In order to do that, let's explore several simple effects included in the system.

Let's start with **Chromatic Aberration**, the one we just used, which, as with most image effects, tries to replicate a particular real-life effect. All game-engine rendering systems use a simple mathematical approximation of how eye vision really works, and because of that, we don't have some effects that occur in the human eyes or camera lenses. A real camera lens works by bending light rays to point them toward the camera sensors, but that bending is not perfect in some lenses (sometimes intentionally), and, hence, you can see a distortion, as shown in the following screenshot:

Figure 13.6: Image without chromatic aberration (left) and the same image with chromatic aberration (right)

This effect will be one of several that we will add to generate a cinematic feeling in our game, simulating the usage of real-life cameras. Of course, this effect won't look nice in every kind of game; maybe a simplistic cartoonish style won't benefit from this one, but you never know: art is subjective, so it's a matter of trial and error.

Also, we have exaggerated the intensity a little bit in the previous example to make the effect more noticeable, but I would recommend using an intensity of `0.25` in this scenario. It is usually recommended to be gentle with the intensity of the effects; it's tempting to have intense effects, but as you will be adding lots of them, after a while, the image will be bloated, with too many distortions. So, try to add several subtle effects instead of a few intense ones. But, again, this depends on the target style you are looking for; there are no absolute truths here (but common sense still applies).

Finally, before moving on to discuss other effects, if you are used to using other kinds of post-processing effects frameworks, you will notice that this version of **Chromatic Aberration** has fewer settings, and that's because the URP version seeks performance, so it will be as simple as possible.

The next effect we are going to discuss is **Vignette**. This is another camera-lens imperfection where the image intensity is lost at the edges of the lens. This can be applied not only to simulate older cameras but also to draw the attention of the user toward the center of the camera—for example, during cinematics.

Also, if you are developing **virtual reality (VR)** applications, this can be used to reduce motion sickness by reducing the peripheral vision of the player. In the following screenshot, you can see an example of vignetting on an old camera:

Figure 13.7: Photo taken with an old camera, with vignetting over the edges

Just to try it, let's apply some vignetting to our scene by doing the following:

1. Select the `PP Volume` GameObject.
2. Add the **Postprocessing | Vignette** effect by clicking on the **Add Override** button.
3. Check the **Intensity** checkbox and set it to `0.3`, increasing the effect.
4. Check the **Smoothness** checkbox and set it to `0.5`; this will increase the spread of the effect. You can see the result in the following figure:

Figure 13.8: Vignette effect

If you want, you can change the color by checking the **Color** checkbox and setting it to another value; in our case, black is okay to reinforce the rainy-day environment. Here, I invite you to check other properties, such as **Center** and **Rounded**. You can create nice effects just by playing with the values.

Another effect we are going to see is **Motion Blur**, and again, it simulates the way the cameras work. A real camera has an exposure time: the time it needs to capture photons into an image. When an object moves fast enough, the same object is placed in different positions during that brief exposure time, so it will appear blurred. In the following screenshot, you can see the effect applied to our scene. In the case of this image, we are rotating the camera up and down fast, with the following result:

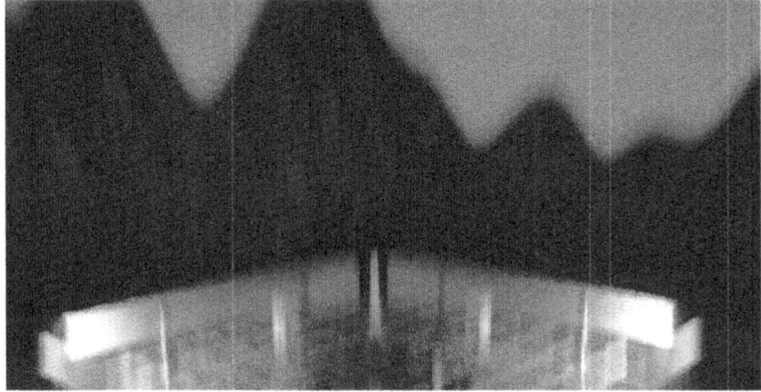

Figure 13.9: Motion Blur being applied to our scene

One thing to consider is that this blur will only be applied to the camera movement and not the movement of the objects (still camera, moving objects), due to the fact that this URP doesn't support motion vectors yet.

In order to use this effect, follow these next steps:

1. Add the **Post-processing | Motion Blur** override with the **Add override** button.
2. Check the **Intensity** checkbox and set it to `0.25`.

3. Rotate the camera while looking at the Game view (not the Scene view). You can click and drag the **X** property of the **Transform** of the camera (not the value—the **X** label), as illustrated in the following screenshot:

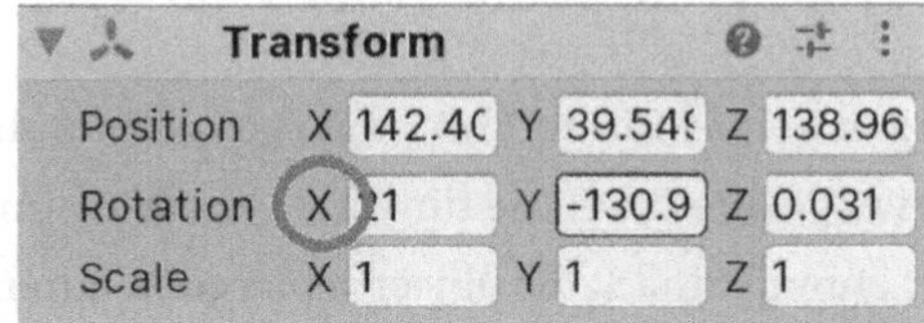

Figure 13.10: Changing rotation

As you can see, this effect cannot be seen in the Scene view, as well as other effects, so take that into account before concluding the effect is not working. Unity does this because it would be very annoying to have that effect while working in the scene.

Finally, we are going to briefly discuss two final simple effects, **Film Grain** and **White Balance**. The first is pretty simple: add it, set the intensity to `1`, and you will get the famous grain effect from the old movies. You can set the **Type** with a different number of sizes to make it more subtle or harsh. **White Balance** allows you to change the color temperature, making colors warmer or cooler depending on how you configure it. In our case, we are working in a cold, dark scene, so you can add it and set the temperature to `-20` to adjust the appearance just slightly and improve the look and feel in this kind of scene.

Now that we have seen a few of the simple effects, let's check out a few of the remaining ones that are affected by some advanced rendering features.

Using advanced effects

The effects we are going to see in this section don't differ a lot from the previous ones; they are just a little bit trickier and need some background to properly use them. So, let's dive into them!

In this section, we are going to see the following advanced effect concepts:

- High Dynamic Range (HDR) and Depth Map
- Applying advanced effects

Let's start by discussing some requirements for some of these effects to work properly.

High Dynamic Range (HDR) and Depth Map

Some effects not only work with the rendered image but also need additional data. We can first discuss the **Depth Map**, a concept we discussed in the previous chapter.

To recap, a Depth Map is an image rendered from the point of view of the camera, but instead of generating a final image of the scene, it renders the scene objects' depth, rendering the objects in shades of gray. The darker the color, the farthest from the camera the pixel is, and vice versa. In the following screenshot, you can see an example of a Depth Map:

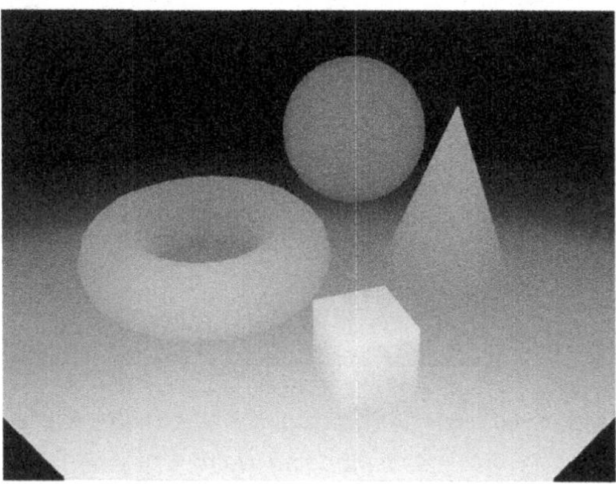

Figure 13.11: Depth map of a few primitive shapes

We will see some effects such as **Depth of Field**, which will blur some parts of the image based on the distance of the camera, but it can be used for several purposes on custom effects (not in the base URP package).

Another concept to discuss here that will alter how colors are treated and, hence, how some effects work is **High Dynamic Range** (**HDR**). In older hardware, color channels (Red, Green, and Blue) were encoded in a 0 to 1 range, 0 being no intensity and 1 being full intensity (per channel), so all lighting and color calculations were done in that range. That seems okay but doesn't reflect how light actually works. You can see full white (all channels set to 1) in a piece of paper being lit by sunlight, and you can see full white when you look directly at a light bulb, but even if both light and paper are of the same color, the latter will, firstly, irritate the eye after a while, and secondly, will have some overglow due to an excess of light. The problem here is that the maximum value (1) is not enough to represent the most intense color, so if you have a high-intensity light and another with even more intensity, both will generate the same color (1 in each channel) because calculations cannot go further than 1. So, that's why **HDR Rendering** was created.

HDR is a way for colors to exceed the 0 to 1 range, so lighting and effects that work based on color intensity have better accuracy in this mode. It is the same idea as the new televisions models' HDR feature, although in this case, Unity will do the calculations in HDR but the final image will still work using the previous color space (0 to 1, or **Low Dynamic Range** (**LDR**), so don't confuse Unity's **HDR Rendering** with the **Display's HDR**.

To convert the HDR calculations back to LDR, Unity (and also TVs) uses a concept called **tone-mapping**. You can see an example of an LDR-rendered scene and tonemapping being used in an HDR scene in the following screenshots:

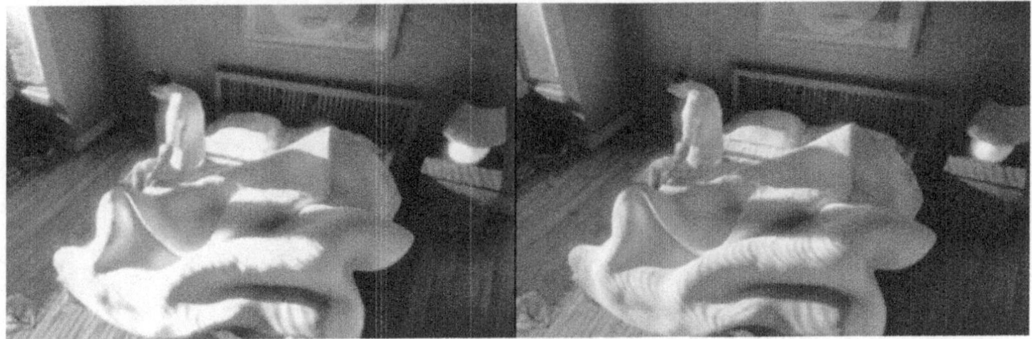

Figure 13.12: An LDR-rendered scene (left) and an HDR scene with corrected overbrights using tonemapping (right)

Tonemapping is a way to bring colors outside the 0-1 range back in to it. It basically uses curves to determine how each color channel should be mapped back.

You can clearly see this in the typical darker-to-lighter scene transition, such as when you exit a building without windows to go out into a bright day. For a time, you will see everything lighter until everything goes back to normal. The idea here is that calculations are not different when you are inside or outside the building; a white wall inside the building will have a color near the 1 intensity, while the same white wall outside will have a higher value (due to sunlight). The difference is that tonemapping will take the higher-than-1 color back to 1 when you are outside the building, and maybe it will increase the lighting of the wall inside if all the scene is darker, depending on how you set it. That feature is called **auto-exposure**.

Even if HDR is enabled by default, let's just see how we can check that, by doing the following:

1. Go to **Edit | Project Settings**.
2. Click on the **Graphics** section in the left panel.
3. Click the asset referenced under the **Scriptable Render Pipeline Settings** property.
4. Click on the highlighted asset in the **Project** panel. Ensure that this panel is visible before clicking the property in the **Graphics** settings. Alternatively, you can double-click the asset reference in the **Graphics** settings to select it.

5. Under the **Quality** section, ensure that **HDR** is checked, as illustrated in the following screenshot:

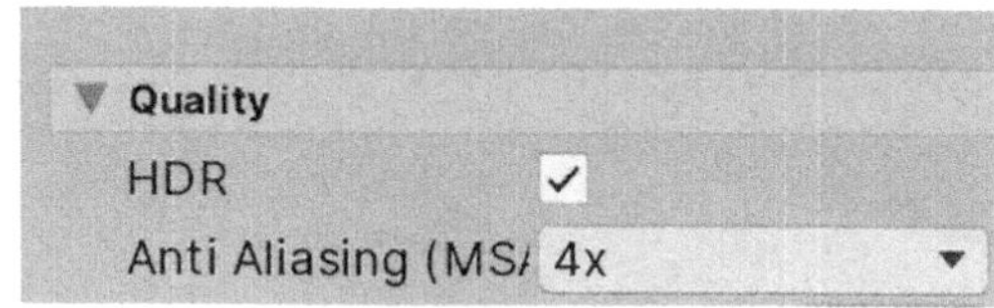

Figure 13.13: Enabling HDR

6. Ensure that the **HDR** property of the **Camera** component in the **Main Camera** GameObject is set to **Use settings from Render Pipeline** to ensure the change in the previous steps is respected.

Of course, the fact that HDR is togglable means that there are scenarios where you don't want to use it. As you can guess, not all hardware supports HDR, and using it incurs a performance overhead, so take that into account. Luckily, most effects work with both HDR and LDR color ranges, so if you have HDR enabled but the user device doesn't support it, you won't get any errors, just different results depending on the effect, such as brighter or darker images, or exaggerated effects, as we will see in the next section, *Applying advanced effects*.

Now that we are sure we have HDR enabled, let's explore some advanced effects that use this and Depth Mapping.

Applying advanced effects

Let's see certain effects that use the previously described techniques, starting with the commonly used **Bloom**. This effect emulates the overglow that happens around a heavily lit object on a camera lens or even the human eye. In *Figure 13.14*, you can see the difference between the default version of our scene and an exaggerated Bloom version.

You can observe how the effect is only applied to the brightest areas of our scene. Have a look at both effects here:

Figure 13.14: The default scene (left) and the same scene with a high-intensity Bloom (right)

This effect is actually very common and simple, but I considered it advanced because the results are drastically affected by HDR. This effect relies on calculating the intensity of each pixel's color to detect areas where it can be applied. In LDR, we can have a white object that isn't overbright, but due to the limitations in this color range, Bloom may cause an overglow over it. In HDR, due to its increased color range, we can detect if an object is white or if the object is maybe light blue but just overbright, generating the illusion that it is white (such as objects near a high-intensity lamp). In *Figure 13.15* screenshot, you can see the difference between our scene with HDR and without it. You will notice that the LDR version will have overglow in areas that are not necessarily overbright. The difference may be very subtle, but pay attention to the little details to note the difference. And remember, I exaggerated the effect here. Have a look at both scenes here:

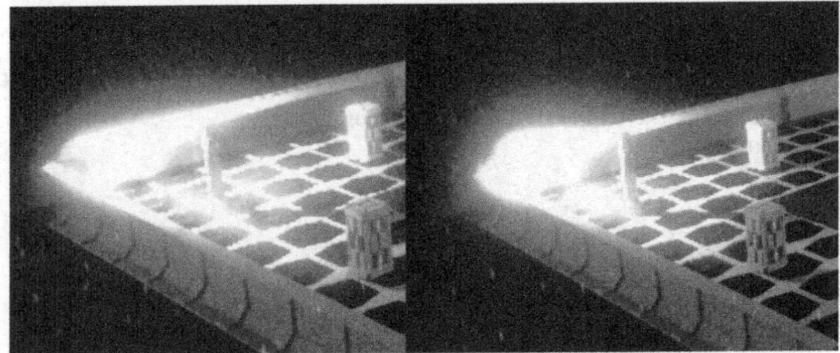

Figure 13.15: Bloom in an LDR scene (left) and Bloom in an HDR scene (right). Notice that the Bloom settings were changed to try to approximate them as much as possible

For now, let's stick with the HDR version of the scene. In order to enable Bloom, do the following:

1. Add the **Bloom** override to the profile, as usual.
2. Enable the **Intensity** checkbox by checking it, and set the value to `0.2`. This controls how much overglow will be applied.
3. Enable **Threshold** and set it to `0.7`. This value indicates the minimum intensity a color needs to have to be considered for overglow. In our case, our scene is somewhat dark, so we need to reduce this value in the Bloom effect settings to have more pixels included. As usual, those values need to be adjusted to your specific scenario.
4. You will notice that the difference is very subtle, but again, remember that you will have several effects, so all those little differences will sum up. You can see both effects in the following screenshots:

Figure 13.16: Bloom effect

As usual, it is recommended that you fiddle with the other values. Some interesting settings I recommend you test are the **Dirt Texture** and **Dirt Intensity** values, which will simulate dirty lenses in the overglow area.

Now, let's move to another common effect, **Depth of Field**. This one relies on the depth map we discussed earlier. It is not that obvious to the naked eye, but when you focus on an object within your sight, the surrounding objects became blurred because they are out of focus. We can use this to focus the attention of the player in key moments of the gameplay. This effect will sample the Depth Map to see if the object is within the focus range; if it is, no blur will be applied, and vice versa.

In order to use it, do the following:

1. This effect depends on the camera positioning of your game. To test it, in this case, we will put the camera near a column to try to focus on that specific object, as illustrated in the following screenshot:

Figure 13.17: Camera positioning

2. Add the **Depth of Field** override.
3. Enable and set the **Mode** setting to **Gaussian**: the cheapest one in terms of performance to use.
4. In my case, I have set **Start** to `10` and **End** to `20`, which will make the effect start at a distance behind the target object. The **End** setting will control how the blur's intensity will increase, reaching its maximum at a distance of `20` meters. Remember to tweak these values to your case.

5. If you want to exaggerate the effect a little bit, set **Max Radius** to `1.5`. The result is shown in the following screenshot:

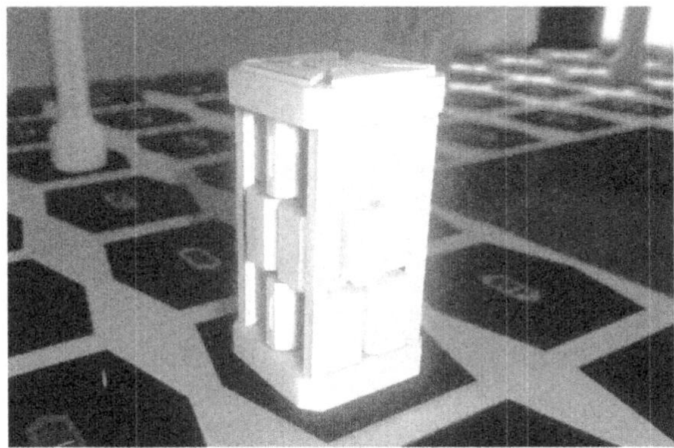

Figure 13.18: Exaggerated effect

Something to consider here is that our game will have a top-down perspective, and unlike the first-person camera where you can see distant objects, here, we will have objects near enough to not notice the effect, so we can limit the use of this effect just for cutscenes in our scenario.

Now, most of the remaining effects are different ways to alter the actual colors of the scene. The idea is that the real color sometimes doesn't give you the exact look and feel you are seeking. Maybe you need the dark zones to be darker to reinforce the sensation of a horror ambiance, or maybe you want to do the opposite: increase the dark areas to represent an open scene. Maybe you want to tint the highlights a little bit to get a neon effect if you are creating a futuristic game, or perhaps you want a sepia effect temporarily to do a flashback. We have a myriad of ways to do this, and in this case, I will use a simple but powerful effect called **Shadow, Midtones, Highlights**.

This effect will apply different color corrections to—well —Shadows, Midtones, and Highlights, meaning that we can modify darker, lighter, and medium areas separately. Let's try it by doing the following:

1. Add the **Shadow Midtones Highlights** override.
2. Let's start doing some testing. Check the three **Shadows**, **Midtones**, and **Highlights** checkboxes.

3. Move the **Shadow** and **Midtones** sliders all the way to the left and the one for **Highlights** to the right. This will reduce the intensity of Shadows and Midtones and increase the intensity of Highlights. We did this so that you can see the areas that **Highlights** will alter, based on their intensity. You can do the same with the rest of the sliders to check the other two areas. You can see the result in the following screenshot:

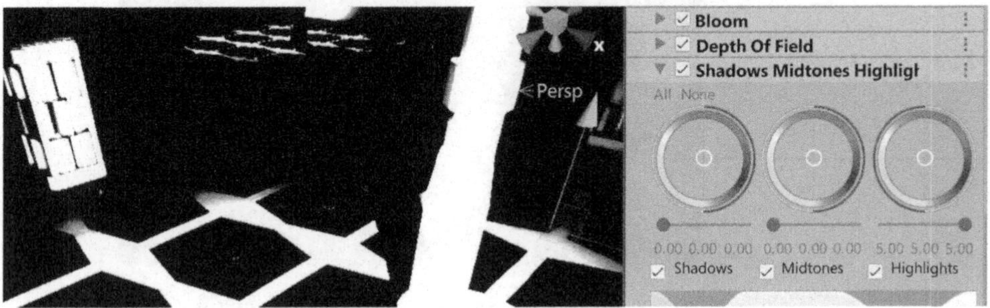

Figure 13.19: Isolating highlights

4. Also, you can test moving the white circle at the center of the colored circle to apply a little bit of tinting to those areas. Reduce the intensity of the highlights by moving the slider a little bit to the left to make the tinting more noticeable. You can see the result in the following screenshot:

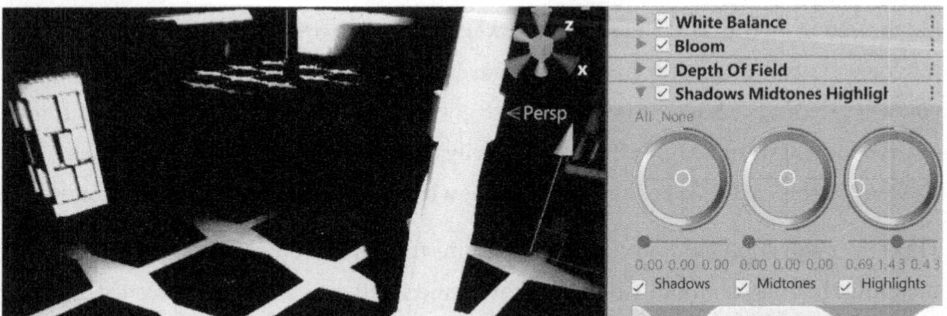

Figure 13.20: Tinting highlights

5. By doing this, you can explore how those controls work, but of course, those extreme values are useful for some edge cases. In our scene, the settings you can see in the following screenshot worked best for me. As always, it is better to use subtler values to not distort too much the original result, as illustrated here:

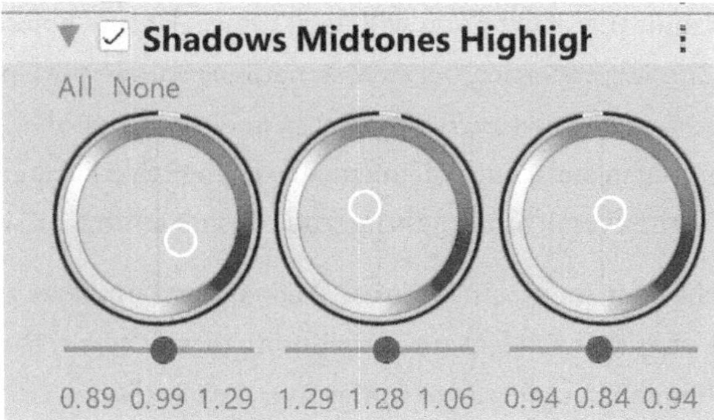

Figure 13.21: Subtle changes

6. You can see the before-and-after effects in the following screenshots:

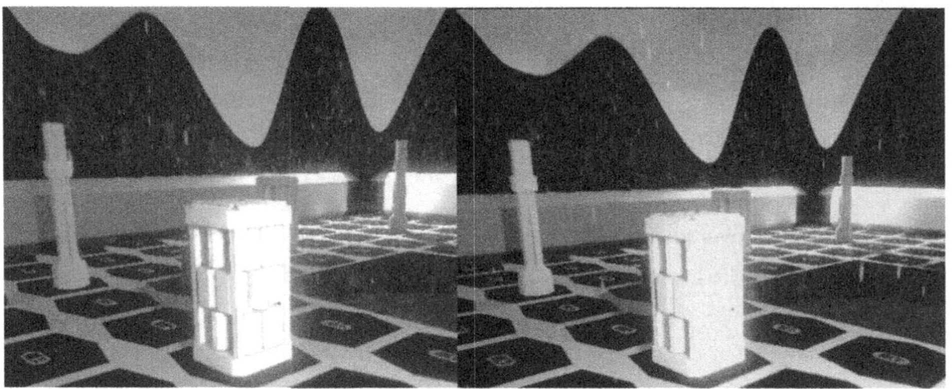

Figure 13.22: Before-and-after effects

You have other simpler options such as **Split Toning**, which does something similar but just with **Shadows** and **Highlights**, or **Color Curves**, which give you advanced control of how each color channel of the scene will be mapped, but the idea is the same—that is, to alter the actual color of the resulting scene to apply a specific color ambiance to your scene. If you remember the movie series *The Matrix* when the characters were in the Matrix, everything had subtle green tinting, and while outside it, the tinting was blue.

Remember that the results of using HDR and not using it regarding these effects are important, so it is better to decide sooner rather than later whether to use HDR, excluding certain target platforms (which may not be important to your target audience), or not to use it (using LDR) and have less control over your scene lighting levels.

Also, take into account that maybe you will need to tweak some objects' settings, such as light intensities and material properties, because sometimes we use post-processing to fix graphics errors that may be caused by wrongly set objects, and that's not okay. For example, increasing the `Ambient Lighting` in our scene will drastically change the output of the effects, and we can use that to increase the overall brightness instead of using an effect if we find the scene too dark.

This has covered the main image effects to use. Remember that the idea is not to use every single one but to use the ones that you feel are contributing to your scene; they are not free in terms of performance (although not that resource intensive), so use them wisely. Also, you can check for the already created profiles to apply them to your game and see how little changes can make a huge difference.

Summary

In this chapter, we discussed basic and advanced full-screen effects to apply in our scene, making it look more realistic in terms of camera-lens effects and more stylish in terms of color distortions. We also discussed the internals of HDR and Depth Maps and how they are important when using those effects, which can immediately increase your game's graphic quality with minimal effort.

Now that we have covered most of the common graphics found in Unity systems, let's start looking at how to increase the immersion of our scene by using sounds.

14

Sound and Music Integration

We have now achieved good enough graphics quality, but we are missing an important part of the game aesthetics: the sound. Often relegated to being the last step in game development, sound is one of those things that if it's there, you won't notice its presence, but if you don't have it, you will feel that something is missing. It will help you to reinforce the ambience you want in your game and must match the graphical setting.

In this chapter, we will examine the following sound concepts:

- Importing audio
- Integrating and mixing audio

We will apply those concepts in our game to import the audio to play in different scenarios—such as when the player shoots—and the music. Later in the programming chapters, we will play sounds, but for now, let's focus on how to import them into our project.

Importing audio

As with graphic assets, it is important to properly set up the import settings for your audio assets, as the import can be resource-intensive if not done properly.

In this section, we will examine the following audio importing concepts:

- Audio types
- Configuring import settings

Let's start by discussing the different kinds of audio we can use.

Audio types

There are different types of audio present in video games, which are the following:

- **Music**: Music used to enhance the player's experience according to the situation.
- **Sound effects (SFX)**: Sounds that happen as a reaction to player or NPC actions, such as clicking a button, walking, opening a door, shooting a gun, and so on.
- **Ambient sound**: A game that uses sounds only in response to events would feel empty. If you are recreating an apartment in the middle of the city, even if the player is just idle in the middle of the room doing nothing, lots of sounds should be heard, and the sources of most of them will be outside the room, such as an airplane flying overhead, a construction site two blocks away, cars in the street, and so on. Creating objects that won't be seen is a waste of resources. Instead, we can place individual sounds all over the scene to recreate the desired ambience, but that would be resource-intensive, requiring lots of CPU and RAM to achieve believable results. Considering that these sounds usually occupy the second plane of the user's attention, we can just combine them all into a single looping track and just play one audio file, and that's exactly what ambient sound is. If you want to create a café scene, you can simply go to a real café and record a few minutes of audio, using that as your ambient sound.

For almost all games, we will need at least one music track, one ambient track, and several SFX to start the production of the audio. As always, we have different sources of audio assets, but we will use the Asset Store. It has three audio categories to search for the assets we need:

Figure 14.1: Audio categories in the Asset Store

In my case, I also used the search bar to further filter the categories, searching for `weather` to find a rain effect. Sometimes, you can't find the exact audio separately; in such cases, you will need to dig into **Packs** and **Libraries**, so have patience here. In my case, I picked the three packages you can see in *Figure 14.2*, but imported just some of the sounds included, as all of them would weigh a lot in the project in terms of size. For ambience, I picked a rain sound file called `Ambience_Rain_Moderate_01_LOOP` in the case of this package, but the name of the rain sound we are looking for can be different if you downloaded another package. Then, I picked **Music – Sad Hope** for music, and for SFX, I picked one gun sound effect package for our future player's hero character. Of course, you can pick other packages to better suit your game's needs:

Figure 14.2: The packages for our game

Now that we have the necessary audio packages, let's discuss how to import them.

Configuring import settings

We have several import settings we can tweak, but the problem is that we need to consider the usage of the audio to properly set it up, so let's see the ideal settings for each case. In order to see the import settings, as always, you can select the asset and see it in the Inspector panel, as in the following figure:

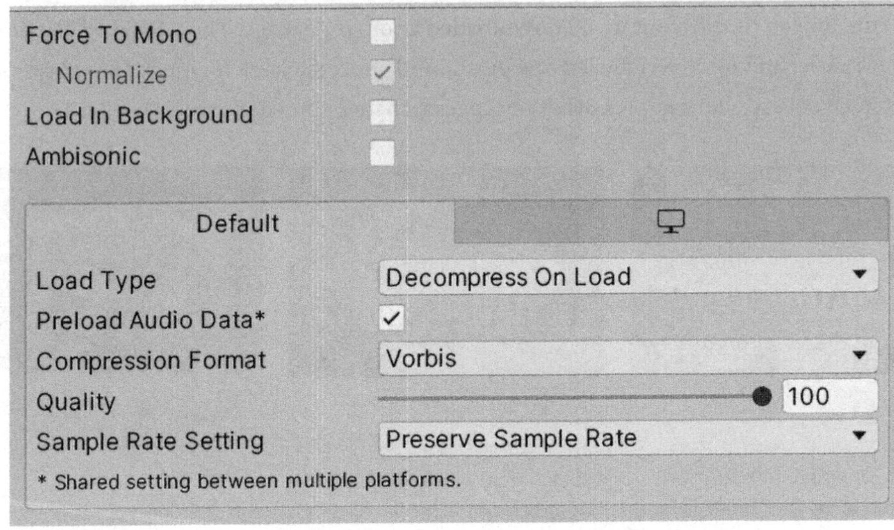

Figure 14.3: Audio Import Settings

Let's discuss the most important ones, starting with **Force To Mono**. Some audio may come with stereo channels, meaning that we have one sound playing in the left ear and another one for the right ear. This means that one piece of audio can actually contain two different audio tracks. Stereo sound is useful for different effects and instrument spatialization in the case of music, so we want that in those scenarios, but there are other scenarios where stereo is not useful. Consider 3D sound effects such as a shooting gun or some walking-pace steps. In those cases, we need the sound to be heard in the direction of the source—if the shooting of a gun happened to my left, I need to hear it coming from my left. In these cases, we can convert stereo audio to mono audio checking the **Force To Mono** checkbox in the audio import settings. This will make Unity combine the two channels into a single one, reducing the audio usually to almost half its size (sometimes more, sometimes less, depending on various aspects).

You can verify the impact of that and other settings at the bottom of the Audio Asset Inspector, where you can see the imported audio size:

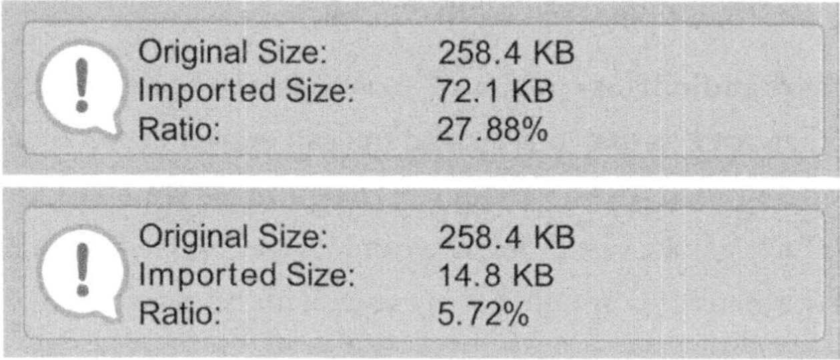

Figure 14.4: Left: audio imported without Force To Mono. Right: same audio with Force To Mono

The next setting to discuss, and an important one at that, is **Load Type**. In order to play some audio, Unity needs to read the audio from disk, decompress it, and then play it. Load Type changes the way those three processes are handled. We have the following three options here:

- **Decompress on Load**: The most memory-intensive option. This mode will make Unity load the audio uncompressed in memory when the scene is loaded. That means that the audio will take lots of space in RAM because we have the uncompressed version loaded. The advantage of using this mode is that playing the audio is easier because we have the raw audio data ready to play in RAM.
- **Streaming**: The total opposite of **Decompress on Load**. This mode never loads audio in RAM. Instead, while the audio is playing, Unity reads a piece of the audio asset from disk, decompresses it, plays it, and repeats, running this process once for each piece of audio playing in **Streaming**. This means that this mode will be CPU intensive, but will consume almost zero bytes of RAM.
- **Compressed in Memory**: The middle ground. This mode will load the audio from disk when the scene is loaded but will keep it compressed in memory. When Unity needs to play the audio, it will just take a piece from the RAM, decompress it, and play it. Remember that reading pieces of the audio asset from RAM is considerably faster than reading from disk.

Maybe if you are an experienced developer, you can easily determine which mode is better suited for which kind of audio, but if this is your first encounter with video games, it may sound confusing. So, let's discuss the best modes for different cases:

- **Frequent short audio**: This could be a shooting gun or the sound of footsteps, which are sounds that last less than one second but can occur in several instances and play at the same time. In such cases, we can use **Decompress On Load.** Uncompressed short audio won't have a huge size difference from its compressed version. Also, since this is the most performant CPU option, having several instances won't have a huge impact on performance.
- **Infrequent large audio**: This includes music, ambient sound, and dialog. These kinds of audio usually have just one instance playing, and they are usually big. Those cases are better suited for **Streaming** mode because having them compressed or decompressed in RAM can have a huge impact on RAM consumption in low-end devices such as mobile devices (on PCs, we can use **Compressed in Memory** sometimes). A CPU can handle having two or three bits of audio playing in Streaming mode, but try to have no more than that.
- **Frequent medium audio**: This includes pre-made voice chat dialog in multiplayer games, character emotes, long explosions, or any audio that is more than 500 KB (that is not a strict rule—this number depends a lot on the target device). Having this kind of audio decompressed in RAM can have a noticeable impact on performance, but due to the fact that this audio is fairly frequently used, we can have it compressed in memory. Their relatively small size means they usually won't make a huge difference in our game's overall size, and we will avoid wasting CPU resources on reading from disk.

There are other cases to consider, but those can be extrapolated based on the previous ones. Remember that the previous analysis was made by taking into account the requirements of the standard game, but this can vary a lot according to your game and your target device. Maybe you are making a game that won't consume lots of RAM but is pretty intensive in terms of CPU resources, in which case you can just put everything in **Decompress on Load**. It's important to consider all aspects of your game and to balance your resources accordingly.

Finally, another thing to consider is the compression format, which will change the way Unity will encode the audio in the published game. Different compression formats will give different compression ratios in exchange for less fidelity with the original audio, or higher decompression times, and all this varies a lot based on the audio patterns and length. We have three compression formats:

- **PCM**: The uncompressed format will give you the highest audio quality, with no noise artifacts, but will result in a bigger asset file size.
- **ADPCM**: Compressing audio this way reduces file size and yields a fast, uncompressing process, but this can introduce noise artifacts that can be noticeable in certain types of audio.
- **Vorbis**: A high-quality compression format that will yield almost zero artifacts but takes longer to decompress, so playing Vorbis audio will be slightly more intensive than for other formats. It also provides a quality slider to select the exact amount of compression aggressiveness.

Which one should you use? Again, that depends on the features of your audio. Short smooth audio can use PCM, while long noisy audio can use ADPCM; the artifacts introduced by this format will be hidden in the audio itself. Maybe long smooth audio where compression artifacts are noticeable could benefit from using Vorbis. Sometimes, it's just a matter of trial and error. Maybe use Vorbis by default and when performance is reduced, try to switch to ADPCM, and if that causes glitches, just switch to PCM. Of course, the problem here is being sure that the audio processing is really what's responsible for the performance issues—maybe switching all audio to ADPCM and checking whether that made a difference is a good way to detect that, but a better approach would be to use the Profiler, a performance measurement tool that we will see later in this book.

We have other settings, such as **Sample Rate Setting**, that again, with a little trial and error, you can use to detect the best setting.

I have set up the audio that I downloaded from the Asset Store as you can see in *Figures 14.5* and *14.6*. The first one shows how I set up the music and ambient audio files (large files):

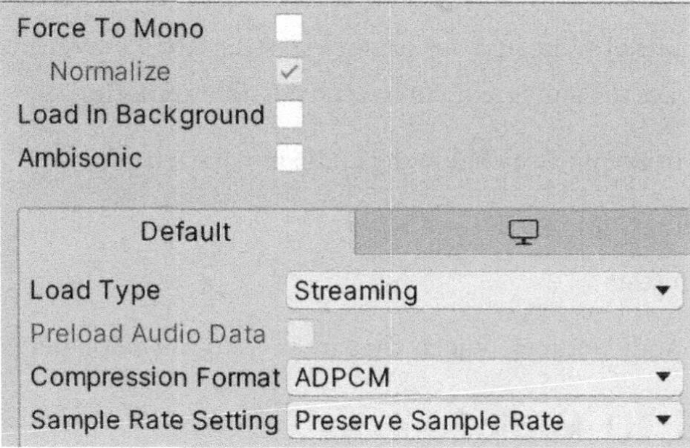

Figure 14.5: Music and ambient settings

The music should be configured as stereo (**Force To Mono** unchecked), use **Streaming Load Type** because they are large and will have just one instance playing, and **ADPCM Compression Format** because **Vorbis** didn't result in a huge size difference.

This second screenshot shows how I set up the SFX files (small files):

Force To Mono	✓
Normalize	✓
Load In Background	☐
Ambisonic	☐

Default

Load Type	Decompress On Load
Preload Audio Data*	✓
Compression Format	Vorbis
Quality	100
Sample Rate Setting	Preserve Sample Rate

Figure 14.6: Shooting SFX settings

The sounds we downloaded will be 3D, so **Force To Mono** should be checked. They will also be short, so the **Load Type** named **Decompress On Load** works better. Finally, choosing the **Vorbis Compression Format** reduced **ADPCM** size by more than a half, which is why we picked it.

Now that we have our pieces of audio properly configured, we can start to use them in our scene.

Integrating and mixing audio

We can just drag our bits of audio into our scene to start using it, but we can dig a little bit further to explore the best ways to configure them to each possible scenario.

In this section, we will examine the following audio integration concepts:

- Using 2D and 3D AudioSources
- Using audio mixers

Let's start exploring AudioSources, objects that are in charge of audio playback.

Using 2D and 3D AudioSources

AudioSources are components that can be attached to GameObjects. They are responsible for emitting sound in our game based on **AudioClips**, which are the audio assets we downloaded previously.

It's important to differentiate an AudioClip from an **AudioSource**; we can have a single explosion AudioClip, but lots of AudioSources playing it, simulating several explosions. An AudioSource can be seen as a CD player that can play AudioClips (our CDs in this analogy), only with the exception that we can have several CD players or AudioSources playing the same CD at the same time (for example, two explosions sounds playing at the same time).

The simplest way to create an **AudioSource** is to pick an **AudioClip** (an audio asset) and drag it to the **Hierarchy** window. Try to avoid dragging the audio into an existing object; instead, drag it between objects, so Unity will create a new object with the **AudioSource** instead of adding it to an existing object (sometimes, you want an existing object to have the **AudioSource**, but let's keep things simple for now):

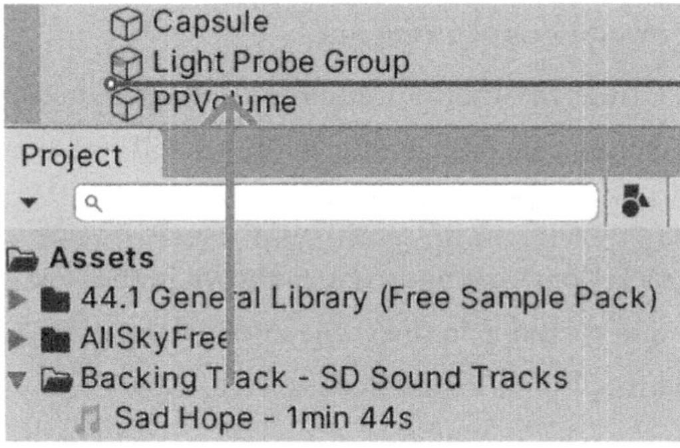

Figure 14.7: Dragging an AudioClip to the Hierarchy window between objects

The following screenshot shows the **AudioSource** generated by dragging the music asset to the scene. You can see that the **AudioClip** field has a reference to the dragged audio:

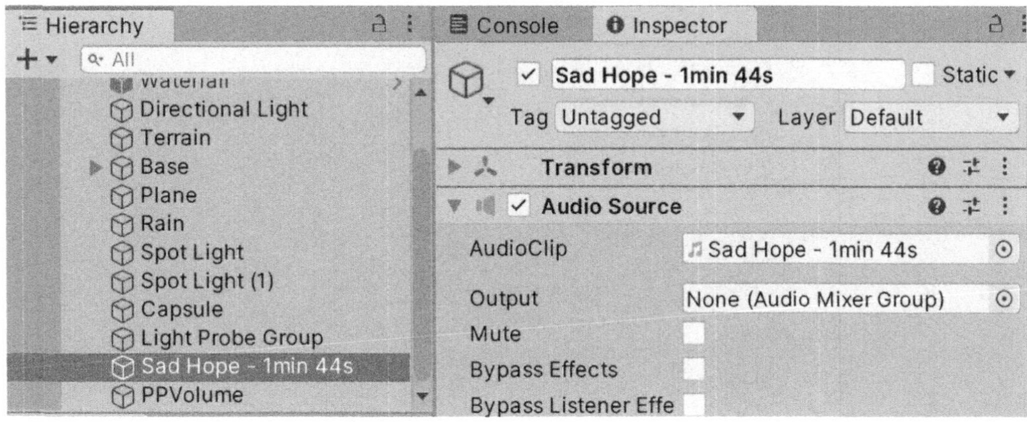

Figure 14.8: AudioSource configured to play our music asset

As you can see, the **AudioSource** has several settings, so let's review the common ones in the following list:

- **Play on Awake**: Determines whether the audio starts playing automatically when the game starts. We can uncheck that and play the audio via scripting, perhaps when the player shoots or jumps (more on that in *Part 3* of the book).
- **Loop**: Will make the audio repeat automatically when it finishes playing. Remember to always check this setting on the music and ambient audio clips. It is easy to forget this because those tracks are long, and we may never reach the end of them in our tests.
- **Volume**: Controls the audio intensity.
- **Pitch**: Controls the audio velocity. This is useful for simulating effects such as slow motion or the increasing revolutions of an engine.
- **Spatial Blend**: Controls whether our audio is 2D or 3D. In 2D mode, the audio will be heard at the same volume at all distances, while 3D will make the audio volume decrease as the distance from the camera increases.

In the case of our music track, I have configured it as shown in the following screenshot. You can drag the ambient rain sound to add it to the scene and use the same settings as these because we want the same ambient effect in all our scenes. In complex scenes, though, you can have different 3D ambient sounds scattered all over the scene to change the sound according to the current environment:

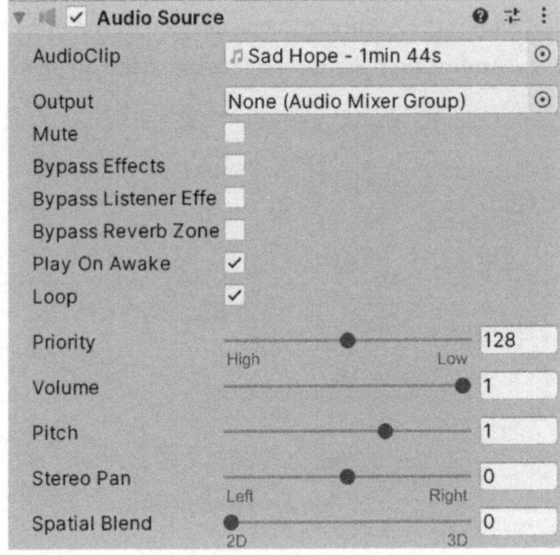

Figure 14.9: Music and ambient settings. This will loop, is set to Play on Awake, and is 2D

Now, you can drag the shooting effect and configure it as shown in *Figure 14.10*. As you can see, the audio, in this case, won't loop because we want the shooting effect to play once per bullet. Remember that, for our game, the bullet will be a Prefab that will spawn each time we press the shoot key, so each bullet will have its own **AudioSource** that will play when the bullet is created. Also, the bullet is set to a 3D **Spatial Blend**, meaning that the effect will be transmitted through different speakers based on the position of the **AudioSource** against the camera position:

Figure 14.10: Sound effect setting. This won't loop and is a 3D sound

Something to consider in the case of 3D sounds is the **Volume Rolloff** setting, which is inside the 3D sound settings section. This setting controls how the volume decays as distance from the camera increases. By default, you can see that this setting is set to **Logarithmic Rolloff**, the way real-life sound works, but sometimes you don't want real-life sound decay, because sounds in real life are usually heard slightly even if the source is very far away.

One option is to switch to **Linear Rolloff** and configure the exact maximum distance with the **Max Distance** setting:

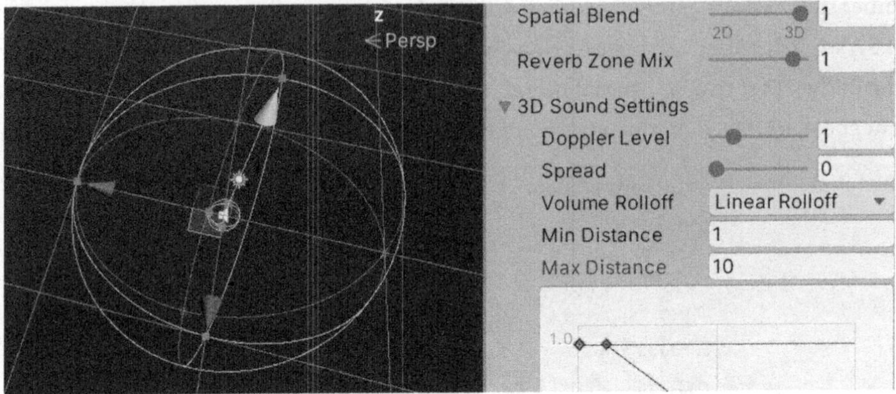

Figure 14.11: A 3D sound with a maximum distance of 10 metres, using Linear Rolloff

Considering we just discussed 3D sounds, it is worth mentioning the **AudioListener** component, one that is created by default in the **MainCamera**, and 99% of the time, this component will be placed in the **MainCamera.** It serves as a way to identify which object represents the ears of the player in the world, with which we can calculate audio directionality. The camera is the logical place to put it given it represents the eyes of the user, and having the eyes and the ears of the player in different places would be confusing. There are no properties to configure in the **AudioListener** component, but it is important to mention that in order for audio to work, we need one, and no more than one; we have just one pair of ears:

Figure 14.12: Audio Listener component in the Main Camera

Now that we can configure individual pieces of audio, let's see how to apply effects to groups of audio instances using an **Audio Mixer**.

Using an Audio Mixer

We will have several audio instances playing all over our game: the footsteps of characters, shooting, bonfires, explosions, rain, and so on. Controlling exactly which sounds are supposed to sound louder or quieter depending on the context, and applying effects to reinforce certain situations, such as being stunned due to a nearby explosion, is called audio mixing—the process of mixing several sounds together in a cohesive and controlled way.

In Unity, we can create an Audio Mixer, an asset that we can use to define groups of sounds. All changes to a group will affect all sounds inside it by raising or lowering the volume, perhaps, or by applying an effect. You can have SFX and music groups to control sounds separately—as an example, you could lower the SFX volume while in the **Pause** menu but not the music volume. Also, groups are organized in a hierarchy, where a group can also contain other groups, so a change in a group will also apply changes to its sub-groups. As a matter of fact, every group you create will always be a child group of the master group, the group that controls every single sound in the game (that uses that mixer).

Let's create a mixer with SFX and music groups:

1. In the Project window, using the + button, select the **Audio Mixer** option. Name the asset as you wish; in my case, I chose `Main Mixer`.
2. Double-click the created asset to open the **Audio Mixer** window:

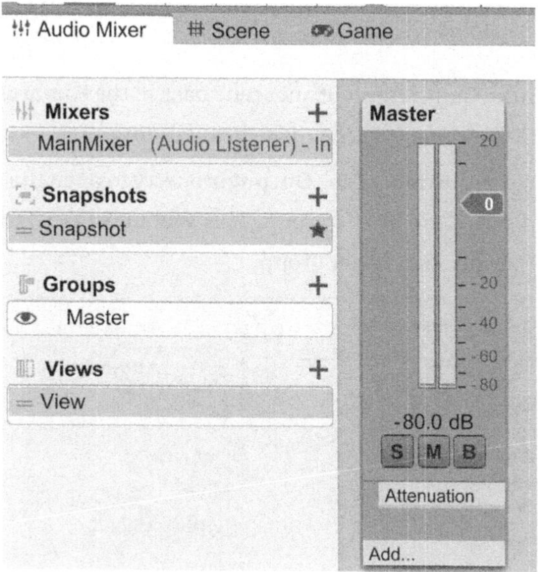

Figure 14.13: Audio Mixer window

3. Click the + button at the right of the **Groups** label to create a child group of the master node. Name it `SFX`:

Figure 14.14: Group creation

4. Click on the **Master** group and click again on the + button to create another master node child group called `Music`. Remember to select the **Master** group before clicking the + button, because if another group is selected, the new group will be a child of that one. Anyway, you can rearrange a group child-parent relationship by dragging the group in the **Groups** panel in the **AudioMixer** window:

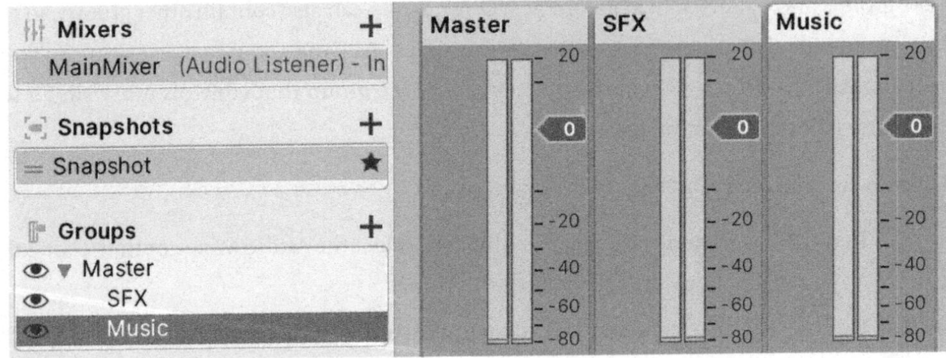

Figure 14.15: The Master, SFX, and Music groups

5. Select the **Music** GameObject of our scene back in the **Hierarchy** window and look for the **AudioSource** component in the **Inspector** window.
6. Click the circle to the right of the **Output** property to open the **AudioMixerGroup** selector window and select the **Music** group. This will make that **AudioSource** affected by the settings on the specified Mixer group:

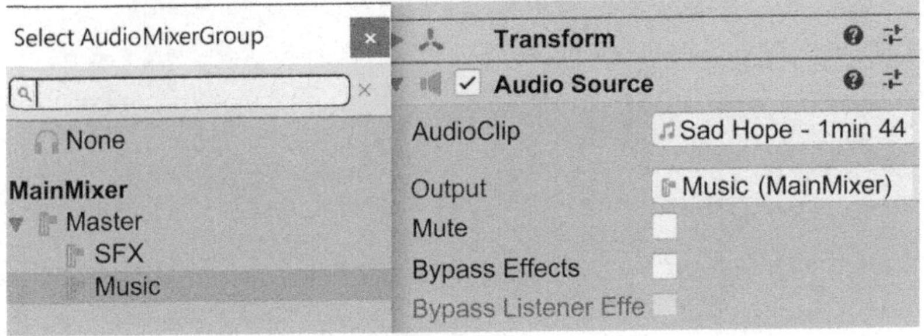

Figure 14.16: Making an AudioSource belong to an Audio Mixer group

7. If you play the game now, you can see how the volume meters in the **Audio Mixer** window start to move, indicating that the music is going through the **Music** group. You will also see that the **Master** group volume meter is also moving, indicating that the sound that is passing through the **Music** group is also passing through the **Master** group (the parent of the **Music** group) before going to the sound card of your computer:

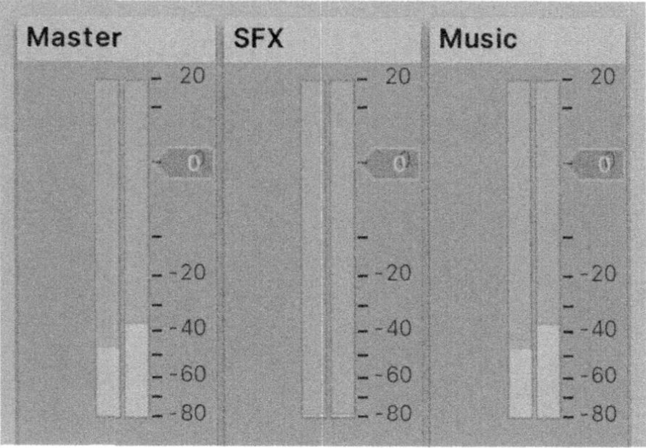

Figure 14.17: Group volumes levels

8. Repeat *steps 5* and *6* for the ambient and shooting sounds to make them belong to the **SFX** group.

Now that we have separated our sounds into groups, we can start adjusting the groups' settings. But, before doing that, we need to take into account the fact that we won't want the same settings all the time, as in the previously mentioned pause menu case, where the SFX volume should be lower. To handle those scenarios, we can create snapshots, which are presets of our mixer that can be activated via scripting during our game. We will deal with the scripting steps in *Part 3* of this book, but we can create a normal snapshot for the in-game settings and a pause snapshot for the pause menu settings.

If you check the **Snapshots** list, you will see that a single snapshot has already been created—that can be our normal snapshot. So, let's create a pause snapshot by doing the following:

1. Click on the + button to the right of the **Snapshots** label and call the snapshot `Pause`. Remember to stop the game to edit the mixer or click the **Edit in Playmode** option to allow Unity to change the mixer during play. If you do the latter, remember that the changes will persist when you stop the game, unlike changes to GameObjects. Actually, if you change other assets during **Play** mode, those changes will also persist—only GameObject changes are reverted.

There are some other cases, like Materials and Animations, changes to which are not reverted after pausing given that they are assets, but we won't discuss them right now:

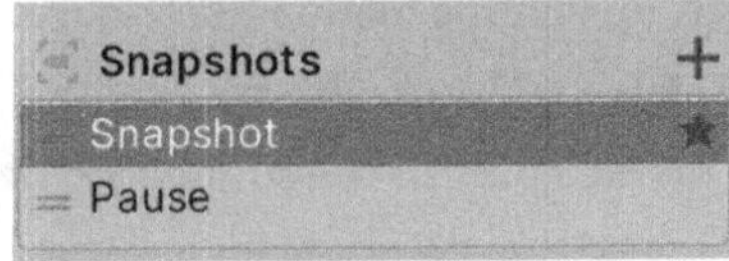

Figure 14.18: Snapshot creation

2. Select the **Pause** snapshot and lower the volume slider of the **SFX** group:

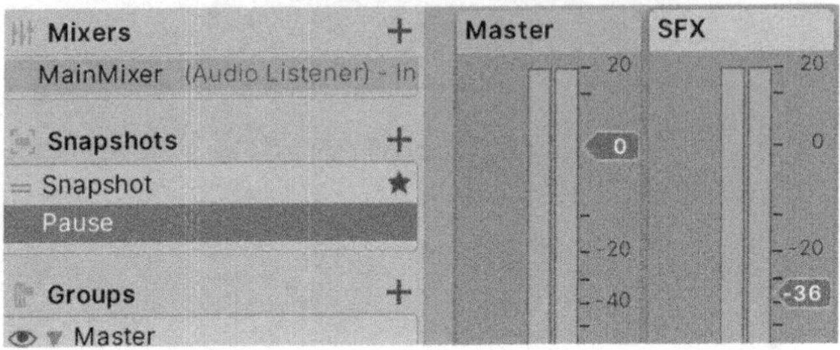

Figure 14.19: Lowering the volume of the Pause snapshot

3. Play the game and hear how the sound is still at its normal volume. That's because the original snapshot is the default one—you can see that by checking for the star to its right. You can right-click any snapshot and make it the default one using the **Set as Start Snapshot** option.
4. Click on **Edit in Playmode** to enable **Audio Mixer** modification during runtime.
5. Click on the **Pause** snapshot to enable it and hear how the **Shooting** and **Ambient** sound volumes have decreased.

As you can see, one of the main uses of the mixer is to control group volume, especially when you see that the intensity of a group's volume is going higher than the 0 mark, indicating that the group is too loud. Anyway, there are other uses for the mixer, such as applying effects. If you've played any war game, you will have noticed that whenever a bomb explodes nearby, you hear the sound differently for a moment, as if the sound were located in another room. That can be accomplished using an effect called **Low Pass**, which blocks high-frequency sounds, and that's exactly what happens with our ears in those scenarios: the stress of the high-volume sound generated by an explosion irritates our ears, making them less sensitive to high frequencies for a while.

We can add effects to any channel and configure them according to the current snapshot, just as we did for the volume, by doing the following:

1. Click on the **Add...** button at the bottom of the **Master** group and select **Lowpass Simple**:

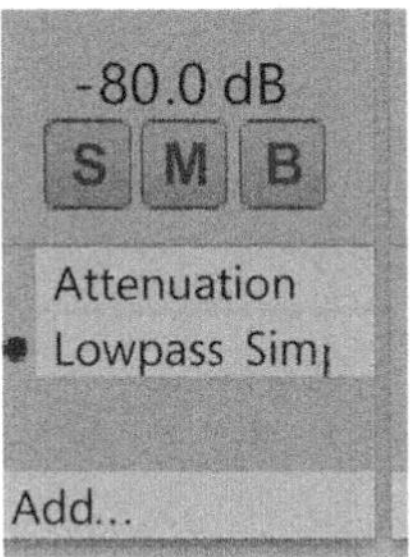

Figure 14.20: The effects list of a channel

2. Select the normal snapshot (the one called `Snapshot`) to modify it.
3. Select the **Master** group and look at the **Inspector** panel, where you will see settings for the group and its effects.
4. Set the **Cutoff freq** property of the **Lowpass Simple** settings to the highest value (`22000`), this will disable the effect.
5. Repeat *steps 3* and *4* for the **Pause** snapshot; we don't want this effect in that snapshot.
6. Create a new snapshot called **Bomb Stun** and select it to edit it.
7. Set **Cutoff freq** to `1000`:

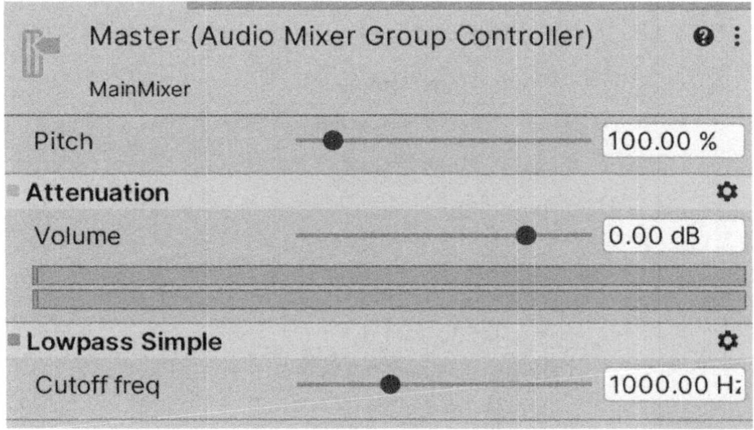

Figure 14.21: Setting the cutoff frequency of the Lowpass Simple effect

8. Play the game and change between snapshots to check the difference.

Aside from the Low Pass filter, you can apply several other filters, such as **Echo**, to create an almost dreamy effect, or a combination of **Send**, **Receive**, and **Duck** to make a group lower its volume based on the intensity of another group (for instance, you may want to lower SFX volume when dialog is happening). I invite you to try those and other effects and check the results to identify potential uses by reading the following documentation: `https://docs.unity3d.com/Manual/class-AudioEffectMixer.html`.

Now that we have integrated the audio, let's see how we can script our audio.

Scripting audio feedback

As with the VFX, audio also needs to react to what is happening to the game to give a better sense of immersion. Let's start adding sound to the explosion effect that enemies spawn when they die, which doesn't necessarily need scripting itself, but is a result of the script that spawned the explosion in the first place:

1. Download an explosion sound effect from the internet or the Asset Store.
2. Select the **Explosion** prefab we spawn when the enemies die and add **Audio Source** to it.
3. Set the downloaded explosion's audio clip as the **AudioClip** property of the audio source.
4. Make sure **Play On Awake** is checked and **Loop** is unchecked under **Audio Source**:

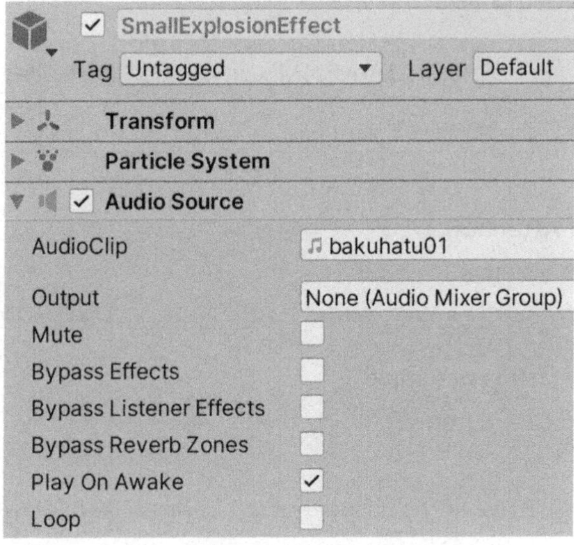

Figure 14.22: Adding sounds to our explosion effect

As you can see here, we didn't need to use any script. As the sound is added to the Prefab, it will be played automatically at the very moment the Prefab is instantiated. Now, let's integrate the shooting sound by doing the following:

1. Download a shooting sound and add it through an audio source to the player's weapon muzzle effect (not the weapon), this time unchecking the **Play On Awake** checkbox.
2. In the `PlayerShooting` script, create a field of the `AudioSource` type called `shootSound`.
3. Select the **Player** in the **Hierarchy** and drag the weapon muzzle effect GameObject to the **Shoot Sound** property in the **Inspector** to connect the script with the `AudioSource` variable in the weapon muzzle effect.
4. In the `if` statement that checks whether we can shoot, add the `shootSound.Play();` line to execute the sound when shooting:

```
public GameObject prefab;
public GameObject shootPoint;
public ParticleSystem muzzleEffect;
public AudioSource shootSound;

public void OnFire(InputValue value)
{
    if (value.isPressed)
    {
        GameObject clone = Instantiate(prefab);

        clone.transform.position = shootPoint.transform.position;
        clone.transform.rotation = shootPoint.transform.rotation;

        muzzleEffect.Play();
        shootSound.Play();
    }
}
```

Figure 14.23: Adding sound when shooting

The Visual Scripting additional nodes would look like this:

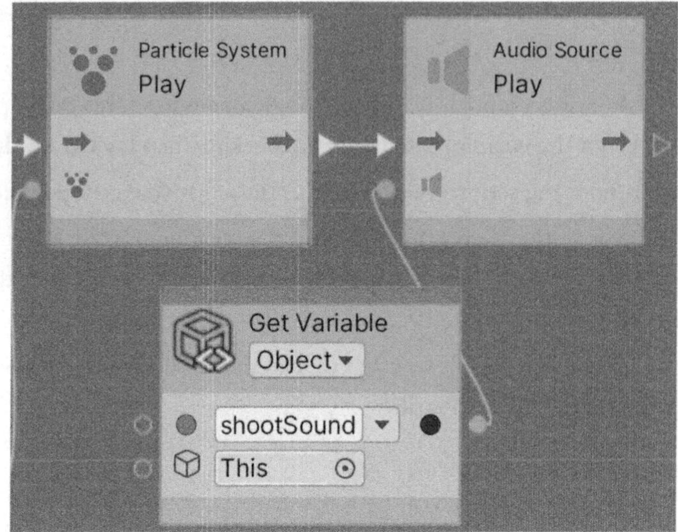

Figure 14.24: Adding sound when shooting in Visual Scripting

As we did with the muzzle effect, we added a GameObject variable called `shootSound` to reference the weapon GameObject that contains the `AudioSource`, and then we called the **Play** method of the `shootSound` variable.

I challenge you to try adding shooting sounds to the enemy AI in both C# and Visual Scripting versions of the scripts. Take as a guide what we did in *Chapter 11, Visual Effects with Particle Systems and Visual Effect Graph*, for the muzzle effect, and in any case, you can always check the Git repository of the book (link can be found in the *Preface*) for the solution.

Another approach to this would be the same as the one we did with the explosion; just add the shooting sound to the bullet, but if the bullet collides with a wall, soon enough the sound will be cut off. Or, if in the future we want an automatic weapon sound, it will need to be implemented as a single looping sound that starts when we press the relevant key and stops when we release it. This way, we prevent too many sound instances from overlapping when we shoot too many bullets. Take into account those kinds of scenarios when choosing the approach to script your feedback.

Summary

In this chapter, we discussed how to import and integrate sounds, considering their impact on memory usage, and we considered how to apply effects to generate different scenarios. Sound is a big part of achieving the desired game experience, so take the proper amount of time to get it right.

Now that we have covered almost all of the vital aesthetic aspects of our game, let's create another form of visual communication, the user interface or UI. We will create the necessary UI to display the player's current score, bullets, life, and lots more info in the next chapter.

15

User Interface Design

Everything that is shown on the screen and transmitted through the speakers of a computer is a form of communication. In previous chapters, we used 3D models to let the user know that they are in a base in the middle of the mountains, and we reinforced that idea with the appropriate sound and music. But for our game, we need to communicate other information, such as the amount of life the player has left and the current score, and sometimes, it is difficult to express these things using the in-game graphics (there are some successful cases that manage to do this, such as *Dead Space*, but let's keep things simple).

In order to transmit this information, we need to add another layer of graphics on top of our scene, which is usually called the **User Interface** (**UI**). This will contain different visual elements, such as text fields, bars, and buttons, to prepare the user to make an informed decision based on things such as fleeing to a safe place when their life is low.

In this chapter, we will visit the following topics:

- Understanding the Canvas and RectTransform
- Canvas object types
- Creating a responsive UI

By the end of this chapter, you will be able to use the Unity UI system to create interfaces capable of informing the user about the state of the game and allowing them to take action by pressing buttons. Let's start by discussing the basic concepts of the Unity UI system—the Canvas and RectTransform.

Understanding the Canvas and RectTransform

We are only going to focus on the in-game UI to communicate different information to the player using the Unity GUI system (or uGUI). At the time of writing this book, a new GUI system called UI Toolkit has been released, but uGUI will still be here for a while, given UI Toolkit will be used mostly in new projects, and is still perfectly capable of handling all types of UI. We will explore UI Toolkit in the next chapter.

If you are going to work with Unity UI, you first need to understand its two main concepts—the **Canvas** and **RectTransform**. The **Canvas** is the master object that will contain and render our UI, and **RectTransform** is the feature in charge of positioning and adapting each UI element on our screen.

In this section, we will be:

- Creating a UI with the Canvas
- Positioning elements with RectTransform

Let's start by using the Canvas component to create our UI.

Creating a UI with the Canvas

In Unity UI, each image, text, and element you see in the UI is a GameObject with a set of proper components, but in order for them to work, they must be a child of a master GameObject with the Canvas component. This component is responsible for triggering the UI generation and drawing iterations over each child object. We can configure this component to specify exactly how that process works and adapt it to different possible requirements.

To start, you can simply create a canvas with the **GameObject** | **UI** | **Canvas** option. After doing that, you will see a rectangle in the scene, which represents the user screen, so you can put elements inside it and preview where they will be located relative to the user's monitor.

You are probably wondering two things here. First, *"Why is the rectangle in the middle of the scene? I want it to always be on the screen!"* Don't worry because that will be exactly the case. When you edit the UI, you will see it as part of the level, as an object inside it, but when you play the game, it will be always projected over the screen, on top of every object. Also, you may be wondering why the rectangle is huge, and that's because one pixel of the screen map corresponds to one meter on the scene when using the default **Canvas Render Mode**, the one called **Screen Space - Overlay**. There are other modes, but discussing them is outside of the scope of this chapter.

Again, don't worry about that; you will see all your UI elements in their proper size and position on the user's screen when you see the game in the **Game** view. Consider setting the **Game** view size prior to editing it in the **Scene** view given that the **Scene** view will follow the **Game** view dimensions. You can do that by clicking the dropdown saying **Free Aspect** at the top part of the **Game** panel and selecting the desired resolution or aspect ratio, **16:9 Aspect** being the most used option:

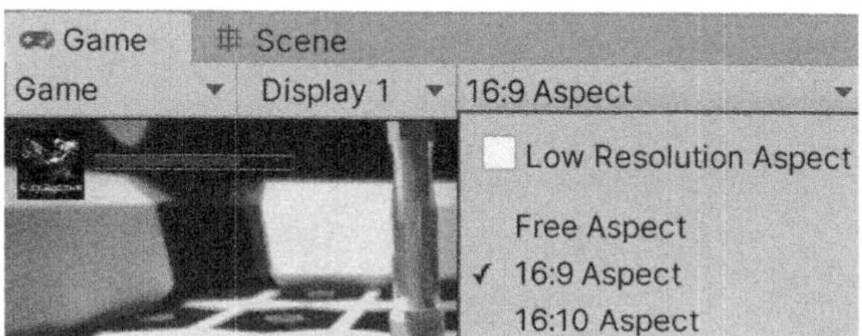

Figure 15.1: A default image UI element—a white box

Before adding elements to our UI, it's worth noting that when you created the UI, a second object was created alongside the Canvas, called **EventSystem**. This object is not necessary to render a UI but is necessary if you want the UI to be interactable, which means including actions such as clicking buttons, introducing text in fields, or navigating the UI with the joystick. The **EventSystem** component is responsible for sampling the user input, such as with a keyboard, mouse, or joystick, and sending that data to the UI to react accordingly. We can change the exact buttons to interact with the UI, but the defaults are OK for now, so just know that you need this object if you want to interact with the UI. If for some reason you delete the object, you can recreate it again in **GameObject | UI | Event System**.

Now that we have the base objects to create our UI, let's add elements to it.

Positioning elements with RectTransform

In Unity UI, each image, text, and element you see in the UI is a GameObject with a set of proper components according to its usage, but you will see that most of them have one component in common—**RectTransform**. Each piece of the UI is essentially a rectangle filled with text or images and has different behavior, so it is important to understand how the **RectTransform** component works and how to edit it.

In order to experiment with this component, let's create and edit the position of a simple white box element for the UI as follows:

1. Go to **GameObject | UI | Image**. After that, you will see that a new GameObject is created within the **Canvas** element. Unity will take care of setting any new UI element as a child of the Canvas; outside it, the element will not be visible:

Figure 15.2: A default image UI element—a white box

2. Click on the 2D button in the top bar of the **Scene** view. This will just change the perspective of the Scene view to one that is better suited to edit the UI (and also 2D games):

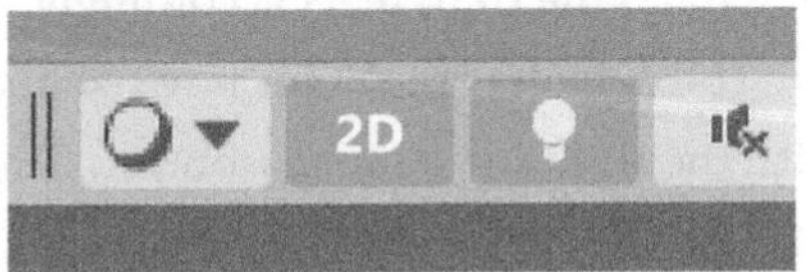

Figure 15.3: The 2D button location

3. Double-click on the Canvas in the **Hierarchy** window to make the UI fit entirely in the Scene view. This will allow us to edit the UI clearly. You can also navigate the UI using the mouse scroll wheel to zoom, and click and drag the scroll wheel to pan the camera.
4. Enable the **RectTransform** tool, which is the fifth button in the top-left part of the Unity Editor (or press the *T* key). This will enable the rectangle gizmo, which allows you to move, rotate, and scale 2D elements without the issues the regular 3D transform gizmos can cause:

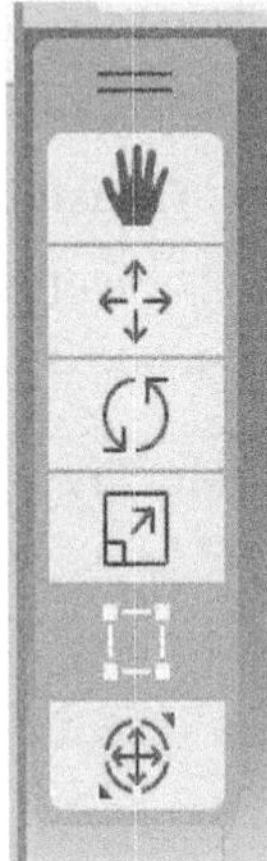

Figure 15.4: The rectangle gizmo button

5. Using the rectangle gizmo, drag the object to move it, use the blue dots to change its size, or locate the mouse in a position near the blue dots until the cursor becomes a curved arrow to rotate it. Consider that resizing the object using this gizmo is not the same as scaling the object, but more on that in a moment:

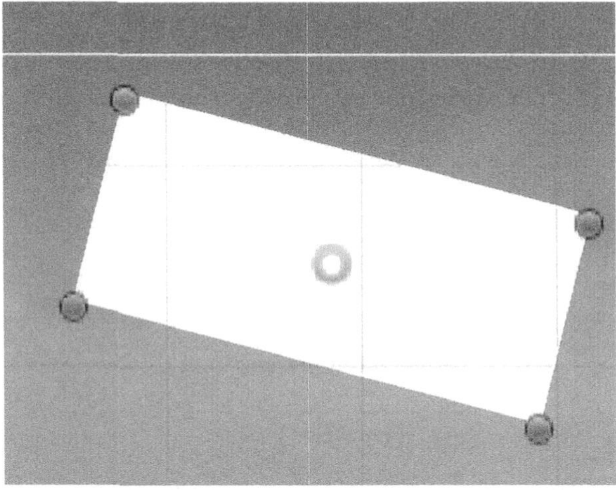

Figure 15.5: The rectangle gizmo for editing 2D elements

6. In the **Inspector** window, notice that after changing the size of the UI element, the **Rect Transform** setting's **Scale** property is still at 1, 1, 1, but you can see how the **Width** and **Height** properties changed. **RectTransform** is essentially a classic transform but with **Width** and **Height** added (among other properties to explore later). You can set the exact values you want here expressed in pixels:

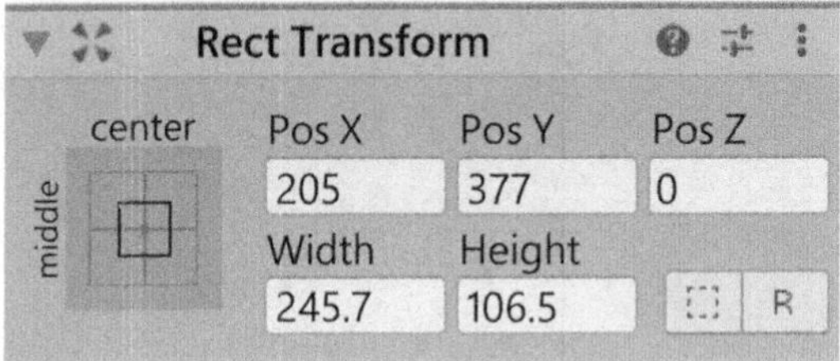

Figure 15.6: The Rect Transform properties

Now that we know the very basics of how to position any UI object, let's explore the different types of elements you can add to the Canvas.

Canvas object types

So far, we have used the simplest Canvas object type—a white box—but there are plenty of other object types we can use, such as images, buttons, and text. All of them use **RectTransform** to define their display area, but each one has its own concepts and configurations to understand.

In this section, we will explore the following Canvas object concepts:

- Integrating assets for the UI
- Creating UI controls

Let's first start exploring how we can integrate images and fonts to use in our Canvas so that we can integrate them in our UI using the **Images** and **Text** UI object types.

Integrating assets for the UI

Before making our UI use nice graphics assets, we need to integrate them properly into Unity. In the following screenshot, you will find the UI design we propose for our game:

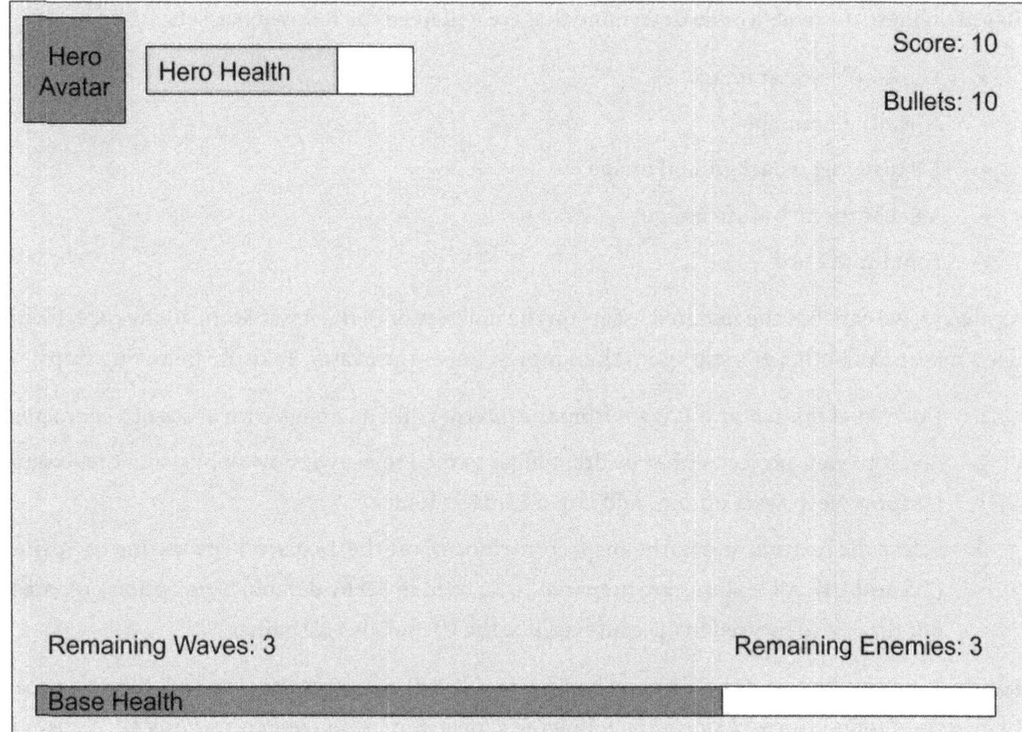

Figure 15.7: UI design

On top of that, we will add a **Pause** menu, which will be activated when the user presses *Esc*. It will look like the following screenshot:

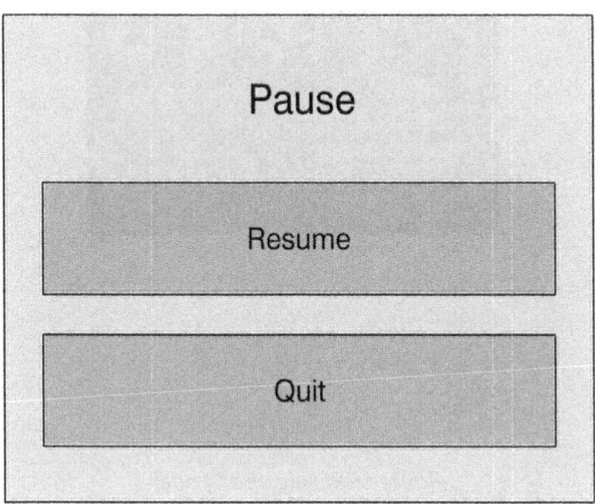

Figure 15.8: The Pause menu design

Based on these designs, we can determine that we will need the following assets:

- The hero's avatar image
- A health bar image
- A **Pause** menu background image
- A **Pause** menu button image
- Font for the text

As always, we can find the required assets on the internet or in the Asset Store. In my case, I will use a mixture of both. Let's start with the simplest one—the avatar. Take the following steps:

1. Download the avatar you want from the internet, like an image with a face of a character.
2. Add it to your project, either by dragging it to the Project window or by using the **Assets | Import New Asset** option. Add it to a `Sprites` folder.
3. Select the texture, and in the Inspector window, set the **Texture Type** setting to **Sprite (2D and UI)**. All textures are prepared to be used in 3D by default. This option prepares our texture to be used in 2D contexts, like the UI and also 2D games.

For the bars, buttons, and the window background, I will use Asset Store to look for a UI pack. In my case, I found the package in the following screenshot a good one to start my UI. As usual, remember that this exact package might not be available right now. In that case, remember to look for another similar package, or pick the sprites from the GitHub repo:

Figure 15.9: Selected UI pack

At first, the package contains lots of images configured the same way, as sprites, but we can further modify the import settings to achieve advanced behavior, which we will need for the buttons. The button asset comes with a fixed size, but what happens if you need a bigger button? One option is to use other button assets with different sizes, but this will lead to a lot of repetitions of the buttons and other assets, such as different-sized backgrounds for different windows, which will unnecessarily consume RAM.

Another option is to use the **9-slices** method, which consists of splitting an image so that the corners are separated from the other parts. This allows Unity to stretch the middle parts of the image to fit different sizes, keeping the corners at their original size, which, when combined with an image prepared for the 9-slices technique, can be used to create almost any size you need.

In *Figure 15.10*, you can see a shape with nine slices in the bottom-left corner, and at the bottom-right corner of the same diagram, you can see the shape is stretched but keeps its corners at their original size. The top-right corner shows the shape stretched without slices. You can see how the non-sliced version is distorted:

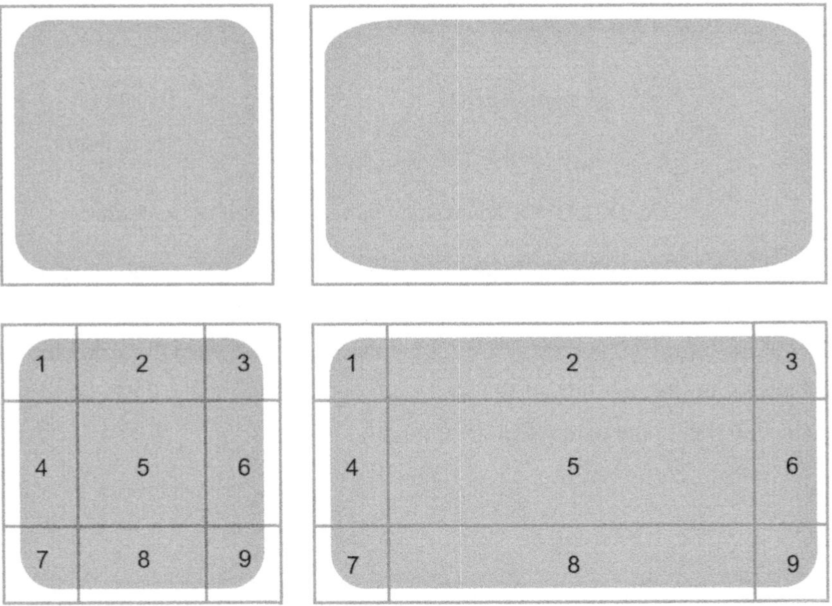

Figure 15.10: Sliced versus non-sliced image stretching

In this case, we can apply the nine slices to the button and the panel background images to use them in different parts of our game. In order to do this, do the following:

1. Open **Package Manager** using the **Window | Package Manager** option.
2. Verify that **Package Manager** is showing all the packages by setting the dropdown to the right of the + button in the top-left part of the window to **Unity Registry** as usual.
3. Install the **2D Sprite** package to enable the sprite editing tools (if it is not already installed).
4. Select the button sprite in the **Project** window and click on the **Sprite Editor** button in the **Inspector** window:

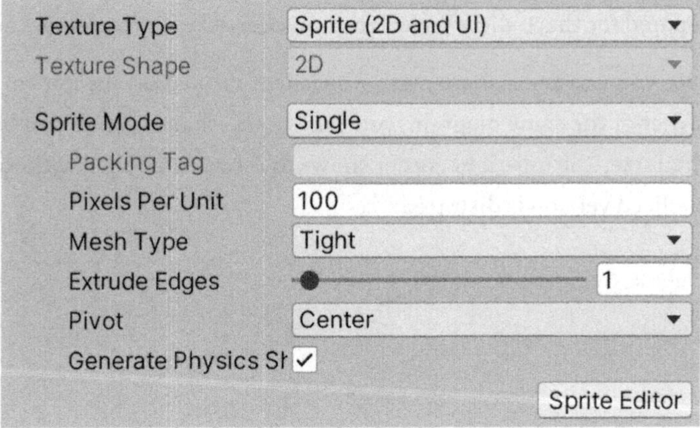

Figure 15.11: The Sprite Editor button in the Inspector window

5. In the **Sprite Editor** window, locate and drag the green dots at the edges of the image to move the slice rulers. Try to ensure that the slices are not located in the middle of the edges of the button. One thing to notice is that in our case, we will work with three slices instead of nine because our button won't be stretched vertically. If you don't see the dots, try clicking the image to make them appear.

6. Notice that after dragging the green dots, the **Border** properties (**L**, **T**, **R**, and **B**, which are left, top, right, and bottom, respectively) in the bottom-right corner changed. Those are the exact values you set by moving the green dots. Feel free to change them to more round numbers to allow the 9 slices to work evenly. In our case, Left and Right became a round 60, and top and bottom 50.
7. Click on the **Apply** button in the top-right corner of the window and close it:

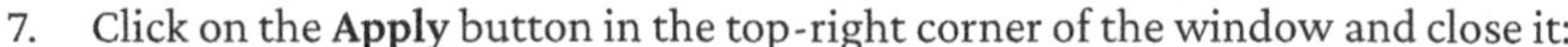

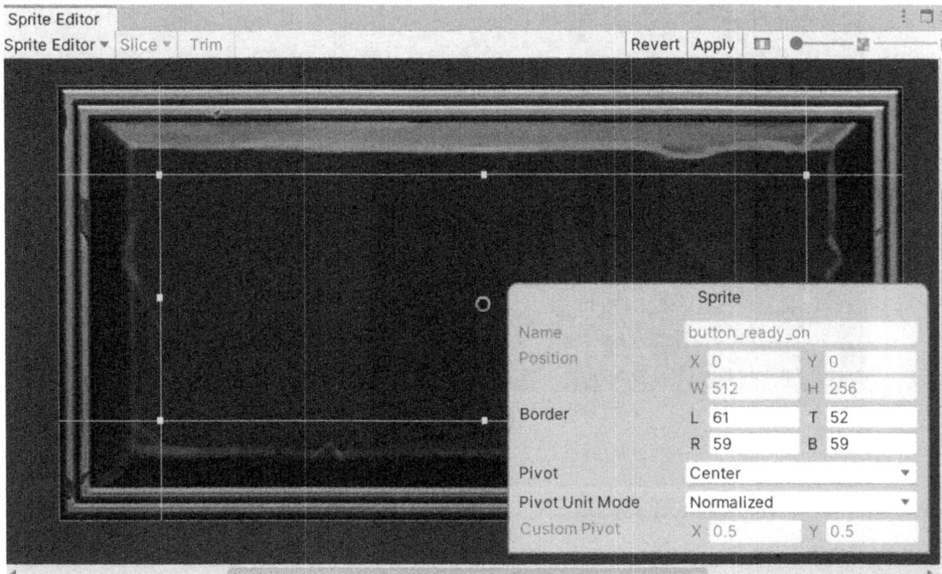

Figure 15.12: Nine slices in the Sprite Editor window

8. Repeat *steps 4* to *6* for the **Background** panel image. In my case, you can see in *Figure 15.13* that this background is not completely prepared with nine slices in mind because all the middle areas of the image can be made smaller to save memory.

When displaying this image with a smaller width, the 9-slicing method will stretch the middle part and will look the same, so essentially is wasted memory:

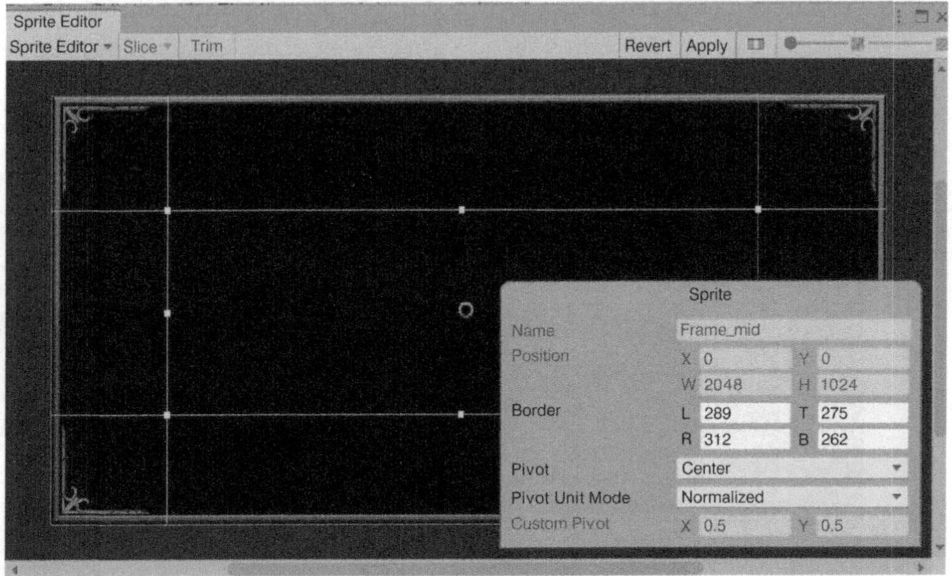

Figure 15.13: Nine slices in the Sprite Editor window

Now that we have prepared our sprites, we can find a font to customize the text of our UI. Before discussing how to import fonts, it is worth mentioning that we will be using **TextMesh Pro**, a Unity package (already included in the project) that provides a text rendering solution much better than the old text component. If you never used that component before, you shouldn't worry about this detail.

You must get fonts in the `.ttf` or `.otf` formats and import them to Unity. You can find lots of good, free font websites on the internet. I am used to working with the classic `DaFont.com` site, but there are plenty of other sites that you can use. In my case, I will work with the `Militech` font:

Figure 15.14: My chosen font from DaFont.com to use in the project

If the font download comes with more than one file, you can just drag them all into Unity and then use the one that you like the most. Also, as usual, try to put the font inside a folder called `Fonts`. Now, these files' format is not compatible with TextMesh Pro, our text rendering solution, so we must convert it using the **Font Asset Creator** window, as depicted in the following steps:

1. Go to **Window | Text Mesh Pro | Font Asset Creator**.
2. If this is the first time you have used Text Mesh Pro in your project, a window will appear. You must click the option **Import TMP Essentials** and wait for the import process to finish:

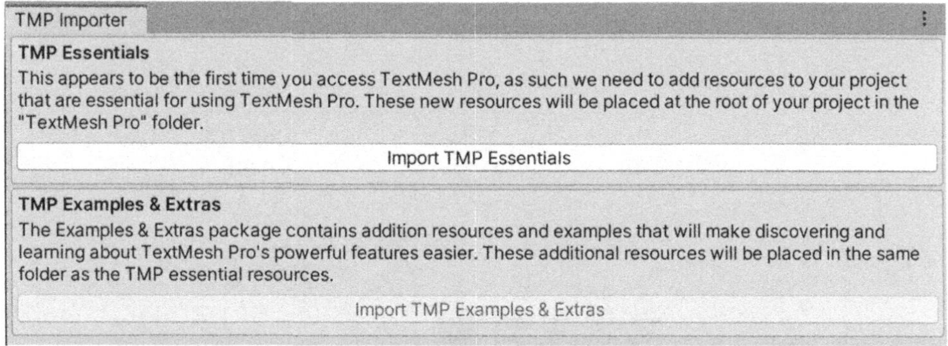

Figure 15.15: TextMesh Pro first run initialization

3. Close the **TMP Importer** window.
4. In **Font Asset Creator**, drag your font from the **Project** view to the **Source Font File**, or select it by clicking the **Target** button at the right (the circle with the point at the center).

5. Click the **Generate Font Atlas** button and wait a moment:

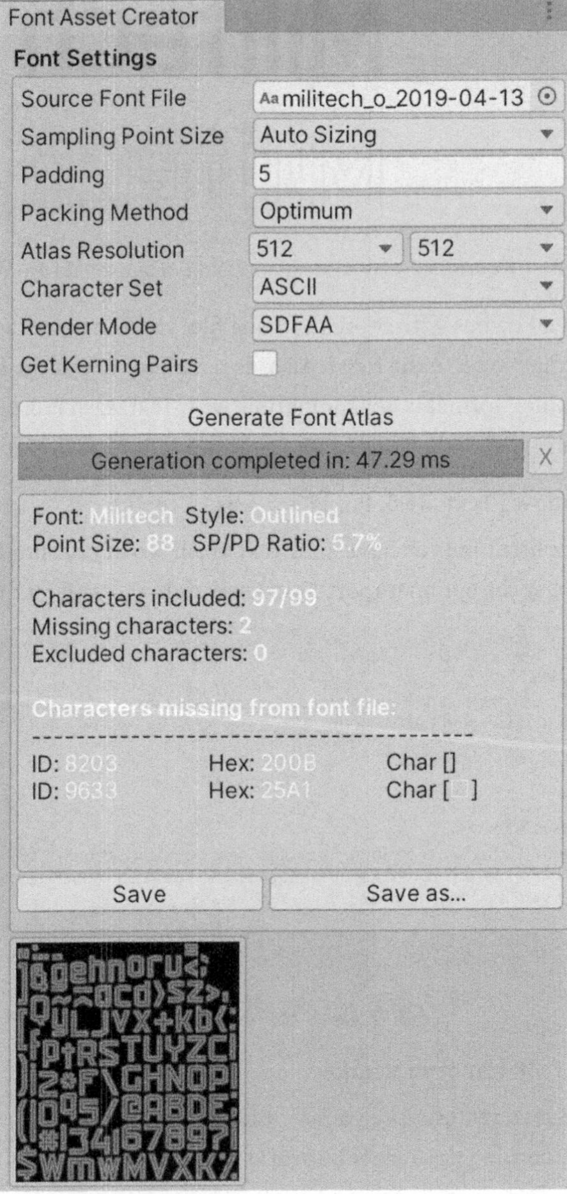

Figure 15.16: Converting font assets to TextMesh Pro

6. Click the **Save** button and save the converted font in the **TextMesh Pro | Resources | Fonts & Materials** folder. Saving here is important so don't forget to pick the proper folder:

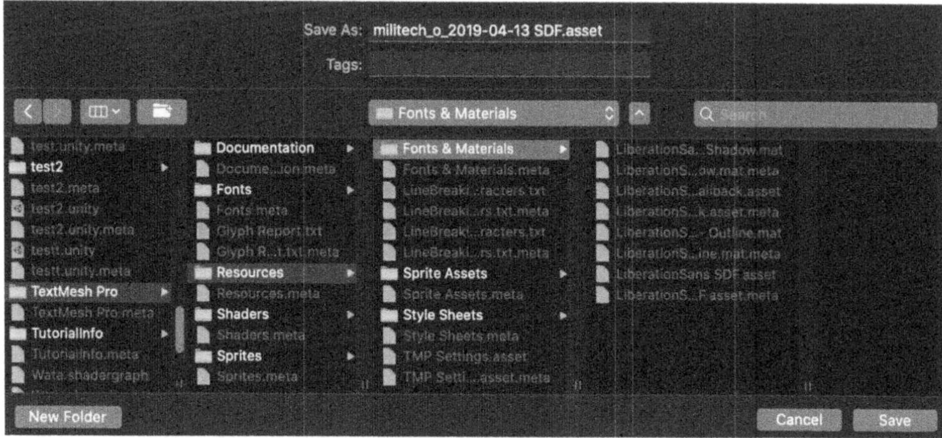

Figure 15.17: Saving the converted font in the proper folder (Mac)

Now that we have all the required assets to create our UI, let's explore the different types of components to create all the required UI elements.

Creating UI controls

Almost every single part of the UI will be a combination of images and texts configured cleverly. In this section, we will explore how to create images, text, and buttons, starting with images. We have already an image in our UI—the white rectangle we created previously. If you select it and look at the **Inspector** window, you will notice that it has an **Image** component, like the one in the following screenshot:

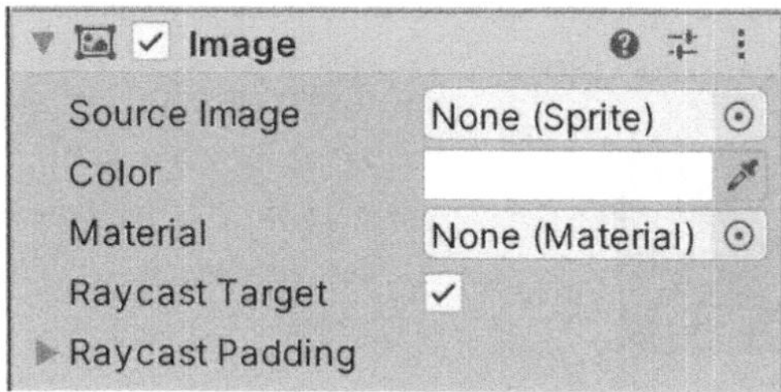

Figure 15.18: The Image component's Inspector window

Let's start exploring the settings of this component, starting with our hero's avatar:

1. Using the rectangle gizmo, move the white rectangle to the top-left part of the UI:

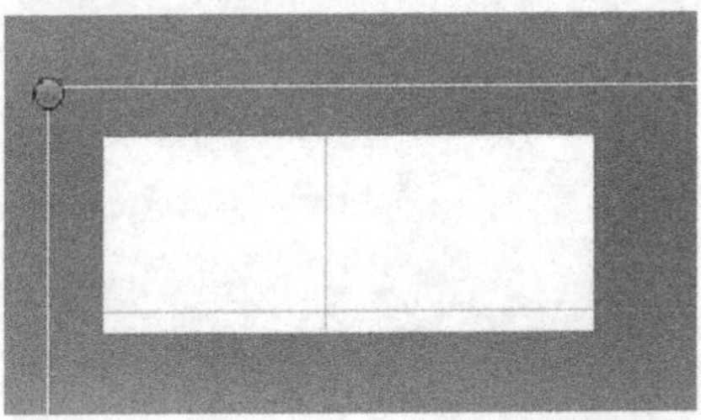

Figure 15.19: The white rectangle located at the top-left part of the UI

2. In the **Inspector** window, click on the circle to the right of the **Source Image** property and pick the downloaded hero avatar sprite:

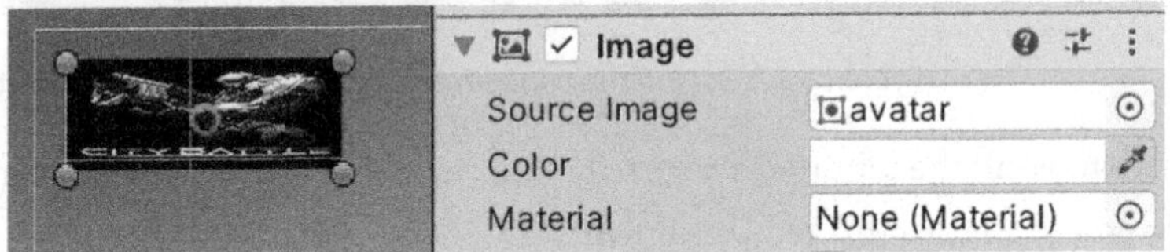

Figure 15.20: Setting the sprite of our Image component

3. We need to correct the aspect ratio of the image to prevent distortion. One way to do this is to click the **Set Native Size** button at the bottom of the **Image** component to make the image use the same size as the original sprite. However, by doing this, the image can become too big, so you can reduce the image size by pressing *Shift* to modify both the **Width** and **Height** values. Another option is to check the **Preserve Aspect** checkbox to make sure the image fits the rectangle without stretching. In my case, I will use both:

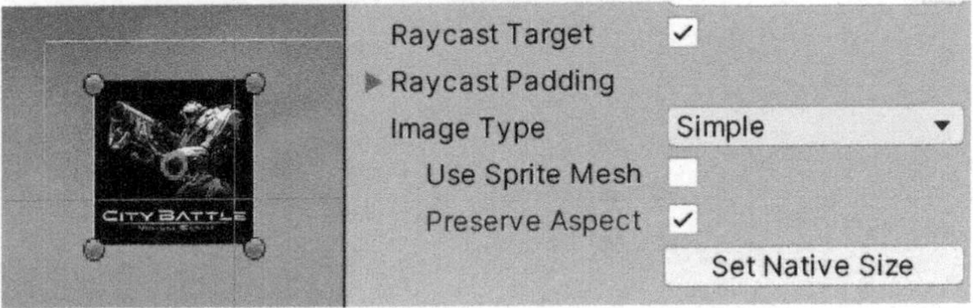

Figure 15.21: The Preserve Aspect and Set Native Size image options

Now, let's create the life bars by doing the following:

1. Create another **Image** component using the **GameObject | UI | Image** option.
2. Set the **Source Image** property to the life bar image you downloaded:

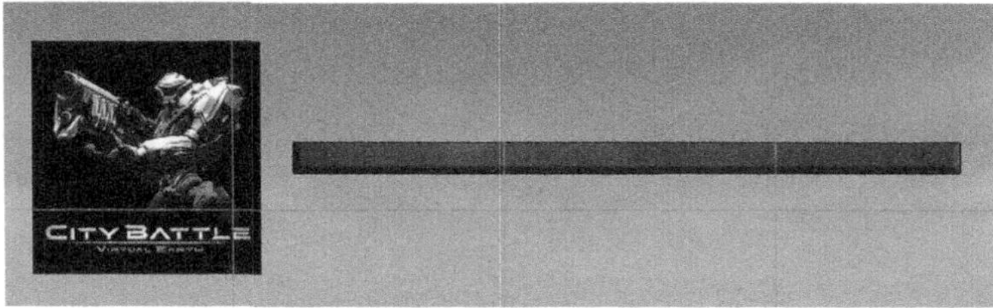

Figure 15.22: The avatar and life bar

3. Set the **Image Type** property to **Filled.**
4. Set the **Fill Method** property to **Horizontal.**
5. Drag the **Fill Amount** slider to see how the bar is cut according to the value of the slider. We will change that value via scripting later in *Chapter 18, Optimization with Profiler, Frame Debugger, and Memory Profiler*:

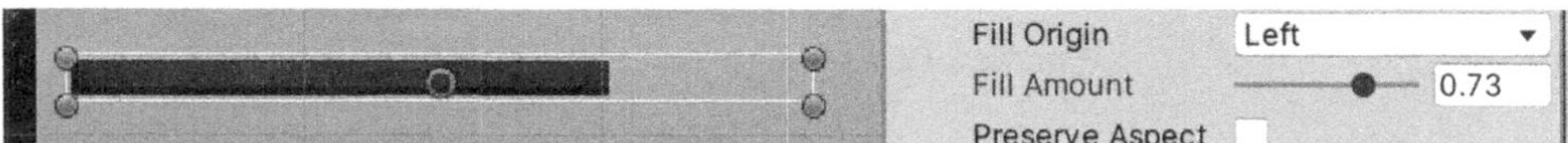

Figure 15.23: The Fill Amount slider, cutting the image width by 73% of its size

6. In my case, the bar image also comes with a bar frame, creating another image, setting the sprite, and positioning it on top of the life bar to frame it. Bear in mind that the order the objects appear in the **Hierarchy** window determines the order in which they will be drawn. So, in my case, I need to be sure the frame GameObject is below the health bar image. Also, consider the bar frame image is not sliced, so there's no need to use the **Sliced Image Type** in this case. Feel free to try slicing it and see the results:

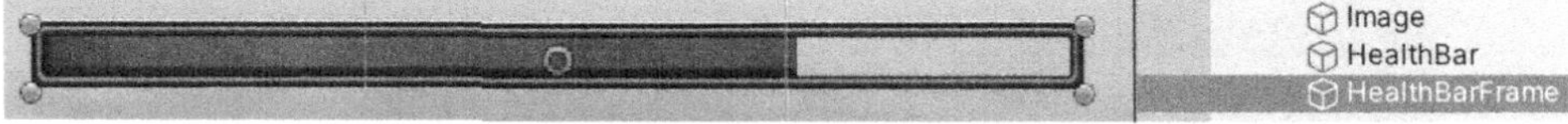

Figure 15.24: Putting one image on top of the other to create a frame effect

7. Repeat *steps 1* to *6* to create the base bar at the bottom, or just copy and paste the bar and the frame and locate it at the bottom of the screen:

Figure 15.25: The Player's and Player's Base health bars

8. Click on the + button in the **Project** window and select the **Sprites** | **Square** option. This will create a simple squared sprite with a 4x4 resolution.
9. Set the sprite as the base bar of the Player's Base health bar instead of the downloaded bar sprite. This time, we will be using a plain-white image for the bar because in my case, the original one is red, and tinting the color of a red image to green is not possible. However, a white image can be easily tinted. Take into account the detail of the original bar—for example, the little shadow in my original bar won't be present here.
10. Select the base health bar and set the **Color** property to green:

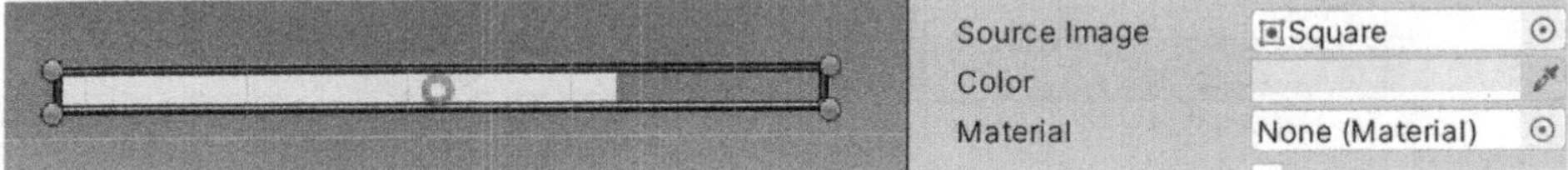

Figure 15.26: A bar with a squared sprite and green tint

11. One optional step would be to convert the bar frame image into a nine-slices image to allow us to change the original width to fit the screen.

Now, let's add the text fields for the **Score**, **Bullets**, **Remaining Waves**, and **Remaining Enemies** labels by doing the following:

1. Create a text label using the **GameObject | UI | Text - Text Mesh Pro** option (avoid the one that only says **Text**). This will be the **Score** label.
2. Position the label at the top-right part of the screen.
3. In the **Inspector** window, set the **Text Input** property to `Score: 0`.
4. Set the **Font Size** property to `20`.
5. Apply the converted font by clicking on the circle to the right of the **Font Asset** property and selecting the desired font.
6. In the **Alignment** property, select the **Horizontal Right Align** icon (third button from the first row) and the **Vertical Center Align** icon (second button from the second row):

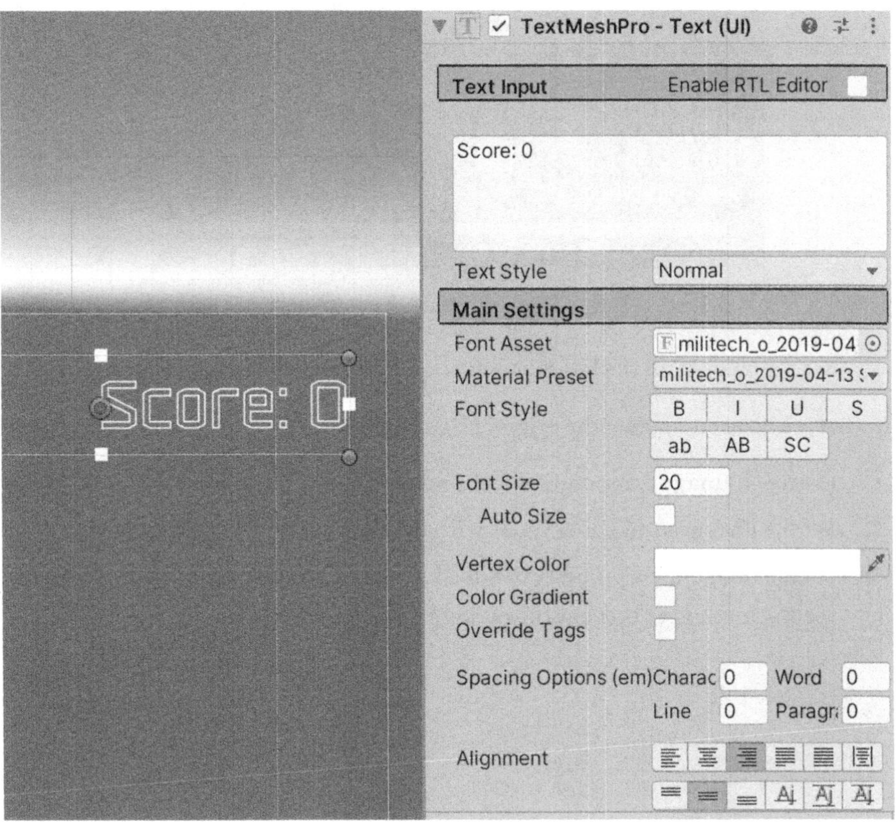

Figure 15.27: The settings for a text label

7. Repeat *steps 1* to *6* to create the other three labels (or just copy and paste the score three times). For the **Remaining Waves** label, you can use the left alignment option to better match the original design:

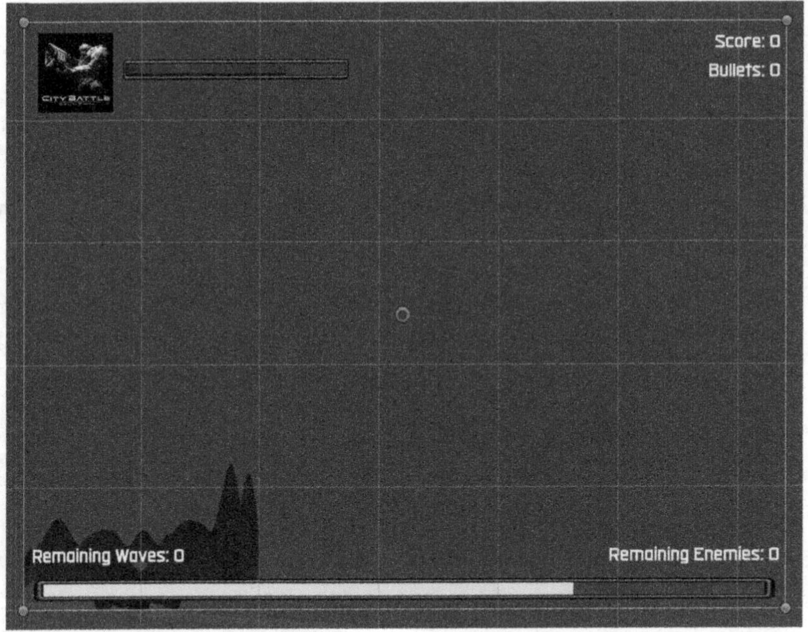

Figure 15.28: All the labels for our UI

8. Set the color of all the labels to white as our scene will be mainly dark.

Now that we have completed the original UI design, we can create the **Pause** menu:

1. Create an **Image** component for the menu's background (**GameObject** | **UI** | **Image**).
2. Set the **Background** panel sprite with the nine slices we made earlier.
3. Set the **Image Type** property to **Sliced** if it is not already. This mode will apply the 9-slice scaling method to prevent the corners from stretching.

4. There's a chance that the image will stretch the corners anyway, which happens because sometimes the corners are quite big compared to the **RectTransform** setting's **Size** property that you are using, so Unity has no option other than to do that. In this scenario, the correct solution is to have an artist that creates assets tailored to your game, but sometimes we don't have that option. This time, we can just increase the **Pixels Per Unit** value of the sprite file, which will reduce the scale of the original image while preserving its resolution. In the following two screenshots, you can see the background image with a **Pixels Per Unit** value of `100` and again with `700`. Remember to only do this for the nine-slices or tiled-image types, or if you don't have an artist to adjust it for you:

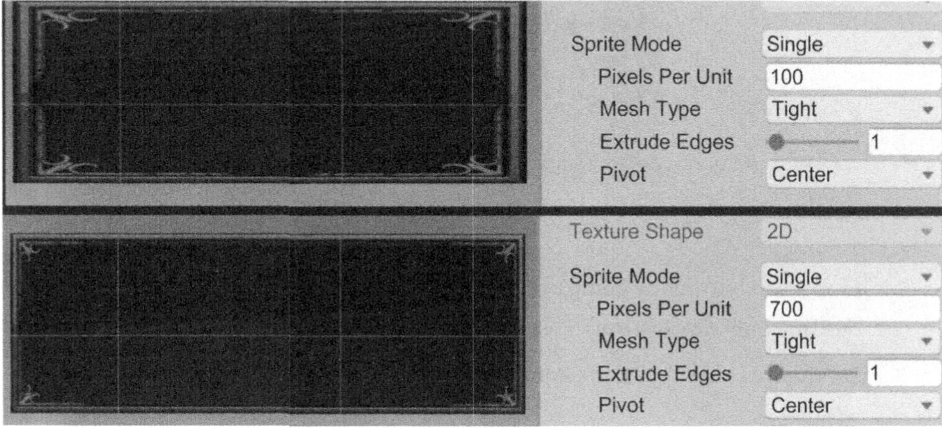

Figure 15.29: On top, a large nine-slices image in a small RectTransform component, small enough to shrink the corners, and on the bottom, the same image with Pixels Per Unit set to 700

5. Create a **TextMesh Pro** text field, position it where you want the **Pause** label to be in your diagram, set it to display the **Pause** text, and set the font. Remember that you can change the text color with the **Color** property.

6. Drag the text field onto the background image. The parenting system in **Canvas** works the same—if you move the parent, the children will move with it. The idea is that if we disable the panel, it will also disable the buttons and all its content:

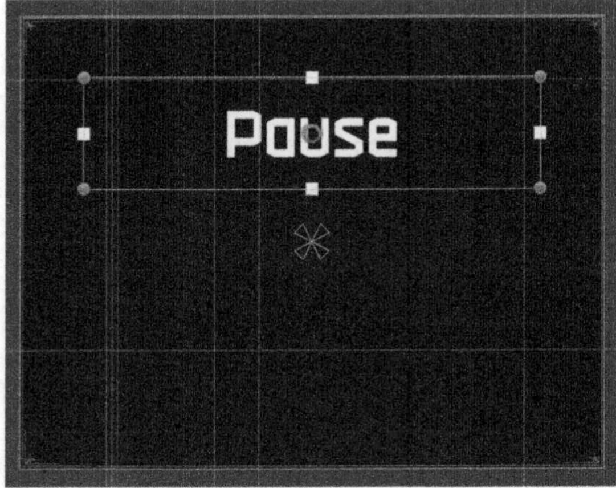

Figure 15.30: The Pause label

7. Create two buttons by going to **GameObject | UI | Button - Text Mesh Pro** (avoid using the one that only says **Button**). Position them where you want them on the background image.
8. Set them as children of the **Pause** background image by dragging them in the **Hierarchy** window.
9. Select the buttons and set the **Source Image** property of their **Image** components to use the button sprite that we downloaded earlier. Remember our **Pixels Per Unit** fix from *step 4* in this list if you have the same problem as before.
10. You will notice that the button is essentially an image with a child **TextMesh Pro** text object. Change the font of each button and the text in each button to `Resume` and `Quit`:

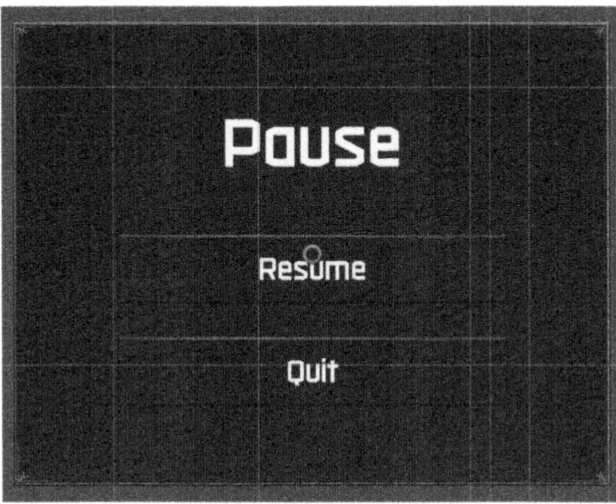

Figure 15.31: The Pause menu implementation

11. Remember that you can hide the panel by unchecking the checkbox to the right of the name of the object in the top part of the **Inspector** window:

Figure 15.32: Disabling a GameObject

In this section, we discussed how to import images and fonts to be integrated through the **Image**, **Text**, and **Button** components to create a rich and informative UI. Having done that, let's discuss how to make them adapt to different devices.

Creating a responsive UI

Nowadays, it is almost impossible to design a UI in a single resolution, and our target audience display devices can vary a lot. A PC has a variety of different kinds of monitors with different resolutions (such as 1080p and 4k) and aspect ratios (such as 16:9, 16:10, and ultra-wide), and the same goes for mobile devices. We need to prepare our UI to adapt to the most common displays, and Unity UI has the tools needed to do so.

In this section, we will explore the following UI responsiveness concepts:

- Adapting object positions
- Adapting object sizes

We are going to explore how the UI elements can adapt their position and size to different screen sizes using advanced features of the **Canvas** and **RectTransform** components, such as **Anchors** and **Scalers**.

Adapting object positions

Right now, if we play our game, we will see how the UI fits nicely onto our screen. But if for some reason we change the **Game** view size, we will see how objects start to disappear from the screen. In the following screenshots, you can see different-sized game windows and how the UI looks nice in one but bad in the others:

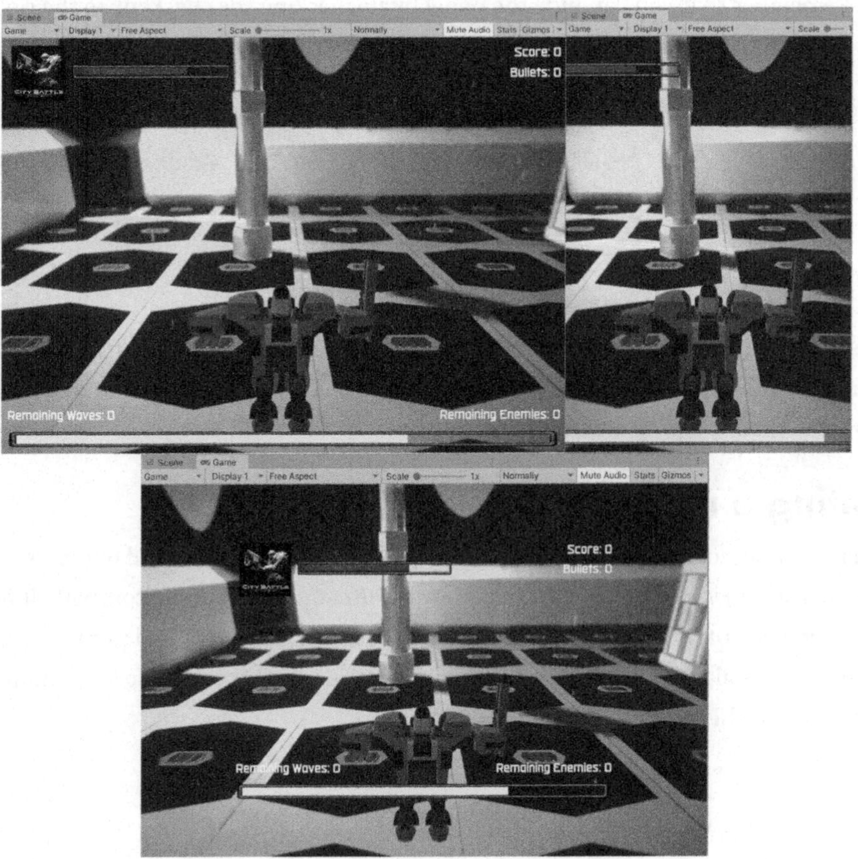

Figure 15.33: The same UI but on different screen sizes

The problem is that we created the UI using whatever resolution we had in the editor, but as soon as we change it slightly, the UI keeps its design for the previous resolution. Also, if you look closely, you will notice that the UI is always centered, such as in the second image, where the UI is cropped at its sides, or in the third image, where extra space is visible along the borders of the screen. This happens because every single element in the UI has its own **Anchor**, a little cross you can see when you select an object, such as the one in the following screenshot:

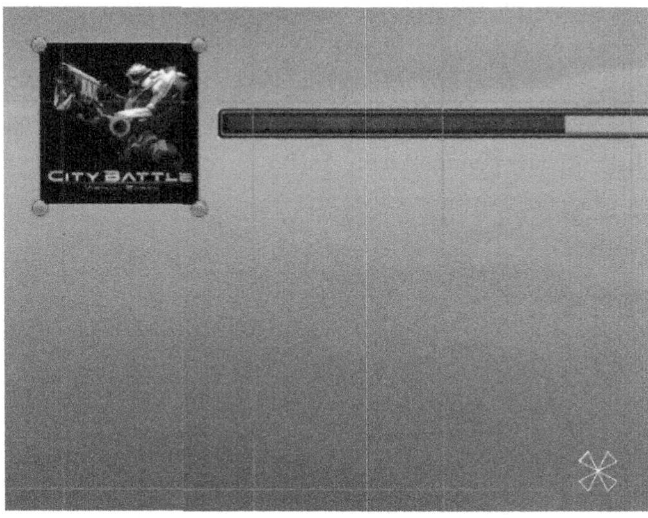

Figure 15.34: An Anchor cross in the bottom-right part of the screen belonging to the hero avatar in the top-left part of the screen

The *x* and *y* position of the object is measured as a distance to that Anchor, and the Anchor has a position relative to the screen, with its default position being at the center of the screen. This means that on an *800 x 600* screen, the Anchor will be placed at the *400 x 300* position, and on a *1920 x 1080* screen, the Anchor will be located at the *960 x 540* position. If the *x* and *y* position of the element (the one in **RectTransform**) is **0**, the object will always be at a distance of 0 from the center. In the middle screenshot of the previous three examples, the hero avatar falls outside of the screen because its distance from the center is greater than half the screen, and the current distance was calculated based on the previous bigger screen size. So, what we can do about that? Move the Anchor!

By setting a relative position, we can position the Anchor at different parts of our screen and make that part of the screen our reference position. In the case of our hero avatar, we can place the Anchor in the top-left corner of the screen to guarantee that our avatar will be at a fixed distance from that corner.

We can do that by following these steps:

1. Select your player avatar.
2. Expand the **RectTranform** component in the **Inspector**, if not expanded yet, in a way that you can see its properties. This will reveal the **Anchors** in the **Scene** view.
3. Drag the Anchor cross with your mouse to the top-left part of the screen. If for some reason the Anchor breaks into pieces when you drag it, undo the change (press *Ctrl* + *Z*, or *Command* + *Z* on Mac) and try to drag it by clicking in the center. We will break the Anchor later. Check the avatar image **RectTransform** component to verify that the **Anchors** property **Min** and **Max** sub-properties have the same values as in *Figure 15.35*, meaning the object has correctly configured the Anchors to be in the top-left part of the screen:

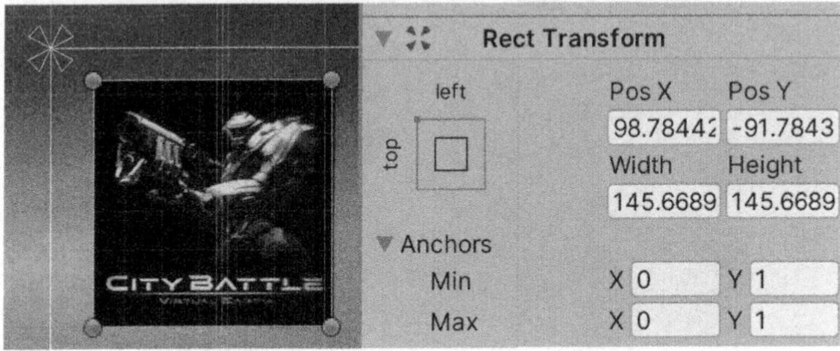

Figure 15.35: An image with an Anchor in the top-left part of the screen

4. Put the Anchor of the **Health Bar** object and its frame in the same position. We want the bar to always be at the same distance from that corner so that it will move alongside the hero avatar if the screen size changes.
5. Place the Anchor in the bottom-center part of the screen for the **Boss Bar** object so that it will always be centered. Later, we will deal with adjusting its size.
6. Put the **Remaining Waves** label in the bottom-left corner, and **Remaining Enemies** in the bottom-right corner:

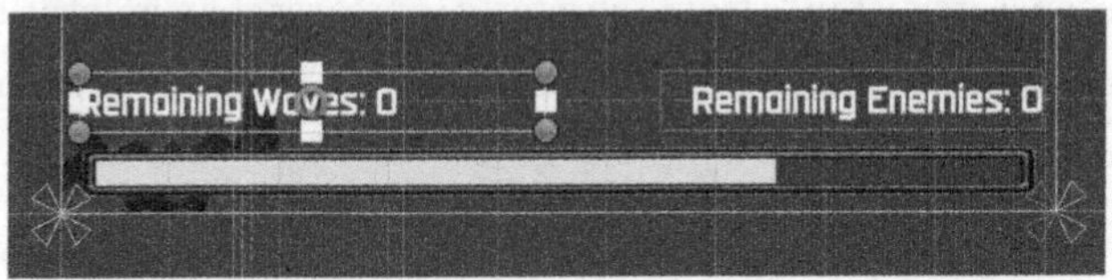

Figure 15.36: The Anchors for the life bar and the labels

7. Put the **Score** and **Bullets** Anchors in the top-right corner:

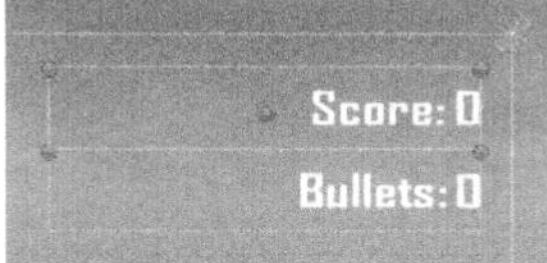

Figure 15.37: The Anchors for the Score and Bullets labels

8. Select any element and drag the sides of the Canvas rectangle with your mouse to preview how the elements will adapt to their positions. Take into account that you must select any object that is a direct child of the Canvas; the text within the buttons won't have that option:

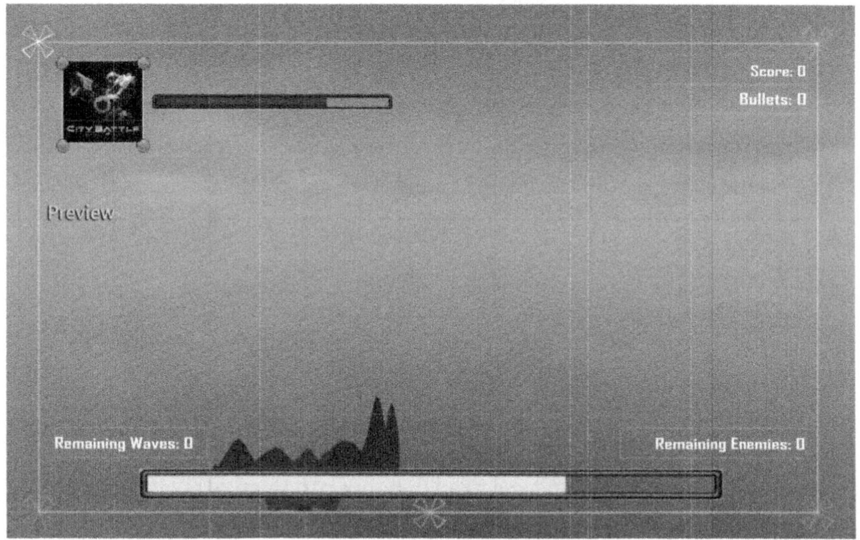

Figure 15.38: Previewing the Canvas resizing

Now that our UI elements have adapted to their positions, let's consider scenarios where the object size must adapt as well.

Adapting object sizes

The first thing to consider when dealing with different aspect ratios is that our screen elements may not only move from their original design position (which we fixed in the previous section) but also, they may not fit into the original design. In our UI, we have the case of the health bar, where the bar clearly doesn't adapt to the screen width when we previewed it on a wider screen. We can fix this by breaking our Anchors.

When we break our Anchors, the position and size of our object are calculated as a distance relative to the different Anchor parts. If we split the Anchor horizontally, instead of having an **X** and **Width** property, we will have a **Left** and **Right** property, representing the distance to the left and right Anchor. We can use this in the following way:

1. Select the health bar and drag the left part of the Anchor all the way to the left part of the screen, and the right part to the right part of the screen.
2. Do the same for the health bar frame:

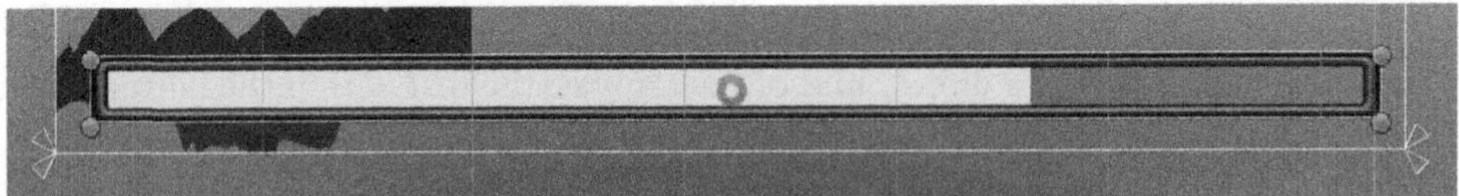

Figure 15.39: The splitter Anchor in the health bar

3. Check the **Rect Transform** setting's **Left** and **Right** properties in the **Inspector** window, which represent the current distance to their respective Anchors. If you want, you can add a specific value, especially if your health bars are displaying outside the screen:

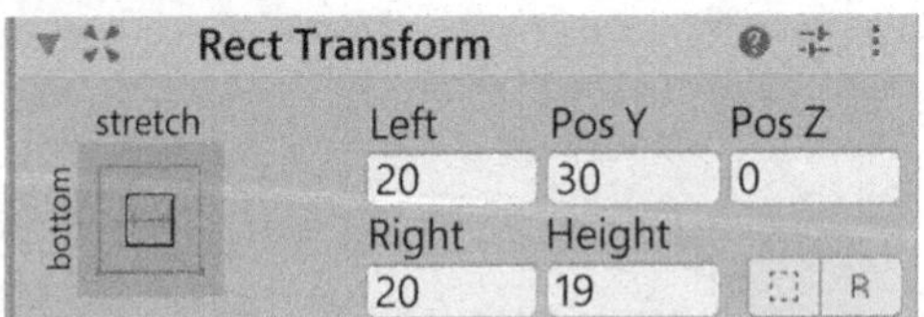

Figure 15.40: The Left and Right properties of a split anchor

This way, the object will always be at a fixed distance of a relative position to the screen—in this case, the sides of the screen. If you are working with a child object, as is the case with the **Text** and **Image** components of the buttons, the Anchors are relative to the parent. If you pay attention to the Anchors of the text, they are not only split horizontally but also vertically. This allows the text to adapt its position to the size of the button, so you won't have to change it manually:

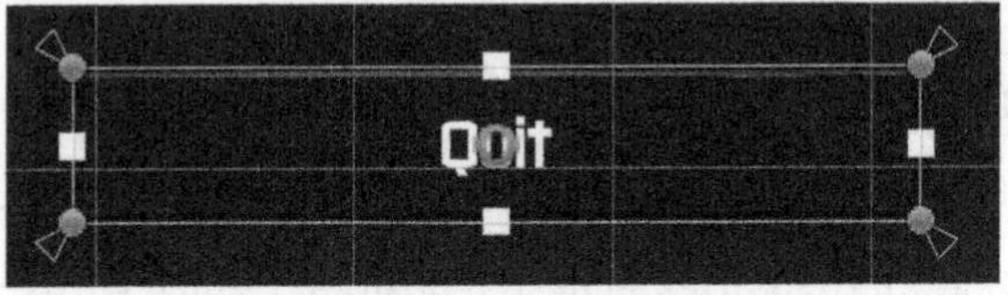

Figure 15.41: The split Anchors of the text of the button

Now, this solution is not suitable for all scenarios. Let's consider a case where the hero avatar is displayed in higher resolution than what it was designed for. Even if the avatar is correctly placed, it will be displayed smaller because the screen has more pixels per inch than screens with lower resolutions and the same physical size. You consider using split Anchors, but the width and height Anchors could be scaled differently in different aspect ratio screens, so the original image becomes distorted. Instead, we can use the **Canvas Scaler** component.

The **Canvas Scaler** component defines what one pixel means in our scenario. If our UI design resolution is 1080p, but we see it in a 4k display (which is twice the resolution of 1080p), we can scale the UI so that a pixel becomes 2, adapting its size to keep the same proportional size as the original design. Basically, the idea is that if the screen is bigger, our elements should also be bigger.

We can use this component by doing the following:

1. Select the **Canvas** object and locate the **Canvas Scaler** component in the **Inspector** window.
2. Set the **UI Scale Mode** property to **Scale with Screen Size**.
3. If working with an artist, set the reference resolution to the resolution in which the artist created the UI, keeping in mind that it must be the highest target device resolution (this isn't the case for us). In our case, we are not sure which resolution the artist of the downloaded assets had in mind, so we can put *1920 x 1080*, which is the full HD resolution size and is very common nowadays.
4. Set the **Match** property to **Height**. The idea of this property is that it sets which side of the resolution will be considered when carrying out the scaling calculation. In our case, if we are playing the game in 1080p resolution, 1 UI pixel equals 1 real screen pixel. However, if we are playing in 720p resolution, 1 UI pixel will be 0.6 real pixels, so the elements will be smaller on smaller resolution screens, keeping the correct size. We didn't choose a **Width** value in this case because we can have extreme widths in screens, such as ultra-wide, and if we picked that option, those screens would scale the UI unnecessarily. Another option is to set this value to `0.5` to consider the two values, but on a PC, this doesn't make too much sense. On a mobile device, you should choose this based on the orientation of the game, setting the height for landscape mode and the width for portrait mode.

5. Try previewing a wider and higher screen and see how this setting works:

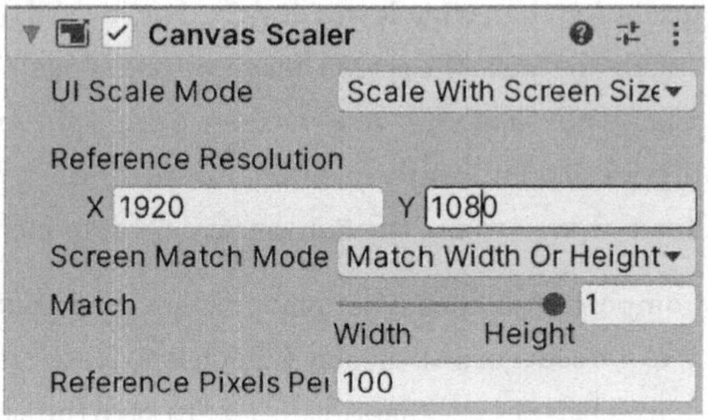

Figure 15.42: Canvas Scaler with the correct settings for standard PC games

You will find that your UI will be smaller than your original design, which is because we should have set these properties before. Right now, the only fix is to resize everything again. Take this into account the next time you try this exercise; we only followed this order for learning purposes.

With this knowledge, you are now ready to start scripting the UI to reflect what's happening in the game.

Scripting the UI

We previously created a UI layout with elements such as bars, text, and buttons, but so far, they are static. We need to make them adapt to the game's actual state. In this section, we are going to discuss the following UI scripting concepts:

- Showing information in the UI
- Programming the Pause menu

We will start by seeing how to display information on our UI using scripts that modify the text and images that are displayed with Canvas elements. After that, we will create the **Pause** functionality, which will be used throughout the UI.

Showing information in the UI

As discussed earlier, we will use the UI to display information to the user to allow them to make informed decisions, so let's start by seeing how we can make the player's health bar react to the amount of life they have left in the `Life` script we created earlier:

1. Add a new script called **Life Bar** to the **HealthBar** Canvas child object, which is the `UI Image` component we created earlier to represent the life bar:

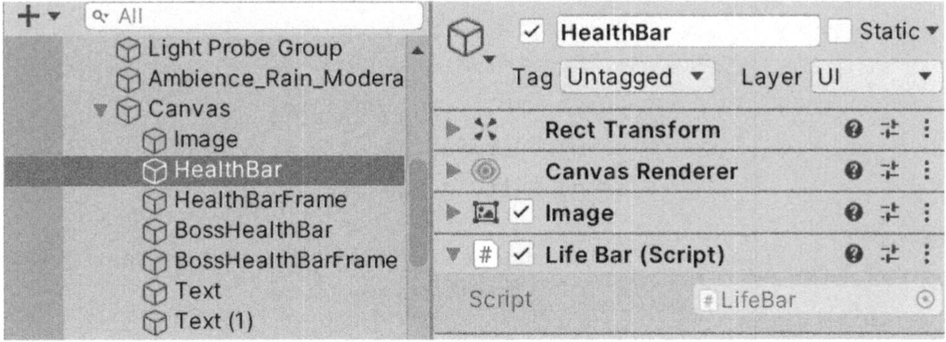

Figure 15.43: The Life Bar component in the player's HealthBar Canvas

2. In the `LifeBar`, the script adds a `Life` type field. This way, our script will ask the editor which `Life` component we will be monitoring. Save the script:

```
public class LifeBar : MonoBehaviour
{
    public Life targetLife;
}
```

Figure 15.44: Editor-configurable reference to a Life component

3. In the editor, drag the `Player` GameObject from the **Hierarchy** window to the `targetLife` property to make the life bar reference the player's life, and remember to have the `HealthBar` object selected before dragging **Player**. This way, we are telling our **LifeBar** script which Life component to check to see how much life the player has remaining. Something interesting here is that the enemies have the same Life component, so we can easily use this component to create life bars for every other object that has a life in our game:

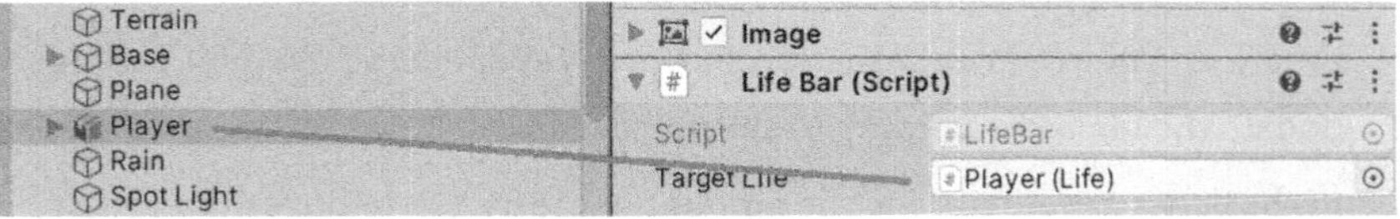

Figure 15.45: Dragging Player to reference its Life component

4. Add the `using UnityEngine.UI;` line right after the `using` statements in the first few lines of the script. This will tell C# that we will be interacting with the UI scripts:

```
using System;
using System.Collections;
using System.Collections.Generic;
using UnityEngine;
using UnityEngine.UI;
```

Figure 15.46: All the using statements in our script. We are not going to use them all but let's keep them for now

5. Create a `private` field (without the `public` keyword) of the `Image` type. We will save the reference to the component here in a moment:

```
Image image;
public Life targetLife;
```

Figure 15.47: Private reference to an image

6. Using `GetComponent` in `Awake`, access the reference to the `Image` component in our GameObject (`HealthBar`) and save it in the `image` field. As usual, the idea is to get this reference just once and save it for later use in the `Update` function. Of course, this will always work when you put this component in an object with an `Image` component. If not, the other option would be to create a public field of the `Image` type and drag the image component into it:

```
void Awake()
{
    image = GetComponent<Image>();
}
```

Figure 15.48: Saving the reference to the Image component in this object

7. Create an `Update` event function in the `LifeBar` script. We will use this to constantly update the life bar according to the player's life.
8. In the `Update` event, divide the amount of life by `100` to have our current life percentage expressed in the `0` to `1` range (assuming our maximum life is `100`), and set the result in the `fillAmount` field of the `Image` component as in the following screenshot. Remember that `fillAmount` expects a value between `0` and `1`, with `0` signaling that the bar is empty and `1` signaling that the bar is at its full capacity:

```
void Update()
{
    image.fillAmount = targetLife.amount / 100;
}
```

Figure 15.49: Updating the fill amount of the LifeBar script's Image component according to the Life component

Remember that putting 100 within the code is considered hardcoding (it is also known as a **magic number**), meaning later changes on that value would require us to look through the code for that value, which is a complicated task in big projects. That's why it is considered bad practice. It would be better to have a **Maximum Life** field in the **Life** component or at least have a constant with this value.

9. Save the script and in the editor, select the player and play the game. During **Play** mode, press *Esc* to regain access to the mouse and change the player's health in the Inspector window to see how the life bar updates accordingly. You can also test this by making the player receive damage somehow, such as by making enemies spawn bullets (more on enemies later):

```
using UnityEngine;
using UnityEngine.UI;

public class LifeBar : MonoBehaviour
{
    Image image;
    public Life targetLife;

    void Awake()
    {
        image = GetComponent<Image>();
    }

    void Update()
    {
        image.fillAmount = targetLife.amount / 100;
    }
}
```

Figure 15.50: Full LifeBar script

In the previous chapter, we explored the concept of events to detect changes in the state of other objects. The life bar is another example of using an event as we can change the fill amount of the image when the life actually changes. I challenge you to try to create an event when the life changes and implement this script using the one we looked at in the previous chapter.

You may be thinking that this UI behavior could be directly coded within the `Life` component, and that's completely possible, but the idea here is to create simple scripts with little pressure to keep our code separated. Each script should have just one reason to be modified, and mixing UI behavior and gameplay behavior in a single script would give the script two responsibilities, which results in two possible reasons to change our script. With this approach, we can also set the player's base life bar at the bottom by just adding the same script to its life bar but dragging the **Base Damage** object, which we created in the previous chapter, as the target life this time.

Regarding the Visual Scripting version, here is what you need to add to your health bar image GameObject:

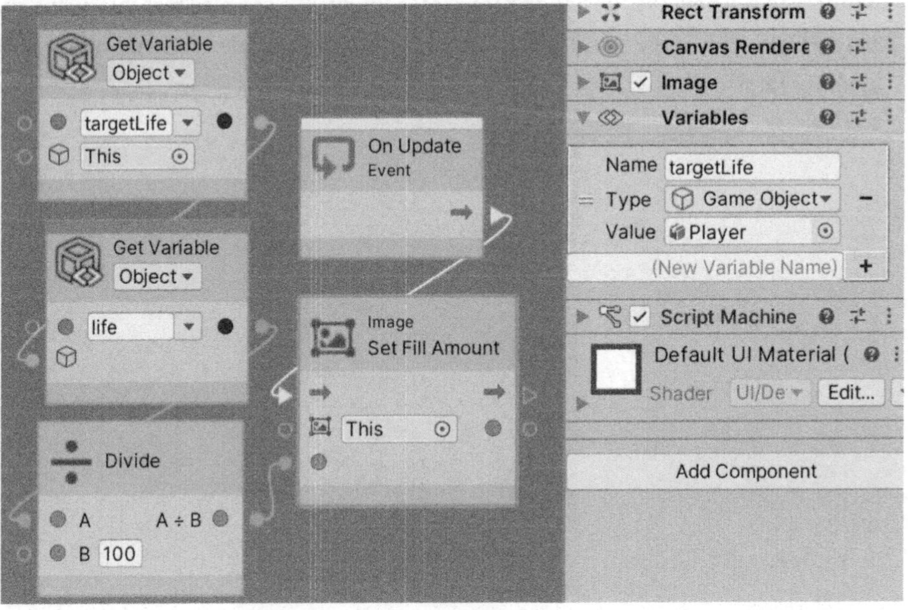

Figure 15.51: Full LifeBar Visual Graph

First, we added a `targetLife` variable of type `GameObject` to the **Variables** component of our life bar image. Then we dragged our **Player** GameObject (called **Robot** so far) to this variable, in a way the life bar now has a reference to the object from which we want to display its life. Then we added a **LifeBar** visual graph; in the **Update** node, it calls the **Set Fill Amount** node in order to update the fill amount of the **Image**. Remember that in this case, just calling the **Set Fill Amount** node will understand we are referring to the image component where this visual graph is located, so no need to use **GetComponent** here. In order to calculate the fill amount, we get the **targetLife** GameObject reference, and, using a second **Get Variable** node, we extract the life variable of that object. Finally, we divide that by 100 (we needed to create a **Float Literal** node in order to represent the value **100**) and pass that to the **Set Fill Amount** node. As usual, you can check the complete version on the GitHub repository.

The single object responsibility principle we just mentioned is one of the five object-oriented programming principles known as **SOLID**. If you don't know what SOLID is, I strongly recommend you search for `SOLID programming principles` on the internet to improve your programming best practices.

Now that we have sorted out the player's life bar, let's make the `Bullets` label update according to the player's remaining bullets. Something to consider here is that our current `PlayerShooting` script has unlimited bullets, so let's change that by following these steps:

1. Add a public `int` type field to the `PlayerShooting` script called `bulletsAmount`.
2. In the `if` statement that checks the pressure of the left mouse button, add a condition to check whether the number of bullets is greater than `0`.

3. Inside the `if` statement, reduce the number of bullets by `1`:

```
public int bulletsAmount;

public void OnFire(InputValue value)
{
    if (value.isPressed && bulletsAmount > 0)
    {
        bulletsAmount--;

        GameObject clone = Instantiate(prefab);

        clone.transform.position = shootPoint.transform.position;
        clone.transform.rotation = shootPoint.transform.rotation;

        muzzleEffect.Play();
        shootSound.Play();
    }
}
```

Figure 15.52: Limiting the number of bullets to shoot

In the Visual Scripting version, the modified shooting condition of the **PlayerShooting** visual graph will look like this:

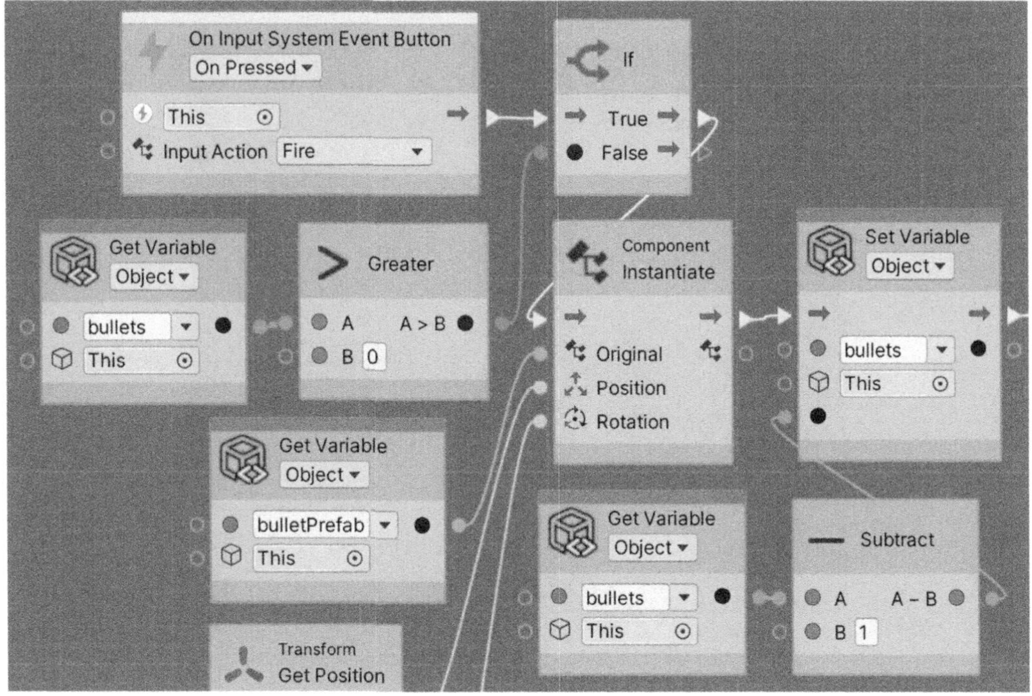

Figure 15.53: Shooting only if bullets are available and reducing the number of bullets after shooting

As you can see, we simply check if the new **bullets** variable we added is greater than zero and then use an **If** node condition for the execution of the **Instantiate** node. Regarding the bullets decrement, it will look like this:

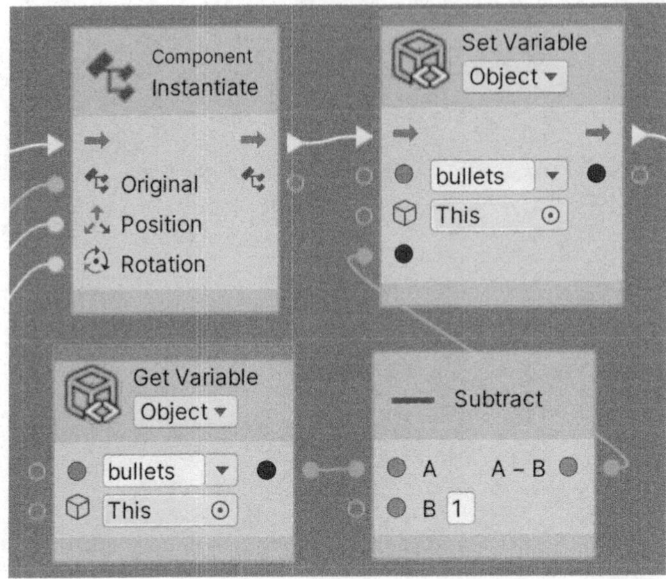

Figure 15.54: Decrementing bullet count in the Visual Graph

We simply subtract one from the bullets variable and set bullets again with this value.

Now that we have a field indicating the number of remaining bullets, we can create a script to display that number in the UI by doing the following:

1. Add a `PlayerBulletsUI` script to the bullet's `Text` GameObject. In my case, I called it `Bullets Label`.
2. Add the `using TMPro;` statement at the beginning of the file, given that we will modify the `Text Mesh Pro` component of our label.

3. Add a private field of the `TMP_Text` type, saving it in the reference to our own `Text` component in `Awake`:

```
using TMPro;
using UnityEngine;

public class PlayerBulletsUI : MonoBehaviour
{
    TMP_Text text;

    void Awake()
    {
        text = GetComponent<TMP_Text>();
    }
}
```

Figure 15.55: Caching the reference to our own Text component

4. Create a `public` field of the `PlayerShooting` type called `targetShooting` and drag `Player` to this property in the Editor. As was the case for the `LifeBar` component, the idea is that our UI script will access the script that has the remaining bullets to update the text, bridging the two scripts (`Text` and `PlayerShooting`) to keep their responsibilities separated.
5. Create an `Update` statement and inside it, set the `text` field of the text reference (I know, confusing) with a concatenation of `"Bullets: "` and the `bulletsAmount` field of the `targetShooting` reference. This way, we will replace the text of the label according to the current amount of bullets:

```
void Update()
{
    text.text = "Bullets: " + targetShooting.bulletsAmount;
}
```

Figure 15.56: Updating the bullet's text label

Remember that concatenating strings allocates memory, so again, I recommend you to only do this when necessary, using events. Also consider having two separated labels, one for the "Bullets: " part, and another for just the number of bullets, so you can only change the number label and avoid concatenation and UI text re-generation costs.

Regarding Visual Scripting, before actually setting the text, we need to add support for TextMeshPro in Visual Scripting. Visual Scripting requires manually specifying which Unity systems and packages we are going to use, and as TextMeshPro is not strictly a core Unity feature, so it might not be included by default. We can add support for TextMeshPro in Visual Scripting by doing the following:

1. Go to **Edit | Project Settings** and select the **Visual Scripting** category.
2. Expand the **Node Library** option using the arrow to its left.
3. Check if you have **Unity.TextMeshPro** in that list. If you do, feel free to skip these steps.
4. Use the + button at the bottom of the list to add a new library.
5. Click where it says **(No Assembly)** and search for **Unity.TextMeshPro**.
6. Click the **Regenerate Nodes** button and wait until the regeneration process is done:

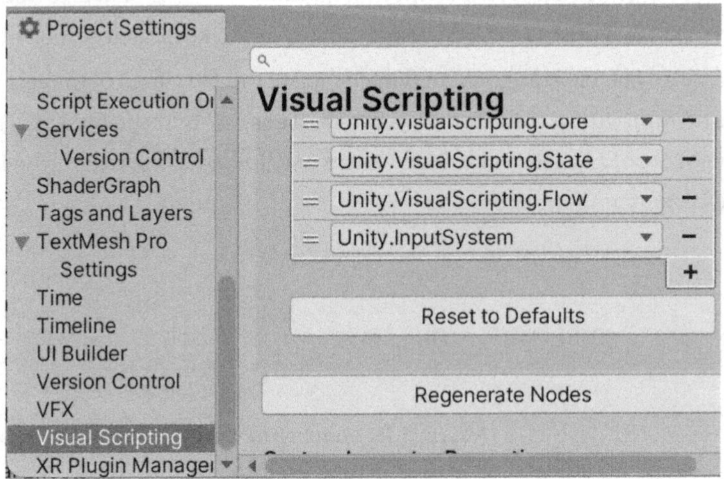

Figure 15.57: Adding TextMeshPro support to Visual Scripting

After setting that, this is what the visual graph to add to the **Bullets** text GameObject will look like:

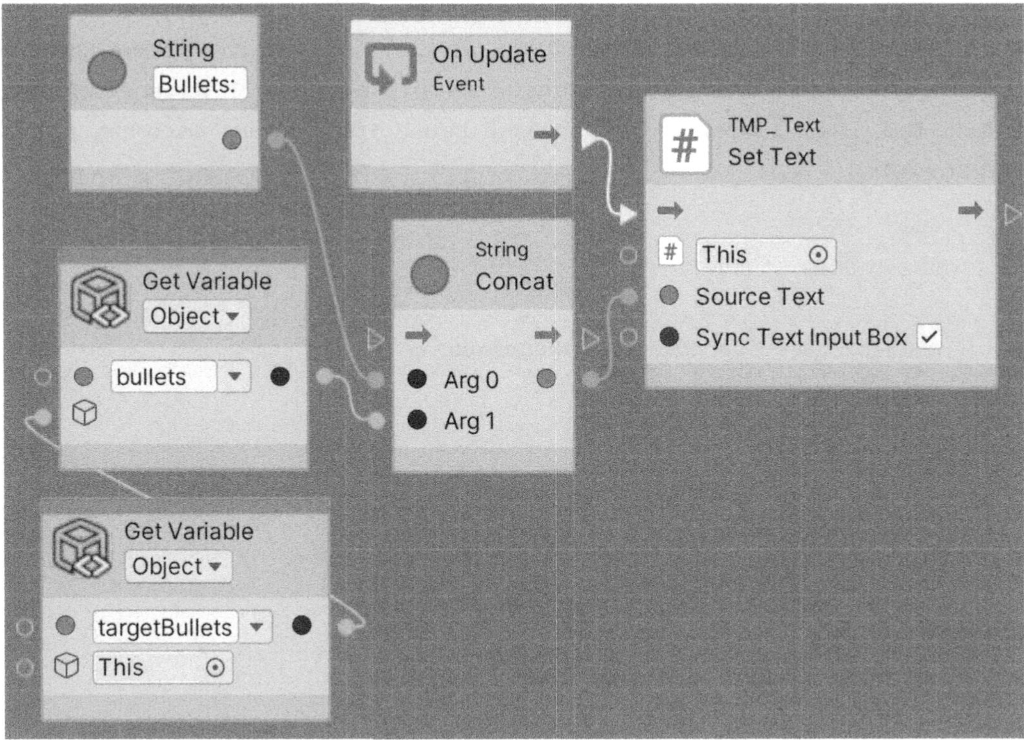

Figure 15.58: Updating the Bullets' text label in Visual Scripting

As usual, we need a reference to the **Player** to check its bullets, so we created a `targetBullets` variable of type **GameObject** and dragged the player there. Then we use a **Get Variable** node to extract the bullets amount from that reference and concatenate the string `"Bullets: "`, using the **String Literal** node, with the amount of bullets using the **Concat** node. That node will do the same as when we added two strings together using the + operator in C#. Finally, we use the **Set Text (Source Text, Sync Text InputBox)** node to update the text of our text field.

If you look at the two scripts, you will find a pattern. You can access the `UI` and `Gameplay` components and update the **UI** component accordingly, and most UI scripts will behave in the same way. Keeping this in mind, I challenge you to create the necessary scripts to make the **Score**, **Enemies**, and **Waves** counters work. Remember to add `using TMPro;` to use the `TMP_Text` component. After finishing this, you can compare your solution with the one in the following screenshot, starting with `ScoreUI`:

```
using TMPro;
using UnityEngine;

public class ScoreUI : MonoBehaviour
{
    TMP_Text text;

    void Awake()
    {
        text = GetComponent<TMP_Text>();
    }

    void Update()
    {
        text.text = "Score: " + ScoreManager.instance.amount;
    }
}
```

Figure 15.59: The ScoreUI script

Also, we need the WavesUI component:

```
using TMPro;
using UnityEngine;

public class WavesUI : MonoBehaviour
{
    TMP_Text text;

    void Start()
    {
        text = GetComponent<TMP_Text>();
        WavesManager.instance.onChanged.AddListener(RefreshText);
    }

    void RefreshText()
    {
        text.text = "Remaining Waves: " + WavesManager.instance.waves.Count;
    }
}
```

Figure 15.60: The WavesUI script

Finally, we need EnemiesUI:

```
using TMPro;
using UnityEngine;

public class EnemiesUI : MonoBehaviour
{
    TMP_Text text;

    void Start()
    {
        text = GetComponent<TMP_Text>();
        EnemyManager.instance.onChanged.AddListener(RefreshText);
    }

    void RefreshText()
    {
        text.text = "Remaining Enemies: " + EnemyManager.instance.enemies.Count;
    }
}
```

Figure 15.61: The EnemiesUI script

Notice how we took advantage of the existence of the **onChanged** events in the **WavesManager** and **EnemyManager** scripts to only update the text fields when needed. Observe how we didn't need to drag a reference to get the values to display, as all these scripts use managers to get that info.

Regarding Visual Scripting, we have the **ScoreUI** script:

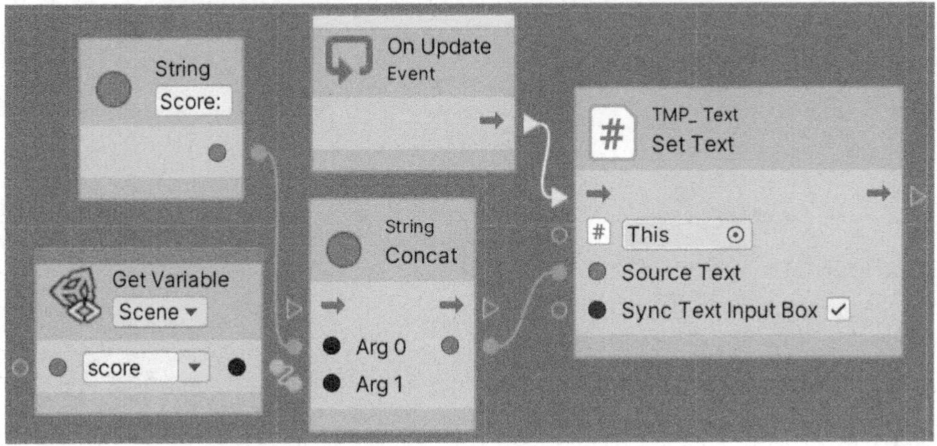

Figure 15.62: The ScoreUI visual script

Then the **WavesUI** script:

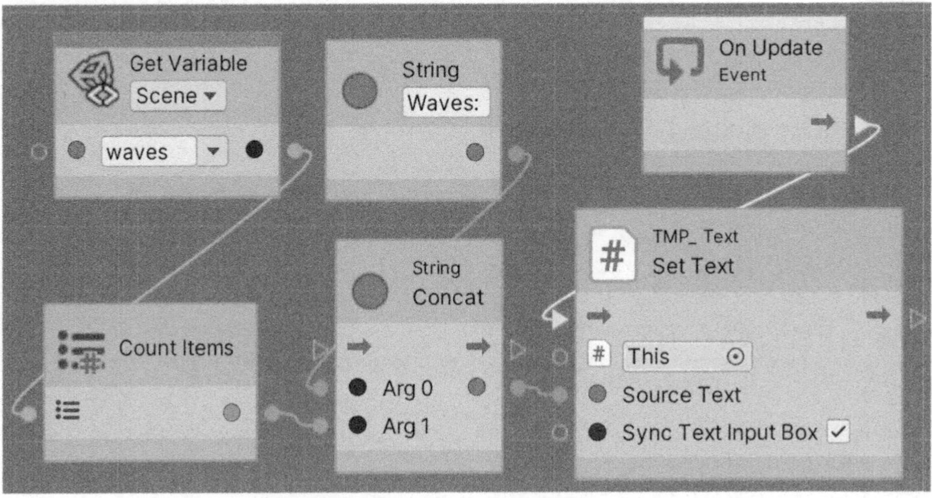

Figure 15.63: The Waves UI visual script

And finally, the **EnemiesUI** script:

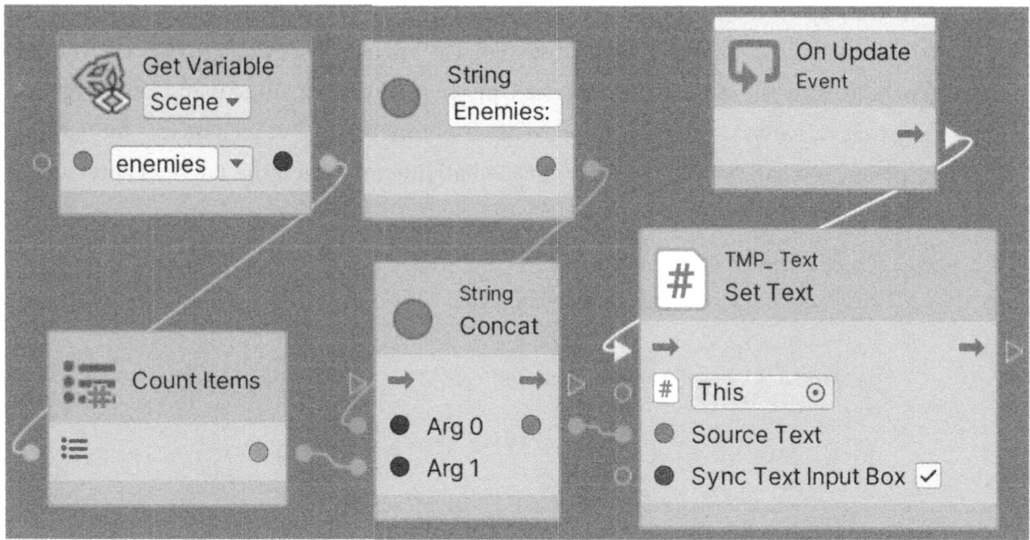

Figure 15.64: The Enemies UI visual script

As you can see, we have used the events already coded in the managers to change the UI only when necessary. Also, observe how we used **Scene** variables to get the info to display. Now that we have coded the UI labels and bars, let's code the `Pause` menu.

Programming the Pause menu

Recall how we created a **Pause** menu in a previous section. It is currently disabled, so let's make it work. First, we need to code the **Pause** feature, which can be quite complicated. So again, we will use a simple approach for pausing most behaviors, which is stopping the time! Remember that most of our movement scripts use time functionality, such as **Delta Time** (the one we discussed in *Chapter 2, Editing Scenes and Game Objects*), as a way to calculate the amount of movement to apply. There is also a way to simulate time going slower or faster, which is by setting `timeScale`. This field will affect Unity's time system's speed, and we can set it to `0` to simulate that time has stopped, which will pause animations, stop particles, and reduce **Delta Time** to `0`, making our movements stop. So, let's do it:

1. Create a script called `Pause` and add it to a new GameObject called `Pause`.
2. Add the `using UnityEngine.InputSystem;` statement at the beginning of the script file to be able to read input.

3. In `Update`, detect when the *Esc* key is pressed. We can add a mapping to our **Player Input** asset file and read the input as we did in *Chapter 2, Editing Scenes and Game Objects*, but to learn a new way of using the input system, we will use the `Keyboard.current` variable to read directly the state of a key in the **Update** method instead of using mapping. Consider that it is always recommended to use input mapping, but let's do this for learning purposes. You can set the `Time.timeScale` variable to `0` when the *Esc* key is pressed, as you can see in the following image:

```
using UnityEngine;
using UnityEngine.InputSystem;

public class Pause : MonoBehaviour
{
    void Update()
    {
        if (Keyboard.current.escapeKey.wasPressedThisFrame)
        {
            Time.timeScale = 0;
        }
    }
}
```

Figure 15.65: Stopping time to simulate a pause

4. Save and test this by playing the game and pressing the *Esc* key. You will notice that almost everything will stop, but you can see how the shoot functionality still works. That's because the `PlayerShooting` script is not time-dependent. One solution here could be to simply check whether `Time.timeScale` is greater than `0` to prevent this:

```
public void OnFire(InputValue value)
{
    if (value.isPressed && bulletsAmount > 0 && Time.timeScale > 0)
    {
        bulletsAmount--;
```

Figure 15.66: Checking Pause in the player shooting script

5. The same needs to be done in our `EnemyFSM` Shoot method, changing it for this:

As usual, we have pursued the simplest way here, but there is a better approach. I challenge you to try to create `PauseManager` with a Boolean indicating whether the game is paused or not, changing `timeScale` in the process.

Now that we have a simple but effective way to pause the game, let's make the **Pause** menu visible to resume the game by doing the following:

1. Add a field of the `GameObject` type called `pauseMenu` in the `Pause` script. The idea is to drag the **Pause** menu here so that we have a reference to enable and disable it
2. In `Awake`, add `pauseMenu.SetActive(false);` to disable the **Pause** menu at the beginning of the game. Even if we disabled the **Pause** menu in the editor, we add this just in case we re-enable it by mistake. It must always start disabled.
3. Using the same function but passing `true` as the first parameter, enable the **Pause** menu in the *Esc* key pressure check:

```
public GameObject pauseMenu;

void Awake()
{
    pauseMenu.SetActive(false);
}

void Update()
{
    if (Keyboard.current.escapeKey.wasPressedThisFrame)
    {
        pauseMenu.SetActive(true);
        Time.timeScale = 0;
    }
}
```

Figure 15.67: Enabling the Pause menu when pressing the Esc key

Now, we need to make the **Pause** menu buttons work. If you recall, we explored the concept of events, implementing them with `UnityEvents` in the different `Managers`. Our **Pause** menu buttons use the same class to implement the `onClick` event, which is an event that informs us that a specific button has been pressed. Let's resume the game when pressing those buttons by doing the following:

1. Create a field of the `Button` type in our `Pause` script called `resumeButton`, and drag `resumeButton` to it; this way, our `Pause` script has a reference to the button.
2. In `Awake`, add a listener function called `OnResumePressed` to the `onClick` event of `resumeButton`.
3. Make the `OnResumePressed` function set `timeScale` to `1` and disable the **Pause** menu, as we did in `Awake`:

```
public GameObject pauseMenu;
public Button resumeButton;

void Awake()
{
    pauseMenu.SetActive(false);
    resumeButton.onClick.AddListener(OnResumePressed);
}

void OnResumePressed()
{
    pauseMenu.SetActive(false);
    Time.timeScale = 1;
}
```

Figure 15.68: Unpausing the game

If you save and test this, you will notice that you cannot click the **Resume** button because we disabled the cursor at the beginning of the game, so make sure you re-enable it while in `Pause` and disable it when you resume:

```
void OnResumePressed()
{
    pauseMenu.SetActive(false);
    Time.timeScale = 1;
    Cursor.visible = false;
    Cursor.lockState = CursorLockMode.Locked;
}

void Update()
{
    if (Keyboard.current.escapeKey.wasPressedThisFrame)
    {
        Cursor.visible = true;
        Cursor.lockState = CursorLockMode.None;
        pauseMenu.SetActive(true);
        Time.timeScale = 0;
    }
}
```

Figure 15.69: Showing and hiding the cursor while in Pause

One final thing to consider is that we want to set the time scale to 1 again on the **OnDestroy** method. This method gets executed when the **Pause** object is destroyed, which will happen when we manually destroy the object via scripting, or most importantly in this case, if we change scenes. The idea is to make sure to resume the time system if we change scenes while being in the **Pause** menu, so the next scene can play the game properly:

```
private void OnDestroy()
{
    Time.timeScale = 1;
}
```

Figure 15.70: Resetting the time scale when leaving the scene

Regarding the Visual Scripting version of the **Pause** script, consider that we don't have an equivalent to `Keyboard.current`, so we will need to do it using the input mappings. In order to add an input mapping for the *Esc* key, do the following:

1. Double-click the **Player Input** asset to edit it. You can find it by selecting the **Player** GameObject, and clicking the box at the right of the **Actions** property of the `PlayerInput` component in the Inspector.
2. Using the + button in the top-right corner of the **Actions** list (the middle list), create a new **Action** called `Pause`:

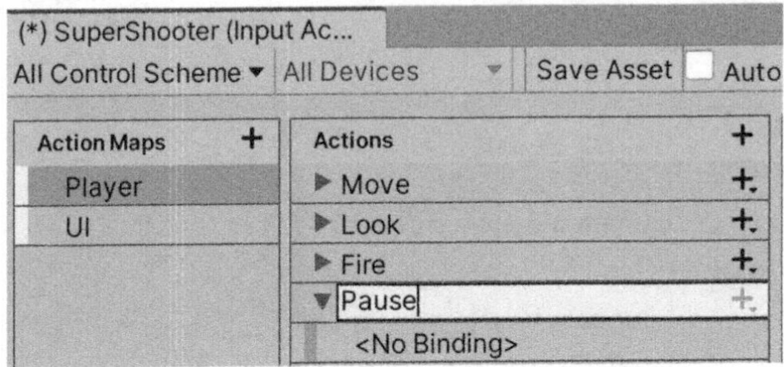

Figure 15.71: Creating a new input mapping

3. Click the <No Binding> item inside the **Pause** action we just created (below it).
4. In the **Path** property in the **Binding Properties** section (at the right side of the screen), click the empty rectangle at its left, and search and select the **Escape [Keyboard]** button:

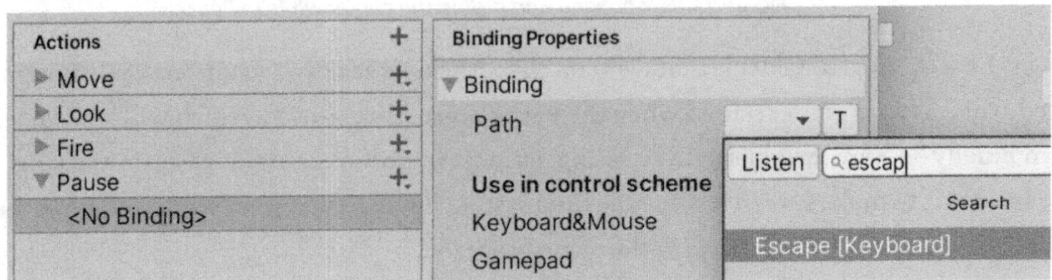

Figure 15.72: Adding a key to the mapping

5. Click the **Save Asset** button in the top-middle part of the screen.

Now, you can add the following graph, this time to the **Player** GameObject, as we need to read input from it:

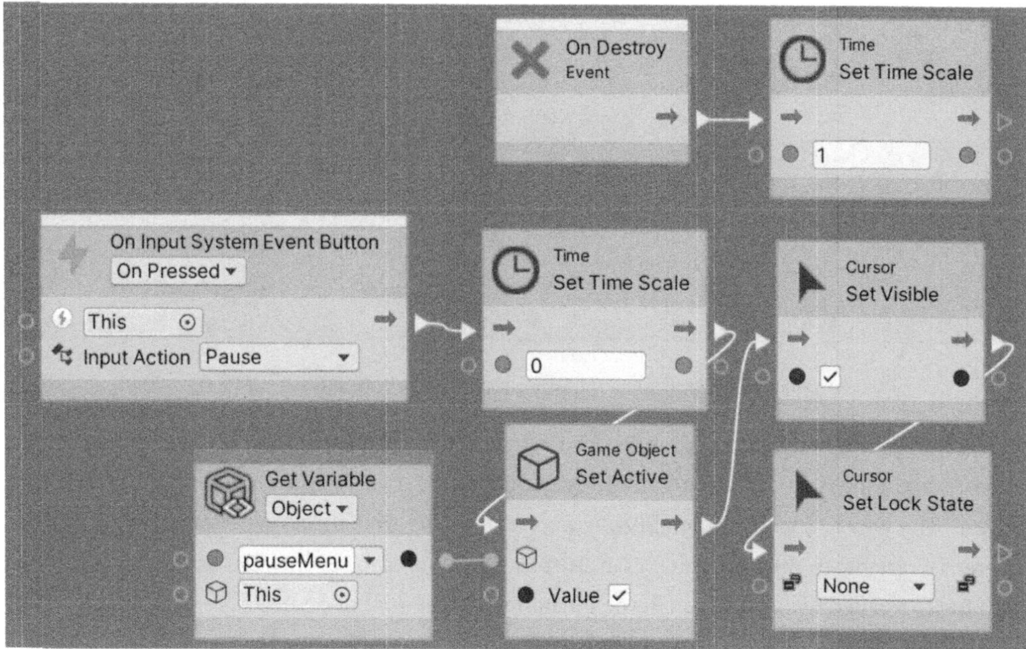

Figure 15.73: Pausing when Esc is pressed

So far nothing new; we detect that *Esc* is pressed and, in such a moment, we call **Set Time Scale** and specify the `0` value. Then we activate the **Pause** menu (having a reference through a variable `pauseMenu` in the **Variables** component), and we enable the cursor. Finally, we set the time scale to 1 when the object is destroyed.

Regarding the **Resume** behavior, the nodes to add to the same **Pause** graph will look like this:

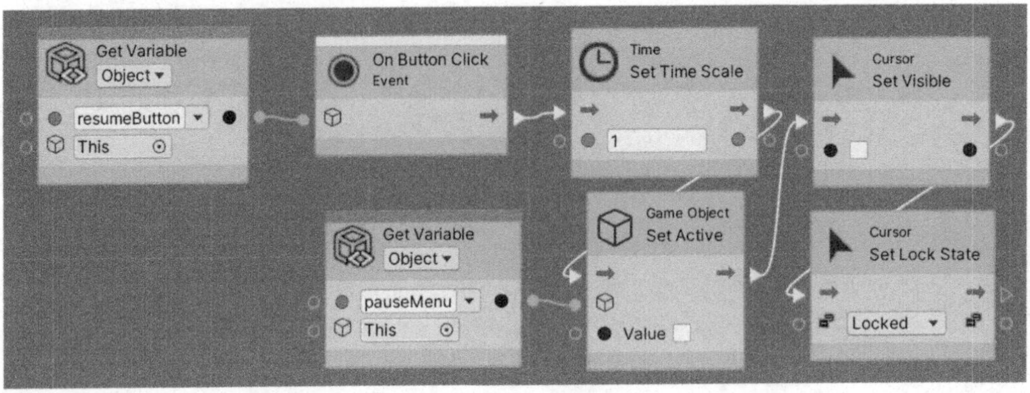

Figure 15.74: Unpausing when the Resume button is pressed

The only new element on this graph is the usage of the **On Button Click** node. As you might expect, that node is an event, and anything connected to it will execute under the pressure of a button. The way to specify which button we are referring to is through connecting the **Button** reference variable to the input pin of **On Button Click**. You can see how we created a variable of type **Button** called `resumeButton` in the **Variables** component to do this.

Now that you know how to code buttons, I challenge you to code the `Exit` button's behavior. Again, remember to add `using UnityEngine.UI`. Also, you will need to call `Application.Quit();` to exit the game but take into account that this will do nothing in the editor; we don't want to close the editor while creating the game. This function only works when you build the game.

So, for now, just call it, and if you want to print a message to be sure that the button is working properly, you can; a solution is provided in the following screenshot:

```
using UnityEngine;
using UnityEngine.UI;

public class QuitButton : MonoBehaviour
{
    Button button;

    void Awake()
    {
        button = GetComponent<Button>();
        button.onClick.AddListener(Quit);
    }

    void Quit()
    {
        print("Quitting");
        Application.Quit();
    }
}
```

Figure 15.75: The Quit button script

This solution proposes that you add this script directly to the **Quit** button GameObject itself so that the script listens to the `onClick` event on its `Button` sibling component, and in that case, executes the `Quit` function. You could also add this behavior to the `Pause` script, and while that will work, remember that if a script can be split into two because it does two unrelated tasks, it is always best to split it so that separate behavior is unrelated. Here, the **Pause** behavior is not related to the **Quit** behavior.

Regarding the Visual Scripting version, the graph to add to the **Quit** button would look like this:

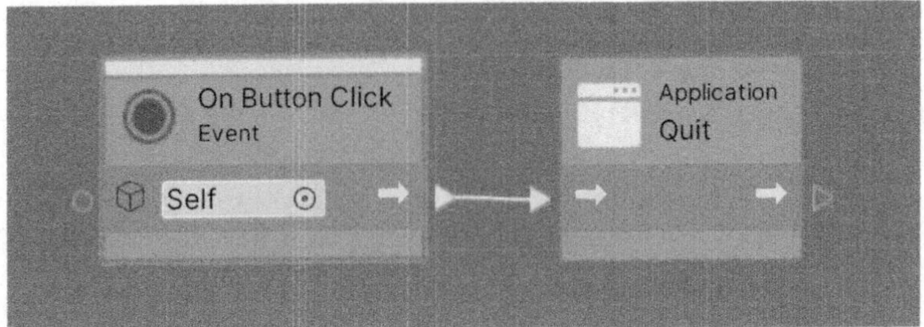

Figure 15.76: The Quit button visual script

Simple, right? As we put this in the `Button` itself, we don't even need to specify which button, as it automatically detects that we are referring to ourselves.

Now that we have our **Pause** system set up using the UI and buttons, let's continue looking at other visual and auditive ways to make our player aware of what has happened.

Summary

In this chapter, we introduced the basics of UI, understanding the **Canvas** and **RectTransform** components to locate objects onscreen and create a UI layout. We also covered different kinds of UI elements, mainly **Image** and **Text**, to give life to our UI layout and make it appealing to the user. Finally, we discussed how to adapt UI objects to different resolutions and aspect ratios to make our UI adapt to different screen sizes, even though we cannot predict the exact monitor our user will be playing the game on. All of this allows us to create any UI we will need in our game using the Canvas.

In the next chapter, we will explore how to create UIs using UI Toolkit instead, another Unity system to create UIs, and compare both the Canvas and UI Toolkit to see where to use which.

Join us on Discord!

Read this book alongside other users, Unity game development experts, and the author himself.

Ask questions, provide solutions to other readers, chat with the author via Ask Me Anything sessions, and much more.

Scan the QR code or visit the link to join the community.

`https://packt.link/handsonunity22`

16

Creating a UI with the UI Toolkit

In the previous chapter, we discussed how to create user interfaces using **uGUI** (also known as **Canvas**), one of the most common Unity UI systems, but as we already mentioned, this is not the only one. While so far, uGUI is the most preferred option, Unity is working on a replacement called **UI Toolkit**, and even if it doesn't have feature parity with uGUI yet, we thought it is worth covering it in this book.

The idea of this chapter is to create the same UI we created previously but with UI Toolkit, so you can get an idea of how creating a UI in Unity will look soon.

In this chapter, we will examine the following UI concepts:

- Why learn UI Toolkit?
- Creating a UI with UI Toolkit
- Making a responsive UI with UI Toolkit

By the end of the chapter, you will know how to use UI Toolkit to create basic UIs for our game, redoing the UI we did in the last chapter as a point of reference. So, let's start by discussing the following question first: why are we using UI Toolkit?

Why learn UI Toolkit?

I know the topic of this chapter might sound a little bit confusing; we just learned how to use a whole Unity system to create our UI, and now we are learning another one! Why didn't we just learn this new one?

Well, the first part of the answer is that UI Toolkit doesn't have feature parity with uGUI yet, meaning that it doesn't have all the features necessary to use it in real production environments. Another thing to take into account is that even if UI Toolkit is stable enough, it's still a relatively new system, and there are still lots of games in development that were created on older Unity versions that don't support it. This means that in order to land a job in this industry, we need to get a decent amount of exposure to uGUI due to most games being created with this technology. This happens because it's not safe or practical to update an already-tested and working game with new technologies; such changes could lead to a major rework of the game to make it compatible with the new versions. Also, this could potentially introduce tons of bugs that could delay the release of new versions—not to mention the time it will take to remake a full app with a new system.

That being said, we believe it's still worth learning the basic concepts of UI Toolkit to be prepared to use it in newer Unity versions, so let's dive into it now.

Creating a UI with UI Toolkit

In this section, we are going to learn how to create UI Documents, an asset that will define the elements our UI has. To do this, we are going to discuss the following concepts:

- Creating UI Documents
- Editing UI Documents
- Creating UI Stylesheets

Let's start by seeing how we can create our first UI Document.

Creating UI Documents

When creating a UI with uGUI, we need to create GameObjects and attach components like **Button, Image**, or **Text**, but with UI Toolkit, we need to create a **UI Document** instead. UI Document is a special kind of asset that will contain the definition of the elements our UI will have and its hierarchy. We will have a GameObject with a **UI Document** component (yes, it's called the same, so pay attention here) that will reference this UI document asset and render its contents. It's like a mesh asset that contains information about the Mesh, and the `MeshRenderer` component that will render it. In this case, the elements to render are contained in an asset and we have a component that reads the asset and renders its content (UI in this case).

UI Documents are actually plain text files. You can open one with a text editor and easily see its contents. If you do that and you are familiar with HTML, you will recognize the XML-like format used to define the elements our UI will be composed of; Unity calls this format **UXML**. With UI Toolkit, Unity is attempting to make it easy for web developers to jump into Unity and create UIs. In the following code, you can see the typical look of an UXML document's file contents:

```
<ui:UXML
   xmlns:ui="UnityEngine.UIElements"
   xsi="http://www.w3.org/2001/XMLSchema-instance"
   engine="UnityEngine.UIElements"
   editor="UnityEditor.UIElements"
   noNamespaceSchemaLocation="../../UIElementsSchema/UIElements.xsd"
   editor-extension-mode="False">
    <ui:Button tabindex="-1" text="Button"
               display-tooltip-when-elided="true" />
    <ui:Scroller high-value="100"
                 direction="Horizontal"
                  value="42" />
    <ui:VisualElement>
        <ui:Label tabindex="-1"
                  text="Label"
                  display-tooltip-when-elided="true" />
        <ui:Label tabindex="-1"
                  text="Label"
                  display-tooltip-when-elided="true" />
    </ui:VisualElement>
</ui:UXML>
```

Don't worry if you don't know XML; we will explain the core concepts in this chapter. Also, don't worry about the UXML format; later in this chapter, we will be using a visual editor called **UI Builder** to edit our UI without writing UXML at all, but it is worth knowing how it actually works.

In order to create a UI Document and add it to the scene, we need to do the following:

1. Click the **+** | **UI Toolkit** | **UI Document** option in the **Project** view to create a UI Document asset and name it `GameHUD`:

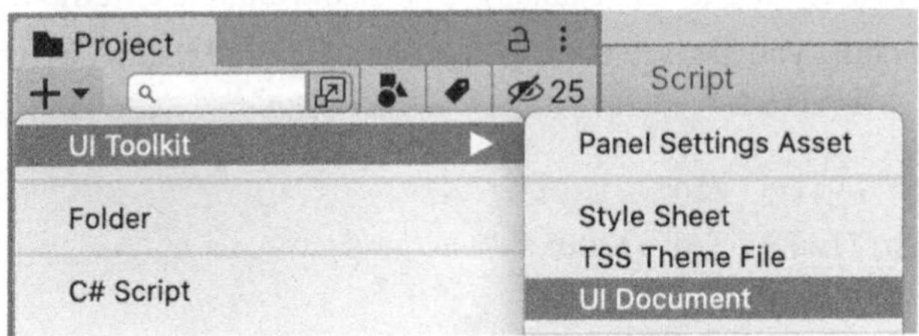

Figure 16.1: Creating the UI Document asset

2. Click the **Game Object** | **UI Tookit** | **UI Document** option to create a GameObject in your scene with the UI Document component, which is capable of rendering the UI Document.
3. Select it and drag the **GameHUD** UI Document asset (the one created in *step 1*) to the **Source Asset** property of the UI Document GameObject (the one created in *step 2*):

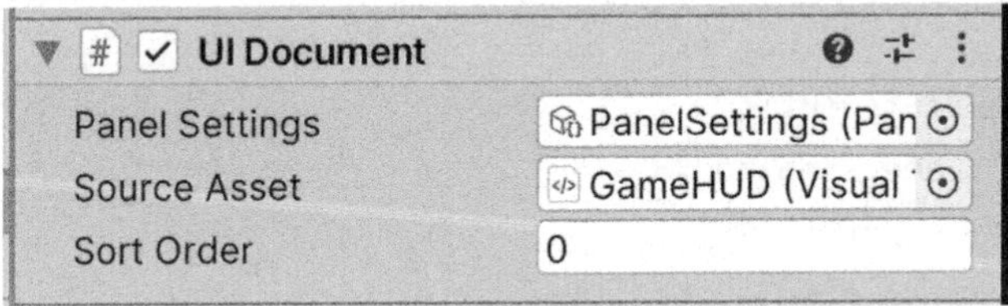

Figure 16.2: Making the UI Document component to render our UI Document asset

And that's it! Of course, we won't see anything yet on our screen as the UI Document is blank, so let's start adding elements to it.

Editing UI Documents

As our goal is to recreate the same UI we created in the last chapter, let's start with the simplest part: adding the player avatar to the top-left corner. One option would be to open the UI Document asset with any text editor and start writing the UXML code, but luckily, we have an easier way, which is using the **UI Builder** editor. This editor allows us to generate the UXML code visually, by dragging and dropping elements.

In order to do that, let's first see how the **UI Builder** window works:

1. Double-click the **GameHUD** asset in the Project view to make **UI Builder** open it:

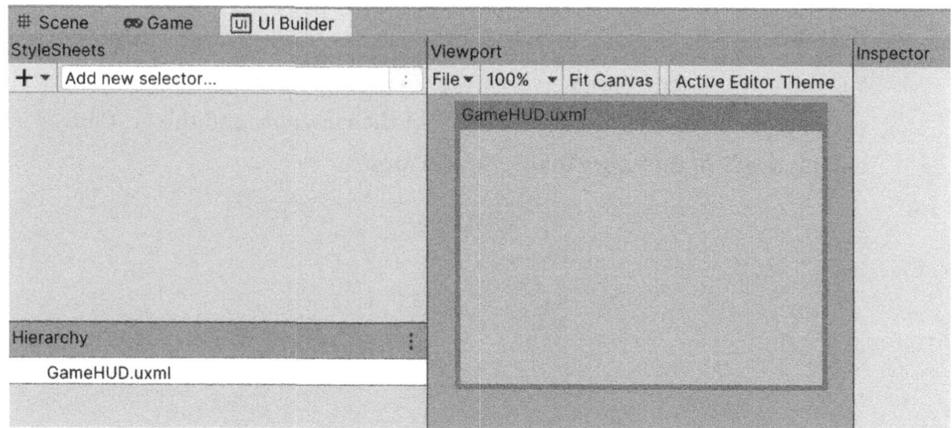

Figure 16.3: The UI Builder editor

2. In the **Hierarchy** panel inside the UI Builder (*not* the **Hierarchy** panel we've used so far in previous chapters), select `GameHUD.uxml`, which is the container element of the UI.

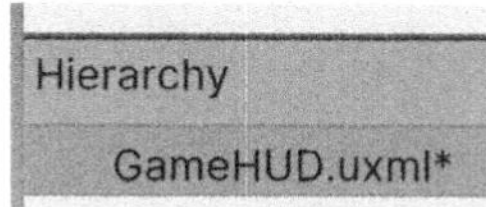

Figure 16.4: Selecting the asset name in Hierarchy to edit the general UI settings

3. Look at the **Inspector** panel at the right of the UI Builder window (*not* the **Inspector** we've used so far to modify GameObjects). Set the **Size** property to a **Width** of `1920` and a **Height** of `1080`. This will allow us to view how our UI will look in this resolution. You can later change this value to see how it adapts to different sizes, but more on that later:

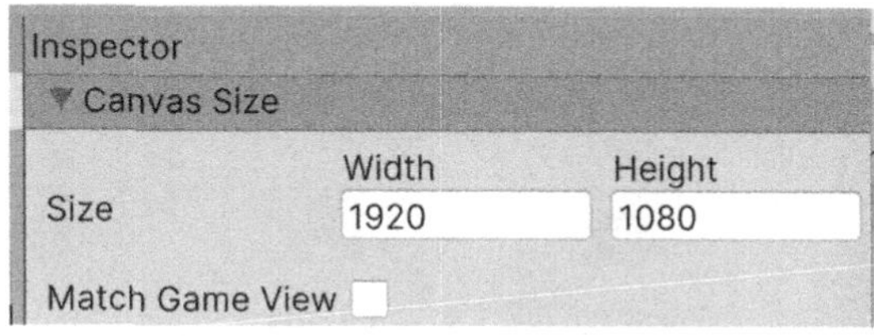

Figure 16.5: Setting the preview UI resolution

4. You can pan the viewport to navigate the UI by pressing the *Mouse Wheel Button* (also known as *Middle Button*) and moving the mouse. On Mac, you can also press *Option + Command* and click and drag any free area of the viewport (places without our UI) to do the same.
5. You can also use the *Mouse Scroll Wheel* to zoom in and out. Finally, you can use the zoom percentage selection at the top-left part of the **viewport** and the **Fit Canvas** button to automatically fit the entire UI in your **viewport**:

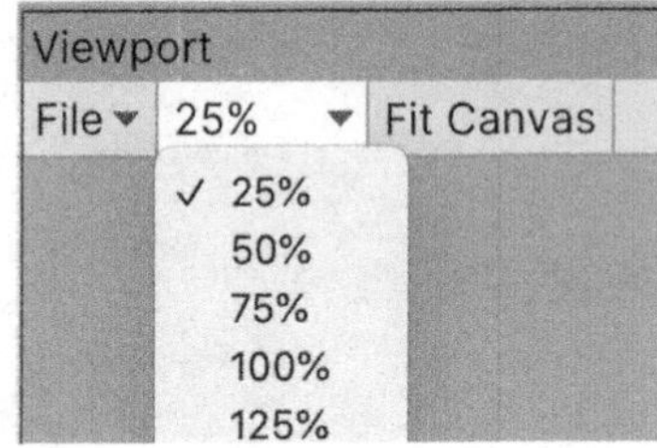

Figure 16.6: Setting the preview zoom

Now that we know the basics of UI Builder, let's add our image to the UI:

1. Drag the **VisualElement** icon from the **Library** at the bottom left to the **Hierarchy** section on the left. This will create a basic UI element capable of rendering an image and much more:

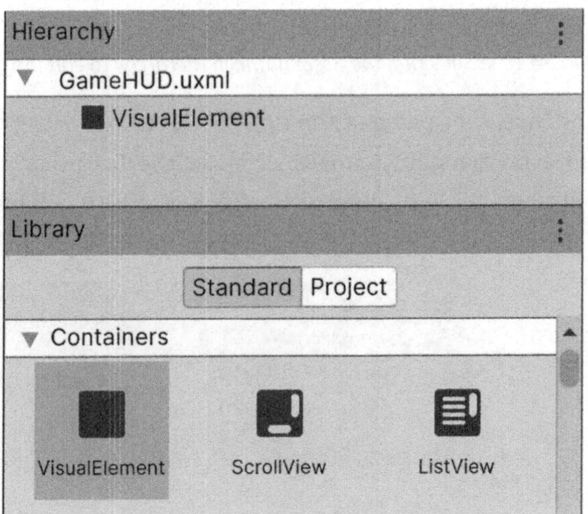

Figure 16.7: Creating a Visual Element

2. Select the **VisualElement** in the **Hierarchy** (under `GameHUD.uxml`) and look at the **Inspector** at the right part of the UI Builder window (again, not the regular Unity Inspector panel) for the **Position** section. Expand it if not already expanded (using the arrow on the left).
3. Set **Position** to **Absolute** in order to allow us to move our element freely around the UI. Later in this chapter, in the *Using relative positions* section, we will explain how **Relative** mode works:

Figure 16.8: Setting our UI Element to be freely moved around

4. Open the **Size** section and set **Width** and **Height** to `100` to make our UI element have a non-zero size. This way, we can see its area in the **Viewport**:

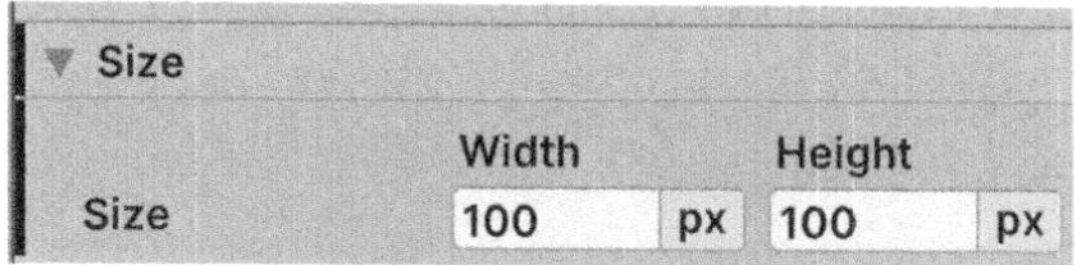

Figure 16.9: Setting our UI Element size

5. In the **Viewport** pane, you can drag your element around and use the blue rectangles in the corners to change its size. Position your element at the top-left corner of the UI. If you don't see your element in the **Viewport**, select it in the **Hierarchy** (the one of UI Builder):

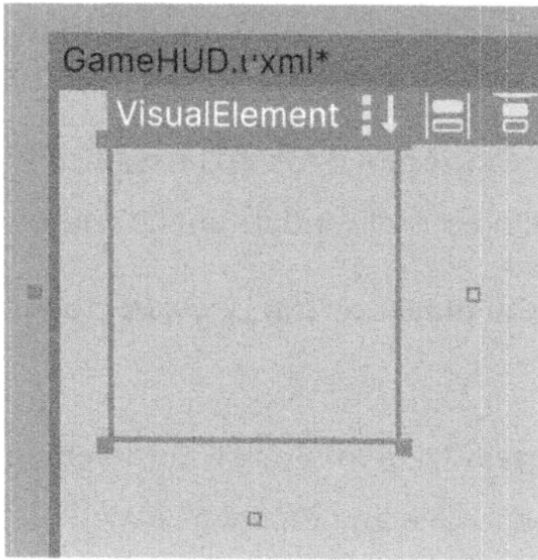

Figure 16.10: Moving VisualElements

6. In order to set an exact position, you can set the **Left** and **Top** values of the **Position** section in the **Inspector** to specify the exact *x* and *y* coordinates respectively, expressed in pixels:

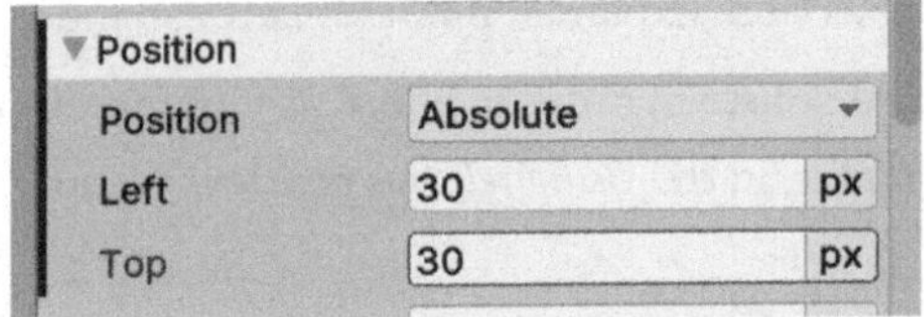

Figure 16.11: Setting the Position

7. In the **Background** section of the **Inspector**, set the **Image** mode to **Sprite** using the combo box at the right of the **Image** property. This allows us to apply a sprite as the background of our element.
8. Drag the sprite asset (the image) of our player avatar we imported in *Chapter 15, User Interface Design*, from the **Project** panel to the **Image** property in order to set it. Also, you can use the target button (circle button with the dot in the middle) to select the sprite asset from the picker window:

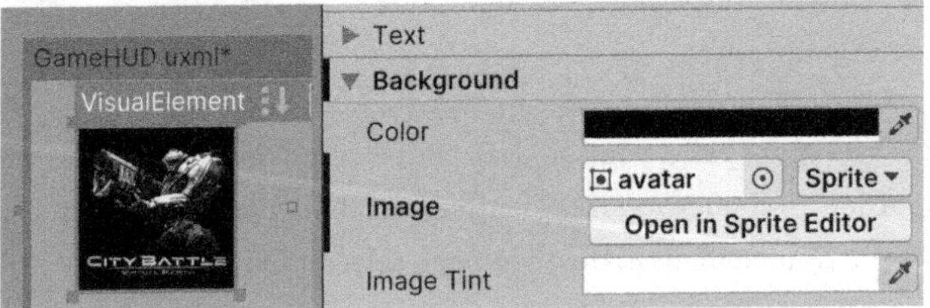

Figure 16.12: Setting the Background image of the element

9. Return to the regular **Game** panel to see the results. If you don't see a change, you can turn off and on the GameObject that renders our UI (the one we created with the UI Document).

Now that we have created the player avatar, we can create the player health bar by doing the following:

1. Repeat the previous *steps 1* to *6* to create a new element that will serve as the player health bar container. It won't have any image as it will just be the container of the rest of the elements that will compose the health bar.

2. Position it right next to the player avatar and set a width and height to resemble a classic health bar. Remember you can do this by dragging the image and the squares at the corners, or through the **Size** and **Position** properties as we did before.
3. Drag a new **VisualElement** to the Hierarchy, as we did in *step 1*, but this time drop it over the element created in *step 1*. This will make this new element a child of it, which will make that element's position and size depend on its parent, the same as what happened when we parented Canvas objects in *Chapter 15*, *User Interface Design*.
4. Select the parent Visual Element and in the **Inspector**, set the **Name** property to `PlayerHealth` to easily identify it. Do the same with the child element, calling it `Filling`:

Figure 16.13: Parenting and naming Visual Elements

5. Select the **Filling** element in the **Hierarchy** and look at the **Inspector**.
6. In the **Background** section, set the **Color** property to red, clicking on the color box and using the **Color Picker**. This will fill our UI Element background with plain red instead of using an image:

Figure 16.14: Setting a pure red background for our element

7. As usual, set the **Position** to **Absolute**, and also the **Left** and **Top** properties to `0`. As this is a child of another element, the position will be relative to its parent position, so by specifying a **Left** and **Top** value of `0`, we are saying that we will be at 0 pixels from the left and top sides of our parent. This means that if our parent moves, this child element will move along with it.

8. Set **Size**'s **Width** and **Height** to `100` and change the unit of measurement from px (pixels) to `%` (percentage) by clicking on the **px** button and selecting **%**. This will make the **Filling** element size the same as its parent (100 percent the parent size):

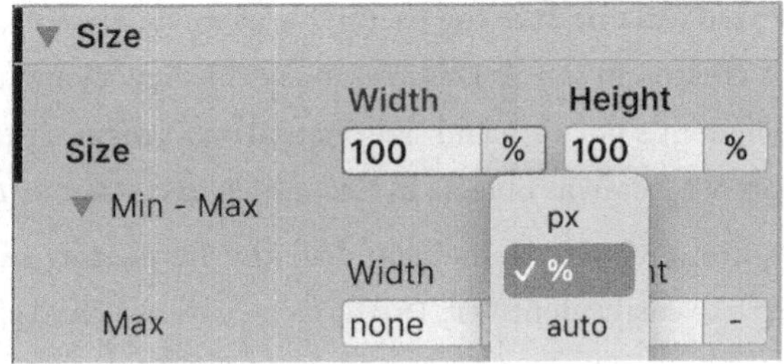

Figure 16.15: Setting our size as the same size as our parent element

9. Add a new **VisualElement** as a child of **PlayerHealth** (a sibling of **Filling**) and call it `Border`.
10. Set the **Position** and **Size** as we did in *steps 7* and *8* for the **Filling** element, but don't set the background color.
11. Set the **Background** section's **Image** property to be the same border image we used in the previous chapter. Remember to set the **Image** mode to **Sprite** instead of **Texture**.
12. Set the **Slice** property in the **Background** section to 15. This applies the nine-slices technique we used in *Chapter 15, User Interface Design*, to expand an object without stretching it:

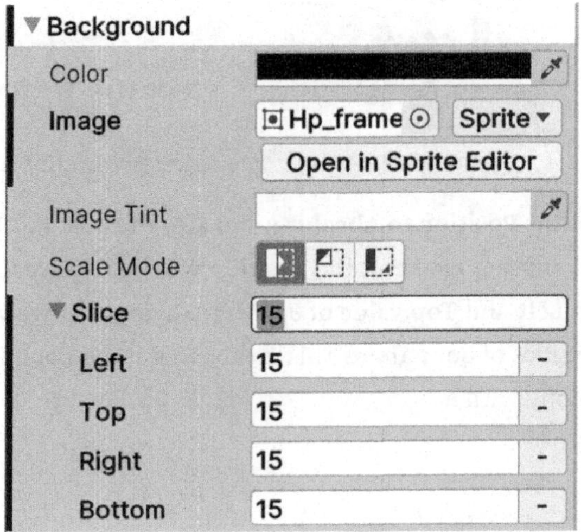

Figure 16.16: Setting the nine-slices sizes in the element directly

13. Select the **Filling** visual element in the **Hierarchy** and set its **Size** section's **Width** property to simulate the **Fill Amount** property of the images we used in *Chapter 11, User Interface Design*. Later, we will change this **Size** to be directly proportional to the player's health number via code:

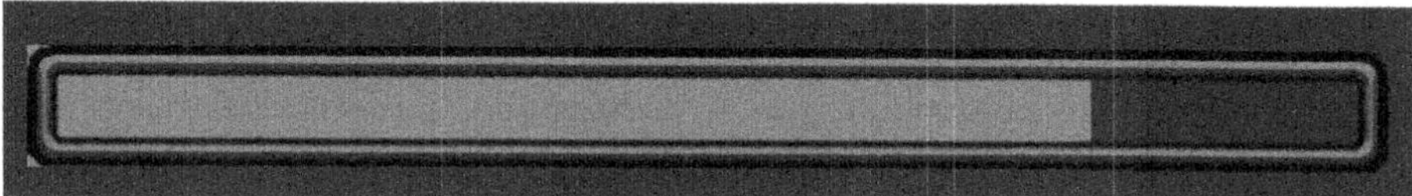

Figure 16.17: Health bar result

14. Repeat *steps 1* to *12* to create the bottom of the **Base Health** bar. Remember the filling must be green this time. Alternatively, you can just copy and paste the **PlayerHealth** container, but I recommend you repeat the steps for learning purposes.

In previous steps, we basically saw how to compose several UI Elements to create a complex object. We needed a parent container element to drive the size of our child's so that the inner elements adapt to it, especially the filling, which requires a percentage value to represent the current player health.

Now we have our Life Bar! Well, not quite yet; those red corners from the filling that our border doesn't cover are pretty rough! We will improve that later in this chapter when discussing how to make our UI responsive, so for now, let's keep it as is.

Finally, let's add text elements to the UI by doing the following, but first, we will need to think about fonts. If you download a TTF font, you will need to create a Font Asset as we did in *Chapter 15, User Interface Design*, for it to be used in UI Toolkit. But with the current release of UI Toolkit, the Font Asset we created in the last chapter is not compatible. We will need to create a Font Asset using the UI Toolkit Font Asset Creator, instead of the Text Mesh Pro one. The reason behind the existence of duplicated tools is that Unity is integrating the Text Mesh Pro package into a new, improved one called Text Core, one of those improvements being compatibility with UI Toolkit and other Unity systems.

Considering this, in order to convert the TTF to a Font Asset compatible with UI Toolkit, you can just right-click the TTF asset in the **Project** panel and select **Create | Text | Font Asset**. This will create a new asset that will be the one we will be using to define the font of our UI Toolkit text.

Having solved this, let's create the UI Element for text, that is, **Label**:

1. Drag the **Label** icon from the **Library** pane of the UI Builder window to its **Hierarchy** panel. This will add a UI element capable of rendering not only an image in its background but also text (yes, you can add a background to the text if you want to).
2. As usual, set its **Position** and **Size**, this time putting it in the top-right corner of the screen. Remember you can simply drag the element; you don't need to set the specific coordinates by hand (although you can if you want to).
3. Change the **Text** property in the **Label** section of the **Inspector** to the needed text; in our case, this will be `Score: 0`:

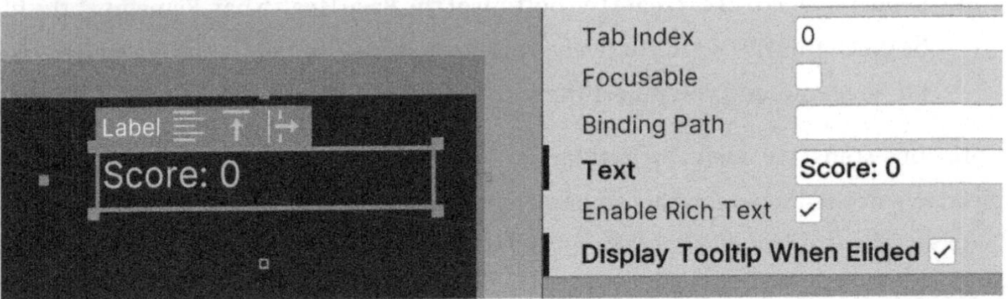

Figure 16.18: Setting the text to display

4. Drag the **Font** asset created just before these steps to the **Font Asset** property in the **Text** section of the **Inspector**. Don't confuse it with the **Font** property (the one above **Font Asset**). That one allows you to drag TTF assets directly, but that will be deprecated soon, so let's stick with the Unity-recommended approach.
5. If you notice your **Font** asset doesn't work, try putting it in the **UI Toolkit** | **Resources** | **Fonts & Materials** folder in the **Project** panel. While this shouldn't be necessary in the latest Unity versions, I've noticed that this solves these sorts of issues in the past. Also, there's a bug that makes the font not recognized sometimes, which can be fixed by deleting and recreating the **Label**.
6. Set the **Size** property of the **Text** section to any size that seems fit:

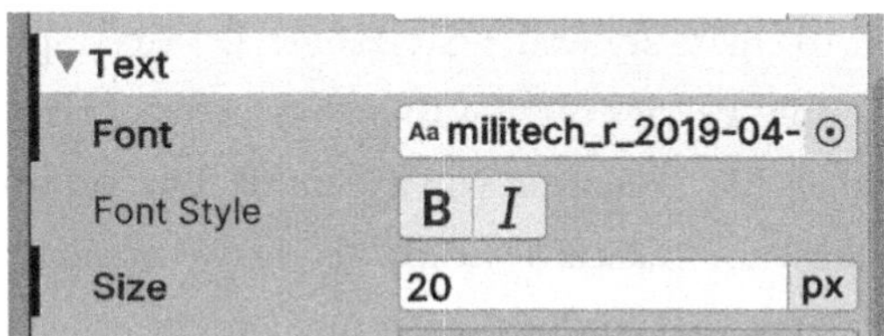

Figure 16.19: Setting the Text Font and Size of a Label

7. Repeat *steps 1* to *6* to add all the remaining **labels** to the UI.
8. One last thing we need to do is save, which can be simply done by pressing *Ctrl + S* (*Command + S* on Mac) or using the **File** | **Save** menu in the top-left part of the **Viewport** section in the **UI Builder** window. Note that previous versions of UI Toolkit had a bug where this could make the Viewport become corrupt. Please close it and reopen UI Builder again if this happens.

Now that we have created our UI, you probably noticed the need to repeat several settings to make several objects look the same, like our health bars and labels. While this is perfectly viable, we could improve our workflow greatly by reusing styles, and **Stylesheets** are the exact feature we need to accomplish that, so let's see them.

Creating UI Stylesheets

When creating UIs, you will find scenarios where several elements throughout the whole game will share the same style, for example, buttons with the same background, font, size, borders, etc. When creating the UI with uGUI, one way to not repeat configurations for each element would be to create a Prefab for the button and create instances (and Prefab variants where necessary). The problem is that here, we don't have GameObjects, hence there are no Prefabs, but luckily, we have **Stylesheets**.

Stylesheets are separated assets that contain a series of styling presets for our UI elements. We can define a set of styles (for example, background, borders, font, size, etc.) and apply those to several elements across different UI Elements. This way, if we change a style in a Stylesheet asset, all UI Elements using that style will change, in a similar way to how materials work.

There are several ways to create styles in a Stylesheet. One example is the selector system. This system allows you to apply a series of rules to pick which elements should have a style applied (if you are thinking this is like CSS, then you are right), but for now, let's stick with the basics, creating **Stylesheet Classes.** A **Class** is basically a style we can apply to any element via its name. For example, we can create a Class called `Button` and add that class to every button in the UI that we want to have that style. Please consider that the concept of Class here is something completely different from what a Class means in coding.

So, in this case, let's create a Class for all the labels in our UI so that the appearance of all of them can be modified by simply changing the style:

1. In the **StyleSheets** panel of the **UI Builder**, click the Add (+) button and click **Create New USS** (Unity StyleSheet). If that doesn't work, try restarting Unity; there's a bug in the current version of UI Toolkit that could cause this:

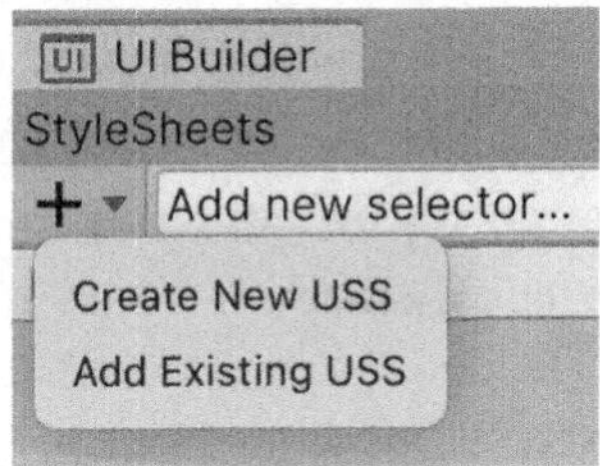

Figure 16.20: Creating a Unity StyleSheet

2. Name the USS as you like (`GameUSS` in my case) and save the file.
3. Select one of the label elements we have in our UI Document and look at the **Inspector**.
4. In the **StyleSheet** pane of the **Inspector**, type `HUDText` in the **Style Class List** input field, but don't press *Enter* yet.
5. Click the **Extract Inlined Styles to New Class** button. This will take all style modifications we did to our Label (position, size, font, etc.) and save them into a new style class called `HUDText`. You can observe that it was added to the list of classes applied to the element (those labels at the bottom of the **StyleSheet** section in the **Inspector**):

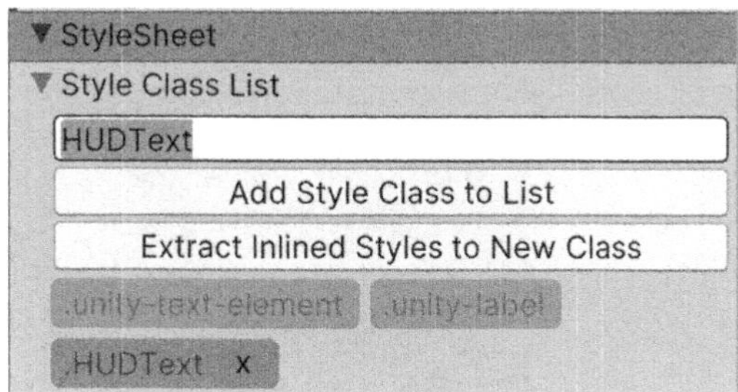

Figure 16.21: Extracting settings into a Style Class

With these steps, we have taken a Label with the style we need to apply to others and extract it into a class named **HUDText**. This way, we can simply add the class **HUDText** to other elements in our UI, and we can even add the same USS asset to other UI Documents (click the + button on the **StyleSheets** pane | **Add Existing USS**) to add this class to the elements in it.

Also, if you select the label again, you can notice how properties that previously were in bold now became normal again; that's because properties in bold represent changed properties, and we have extracted them, so the default values became whatever the style classes define. Luckily, not everything is extracted to the new USS Class; for example, the **Text** field still has our specific desired text, as it is highly unlikely you would want to put the same text in other objects.

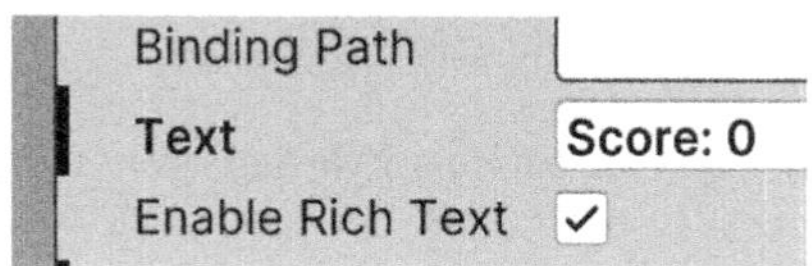

Figure 16.22: The Text property is bold, indicating it is different from the default values. On the other end, Enable Rich Text is not bold, meaning it follows the default values and the Classes ones

If you forgot some change in the style when extracting the class, you can easily modify it by selecting it in the **StyleSheets** section at the top-left part of the **UI Builder**. Then, select the class **HUDText** in the list. If you don't see it, try expanding the **GameUSS.uss** section.

Once selected, you can change it in the Inspector panel, similarly to when we change the properties of a UI Element:

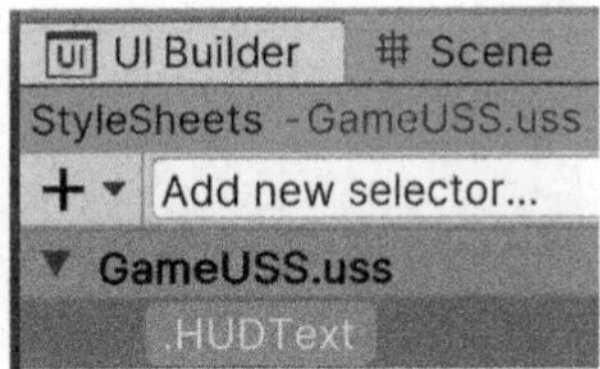

Figure 16.23: Selecting a Style Class for modification

This way, we have edited our `HUDText` class. If other elements had this class applied, they would have these changes applied also. Consider that another option would be to create the Class first, typing the name in the **StyleSheets** input field and pressing *Enter*, and then applying it to UI elements. This way, you will avoid needing to revert unwanted changes, but if you created the element first, it's convenient to have the option to revert:

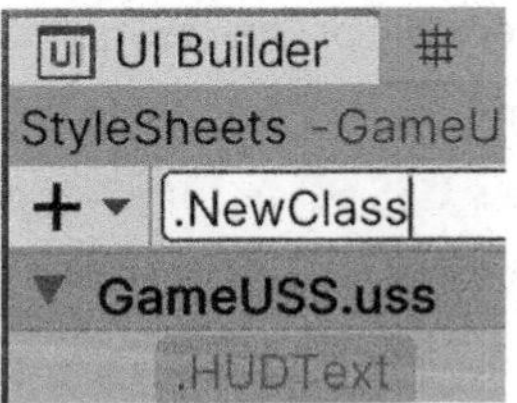

Figure 16.24: Creating a Style Class from scratch

Now that we have our Style Class, let's apply it to other elements by doing the following:

1. Select another label of our UI.
2. Drag the **HUDText** style from the **Stylesheet** pane at the top-left part of the UI Builder window all the way to our element on the Viewport. You can also drag it to the **Hierarchy** element if you prefer:

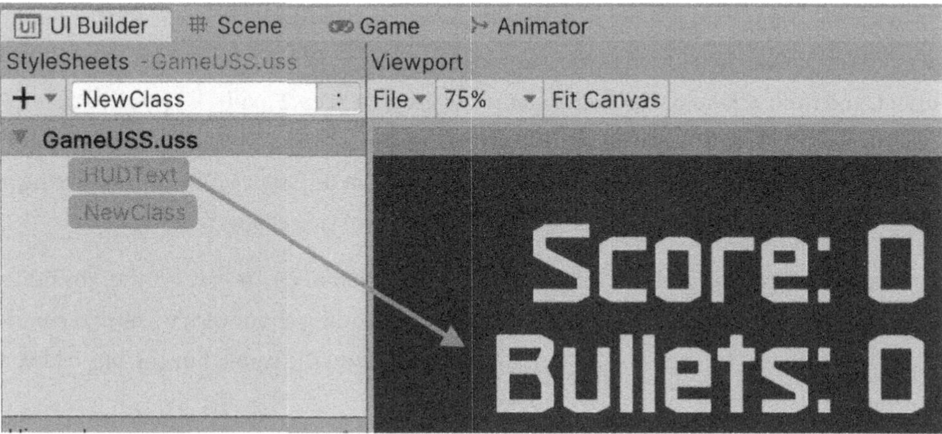

Figure 16.25: Applying a Class to an element

3. Select the **Label** and check how the **HUDText** class has been added to the **StyleSheet** section on the **Inspector**.

Now, consider that even if the element now has the class applied, the element itself has changes to the text we did in previous steps, overriding the style in our class. You can easily check this by selecting the class again (in the **StyleSheets** section at the top-left part of the **UI Builder** window) and changing any setting, like the size, and seeing how not all elements have changed. This shows how the override system works; the changes on the element take precedence over the ones in the classes it has applied.

If you want to remove these overrides, you can simply select the element (not the class), right-click on the overridden properties, and unset the changes by right-clicking and then selecting **Unset**. In the case of our **Label**, we can unset the entire **Text** section and probably the **Absolute** position (as the desired values are already contained in the class).

Figure 16.26: Reverting an override to use the default values of the Classes applied to the element

So, with these steps, we created a new **StyleSheet** asset and added it to the UI Document for it to use it. We have created a new Style Class in it, extracting the changes of an existing UI Element into it, and then adjusted which changes we wanted to keep. Finally, we applied that style to another element. With this, we just scratched the surface of the real power of StyleSheets. We can start doing things like combining different classes from different StyleSheets or using selectors to dynamically set styles, but that's outside the scope of this chapter.

Something interesting is that even if the documentation of UI Toolkit is pretty basic at the moment, all these advanced concepts can be learned by reading about CSS, the web technology that Unity based the stylesheet system on. It won't be exactly the same, but the basic idea and best practices still apply.

Now, the UI looks almost exactly the same as it does in *Chapter 15, User Interface Design*, but it won't behave in the same way. If you try changing the size of the viewport (selecting **GameHUD.uxml** in the Hierarchy and changing **Width** and **Height** as we did at the beginning of the chapter), you will see the UI won't adapt properly, so let's fix this.

Making a responsive UI

In this section, we are going to learn how to make the UI we created previously adapt to different screen sizes. We are going to discuss the following concepts:

- Dynamic positioning and sizing
- Dynamic scaling
- Using relative positions

Let's start by discussing how we can make the **Position** and **Size** of our objects adapt to the screen size.

Dynamic positioning and sizing

So far, we have used the **Left** and **Top** position attributes in order to specify the *x* and *y* positions of our elements with respect to the top-left corner of the screen, and then **Width** and **Height** to define the **Size**. While essentially that's all that's needed to define an object's position and size, it is not very useful in all cases, especially when we need to adapt to different screen sizes.

For example, if you need to place an object in the top-right corner of the screen, knowing its size is `100x100` pixels and the screen size is `1920x1080` pixels, we can put the **Left** and **Right** position attributes as `1820x980` pixels, and this will work, but only for that specific resolution.

So, what happens if the user runs the game at `1280x720` pixels? The object will be outside the screen! In uGUI, we used **Anchors** to solve this issue, but we don't have them here. Luckily, we have **Right** and **Bottom** to help.

As **Left** and **Top** attributes, **Right** and **Bottom** define distances from the parent element's sides (if there is no parent, then just from the entire screen). Right now, we have both set to **auto**, meaning that the position will be driven by **Left** and **Right** exclusively, but interesting things can happen by changing those values, so let's use them to make our **Score** and **Bullet** labels stick to the top-right corner of the screen instead, by doing the following:

1. Put the cursor in the bottom part of the UI in the **Viewport** until a white bar appears.
2. Drag that bar to resize the screen and see how our adapts (or not) to the different size.
3. Do the same on the laterals to also see how it adapts to different screen widths:

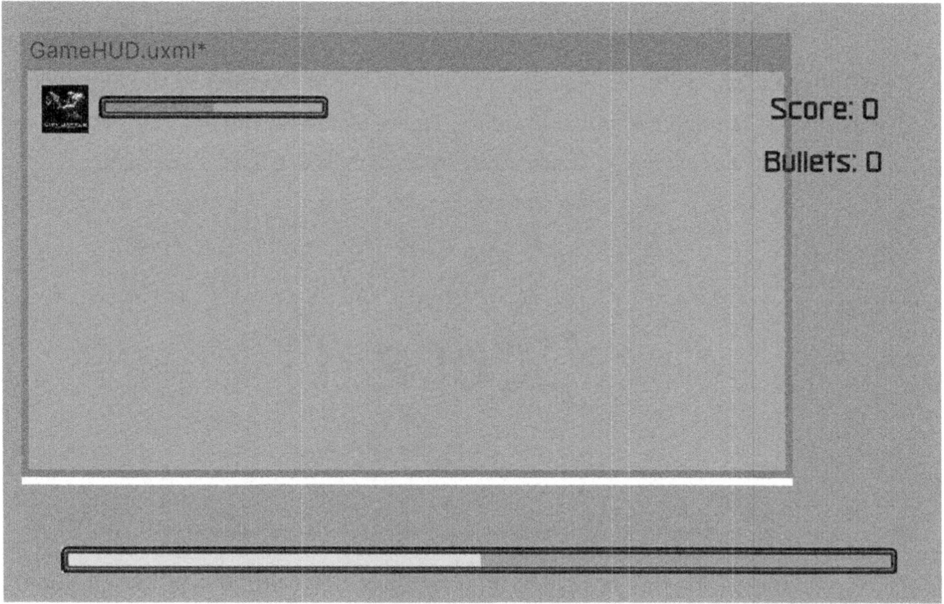

Figure 16.27: UI not adapting to different screen sizes

4. Select the score label on the **Viewport** and look at the **Inspector**.
5. Set the **Top** and **Right** values in the **Position** section to `30`.

6. Set the **Left** and **Bottom** values to auto by clicking the **px** button at the right of each attribute and selecting auto:

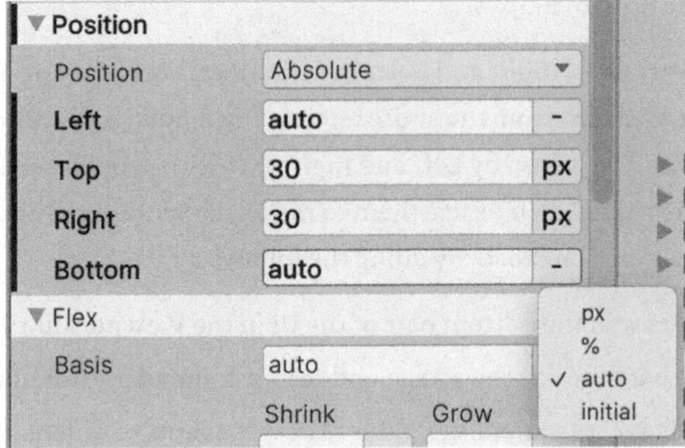

Figure 16.28: Changing the unit type of the Position attributes to auto mode

7. Notice the right and top golden-colored squares at the sides of the label became filled, while the left and bottom are hollow. This means that the left and bottom are in **auto** mode. You can also toggle **auto** mode by clicking those boxes if needed:

Figure 16.29: Toggling auto mode of our element position attributes

8. Try changing the size of the UI container again as we did in *steps 1* and *2* to see how our **Score** label is always aligned to the top-right corner.
9. Repeat *steps 4* to *6* for the **Bullets** label, this time setting the **Top** property to `140`.

What we did with these steps was essentially make the position of the object expressed as a distance in pixels against the **Top** and **Right** sides of the UI, or the top-right corner of the screen. We needed to set the other sides to auto mode, so they won't participate in the position calculations.

Now, we can use the **Position** attribute in other ways as well. As you might imagine by now, we can start combining **Left** and **Right** and **Top** and **Bottom** if we wish. In such cases, **Left** and **Top** will take precedence in defining the position, but then, what do **Right** and **Bottom** do? They define the size of the element.

For example, if we have an element with **Left** and **Right** attributes set to `100px` each and we are seeing our UI on a screen with a width of `1920` pixels, the final width of our element will be `1720` (`1920` minus `100` from **Left** minus `100` from **Right**). This way, the **Position** attributes represent the distances of the sides of our element from the sides of the screen (or the parent element).

Let's see this in action by making the bottom health bar adapt to the screen width while preserving its position relative to the bottom of the screen by doing the following:

1. Select the bottom health bar parent in the **Hierarchy**. Don't select it in the **Viewport** as you will only be selecting its filling or border.
2. Set **Left**, **Right**, and **Bottom** to `50px`.
3. Set **Top** to auto (click on the **px** button at the right and select **auto**).
4. In the **Size** section, set **Width** to **auto** also.
5. Set **Height** to `35px`:

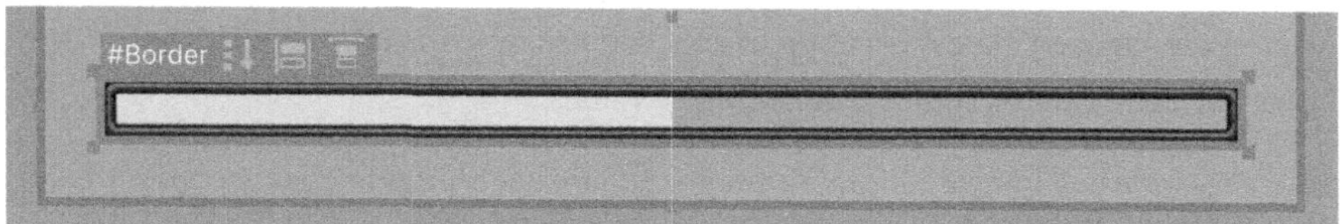

Figure 16.30: Making the player's base health bar adapt to the screen width

6. Change the size of the UI to see how it adapts.

With these steps, we defined the bar distance from the sides of the screen as `50` pixels for it to adapt to any screen width, while keeping the distance from the border and height fixed. We basically achieved the same behavior as split anchors in uGUI! Consider that we needed to set **Size**'s **Width** attributes to **auto** to let the **Left** and **Right** attributes drive the position; if you don't do that, the **Width** attributes take precedence and **Right** won't have any effect. I invite you to experiment with other combinations of **px**/**auto**.

One last trick we can do here is to use negative values in the **Left**, **Top**, **Right**, and **Bottom Position** attributes of the health bar borders to make the borders slightly bigger than the container and cover the filling borders. Just set **Left**, **Top**, **Right**, and **Bottom** to `-15px` in this case and remember to set both the **Size Width** and **Height** attributes to **auto**. You might want to reduce the **Height** of the bar container (not the border) a little bit, as now it will look thicker due to this change:

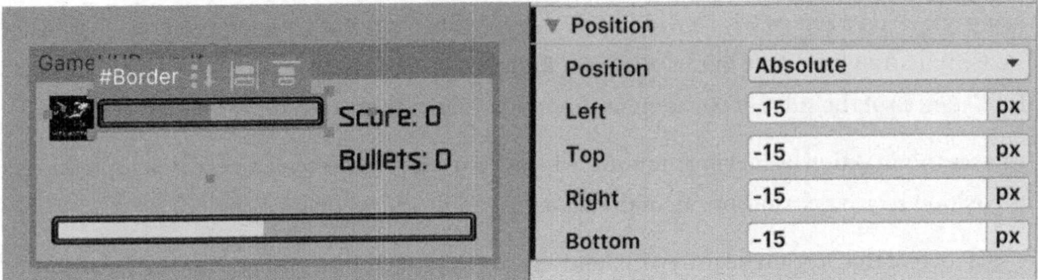

Figure 16.31: Using negative Position attributes to cover the filling

Another mode aside from **px** (pixels) or **auto** mode is the percentual (%) mode, which allows us to represent values as percentages relative to the screen (or parent element if present) size. For example, if we set **Top** and **Bottom** to 25%, this means that our element will be vertically centered with a size of 50% of the Screen height (remember to set **Height** mode to `auto` here). We could achieve the same result if we set **Top** to `25%`, **Bottom** to `Auto`, and **Height** to `50%`; as you can see, we can achieve a clever combination of those values.

In our case, we will use percentual values in our Life Bar fillings so that we can express its size in percentages. We need this as later in the code, we can specify the width of the bar as a percentage of the player's life (for example, a player with 25 life points and a max of `100` points has `25%` life).

Now, while we solved the positioning adaption to the screen size with the usage of the **Left**, **Top**, **Right**, and **Bottom** properties, we still didn't solve the dynamic sizing of the elements. With sizing this time, we are referring to screens with a different number of **DPI** (**dots per inch**), so let's discuss how we can achieve that with the **Panel Settings** asset.

Dynamic scaling

We used `1920x1080` as the UI base resolution to position and size our elements so that they look nice in that resolution. We also changed the UI size to see how the elements adapt their position with different screen sizes, and while that worked nicely, you can notice how the elements looked bigger or smaller while doing that.

While having a base reference resolution is good to design our UI, we should consider the sizing of elements on different resolutions, especially on screens with high DPI. Sometimes, you can have screens with higher resolution but the same physical size in centimeters. This means pixels are smaller in the ones with higher resolution, hence they have a larger DPI, so elements can seem smaller if not scaled properly.

In the past, we used the **Canvas Scaler** component of the **Canvas** to make the UI scale the size of its elements according to the screen resolution. We have the exact same settings here as in the **Panel Settings** asset referenced in our UI Document component, so let's configure it by doing the following:

1. Look for the **Panel Settings** asset in the **Project** panel and select it. Another option would be to select the `UI Document` GameObject in the Main Editor Hierarchy and click the asset referenced in the **Panel Settings** property:

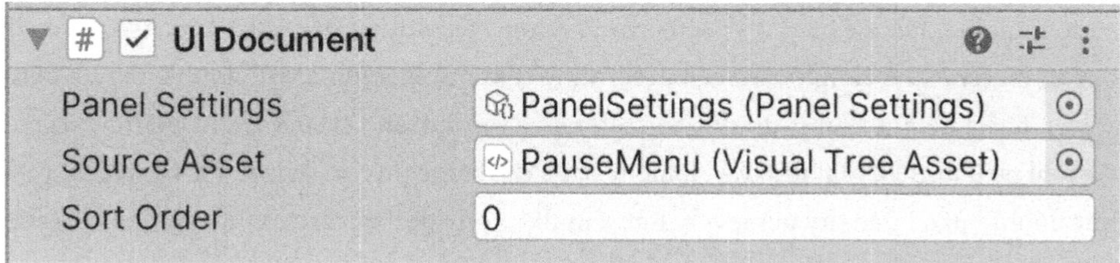

Figure 16.32: Panel Settings being referenced in the UI Document component

2. Set **Scale Mode** to **Scale With Screen Size.**
3. Set **Screen Match Mode** to **Match Width Or Height**.
4. Set the **Reference Resolution X** value to `1920` and **Y** to `1080`.
5. Move the **Match** slider all the way to the right, toward the end labeled **Height**:

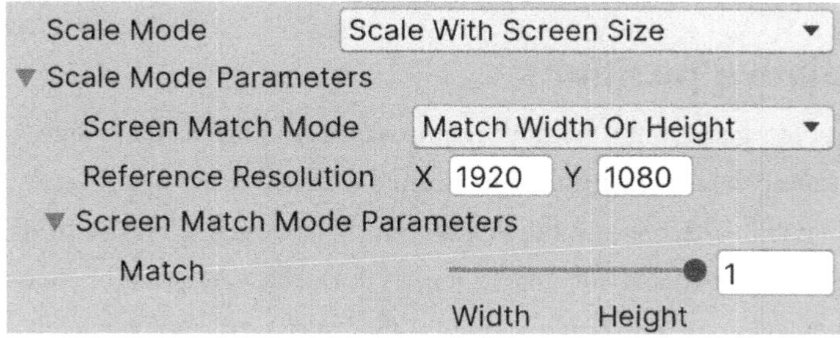

Figure 16.33: Setting the scaling of our UI

6. Observe how changing the height of the **Game** panel of the Unity editor will make the UI adapt its element sizes accordingly (change the whole Unity editor window height).

What we did with those changes was first set **Reference Resolution** to whatever resolution we designed our UI, in our case, `1920x1080`. Then, we set **Screen Match Mode** to allow us to scale our elements according to one of the sides, **Width**, **Height**, or a combination of the two if we prefer. In our case, we chose **Height**, mainly because our game is targeted at PC, where the screens are wide rather than tall. This means that on different screen widths, the elements will look the same size, but on different heights, the elements will be bigger or smaller.

With these settings, we can do some math to understand the values. If our screen is the same as the reference resolution (`1920x1080`), the element sizes will be the same as we specified in the size of our elements in pixels, so for the case of our player avatar, it will be `150x150` pixels. Remember that the physical size in centimeters depends on the DPI of the screen.

Now, imagine that we have a 4k screen, meaning a resolution of `3840x2160`. As we specified that our UI matches via **Height**, we can determine that our elements will double in size because our screen has a height that is double the reference resolution (`2160` divided `1080`). Our player avatar will be `300x300`, making the element have the same physical size in a 4k screen, double size but double pixel density achieves that. Finally, consider an ultra-wide standard resolution of `2560×1080` (yes, very wide screens), in which case the elements will be the same size as the only change is the width; the only difference is that the elements will have more horizontal separation due to the screen size. I know these calculations can be confusing but keep experimenting with the values of the **Panel Settings** and **Game View** sizes to understand them better.

Great, now we really have the same HUD. We could start applying the concepts seen so far to the **Options** menu, but let's take the opportunity to do it in a different way, using **relative positions**, a way to create a flow of elements where the elements' positions depend on each other.

Using relative positions

In the HUD of our game, each element requires its own **Position** and **Size**, and the different elements' positions can be resized and repositioned without affecting others. We might observe the case of the player health bar and the avatar, but the changes would be trivial in this case. There are other cases where this is not that trivial, as in the case of a **List** of elements (for example, a list of matches to join in a multiplayer game) that needs to adapt vertically or horizontally, and here is where **relative positions** help us.

Relative positions allow us to make the positions of the elements relative to each other; in a way, the position of one element will depend on the position of the previous one, and that one to its previous, and so on, forming a chain or **flow**. This works like **Vertical** and **Horizontal Layouts** on uGUI. In our case, we will make the **Pause** label and the **Options** and **Exit** buttons of our options menu be vertically aligned and centered along its parent using those.

Let's start creating the menu by doing the following:

1. Create a new UI Document (click the + button after going to **Project View | UI Tookit | UI Document**) and call it `OptionsMenu`. We can work on the previous UI Document but let's keep those pieces of UI separated for easy activation and deactivation, and general assets organization.
2. Double-click the asset to set it as the current UI being edited by the **UI Builder**.
3. Select the root object (**OptionsMenu.uxml** in the **Hierarchy**) and set the **Width** and **Height Inspector** properties to `1920x1080` pixels.
4. Create a new GameObject with the UI Document component (**GameObject | UI Toolkit | UI Document**) and drag the asset for this object to render it (as we did with the HUD created earlier in the chapter).
5. Double-click the UI Document asset to open the **UI Builder** window to edit it, and in that window, drag a new **Visual Element** to the **Hierarchy** or **Viewport** and call it `Container` (the **Name** property in the **Inspector** in **UI Builder**).
6. Set the **Left**, **Right**, **Top**, and **Right Position** attributes to `0px`.
7. Set **Position** to **Absolute**.
8. Set **Width** and **Height** in the **Size** section to **auto**. This will make the container fit the entire screen.
9. Drag a new **Visual Element** to be a child of the **Container** and call it `Background`.
10. Leave **Position** as **Relative** this time.
11. Set **Size**'s **Width** and **Height** to `500px`.
12. Set the **Background Image** of the **Background** object to use the same background sprite used in the previous chapter.
13. Select the **Container** parent object (not the **Background**).
14. In the **Inspector**, set the **Align Items** property of the **Align** section to `center`, which is the third button. If you hover the mouse over the icons, they will show their names in a tooltip.

15. Set **Justify Content** to **Center** (second button):

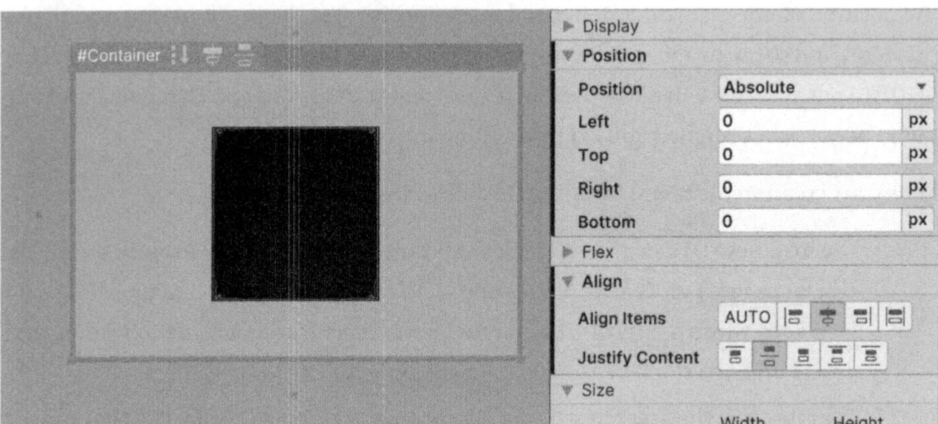

Figure 16.34: Preparing the UI background to host elements inside

16. Change the size of the UI using the white bars at the sides to see how the background is always centered.

Even if we have only one element, we can start seeing how the relative positions work. First, we created an empty object that will always adapt to the screen size, allowing us to make the children's elements depend on the full screen size. Then, we created an image element with a fixed size, but with relative position, meaning its position will be calculated by the parent container. Finally, we told the **Container** to make its child objects aligned to its horizontal and vertical center, so the background immediately became centered whatever the screen size is. When working with absolute positions, the Align properties didn't work, so this is one of the first benefits of **relative** positioning.

But **relative** positioning becomes more powerful with multiple elements, so let's add the **Label** and **Buttons** to our **Background** element to explore this concept further by doing the following:

1. From the **Library** pane at the bottom left of **UI Builder**, drag a **Label** and two **Button** elements inside the **Background** in the **Hierarchy**. Note that there's a bug where sometimes, even if you drag and drop a new element inside the desired object, it won't be its child. Just drag the one created in the Hierarchy this time:

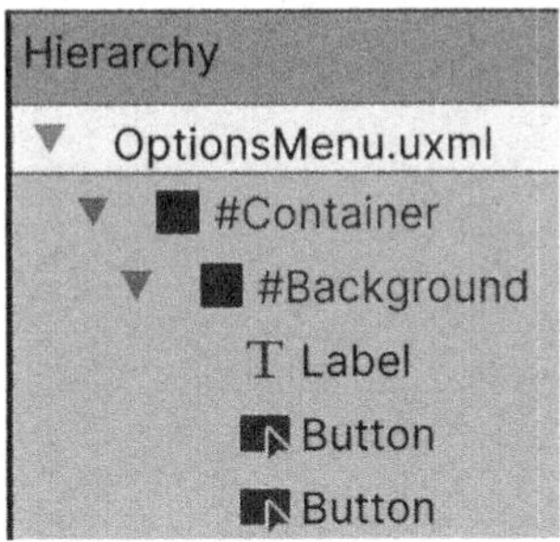

Figure 16.35: Adding elements inside the menu background

2. Observe how by default, the elements became vertically aligned one on top of the other due to the relative position's default settings:

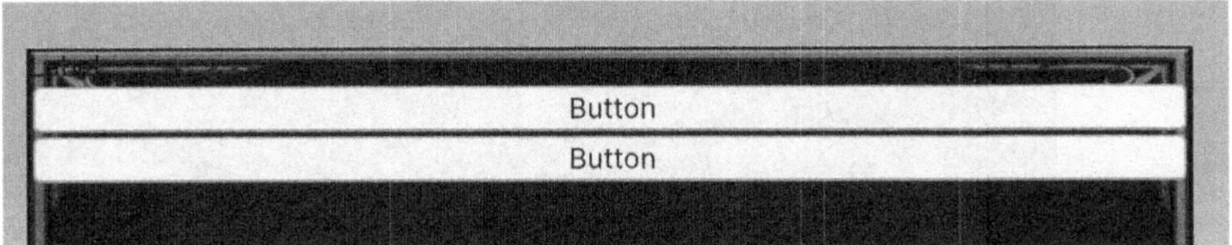

Figure 16.36: Automatic relative vertical positioning

3. Select the **Background** element and set **Justify Content** to `space-around` (fifth button). This will spread the elements along the background.

4. Set **Align Items** to **center** (third option) to center elements horizontally:

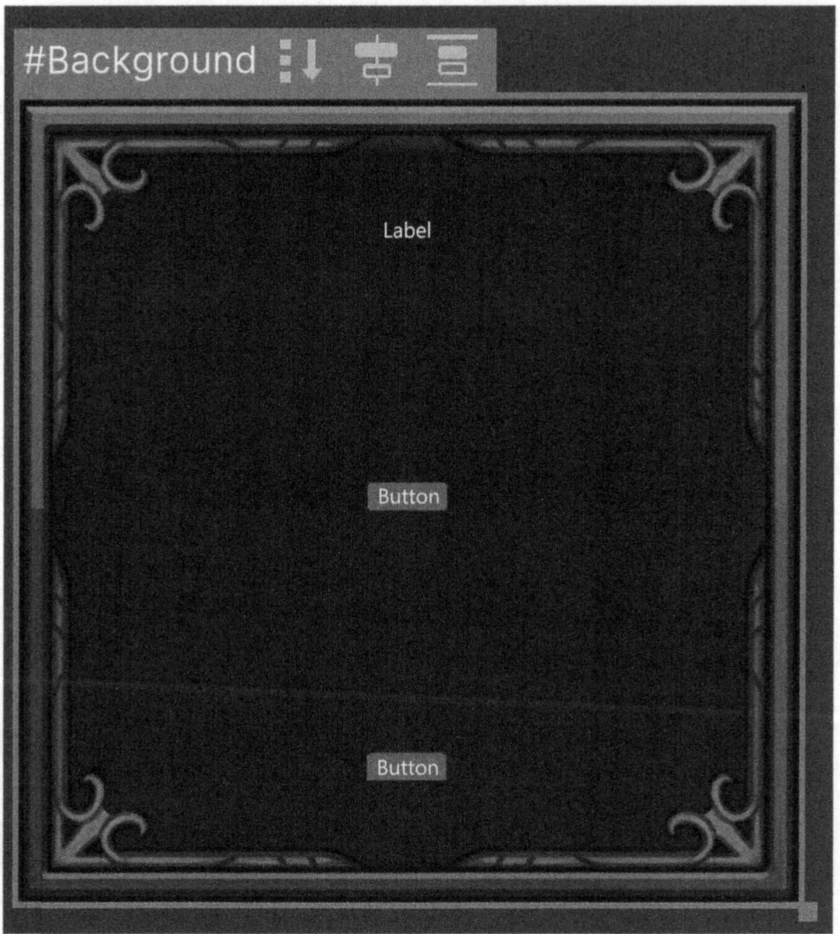

Figure 16.37: Automatic relative vertical positioning

There is a similar mode for **Justify Content** called "space-between" (the fourth button in Justify Content) that will also spread the elements along the vertical axis but won't leave space on top of the first element or the bottom of the last one. Also, **Align Items** has an option called **stretch** (the fifth option) that, like **center**, will center elements horizontally, but also stretch them instead of respecting each element's width. I recommend experimenting with the different aligning modes to discover all opportunities.

5. Set the **Label Text**'s **Font** and **Size** attributes to whatever seems fit. In my case, I used the imported font and a size of `60px`. Remember to also set the **Text** to `Pause`.
6. Set the **Buttons Background Image** to use the same used for the button in the last chapter.
7. Set the **Color** property of the **Background** section to a color with no alpha. You can achieve this by clicking the color rectangle and reducing the **A** channel in the color picker to `0`. The idea of this color is to act as a background for our image, but we don't need it, so we made it completely transparent.
8. Set the Buttons **Text**'s **Font**, **Size**, and **Color** to whatever seems fit to you. In my case, I'm using `50` and gray color.
9. In the **Margin and Padding** section, set **Padding** to have some spacing between the text and the borders of the button. In my case, `30px` did the trick:

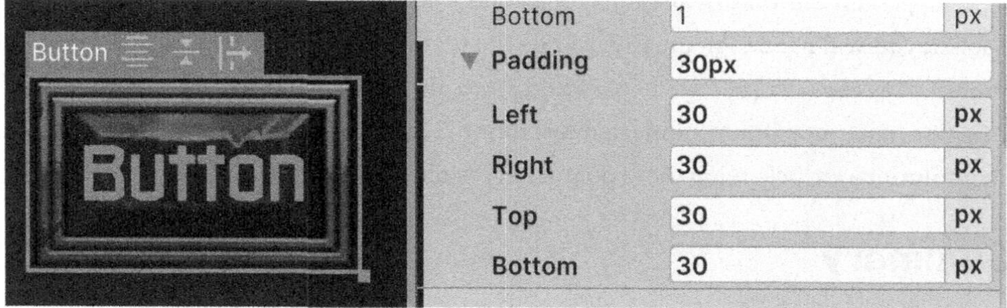

Figure 16.38: Adding inner padding to the button contents (the text in this case)

10. Also, set the **Top** and **Bottom Padding** of the **Background** to allow some space between the borders of the window and its elements. In my case, it is `40px` each.

As you can see, we changed different settings to set the size of the elements dynamically, like font sizes and paddings, and the relative system along with the align settings took the role of determining the position of the elements automatically. We can rearrange the order of the elements by dragging them in the Hierarchy and they will be accommodated automatically. We could have also set the size of the elements with the **Size** property, and we can also apply some offsets if desired using the **Position** properties, but I encourage you to see how these properties behave in Relative mode on your own.

One last setting I want you to explore is the **Direction** attribute of the **Flex** section, which, as you can imagine, will determine the orientation the elements will follow, vertically from top to bottom or bottom to top, and horizontally from left to right or right to left. For example, you could set **Direction** to distribute the elements from left to right using the **row** mode (third button) and make the background wider to have a horizontal options menu if you wish.

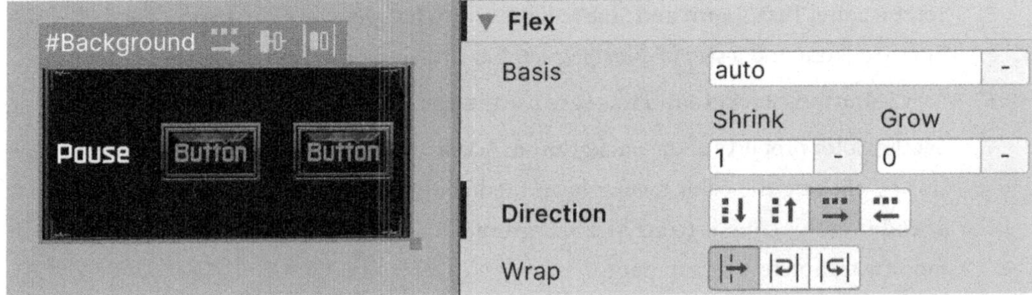

Figure 16.39: Changing to a vertical orientation of elements

As a side note, you might notice that the images for the background and buttons will look bigger than the options menu done in the last chapter. That's because the **Pixels per Unit** setting that we changed on the **Texture** assets to control the scaling of the textures won't take effect in UI Toolkit; you will need to manually change the texture file size in any image editor to give it its proper size. The best practice here would be to always create the images with a size that will look fine in our maximum supported resolution. Usually, this is `1920x1080` on PC but note that 4k resolutions are becoming more popular every day.

Summary

In this chapter, we had an introduction to the key concepts of UI Toolkit and how to create UI Documents and Stylesheets. Regarding UI Documents, we learned how to create different elements like images, text, and buttons and how to position and size them using different methods, like absolute and relative positioning, and pixel or percentual units. Also, we saw how to make the UI adapt to different sizes using different combinations of **Position** attributes. Finally, we learned how to use USS Stylesheets to share styles between different elements to easily manage our whole UI skinning.

Essentially, we learned again how to make UIs with a different system. Again, please note that this system is still in the experimental phase and is not recommended for real production projects. We used all these concepts to recreate the same UI created in *Chapter 15, User Interface Design.*

In the next chapter, we are going to see how to add animations to our game to make our character move. We will also see how to create cut-scenes and dynamic cameras.

17

Creating Animations with Animator, Cinemachine, and Timeline

Sometimes, we need to move objects in a predetermined way, such as with cutscenes, or specific character animations, such as jumping, running, and so on. In this chapter, we will go over several Unity animation systems to create all the possible movements of objects we can get without scripting.

In this chapter, we will examine the following animation concepts:

- Using Skinning Animation with Animator
- Scripting animations
- Creating dynamic cameras with Cinemachine
- Creating cutscenes with Timeline

By the end of this chapter, you will be able to create cutscenes to tell the history of your game or highlight specific areas of your level, as well as create dynamic cameras that are capable of giving an accurate look to your game, regardless of the situation.

Using Skinning Animation with Animator

So far, we have used what are called static meshes, which are solid three-dimensional models that are not supposed to bend or animate in any way (aside from moving separately, like the doors of a car).

We also have another kind of mesh, called skinned meshes, which are meshes that have the ability to bend based on a skeleton, so they can emulate the muscle movements of the human body. We are going to explore how to integrate animated humanoid characters into our project to create enemy and player movements.

In this section, we will examine the following skeletal mesh concepts:

- Understanding skinning
- Importing skinned meshes
- Integration using Animator Controllers
- Using Avatar Masks

We are going to explore the concept of skinning and how it allows you to animate characters. Then, we are going to bring animated meshes into our project to finally apply animations to them. Let's start by discussing how to bring skeletal animations into our project.

Understanding skinning

In order to get an animated mesh, we need to have four pieces, starting with the mesh that will be animated, which is created the same way as any other mesh. Then, we need the skeleton, which is a set of bones that will match the desired mesh topology, such as the arms, fingers, feet, and so on. In *Figure 17.1*, you can see an example of a set of bones aligned with our target mesh:

Figure 17.1: A ninja mesh with a skeleton matching its default pose

Once the artist has created the model and its bones, the next step is to do skinning, which is the act of associating every vertex of the model to one or more bones. This way, when you move a bone, the associated vertices will move with it. In *Figure 17.2*, you can see the triangles of a mesh being painted according to the color of the bone that affects it as a way to visualize the influence of the bones. You will notice blending between colors, meaning that those vertexes are affected differently by different bones to allow the vertexes near an articulation to bend nicely. Also, *Figure 17.2* illustrates an example of a two-dimensional mesh used for two-dimensional games, but the concept is the same:

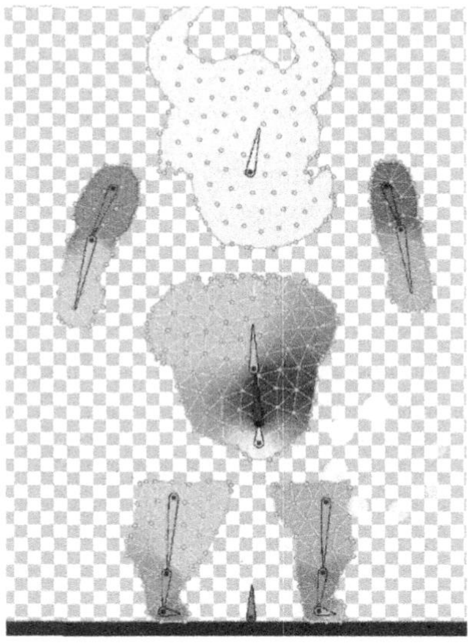

Figure 17.2: Mesh skinning weights visually represented as colors

Finally, the last piece you need is the actual animation, which will simply consist of a blending of different poses of the mesh bones. The artist will create keyframes in an animation, determining which pose the model needs to have at different moments, and then the animation system will simply interpolate between them. Basically, the artist will animate the bones, and the skinning system will apply this animation to the whole mesh.

In order to get the four parts, we need to get the proper assets containing them. The usual format in this scenario is **Filmbox (FBX)**, which we used previously to import 3D models. This format can contain every piece we need—the model, the skeleton with the skinning, and the animations—but usually those pieces will come split into several files to be re-utilized.

Imagine a city simulator game where we have several citizen meshes with different aspects and all of them must be animated. If we have a single FBX per citizen containing the mesh, the skinning, and the animation, it will cause each model to have its own animation, or at least a clone of the same one, repeating them. When we need to change that animation, we will need to update all the mesh citizens, which is a time-consuming process. Instead of this, we can have one FBX per citizen, containing the mesh and the bones with the proper skinning based on that mesh, as well as a separate FBX for each animation, containing the same bones that all the citizens have with the proper animation, but without the mesh. This will allow us to mix and match the citizen FBX with the animation's FBX files. You may be wondering why both the model FBX and the animation FBX must have the mesh. This is because they need to match in order to make both files compatible. In *Figure 17.3*, you can see how the files should look:

Figure 17.3: The animation and model FBX files of the package we will use in our project

Also, it is worth mentioning a concept called retargeting. As we said before, in order to mix a model and an animation file, we need them to have the same bone structure, which means the same number of bones, hierarchy, and names.

Sometimes, this is not possible, especially when we mix custom models created by our artist with external animation files that you can record from an actor using motion-capture techniques, or just by buying a mocap (motion-capture) library, a set of animations captured on real humans using specific mocap hardware. In such cases, it is highly likely that you will encounter different bone structures between the one in the mocap library and your character model, so here is where retargeting kicks in. This technique allows Unity to create a generic mapping between two different humanoid-only bone structures to make them compatible. In the next section, *Importing skeletal animations*, we will see how to enable this feature.

Now that we understand the basics behind skinned meshes, let's see how we can get the model's assets with bones and animations.

Importing skeletal animations

We can download a character model by searching for it in the Asset Store, under the **3D** | **Characters** | **Humanoids** section. You can also use external sites, such as the website called Mixamo, to download them. Note that sometimes you will need to download several packages because sometimes packages come only with the skinned model, and others with animation only. Luckily the one we downloaded already contains the skinned meshes and the animations.

In my package content, I can find the animation's FBX files in the `Animations` folder and the FBX file of my model called `Polyart_Mesh` in the `Mesh` folder. Remember that sometimes you won't have them separated like this, and the animations may be located in the same FBX as the model, if any animations are present at all. Now that we have the required files, let's discuss how to properly configure them.

Let's start selecting the **Model** file and checking the **Rig** tab. Within this tab, you will find a setting called **Animation Type**, as shown in *Figure 17.4*:

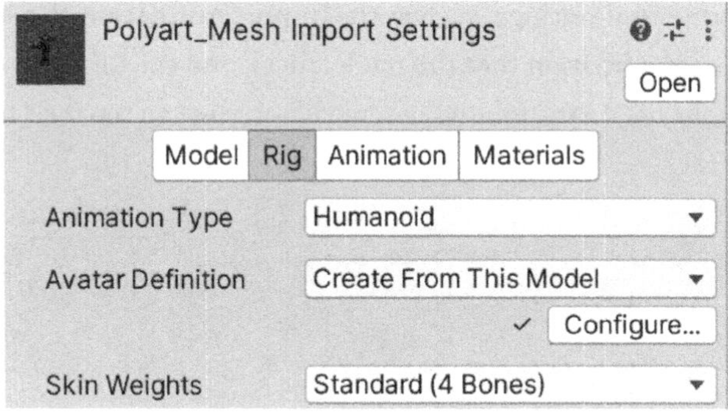

Figure 17.4: The Rig properties

This property contains the following options:

- **None**: Mode for non-animated models; every static mesh in your game will use this mode.
- **Legacy**: The mode to be used in old Unity Projects and models; do not use this in new projects.

- **Generic**: A new animation system that can be used in all kinds of models but is commonly used in non-humanoid models, such as horses, octopuses, and so on. If you use this mode, both the model and animation FBX files must have the exact same bone names and structure, thereby reducing the possibility of combining animation from external sources.
- **Humanoid**: New animation systems designed to be used in humanoid models. It enables features such as retargeting and **Inverse Kinematics** (**IK**). This allows you to combine models with different bones than the animation because Unity will create a mapping between those structures and a generic one, called the avatar. Take into account that sometimes the automatic mapping can fail, and you will need to correct it manually; so, if your generic model has everything you need, I recommend you stick to **Generic** if that's the default configuration of the FBX.

In my case, the FBX files in my package have the modes set to **Humanoid**, so that's good, but remember, only switch to other modes if it is absolutely necessary (for example, if you need to combine different models and animations). Now that we have discussed the **Rig** settings, let's talk about the **Animation** settings.

In order to do this, select any animation FBX file and look for the **Animation** tab in the Inspector window. You will find several settings, such as the **Import Animation** checkbox, which must be marked if the file has an animation (not the model files), and the **Clips** list, where you will find all the animations in the file. In the following screenshot, you can see the **Clips** list for one of our animation files:

Figure 17.5: A Clips list in the Animation settings

An FBX file with animations usually contains a single large animation track, which can contain one or several animations. Either way, by default, Unity will create a single animation based on that track, but if that track contains several animations, you will need to split them manually. In our case, our FBX contains a single animation, but in order to learn how to split it in other cases, do the following:

1. From the **Clips** list, select any animation that you want to recreate; in my case, I will choose `Run_guard_AR`.

2. Take a look at the **Start** and **End** values below the animation timeline and remember them; we will use them to recreate this clip:

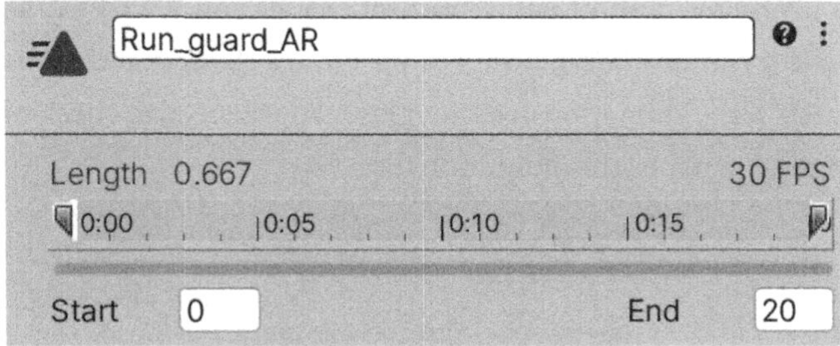

Figure 17.6: The clip settings

3. Use the + button to create a new clip and select it.
4. Rename it to something similar to the original using the input field that currently says something like `Take 001`. In my case, I will name it `Run`.
5. Set the **End** and **Start** properties with the values we needed to remember in *step 2*. In my case, I have `20` for **End** and `0` for **Start**. This information usually comes from the artist that made the animation, but you can just try the number that works best or simply drag the blue markers in the timeline on top of these properties.
6. If an animation needs to loop, check the **Loop Time** checkbox to guarantee that. This will make the animation repeat constantly, which is required in most animations like **Walk** or **Run**. If not, the animation will play once and never repeat:

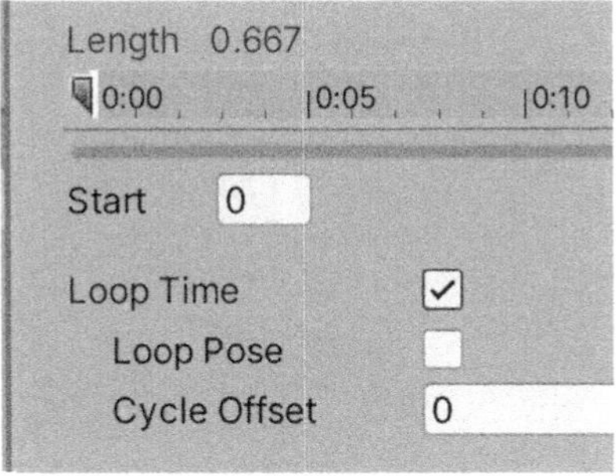

Figure 17.7: Looping the animation

7. Preview the clip by clicking on the bar titled for your animation (**Run**, in my case) at the very bottom of the Inspector window and click on the **Play** button. You can see the default Unity model in some cases, but you can see your own by dragging the model file to the preview window because it is important to check whether our models are properly configured. If the animation does not play, you will need to check whether the **Animation Type** setting matches the animation file:

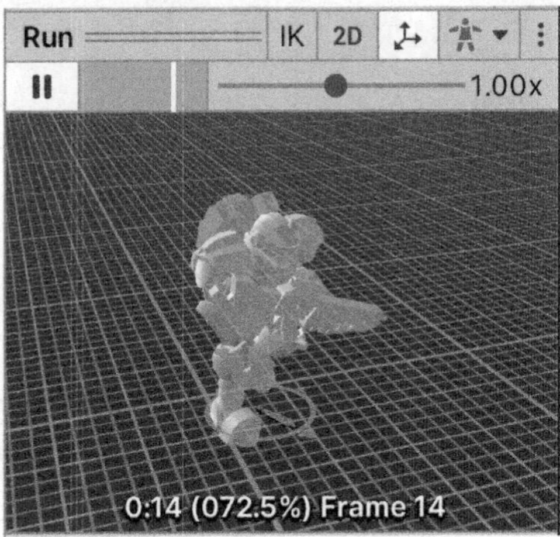

Figure 17.8: Animation preview

8. Open the animation asset (the FBX) by clicking the arrow on its left, and check the sub-assets. You will see that there is an asset with the same title as your animation:

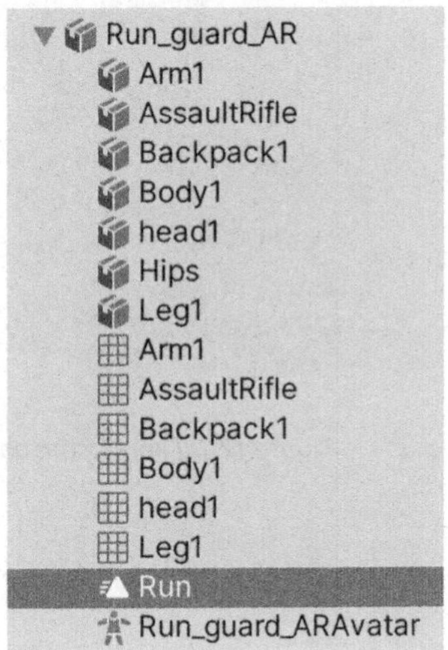

Figure 17.9: Generated animation clips

9. Remember that there are plenty of other settings aside from the **Init** frame, **End** frame, and **Loop Time**. The character I downloaded required other settings like **Root Transform Rotation**, **Root Transform Position**, and **Mask** to make it work, and the mileage may vary between character packages. If you are recreating an existing animation, consider copying all settings as they were, or just use the default one. These mentioned settings are beyond the scope of the book, but you can always consult them in the Unity documentation at `https://docs.unity3d.com/Manual/class-AnimationClip.html`.

Now that we have covered the basic configuration, let's learn how to integrate animations.

Integration using Animation Controllers

When adding animations to our characters, we need to think about the flow of the animations, which means thinking about which animations must be played, when each animation must be active, and how transitions between animations should happen. In previous Unity versions, you needed to code that manually, generating complicated scripts of C# code to handle complex scenarios; but now, we have **Animation Controllers**.

Animation Controllers are a state machine-based asset where we can diagram the transition logic between animations with a visual editor called **Animator**. The idea is that each animation is a state and our model will have several of them. Only one state can be active at a time, so we need to create transitions in order to change them, which will have conditions that must be met in order to trigger the transition process. Conditions are comparisons of data about the character to be animated, such as its velocity, whether it's shooting or crouched, and so on.

So, basically, an Animation Controller or state machine is a set of animations with transition rules that will dictate which animation should be active. Let's start creating a simple Animation Controller by doing the following:

1. Click the + button under the **Project** view, click on **Animator Controller**, and call it `Player`. Remember to locate your asset within a folder for proper organization; I will call mine `Animations`.
2. Double-click on the asset to open the **Animator** window. Don't confuse this window with the **Animation** window; the **Animation** window serves to create new Animations, but for now, we will stick with the downloaded ones.

3. Search for the **Idle** animation clip of your character in the **Animations** folder of your characters package and drag it into the **Animator** window. In my case it was called **Idle_guard_ar**. Remember to drag the sub-asset, not the entire file. This will create a box in the Controller representing the animation that will be connected to the entry point of the Controller, indicating that the animation will be the default one because it is the first one that we dragged. If you don't have an **Idle** animation, I encourage you to download one from the Asset Store, maybe searching in other characters' packages. We will need at least one **Idle** and one **walking/running** animation clip:

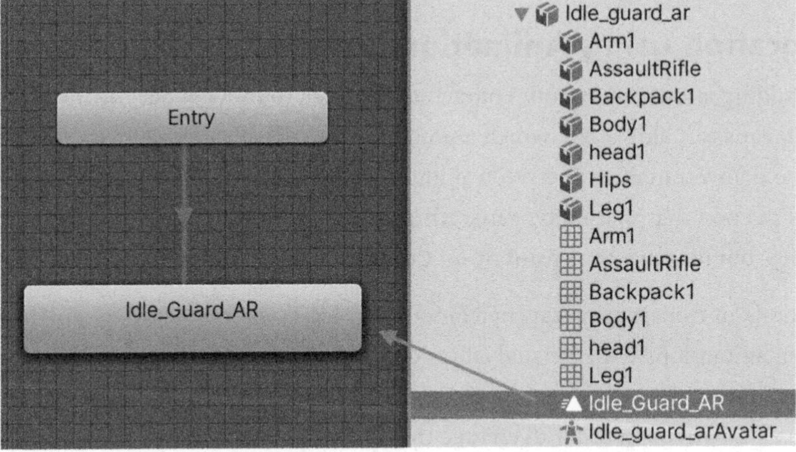

Figure 17.10: Dragging an animation clip from an FBX asset into an Animator Controller

4. Drag the running animation in the same way, which is **Run_guard_AR** in my case.
5. Right-click on the **Idle** animation box in the **Animator** window, select **Make Transition**, and left-click on the **Run** animation. This will create a transition between **Idle** and **Run**.
6. Create another transition from **Run** to **Idle** in the same way:

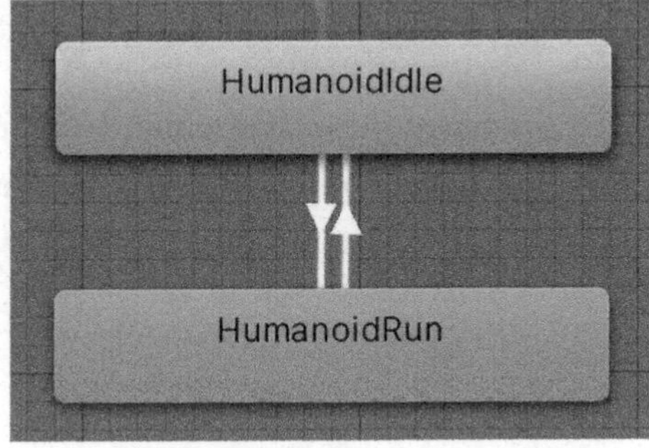

Figure 17.11: Transitions between two animations

Transitions must have conditions in order to prevent animations from swapping constantly, but in order to create conditions, we need data to make comparisons. We will add properties to our Controller, which will represent data used by the transitions. Later, in the *Scripting Animations* section of this chapter, we will set that data to match the current state of our object. But for now, let's create the data and test how the Controller reacts to different values. In order to create conditions based on properties, do the following:

1. Click on the **Parameters** tab in the top-left part of the **Animator** window. If you don't see it, click on the button that looks like an eye crossed by a line to display the tabs. The icon will change to an uncrossed eye.
2. Click on the + button and select **Float** to create a number that will represent the velocity of our character, naming it `Velocity`. If you missed the renaming part, just left-click on the variable and rename it:

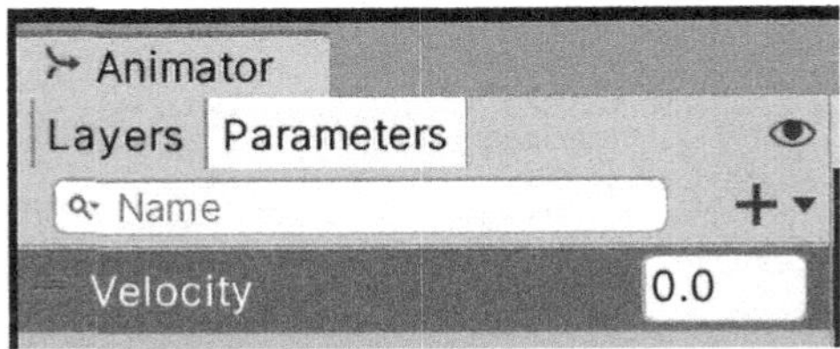

Figure 17.12: The Parameters tab with a float Velocity property

3. Click on the **Idle to Run** transition (the white line with an arrow in the middle) and look at the Conditions property in the Inspector window.
4. Click on the + button at the bottom of the list, which will create a condition that will rule the transition. The default setting will take the first parameter of our animator (in this case, it is **Velocity**) and will set the default comparer, in this case, **Greater**, to a value of `0`. This tells us that the transition will execute from **Idle** to **Run** if **Idle** is the current animation and the velocity of the Player is greater than `0`. I recommend you set a slightly higher value, such as `0.01`, to prevent any float rounding errors (a common CPU issue). Also, remember that the actual value of **Velocity** needs to be set manually via scripting, which we will do in this chapter's *Scripting animations* section:

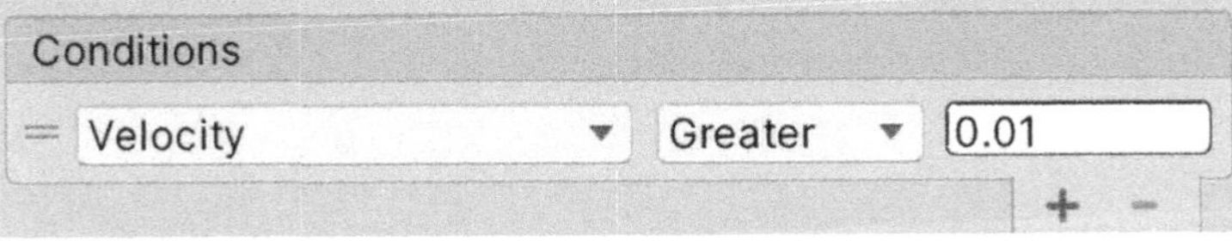

Figure 17.13: Condition to check whether the velocity is greater than 0.01

5. Do the same to the **Run** to **Idle** transition, but this time, change **Greater** to **Less** and again set the value to `0.01`:

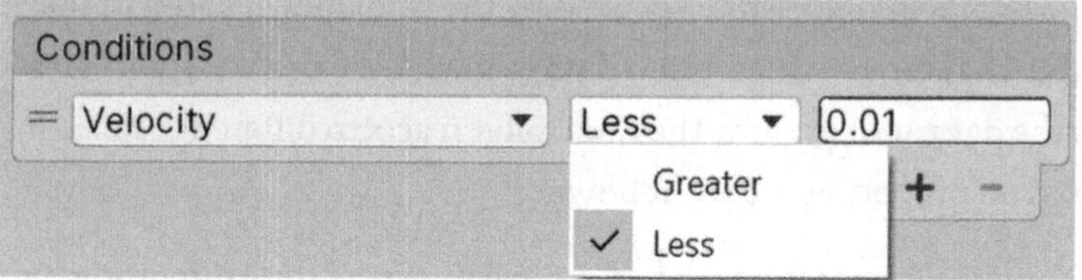

Figure 17.14: Condition to check whether a value is less than 0.01

Now that we have our first Animator Controller set up, it's time to apply it to an object. In order to do that, we will need a series of components. First, when we have an animated character, rather than a regular Mesh Renderer, we use the **Skinned Mesh Renderer**. If you select your player or enemy characters and view their children, GameObjects, you will see the Skinned Mesh Renderer in one or more of them:

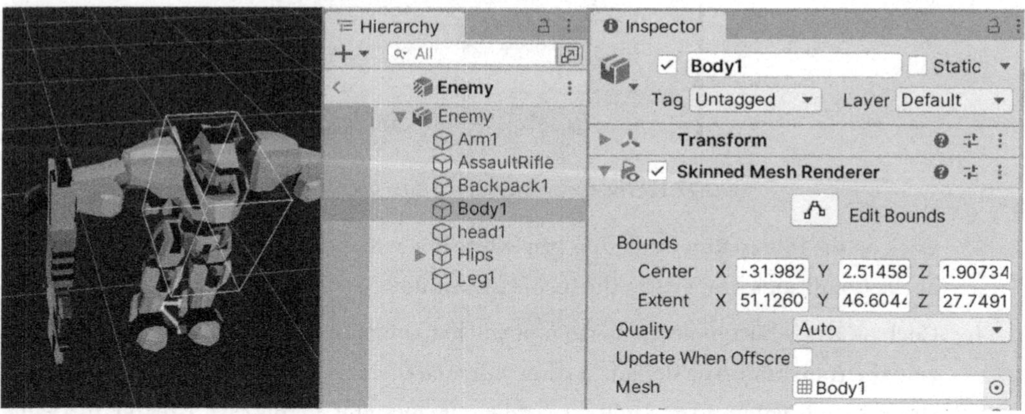

Figure 17.15: A Skinned Mesh Renderer component

This component will be in charge of applying the bones' movements to the mesh. If you search the children of the model, you will find some bones; you can try rotating, moving, and scaling them to see the effect, as shown in the following screenshot. Bear in mind that your bone hierarchy might be different from mine if you downloaded another package from the Asset Store:

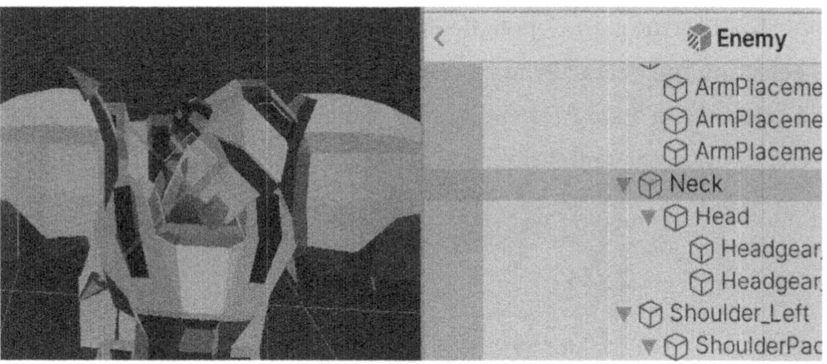

Figure 17.16: Rotating the neckbone

The other component that we need is **Animator**, which is automatically added to the skinned meshes at its root GameObject. This component will be in charge of applying the state machine that we created in the Animator Controller if the animation FBX files are properly configured, as we mentioned earlier. In order to apply the Animator Controller, do the following:

1. Select the player in the **Hierarchy** and locate the **Animator** component in the root GameObject.
2. Click on the circle to the right of the **Controller** property and select the **Player** controller we created earlier. You can also just drag it from the **Project** window.
3. Make sure that the **Avatar** property is set to the avatar inside the FBX model of the character (`Polyart_Mesh` being the FBX model in our example project); this will tell the animator that we will use that skeleton. You can identify the avatar asset by its icon of a person, as shown in the following screenshot. Usually, this property is correctly set automatically when you drag the FBX model to the scene:

Figure 17.17: Animator using the Player controller and the robot avatar

4. Without stopping the game, open the Animator Controller asset again by double-clicking it and selecting the character in the **Hierarchy** pane. By doing this, you should see the current state of the animation being played by that character, using a bar to represent the current part of the animation:

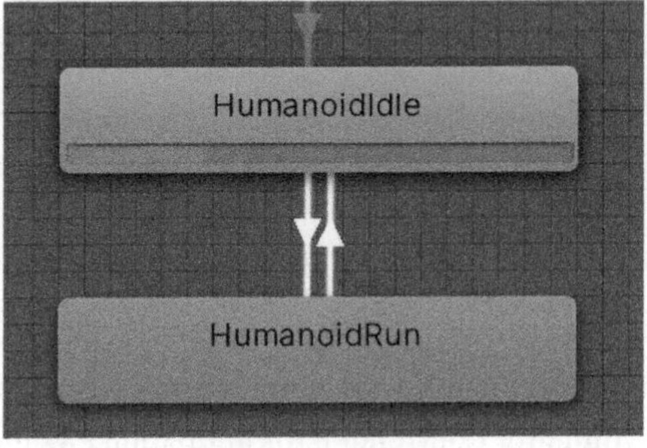

Figure 17.18: The Animator Controller in Play mode while an object is selected, showing the current animation and its progress

5. Using the **Animator** window, change the value of **Velocity** to `1.0` and see how the transition will execute. Feel free to disable the **WaveSpawners** to test this, given they will probably kill the player before we can safely do so:

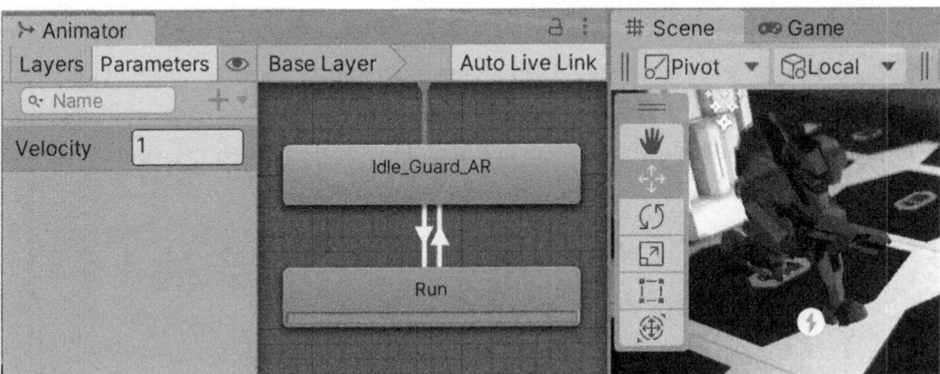

Figure 17.19: Setting the velocity of the Controller to trigger a transition

6. Depending on how the **Run** animation was set, your character might start to move instead of executing the animation in place. This is caused by root motion, a feature that will move the character based on the animation movement. Sometimes, this is useful, but due to the fact that we will fully move our character using scripting, we want that feature to be turned off. You can do that by unchecking the **Apply Root Motion** checkbox in the **Animator** component of the **Character** object, as seen in *Figure 17.17*.

7. You will also notice a delay between changing the Velocity value and the start of the animation transition. That's because, by default, Unity will wait for the original animation to end before executing a transition, but in this scenario, we don't want that. We need the transition to start immediately. In order to do this, select each transition of the Controller, and in the Inspector window, uncheck the **Has Exit Time** checkbox. When this property is checked, a hidden condition for the transition to execute is waiting for the animation to end. But with this unchecked, the transition can execute at any moment during the animation, which we want, given that we don't want any delay between the player being idle and running:

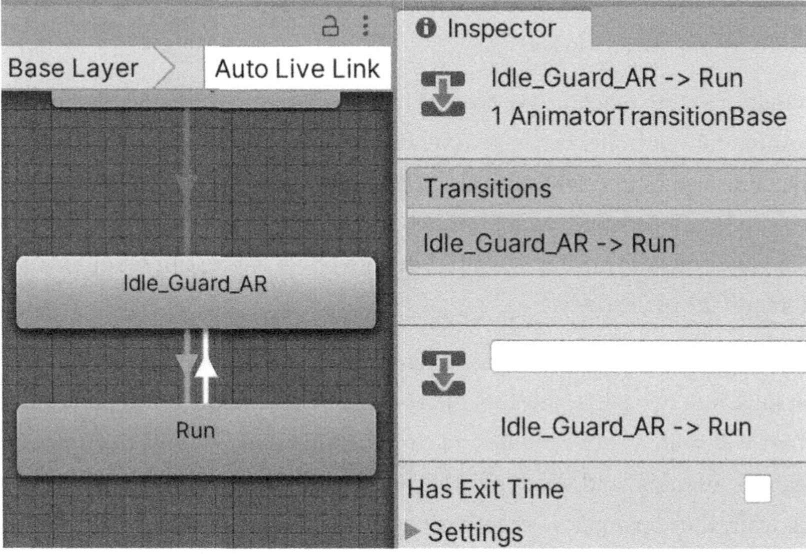

Figure 17.20: Disabling the Has Exit Time checkbox to execute the transition immediately

You can start dragging other animations into the Controller and create complex animation logic, such as adding jump, fall, or crouched animations. I invite you to try other parameter types, such as a Boolean, that use checkboxes instead of numbers. Also, as you develop your game further, your Controller will grow in its number of animations. To manage that, there are other features worth researching, such as **Blend Trees** and sub-state machines, but that's beyond the scope of this book.

In this section, we learned how to integrate animation clips into our character through Animator Controllers. We added all needed animations and created the necessary transitions between them to react to the game circumstances, like the character velocity changes.

Now that we have integrated the idle and run animations, let's integrate the shoot animation, which requires us to use **Avatar Masks**.

Using Avatar Masks

At first, this case seems as simple as dragging a shoot animation and making transitions that use the `Shooting` Boolean parameter as a condition. Consider, however, that we can shoot while walking and while running, so that leads to two shooting animations, **Walking Shooting** and **Idle Shooting**. If you follow this logic, you can think of shooting while falling, jumping, etc., which leads to a greater number of animation combinations. Imagine having different shooting animations for different weapons! Luckily, we have a better solution: a way to combine several animations, using Avatar Masks.

The animations state machine we created in the Animator Controller is what is called a **layer**, and an Animator Controller can have several layers. This means that we can have more than one state machine in an Animator Controller. There are several reasons to use this, but the common one is to combine layers with Avatar Masks, an asset that allows us to make a specific Animator Controller layer or state machine to affect certain bones, so we can set different state machines for different parts of the body.

We can use this to solve the shooting scenario we discussed previously, splitting our player animation logic into two parts, the upper part of the body, and the lower part. The idea is that the lower part will switch between idle and running animations, while the upper part can switch between idle, running, and shooting. This allows us to have scenarios where the lower part is running while the upper part is shooting, or the lower part is idle and the upper part also, or any combination we can imagine.

Let's start by creating the second layer by doing the following:

1. Download a shooting animation from the internet or the Asset Store if you don't have one already. In our case we already have several shooting animations, and we are going to pick the one called `Idle_Shoot_ar`.
2. In the Animator Controller, do a single click in **Base Layer** and rename it **LowerBody**. If you don't see the layers list, click the **Layers** button at the top-left part of the **Animator** window:

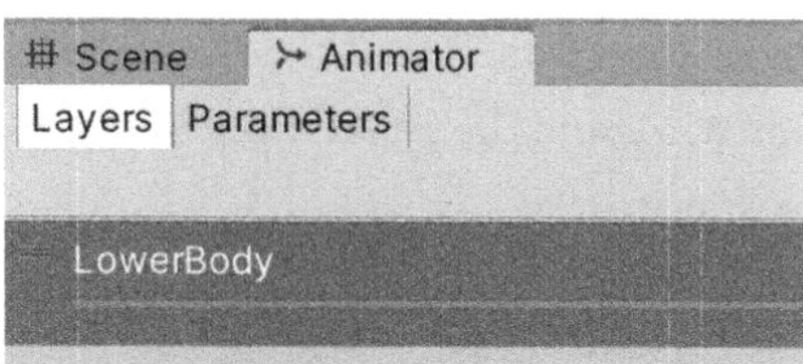

Figure 17.21: Renaming the base layer

3. Add a second layer to the Controller using the + button and rename it `UpperBody`.
4. Select the layer and add the **Idle**, **Run**s, and **Shoot** animations to it, connecting the states with transitions. Remember to uncheck **Has Exit Time** in each transition:

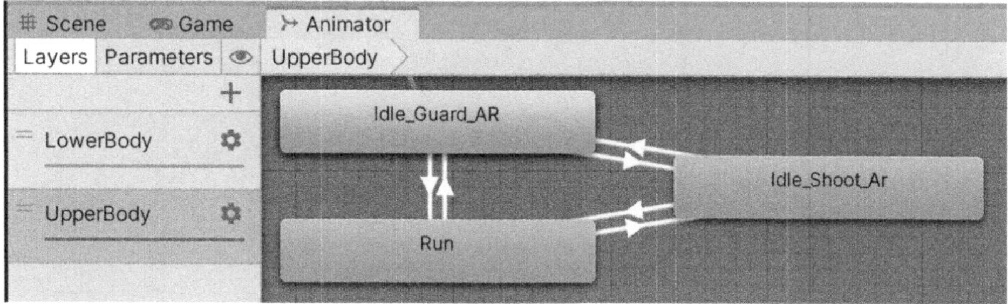

Figure 17.22: UpperBody state machine

5. Add the same transition logic between **Idle** and **Run** used before, using **Velocity** as the parameter for the conditions, as before.
6. For the shooting transitions, create a Boolean parameter called **Shooting**:

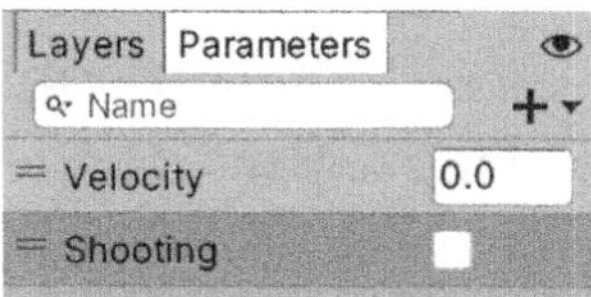

Figure 17.23: Shooting Boolean

7. Make both transitions to shooting (**Idle** to **Shoot** and **Run** to **Shoot**) execute when the **Shooting** Boolean is **true**.

8. Make the return transition from **Shoot** to **Idle** when the **Shooting** Boolean is false and **Velocity** is less than `0.01`, and the return from **Shoot** to **Run** when **Shooting is true** and **Velocity** is greater than `0.01`:

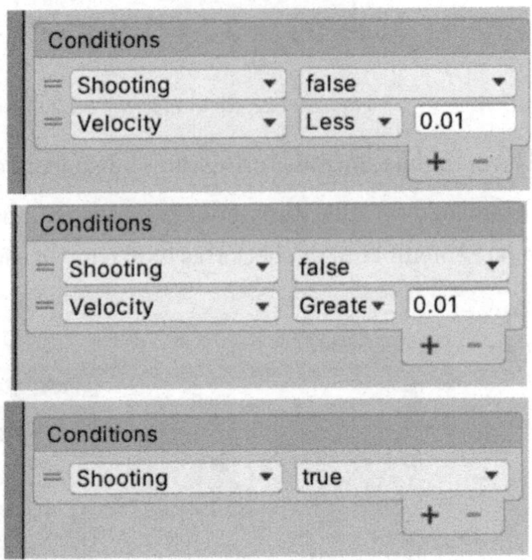

Figure 17.24: The Shoot to Idle transition at the top, the Shoot to Run transition in the middle, and both the Idle to Shoot and Run to Shoot transitions at the bottom

Now that we have the layers created, let's apply the Avatar Masks to them:

1. Create an Avatar Mask using the + button in the **Project View**, and name the first one `UpperBodyMask`.
2. Select the `UpperBodyMask` asset in the **Inspector** and click the arrow on the left where it says **Humanoid to expand this section.**
3. Click the lower parts of the body displayed in the **Inspector** until they become red:

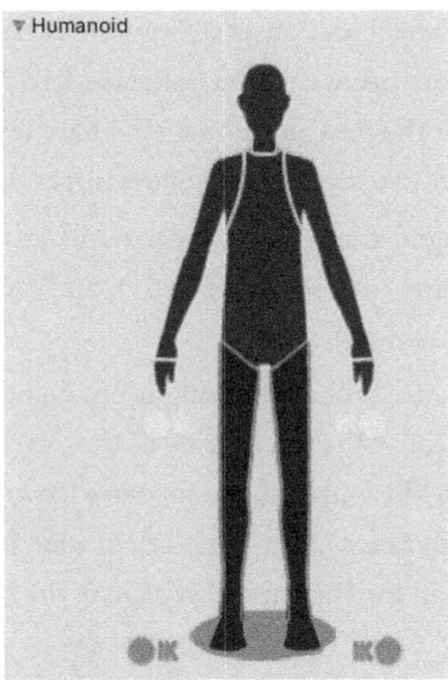

Figure 17.25: UpperBodyMask asset configs

4. In the Animator Controller, select the **UpperBody** layer and click on the wheel to its right to display some options.
5. Click at the circle at the right of the **Mask** property and select the **UpperBodyMask** asset in the window that appears.
6. Click again at the wheel of the **UpperBody** layer and set its **Weight** to 1. Since the two layers are affecting different parts of the body, both of them have the same priority. In scenarios where two layers affect the same bones, the weight is used to calculate which one has more influence:

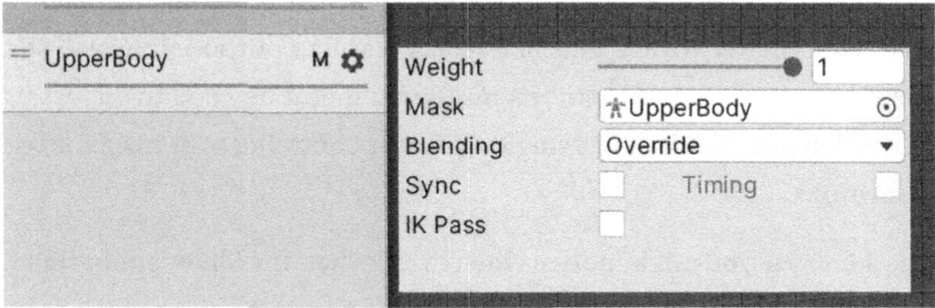

Figure 17.26: Setting the Weight and the Mask of a layer

7. Click again on the wheel and observe how the **Blending** parameter is set to **Override**, meaning that the bones that this layer affects (driven by the Avatar Mask) will override whatever animation the base layer has—the base layer, in this case, being **LowerBody**. That's how this layer takes ownership of the upper part of the body.
8. Test this again, changing the values of the parameters while in **Play** mode. For example, try checking **Shooting** and then set **Velocity** to `1`, and then to `0`, to finally uncheck **Shooting**, and see how the transitions execute.
9. You might notice that our character might not be pointing in the right direction when shooting. This is because the orientation of the character is modified for this **Shoot** animation compared to **Idle** and **Run**, but the **Base Layer** still has ownership of that. We can make the **UpperBodyMask** control the orientation by clicking the circle at the bottom of the human figure in the **Humanoid** section of the Avatar Mask until it becomes green:

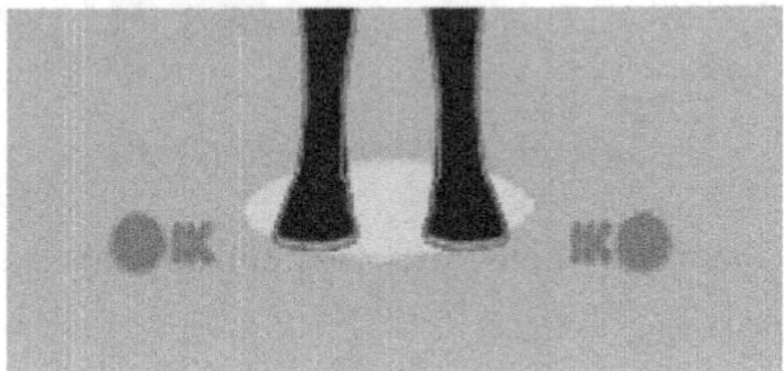

Figure 17.27: Giving the mask authority over the player orientation

The issue here is that you will now see the character moving the feet sideways when running and shooting. There's no easy solution here other than to modify the original animations. In this case, this character has Idle, Idle Shooting, Run and Run Shooting animations, so it clearly has been created without having Avatar Masks in mind, instead just having all possible animation combinations. An alternative is to find another package that works better with Avatar Masks. For learning purposes, we will stick with this, but note that Avatar Masks are not a must; you might be good to go just using all possible animation permutations in a single Animator Controller state machine with all the needed transitions.

Another issue you might notice when firing when the Shoot animation is playing is that the muzzle effect will stay in the original position of the weapon. Since the weapon mesh is affected by the skinning animation but not its Transform position, the muzzle cannot follow it. In order to solve this, you can reparent the Muzzle Effect to one of the bones of the weapons—in this case, the GameObject called Trigger_Right, one of the children of the Hips GameObject. Not all animations will have bones for the weapons, so this is one of the possible scenarios you could face:

Figure 17.28: Reparenting the Muzzle Effect to one of the weapon's bones

10. Remember to apply the same changes we made to our player to the enemy, which means adding and setting the Player Animator Controller to its **Animator** component and changing the `Muzzle effect` parent.

Now that we have a fully functional Animator Controller, let's make it reflect the player movement through scripting.

Scripting animations

With our player's Animator ready, it is time to do some scripting to make these parameters be affected by the actual behavior of the player and match the player's. In this section we will do the following to achieve this:

- Script shooting animations
- Script movement animations

Let's start making our characters execute the **Shoot** animation when necessary.

Scripting player shooting animations

So far, we have created a behavior to shoot each time we press a key, but the animation is prepared for sustained fire. We can make our `PlayerShooting` script shoot a bullet every X number of seconds while we keep the **Fire** key pressed to match the animation, instead of having to press the key repeatedly.

Let's see how to do this:

1. In the **PlayerShooting** script, add a public float field called **fireRate**, which will measure the seconds between bullet spawns. Remember to set this value in the **Inspector** of the player.
2. Change the **OnFire** method to the code seen in *Figure 17.29*. The idea is to start a repeating action when we press the key and stop it when we release the key. We are using **InvokeRepeating** to repeatedly execute a function called **Shoot,** which we will be creating in the next step. The rate of execution will be controlled by the **fireRate** field we created in *step 1*:

```
public void OnFire(InputValue value)
{
    if (value.isPressed)
    {
        InvokeRepeating("Shoot", fireRate, fireRate);
    }
    else
    {
        CancelInvoke();
    }
}
```

Figure 17.29: OnFire changes needed for sustained fire

3. Add the **Shoot** method as seen in *Figure 17.30* to our **PlayerShooting** script. This is essentially the same code we had before in the **OnFire** method but separated in a function, so we can execute it several times with the **InvokeRepeating** function:

```
private void Shoot()
{
    if (bulletsAmount > 0 && Time.timeScale > 0)
    {
        bulletsAmount--;

        GameObject clone = Instantiate(prefab);

        clone.transform.position = shootPoint.transform.position;
        clone.transform.rotation = shootPoint.transform.rotation;

        muzzleEffect.Play();
        shootSound.Play();
    }
}
```

Figure 17.30: OnFire changes needed for sustained fire

If you try these changes now, you will notice the bullets will never stop shooting once we click the **Fire** button. Even worse, as we press repeatedly, more and more bullets will be shot. With some debugging or educated guessing, you might figure out that the **CancelInvoke** method is not being executed. The reason behind this is that the **Fire** input mapping is not configured by default to inform us about the release of keys, just when they were pressed. Luckily the solution is pretty simple:

1. Double-click the **SuperShooter** inputs asset, the one we created in *Chapter 6, Implementing Movement and Spawning*, that contains all the inputs our game supports.
2. Select the **Fire** action in the **Actions** list (the middle column).
3. Click the + button at the right of the **Interactions** section and click **Press**.

4. Set the **Trigger Behavior** of the **Press** section to **Press And Release**:

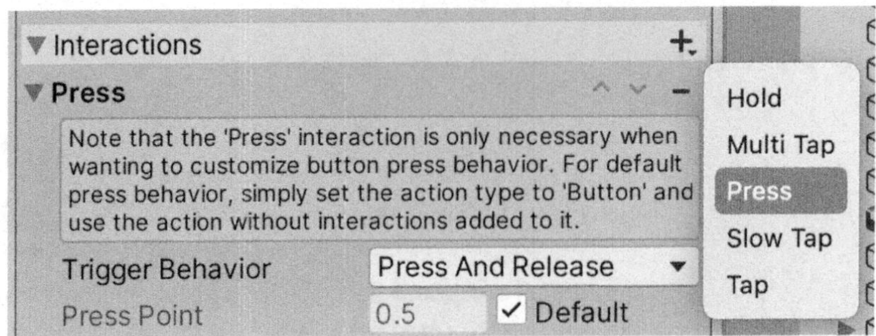

Figure 17.31: OnFire changes needed for sustained fire

5. With this we have configured the Input to not only tell us when the key was pressed but also when it was released, making our **CancelInvoke** method execute now.

Now that we have our constant fire behavior, we can do the following to make the animation reflect this:

1. Add a reference to Animator using **GetComponent** in **Awake** and cache it in a field, as seen in *Figure 17.32*:

```
Animator animator;

private void Awake()
{
    animator = GetComponent<Animator>();
}
```

Figure 17.32: Caching the Animator reference

2. Add the line `animator.SetBool("Shooting", value.isPressed);` at the beginning of the **OnFire** method:

```
public void OnFire(InputValue value)
{
    animator.SetBool("Shooting", value.isPressed);

    if (value.isPressed)
    {
```

Figure 17.33: Setting the Shooting animation parameter to reflect input

3. The idea behind this change is to make sure the **Shooting** animation parameter reflects the state of the fire key, meaning that the `Shoot` animation will play as long as the **Fire** button is pressed, and will stop when we release it.

One thing you will notice is that the bullets are still being shot from the player's chest because our **ShootPoint** GameObject, the one that defines the shooting position, is not positioned in front of the weapon. Just re-parent the **ShootPoint** to the weapon bone (**Trigger_Right** in our case) and position it to be in front of the weapon. Remember to make the forward vector (the blue arrow in the **Scene** view) point along the weapon:

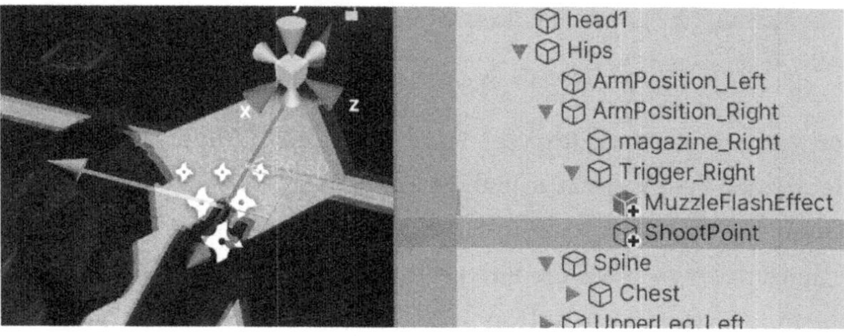

Figure 17.34: Adapting the ShootPoint to follow the animation

For the Visual Scripting version, in order to make the bullet get shot constantly, you should change the **Input** nodes of **PlayerShooting** like in *Figure 17.35*:

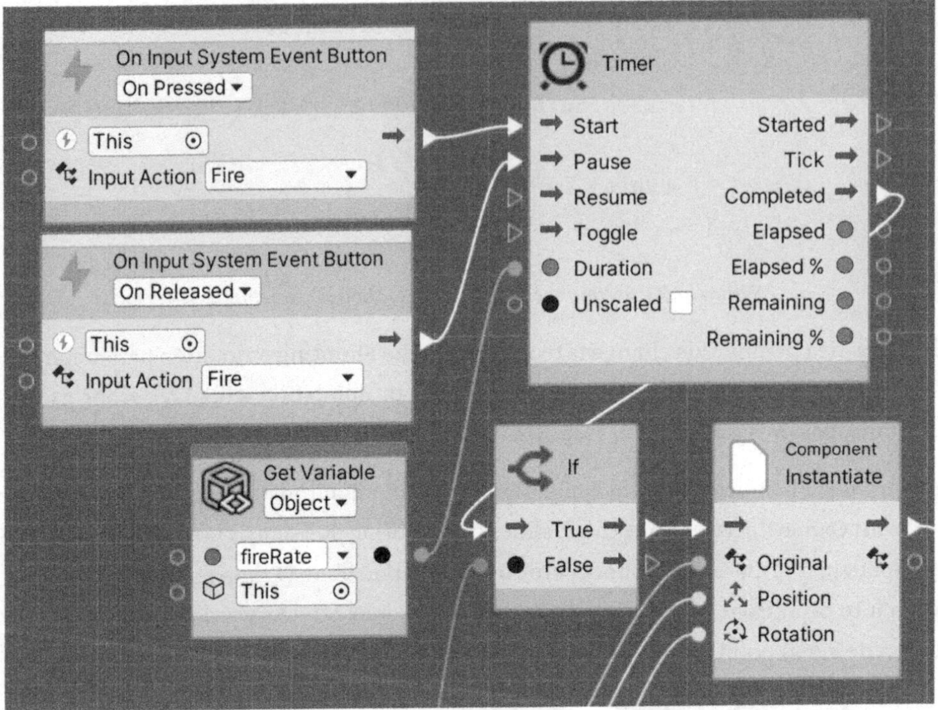

Figure 17.35: Creating a shoot loop

As you can see, we used a new node called **Timer**. The idea of **Timer** is similar to the **Wait For Seconds** node we used before, because it allows us to delay the execution of one action. One of the main differences is that it allows us to cancel the timer before it executes again, meaning we can start the timer when we press the **Fire** key, and stop it when we release it. We did that by connecting the **InputSystemEventButton** node that has the **OnPressed** mode to the **Start** pin of the **Timer**, and the one with the **OnReleased** mode to the **Pause** pin. Also, we created a new variable called **fireRate** and connected it to the **Duration** pin of the **Timer**, so we need to specify how much time the **Timer** will wait before instantiating our bullets. See how we connected the **Completed** pin of the **Timer** to the **If** node that checks if we have enough bullets to instantiate; we used to connect to the input node here before.

One little missing detail here is that when we press a key, time will pass (**fireRate**) and then a bullet will be instantiated, but then nothing else. We need to connect the end of the **Bullet** shoot sequence (the **AudioSource: Play** node in this case) of nodes again to the **Start** pin of the **Timer** to create a spawn loop. That loop will be interrupted when we release the key, to prevent it from being executed forever:

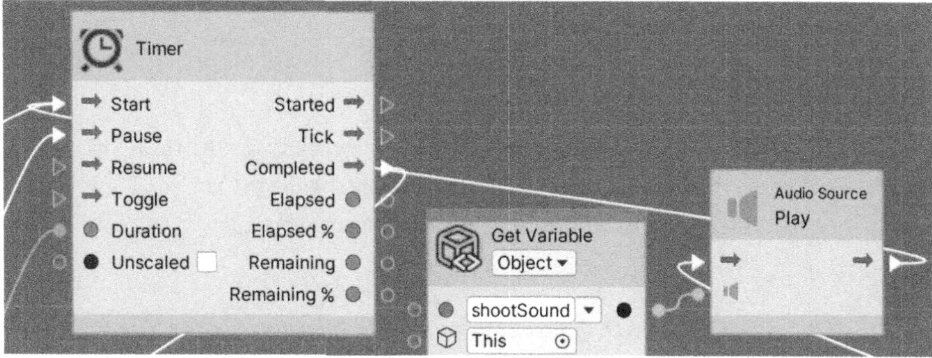

Figure 17.36: Completing the shoot loop

Finally, we need to add the proper `Animator: SetBool(Name, Value)` node to the Input nodes to turn on and off the Boolean and trigger the animation:

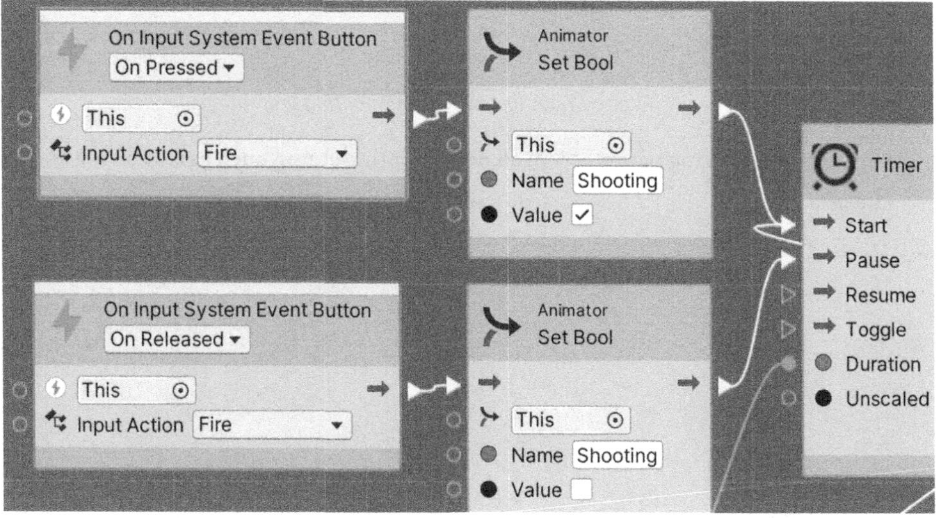

Figure 17.37: Executing the Shoot animation

Now that we have handled the **Shoot** animations of the player, let's handle the one of the enemy by doing the following:

1. Cache a reference to the parent animator in the **EnemyFSM** script using **GetComponentInParent** as we did with the **NavMeshAgent**:

```
Animator animator;

void Awake()
{
    baseTransform = GameObject.Find("BaseDamagePoint").transform;
    agent = GetComponentInParent<NavMeshAgent>();
    animator = GetComponentInParent<Animator>();
}
```

Figure 17.38: Accessing the parent's Animator reference

2. Turn on the **Shooting** animator parameter inside the **Shoot** function to make sure that every time we shoot, that parameter is set to **true** (checked):

```
void Shoot()
{
    animator.SetBool("Shooting", true);
```

Figure 17.39: Turning on the shooting animation

3. Turn off the `Shooting` parameter in all non-shooting states, such as **GoToBase** and **ChasePlayer**:

```
void GoToBase()
{
    animator.SetBool("Shooting", false);
    agent.isStopped = false;

    agent.SetDestination(baseTransform.position);

    if (sightSensor.detectedObject != null)
        currentState = EnemyState.ChasePlayer;

    float distanceToBase = Vector3.Distance(
        transform.position,
        baseTransform.position);

    if (distanceToBase <= baseAttackDistance)
        currentState = EnemyState.AttackBase;
}

void ChasePlayer()
{
    animator.SetBool("Shooting", false);
    agent.isStopped = false;
```

Figure 17.40: Turning off the shooting animation

4. Regarding the Visual Scripting version, the **GoToBase** state in the **EnemyFSM** will look like this:

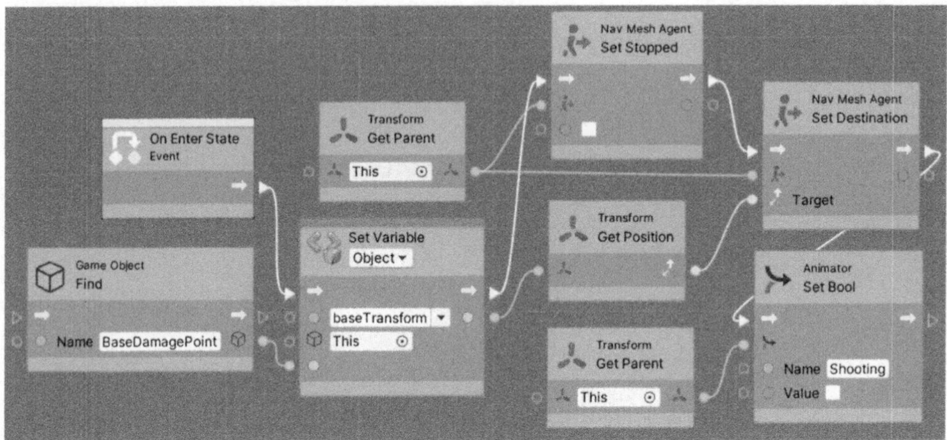

Figure 17.41: GoToBase state

5. Note that we needed again the **GetParent** node to access the enemy's parent **Transform** (the **root**), which we connected to the **Animator: SetBool** node in order to access the Animator in the enemy's root. Then the **ChasePlayer** state actions will look like this:

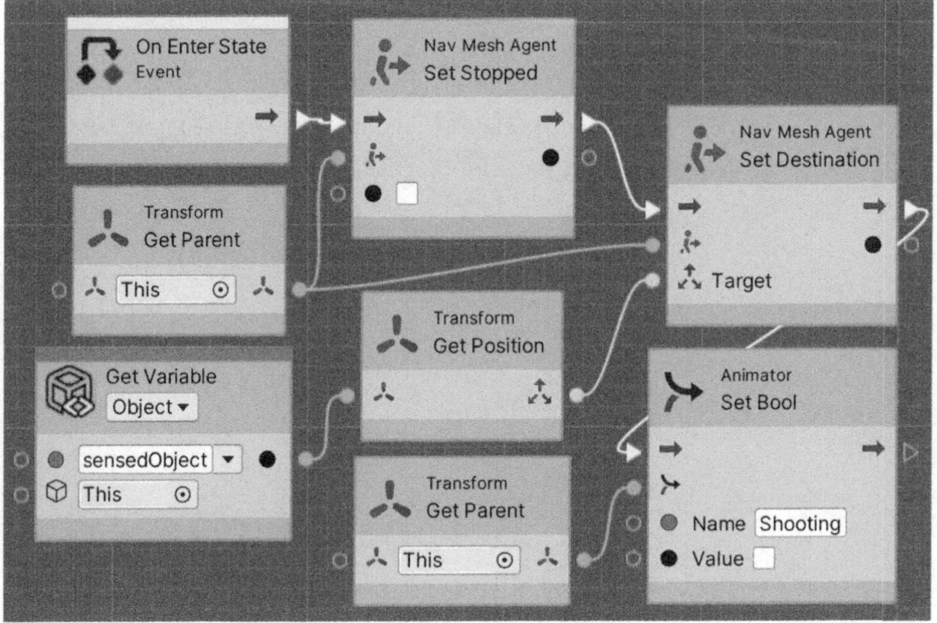

Figure 17.42: ChasePlayer state

6. Then both the **AttackBase** and **AttackPlayer** initial actions will look like this:

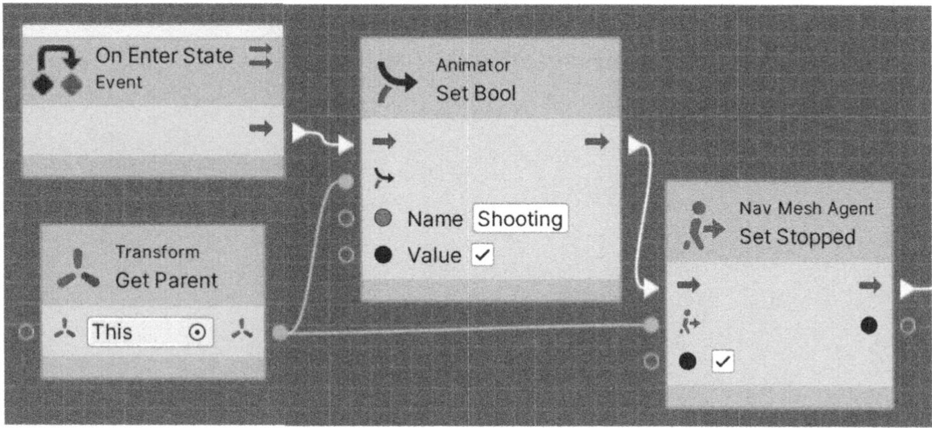

Figure 17.43: Attack Base state

With this, both our player and enemies have a constant shooting behavior and a **Shoot** animation to reflect this. Now let's handle the movement animations for both.

Scripting movement animations

For the animator controller's **Velocity** parameter, we can detect the magnitude of the velocity vector of **Rigidbody**, the velocity in meters per second, and set that as the current value. This can be perfectly separated from the **PlayerMovement** script, so we can reuse this if necessary, in other scenarios. So, we need to create a script such as the one in the following image, which just connects the **Rigidbody** component's velocity with the animator **Velocity** parameter, and adds it to the **Player** GameObject:

```
using UnityEngine;

public class VelocityAnimator : MonoBehaviour
{
    Rigidbody rb;
    Animator animator;

    void Awake()
    {
        rb = GetComponent<Rigidbody>();
        animator = GetComponent<Animator>();
    }

    void Update()
    {
        animator.SetFloat("Velocity", rb.velocity.magnitude);
    }
}
```

Figure 17.44: Setting VelocityAnimator variables

And regarding the Visual Scripting version, this is what it would look like:

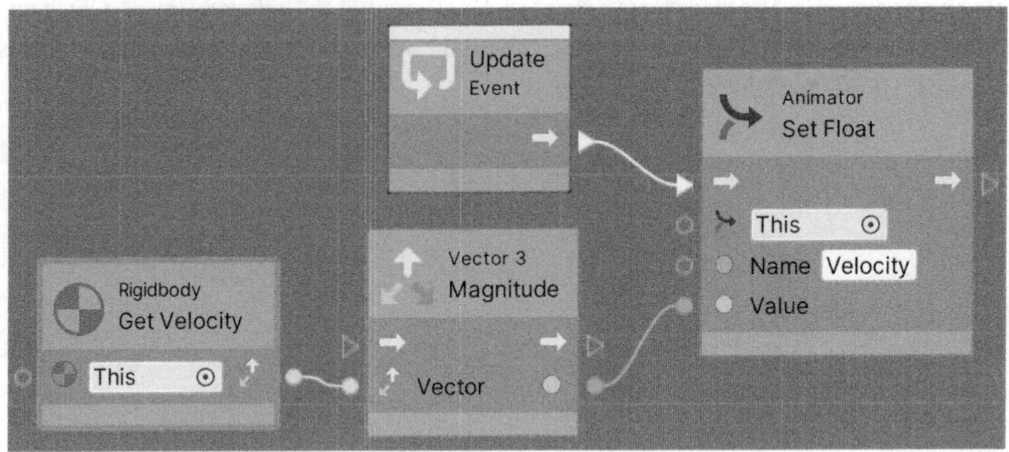

Figure 17.45: Setting Velocity Animator variables in Visual Scripting

You may need to increase the `0.01` transitions threshold used so far in the conditions of the transitions of the animator controller because **Rigidbody** keeps moving after releasing the keys. Using 1 worked perfectly for me. Another option would be to increase the drag and the velocity of the player to make the character stop faster. Pick whatever method works best for you. Remember the transitions of both layers (**UpperBody** and **LowerBody**).

Now we can add the movement animations to the enemy. Create and add a script to the Enemy prefab called **NavMeshAnimator**, which will take the current velocity of its **NavMeshAgent** and will set it to the Animator Controller. This will work similarly to the **VelocityAnimator** script but this time checking the velocity of the **NavMeshAgent**. We didn't use **VelocityAnimator** here because our AI doesn't use **Rigidbody** to move, so it won't work:

```
using UnityEngine;
using UnityEngine.AI;

public class NavMeshAnimator : MonoBehaviour
{
    NavMeshAgent navMesh;
    Animator animator;

    void Awake()
    {
        navMesh = GetComponent<NavMeshAgent>();
        animator = GetComponent<Animator>();
    }

    void Update()
    {
        animator.SetFloat("Velocity", navMesh.velocity.magnitude);
    }
}
```

Figure 17.46: Connecting the NavMeshAgent to our Animator Controller

The Visual Scripting version will look like this:

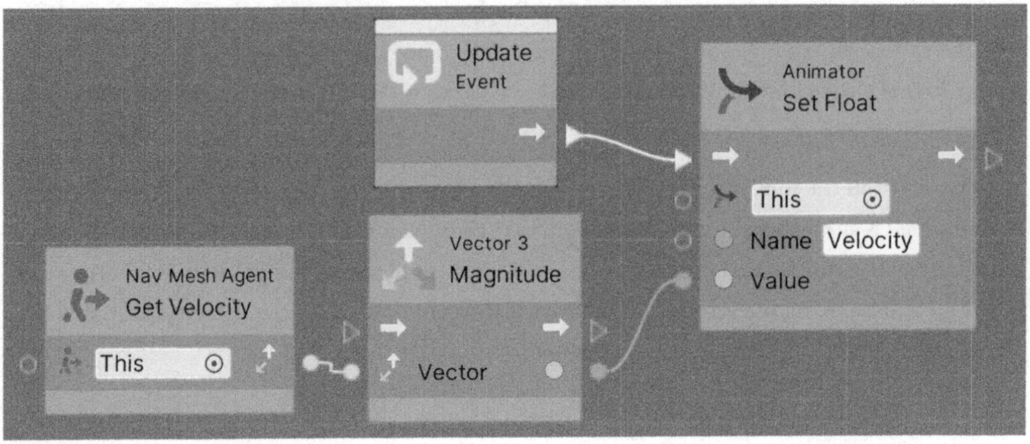

Figure 17.47: Setting the animator velocity parameter the same as our NavMeshAgent

Notice here we don't need the **GetParent** node, given that this graph is located at the Enemy's root object alongside the **Animator** and the **NavMeshAgent**. With that, we have scripted our Player and Enemies animations. We are ready to keep learning about animations using Cinemachine to create cutscene cameras and much more.

Creating dynamic cameras with Cinemachine

Cameras are a very important subject in video games. They allow the player to see their surroundings to make decisions based on what they see. The game designer usually defines how it behaves to get the exact gameplay experience they want, and that's no easy task. A lot of behaviors must be layered to get the exact feeling. Also, for cutscenes, it is important to control the path that the camera will be traversing during it and where the camera is looking to focus the action during those constantly moving scenes.

In this chapter, we will use the `Cinemachine` package to create both the dynamic cameras that will follow the player's movements, which we will code in *Part 3*, and also, the cameras to be used during cutscenes.

In this section, we will examine the following Cinemachine concepts:

- Creating camera behaviors
- Creating dolly tracks

Let's start by discussing how to create a Cinemachine-controlled camera and configure behaviors in it.

Creating camera behaviors

Cinemachine is a tech library containing a collection of different behaviors that can be used in a camera, which when properly combined can generate all kinds of common camera types in video games, including following the player from behind, first-person cameras, top-down cameras, and so on. In order to use these behaviors, we need to understand the concept of brains and virtual cameras.

In Cinemachine, we will only keep one main camera, as we have done so far, and that camera will be controlled by virtual cameras, separated GameObjects that have the aforementioned behaviors. We can have several virtual cameras and swap between them at will, but the active virtual camera will be the only one that will control our main camera. This is useful for switching cameras at different points of the game, such as switching between our player's third-person camera and a cutscene camera. In order to control the main camera with the virtual cameras, it must have a **Brain** component, which will monitor all active virtual cameras and pick the proper position to use them.

To start using Cinemachine, first, we need to check if it is installed in the Package Manager, as we did previously with other packages. If you don't remember how to do this, just do the following:

1. Go to **Window | Package Manager**.
2. Ensure that the **Packages** option in the top-left part of the window is set to **Unity Registry**:

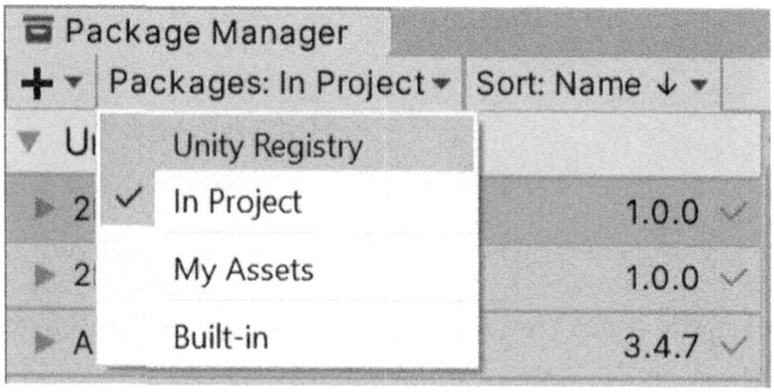

Figure 17.48: The Packages filter mode

3. Wait a moment for the left panel to populate all packages from the servers (the internet is required).

4. Look for the **Cinemachine** package from the list and select it. At the moment of writing this book the latest available version is 2.8.6, but you can use newer versions if you prefer, always ensuring that the following steps work as expected; if not, you can always install the closest version to ours.
5. If you see the **Install** button in the bottom-right corner of the screen it means it is not installed. Just click that button.

Now that we have it installed, we can start creating a virtual camera to follow the player. So far, we just simply parented the camera to the player for it to follow them, but now we will unparent the camera and let Cinemachine handle it to learn how to use this tool:

1. Select the **MainCamera** inside the player and unparent it (drag it outside the player) in such a way that it becomes a root object of our scene, having no parent at all.
2. Click **GameObject | Cinemachine | Virtual Camera**. This will create a new object called `CM vcam1`:

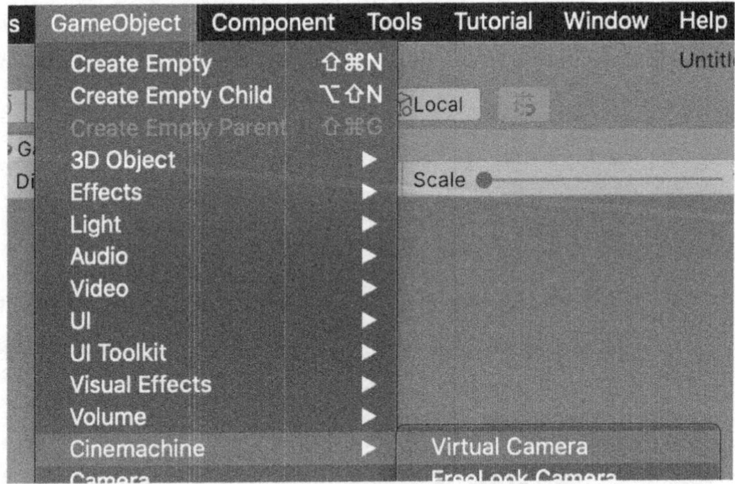

Figure 17.49: Virtual camera creation

3. If you select the main camera from the **Hierarchy** pane, you will also notice that a `CinemachineBrain` component has been automatically added to it, making our main camera follow the virtual camera. Try to move the created virtual camera, and you will see how the main camera follows it:

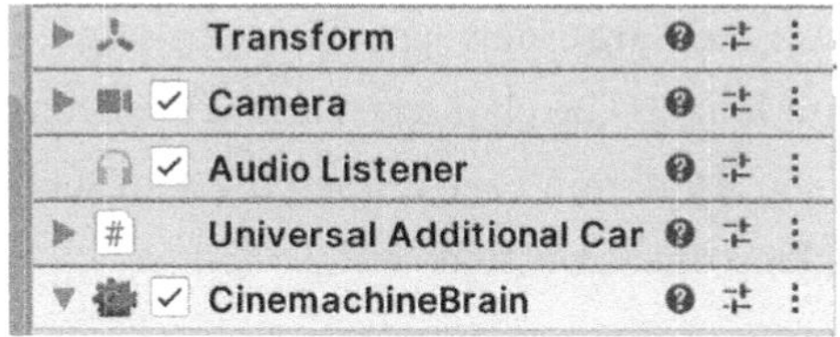

Figure 17.50: The CinemachineBrain component

4. Select the virtual camera (`CM vcam1`) and drag the character to the **Follow** and **Look At** properties of the **CinemachineVirtualCamera** component. This will make the movement and looking behaviors use that object to do their jobs:

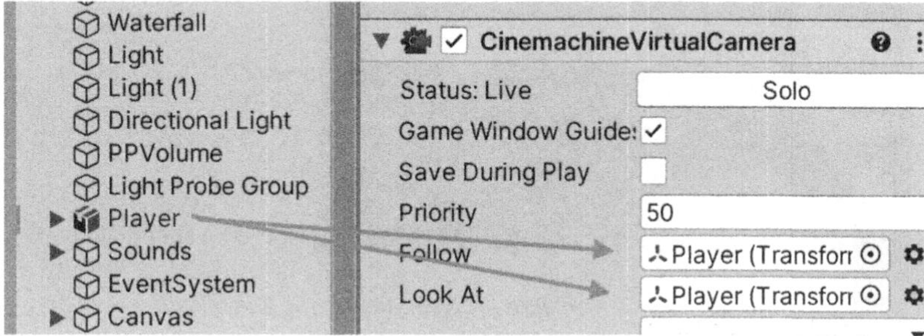

Figure 17.51: Setting the target of our camera

5. You can see how the **Body** property of the virtual camera is set to **Transposer**, which will move the camera relative to the target set at the **Follow** property—in our case, the character. You can open the **Body** options (the arrow to its left), change the **Follow Offset** property, and set it to the desired distance you want the camera to have from the target. In my case, I used the `0`, `3`, and `-3` values:

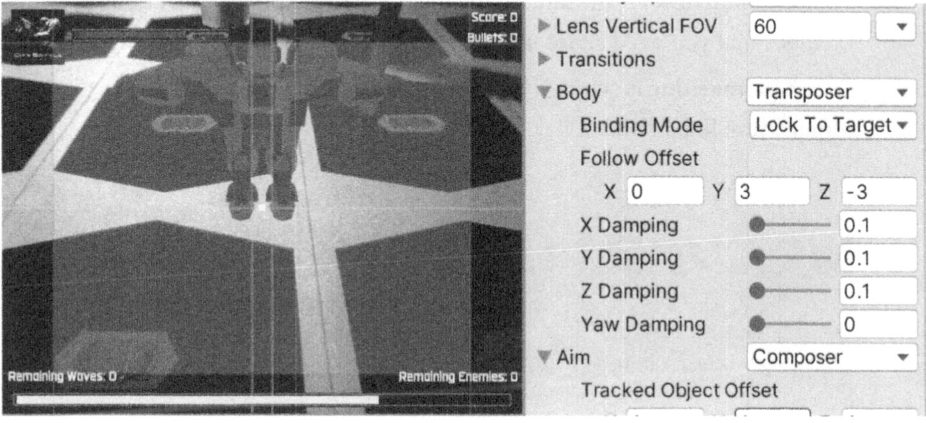

Figure 17.52: The camera following the character from behind

6. *Figure 17.50* shows the **Game** view; you can see a small, yellow rectangle indicating the target position to look at the character, and it's currently pointing at the pivot of the character—its feet. If you don't see it open the **Aim** section of the virtual camera in the Inspector by clicking the arrow to its left.
7. We can apply an offset in the **Tracked Object Offset** property of the **Aim** section of the virtual camera. In my case, a value of `0`, `1.8`, and `0` worked well to make the camera look at the head instead:

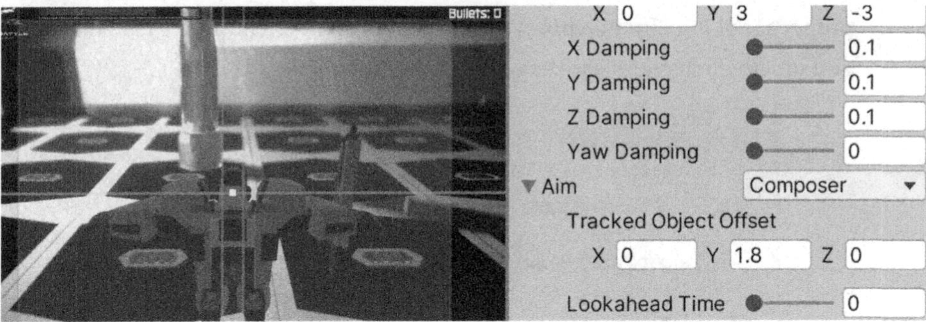

Figure 17.53: Changing the Aim offset

As you can see, using Cinemachine is pretty simple, and in our case, the default settings were mostly enough for the kind of behavior we needed. However, if you explore the other **Body** and **Aim** modes, you will find that you can create any type of camera for any type of game. We won't cover the other modes in this book, but I strongly recommend you look at the documentation for Cinemachine to check what the other modes do. To open the documentation, follow these steps:

1. Open the **Package Manager** by going to **Window | Package Manager**.
2. Find **Cinemachine** in the left-hand side list. Wait a moment if it doesn't show up. Remember that you need an internet connection for it to work.
3. Once **Cinemachine** is selected, scroll down in the right panel until you see the **View documentation** link in blue. Click on it:

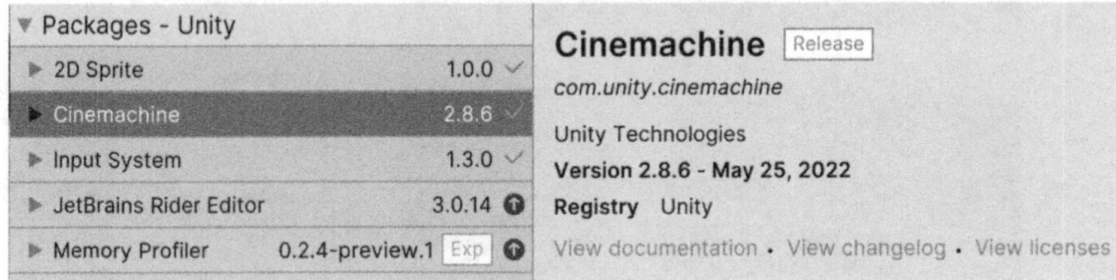

Figure 17.54: The Cinemachine documentation link

4. You can explore the documentation using the navigation menu on the left:

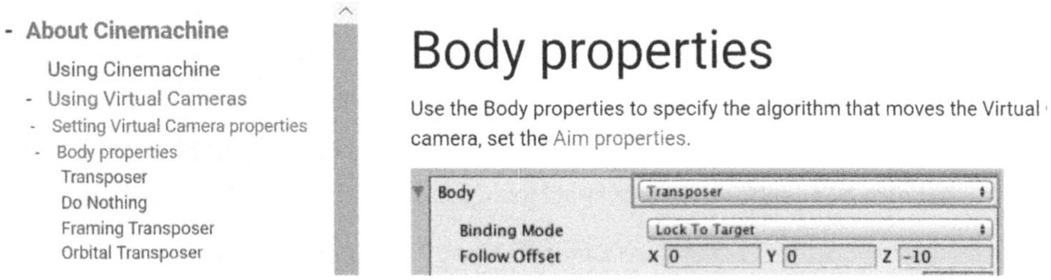

Figure 17.55: The Cinemachine documentation

As you did with Cinemachine, you can find other packages' documentation in the same way. Now that we have achieved the basic camera behavior that we need, let's explore how we can use Cinemachine to create a camera for our intro cutscene.

Creating dolly tracks

When the player starts the level, we want a little cutscene with a pan over our scene and the base before entering the battle. This will require the camera to follow a fixed path, and that's exactly what Cinemachine's dolly camera does. It creates a path where we can attach a virtual camera so that it will follow it. We can set Cinemachine to move automatically through the track or follow a target to the closest point to the track; in our case, we will use the first option.

In order to create a dolly camera, follow these steps:

1. Let's start creating the track with a cart, which is a little object that will move along the track, which will be the target to follow the camera. To do this, click on **GameObject | Cinemachine | Dolly Track with Cart**:

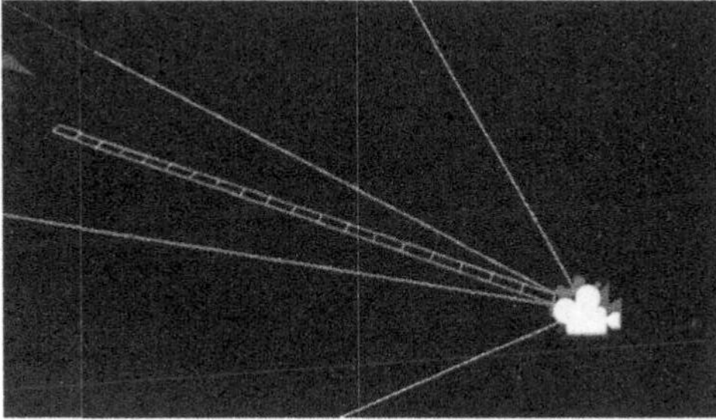

Figure 17.56: A dolly camera with a default straight path

2. If you select the `DollyTrack1` object, you can see two circles with the numbers `0` and `1` in the **Scene** view. These are the control points of the track. Select one of them and move it as you move other objects, using the arrows of the translation gizmo. If you don't see them press the *W* key to enable the **Translation** gizmo.
3. You can create more control points by clicking the + button at the bottom of the **Waypoints** list of the `CinemachineSmoothPath` component of the `DollyTrack1` object:

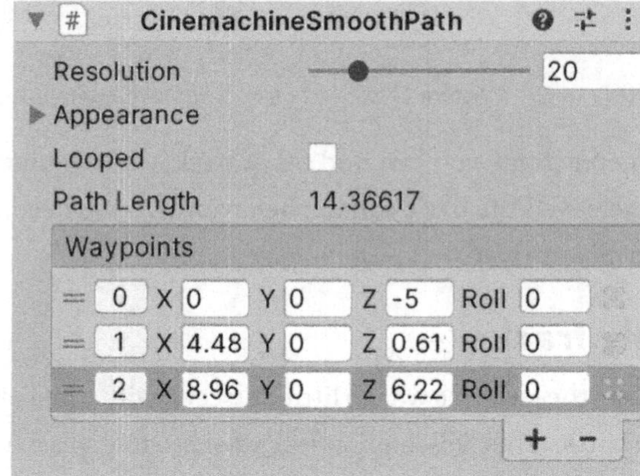

Figure 17.57: Adding a path control point

4. Create as many waypoints as you need to create a path that will traverse the areas you want the camera to oversee in the intro cutscene. Remember, you can move the waypoints by clicking on them and using the translation gizmo:

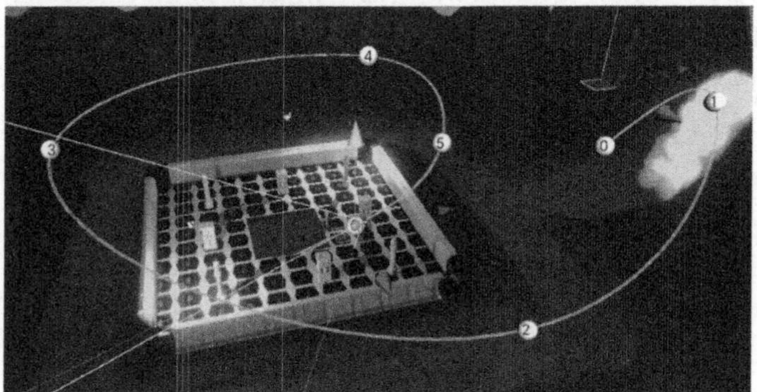

Figure 17.58: A dolly track for our scene. It ends right behind the character

5. Create a new virtual camera. If you go to the **Game** view after creating it, you will notice that the character camera will be active. In order to test how the new camera looks, select the previous one (**CM vcam1**) and temporarily disable it by clicking the checkbox to the left of the GameObject's name in the Inspector.
6. Set the **Follow** target this time to the `DollyCart1` object that we previously created with the track.
7. Set **Follow Offset** of the **Body** section to `0`, `0`, and `0` to keep the camera in the same position as the cart.
8. Set **Aim** to **Same As Follow Target** to make the camera look in the same direction as the cart, which will follow the track curves:

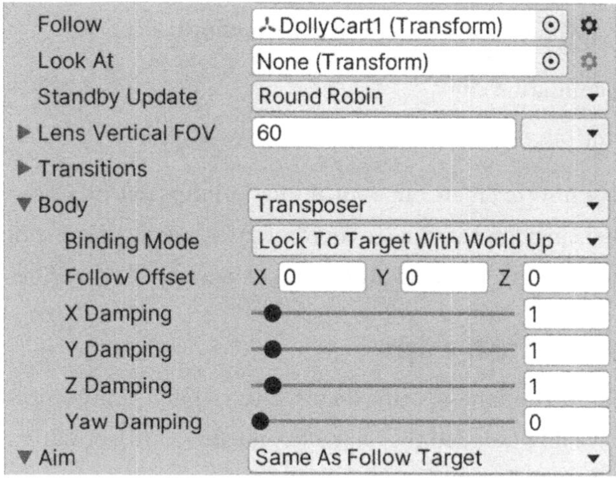

Figure 17.59: Configuration to make the virtual camera follow the dolly track

9. Select the **DollyCart1** object and change the **Position** value to see how the cart moves along the track. Do this while the game window is focused and **CM vcam2** is in solo mode to see how the camera will look:

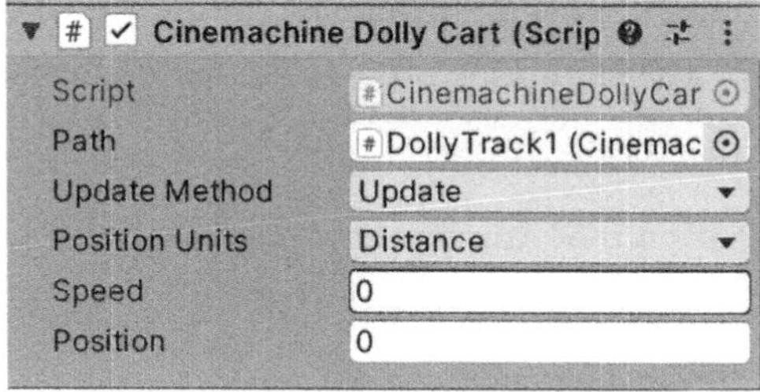

Figure 17.60: The dolly cart component

10. Re-enable `CM vcam1`.

With the dolly track properly set, we can create our cutscene using **Timeline** to sequence it.

Creating cutscenes with Timeline

We have our intro camera, but that's not enough to create a cutscene. A proper cutscene is a sequence of actions happening at the exact moment that they should happen, coordinating several objects to act as intended. We can have actions such as enabling and disabling objects, switching cameras, playing sounds, moving objects, and so on. To do this, Unity offers **Timeline**, which is a sequencer of actions to coordinate those kinds of cutscenes. We will use **Timeline** to create an intro cutscene for our scene, showing the level before starting the game.

In this section, we will examine the following Timeline concepts:

- Creating animation clips
- Sequencing our intro cutscene

We are going to see how to create our own animation clips in Unity to animate our GameObjects and then place them inside a cutscene to coordinate their activation, using the Timeline sequencer tool. Let's start by creating a camera animation to use later in Timeline.

Creating animation clips

This is actually not a Timeline-specific feature but rather a Unity feature that works great with Timeline. When we downloaded the character, it came with animation clips that were created using external software, but you can create custom animation clips using Unity's **Animation** window. Don't confuse it with the **Animator** window, which allows us to create animation transitions that react to the game situation. This is useful to create small object-specific animations that you will coordinate later in Timeline with other objects' animations.

These animations can control any value of an object's component properties, such as the positions, colors, and so on. In our case, we want to animate the dolly track's **Position** property to make it go from start to finish in a given time. In order to do this, do the following:

1. Select the `DollyCart1` object.
2. Open the **Animation** (not **Animator**) window by going to **Window | Animation | Animation**.

3. Click on the **Create** button at the center of the **Animation** window. Remember to do this while the dolly cart (not track) is selected:

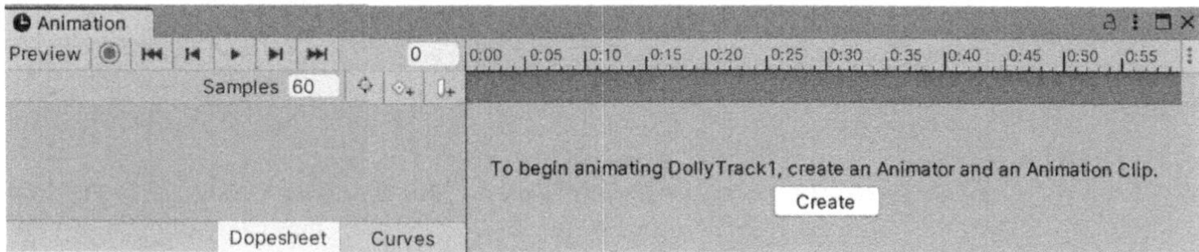

Figure 17.61: Creating a custom animation clip

4. After doing this, you will be prompted to save the animation clip somewhere. I recommend you create an `Animations` folder in the project (inside the `Assets` folder) and call it `IntroDollyTrack`.

If you pay attention, the dolly cart now has an **Animator** component with an Animator Controller created, which contains the animation we just created. As with any animation clip, you need to apply it to your object with an Animator Controller; custom animations are no exception. So, the **Animation** window created them for you.

Animating in this window consists of specifying the value of its properties at given moments. In our case, we want Position to have a value of 0 at the beginning of the animation, at 0 seconds on the timeline, and have a value of 254 at the end of the animation, at 5 seconds. I chose 254 because that's the last possible position in my cart, but that depends on the length of your dolly track. Just test which is the last possible position in yours. Also, I chose 5 seconds because that's what I feel is the correct length for the animation, but feel free to change it as you wish. Now, whatever happens between the animation's 0 and 5 seconds is an interpolation of the 0 and 254 values, meaning that in 2.5 seconds, the value of Position will be 127. Animating always consists of interpolating different states of our object at different moments.

In order to do this, follow these steps:

1. In the **Animation** window, click on the record button (the red circle in the top-left section). This will make Unity detect any changes in our object and save them to the animation. Remember to do this while you have selected the dolly cart.
2. Set the **Position** setting of the dolly cart to `1` and then `0`. Changing this to any value and then to `0` again will create a keyframe, which is a point in the animation that says that at `0` seconds, we want the **Position** value to be `0`. We need to set it first to any other value if the value is already at `0`.

You will notice that the **Position** property has been added to the animation:

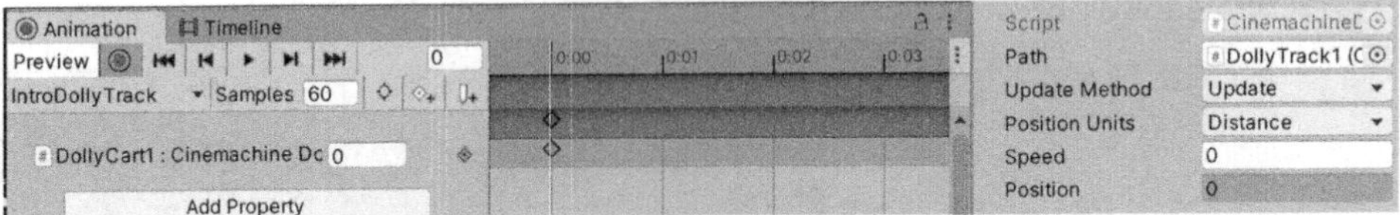

Figure 17.62: The animation in Record mode after changing the Position value to 0

3. Using the mouse scroll wheel, zoom out the timeline to the right of the **Animation** window until you see **5:00** seconds in the top bar:

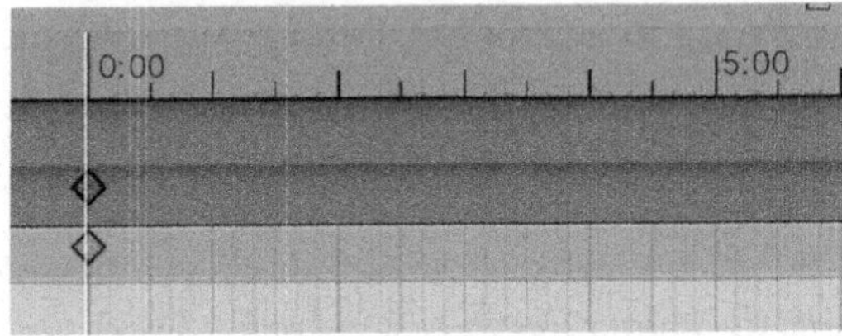

Figure 17.63: The timeline of the Animation window seeing 5 seconds

4. Click on the **5:00**-second label in the top bar of the timeline to position the playback header at that moment. This will locate the next change we do at that moment.
5. Set the **Position** value of the dolly track to the highest value you can get; in my case, this is `240`. Remember to have the **Animation** window in **Record** mode:

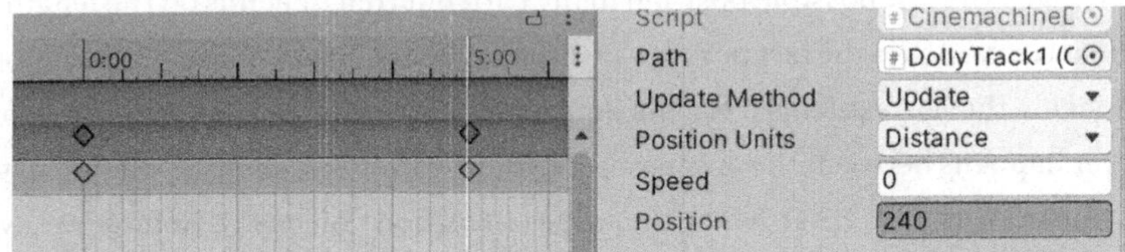

Figure 17.64: Creating a keyframe with the 240 value 5 seconds into the animation

6. Hit the play button in the top-left section of the **Animation** window to see the animation playing. Remember to view it in the **Game** view while `CM vcam1` is disabled.

Now, if we hit **Play**, the animation will start playing, but that's something we don't want. In this scenario, the idea is to give control of the cutscene to the cutscene system, Timeline, because this animation won't be the only thing that needs to be sequenced in our cutscene. One way to prevent the **Animator** component from automatically playing the animation we created is to create an empty animation state in the Controller and set it as the default state by following these steps:

1. Search the Animator Controller that we created at the same time as the animation and open it. If you can't find it, just select the dolly cart and double-click on the **Controller** property of the **Animator** component on our GameObject to open the asset.
2. Right-click on an empty state in the Controller and select **Create State | Empty**. This will create a new state in the state machine as if we created a new animation, but it is empty this time:

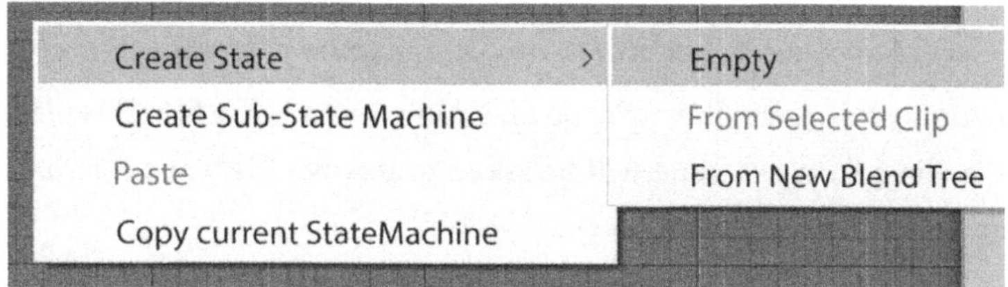

Figure 17.65: Creating an empty state in the Animator Controller

3. Right-click on **New State** and click on **Set as Layer Default State**. The state should become orange:

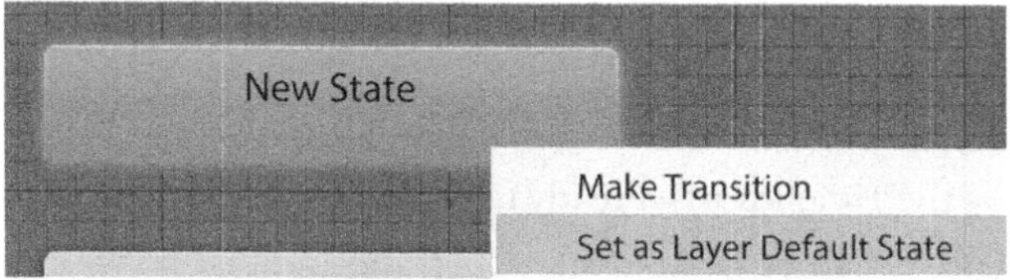

Figure 17.66: Changing the default animation of the Controller to an empty state

4. Now, if you hit **Play**, no animation will play as the default state of our dolly cart is empty. No transition will be required in this case.

Now that we have created our camera animation, let's start creating a cutscene that switches from the intro cutscene camera to the player camera by using Timeline.

Sequencing our intro cutscene

Timeline is already installed in your project, but if you go to the Package Manager of Timeline, you may see an **Update** button to get the latest version if you need some of the new features. In our case, we will keep the default version included in our project (1.5.2, at the time of writing this book).

The first thing we will do is create a cutscene asset and an object in the scene responsible for playing it. To do this, follow these steps:

1. Create an empty GameObject using the **GameObject | Create Empty** option.
2. Select the empty object and call it `Director`.
3. Go to **Window | Sequencing | Timeline** to open the **Timeline** editor.
4. Click the **Create** button in the middle of the **Timeline** window while the **Director** object is selected to convert that object into the cutscene player (or director).
5. After doing this, a window will pop up asking you to save a file. This file will be the cutscene or timeline; each cutscene will be saved in its own file. Save it in a `Cutscenes` folder in your project (the `Assets` folder).
6. Now, you can see that the **Director** object has a **Playable Director** component with the **Intro** cutscene asset saved in the previous step set for the **Playable** property, meaning this cutscene will be played by the Director:

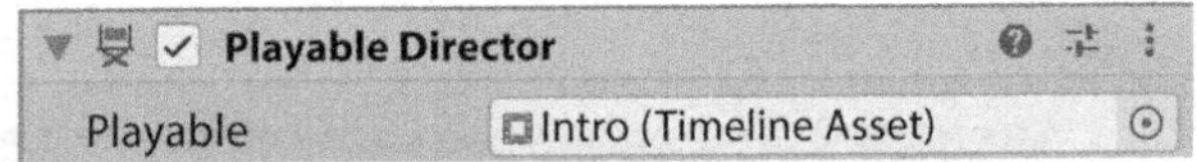

Figure 17.67: Playable Director prepared to play the Intro Timeline asset

Now that we have the Timeline asset ready to work with, let's make it sequence actions. To start, we need to sequence two things—first, the cart position animation we did in the last step and then the camera swap between the dolly track camera (`CM vcam2`) and the player cameras (`CM vcam1`). As we said before, a cutscene is a sequence of actions executing at given moments, and in order to schedule actions, you will need tracks. In Timeline, we have different kinds of tracks, each one allowing you to execute certain actions on certain objects. We will start with the animation track.

The animation track will control which animation a specific object will play; we need one track per object to animate. In our case, we want the dolly track to play the **Intro** animation that we created, so let's do that by following these steps:

1. Add an Animation track by clicking **the plus button (+)** and then **Animation Track**:

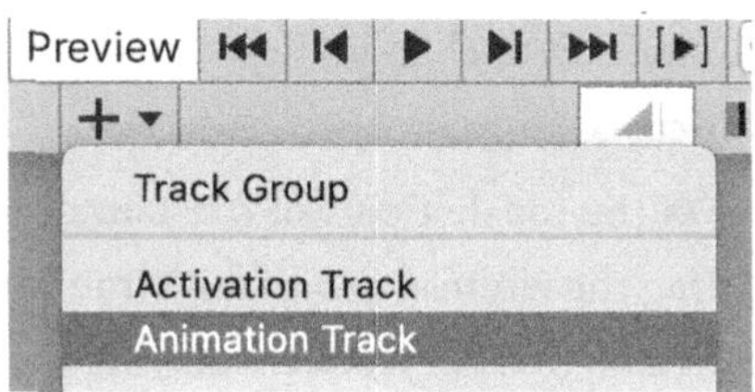

Figure 17.68: Creating an animation track

2. Select the **Director** object and check the **Bindings** list of the **Playable Director** component in the **Inspector** window.
3. Drag the **Cart** object to specify that we want the animation track to control its animation:

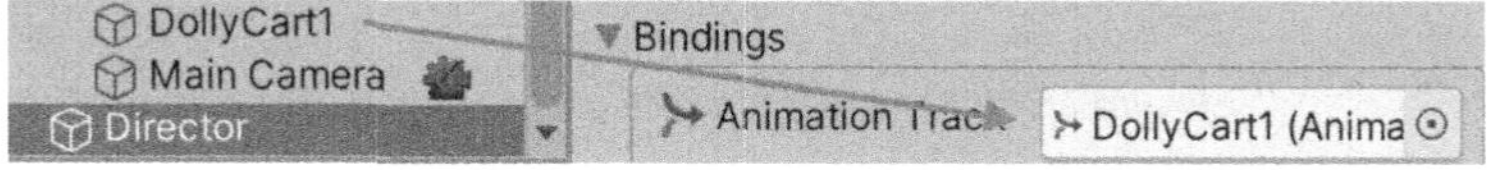

Figure 17.69: Making the animation track control the dolly cart animation in this Director

Timeline is a generic asset that can be applied to any scene, but as the tracks control specific objects, you need to manually bind them in every scene. In our case, we have an animation track that expects to control a single animator, so in every scene, if we want to apply this cutscene, we need to drag the specific animator to control it in the **Bindings** list.

4. Drag the **Intro** animation asset that we created to the animation track in the **Timeline** window. This will create a clip in the track showing when and for how long the animation will play. You can drag as many animations as possible that the cart can play into the track to sequence different animations at different moments, but right now, we want just that one:

Figure 17.70: Making the animator track play the intro clip

5. You can drag the animation to change the exact moment you want it to play. Drag it to the beginning of the track.
6. Hit the **Play** button in the top-left part of the **Timeline** window to see it in action. You can also manually drag the white arrow in the **Timeline** window to view the cutscene at different moments. If that doesn't work try playing the game and then stopping:

Figure 17.71: Playing a timeline and dragging the playback header

7. Now, we will make our **Intro** timeline asset tell the `CinemachineBrain` component (the main camera) which camera will be active during each part of the cutscene, switching to the player camera once the camera animation is over. We will create a second track—a Cinemachine track—which is specialized in making a specific `CinemachineBrain` component to switch between different virtual cameras. To do this, follow these steps:
8. Click the + button again and click on **Cinemachine Track**. Note that you can install Timeline without **Cinemachine**, but this kind of track won't show up in that case:

Figure 17.72: Creating a new Cinemachine track

9. In the **Playable Director** component's **Bindings** list, drag the main camera to **Cinemachine Track** to make that track control which virtual camera will control the main camera at different moments of the cutscene:

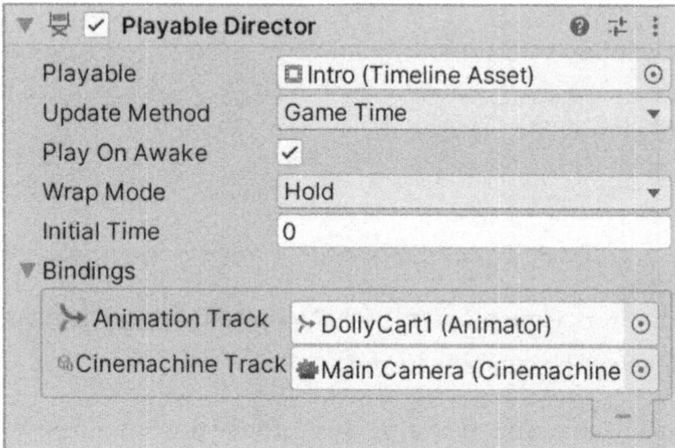

Figure 17.73: Binding the main camera to the Cinemachine track

10. The next step indicates which virtual camera will be active during specific moments of the timeline. To do so, our Cinemachine track allows us to drag virtual cameras to it, which will create virtual camera clips. Drag both **CM vcam2** and **CM vcam1**, in that order, to the Cinemachine track:

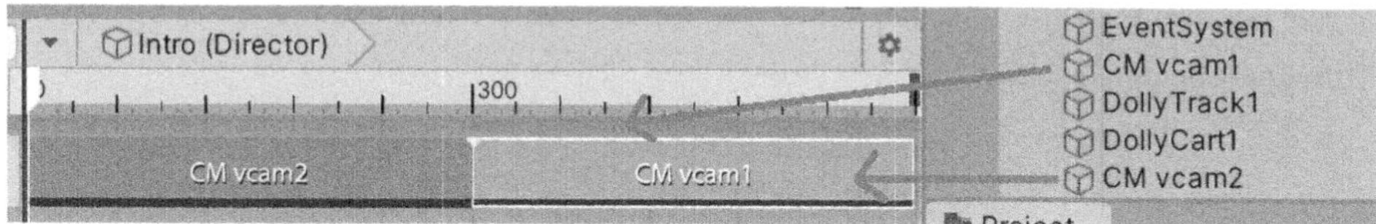

Figure 17.74: Dragging virtual cameras to the Cinemachine track

11. If you hit the **Play** button or just drag the **Timeline Playback** header, you can see how the active virtual camera changes when the playback header reaches the second virtual camera clip. Remember to view this in the **Game** view.
12. If you place the mouse near the ends of the clips, a resize cursor will show up. If you drag them, you can resize the clips to specify their duration. In our case, we will need to match the length of the `CM vcam2` clip to the **Cart** animation clip and then put `CM vcam1` at the end of it by dragging it so that the camera will be active when the dolly cart animation ends. In my case, they were already the same length, but just try to change it anyway to practice. Also, you can make the `CM vcam1` clip shorter; we just need to play it for a few moments to execute the camera swap.

13. You can also overlap the clips a little bit to make a smooth transition between the two cameras, instead of a hard switch, which will look odd:

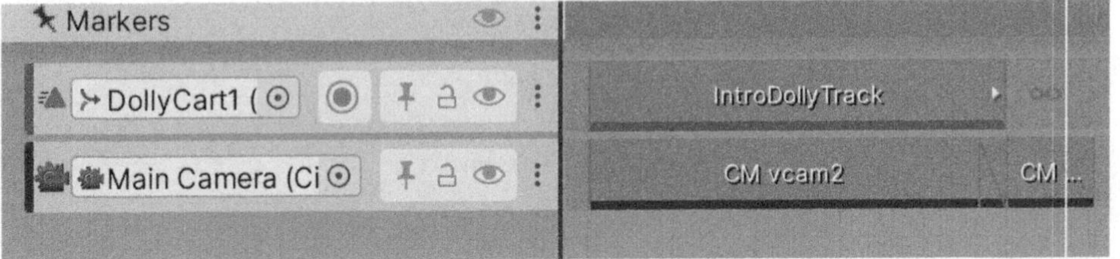

Figure 17.75: Resizing and overlapping clips to interpolate them

14. Increase the **Start Time** property of the **WaveSpawners** to prevent the enemies from being spawned before the cutscene begins.

If you wait for the full cutscene to end, you will notice how at the very end, `CM vcam2` becomes active again. You can configure how Timeline will deal with the end of the cutscene, as by default, it does nothing. This can cause different behavior according to the type of track–in our case, again giving control to pick the virtual camera to the `CinemachineBrain` component, which will pick the virtual camera with the highest **Priority** value. We can change the **Priority** property of the virtual cameras to be sure that **CM vcam1** (the player camera) is always the more important one, or set **Wrap Mode** of the **Playable Director** component to **Hold**, which will keep everything as the last frame of the timeline specifies. In our case, we will use the latter option to test the Timeline-specific features:

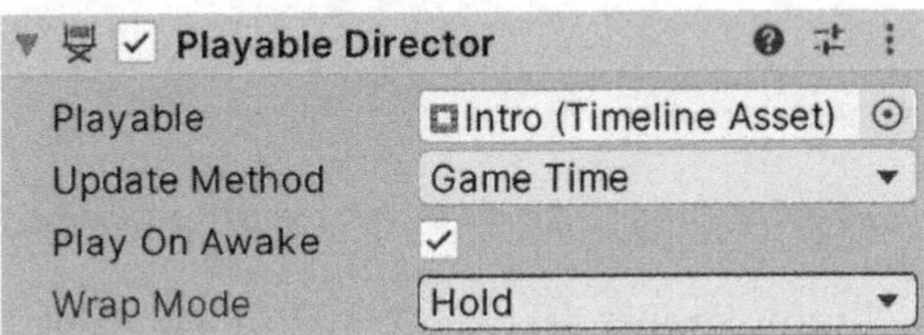

Figure 17.76: Wrap Mode set to Hold mode

Most of the different kinds of tracks work under the same logic; each one will control a specific aspect of a specific object using clips that will execute during a set time. I encourage you to test different tracks to see what they do, such as **Activation**, which enables and disables objects during the cutscene. Remember, you can check out the documentation of the Timeline package in the Package Manager.

Summary

In this chapter, we introduced the different animation systems that Unity provides for different requirements. We discussed importing character animations and controlling them with Animation Controllers. We also saw how to make cameras that can react to the game's current situation, such as the player's position, or that can be used during cutscenes. Finally, we looked at Timeline and the animation system to create an intro cutscene for our game. These tools are useful for making the animators in our team work directly in Unity without the hassle of integrating external assets (except for character animations) and also preventing the programmer from creating repetitive scripts to create animations, wasting time in the process.

Now, you are able to import and create animation clips in Unity, as well as apply them to GameObjects to make them move according to the clips. Also, you can place them in the Timeline sequencer to coordinate them and create cutscenes for your game. Finally, you can create dynamic cameras to use in-game or in cutscenes.

With this, we end *Part 2*, where we learned about different Unity Systems to improve several artistic aspects of our game. In the next chapter, the first chapter of *Part 3*, we will wrap up the development of our game, seeing how to build and optimize our game, and also provide a quick intro to augmented reality applications.

18

Optimization with Profiler, Frame Debugger, and Memory Profiler

Welcome to the fourth part of this book—I am glad you have reached this part as it means that you have almost completed a full game! In this chapter, we are going to discuss optimization techniques to review your game's performance and improve it, as having a good and constant framerate is vital to any game.

Performance is a broad topic that requires a deep understanding of several Unity systems and could span several books. We are going to look at how to measure performance and explore the effects of our changes to systems to learn how they work through testing.

In this chapter, we will examine the following performance concepts:

- Optimizing graphics
- Optimizing processing
- Optimizing memory

By the end of this chapter, you will be able to gather performance data of the three main pieces of hardware that run your game—the GPU, CPU, and RAM. You will be able to analyze that data to detect possible performance issues and understand how to solve the most common ones.

We will start by learning how to optimize the graphics side of our game.

Optimizing graphics

The most common cause of performance issues is related to the misuse of assets, especially on the graphics side, due to not having enough knowledge of how Unity's graphics engines work. We are going to explore how a GPU works at a high level and how to improve its usage.

In this section, we will examine the following graphics optimization concepts:

- Introduction to graphics engines
- Using Frame Debugger
- Using batching
- Other optimizations

We will start by looking at a high-level overview of how graphics are rendered to better understand the performance data that we will gather later in Frame Debugger. Based on the debugger's results, we are going to identify the areas where we can apply **batching** (which is a technique to combine the rendering process of several objects, reducing its cost), along with other common optimizations to keep in mind.

Introduction to graphics engines

Nowadays, every gaming device, whether it is a computer, a mobile device, or a console, has a video card—a set of hardware that specializes in graphics processing. It differs from a CPU in a subtle but important way. Graphics processing involves the processing of thousands of mesh vertices and the rendering of millions of pixels, so the GPU is designed to run short programs a massive number of times, while the CPU can handle programs of any length but with limited parallelization capabilities. The reason for having those processing units (CPU and GPU) is so that our program can use each one when needed.

The problem here is that graphics don't just rely on the GPU. The CPU is also involved in the process, making calculations and issuing commands to the GPU, so they must work together. For that to happen, both processing units need to communicate, and because they are (usually) physically separated, they need another piece of hardware to allow this: a bus, the most common type being the **Peripheral Component Interconnect Express (PCI Express)** bus.

PCI Express is a type of connection that allows massive amounts of data to be moved between the GPU and CPU, but the problem is that even if it's very fast, the communication time can be noticeable if you issue a lot of commands between both units. So, the key concept here is that graphics performance is improved mainly by reducing the communications between the GPU and CPU:

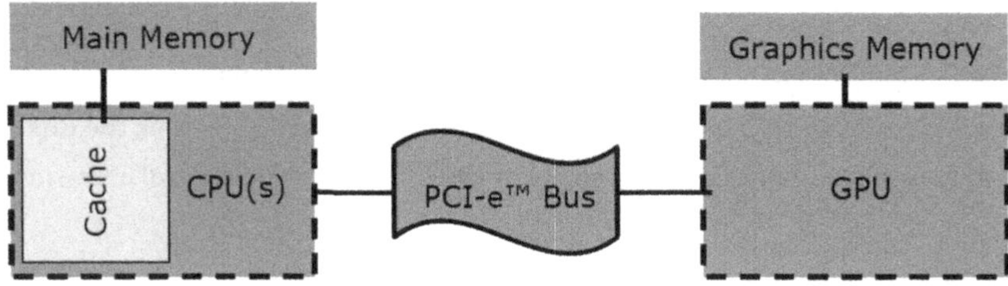

Figure 18.1: CPU/GPU communication through a PCI Express bus

Nowadays, new hardware architecture allows the CPU and GPU to coexist in the same chipset, reducing communication time and even sharing memory. Sadly, that architecture doesn't allow the processing power needed for video games, as having those two pieces separated allows them to have enough space for a large number of cores.

The basic algorithm of a graphics engine is to determine which objects are visible using culling algorithms, sorting and grouping them according to their similarities, and then issuing drawing commands to the GPU to render those groups of objects, sometimes more than once. The main form of communication between the CPU and GPU are the **drawing commands**, usually called **draw calls**, and our main task when optimizing graphics is to reduce them as much as we can. The problem is that there are several sources of draw calls that need to be considered, such as the lighting or certain special effects. Studying every single one of them will take a long time, and even so, new versions of Unity can introduce new graphics features with their own draw calls. Instead, we will explore a way to discover these draw calls using Frame Debugger.

Using Frame Debugger

Frame Debugger is a tool that allows us to see a list of all the draw calls that the Unity rendering engine sends to the GPU. It not only lists them but also provides information about each draw call, including the data needed to detect optimization opportunities. By using Frame Debugger, we can see how our changes modify the number of draw calls, giving us immediate feedback on our efforts.

Note that reducing draw calls is sometimes not enough to improve performance, as each draw call can have different processing times; but usually, that difference is not big enough to consider. Also, in certain special rendering techniques, such as ray tracing or ray marching, a single draw call can drain all of our GPU power. This won't be the case in our game, so we won't take that into account right now.

Let's use Frame Debugger to analyze the rendering process of our game by doing the following:

1. Open Frame Debugger (**Window** | **Analysis** | **Frame Debugger**).
2. Play the game and when you want to analyze the performance, click the **Enable** button in the top-left corner of **Frame Debugger** (press *Esc* to regain control of the mouse while playing):

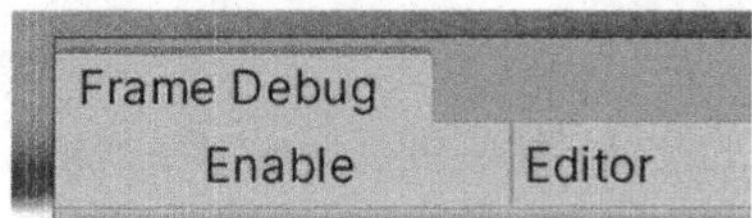

Figure 18.2: Enabling Frame Debugger

3. Click on the **Game** tab to open the Game view.
4. Drag the slider to the right of the **Disable** button slowly from left to right to see how the scene is rendered. Each step is a draw call that is being executed in the CPU for that given game frame. You can also observe how the list in the left part of the window highlights the name of the executed draw call at that moment:

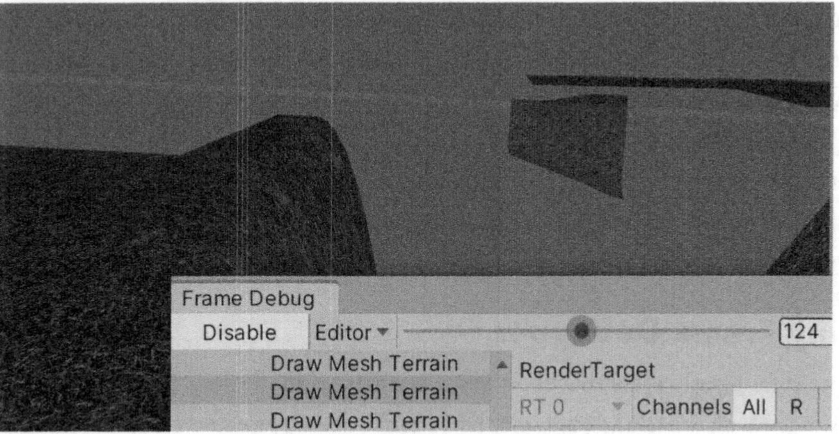

Figure 18.3: Analyzing our frame's draw calls

5. If some of the draw calls in the list output a gray image in the Game panel, alongside a warning in the console, a temporary fix for this is selecting your scene's Main Camera and setting the **MSAA** property in the **Output** section of its **Camera** component to **Off**. Remember to revert this change afterward using Frame Debugger.

6. Click on any draw call from the list and observe the details in the right part of the window.

   Most of them can be confusing to you if you are not used to code engines or shaders, but you can see that some of them have a human-readable part that says **Why this draw call can't be batched with the previous one**, which tells you why two objects weren't drawn together in a single draw call. We will examine those reasons later:

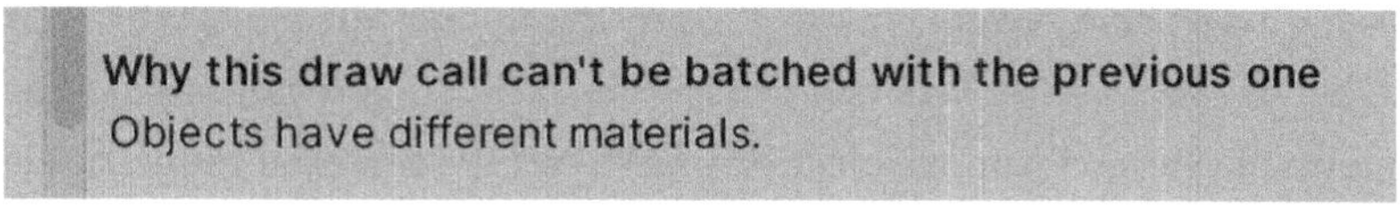

   Why this draw call can't be batched with the previous one
   Objects have different materials.

   Figure 18.4: The batching break reasons in Frame Debugger

7. With the window open in **Play** mode, disable the terrain and see how the amount of draw calls changes immediately. Sometimes, just turning objects on and off can be enough to detect what is causing performance issues. Also, try disabling postprocessing and other graphics-related objects, such as particles.

Even if we are not fully aware of where each one of these draw calls came from, we can at least start by modifying the settings throughout Unity to see the impact of those changes. There's no better way of discovering how something as massive as Unity works than going through every toggle and seeing the impact of those changes through a measuring tool. Of course, sometimes we just need to pay the price of certain draw calls to achieve certain effects, like in the case of the terrain, although you can always wonder if it's worth it or not, but that would require a case-by-case analysis.

Even if Frame Debugger gives us lots of info, sometimes you can take an extra step and use more advanced tools, like RenderDoc or Nvidia Nsight to mention some of them, which work similarly to Frame Debugger in the sense that they show all the draw calls, but also show info like the timings of each draw call, meshes, shaders, textures being used by each one of them, and much more.

Now, let's discuss the basic techniques for reducing draw calls and see their effects in Frame Debugger.

Using batching

We discussed several optimization techniques in previous chapters, with lighting being the most important one. If you measure the draw calls as you implement the techniques, you will notice the impact of those actions on the draw call count. However, in this section, we will focus on another graphics optimization technique known as batching. **Batching** is the process of grouping several objects to draw them together in a single draw call.

You may be wondering why we can't just draw everything in a single draw call, and while that is technically possible, there is a set of conditions that need to be met in order to combine two objects, the usual case being combining materials.

Remember that materials are assets that act as graphics profiles, specifying a **Material** mode or shader and a set of parameters to customize the aspect of our objects, and remember that we can use the same material in several objects. If Unity has to draw an object with a different material than the previous one, a `SetPass` call needs to be called before issuing its draw call, which is another form of CPU/GPU communication used to set the **Material** properties in the GPU, such as its textures and colors. If two objects use the same materials, this step can be skipped. The `SetPass` call from the first object is reused by the second, and that opens the opportunity to batch the objects. If they share the same settings, Unity can combine the meshes into a single one in the CPU, and then send the combined mesh in a single draw call to the GPU.

There are several ways to reduce the number of materials, such as removing duplicates, but the most effective way is through a concept called **texture atlasing**. This means merging textures from different objects into a single one. This way, several objects can use the same material due to the fact that the texture used there can be applied to several objects and an object that has its own texture requires its own material. Sadly, there's no automatic system in Unity to combine the textures of three-dimensional objects, such as the Texture Atlas object we used in 2D. There are probably some systems in the Asset Store, but automatic systems can have several side effects. This work is usually done by an artist, so just keep this technique in mind when working with a dedicated 3D artist (or if you are your own artist):

Figure 18.5: Pieces of different metallic objects

Let's explore batching with Frame Debugger by doing the following:

1. Go to **Edit | Preferences | Core Render Pipeline** and set **Visibility** to **All Visible**. This will allow us to see both basic and advanced graphics settings:

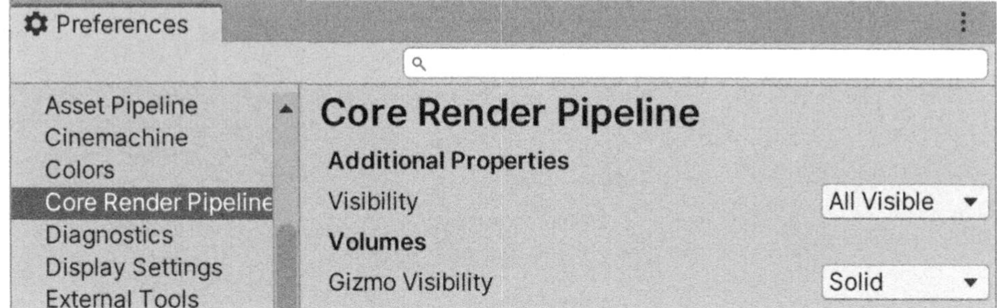

Figure 18.6: Enable the display of all available graphics settings

2. Search for the **Scriptable Render Pipeline Settings** asset that we currently want to use (**Edit | Project Settings | Graphics | Scriptable Render Pipeline Settings**):

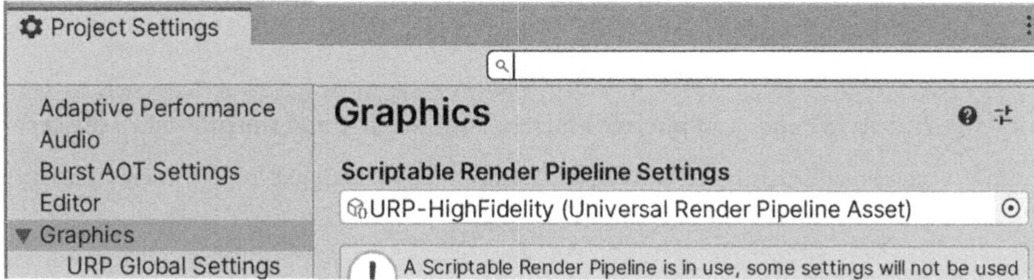

Figure 18.7: Scriptable Render Pipeline Settings

3. Uncheck **SRP Batcher** in the **Rendering** section and check **Dynamic Batching**. We will discuss **SRP Batcher** later in this chapter:

Figure 18.8: Disabling SRP Batcher

4. Create a new empty scene for testing (**File** | **New Scene**).
5. Create two materials of different colors.
6. Create two cubes and put one material into the first and the other into the second.
7. Open Frame Debugger and click **Enable** to see the call list for the draw calls of our cubes:

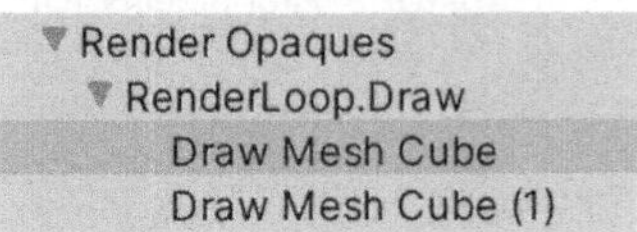

Figure 18.9: The draw calls for the cubes

8. Select the second **Draw Mesh Cube** call and look at the batch-breaking reason. It should say that the objects have different materials.
9. Use one of the materials on both cubes and look at the list again. You will notice that now we just have one **Draw Mesh Cube** call. You might need to disable and enable Frame Debugger again for it to refresh properly if you are not playing the game.

Now, I challenge you to try the same steps but create spheres instead of cubes. If you do that, you will probably notice that even with the same materials, the spheres are not batched! Here is where we need to introduce the concept of **dynamic batching**.

Remember that GameObjects have a **Static** checkbox, which serves to notify several Unity systems that the object won't move so that they can apply several optimizations. Objects that don't have this checkbox checked are considered dynamic. So far, the cubes and spheres we used for our tests have been dynamic, so Unity needed to combine them in every frame because they can move and combining is not "free." Its cost is associated directly with the number of vertices in the model. You can get the exact numbers and all the required considerations from the Unity manual, which will appear if you search `Unity Batching` on the internet or can be accessed with this link: `https://docs.unity3d.com/Manual/DrawCallBatching.html`. However, it is enough to say that if the number of vertices of an object is big enough, that object won't be batched, and doing so would require more than issuing two draw calls. That's why our spheres weren't batched; a sphere has too many vertices.

Now, things are different if we have static objects because they use a second batching system—the **static batcher**. The concept of this is the same. Merge objects to render them in one draw call, and again these objects need to share the same material. The main difference is that this batcher will batch more objects than the dynamic batcher because the merging is done once at the time that the scene loads and is then saved in memory to use in the next frames, costing memory but saving lots of processing time with each frame. You can use the same approach we used to test the dynamic batcher to test the static version just by checking the **Static** checkbox of the spheres this time and seeing the result in **Play** mode; in **Edition** mode (when it is not playing), the static batcher won't work:

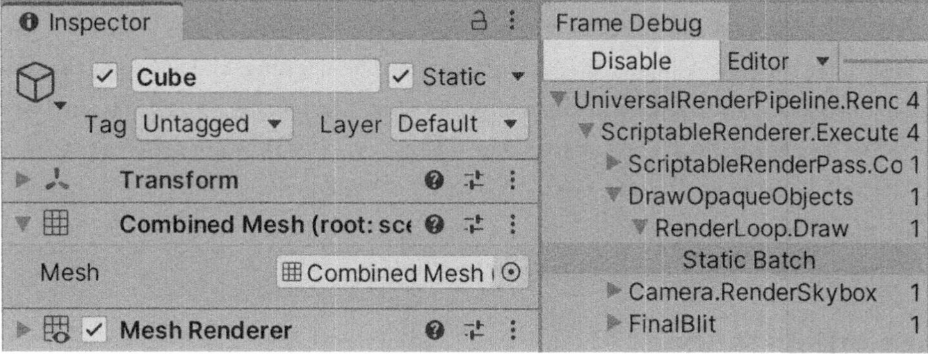

Figure 18.10: A static sphere and its static batch

Before moving on, let's discuss why we disabled SRP Batcher and how that changes what we just discussed. In its 2020 edition, Unity introduced **Universal Render Pipeline** (**URP**), a new Render Pipeline.

Along with several improvements, one that is relevant right now is SRP Batcher, a new batcher that works on dynamic objects with no vertex or material limits (but with other limits). Instead of relying on sharing the same material with batch objects, SRP Batcher can have a batch of objects with materials that use the same shader, meaning we can have, for example, 100 objects with 100 different materials for each one, and they will be batched regardless of the number of vertices, as long as the material uses the same shader and Variant:

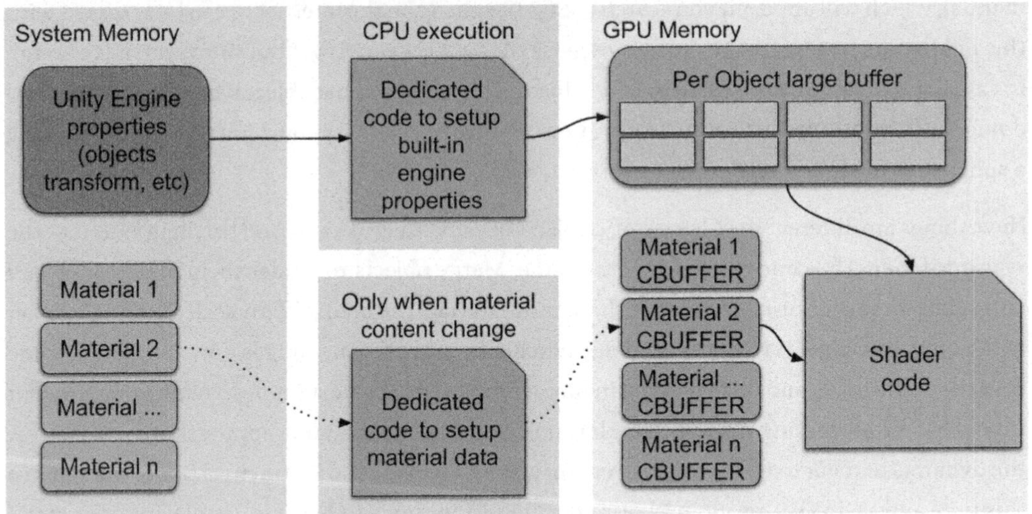

Figure 18.11: GPU data persistence for materials, which allows SRP Batcher to exist

One shader can have several versions or Variants, and the selected Variant is chosen based on the settings. We can have a shader that doesn't use normal mapping, and a Variant that doesn't calculate normals will be used, so that can affect SRP Batcher. So, there's basically no drawback to using SRP Batcher, so go ahead and turn it on again. Try creating lots of spheres with as many materials as you can and check the number of batches it will generate in Frame Debugger. Just consider that if you need to work on a project done in a pre-URP era, this won't be available, so you will need to know the proper batching strategy to use.

Other optimizations

As mentioned before, there are lots of possible graphics optimizations, so let's discuss briefly the basic ones, starting with **Level of Detail (LOD)**. LOD is the process of changing the mesh of an object based on its distance to the camera. This can reduce draw calls if you replace, for example, a house with several parts and pieces with a single combined mesh with reduced detail when the house is far. Another benefit of using LOD is that you reduce the cost of a draw call because of the reduction in the vertex count.

To use this feature, do the following:

1. Create an empty object and parent the two versions of the model. You need to use models that have several versions with different levels of detail, but for now, we are just going to test this feature using a cube and a sphere:

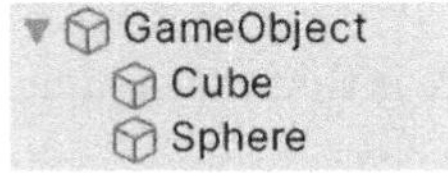

Figure 18.12: A single object with two LOD meshes

2. Add a **LOD group** component to the parent.
3. The default **LOD group** is prepared to support three LOD meshes groups, but as we only have two, right-click on one and click **Delete**. You can also select **Insert Before** to add more LOD groups:

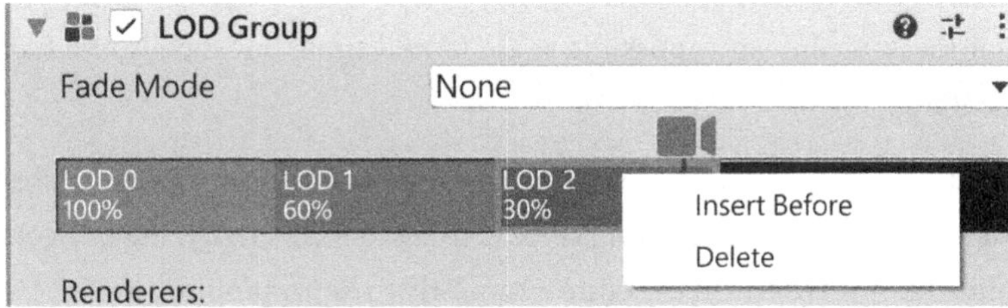

Figure 18.13: Removing a LOD group

4. Select **LOD 0**, the highest-detail LOD group, and click on the **Add** button in the **Renderers** list below this to add the sphere to that group. You can add as many mesh renderers as you want.
5. Select **LOD 1** and add the cube:

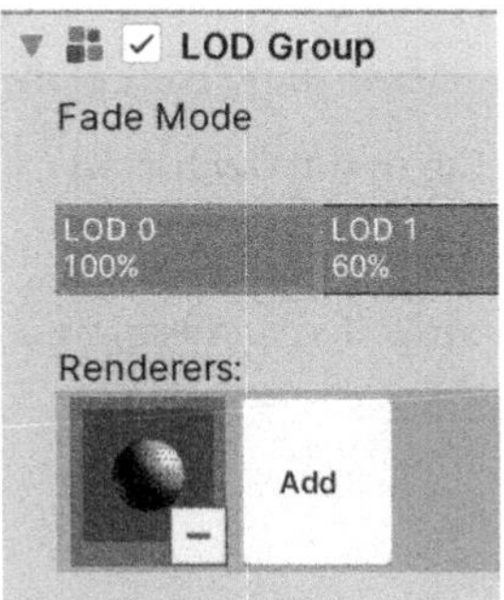

Figure 18.14: Adding renderers to LOD groups

6. Drag the line between the two groups to control the distance range that each group will occupy. As you drag it, you will see a preview of how far the camera needs to be to switch groups. Also, you have the **Culled** group, which is the distance from where the camera will not render any group.
7. Just move around the scene in the **Scene** panel to see how the meshes are swapped.
8. Something to consider here is that the colliders of the objects won't be disabled, so just have the renderers in the LOD sub-objects. Put the collider with the shape of LOD 0 in the parent object, or just remove the colliders from the LOD group objects, except group 0.

Another optimization to consider is **frustum culling**. By default, Unity will render any object that falls into the view area or frustum of the camera, skipping the ones that don't. The algorithm is cheap enough to always use, and there's no way to disable it. However, it does have a flaw. If we have a wall hiding all the objects behind it, even if they are occluded, they fall inside the frustum, so they will be rendered anyway. Detecting whether every pixel of a mesh occludes every pixel of the other mesh is almost impossible to do in real time, but luckily, we have a workaround: occlusion culling.

Occlusion culling is a process that analyzes a scene and determines which objects can be seen in different parts of the scene, dividing them into sectors and analyzing each one. As this process can take quite long, it is done in the editor, similarly to lightmapping. As you can imagine, it only works on static objects given its calculated in editor time. To use it, do the following:

1. Mark the objects that shouldn't move as static, or if you only want this object to be considered static for the occlusion culling system, check the **Occluder Static** and **Ocludee Static** checkboxes of the arrow to the right of the **Static** checkbox.
2. Open the **Occlusion Culling** window (**Window | Rendering | Occlusion Culling**).
3. Save the scene and hit the **Bake** button at the bottom of the window, and then wait for the baking process. If you don't save the scene before the baking process, it won't be executed.
4. Select the **Visualization** tab in the **Occlusion Culling** window.
5. With the **Occlusion Culling** window visible, select the camera (or Virtual Camera in the case of a Cinemachine controlled camera) and drag it around, seeing how objects are occluded as the camera moves:

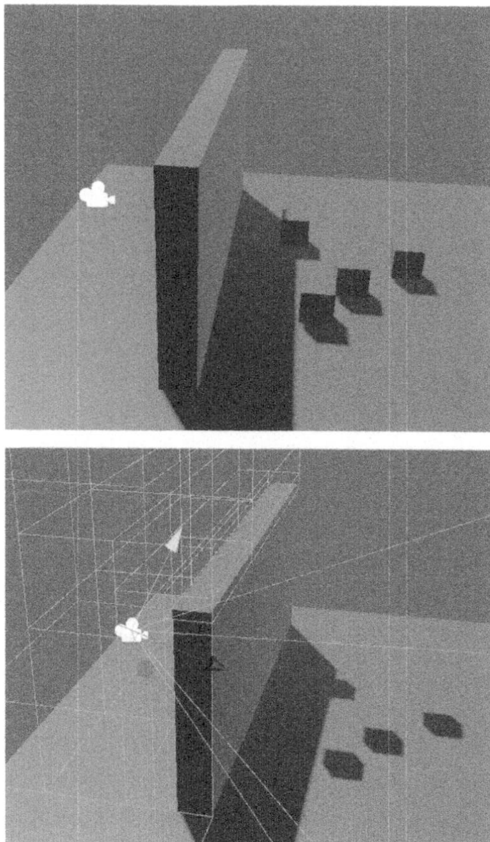

Figure 18.15: On the left is the normal scene and on the right is the scene with occlusion culling

Take into account that if you move the camera outside the calculated area, the process won't take place, and Unity will only calculate areas near the static objects. You can extend the calculation area by creating an empty object and adding an **Occlusion Area** component, setting its position and size to cover the area that the camera will reach, and, finally, rebaking the culling. Try to be sensible with the size of the cube. The larger the area to calculate, the larger the space needed in your disk to store the generated data.

You can use several of these areas to be more precise—for example, in an L-shaped scene, you can use two of them:

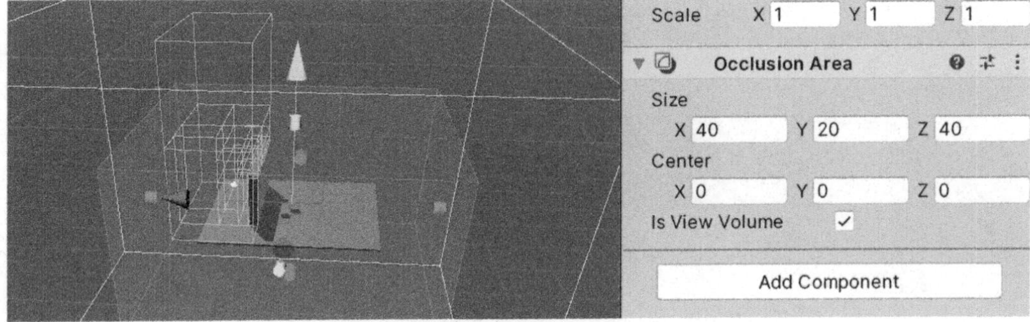

Figure 18.16: Occlusion Area

If you see that the objects are not being occluded, it can be that the occluder object (the wall in this case) is not big enough to be considered. You can increase the size of the object or reduce the **Smallest Occluder** setting in the **Bake** tab of the window. Doing that will subdivide the scene further to detect small occluders, but that will take more space in the disk to store more data. So again, be sensible with this setting.

There are still some more techniques that we can apply to our game, but the ones we have discussed are enough for our game. So, in this section, we learned about the process of rendering graphics in a video card, the concept of batches, how to profile them to know exactly how many of them we have and what they are doing, and finally, how to reduce them as much as we can. Now, let's start discussing other optimization areas, such as the processing area.

Optimizing processing

While graphics usually take up most of the time that a frame needs to be generated, we should never underestimate the cost of badly optimized code and scenes. There are several parts of the game that are still calculated in the CPU, including part of the graphics process (such as the batching calculations), physics, audio, and our code. Here, we have a lot more causes of performance issues than on the graphics side, so again, instead of discussing every optimization, let's learn how to discover them.

In this section, we will examine the following CPU optimization concepts:

- Detecting CPU- and GPU-bound
- Using the **CPU Usage** Profiler
- General CPU optimization techniques

We will start by discussing the concepts of CPU- and GPU-bound, which focus on the optimization process, determining whether the problem is GPU- or CPU-related. Later, as with the GPU optimization process, we will look at how to gather the performance data of the CPU and interpret it to detect possible optimization techniques to be applied.

Detecting CPU- and GPU-bound

As with Frame Debugger, the Unity Profiler allows us to gather data about the performance of our game through a series of Profiler modules, each one designed to gather data about different Unity systems per frame, such as physics, audio, and, most importantly, **CPU usage**. This last module allows us to see the most important operations that Unity executed to process the frame—which range from our scripts to systems such as physics and graphics (the CPU part).

Before exploring the **CPU usage**, one important bit of data that we can gather in this module is whether we are CPU or GPU bound. As explained before, a frame is processed using both the CPU and GPU, and those pieces of hardware can work in parallel. While the GPU is executing drawing commands, the CPU can execute physics and our scripts in a very efficient way. But now, let's say that the CPU finishes its work while the GPU is still working. Can the CPU start to work on the next frame? The answer is no. This would lead to a de-synchronization, so in this scenario, the CPU will need to wait. This is known as CPU-bound, and we also have the opposite case, GPU-bound, when the GPU finishes earlier than the CPU.

It is important to concentrate our optimization efforts, so if we detect that our game is GPU-bound, we will focus on GPU graphics optimization (like reduction of mesh and shader complexity), and if it is CPU-bound, then we will focus on the rest of the systems and the CPU side of graphics processing. To detect whether our game is one or the other, do the following:

1. Open **Profiler (Window | Analysis | Profiler)**.
2. In the **Profiler Modules** dropdown in the top-left corner, tick **GPU** to enable the GPU profiler:

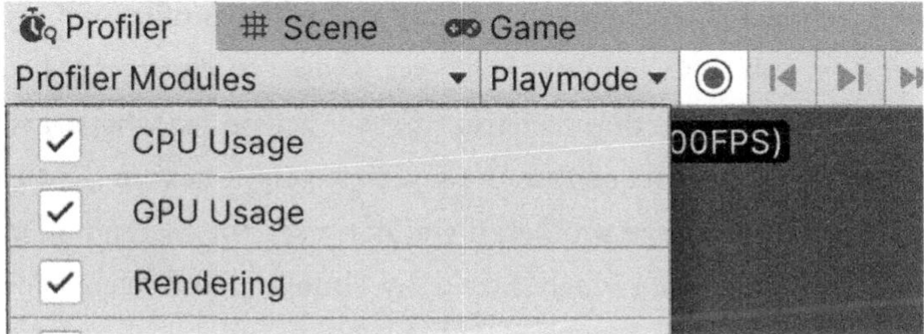

Figure 18.17: Enabling the GPU profiler

3. Play the game and select the **CPU Usage** profiler, clicking on its name in the left part of the **Profiler** window.
4. Click the **Last Frame** button, the one with the double arrow pointing to the right, to always display info of the last frame being rendered:

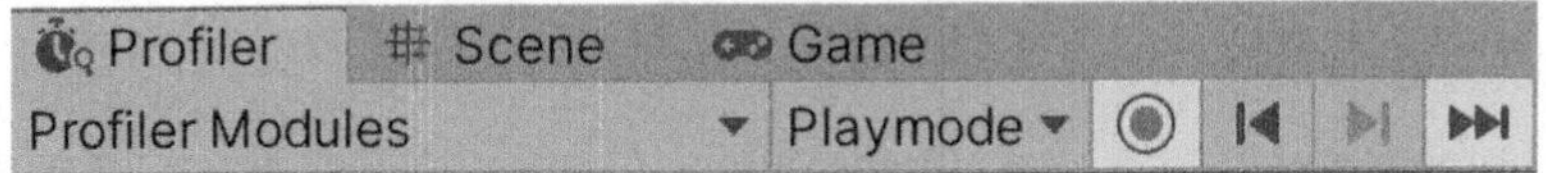

Figure 18.18: Last frame button (double arrow to the right)

5. Also click the **Live** button to enable Live mode, which allows you to see the results of profiling in real time. This can have an impact on performance, so you can disable it later:

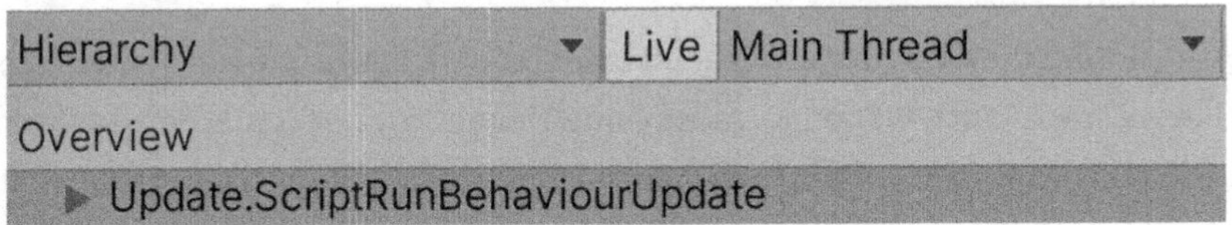

Figure 18.19: Enabling Live mode

6. Observe the bar with the **CPU** and **GPU** labels in the middle of the window. It should say how many milliseconds are being consumed by the CPU and GPU. The one with the higher number will be the one that is limiting our framerate and will determine whether we are GPU- or CPU-bound:

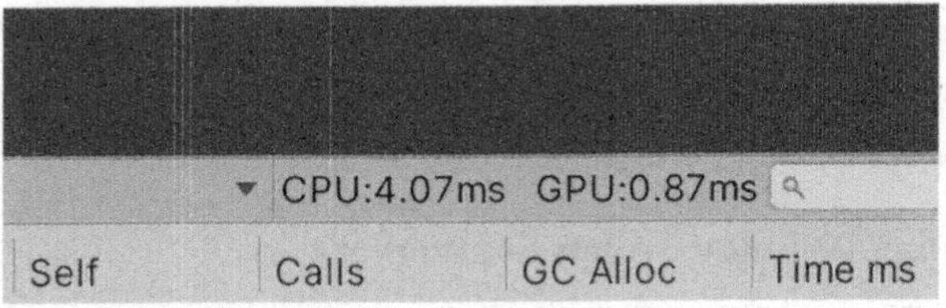

Figure 18.20: Determining whether we are CPU- or GPU-bound

7. There is a chance that when you try to open the GPU profiler, you will see a not supported message, and this can happen in certain cases (such as on Mac devices that use the Metal graphics API). In that scenario, another way to see whether we are GPU-bound is by searching `waitforpresent` in the search bar right next to the CPU/GPU labels while selecting the **CPU Usage** profiler. If you don't see the search bar, click the drop-down menu at the left of **Live** (which should say **Timeline**) and select **Hierarchy**:

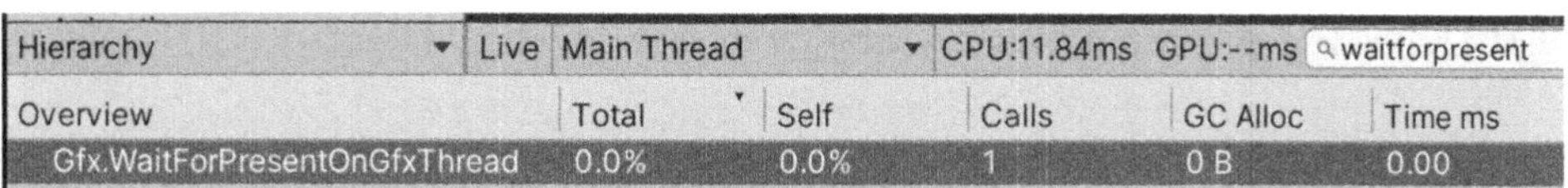

Hierarchy	Live	Main Thread	CPU:11.84ms	GPU:--ms	waitforpresent
Overview	Total	Self	Calls	GC Alloc	Time ms
Gfx.WaitForPresentOnGfxThread	0.0%	0.0%	1	0 B	0.00

Figure 18.21: Searching waitforpresent

8. Here, you can see how long the CPU has been waiting for the GPU. Check the **Time ms** column to get the number. If you see **0.00**, it is because the CPU is not waiting for the GPU, meaning we are CPU-bound. In the preceding screenshot, you can see that my screen displays **0.00** while the CPU is taking **9.41ms** and the GPU is taking **6.73ms**. So, my device is CPU-bound, but consider your device and project can bring different results.

Now that we can detect whether we are CPU- or GPU-bound, we can focus our optimization efforts. So far, we discussed how to profile and optimize part of the GPU process in the *Optimizing graphics* section. Now, if we detect that we are CPU-bound, let's see how to profile the CPU.

Using the CPU Usage Profiler

Profiling the CPU is done in a similar way to profiling the GPU. We need to get a list of actions the CPU executes and try to reduce the number of them, or at least reduce their cost. Here is where the **CPU Usage Profiler** module comes in—a tool that allows us to see all the instructions that the CPU executed in one frame. The main difference is that the GPU mostly executes draw calls, and we have a few types of them, while the CPU can have hundreds of different instructions to execute, and sometimes some of them cannot be deleted, such as physics or audio processing. In these scenarios, we are looking to reduce the cost of these functions in case they are consuming too much time. So, again, an important note here is to detect which function is taking too much time and then reduce its cost or remove it, which requires a deeper understanding of the underlying system. Let's start detecting the function first.

When you play the game with the **Profiler** tab opened, you will see a series of graphics showing the performance of your game, and in the **CPU Usage** profiler, you will see that the graphic is split into different colors, each one referring to different parts of frame processing. You can check the information to the left of the Profiler to see what each color means, but let's discuss the most important ones.

In the following screenshot, you can see how the graphic should look:

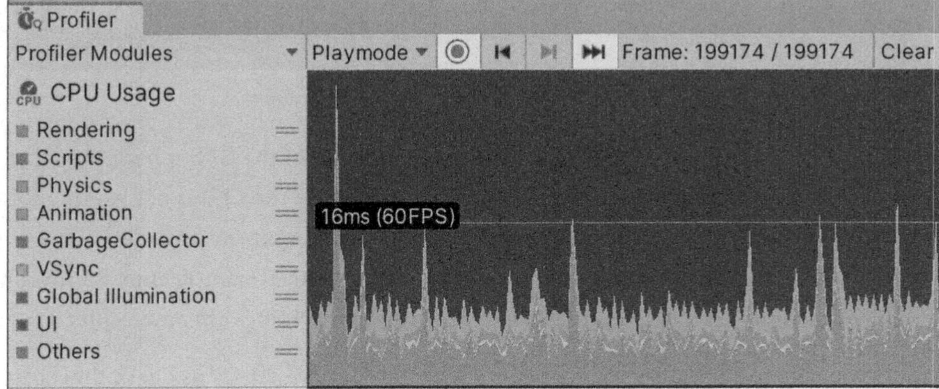

Figure 18.22: Analyzing the CPU Usage graph

If you see the graphic, you will probably assume that the dark-green part of the graph is taking up most of the performance time, and while that is true, you can also see from the legend that dark green means **Others**, and that's because we are profiling the game in the editor. The editor won't behave exactly like the final game. In order for it to run, it has to do lots of extra processing that won't be executed in the game, so the best you can do is profile directly in the build of the game. There, you will gather more accurate data. We are going to discuss how to do builds in the next chapter, so for now, we can ignore that area. What we can do now is simply click on the colored square to the left of the **Others** label to disable that measurement from the graph in order to clean it up a little bit. If you also see a large section of yellow, it is referring to **VSync**, which is basically the time spent waiting for our processing to match the monitor's refresh rate. This is also something that we can ignore, so you should also disable it. In the next screenshot, you can check the graphic color categories and how to disable them:

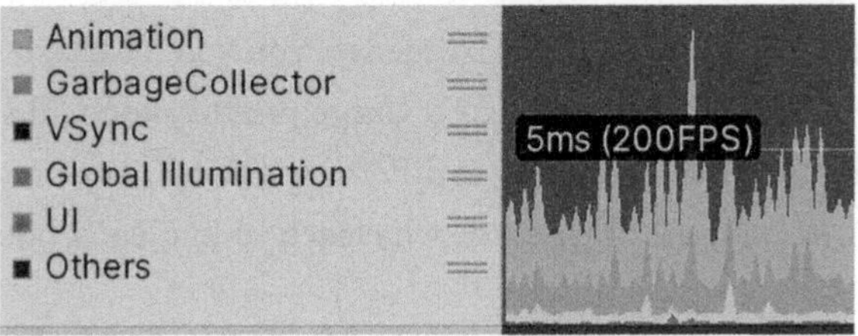

Figure 18.23: Disabling VSync and Others from the Profiler

Now that we have cleaned up the graph, we can get a good idea of our game's potential framerate by looking at the line with the **ms** label (in our case, **5ms (200FPS)**), which indicates that frames below that line have more than 200 FPS, and frames above that line have less.

In my case, I have excellent performance, but remember, I am testing this on a powerful machine. The best way to profile is not only in the build of the game (as an executable) but also in the target device, which should be the lowest-spec hardware we intend our game to run on. Our target device depends a lot on the target audience of the game. If we are making a casual game, we are probably targeting mobile devices, so we should test the game on the lowest-spec phone we can, but if we are targeting hardcore gamers, they will probably have a powerful machine to run our game on.

If you are targeting hardcore gamers, of course, this doesn't mean that we can just make a very unoptimized game because of that, but it will give us enough processing space to add more detail. Anyway, I strongly recommend you avoid those kinds of games if you are a beginner as they are more difficult to develop, which you will probably realize. Stick to simple games to begin with.

Looking at the graphics colors, you can observe the cost on the CPU side of rendering in light green, which the graph shows is taking up a significant portion of the processing time, which is actually normal. Then, in blue, we can see the cost of our scripts' and others systems' execution, which is also taking up a significant portion, but again, this is quite normal. Also, we can observe a little bit of orange, which is physics, and also a little bit of light blue, which is animations. Remember to check the colored labels in the Profiler to remember which color refers to what.

Now, those colored bars represent a group of operations, so if we consider the **Rendering** bar to be representing 10 operations, how do we know which operations that includes? Also, how do we know which of these operations is taking up the most performance time? Out of those 10 operations, a single one could be causing these issues. Here is where the bottom part of the profiler is useful. It shows a list of all the functions being called in the frame. To use it, do the following:

1. Click any part of the *CPU Usage* section in the Profiler and check that the button at the top-left part of the bottom bar of the Profiler says **Hierarchy**. If not (for example, if it says **Timeline**), click it and select **Hierarchy**.
2. Clear the search bar we used earlier. It will filter function calls by name, and we want to see them all.
3. Click on the **Time ms** column until you see an arrow pointing downward. This will order the calls by cost in descending order.
4. Click on a frame that catches your attention in the graph—probably one of the ones with the biggest height that consume more processing time. This will make the Profiler stop the game straight away and show you information about that frame.

There are two things to consider when looking at the graph. If you see peaks that are significantly higher than the rest of the frames, that can cause a hiccup in your game—a very brief moment where the game is frozen—which can break the performance. Also, you can look for a long series of frames with higher time consumption. Try to reduce them as well. Even if this is only temporary, the impact of it will be easily perceived by the player, especially in VR games, as that could induce nausea.

5. **PlayerLoop** will probably appear as the most time-consuming frame, but that's not very informative. You can explore it further by expanding it by clicking on the arrow to its left.
6. Click on each function to highlight it in the graph. Functions with higher processing times will be highlighted with thicker bars, and those are the ones we will focus on:

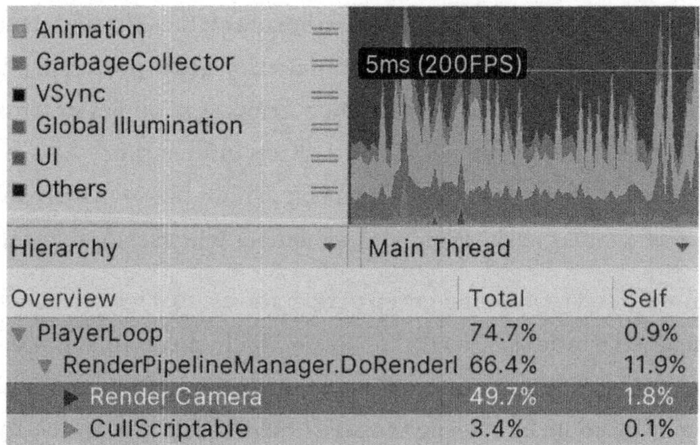

Figure 18.24: The Render Camera function highlighted in the graph

7. You can keep clicking on the arrows to further explore the functions until you hit a limit. If you want to go deeper, enable the **Deep Profile** mode in the top bar of the Profiler. This will give you more details, but take into account that this process is expensive and will make the game go slower, altering the time shown in the graph, making it appear much higher than the real time. Here, ignore the numbers and look at how much of the process a function is taking up based on the graph. You will need to stop, enable **Deep Profile**, and play it again to make it work:

Clear on Play | Deep Profile

Figure 18.25: Enabling Deep Profile

With this knowledge, we can start improving our game performance (if it's below the target framerate), but each function is called by the CPU and is improved in its own unique way, which requires greater knowledge about Unity's internal workings. That could span several books, and anyway, the internals change on a version-to-version basis. Instead, you could study how each function works by looking up data about that specific system on the internet and official documentation, or again, by just disabling and enabling objects or parts of our code to explore the impact of our actions, as we did with Frame Debugger. Profiling requires creativity and inference to interpret and react accordingly to the data obtained, so you will need some patience here.

Now that we have discussed how to get the profiling data relating to the CPU, let's discuss some common ways to reduce **CPU usage**.

General CPU optimization techniques

In terms of CPU optimizations, there are lots of possible causes of high performance, including the abuse of Unity's features, a large number of physics or audio objects, improper asset/object configurations, and so on. Our scripts can also be coded in an unoptimized way, abusing or misusing expensive Unity API functions. So far, we have discussed several good practices of using Unity systems, such as audio configurations, texture sizes, batching, and finding functions such as `GameObject.Find` and replacing them with managers. So, let's discuss some specific details about common cases.

Let's start by seeing how a large amount of objects impacts our performance. Here, you can just create lots of objects with `Rigidbody` (at least 200) configured in **Dynamic Profile**, and observe the results in the Profiler.

You will notice, in the following screenshot, how the orange part of the profiler just got bigger and that the `Physics.Processing` function is responsible for this increase:

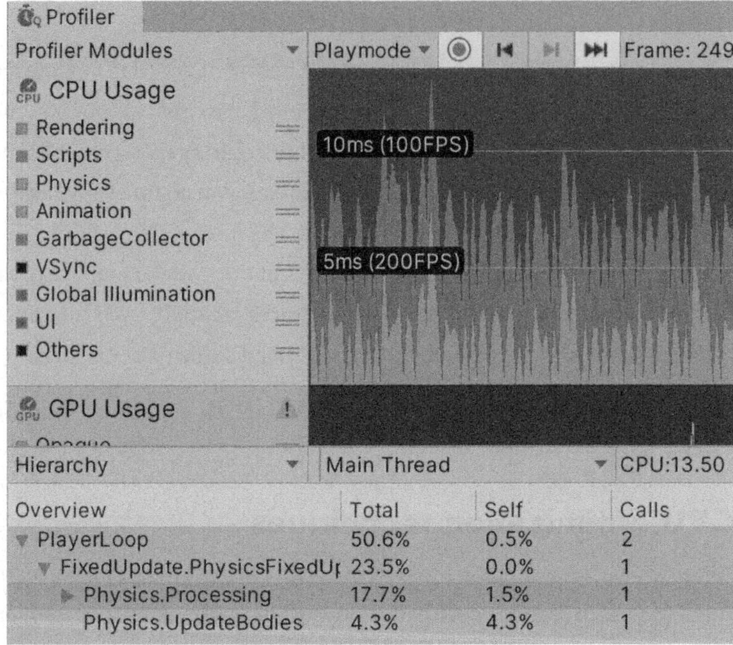

Figure 18.26: The Physics processing of several objects

Remember that the Profiler has other modules that you can activate by clicking the **Profiler Modules** button, and there's one for physics. Consider enabling it and checking the info it gives you. Also check the official documentation for the profiler for more info on those modules.

Another test to see the impact of several objects could be creating lots of audio sources. In the following screenshot, you can see that we needed to re-enable **Others** because part of the audio processing comes under that category. We mentioned earlier that **Others** belongs to the editor, but it can encompass other processes as well, so keep that in mind:

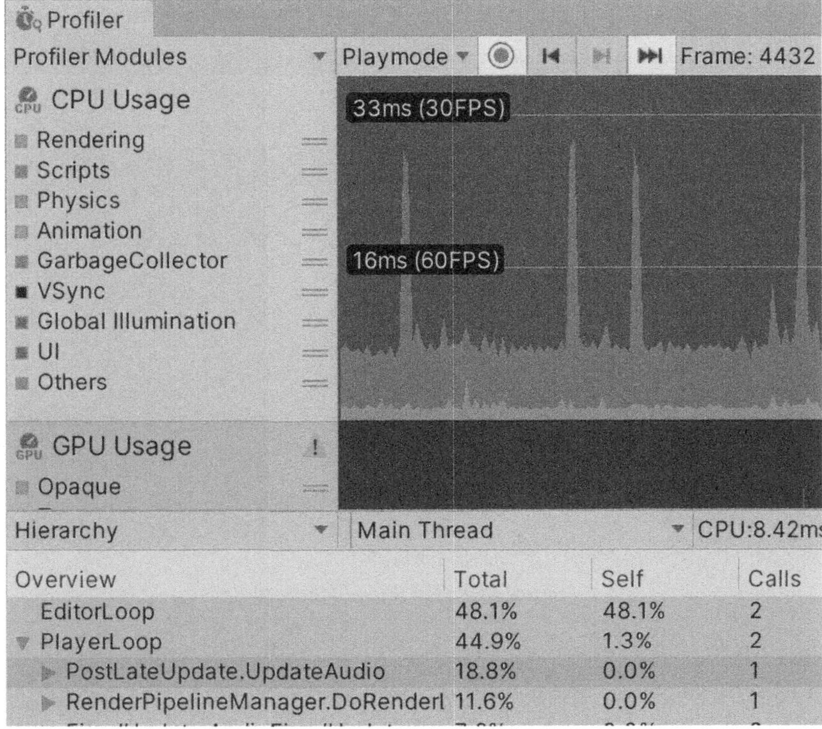

Figure 18.27: The Physics processing of several objects

So, to discover these kinds of problems, you can just start disabling and enabling objects and see whether they increase the time or not. A final test is on particles. Create a system that spawns a big enough number of particles to affect our framerate and check the Profiler.

In the following screenshot, you can check how the particle processing function is highlighted in the graph, showing that it takes a large amount of time:

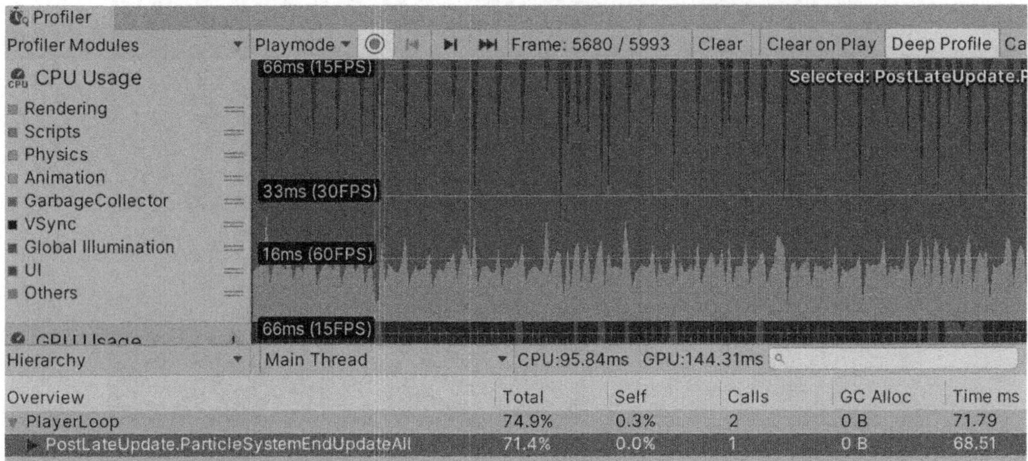

Figure 18.28: Particle processing

Then, on the scripting side, we have other kinds of things to consider, some of which are common to all programming languages and platforms, such as iterating long lists of objects, the misuse of data structures, and deep recursion. However, in this section, I will mainly be discussing Unity-specific APIs, starting with `print` or `Debug.Log`.

This function is useful to get debugging information in the console, but it can also be costly because all logs are written onto the disk immediately to avoid losing valuable information if our game crashes. Of course, we want to keep those valuable logs in the game, but we don't want it to affect the performance, so what can we do?

One possible approach is to keep those messages but disable the non-essential ones in the final build, such as informative messages, keeping the error-reporting function active. One way to do this is through compiler directives, such as the ones used in the following screenshot. Remember that this kind of `if` statement is executed by the compiler and can exclude entire portions of code when compiling if its conditions are not met:

```
#if UNITY_EDITOR || DEVELOPMENT_BUILD
print("Informative message");
#endif
```

Figure 18.29: Disabling code

In the preceding screenshot, you can see how we are asking whether this code is being compiled by the editor or for a development build, which is a special kind of build intended to be used for testing (more on that in the next chapter). You can also create your own kind of logging system with functions with the compiler directives, so you don't need to use them in every log that you want to exclude.

In this section, we learned about the tasks a CPU faces when processing a video game, how to profile them to see which ones are not necessary, and how to reduce the impact of those processes. There are a few other script aspects that can affect performance not only on the processing side but also on the memory side, so let's discuss them in the next section.

Optimizing memory

We discussed how to profile and optimize two pieces of hardware—the CPU and GPU—but there is another piece of hardware that plays a key role in our game—RAM. This is the place where we put all of our game's data. Games can be memory-intensive applications, and unlike several other applications, they are constantly executing code, so we need to be especially careful about that.

In this section, we will examine the following memory optimization concepts:

- Memory allocation and the garbage collector
- Using the Memory Profiler

Let's start discussing how memory allocation works and what role garbage collection plays here.

Memory allocation and the garbage collector

Each time we instantiate an object, we are allocating memory in RAM, and in a game, we will be allocating memory constantly. In other programming languages, aside from allocating the memory, you need to manually deallocate it, but C# has a garbage collector, which is a system that tracks unused memory and cleans it. This system works with a reference counter, which tracks how many references to an object exist, and when that counter reaches `0`, it means all references have become null and the object can be deallocated. This deallocation process can be triggered in several situations, the most common situation being when we reach the maximum assigned memory and we want to allocate a new object. In that scenario, we can release enough memory to allocate our object, and if that is not possible, the memory is expanded.

In any game, you will probably be allocating and deallocating memory constantly, which can lead to memory fragmentation, meaning there are small spaces between alive object memory blocks that are mostly useless because they aren't big enough to allocate an object, or maybe the sum of the spaces is big enough, but we need continuous memory space to allocate our objects. In the following diagram, you can see a classic example of trying to fit a big chunk of memory into the little gaps generated by fragmentation:

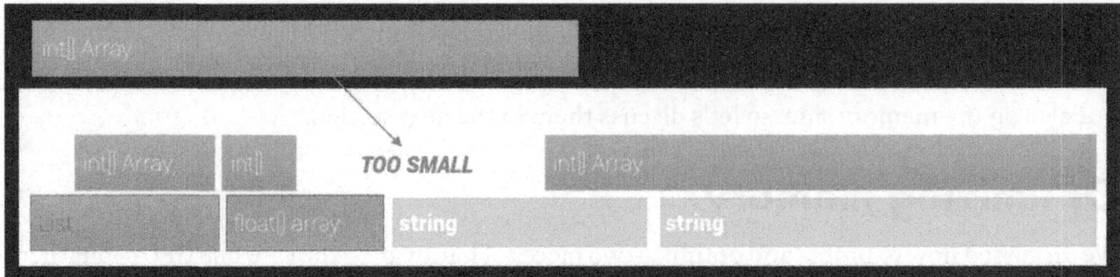

Figure 18.30: Trying to instantiate an object in a fragmented memory space

Some types of garbage collection systems, such as the one in regular C#, are generational, meaning memory is split into generation buckets according to the "age" of its memory. Newer memory will be placed in the first bucket, and this memory tends to be allocated and deallocated frequently. Because this bucket is small, working within it is fast. The second bucket has the memory that survived a previous deallocation sweep process in the first bucket. That memory is moved to the second bucket to prevent it from being checked constantly if it survived the process, and it is possible that that memory will last the length of our program's lifetime. The third bucket is just another layer of bucket 2. The idea is that most of the time, the allocation and deallocation system will be working in bucket 1, and as it is small enough, it is quick to allocate, deallocate, and compact memory in a continuous fashion.

The problem here is that Unity uses its own version of the garbage collection system, and that version is non-generational and non-compacting, meaning memory is not split into buckets and memory won't be moved to fill the gaps. This suggests that allocating and deallocating memory in Unity will still result in the fragmentation problem, and if you don't regulate your memory allocation, you might end up with an expensive garbage collection system being executed very often, producing hiccups in our game, which you can see in the **Profiler CPU Usage** module as a pale-yellow color.

One way to deal with this is by preventing memory allocation as much as you can, avoiding it when it is not necessary. There are a few tweaks here and there that you can make to prevent memory allocation, but before looking at those, again, it is important to first get data about the problem before you start fixing things that may not be an issue. This advice applies to any type of optimization process. Here, we can still use the **CPU Usage** profiler to see how much memory is allocated to each function call that the CPU executes in each frame, and that is simply done by looking at the **GC Alloc** column, which indicates the amount of memory that the function allocated:

Overview	Total	Self	Calls	GC Alloc
▼ Update.ScriptRunBehaviourUpdate	6.4%	0.0%	1	2.3 KB
▼ BehaviourUpdate	6.4%	1.2%	1	2.3 KB
▼ Sight.Update()	2.0%	0.5%	69	2.2 KB
Physics.OverlapSphere	1.4%	1.4%	69	0 B
GC.Alloc	0.0%	0.0%	69	2.2 KB
Physics.Raycast	0.0%	0.0%	1	0 B

Figure 18.31: The memory allocation of the Update event function of Sight

In the preceding screenshot, we can see how our function is allocating too much memory, which is produced because there are many enemies in the scene. But that's no excuse; we are allocating that much RAM at every frame, so we need to improve this. There are several things that can contribute to our memory being claimed by allocations, so let's discuss the basic ones, starting with array-returning functions.

If we review the `Sight` script code, we can see that the only moment where we are allocating memory is in the call to `Physics.OverlapSphere`, and that is evident because it is an array-returning function, which is a function that returns a varying amount of data. To do this, it needs to allocate an array and return that array to us. This needs to be done on the side that created the function, Unity, but in this case, Unity gives us two versions of the function—the one that we are using and the `NonAlloc` version. It is usually recommended to use the second version, but Unity uses the other one to make coding simpler for beginners.

The NonAlloc version looks as in the following screenshot:

```
static Collider[] colliders = new Collider[100];

void Update()
{
    int detectedAmount = Physics.OverlapSphereNonAlloc(
        transform.position,
        distance,
        colliders,
        objectsLayers);

    detectedObject = null;
    for (int i = 0; i < detectedAmount; i++)
    {
        Collider collider = colliders[i];
```

Figure 18.32: Memory allocation of the Update event function of Sight

This version requires us to allocate an array with enough space to save the largest amount of colliders our OverlapSphere variable can find and pass it as the third parameter. This allows us to allocate the array just once and reuse it on every occasion that we need it. In the preceding screenshot, you can see how the array is static, which means it is shared between all the Sight variables as they won't execute in parallel (no Update function will). This will work fine. Keep in mind that the function will return the number of objects that were detected, so we just iterate on that count. The array can have previous results stored within it.

Now, check your Profiler and notice how the amount of memory allocated has been reduced greatly. There might be some remaining memory allocation within our function, but sometimes there is no way to keep it at 0. However, you can try to look at the reasons for this using deep profiling or by commenting some code and seeing which comment removes the allocation. I challenge you to try this. Also, OverlapSphere is not the only case where this could occur. You have others, such as the GetComponents functions family, which, unlike GetComponent, finds all the components of a given type, not just the first one, so pay attention to any array-returning function of Unity and try to replace it with a non-allocating version, if there is one.

Another common source of memory allocation is string concatenation. Remember that strings are immutable, meaning they cannot change if you concatenate two strings. A third one needs to be generated with enough space to hold the first ones. If you need to concatenate a large number of times, consider using `string.Format` if you are just replacing placeholders in a template string, such as putting the name of the player and the score they got in a message or using `StringBuilder`, a class that just holds all the strings to be concatenated in a list and, when necessary, concatenates them together, instead of concatenating them one by one as the + operator does. Also, consider using the new string interpolation functionality of C#. You can see some examples in the following screenshot:

```
string name = "John";
string score = "100";
string template = "{0} has won {1} points";

//both will print: John has won 100 points
print(string.Format(template, name, score));
print($"{name} has won {score} points.");

StringBuilder builder = new StringBuilder();
builder.Append("My ");
builder.Append("name ");
builder.Append("is ");
builder.Append("Neo.");

print(builder.ToString()); //My name is Neo.
```

Figure 18.33: String management in C#

Finally, a classic technique to consider is object pooling, which is suitable in cases where you need to instantiate and destroy objects constantly, such as with bullets or effects. In that scenario, the use of regular `Instantiate` and `Destroy` functions will lead to memory fragmentation, but object pooling fixes that by allocating the maximum amount of required objects possible. It replaces `Instantiate` by taking one of the preallocated functions and it replaces `Destroy` by returning the object to the pool.

A simple pool can be seen in the following screenshot:

```
public class Pool : MonoBehaviour
{
    List<GameObject> storedObjects = new List<GameObject>();

    [SerializeField] private GameObject prefab;

    public GameObject Get()
    {
        if (storedObjects.Count > 0)
        {
            var obj :GameObject = storedObjects[0];
            storedObjects.RemoveAt(0);
            obj.SetActive(true);
            return obj;
        }
        else
        {
            return Instantiate(prefab);
        }
    }

    public void Return(GameObject obj)
    {
        obj.SetActive(false);
        storedObjects.Add(obj);
    }
}
```

Figure 18.34: A simple object pool

There are several ways to improve this pool, but it is fine as it is for now. Note that objects need to be reinitialized when they are taken out of the pool, and you can do that with the `OnEnable` event function or by creating a custom function to inform the object to do so. Also, note that Unity has recently added an Object Pool class that you can investigate at the following link: `https://docs.unity3d.com/2022.1/Documentation/ScriptReference/Pool.ObjectPool_1.html`, but I still recommend making your own first to grasp the idea of pools.

Now that we have explored some basic memory allocation reduction techniques, let's look at the new **Memory Profiler** tool, introduced in the latest version of Unity, to explore memory in greater detail.

Using the Memory Profiler

With this Profiler, we can detect memory allocated on a frame-per-frame basis, but it won't show the total memory allocated so far, which would be useful to study how we are using our memory. This is where the **Memory Profiler** can help us. This relatively new Unity package allows us to take memory snapshots of every single object allocated both on the native and managed side—native meaning the internal C++ Unity code and managed meaning anything that belongs to the C# side (that is, both our code and Unity's C# engine code). We can explore snapshots with a visual tool and rapidly see which type of object is consuming the most RAM and how they are referenced by other objects.

To start using the **Memory Profiler**, do the following:

1. Open the **Package Manager** (**Window** | **Package Manager**) and enable preview packages (**Wheel Icon** | **Project Settings** | **Enable Pre-release Packages**):

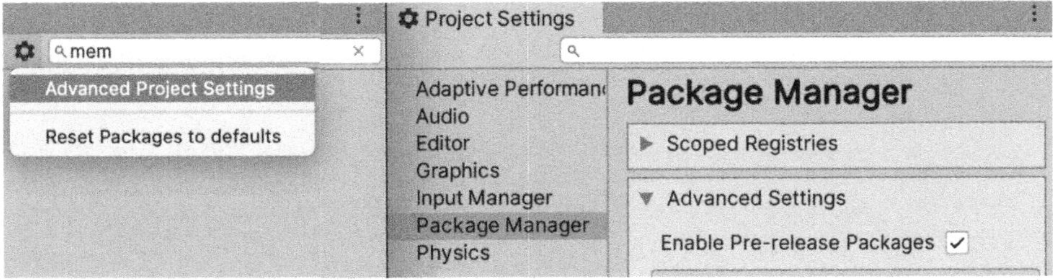

Figure 18.35: Enabling preview packages

2. Click the + button and select **Add package by name...**:

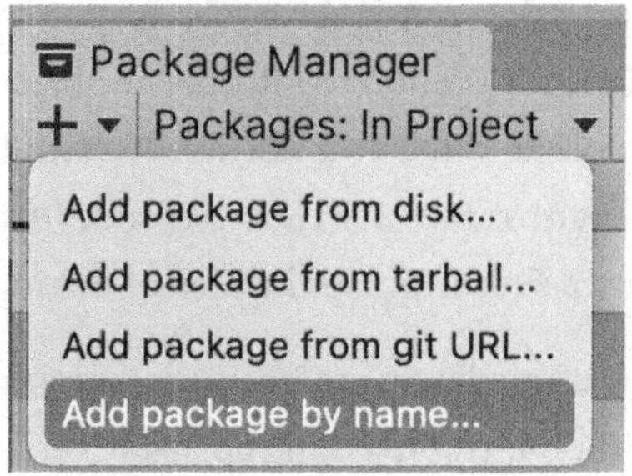

Figure 18.36: Installing packages from Git URLs

3. In the dialog box, write `com.unity.memoryprofiler` and click **Add**. We need to add the package this way as it's still an experimental one:

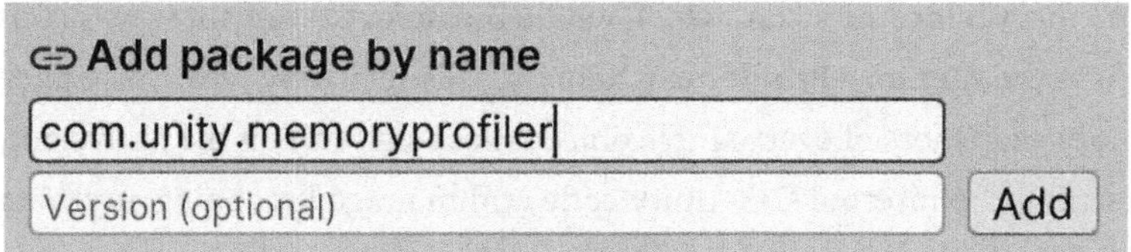

Figure 18.37: Installing the Memory Profiler

4. Once installed, open the **Memory Profiler** in **Window** | **Analysis** | **Memory Profiler**.
5. Play the game and click on the **Capture** button in the **Memory Profiler** window:

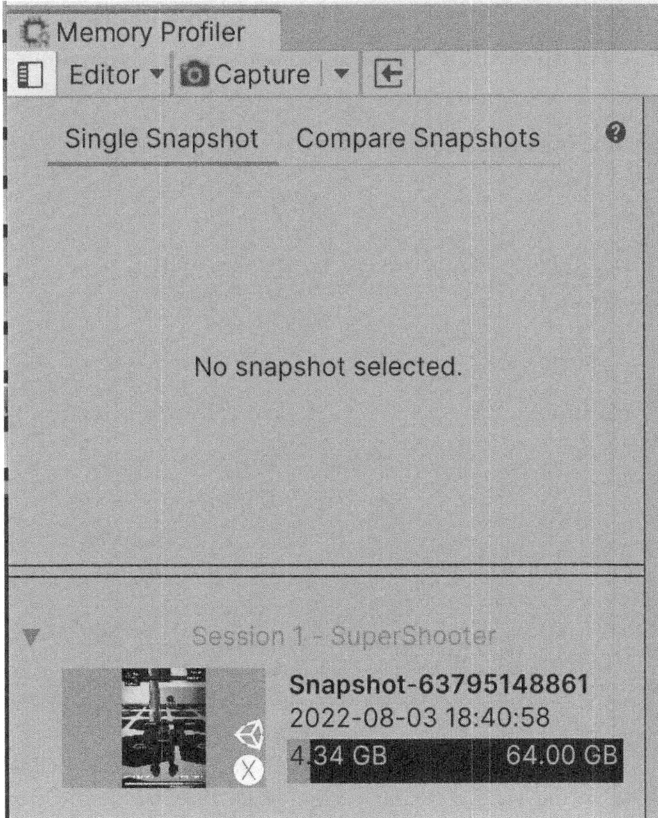

Figure 18.38: Capturing a snapshot

6. Click on the snapshot that appeared in the list (the one below the **Session 1** label) to see a summary of the memory consumption at the moment of taking a snapshot:

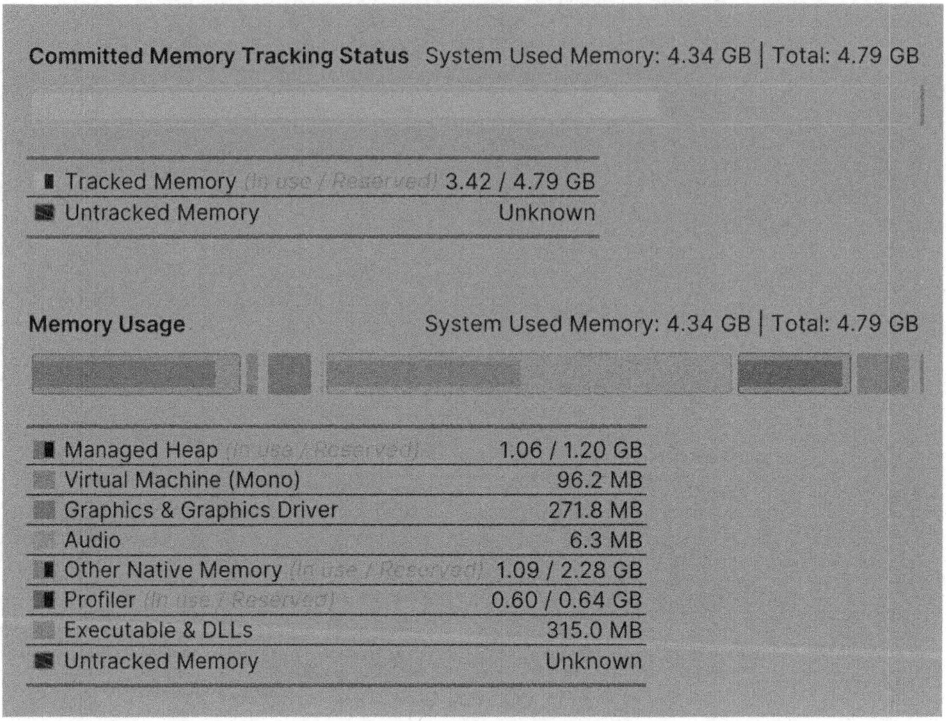

Figure 18.39: Memory summary

7. In our case, we can see that we are consuming 4.79 GB of memory, split between **Managed Heap** (C# code variables), **Other Native Memory** (Unity's C++ memory), **Graphics & Graphics Driver**, **Audio**, and much more. There are different things that are accounted for in these categories, but for now, we are good. Open the package documentation in the Package Manager to get more info about them.
8. Click the **Tree Map** button at the top part of the middle section of the **Memory Profiler** window. This will open the **Tree View**, which allows you to visually see which types of assets are the more demanding in terms of memory:

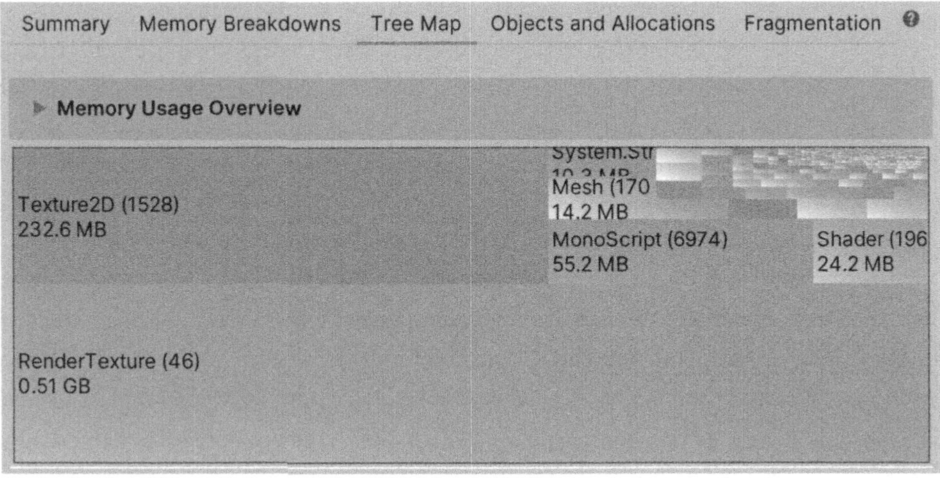

Figure 18.40: Memory tree view

9. In our case, we can see that `RenderTexture` uses up the most memory, which belongs to the image that is displayed in the scene, as well as some textures used by postprocessing effects. Try to disable the `PPVolume` object and take another snapshot to detect the difference.
10. In my case, that dropped off 130 MB. There are other textures needed for other effects, such as HDR. If you want to explore where those remaining MB came from, click on the **RenderTexture** block to subdivide it into its objects and take your own guesses based on the names of the textures:

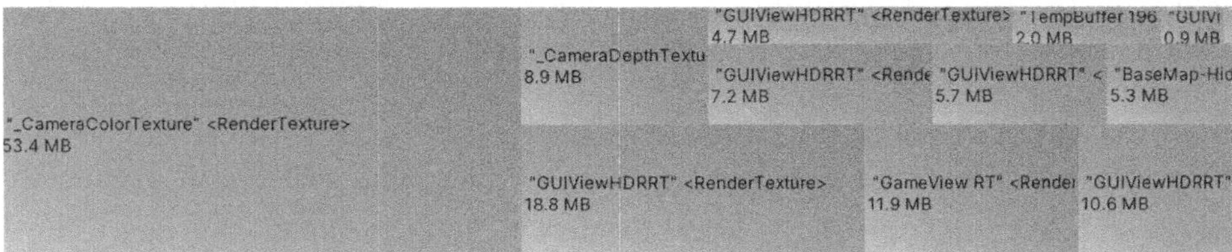

Figure 18.41: Memory blocks in detail

11. You can repeat the same process in the `Texture2D` block type, which belongs to the textures used in the materials of our models. You can look at the biggest one and detect its usage—maybe it is a big texture that is never seen close enough to justify its size. Then, we can reduce its size using the **Max Size of the Texture** import settings.

As with any profiler, it is always useful to carry out the profiling directly in the build (more on that in the next chapter) because taking snapshots in the editor will capture lots of memory that is used by the editor and will not be used in the build. An example of this is the loading of unnecessary textures because the editor probably loaded them when you clicked them to see their previews in the **Inspector** window.

Take into account that due to the **Memory Profiler** being a package, its UI can change often, but its basic idea will remain. You can use this tool to detect whether you are using the memory in unexpected ways. Something useful to consider here is how Unity loads assets when loading a scene, which consists of loading all assets referenced in the scene at load time. This means that you can have, as an example, an array of prefabs that have references to materials that have references to textures, and even if you don't instantiate a single instance of them, the prefabs must be loaded in memory, causing them to occupy space. In this scenario, I recommend that you explore the use of `Addressables`, which provide a way to load assets dynamically. But let's keep things simple for now.

Summary

Optimizing a game is not an easy task, especially if you are not familiar with the internals of how each Unity system works. Sadly, this is a titanic task, and no one knows every single system down to its finest details, but with the tools learned in this chapter, we have a way to explore how changes affect systems through exploration. We learned how to profile the CPU, GPU, and RAM and what the key hardware in any game is, as well as covered some common good practices to avoid abusing them.

Now, you are able to diagnose performance issues in your game, gathering data about the performance of the three main pieces of hardware—the CPU, GPU, and RAM—and then using that data to focus your optimization efforts on applying the correct optimization technique. Performance is important as your game needs to run smoothly to give your users a pleasant experience.

In the next chapter, we are going to see how to create a build of our game to share with other people, without needing to install Unity. This is also very useful for profiling, given profiling builds are going to give us more accurate data than profiling in the editor.

Join us on Discord!

Read this book alongside other users, Unity game development experts, and the author himself.

Ask questions, provide solutions to other readers, chat with the author via Ask Me Anything sessions, and much more.

Scan the QR code or visit the link to join the community.

`https://packt.link/handsonunity22`

19

Generating and Debugging an Executable

So, we have reached a point where the game is in good enough shape to test it with real people. The problem is that we can't pretend people will install Unity, open a project, and hit **Play**. They want to receive a nice executable file to double-click and play right away. In this chapter, we are going to discuss how we can convert our project into an easy-to-share executable format, seeing how to do that in the first section, and then in the second section, we will see how to apply the profiling and debugging techniques learned in *Chapter 18, Scene Performance Optimization*, but this time on the build. After reading this chapter, you will be able to detect potential performance bottlenecks and how to tackle the most common ones, leading to an increase in your game's framerate.

In this chapter, we will examine the following build concepts:

- Building a project
- Debugging the build

Let's start by seeing how we can build the project to get a shareable executable.

Building a project

In software development (including video games), the process of taking the source files of our project and converting them into an executable format is called a **build**. The generated executable files are optimized to achieve the maximum performance possible given the configuration of the project. We can't judge performance while editing the game due to the changing nature of a project. It would be time-consuming to prepare the assets in their final form while editing the game.

Also, the generated files are in a difficult-to-read format. They won't have the textures, audio, and source code files just there for the user to look at. They will be formatted in custom file structures, so in a way, they're protected from users stealing them.

Actually, there are several tools to extract source files from video games, especially from a widely used engine such as Unity. You can extract assets such as textures and 3D models, and there are even programs that extract those assets directly from the VRAM, so we cannot guarantee that the assets won't be used outside the game. In the end, users have the data of those assets on their disks.

The build process is pretty simple when you target desktop platforms such as PC, Mac, or Linux, but there are a few settings we need to keep in mind before building. The first configuration we are going to see is the scenes list. We have already discussed this, but it's a good moment to remember that it is important to set the first element of this list to the scene that will be loaded first. Remember, you can do this by going to **File | Build Settings** and dragging your desired starter scene to the top of the list. In our case, we defined the game scene as the first scene, but in a real game, it would be ideal to create a **Main Menu** scene using UI and some graphics:

Build Settings

Scenes In Build

✓ ProjectScenes/Game
✓ ProjectScenes/LoseScreen
✓ ProjectScenes/WinScreen

Figure 19.1: The Scenes in Build list order

Another setting you can change here is the target platform, the target operating system that the build will be created for. Usually, this is set as the same operating system you are developing on, but in case you are, as an example, developing on a Mac, and you want to build for Windows, just set the **Target Platform** setting to **Windows**. That way, the result will be an .exe file (a Windows executable file) instead of an .app file (the Mac executable file). You may see Android and iOS as other target platforms, but making mobile games requires other considerations that we are not going to discuss in this book:

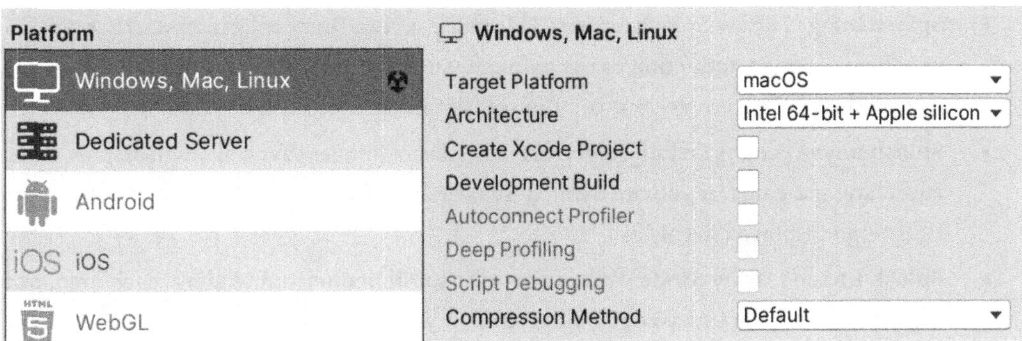

Figure 19.2: Target Platform

In the same window, you can click the **Player Settings** button at the bottom left, or just open the **Edit** | **Project Settings** window and click on the **Player** category to access the rest of the **Build Settings**. Unity calls the generated executable the `Player`. Here, we have a set of configurations that will affect how the build or player behaves, and here is a list of the basic ones:

- **Company Name**: This is the name of the company that developed the game, which is used by Unity to create certain file paths and will be included in the executable information.
- **Product Name**: This is the name of the game in the window title bar and executable file.
- **Default Icon**: Here, you can select a texture to act as the executable icon.
- **Default Cursor**: You can set a texture to replace the regular system cursor. In case you do that, remember to set the **Cursor Hotspot** property to the pixel of the image you want the cursor to click on.
- **Resolution and Presentation**: These are settings for how our game's resolution is going to be handled.
- **Resolution and Presentation** | **Fullscreen Mode**: You can select if your game will start **Windowed** or in different modes of **Fullscreen**. You can change that later via scripting if necessary.
- **Resolution and Presentation** | **Default is Native Resolution**: When this option is checked and **Fullscreen Mode** is set to use any **Fullscreen** option, the resolution currently used by the system will be the one used by Unity. You can uncheck this and set your desired resolution.
- **Splash Image**: These are settings for the splash image the game will show after loading for the first time.

- **Splash Image | Show Splash Screen**: This will enable a Unity splash screen that will display logos as an introduction to the game. If you have the Unity Plus or Pro license, you can uncheck this to create your custom splash screen, if you want.
- **Splash Image | Logos List**: Here, you can add a set of images that Unity will display when launching the game. If you are using a free version of Unity, you are forced to have the Unity logo displayed in this list.
- **Splash Image | Draw Mode**: You can set this to **All Sequential** to show each logo, one after the other, or to **Unity Logo Below** to show your custom introductory logos with the Unity logo always present below yours:

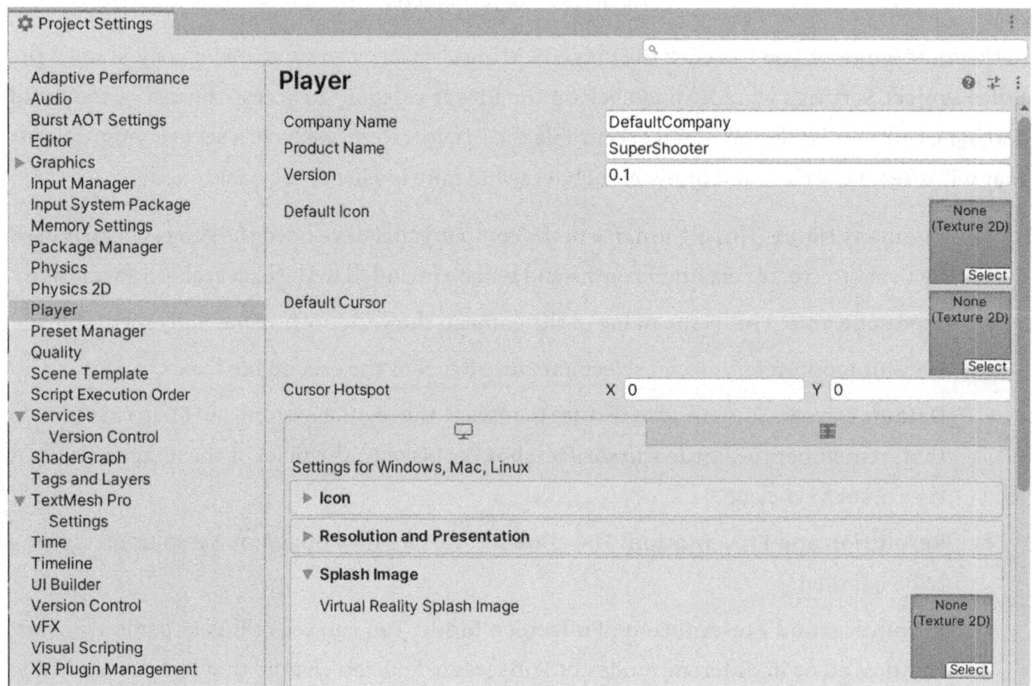

Figure 19.3: Player settings

After configuring these settings as you wish, the next step is to do the actual build, which can be accomplished by hitting the **Build** button in the **File | Build Settings** window. This will ask you to set where you want the build files to be created. I recommend you create an empty folder on your desktop to have easy access to the result. Be patient—this process can take a while depending on the size of the project:

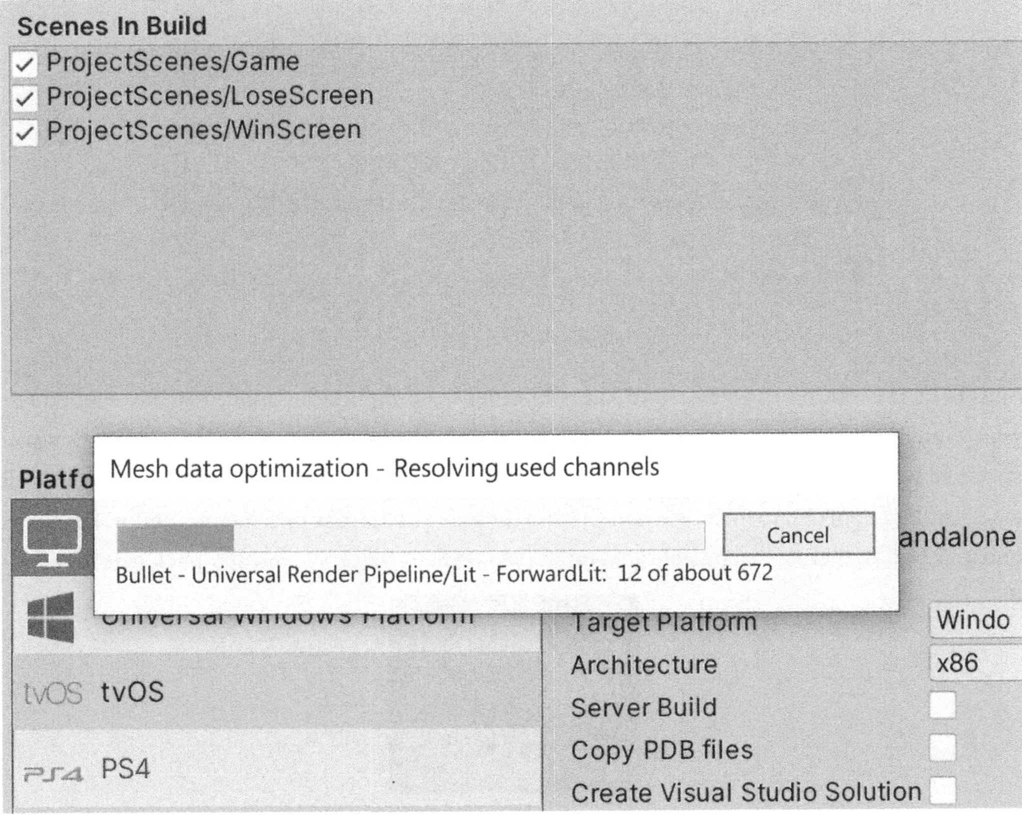

Figure 19.4: Building the game

Something that can fail here is having non-build-compatible scripts—scripts that are intended to be executed only in the Editor, mostly Editor extensions. We haven't created any of those, so if you have an error message in the console after building, similar to the following screenshot, that can happen because of some script in an Asset Store package. In that case, just delete the files that are shown in the console before the **Build Error** message. If, by any chance, there is one of your scripts there, be sure you don't have any `using UnityEditor;` lines in any of your scripts.

That would try to use the Editor namespace, the one that is not included in the build compilation to save space on the disk:

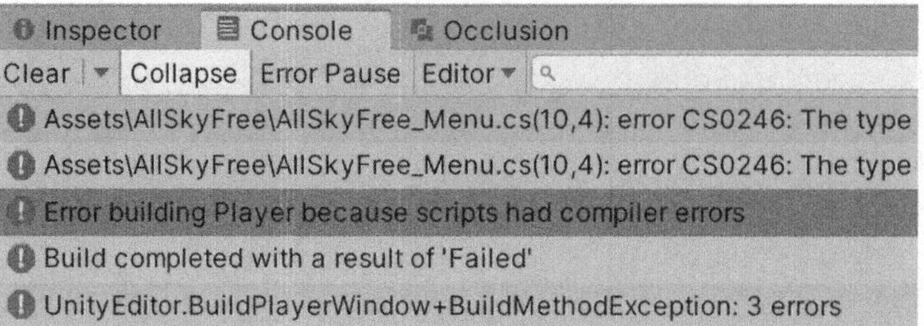

Figure 19.5: Build errors

And that's the minimum you need to know in order to configure the build. You have generated your game! Something to take into account is that every file that was created in the folder that you specified when building must be shared, not only the executable file. The data folder contains all assets and is important to include when sharing the game in the case of Windows builds. For Linux and Mac builds, there is just one file generated (`x86/x86_64` for Linux and `app packages` for Mac):

Figure 19.6: A Windows-generated folder

Now that we have the build, you can test it by double-clicking the executable file. We can now discuss how we use the same debug and profiling tools we used in the Editor to debug our build.

Debugging the build

In an ideal world, the Editor and the build would behave the same, but sadly that isn't true. The Editor is prepared to work in a fast-iteration mode. Code and assets have minimum processing prior to being used to make changes often and fast, so we can test our game easily. When the game is built, a series of optimizations and differences from the Editor project will be applied to ensure the best performance we can get, but those differences can cause certain parts of the game to behave differently, making the profiling data of the player differ from the Editor. That's why we are going to explore how we can debug and profile the game we have built.

In this section, we will examine the following build debugging concepts:

- Debugging code
- Profiling performance

Let's start discussing how to debug the code of a build.

Debugging code

As player code is compiled differently, we can get errors in the build that didn't happen in the Editor, and we need to debug it somehow. We have two main ways to debug—by printing messages and through breakpoints. So, let's start with the first one, messages. If you ran your executable file, you may have noticed that there's no console available. It's just the **Game View** in fullscreen, which makes sense; we don't want to distract the user with annoying testing messages. Luckily, the messages are still being printed, but in a file, so we can just go to that file and look for them.

The location varies according to the operating system. In this list, you can find the possible locations:

- **Linux:** `~/.config/unity3d/CompanyName/ProductName/Player.log`
- **Mac:** `~/Library/Logs/Company Name/Product Name/Player.log`
- **Windows:** `C:\Users\username\AppData\LocalLow\CompanyName\ProductName\Player.log`

In these paths, you must change `CompanyName` and `ProductName` to the values of the properties in the `Player` settings we set before, which are called the same, **Company Name** and **Product Name**. In Windows, you must replace `username` with the name of the Windows account you are executing the game in. Consider that the folders might be hidden, so enable the option to show hidden files in your operating system. Inside that folder, you will find a file called `Player`; you can open it with any text editor and look at the messages.

Aside from downloading any custom package from the Asset Store, there is a way to see the messages of the console directly in the game, at least the error messages: by creating a development build. This is a special build that allows extended debugging and profiling capabilities in exchange for not fully optimizing the code as the final build does, but it will be enough for general debugging.

You can create this kind of build just by checking the **Development Build** checkbox in the **File | Build Settings** window:

Windows, Mac, Linux

Target Platform	macOS
Architecture	Intel 64-bit + Apple silicon
Create Xcode Project	☐
Development Build	☑

Figure 19.7: The Development Build checkbox

Remember that just the error messages will be displayed here, so a little trick you can do is replace `print` and `Debug.Log` function calls with `Debug.LogError`, which will also print the message in the console but with a red icon. Consider that using `Debug.LogError` to show non-error messages is not a good practice, so limit the usage of this kind of message for temporal debugging. For permanent logging, use the log file or find a custom debugging console for runtime in the Asset Store.

```
public class PlayerShooting : MonoBehaviour
{
    private void Start()
    {
        Debug.LogError("Testing Player Shooting Start");
    }
```

Figure 19.8: Debugging error messages

Something interesting regarding **development builds** is that, unlike regular builds, the error messages are displayed directly in the build, allowing you to properly debug your project. In the next screenshot, you can see the error displayed in the runtime:

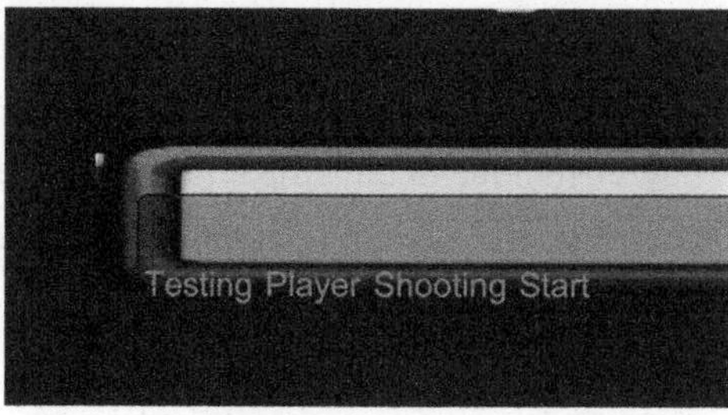

Figure 19.9: Error messages in a development build

You will notice that, aside from showing the error message, there's an **Open Log File** button on the right, allowing you to see the log file. This is a text file containing detailed info regarding all the messages and logs that happened in this run of the game to pinpoint the issue. Essentially, it is the same info the **Console** panel shows in the editor.

Remember that for **development builds** to work, you need to build the game again; luckily, the first build is the one that takes the most time, and the next will be faster. This time, you can just click the **Build and Run** button to do the build in the folder in which you did the previous build.

Also, you can use regular breakpoints the same way as we explained in *Chapter 5, Introduction to C# and Visual Scripting*. Attaching the IDE to the player, it will show up in the list of targets. But for that to work, you must not only check **Development Build** in the **Build** window but also **Script Debugging**. Here, you have an additional option shown when that is checked that allows you to pause the entire game until a debugger is attached, the one called **Wait For Managed Debugger**. This is useful in case you want to test something that happens immediately at the beginning and doesn't allow you enough time to attach the debugger:

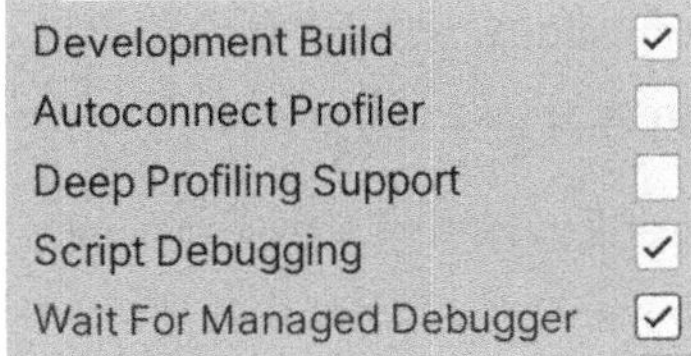

Figure 19.10: Enabling script debugging

We have another way to see the messages, but that will require the Profiler to work, so let's use this as an excuse to also discuss how to profile the editor.

Profiling performance

We are going to use the same tools as we saw in the previous chapter, but to profile the player this time. Luckily, the difference is minimal. As we did in the previous section, you need to build the player in **Development** mode, checking the **Development Build** checkbox in the **Build** window, and then the Profilers should automatically detect it.

Let's start using the Profiler on the build by doing the following:

1. Play the game through the build.
2. Switch to Unity using *Alt* + *Tab* (*Cmd* + *Tab* on Mac).
3. Open the Profiler.

4. Click the menu that says **Play Mode** and select the item that contains **Player** in it. Because I have used Mac, it says **OSXPlayer**, and the name will vary according to the build platform (for example, a Windows build will say **WindowsPlayer**):

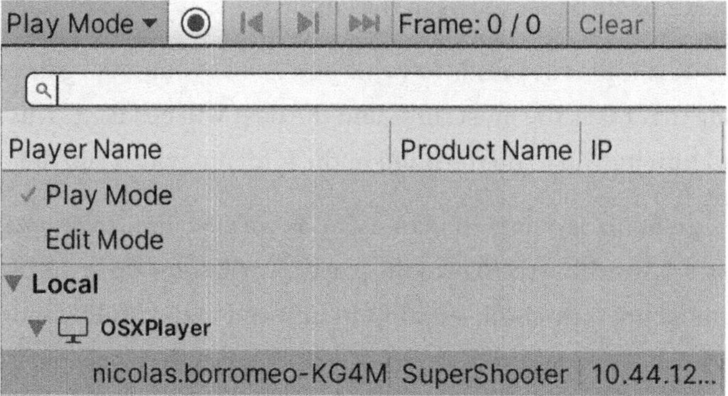

Figure 19.11: Profiling the player

Notice that when you click a frame, the game won't stop like in the Editor. If you want to focus your attention on the frames at a specific moment, you can click the record button (the red circle) to make the Profiler stop capturing data, so you can analyze the frames captured so far.

Also, you can see that when the Profiler is attached to the player, the console will also be attached, so you can see the logs directly in Unity. Consider that this version requires Unity to be opened, and we cannot expect our friends who are testing our game to have it. You might need to click on the **Player** button that appears on the **Console** and check **Player Logging** for this to work:

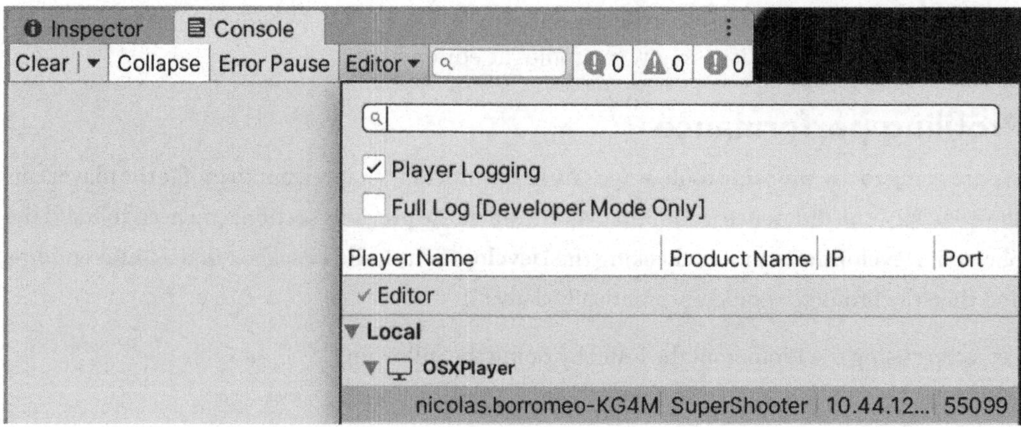

Figure 19.12: Enabling Player Logging after attaching the Profiler

The **Frame Debugger** is also enabled to work with the player. You need to click the **Editor** button in the **Frame Debugger** and again, you will see the player in the list of possible debugging targets; after selecting it, hit **Enable** as usual. Consider that the preview of the **Draw Calls** won't be seen in the **Game View** but in the build itself. If you are running the game in fullscreen mode, you might need to switch back and forth between Unity and the build:

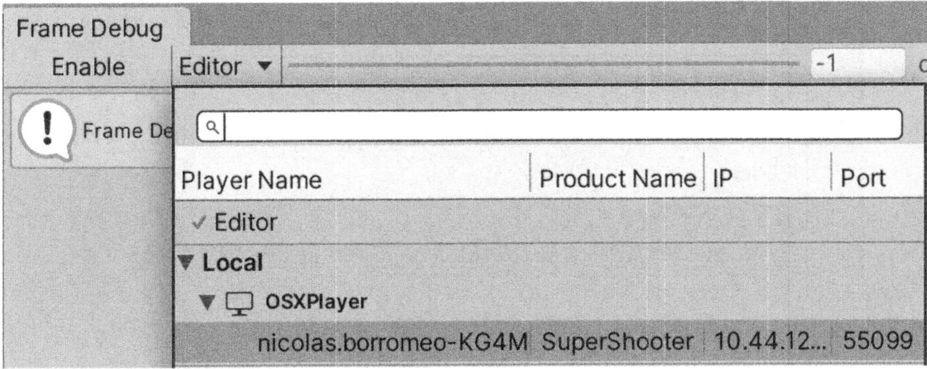

Figure 19.13: Debugging the frames of our game's Player

You may also run the game in **Windowed** mode, setting the **Fullscreen Mode** property in the player settings to **Windowed**, and establishing a default resolution that is smaller than your desktop resolution, to have both Unity and the player visible:

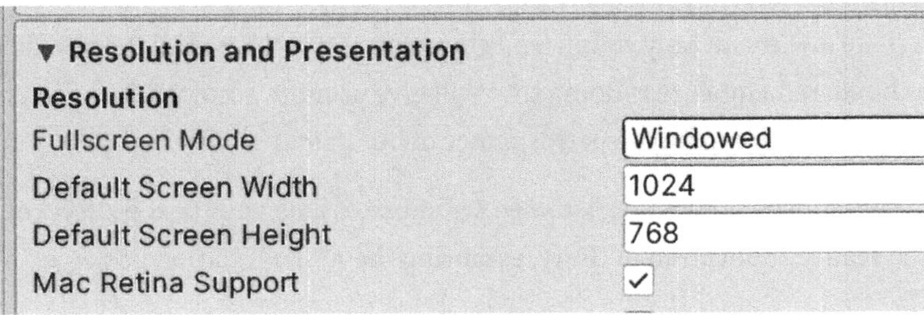

Figure 19.14: Enabling Windowed mode

Finally, the **Memory Profiler** also supports profiling the player, and as you might guess, you can just select the player in the list that is displayed when you click the **Editor** button on the top bar of the window and then click **Capture**:

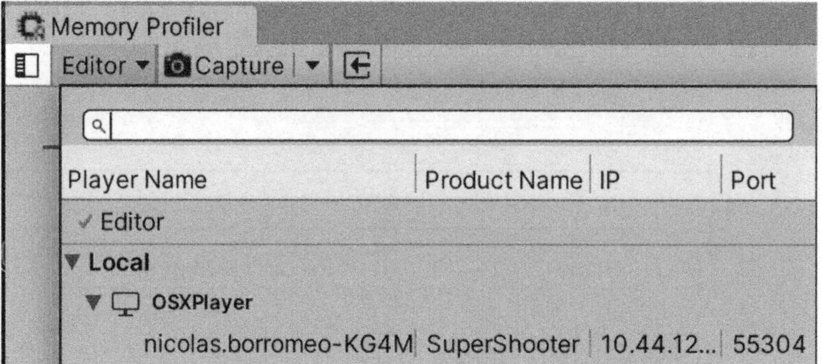

Figure 19.15: Taking memory snapshots of the player

And that is it. As you can see, Unity Profilers are designed to be easily integrated with the player. If you start to take data from them, you will see the difference compared to editor profiling, especially in the **Memory Profiler**.

Summary

In this chapter, we learned how to create an executable version of the game and properly configure it so you can share it with not only your friends but potentially the world! We also discussed how to profile our build; remember that doing that will give us more accurate data than profiling the editor, so we can better improve the performance of our game.

Now that we have finished our game, let's see a glimpse of how your next project could easily be an augmented reality application in Unity, exploring the AR Foundation package.

20

Augmented Reality in Unity

Nowadays, new technologies expand the fields of the application of Unity, from gaming to all kinds of software, such as simulations, training, apps, and so on. In the latest versions of Unity, we saw lots of improvements in the field of augmented reality, which allows us to add a layer of virtuality on top of our reality, thereby augmenting what our device can perceive to create games that rely on real-world data, such as the camera's image, our real-world position, and the current weather. This can also be applied to work environments, such as when viewing the building map or checking the electrical ducts inside a wall. Welcome to the extra section of this book, where we are going to discuss how to create **Augmented Reality** (**AR**) applications using Unity's AR Foundation package.

In this chapter, we will examine the following AR Foundation concepts:

- Using AR Foundation
- Building for mobile devices
- Creating a simple AR game

By the end of this chapter, you will be able to create AR apps using AR Foundation and will have a fully functional game that uses its framework so that you can test the framework's capabilities.

Let's start by exploring the AR Foundation framework.

Using AR Foundation

When it comes to AR, Unity has two main tools to create applications: **Vuforia** and **AR Foundation**. Vuforia is an AR framework that can work in almost any mobile device and contains all the needed features for basic AR apps, but with a paid subscription, we get more advanced features. On the other hand, the completely free AR Foundation framework supports the latest AR native features of our devices but is supported only in newer ones. Picking between one or the other depends a lot on the type of project you're going to build and the target audience. However, since this book aims to discuss the latest Unity features, we are going to explore how to use AR Foundation to create our first AR app for detecting the positions of images and surfaces in the real world. So, we'll start by exploring its API.

In this section, we will examine the following AR Foundation concepts:

- Creating an AR Foundation project
- Using tracking features

Let's start by discussing how to prepare our project so that it can run AR Foundation apps.

Creating an AR Foundation project

Something to consider when creating AR projects is that we will not only change the way we code our game, but also the game design aspect. AR apps have differences, especially in the way the user interacts, and also limitations, such as the user being in control of the camera all the time. We cannot simply port an existing game to AR without changing the very core experience of the game. That's why, in this chapter, we are going to work on a brand-new project; it would be too difficult to change the game we've created so far so that it works well in AR.

In our case, we are going to create a game where the user controls a player moving a "marker," a physical image you can print that will allow our app to recognize where the player is in the real world. We will be able to move the player while moving that image, and this virtual player will automatically shoot at the nearest enemy. Those enemies will spawn from certain spawn points that the user will need to place in different parts of the home. As an example, we can put two spawn points on the walls and place our player marker on a table in the middle of the room so that the enemies will go toward them. In the following image, you can see a preview of what the game will look like:

Figure 20.1: Finished game. The Cylinder is an enemy spawner, the Capsule is the enemy, and the Cube is the player. These are positioned in a marker image displayed by the cellphone

We'll start creating a new URP-based project in the same manner we created our first game. Something to consider is that AR Foundation works with other pipelines, including built-in ones, in case you want to use it in already existing projects. If you don't remember how to create a project, please refer to *Chapter 1, Creating a Unity Project.*

Once you're in your new blank project, install the AR Foundation package from the Package Manager, just like we've installed other packages previously—that is, from **Window | Package Manager**. Remember to set the Package Manager so that it shows all packages, not only the ones in the project (the **Packages** button at the top-left part of the window needs to be set to **Unity Registry**) and also the preview versions (click on the wheel icon, then **Project Settings**, and check **Enable Pre-release Packages** on the window that appears).

At the time of writing this book, the latest stable release is 4.2.3, but we are going to explore the 5.0.0 preview 13 version. Remember to open the package version list by clicking the triangle button at the left to see the preview versions. If you find a newer version than mine, you can try using that one, but as usual, if something works differently from what we want, please install 5.0.0-pre.13. As usual, if a warning prompting you to enable the new input system appears, click **Yes**:

All Services
Packages - Unity
AR Foundation 5.0.0-pre.13 Pre
JetBrains Rider Editor 3.0.14
Test Framework 1.1.31
TextMeshPro 3.0.6
AR Foundation Pre-Release
com.unity.xr.arfoundation
Unity Technologies
Version 5.0.0-pre.13 - August 01, 2022
Registry Unity

Figure 20.2: Installing AR Foundation

Before we install any other needed packages, now is a good moment to discuss some core ideas of the AR Foundation framework. This package, by itself, does nothing; it defines a series of AR features that mobile devices offer, such as image tracking, cloud points, and object tracking, but the actual implementation of how to do that is contained in the **Provider** packages, such as **Apple ARKit XR Plugin** and **Google ARCore XR plugin** packages. This is designed like this because, depending on the target device you want to work with, the way those features are implemented changes. As an example, in iOS, Unity implements those features using AR Kit, while in Android, it uses AR Core; they are platform-specific frameworks. Remember to install the same version of these platform packages as the AR Foundation one (5.0.0 preview 13 in this case).

Something to consider here is that not all iOS or Android devices support AR Foundation apps. You might find an updated list of supported devices when searching for AR Core- and AR Kit-supported devices on the internet. At the time of writing, the following links provide the supported devices lists:

- **iOS:** `https://www.apple.com/lae/augmented-reality` (at the bottom of the page)
- **Android:** `https://developers.google.com/ar/devices`

Also, there isn't a PC Provider package, so the only way to test AR Foundation apps so far is directly on the device, but testing tools are going to be released soon. In my case, I will be creating an app for iOS, so aside from the **AR Foundation** package, I need to install the **ARKit XR** plugin.

However, if you want to develop for Android, install the **ARCore XR** plugin instead (or both if you're targeting both platforms). Also, I will be using the 4.1.7 version of these packages. Usually, the versions of the **AR Foundation** and **Provider** packages match but apply the same logic as when you picked the **AR Foundation** version. In the following screenshot, you can see the **ARKit** package in the **Package Manager**:

Now that we have the needed plugins, we need to prepare a scene for AR, as follows:

1. Create a new Scene in **File | New Scene** and select the **Basic (URP)** template.
2. Delete **Main Camera**; we are going to use a different one.
3. In the **GameObject | XR** menu, create an **AR Session** GameObject.
4. In the same menu, create an **XR Origin (Mobile AR)** object that has a **Camera** inside it.
5. Select the Main Camera inside **XR Origin**.
6. Set the **Render Mode** property of the **AR Camera Manager** component to **After Opaques**. This is a workaround for a bug that prevents the camera from being rendered properly in another mode in the current versions.

7. Your hierarchy should look as follows:

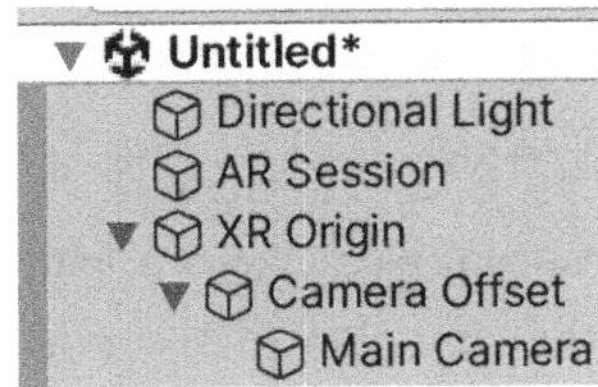

Figure 20.3: Starter AR Scene

The **AR Session** object will be responsible for initializing AR Framework and will handle all the update logic for the AR systems. The **XR Origin** object will allow the framework to locate tracked objects such as images and point clouds in a relative position to the scene. The devices inform the positions of tracked objects relative to what the device considers "the origin." This is usually the first area of your house you were pointing at when the app started detecting objects, so the **XR Origin** object will represent that point in your physical space. Finally, you can check the camera inside the origin, which contains some extra components, with the most important being **Tracked Pose Driver**, which will make your **Camera** object move along with your device. Since the device's position is relative to the Session Origin object's point, the camera needs to be inside the origin object.

One extra step in case you are working on a URP project (our case) is that you need to set up the render pipeline so that it supports rendering the camera image in the app. To do that, go to the `Settings` folder that was generated when we created the project, look for the `URP-HighFidelity-Renderer` file, and select it. In the **Renderer Features** list, click the **Add Renderer Feature** button and select **AR Background Renderer Feature**. In the following screenshot, you can see what the Forward Renderer asset should look like:

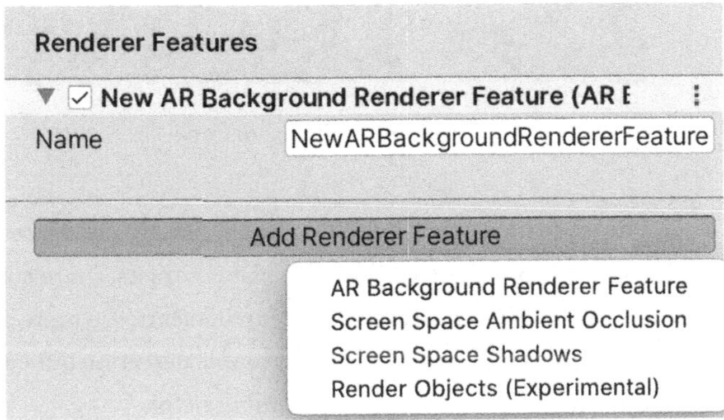

Figure 20.4: Adding support for URP

And that's all! We are ready to start exploring the AR Foundation components so that we can implement tracking features.

Using tracking features

For our project, we are going to need two of the most common tracking features in AR (but not the only ones): image recognition and plane detection. The first one consists of detecting the position in the real world of a specific image so that we can place digital objects on top of it, such as the player. The second one, plane detection, consists of recognizing real-life surfaces, such as floors, tables, and walls, so that we have a reference of where we can put objects, such as the enemy's spawn points. Only horizontal and vertical surfaces are recognized (just vertical surfaces on some devices).

The first thing we need to do is tell our app which images it needs to detect, as follows:

1. Add an image to the project that you can print or display on a mobile device. Having a way to display the image in the real world is necessary to test this. In this case, I will use the following image:

Figure 20.5: Image to track

> Try to get an image that contains as many features as you can. This means an image with lots of little details, such as contrasts, sharp corners, and so on. Those are what our AR systems use to detect it; the more detail, the better the recognition. If your device has trouble detecting our current image, try other images (the classic QR code might help).

2. Consider that some devices might have trouble with certain images, such as the image suggested in this book. If this generates issues when testing, please try using another one. You will be testing this on your device in the upcoming sections of this chapter, so just keep this in mind.
3. Create a **Reference Image Library**, an asset containing all the images we wish our app to recognize, by clicking the + button in **Project Panel** and selecting **XR | Reference Image Library**:

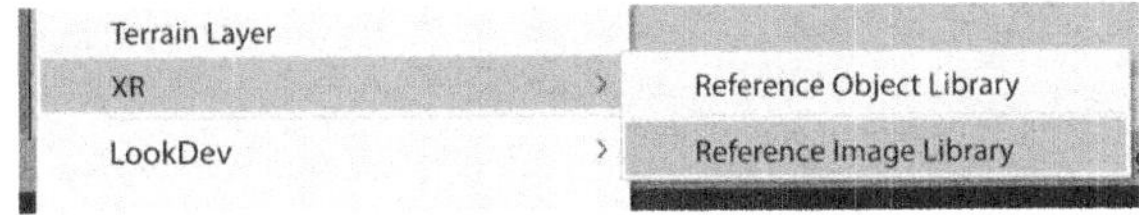

Figure 20.6: Creating a Reference Image Library

4. Select the **Reference Image Library** asset we created and click the **Add Image** button to add a new image to the library.
5. Drag the texture to the texture slot (the one that says **None**).
6. Turn **Specify Size** on and set **Physical Size** to the size that your image will be printed in real life, in meters. Try to be accurate here; on some devices not having this value right might result in the image not being tracked:

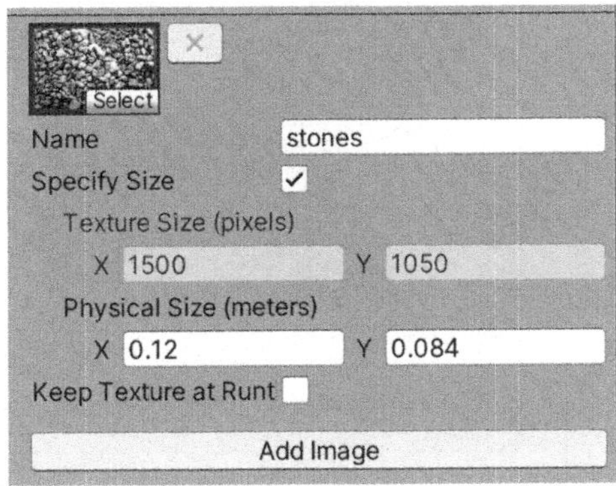

Figure 20.7: Adding an image to be recognized

Now that we've specified the images to be detected, let's test this by placing a cube on top of the real-life image:

1. Create a Prefab of a cube and add the **AR Tracked Image** component to it.
2. Remember to set a small scale, like 0.1, on each axis, given that the default cube will be 1 meter by 1 meter, which will be huge in AR.

3. Add the **AR Tracked Image Manager** component to the **XR Origin** object. This will be responsible for detecting images and creating objects in its position.
4. Drag the **Image Library** asset created in the previous steps to the **Serialized Library** property of the component to specify the images to recognize.
5. Drag the **Cube** Prefab to the **Tracked Image Prefab** property of the component:

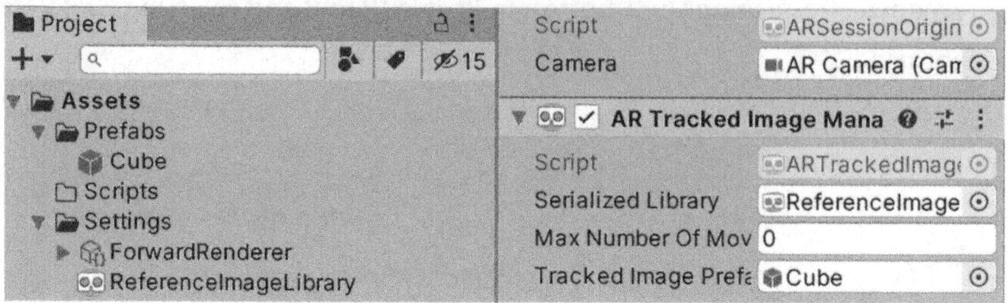

Figure 20.8: Setting up the Tracked Image Manager

And that's all! Later in the *Building for mobile* section in this chapter, when we will create an iOS or Android build, we will see a cube spawning in the same position that the image is located in the real world. Remember that you need to test this in the device, which we will do in the next section, so for now, let's keep coding our test app:

Figure 20.9: Cube located on top of the image being displayed by the cellphone

Let's also prepare our app so that it can detect and display the plane surfaces the camera has recognized. This is simply done by adding the **AR Plane Manager** component to the **XR Origin** object.

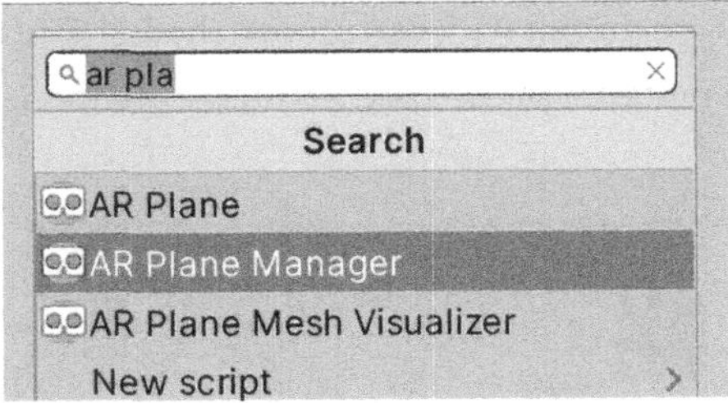

Figure 20.10: Adding the AR Plane Manager component

This component will detect surface planes over our house as we move the camera over it. It can take a while to detect them, so it's important to visualize the detected areas to get feedback about this to ensure it's working properly. We can manually get information about the plane from a component reference to the AR Plane Manager, but luckily, Unity allows us to visualize planes easily. Let's take a look:

1. Create a Prefab of a plane, first by creating the plane in **GameObject | 3D Object | Plane**.
2. Add a **Line Renderer** to it. This will allow us to draw a line over the edges of the detected areas.
3. Set the **Width** property of **Line Renderer** to a small value such as `0.01`, the **Color** gradient property to black, and uncheck **Use World Space**:

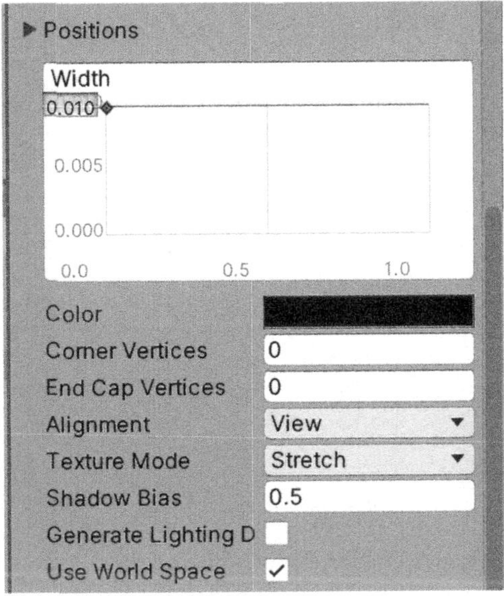

Figure 20.11: Setting the Line Renderer

4. Remember to create a material with the proper shader (**Universal Render Pipeline/Unlit**) and set it as the material of the **Line Renderer** component under the **Materials** list property:

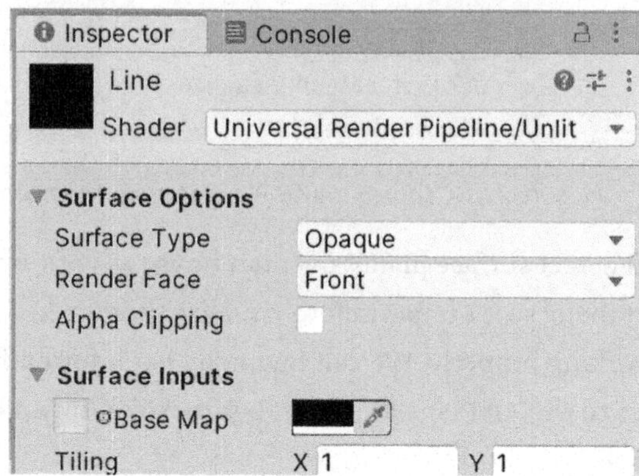

Figure 20.12: Creating the Line Renderer material

5. Also, create a transparent material and use it in the **MeshRenderer** plane. We want to see through it so that we can easily see the real surface beneath:

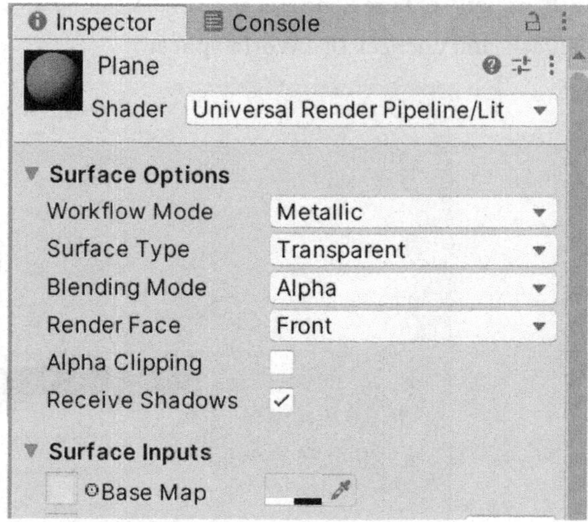

Figure 20.13: Material for the detected plane

6. Add the **AR Plane** and **AR Plane Mesh Visualizer** components to the **Plane** Prefab.

7. Drag the Prefab to the **Plane Prefab** property of the **AR Plane Manager** component of the **XR Origin** object:

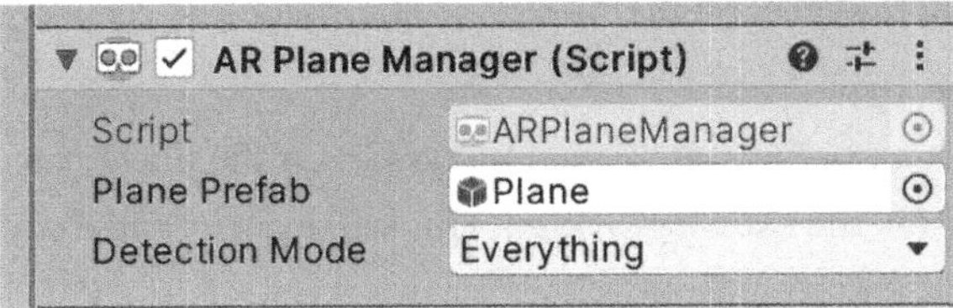

Figure 20.14: Setting the plane visualization Prefab

Now, we have a way to see the planes, but seeing them is not the only thing we can do (sometimes, we don't even want them to be visible). The real power of planes resides in placing virtual objects on top of real-life surfaces, tapping into a specific plane area, and getting its real-life position. We can access the plane data using the **AR Plane Manager** or by accessing the **AR Plane** component of our visualization planes, but something easier is to use the **AR Raycast Manager** component.

The **AR Raycast Manager** component provides us with the equivalent to the `Physics.Raycast` function of the Unity Physics system, which, as you may recall, is used to create imaginary rays that start from one position and go toward a specified direction in order to make them hit surfaces and detect the exact hit point. The version provided by **AR Raycast Manager**, instead of colliding with physics colliders, collides with tracked objects, mostly Point Clouds (we are not using them) and the "planes" we are tracking. We can test this feature by following these steps:

1. Add the **AR Raycast Manager** component to the **XR Origin** object.
2. Create a custom script called `SpawnerPlacer` in the **XR Origin** object.
3. In the **Awake** cache, add the reference to `ARRaycastManager`. You will need to add the `using UnityEngine.XR.ARFoundation;` line to the top of the script for this class to be usable in our script.
4. Create a private field of the `List<ARRaycastHit>` type and instantiate it; the Raycast function is going to detect every plane our ray hit, not just the first one:

```
List<ARRaycastHit> hits = new List<ARRaycastHit>();
```

Figure 20.15: List to store hits

5. Under **Update**, check if the touch screen is pressed (`Touchscreen.current.primaryTouch.press.isPressed`). You will need the `using UnityEngine.InputSystem;` using at the top of the file to use the new input system.

6. Inside the `if` statement from the previous step, add another condition for calling the `Raycast` function of **AR Raycast Manager**, passing the position of the touch as the first parameter and the list of hits as the second (`Touchscreen.current.primaryTouch.position.ReadValue()`).
7. This will throw a Raycast toward the direction the player touches the screen and store the hits inside the list we provided. This will return `true` if something has been hit, and `false` if not.
8. Add a public field to specify the Prefab to instantiate in the place we touched. You can just create a Sphere Prefab and assign it to this field to test this; there's no need to add any special component to the Prefab here. Remember to set a small scale.
9. Instantiate the Prefab in the **Position** and **Rotation** fields of the **Pose** property of the first hit stored in the list. The hits are sorted by distance, so the first hit is the closest one. Your final script should look as follows:

```
using UnityEngine;
using UnityEngine.XR.ARFoundation;
using System.Collections.Generic;
using UnityEngine.InputSystem;

public class SpawnerPlacer : MonoBehaviour
{
    ARRaycastManager raycastManager;
    List<ARRaycastHit> hits = new List<ARRaycastHit>();
    public GameObject spawnerPrefab;

    private void Awake()
    {
        raycastManager = GetComponent<ARRaycastManager>();
    }

    void Update()
    {
        var touchPos :Vector2 =
            Touchscreen.current.primaryTouch.position.ReadValue();

        if (Touchscreen.current.primaryTouch.press.wasPressedThisFrame &&
            raycastManager.Raycast(touchPos, hits))
        {
            Instantiate(spawnerPrefab,
                hits[0].pose.position,
                hits[0].pose.rotation);
        }
    }
}
```

Figure 20.16: Raycaster component

In this section, we learned how to create a new AR project using AR Foundation. We discussed how to install and set up the framework, as well as how to detect real-life image positions and surfaces, and then how to place objects on top of them.

As you may have noticed, we never hit **Play** to test this, and sadly at the time of writing this book, we cannot test this in the Editor. Instead, we need to test this directly on the device. Due to this, in the next section, we are going to learn how to do builds for mobile devices such as Android and iOS.

Building for mobile devices

Unity is a very powerful tool that solves the most common problems in game development very easily, and one of them is building the game for several target platforms. Now, the Unity part of building our project for such devices is easy to do, but each device has its non-Unity-related nuances when installing development builds. In order to test our AR app, we need to test it directly on the device. So, let's explore how we can make our app run on Android and iOS, the most common mobile platforms.

Before diving into this topic, it is worth mentioning that the following procedures change a lot over time, so you will need to find the latest instructions on the internet. The Unity Learn portal site (`https://learn.unity.com/tutorial/how-to-publish-to-android-2`) may be a good alternative in case the instructions in this book fail but try the steps here first.

In this section, we will examine the following mobile building concepts:

- Building for Android
- Building for iOS

Let's start by discussing how to build our app so that it runs on Android phones.

Building for Android

Creating Android builds is relatively easy compared to other platforms, so we'll start with Android. Remember that you will need an Android device capable of running AR Foundation apps, so please refer to the link regarding Android-supported devices we mentioned in the *Using AR Foundation* section of this chapter. The first thing we need to do is check if we have installed Unity's Android support and configured our project to use that platform. To do that, follow these steps:

1. Close Unity and open **Unity Hub**.
2. Go to the **Installs** section and locate the Unity version you are working on.

3. Click the wheel icon button at the top-right corner of the Unity version you are using and click **Add Modules**:

Figure 20.17: Adding modules to the Unity version

4. Make sure **Android Build Support** and the sub-options that are displayed when you click the arrow on its left are checked. If not, check them and click the **Continue** button at the bottom-right to install them:

Figure 20.18: Adding Android support to Unity

5. Accept all the terms and conditions prompts by checking the **Accept Terms** checkbox and clicking the **Continue** button.
6. Open the AR project we created in this chapter.
7. Go to **Build Settings (File | Build Settings)**.
8. Select the **Android** platform from the list and click the **Switch Platform** button at the bottom-right part of the window:

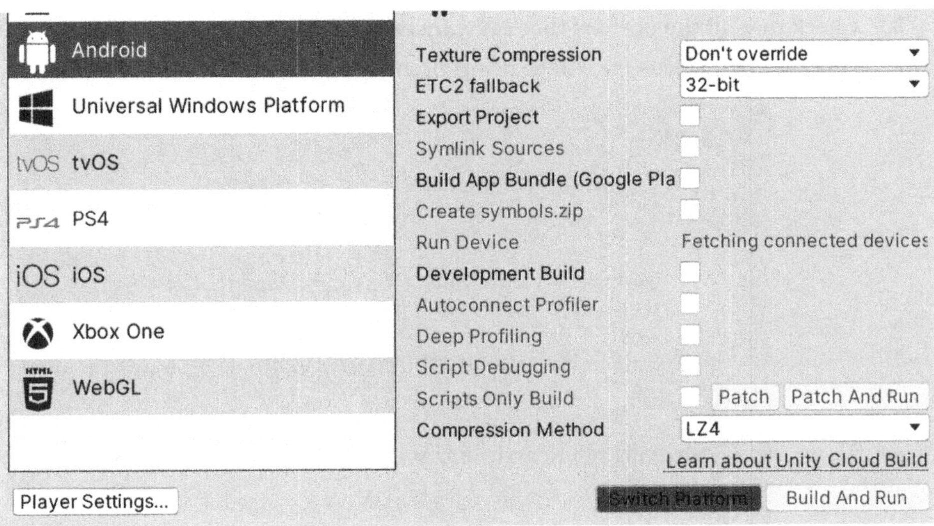

Figure 20.19: Switching to Android builds

To build an app on Android, there are some requirements we need to meet, such as having the Java SDK (not the regular Java runtime) and Android SDK installed, but luckily, the new versions of Unity take care of that. Just to double-check that we have installed the needed dependencies, follow these steps:

1. Go to **Unity Preferences** (**Edit** | **Preferences** on Windows or **Unity** | **Preferences** on Mac).
2. Click **External Tools.**

3. Check that all the options that say **...Installed with Unity** on the Android section are checked. This means we will be using all the dependencies installed by Unity:

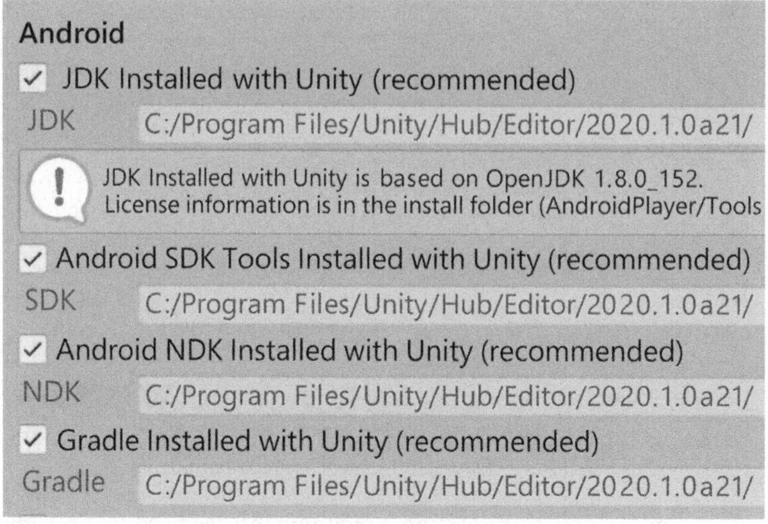

Figure 20.20: Using installed dependencies

There are some additional Android ARCore-specific related settings to check that you can find at `https://developers.google.com/ar/develop/unity-arf/quickstart-android`. These can change if you are using newer versions of AR Core. You can apply them by following these steps:

1. Go to **Player Settings** (**Edit** | **Project Settings** | **Player**).
2. Uncheck **Multithreaded Rendering** and **Auto Graphics API** from the **Other Settings** section.
3. Remove **Vulkan** from the **Graphics APIs** list if it's there.

4. Set **Minimum API Level** to **Android 7.0**:

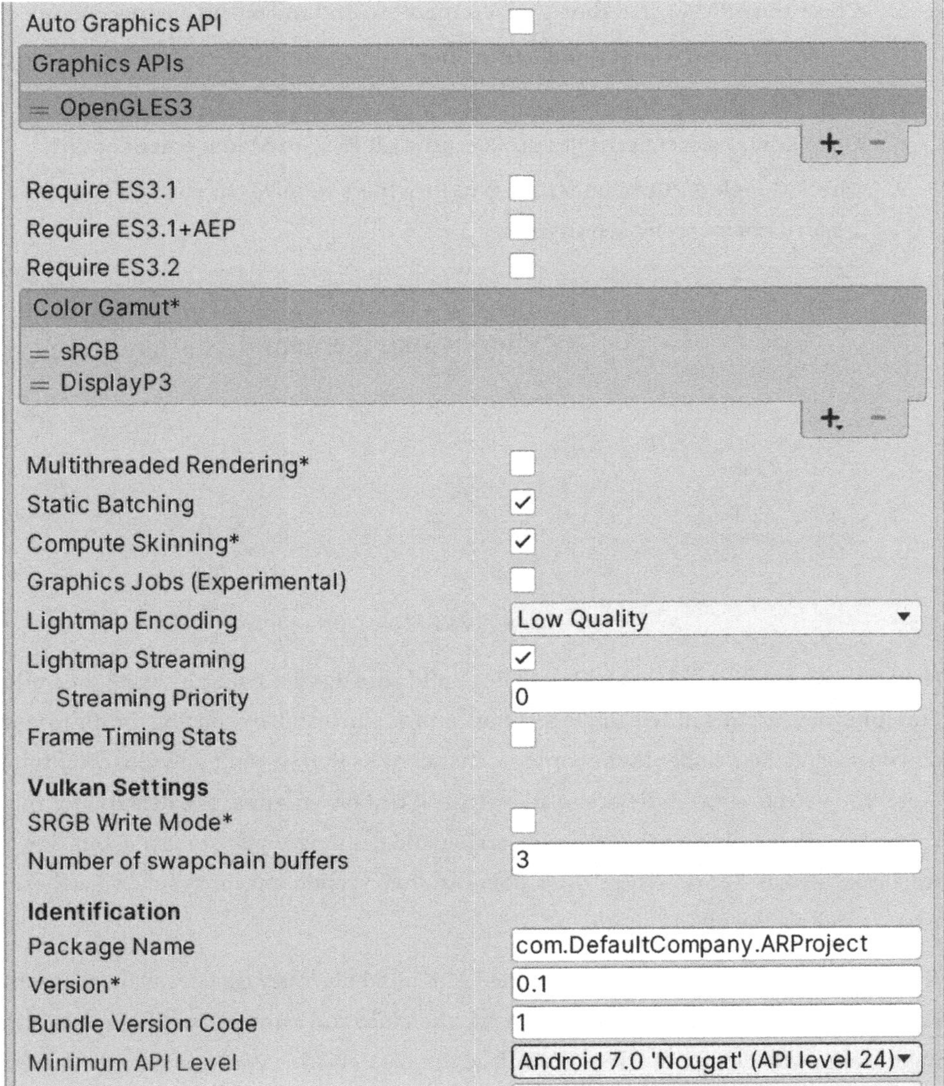

Figure 20.21: AR Core settings

5. Set the Scripting Backend to **IL2CPP**.
6. Check the **ARM64** checkbox to give support to Android 64-bit devices.
7. Check **Override Default Bundle Identifier** and set something custom, like `com.MyCompany.MyARApp`.
8. Go to **Edit | Project Settings** and select the **XR Plug-in Management** option.
9. Check **Google ARCore** under **Plug-in Providers** to make sure it will be enabled in our build; if not we won't see anything:

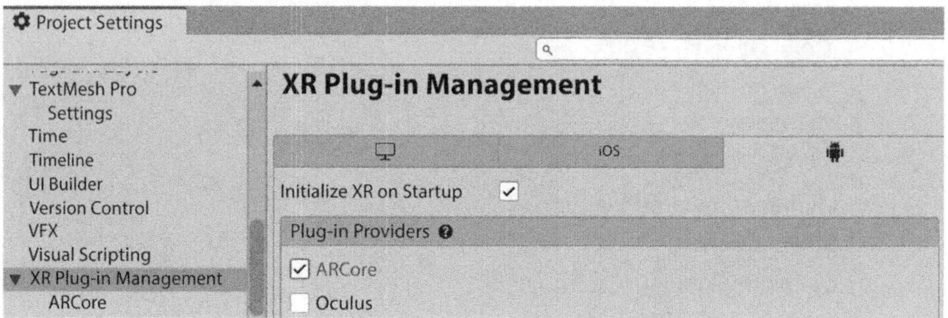

Figure 20.22: ARCore plugin enabled

Now, you can finally build the app from **File | Build Settings** like usual, by using the **Build** button. This time, the output will be a single APK file that you can install by copying the file to your device and opening it. Remember that in order to install APKs that weren't downloaded from the Play Store, you need to set your device to allow **Install Unknown Apps**. The location for that option varies a lot, depending on the Android version and the device you are using, but this option is usually located in the **Security** settings. Some Android versions prompt you to view these settings when installing the APK.

Now, we can copy and install the generated APK build file every time we want to create a build. However, we can let Unity do that for us using the **Build and Run** button. This option, after building the app, will look for the first Android device connected to your computer via USB and will automatically install the app. For this to work, we need to prepare our device and PC, as follows:

1. On your device, find the build number in the **Settings** section of the device, whose location, again, can change depending on the device. On my device, it is located in the **About Phone | Software Information** section:

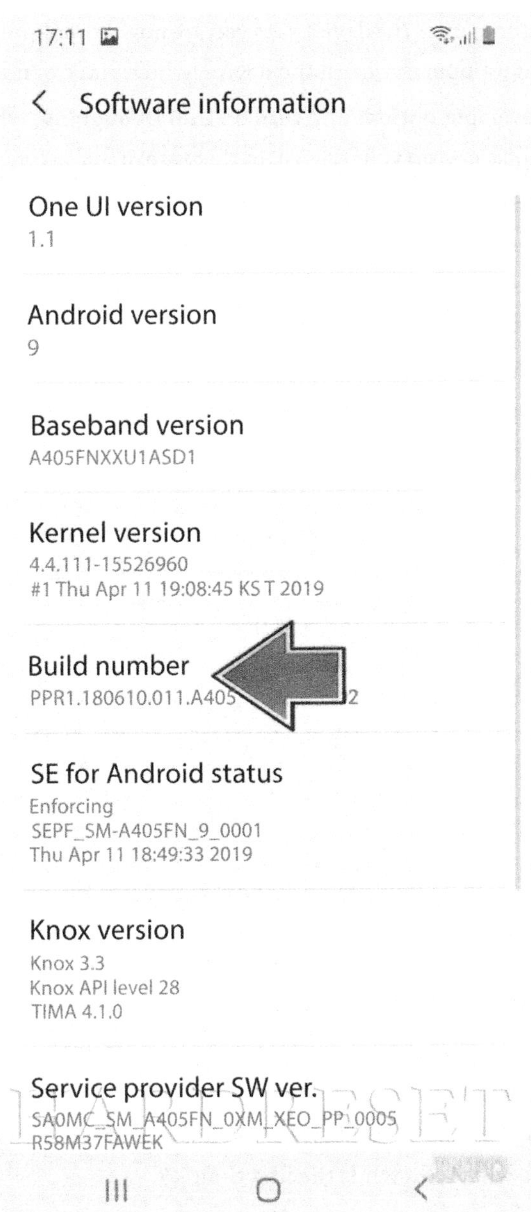

Figure 20.23: Locating the build number

2. Tap it a few times until the device says you are now a programmer. This procedure enables the hidden developer option in the device, which you can now find in the settings.
3. Open the developer options and turn on **USB Debugging**, which allows your PC to have special permissions on your device. In this case, it allows you to install apps.
4. Install the USB drivers from your phone manufacturer's site onto your computer if using Windows. For example, if you have a Samsung device, search for `Samsung USB Driver`. Also, if you can't find that, you can look for `Android USB Driver` to get the generic drivers, but that might not work if your device manufacturer has their own. On Mac, this step is usually not necessary.
5. Connect your device (or reconnect it if it's already connected). The option to **Allow USB Debugging** for your computer will appear on the device. Check **Always Allow** and click **OK**:

Figure 20.24: Allowing USB debugging

6. Accept the **Allow Data** prompt that appears.
7. If these options don't appear, check that the **USB Mode** of your device is set to **Debugging** and not any other.
8. In Unity, build with the **Build and Run** button, and save the `apk` into a folder. Be patient because this will take a while the first time.

Please remember to try another image if you have trouble detecting the image where we instantiate the player (the Unity logo, in my case). This might vary a lot, according to your device's capabilities.

And that's all! Now that you have your app running on your device, let's learn how to do the same for the iOS platform.

Building for iOS

When developing on iOS, you will need to spend some money. You will need to run XCode, a piece of software you can only run on macOS X. Due to this, you'll need a device that can run it, such as a MacBook, a Mac mini, and so on. There may be ways to run macOS X on PCs, but you will need to find this out and try it for yourself. Besides spending on a Mac and an iOS device (iPhone, iPad, iPod, and so on), you'll need to pay for an Apple Developer account, which costs 99 USD per year, but only if you are planning to release the game; for testing purposes, you can continue without it.

To create an AR Foundation iOS build, you should do the following:

1. Get a Mac computer and an iOS device.
2. Create an Apple Developer account (at the time of writing this book, you can create one at `https://developer.apple.com/`).
3. Install the latest XCode from the App Store onto your Mac.
4. Check if you have iOS build support in Unity Install on the Unity Hub. Please refer to the *Building for Android* section for more information about this step.
5. Switch to the iOS platform under **Build Settings**, by selecting iOS and clicking the **Switch Platform** button:

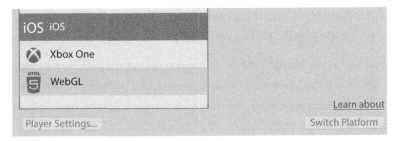

Figure 20.25: Switching to iOS build

6. Go to **Edit | Project Settings** and select the **Player** option.

7. In **Other Settings**, set the **Camera Usage Description** property if not already. This will be a message shown to the user to tell them why we need access to their camera:

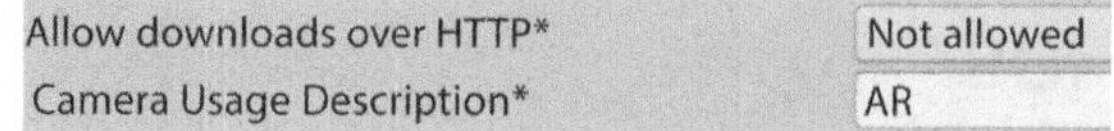

Figure 20.26: Message regarding camera usage

8. Go to **Edit | Project Settings** and select the **XR Plug-in Management** option.
9. Check **Apple ARKit** under **Plug-in Providers** to make sure it will be enabled in our build; if not, we won't see anything:

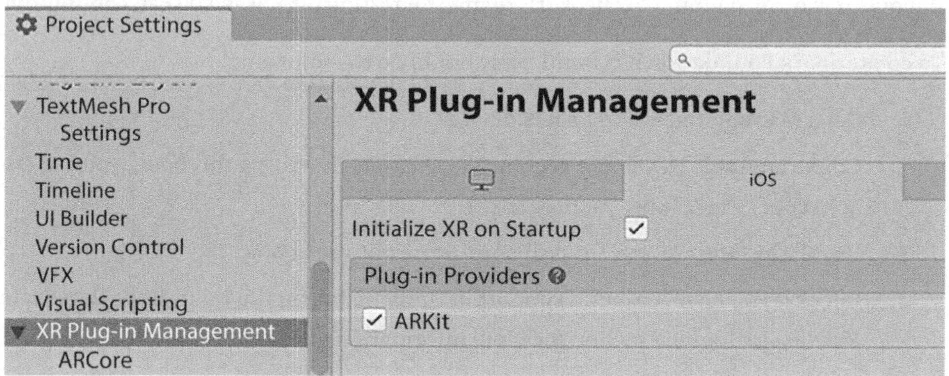

Figure 20.27: ARKit plugin enabled

10. Click the **Build** button in the **Build Settings** window, create a folder for the build, and wait for the build to finish. A folder containing the generated files should open when finished.

You will notice that the result of the build process will be a folder containing an XCode project. Unity cannot create the build directly, so it generates a project you can open with the XCode software we mentioned previously. The step you need to follow to create a build with the XCode version being used in this book (13.4.1) are as follows:

1. Double-click the `.xcodeproj` file inside the generated folder:

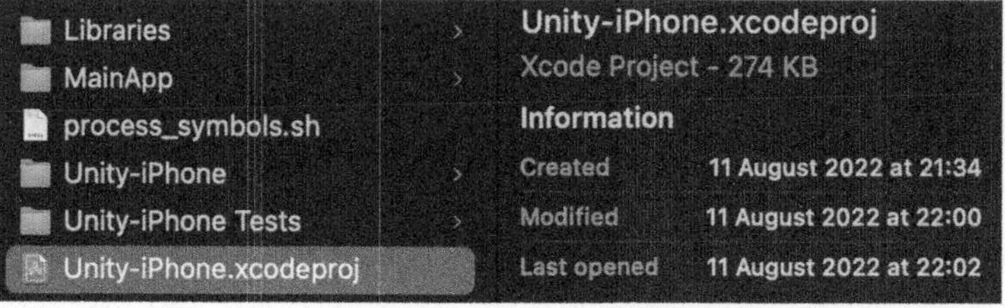

Figure 20.28: XCode project file

2. Go to **XCode | Preferences**.
3. In the **Accounts** tab, hit the + button at the bottom-left part of the window and log in with the Apple account you registered as an Apple developer:

Figure 20.29: Account settings

4. Connect your device and select it from the top-left part of the window, which should now say **Any iOS device**. You might need to unblock your device first, click on the **Trust** button, and wait for XCode to finish setting up your device to see your device in the list:

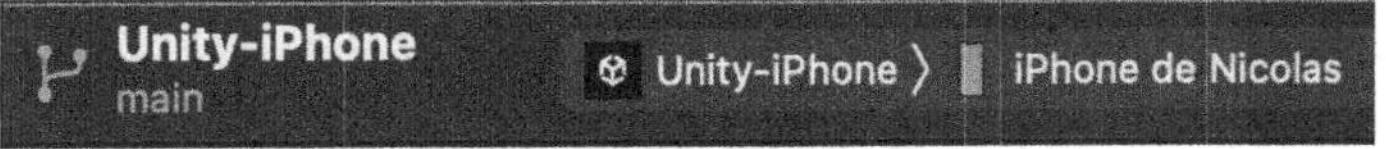

Figure 20.30: Selecting the device

5. XCode might ask you to install certain updates to support your device; please install them if needed.
6. In the left panel, click the folder icon and then the **Unity-iPhone** settings to display the project settings.
7. From the **TARGETS** list, select **Unity-iPhone** and click on the **Signing & Capabilities** tab.
8. Check **Automatically manage signing** and click on the **Enable Automatic** button on the prompt.
9. In the **Team** settings, select the option that says **Personal Team**.
10. If you see a **Failed to register bundle identifier** error, just change the **Bundle Identifier** setting for another one, always respecting the format (`com.XXXX.XXXX`), and then click on **Try Again** until it is solved.

Once you find one that works, set it in Unity (**Bundle Identifier** under **Player Settings**) to avoid needing to change it in every build:

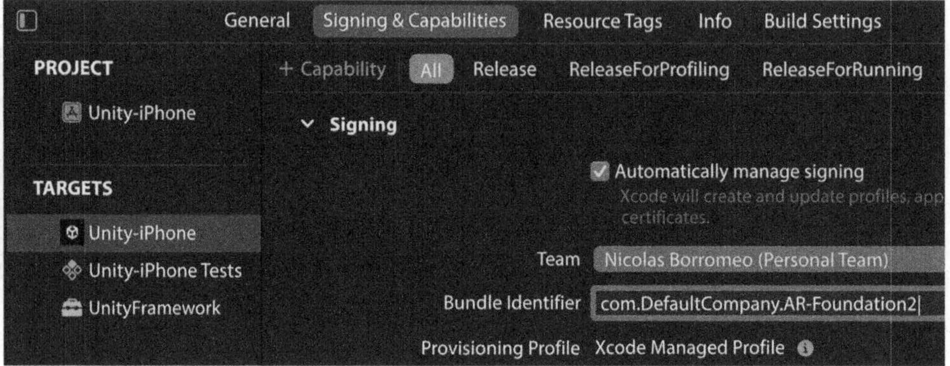

Figure 20.31: Setting up your iOS project

11. Hit the **Play** button at the top-left part of the window and wait for the build to complete. You might be prompted to enter your password a couple of times in the process, so please do so.
12. When the build completes, remember to unlock the device. A prompt will ask you to do that. Note that the process won't continue unless you unlock the phone. If that fails click **Cancel Running** and try again, this time with the device unlocked; remember to select your device in the list again. Also, try to use the latest XCode available to support the latest iOS versions installed on your device.
13. If you see a **Fetching Debug Symbols** prompt that never ends, restart your device.
14. After completion, you may see an error saying that the app couldn't be launched but that it was installed anyway. If you try to open it, it will say you need to trust the developer of the app, which you can do by going to the settings of your device.
15. From there, go to **General | VPN & Device Management** and select the first developer in the list.
16. Click the blue **Trust...** button and then **Trust**.
17. Try to open the app again.
18. Please remember to try another image if you're having trouble detecting the image where we instantiate the player (the pebbles image, in my case). This might vary a lot, depending on your device's capabilities.

In this section, we discussed how to build a Unity project that can run on iOS and Android, thus allowing us to create mobile apps—AR mobile apps, specifically. Like any build, there are methods we can follow to profile and debug, as we saw when we looked at PC builds, but we are not going to discuss that here. Now that we have created our first test project, we will convert it into a real game by adding some mechanics to it.

Creating a simple AR game

As we discussed previously, the idea is to create a simple game where we can move our player while moving a real-life image, and also put in some enemy spawners by just tapping where we want them to be, such as a wall, the floor, a table, and so on. Our player will automatically shoot at the nearest enemy, and the enemies will shoot directly at the player, so our only task will be to move the player so that they avoid bullets. We are going to implement these game mechanics using scripts very similar to the ones we used in this book's main project.

In this section, we will develop the following AR game features:

- Spawning the player and enemies
- Coding the player and enemy behavior

First, we are going to discuss how to make our player and enemies appear on the app, specifically in real-world positions, and then we will make them move and shoot each other to create the specified gameplay mechanics. Let's start with **spawning**.

Spawning the player and enemies

The first thing we need to do in order to implement our game's gameplay is to spawn objects to interact with. Let's start with the player, since that's the easiest one to deal with: we will create a Prefab with the graphics we want the player to have (in my case, just a cube), a `Rigidbody` with **Is Kinematic** checked (the player will move), and an **AR Tracked Image** script. We will set that Prefab as them **Tracked Image Prefab** of the **AR Tracked Image Manager** component in the **XR Origin** object. This will put the player on the tracked image. Remember to set the size of the player in terms of real-life sizes. In my case, I scaled the player to `0.05`, `0.05`, `0.05`. Since the original cube is 1 meter in size, this means that my player will be *5x5x5* centimeters.

Your **Player** Prefab should look as follows:

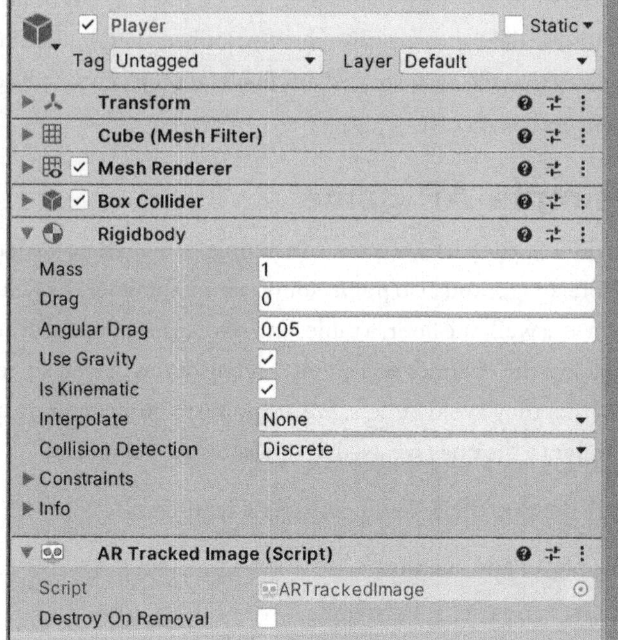

Figure 20.32: The starting "Player" Prefab

The enemies will require a little bit more work, as shown here:

1. Create a Prefab called `Spawner` with the graphic you want your spawner to have (in my case, a cylinder) and its real-life size (small scale).
2. Add a custom script that spawns a Prefab every few seconds, such as the one shown in the following screenshot.
3. You will notice the usage of `Physics.IgnoreCollision` to prevent the `Spawner` GameObject from colliding with the spawned GameObject, getting the colliders of both objects, and passing them to the function. You can also use the **Layer Collision Matrix** to prevent collisions, just like we did in this book's main project, if you prefer to:

```
using UnityEngine;

public class Spawner : MonoBehaviour
{
    public GameObject prefab;
    public float frequency;

    void Awake()
    {
        InvokeRepeating("Spawn", frequency, frequency);
    }

    void Spawn()
    {
        var obj :GameObject = Instantiate(prefab,
            transform.position,
            transform.rotation);

        var myCollider = GetComponentInChildren<Collider>();
        var spawnedCol = obj.GetComponentInChildren<Collider>();

        //Check if both objects have collider
        if (myCollider != null && spawnedCol != null)
        {
            Physics.IgnoreCollision(myCollider, spawnedCol);
        }
    }
}
```

Figure 20.33: Spawner script

4. Create an `Enemy` Prefab with the desired graphic (a capsule, in my case) and a `Rigidbody` component with the **Is Kinematic** checkbox checked. This way, the enemy will move but not with physics. Remember to consider the real-life size of the enemy.
5. Set the **Prefab** property of the Spawner so that it spawns our enemy at our desired time frequency:

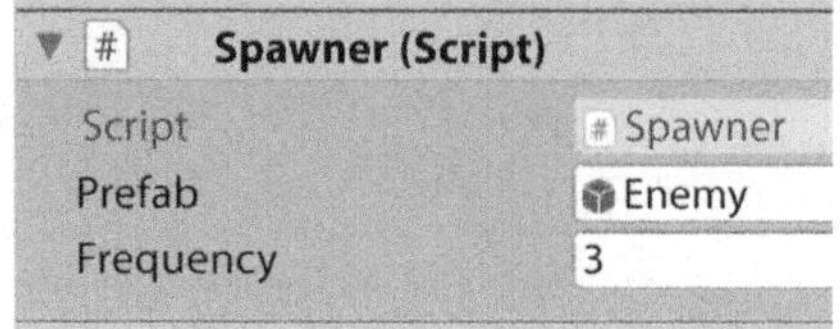

Figure 20.34: Configuring the Spawner

6. Set the Prefab of `SpawnerPlacer` in the XR Origin object so that it spawns the **Spawner** Prefab we created earlier.

And that's all for the first part. If you test the game now, you will be able to tap on the detected planes in the app and see how the Spawner starts creating enemies. You can also look at the target image and see our cube player appear.

Now that we have the objects in the scene, let's make them do something more interesting, starting with the enemies.

Coding the player and enemy behavior

The Enemy must move toward the player in order to shoot at them, so it will need to have access to the player's position. Since the enemy is instantiated, we cannot drag the player reference to the Prefab. However, the player has also been instantiated, so we can add a `PlayerManager` script to the player that uses the `Singleton` pattern (as we did in *Chapter 8, Win and Lose Conditions*).

To do that, follow these steps:

1. Create a `PlayerManager` script similar to the one shown in the following screenshot and add it to the player:

```
using UnityEngine;

public class PlayerManager : MonoBehaviour
{
    public static PlayerManager instance;

    void Awake()
    {
        instance = this;
    }
}
```

Figure 20.35: Creating the PlayerManager script

2. Now that the enemy has a reference to the player, let's make them look at the player by adding a `LookAtPlayer` script, as shown here:

```
using UnityEngine;

public class LookAtPlayer : MonoBehaviour
{
    void Update()
    {
        if(PlayerManager.instance == null) return;

        var playerPos :Vector3 = PlayerManager.instance.transform.position;
        transform.forward = playerPos - transform.position;
    }
}
```

Figure 20.36: Creating the LookAtPlayer script

3. Also, add a simple `MoveForward` script like the one shown in the following screenshot to make the **enemy** not only look at the player but also move toward them. Since the `LookAtPlayer` script is making the enemy face the player, this script moving along the *Z* axis is just enough:

```
using UnityEngine;

public class MoveForward : MonoBehaviour
{
    public float speed;

    void Update()
    {
        transform.Translate(0, 0, speed * Time.deltaTime);
    }
}
```

Figure 20.37: Creating the MoveForward script

Now, we will take care of the player movement. Remember that our player is controlled by moving the image, so here, we are actually referring to the rotation, since the player will need to automatically look and shoot at the nearest enemy. To do this, follow these steps:

1. Create an `Enemy` script and add it to the **Enemy** Prefab.
2. Create an `EnemyManager` script like the one shown in the following screenshot and add it to an empty `EnemyManager` object in the scene:

```
using System.Collections.Generic;
using UnityEngine;

public class EnemyManager : MonoBehaviour
{
    public static EnemyManager instance;

    public List<Enemy> all = new List<Enemy>();

    void Awake()
    {
        instance = this;
    }
}
```

Figure 20.38: Creating the EnemyManager script

3. In the `Enemy` script, make sure to register the object in the **all** list of `EnemyManager`, as we did previously with `WavesManager` in this book's main project:

```
using UnityEngine;

public class Enemy : MonoBehaviour
{
    void OnEnable()
    {
        EnemyManager.instance.all.Add(this);
    }

    void OnDisable()
    {
        EnemyManager.instance.all.Remove(this);
    }
}
```

Figure 20.39: Creating the Enemy script

4. Create a `LookAtNearestEnemy` script like the one shown in the following screenshot and add it to the **Player** Prefab to make it look at the nearest enemy:

```
using UnityEngine;

public class LookAtNearestEnemy : MonoBehaviour
{
    void Update()
    {
        if(EnemyManager.instance.all.Count == 0) return;

        var nearestEnemy = EnemyManager.instance.all[0];

        for (var i = 1; i < EnemyManager.instance.all.Count; i++)
        {
            var enemy = EnemyManager.instance.all[i];
            var enemyPos :Vector3 = enemy.transform.position;
            var nearEnemyPos :Vector3 = nearestEnemy.transform.position;

            var distToNear :float = Vector3.Distance(nearEnemyPos, transform.position);
            var distToEnemy :float = Vector3.Distance(enemyPos, transform.position);

            if (distToEnemy < distToNear)
                nearestEnemy = enemy;
        }

        transform.forward = nearestEnemy.transform.position - transform.position;
    }
}
```

Figure 20.40: Looking at the nearest Enemy

Now that our objects are rotating and moving as expected, the only thing missing is shooting and damaging:

1. Create a `Life` script like the one shown in the following screenshot and add it to both the **Player** and **Enemy** components. Remember to set a value for the amount of life field. You will see this version of `Life` instead of needing to check if the life reached zero every frame. We have created a `Damage` function to check that damage is dealt (the `Damage` function is executed), but the other version of this book's project also works:

```
using UnityEngine;

public class Life : MonoBehaviour
{
    public int amount;

    public void Damage(int damageAmount)
    {
        amount -= damageAmount;
        if(amount <= 0)
            Destroy(gameObject);
    }
}
```

Figure 20.41: Creating a Life component

2. Create a `Bullet` Prefab with the desired graphics, the collider with the **Is Trigger** checkbox on the collider checked, a `Rigidbody` component with **Is Kinematic** checked (a kinematic trigger collider), and the proper real-life size.
3. Add the `MoveForward` script to the **Bullet** Prefab to make it move. Remember to set the speed.
4. Add a `Spawner` script to both the **Player** and the **Enemy** components and set the **Bullet** Prefab as the Prefab to spawn, as well as the desired spawn frequency.
5. Add a `Damager` script like the one shown in the following screenshot to the **Bullet** Prefab to make bullets inflict damage on the objects they touch. Remember to set the damage:

```
using UnityEngine;

public class Damager : MonoBehaviour
{
    public int amount;

    void OnTriggerEnter(Collider other)
    {
        other.GetComponent<Life>()?.Damage(amount);
        Destroy(gameObject);
    }
}
```

Figure 20.42: Creating a Damager script – part 1

6. Add an `AutoDestroy` script like the one shown in the following screenshot to the **Bullet** Prefab to make it despawn after a while. Remember to set the destroy time:

```
using UnityEngine;

public class AutoDestroy : MonoBehaviour
{
    public float time;

    void Awake()
    {
        Destroy(gameObject, time);
    }
}
```

Figure 20.43: Creating a Damager script – part 2

And that's all! As you can see, we basically created a new game using almost the same scripts we used in the main game, mostly because we designed them to be generic (and the game genres are almost the same). Of course, this project can be improved a lot, but we have a nice base project to create amazing AR apps.

Summary

In this chapter, we introduced the AR Foundation Unity framework, explored how to set it up, and how to implement several tracking features so that we can position virtual objects on top of real-life objects. We also discussed how to build our project so that it can run on both iOS and Android platforms, which is the only way we can test our AR apps at the time of writing. Finally, we created a simple AR game based on the game we created in the main project but modified it so that it's suitable for use in AR scenarios.

With this new knowledge, you will be able to start your path as an AR app developer, creating apps that augment real objects with virtual objects by detecting the positions of the real objects. This can be applied to games, training apps, and simulations. You may even be able to find new fields of usage, so take advantage of this new technology and its new possibilities!

Well, this is the end of this journey through Unity 2022. I'm really glad you reached this point in the book. I hope this knowledge will help you to improve or start your game development career with one of the most versatile and powerful tools on the market: Unity. I hope to see your creations someday! See you on the road!

packt.com

Subscribe to our online digital library for full access to over 7,000 books and videos, as well as industry leading tools to help you plan your personal development and advance your career. For more information, please visit our website.

Why subscribe?

- Spend less time learning and more time coding with practical eBooks and Videos from over 4,000 industry professionals
- Improve your learning with Skill Plans built especially for you
- Get a free eBook or video every month
- Fully searchable for easy access to vital information
- Copy and paste, print, and bookmark content

At www.packt.com, you can also read a collection of free technical articles, sign up for a range of free newsletters, and receive exclusive discounts and offers on Packt books and eBooks.

Other Books You May Enjoy

If you enjoyed this book, you may be interested in these other books by Packt:

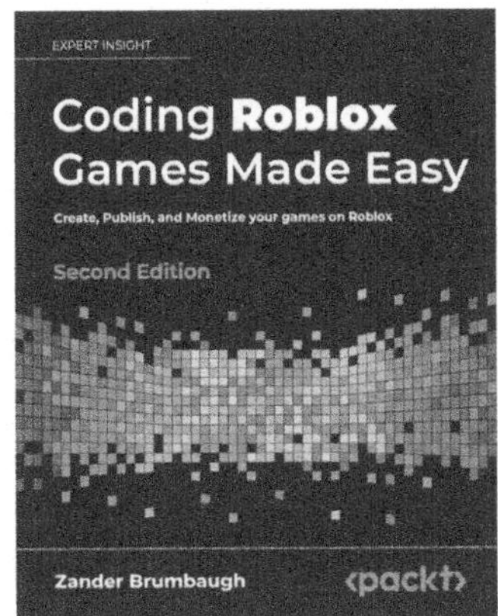

Coding Roblox Games Made Easy, Second Edition

Zander Brumbaugh

ISBN: 9781803234670

- Use Roblox Studio and other free resources
- Learn coding in Luau: basics, game systems, physics manipulation, etc
- Test, evaluate, and redesign to create bug-free and engaging games
- Use Roblox programming and rewards to make your first game
- Move from lobby to battleground, build avatars, locate weapons to fight
- Character selection, countdown timers, locate escape items, assign rewards
- Master the 3 Ms: Mechanics, Monetization, Marketing (and Metaverse)
- 50 cool things to do in Roblox

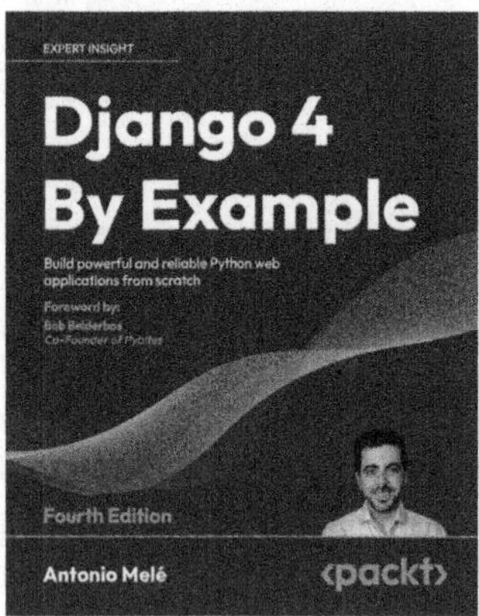

Django 4 By Example – Fourth Edition

Antonio Melé

ISBN: 9781801813051

- Learn Django essentials, including models, ORM, views, templates, URLs, forms, authentication, signals and middleware
- Implement different modules of the Django framework to solve specific problems
- Integrate third-party Django applications into your project
- Build asynchronous (ASGI) applications with Django
- Set up a production environment for your projects
- Easily create complex web applications to solve real use cases

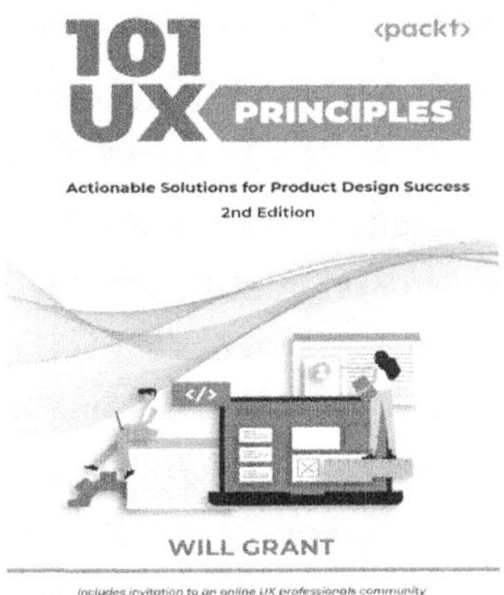

101 UX Principles, Second Edition

Will Grant

ISBN: 9781803234885

- Work with user expectations, not against them
- Make interactive elements obvious and discoverable
- Optimize your interface for mobile
- Streamline creating and entering passwords
- Use animation with care in user interfaces
- How to handle destructive user actions

Packt is searching for authors like you

If you're interested in becoming an author for Packt, please visit `authors.packtpub.com` and apply today. We have worked with thousands of developers and tech professionals, just like you, to help them share their insight with the global tech community. You can make a general application, apply for a specific hot topic that we are recruiting an author for, or submit your own idea.

Share your thoughts

Now you've finished *Hands-On Unity 2022 Game Development, Third Edition*, we'd love to hear your thoughts! Scan the QR code below to go straight to the Amazon review page for this book and share your feedback or leave a review on the site that you purchased it from.

https://packt.link/r/1803236914

Your review is important to us and the tech community and will help us make sure we're delivering excellent quality content.

Index

Symbols

3D Cartesian coordinate system 23

3D Spatial Blend 439

A

Action 241

advanced effects
- applying 421-428
- Depth Map 419
- High Dynamic Range (HDR) 419
- using 418

AI techniques
- bulletPrefab field, adding 291-298

AI techniques, with sensors 244
- debugging, with Gizmos 255-263
- three-filter sensors, creating with C# 244-250
- three-filter sensors, creating with Visual Scripting 251-255

ambient lighting
- configuring, with skyboxes 377-382

Android
- building 651-659
- reference link 642

Animation Controllers 545
- integrating 545-551

Animator 545
- Skinning Animation, using 537, 538

AR Foundation
- project, creating 640-644
- tracking features, using 644-651
- using 640

AR game
- creating 663
- player and enemies, spawning 663-666
- player and enemy behavior, coding 666-672

assets 11, 17
- configuring 99
- importing 79
- importing, from Asset Store 82-89
- importing, from internet 80-82
- importing, from Unity Packages 90
- integrating 91
- meshes, configuring 99-101
- meshes, integrating 94, 95
- prototype base, replacing 103-106
- terrain textures, integrating 91-94
- textures, configuring 101, 102
- textures, integrating 95-98

Asset Store 79
- used, for importing assets 82-89

audio
- importing 429

importing, concepts 429
import settings, configuring 432-436
integrating 436
mixing 436
types 430, 431

AudioClips 436

audio feedback
scripting 446-448

Audio Mixer
using 441-446

audio mixing 441

AudioSources 436
2D mode 438-440
3D mode 438-440
settings 438

audio types
ambient sound 430
music 430
sound effects (SFX) 430

Avatar Masks 552
using 552-557

axis gizmo 23

B

baked lighting 395

Baked mode 400

batching 590, 593
using 593-598

Blackboard 121

Bloom effect 421
enabling 423

Box Collider 29

breakpoints
using 125, 126

build 627, 628
code, debugging 633-635
debugging 632
performance, profiling 635-638

Built-in Renderer Pipeline (BIRP) 304

C

C# 112
Finite State Machines (FSMs), creating 264-267
used, for creating three-filter sensors 244-250

Canvas 452
used, for creating User Interface (UI) 452, 453

Canvas object types 456
graphics assets, integrating for UI 456-465
UI controls, creating 465-473

Canvas Scaler component 479

central processing unit (CPU) 32

Chromatic Aberration effect 414, 415

Cinemachine
camera behaviors, creating 571-575
dolly tracks, creating 575-578
used, for creating dynamic cameras 570

Collision reaction 193

collisions
detecting 193
filtering 190, 191, 192

Color Curves 427

complex simulations
creating, with Visual Effect Graph 349, 350

components 27-29
manipulating 29-34

compression formats
ADPCM 435
PCM 435
Context 355
initialize particle 355
output particle quad 355
update particle 355
C# Script
common beginner errors 132-134
creating 112-115
Cubemap 380
cutscenes
creating, with Timeline 578

D

Deferred Rendering 371, 375-377
Delta Time 148, 495
depth bias 389
Depth Map 419
Depth of Field 419, 423, 424
Development Builds 634
Direct Lights 377, 382
dots per inch (DPI) 528
draw call 374
draw calls 591
dynamic batching 596
dynamic cameras
creating, with Cinemachine 570

E

events
Collision events 193
in C# 122-124
in Visual Scripting 126-129
Trigger events 193
event system 122
executable format
building 627-632

F

fields
using, in instructions 129-132
Filmbox (FBX) 539
Film Grain 418
Finite State Machines (FSMs) 243, 264
creating, in C# 264-267
creating, in Visual Scripting 272-282
decision making 264
transitions, creating 267-272
first-person-shooter (FPS) 102
fluid simulations
bonfire effect, creating 346-349
creating 344
waterfall effect, creating 344-346
Forward Rendering 371
Forward Vector 24
Frame Debugger 591, 637
using 591-593
frames per second (FPS) 32, 349, 394
frustum culling 600
FSM actions
executing 283
NavMesh, calculating 283-285
Pathfinding, using 286-291

G

game concept
defining 47, 48

Game Mode Object
creating 224-231
GameObjects 18
adding, to scene 20, 21
manipulating 22-27
garbage collector 613-619
G-Buffer 375
Gizmos 255
used, for debugging AI techniques with sensors 255-263
GLSL 300
graphics engines 590, 591
graphics optimization 590, 598-602
CPU-bound, detecting 603, 604
CPU optimization techniques 609-613
CPU Usage Profiler, using 605-609
feature 599, 600
GPU-bound, detecting 603, 604
processing 602, 603
gray-boxing 21

H

HDR Rendering 419
Height Maps 49, 50
authoring 53-57
configuring 50-53
creating 50-53
details, adding 57-60
High Definition Render Pipeline (HDRP) 304, 371
High Dynamic Range (HDR) 419
enabling 420, 421
Highlights effect 425

I

Importing Assets process 16
import setting configuration
compressed in memory 433
decompress on load 433
streaming 433
Indirect Light 377
Input System
input mapping, creating 170-173
installing 168-170
mapping, using in scripts 174-179
using 168
Inspector tool 29
instructions
fields, using in 129-132
in C# 123
in Visual Scripting 126-129
Integrated Development Environment (IDE) 109
intelligent pathfinding 243
Inverse Kinematics (IK) 542
iOS
building 659-663
reference link 642

J

JetBrains Rider Editor package 125
Joint Photographic Experts Group (JPG) 16

K

Kinematic Collider 186

L

layer 190, 552

Layer Collision Matrix 190

Level of Detail (LOD) 598

lighting 371

ambient lighting, configuring with skyboxes 377-382

applying 371, 372

configuring in URP 382-385

methods 372-377

optimizing 395

Lightmapping UVs 397

lightmaps 395

baking 396-404

reference link 404

Light Probes 405

long-term support (LTS) 2

Low Dynamic Range (LDR) 419

M

managers

creating 216-224

memory allocation 613-619

memory optimization 613

Memory Profiler 638

using 619-624

Mesh Collider 182

MeshFilter component 29

Midtones effect 425

Mixed mode 400

mobile devices

Android, building 651-659

building 651

iOS, building 659-663

modes

for frequent medium audio 434

for frequent short audio 434

for infrequent large audio 434

Motion Blur effect 417

movement

Delta Time 148-150

implementing 137, 138

objects, moving through Transform 138-141

Player Input, using 141-148

Movement Animations

scripting 567-570

MPEG Audio Layer 3 (MP3) 16

Multi-Pass Forward Renderer 372-374

versus Single Pass Forward Renderer 375

N

normal bias 390

Normals 375, 376

O

object hierarchies 34

uses 36

object managers

creating 207, 208

Object Pool class

reference link 619

Object Pooling 216

objects

modifying 196-200

parenting 34, 35

Object Variables 214

occlusion culling 600

OnDrawGizmos function 256

Overlap Sphere 251

P

panels 18

Panel Settings asset 529

parenting
  of objects 34, 35

particle systems 335

performant shadows
  configuring 391-394

Peripheral Component Interconnect Express (PCI Express) 590

physics
  forces, applying 200-203
  tweaking 203-205
  used, for producing movements 200

Physics Collider 186

physics configuration 182
  collisions, filtering 190-192
  object types 186-190
  shapes, setting 182-185

Physics events 193

Pixel Lighting 374

PlayerMovement script 138

Player Shooting Animations
  scripting 557-567

Point Light 383

Portable Network Graphics (PNG) 16

Post-processing
  using 411, 412

Post Processing Stack version 2 (PPv2) 412

precalculating shadows 395

Prefab-instance relationship 39-42

Prefabs 37, 38
  creating 38, 39

Prefab variant 43, 44

primitive types
  Box 182
  Capsule 182
  Sphere 182

ProBuilder 60
  details, adding 72-76
  installing 61-63
  mesh, manipulating 65-72
  shape, creating 64, 65
  used, for creating shapes 60

Profiler
  using, on Build 635-637

R

real-time lighting 395

Realtime mode 400

RectTransform 452
  used, for positioning elements 453-456

relative positions
  using 530-536

Render Pipeline 303-305

Responsive UI
  creating 524
  dynamic positioning and sizing 524-528
  Dynamic Scaling 528-530
  relative positions, using 530-536

Right Vector 24

Rigidbody 30

S

scene 17
  GameObjects, adding to 20, 21
  purpose 18
  saving 44

scene files
saving 45
scene template 20
Scene variables 213
Scene View 18-20
navigating 21, 22
ScoreOnDeath 211
Scriptable Render Pipeline (SRP) 304
Script Asset 118
Script Graph 118
scripting animations 557
Movement Animations, scripting 567-570
Player Shooting Animations, scripting 557-567
scripts
creating 108
fields, adding 116-118
initial setup 109-112
shader 299, 300
Shader Graph 300, 301, 310
creating 310-315
Textures, combining 325-328
Textures, using 316-325
transparency, applying 328-331
used, for creating shaders 310
Vertex Effects, creating 331-334
Shader Pipeline 300-303
Shader Pipeline, stages
blending 303
culling 301
Depth Testing 302
Fragment Shader 302
Input Assembler 301
rasterizer 302
Vertex Shader 301
Shadow Acne 388
Shadow Cascades 391
Shadow effect 425
Shadow Map 386
shadows
applying 386
calculations 386-391
performant shadows, configuring 39-394
shapes
setting 182-185
Shuriken particle systems 335, 336
advanced module, using 342-344
creating 336-341
Single Pass Forward Renderer 372
versus Multi-Pass Forward Renderer 375
Singleton design pattern
used, for sharing variables 208-213
skeletal animations
importing 541-545
skinned meshes 538
Skinned Mesh Renderer 548
skinning 538-540
Skinning Animation
using, with Animator 537, 538
skyboxes
used, for configuring ambient lighting 377-382
Soft Shadows 388
spawning 663
implementing 150, 151
object, destroying 166-168
object, spawning 151-160
timing actions 161-165
Split Toning 427
Spotlight 383
static batcher 597

Static Collider 186

static lighting 395, 396
  applying, to static objects 404-408

static meshes 537

Streaming 433

Stylesheet Classes 520

subscribing 233, 238

System 355

T

Terrain tool
  Height Maps 49, 50
  Height Maps, authoring 53-57
  Height Maps, configuring 50-53
  Height Maps, creating 50-53
  Height Maps, details adding 57-60
  used, for creating landscape 48

TextMesh Pro 462

Textures
  combining 325-328
  using 316-325

three-filter sensors
  creating, with C# 244-250
  creating, with Visual Scripting 251-255

Timeline
  animation clips, creating 57-581
  intro cutscene, sequencing 581-586
  used, for creating cutscenes 578

tonemapping 420

Transform 28, 138

Transform Gizmo 23

Transform relationship 34

transparency
  applying 328-331

Trigger events
  detecting 193-196

Trigger Kinematic Collider 187

Trigger Static Collider 186, 187

U

UI Builder 509

UI Documents
  creating 508-510
  editing 510-519

UI responsive
  creating 473
  object positions, adapting 474-477
  object sizes, adapting 477-480

UI scripting 480
  information, displaying 480-485, 488-495
  Pause menu, programming 495-504

UI Stylesheets
  creating 519-524

UI Toolkit 452, 507, 508
  used, for creating UI 508

Uniform Scaling 26

Unity
  installing 1
  installing, with Unity Hub 3-11
  technical requirements 2
  versioning 2, 3

Unity Download Archive 7

Unity Editor 18, 19

Unity event functions
  used, for improving code 231-241

Unity Hub
  folder structure, exploring 14-16
  Unity, installing with 3-11
  used, for creating project 11-14

Unity Packages
used, for importing assets 90
Unity Profilers 638
Universal Render Pipeline (URP) 12, 95, 299, 300, 303-305, 350, 412, 597
built-in shaders 305-310
lighting, configuring 382-385
Up Vector 24
URP Post-processing
basic effects, using 414-418
profile, setting up 412-414
User Interface (UI) 451
creating, with Canvas 452, 453
creating, with UI Toolkit 508

V

variables
scopes 214
sharing, with Singleton design pattern 208-213
sharing, with Visual Scripting 213-216
Vertex Effects
creating 331-334
Vertex Lighting 375
Vertex Snapping 104
Vignette effect 415-417
Visual Effect
scripting 363-369
Visual Effect Graph 349, 350
analyzing 352-356
creating 352-356
installing 350-352
rain effect, creating 356-362
reference link 362
used, for creating complex simulations 349, 350
Visual Script
creating 119-121
Visual Scripting graph 107
Finite State Machines (FSMs), creating 272-282
used, for creating three-filter sensors 251-255
used, for sharing variables 213-216
Visual Scripting package 109
Visual Studio Editor package 125
VSync 606

W

Waveform Audio File Format (WAV) 16
White Balance 418
WYSIWYG (What You See Is What You Get) 20

Z

Z-Fighting 65

Download a free PDF copy of this book

Thanks for purchasing this book!

Do you like to read on the go but are unable to carry your print books everywhere?

Is your eBook purchase not compatible with the device of your choice?

Don't worry, now with every Packt book you get a DRM-free PDF version of that book at no cost.

Read anywhere, any place, on any device. Search, copy, and paste code from your favorite technical books directly into your application.

The perks don't stop there, you can get exclusive access to discounts, newsletters, and great free content in your inbox daily

Follow these simple steps to get the benefits:

1. Scan the QR code or visit the link below

`https://packt.link/free-ebook/9781803236919`

2. Submit your proof of purchase
3. That's it! We'll send your free PDF and other benefits to your email directly